EU ANTI-DISCRIMINATION LAW BEYOND GENDER

The EU has slowly but surely developed a solid body of equality law that prohibits different facets of discrimination. While the Union had initially developed anti-discrimination norms that served only the commercial rationale of the common market, focusing on nationality (of a Member State) and gender as protected grounds, the Treaty of Amsterdam (1997) supplied five additional prohibited grounds of discrimination to the EU legislative palette, in line with a much broader egalitarian rationale. In 2000, two EU Equality Directives followed, one focusing on race and ethnic origin, the other covering the remaining four grounds introduced by the Treaty of Amsterdam, namely religion, sexual orientation, disabilities and age.

Eighteen years after the adoption of the watershed Equality Directives, it seems timely to dedicate a book to their limits and prospects, to look at the progress made, and to revisit the rise of EU anti-discrimination law beyond gender. This volume sets out to capture the striking developments and shortcomings that have taken place in the interpretation of relevant EU secondary law. Firstly, the book unfolds an up-to-date systematic reappraisal of the five 'newer' grounds of discrimination, which have so far received mostly fragmented coverage. Secondly, and more generally, the volume captures how and to what extent the Equality Directives have enabled or, at times, prevented the Court of Justice of the European Union from developing even broader and more refined anti-discrimination jurisprudence. Thus, the book offers a glimpse into the past, present and – it is hoped – future of EU anti-discrimination law as, despite all the flaws in the Union's 'Garden of Earthly Delights', it offers one of the highest standards of protection in comparative anti-discrimination law.

EU Anti-Discrimination Law Beyond Gender

Edited by
Uladzislau Belavusau
and
Kristin Henrard

•HART•
OXFORD • LONDON • NEW YORK • NEW DELHI • SYDNEY

HART PUBLISHING

Bloomsbury Publishing Plc

Kemp House, Chawley Park, Cumnor Hill, Oxford, OX2 9PH, UK

1385 Broadway, New York, NY 10018, USA

HART PUBLISHING, the Hart/Stag logo, BLOOMSBURY and the Diana logo are trademarks of Bloomsbury Publishing Plc

First published in Great Britain 2019

Reprinted 2019, 2020

A catalogue record for this book is available from the British Library.

Library of Congress Cataloging-in-Publication data

Names: Belavusau, Uladzislau, editor. | Henrard, Kristin, editor.

Title: EU anti-discrimination law beyond gender / edited by Uladzislau Belavusau and Kristin Henrard.

Other titles: European Union anti-discrimination law beyond gender

Description: Oxford, UK ; Portland, Oregon : Hart Publishing, 2019.

Identifiers: LCCN 2018026328 (print) | LCCN 2018027308 (ebook) | ISBN 9781509915026 (Epub) | ISBN 9781509915019 (hardback : alk. paper)

Subjects: LCSH: Discrimination—Law and legislation—European Union countries. | Equality before the law—European Union countries. | Sex discrimination against women—Law and legislation—European Union countries. | Race discrimination—Law and legislation—European Union countries. | Treaty on European Union (1992 February 7). Protocols, etc. (1997 October 2)

Classification: LCC KJE5142 (ebook) | LCC KJE5142 .E73 2018 (print) | DDC 342.408/5—dc23

LC record available at https://lccn.loc.gov/2018026328

ISBN: HB: 978-1-50991-501-9
ePDF: 978-1-50991-500-2
ePub: 978-1-50991-502-6

Typeset by Compuscript Ltd, Shannon
Printed and bound in Great Britain by TJ International Ltd, Padstow, Cornwall

To find out more about our authors and books visit www.hartpublishing.co.uk. Here you will find extracts, author information, details of forthcoming events and the option to sign up for our newsletters.

FOREWORD

Originally, EU anti-discrimination law did not occupy centre stage in the process of European integration, being seen merely as a means of facilitating the establishment of the EU internal market. The prohibition against discrimination based on nationality sought to protect free movement rights by guaranteeing equal access to the market of the host Member State. For its part, the principle of equal pay for equal work was seen as a way of prohibiting regulatory measures that, in seeking to make undertakings more competitive, had the undesirable – and indeed counterproductive – effect of discriminating against women who joined the workforce.

However, EU anti-discrimination law has progressively grown beyond its internal market origins. That law is no longer a means to an end but an end in itself which implements the value of equality on which the EU is founded. As the editors to this volume posit, one may distinguish three key moments in the evolution of EU anti-discrimination law that contributed to its emergence as a fully-fledged independent discipline.

First, in the 1970s, the case law of the Court of Justice of the European Union (CJEU) played a key role in giving real substance to the principle of gender equality, notably by holding that ex Article 119 EEC (now Article 157 TFEU) could produce horizontal direct effect. That case law was accompanied by the adoption of a series of directives that sought actively to foster gender equality. Second, the entry into force of the Treaty of Amsterdam changed the narrative of EU anti-discrimination law. It introduced a new legal basis (i.e. ex Article 13 EC (now Article 19 TFEU), that enables the EU legislator to fight discrimination based on five new grounds, namely racial or ethnic origin, religion or belief, disability, age and sexual orientation). That new legal basis constituted a quantum leap forward for EU anti-discrimination law as it provided the EU with the constitutional authority to combat discrimination above and beyond the internal market. In that regard, two landmark Directives were adopted in 2000, namely the Framework Equality Directive and the Race Equality Directive (the '2000 Equality Directives'), that have ever since shaped how anti-discrimination law going beyond gender is to be understood at EU level. Last, but not least, with the entry into force of the Treaty of Lisbon, it was made clear that, as a fundamental right recognised by the Charter of Fundamental Rights of the European Union, the principle of equality pervades the entire corpus of EU law and stands at the apex of the hierarchy of EU norms.

Today, 18 years after the adoption of the 2000 Equality Directives, it appears that the time is right to examine the way in which EU anti-discrimination law beyond gender has developed into a mature and complex body of EU law. Edited by Dr Belavusau and Dr Henrard, this volume succeeds in undertaking that examination, thereby making a hugely valuable contribution to the existing literature on EU anti-discrimination law. By bringing together the expertise of its contributors, it does not come as a surprise that the book is an outstanding piece of scholarly work, providing incisive and thought-provoking insights to the way in which the principle of equality applies to race and ethnicity, religion, sexual orientation, age and disability.

Divided into six parts, this book provides a holistic study of EU anti-discrimination law beyond gender. This is, first, because it puts forward a series of chapters that examine the most salient theoretical and procedural aspects of EU anti-discrimination law. Second, for every new ground of discrimination that is given concrete expression in the 2000 Equality Directives, the book contains two specific chapters that examine the underlying rationale of the ground in question, whilst providing the reader with an overview of the major developments in the case law of the CJEU. Most importantly, throughout the book, the contributors do not limit themselves to describing the current legislation and case law, but also provide thorough explanations as to the reasons why they believe that the EU legislator and the CJEU, respectively, reached a given outcome and, where appropriate, suggestions as to how the law might be developed in the future.

Written in a clear and entertaining style, this book succeeds in encapsulating both the past and present of EU anti-discrimination law, whilst providing a solid analytical basis for future debates about that field of law. It is a thoughtful and rigorous work that addresses a challenging set of questions that are of interest to scholars and students. Overall, it is an excellent contribution to the legal literature on European Union law and I warmly congratulate both the editors and contributors for it.

Prof. Dr. Koen Lenaerts
President of the Court of Justice of the European Union

ACKNOWLEDGEMENTS

Many people and several institutions have supported us on this journey of reviewing the eighteen years of EU Equality Directives. We are grateful to the Amsterdam Centre for Contemporary European Studies (*ACCESS-Europe*) and, in particular, to Gareth Davies, Gijs van der Starre and Jonathan Zeitlin for sponsoring our conference that gathered most of the authors of this volume for a critical discussion about their draft chapters in the beautiful Dutch capital. Dion Kramer provided splendid assistance during this event. We are also very thankful to David Oppenheimer for initiating and running the Berkeley Comparative Equality & Anti-Discrimination Study Group. The events and publications within this group have been of great comparative inspiration for our book. In this volume, we explore EU anti-discrimination law as a part of a broader phenomenon, marking the rise of equality law in various jurisdictions, and foremost emphasising the indispensable mutual influence between US and European thinking.

We are much obliged to a number of prominent colleagues who have generously shared their advice including, though not limited to, Mark Bell (Dublin), Bruno De Witte (Florence), Laurence W Gormley (Groningen), Eric Heinze (London), Rikki Holtmaat (Leiden), Magldalena Jozwiak (Amsterdam), Dimitry Kochenov (Groningen), Elise Muir (Leuven), Christophe Paulussen (The Hague), Daša Słabčanka (Amsterdam), Christa Tobler (Leiden), Ioanna Tourkochoriti (Galway), Snježana Vasiljević (Zagreb), and Lisa Waddington (Maastricht). We are particularly honoured and thankful to Prof Koen Lenaerts, President of the Court of Justice for his Foreword to our volume.

The volume would not be possible without the invaluable assistance of Aylin Gayibli. An extremely talented recent graduate from Leiden University and an intern at the T.M.C. Asser Institute in The Hague, Aylin has been our right hand during this long, but intellectually rewarding, work on the volume. In addition, Uladzislau Belavusau would like to express his wholehearted gratitude to Janne Nijman, academic director of the Asser Institute who has facilitated a welcoming working environment for him, which has been crucial for the finalisation of this project. He would like to extend his gratitude to Daniele Gallo for inviting and hosting him as a Visiting Professor at the LUISS Guido Carli University (Rome) in 2017, as well as to Rosann Greenspan and Jonathan Simon for arranging his 2018 stay as a Visiting Scholar at the Center for the Study of Law & Society – University of California, Berkeley, where the finishing touches on this book were completed. Likewise, Kristin Henrard would like to thank Sanne Taekema for the generous financial support she, as head of the Rule of Law Research Programme at Erasmus School of Law, granted for language editing the book proposal and for the copyrights of one author in the volume. Kristin Henrard is also very grateful to Professor Jan Wouters for hosting her as visiting scholar at the Leuven Centre for Global Governance Studies during her sabbatical in the Fall–Winter of 2017, when (somewhat unexpectedly) substantial editing work was still ongoing.

Finally, we wish to thank everyone at Hart – Bloomsbury and, in particular, Emily Braggins and Savannah Rado for their friendly and patient editorship. Last, but not least, deepest gratitude goes to our authors for perservering in spite of the lengthy editing process. We are indebted for your endurance, advice and loyalty!

Kristin and Ulad
Rotterdam and Berkeley, May 2018

CONTENTS

PART III
RELIGION

PART IV
SEXUAL ORIENTATION

PART V
AGE

PART VI
DISABILITY

LIST OF CONTRIBUTORS

Editors

Uladzislau Belavusau is a Senior Researcher in European law at the T.M.C. Asser Institute (The Hague) – University of Amsterdam (the Netherlands). Previously, he was an Assistant Professor at the *Vrije Universiteit Amsterdam* (2011–2015) and holds his PhD from the European University Institute (Florence, Italy). He has published extensively on EU anti-discrimination law, human rights, comparative constitutional law, and memory politics. In 2015, Dr Belavusau received the *Marco Biagi Award* for the best article from the International Association of Labour Law Journals. He is the author of a monograph *Freedom of Speech: Importing European and US Constitutional Models in Transitional Democracies* (Routledge, 2013) and co-editor of a book *Law and Memory: Towards Legal Governance of History* (Cambridge University Press, 2017).

Kristin Henrard is a Professor of Fundamental Rights, in particular pertaining to vulnerable groups, including minorities, at the Erasmus University of Rotterdam (EUR). Prof Henrard has held visiting fellowships at the Leuven Centre for Global Governance Studies (Leuven, Belgium); the Max Planck Institute on Ethnic and Religious Diversity (Göttingen, Germany); the Centre d'Etudes Ethniques des Universités Montréaloises (Québec, Canada), and the African Centre for Migration and Society (Johannesburg, South Africa). In addition, she is a senior non-resident researcher at the European Centre on Minority Issues (Flensburg, Germany). Her research over the past 20 years has continuously branched out to more general doctrines of fundamental rights, the right to equal treatment, the legitimacy quest of international courts, and multi-disciplinary legal research regarding integration and nationality. Prof Henrard has won a prestigious VIDI grant of the Dutch Council for Scientific Research to work on a research project on the implications for minority protection of the Race Equality Directive (2005–2010).

Authors

Phillip Ayoub is an Associate Professor of Diplomacy and World Affairs at Occidental College (Los Angeles, USA).

Mark Bell is the Regius Professor of Laws at Trinity College Dublin (Ireland).

Bruno De Witte is a Professor of European Law at Maastricht University (the Netherlands), and a part-time Professor of Law at the European University Institute (Florence, Italy).

Morag Goodwin is the Professor of Global Law and Development at Tilburg Law School (Netherlands).

Beryl ter Haar is an Assistant Professor at the University of Leiden (Netherlands).

Rachel Horton is a Lecturer in Law at the University of Reading (UK).

Dimitry Kochenov is a Professor of EU Constitutional Law at the University of Groningen (Netherlands).

Luísa Lourenço is a Legal Secretary at the chambers of the President of the EFTA Court (Luxembourg).

Mathias Möschel is an Associate Professor and the Director of the Legal Studies Department's Doctoral Program at Central European University (Budapest, Hungary).

Pekka Pohjankoski is a Legal Secretary at the Court of Justice of the European Union (Luxembourg).

Eugenia Relaño Pastor is a Senior Researcher at the Max Planck Institute for Social Anthropology (Halle, Germany).

Anna Śledzińska-Simon is an Assistant Professor of Constitutional Law at the University of Wrocław and the national expert in the research project on 'Proportionality and Public Policy' at the Israel Democracy Institute (Poland).

Alina Tryfonidou is a Professor in EU Law at the School of Law, University of Reading (UK).

Lisa Waddington is the European Disability Forum Chair in European Disability Law at Maastricht University (Netherlands).

Raphaële Xenidis is a PhD Candidate at the Law Department of the European University Institute (Florence, Italy).

LIST OF ABBREVIATIONS

CFR	Charter of Fundamental Rights of the European Union
CJEU	Court of Justice of the European Union
CRDP	Convention on the Rights of Persons with Disabilities
ECHR	European Convention of Human Rights
ECtHR	European Court of Human Rights
EEC	European Economic Community
EU	European Union
FED	Framework Equality Directive (2000/78/EC)
FRA	Fundamental Rights Agency
OSCE	Organization for Security and Cooperation in Europe
RED	Race Equality Directive (2000/43/EC)
TEU	Treaty on the European Union
TFEU	Treaty on the Functioning of the European Union
UK	United Kingdom of Great Britain and Northern Ireland
UN	United Nations
US	United States of America

1

The Impact of the 2000 Equality Directives on EU Anti-Discrimination Law

Achievements and Pitfalls

ULADZISLAU BELAVUSAU AND KRISTIN HENRARD

I. Introduction

The Ancient Greeks, arguably the historical 'fathers' of our European non-discrimination paradigm, had a very rich understanding of equality that distinguished between its many different dimensions, *inter alia*, discerning equality in various spheres of life.[1] Originally, the European Economic Community (the predecessor of the European Union (EU)) was only concerned with one dimension of equality: equality of economic opportunity. Indeed, the EU has been deemed to foster fully fledged equality of economic opportunity amongst citizens commuting between its various Member States, to ensure their maximum prosperity and economic well-being. However, as the Union developed slowly but surely from an organisation predominantly concerned with economic integration into one with a broader political agenda, and concomitant areas of competence, its ambitions

[1] See H Glykatzi-Ahrweiler, 'European Community as an Idea: The Historical Dimension' in E Chrysos, PM Kitromilides and C Svopoulos (eds), *The Idea of European Community in History*, Conference Proceedings, Vol 1, National and Capodistrian University of Athens, 2003, 25; P Cartledge, *Ancient Greek Political Thought in Practice* (Cambridge, Cambridge University Press, 2009) 8–9. While ancient Greeks admittedly did not have the same concept of egalitarian equality, as we share in modernity after the French Revolution (e.g. excluding women) they did distinguish between equal rights of birth (*isogonia*), equality before the law (*isopoliteia*), equality in the body politics (*isonomia*), equality in economic distribution (*isomoiria*), equal prosperity and well-being (*eudaimonia*), and even equality regarding freedom of speech (*isegoria*). Rediscovered and philosophised *ab novo* during the Enlightenment and eighteenth-century revolutions, the principle of equal treatment gained serious trans-national recognition after World War II in a number of international instruments (eg Universal Declaration of Human Rights, ICCPR, ICESCR, CEDAW, CERD, CRDPD, ECHR, etc).

in the field of equal treatment similarly expanded towards more encompassing visions of justice.[2]

At the turn of the millennium, the year 2000 marked the birth of EU anti-discrimination law[3] as a field in its own right, with the adoption of two major 'Equality Directives'.[4] Not only did they extend the prohibition of discrimination with five 'additional' grounds but also – albeit only for the grounds of 'race and ethnicity' – significantly expanded the material scope of equality regulation.[5] These directives can be seen as launching the transition from the Garden of Earthly Delights opened for mobile EU citizens into a European Garden of Equal Delights, with the anti-discrimination norm increasingly regulating human interactions in wholly internal situations.[6]

The present book zooms in on these 2000 Equality Directives, as well as on the 'new' grounds of discrimination planted therein, namely *race and ethnicity* (the grounds introduced by the Race Equality Directive), *religion, sexual orientation,*[7] *age*, and *disability* (the grounds introduced by Framework Equality Directive) and the related jurisprudence of European courts. Having reached its eighteenth birthday – the age when most Europeans are deemed to reach full adulthood according to civil and criminal law – in the year 2018, EU anti-discrimination law can now celebrate its adulthood. Yet, several problems threaten to undermine this 'maturity'.[8] In the first place, as is well demonstrated by the Commission's reports,[9] a number of countries have delayed the implementation of these

[2] D Kochenov, G de Búrca and A Williams (eds), *Europe's Justice Deficit?* (Cambridge, Cambridge University Press, 2015).

[3] Although the term 'anti-discrimination law' originates from the US doctrine, it has since gained sufficient currency in literature and law courses around the globe to justify our decision to adopt this terminology for the present volume. Alternative terminology in recent literature for the same concept include 'EU law of equal opportunities', 'EU equality law', 'EU non-discrimination law' and even 'EU antidiscrimination law', where antidiscrimination is spelt as one word.

[4] Directive 2000/43 implementing the principle of equal treatment between persons irrespective of racial or ethnic origin [2000] OJ L180/22 (Race Equality Directive or RED); Directive 2000/78 establishing a general framework for equal treatment in employment and occupation [2000] OJ L3030/16 (Framework Equality Directive or FED).

[5] See, e.g. D Schiek, 'From European Union Anti-Discrimination Law towards Multidimensional Equality Law for Europe' in D Schiek and V Chege (eds), *European Union Non-Discrimination Law: Comparative Perspectives on Multidimensional Equality Law* (Abingdon, Routledge, 2009) 3–4.

[6] This is the reason why we symbolically chose a panel of the famous triptych by a Dutch painter Hieronymus Bosch, The Garden of Earthly Delights, as the cover image for this volume.

[7] As will be explained in more detail below, EU law has been treating rights of transsexuals within the cloisters of gender equality (Art 157 TFEU). Hence, this volume – which looks beyond gender jurisprudence – will focus mainly on gay and lesbian rights, and much less on the law regarding transsexuality. For latest account of the latter, see, *inter alia*, P Dunne, 'Towards Trans and Intersex Equality: Conflict or Complementarity?' in T Helms, A Dutta and J Scherpe (eds), *The Legal Status of Intersex Persons* (Antwerpen, Intersentia, 2018); J Scherpe (ed), *The Legal Status of Transgender and Transsexual Persons* (Antwerpen, Intersentia, 2015).

[8] Technically, the assessment should start from July 2003, when Member States undertook the obligation to transpose these instruments into national legislation.

[9] See European Commission, EU Action Against Discrimination: Activity Report 2007–2008 (Luxembourg, Office for Official Publications of the European Communities, 2009) Part 2.1.1. As noted

directives for many years.[10] Second, an impressive number of countries have joined the EU in the meantime (in 2004, 2007 and 2013), further complicating our assessment of maturity. Some of the new Member States have demonstrated notorious resistance to the Equality Directives, manifesting in a very long process of transposition.[11] Third, as will be demonstrated in this volume, the Court of Justice of the European Union (CJEU), the guardian of the European garden of equal delights, has – for a variety of reasons – delivered a rather modest number of cases on some of the newly introduced grounds (race and religion).[12]

Nevertheless, 18 years surely marks the arrival of an appropriate term to look back and ask the central question of this book – how EU anti-discrimination law has developed in relation to these grounds of discrimination that were added to gender and nationality, to cultivate what we term the 'Garden of Equal Delights'.[13] This volume, therefore, sets out to capture the striking developments and shortcomings that have emerged regarding the interpretation and implementation of relevant EU secondary law during the first two decades of the twenty-first century. Firstly, the book unfolds an up-to-date systemic appraisal of the state of (anti-discrimination) law regarding the five 'newer' grounds of discrimination, which have so far received mostly fragmented coverage. Secondly, and more generally, the volume captures the ways and the extent to which the Equality Directives have enabled or, at times prevented, the Court of Justice from developing an even broader and more refined anti-discrimination jurisprudence. Thus, the book offers a glimpse into the past, present and – hopefully – future of EU anti-discrimination law. Despite all the flaws in the Union's garden of equality delights, it still offers one of the highest standards of protection in comparative anti-discrimination law.[14]

Part 2 of this introductory chapter will first outline the genesis and main stages in the development of EU anti-discrimination law. The latter is by now undoubtedly an independent discipline within the narrative of EU law, not merely

by Barbara Havelková, for example, the Czech Anti-Discrimination Act which should have been in place at the time of accession by the Czech Republic to the EU in 2004, was only adopted and entered into force in 2009. See B Havelková, 'Resistance to Anti-Discrimination Law in Central and Eastern Europe: A Post-Communist Legacy?' (2016) 17 *German Law Journal* 627, 629.

[10] See also 'The Politics of Transposition in Britain, France, and Germany' in TE Givens and R Evans *Case, Legislating Equality: The Politics of Antidiscrimination Policy in Europe* (Oxford, Oxford University Press, 2014) 92–117.

[11] Havelková (n 9).

[12] The Court has delivered only two preliminary rulings regarding race and ethnic origin, and two regarding religious discrimination, the latter only in 2017.

[13] Since the Treaty of Amsterdam (1997), which first provided the grounds to legislate in this area on the EU level, and the Equality Directives 2000 that have followed.

[14] Many would even find this garden more fruitful than its American counterpart at the moment. See G De Burca, 'The Trajectories of European and American Antidiscrimination Law' (2012) 60 *American Journal of Comparative Law* 1. See also Croon's piece dismantling the myth about the terribly inconsistent application of the equality principle by the Court of Justice, in J Croon, 'Comparative Institutional Analysis, the European Court of Justice and the General Principle of Non-Discrimination – or – Alternative Tales on Equality Reasoning' (2013) 19 *European Law Journal* 153.

a component of EU labour law or an emanation of EU 'social rights'.[15] The Rome (1957), Amsterdam (1997) and Lisbon Treaties (2007) mark the central stages of our historical overview. Part 3 will focus on the major normative and practical themes emerging in EU anti-discrimination law after 2000. The themes that are picked up in this volume include the personal and material scope of the directives, new forms of discrimination and mechanisms to counteract discrimination (e.g., duty of reasonable accommodation) as well as the *proceduralisation* of EU anti-discrimination law, in particular through the proliferation of equality bodies. In addition, the limits of the current EU equality framework are discussed, such as in the areas of multiple discrimination, linguistic and Roma rights. The fourth part will summarise various accounts presented by our authors in their book chapters, considering wider normative problems and/or specific ground-related issues. Thoughts about the nature, achievements, challenges and limits of the current framework of the post-2000 EU anti-discrimination law are woven throughout the introduction, and are further reflected upon by Bruno de Witte in his epilogue.

II. A Brief History of EU Anti-Discrimination Law

It is common knowledge that the EU did not start as an organisation focused on fundamental rights.[16] Nor did it have or envisage developing a fully fledged system of anti-discrimination law, encompassing the complete panoply of dimensions stemming from the right to equal treatment and covering the full range of discrimination grounds.[17] It is equally obvious that the EU has come a long way since then, partly due to changes in the founding treaties that have enabled adoption of Equality Directives, partly due to the jurisprudence of the CJEU, interpreting the treaty and directive provisions and developing a 'daring' jurisprudence, as the principle of equal treatment is held to be a general principle of EU law.[18]

[15] The demarcation of EU anti-discrimination law beyond traditional French and German obsession with *droits sociaux* actually invites left-wing critique which insists on a more re-distributionist and de-commodifying approach to empower the poor, immunising them from market dependency. For a prominent example of this critique, see A Somek, *Engingeering Equality: An Essay on European Anti-Discrimination Law* (Oxford, Oxford University Press, 2011).

[16] See also S Smismans, 'The European Union's Fundamental Rights Myth' (2010) 48 *Journal of Common Market Studies* 45; P Alston, *The EU and Human Rights* (Oxford, Oxford University Press, 1999).

[17] See below for a more detailed account of the gradual expansion of grounds of discrimination in EU law. The absence of the prohibition of discrimination on grounds of race or ethnic origin when the Treaty of Rome created the European Economic Community in 1957 was only 'natural', given that half of its Member States (and a number of subsequently acceding) countries remained colonial empires at that time. About this aspect and the initially envisaged project of Eurafrique, see 'The Euroafrican Relaunch: The Rome Treaty Negotiations, 1955–1957' in P Hansen and S Jonsson, *The Unfolded History of European Integration and Colonialism* (London, Bloomsbury, 2010).

[18] See also S Prechal, 'Competence Creep and General Principles of Law' (2010) 3 *Review of European Administrative Law* 20.

This general principle of equality embodies Aristotle's formula of equal treatment, namely that one should treat like things alike, and unlike things differently to the extent of the difference.[19] This formula aptly captures the fact that, in some respects, one wants to be treated alike, while in others, one wants to be treated differently. In other words, sometimes differential treatment should be contested to vindicate the right to be treated the same, while in some circumstances being treated differently ensures that one's special characteristics are taken into account.[20] Regarding the former, it is essential to devise criteria to distinguish between legitimate differential treatment and prohibited discrimination. In this respect, EU law has famously chosen to develop different tracks for *direct* and *indirect* discrimination. Due to the different avenues of justification, the exact dividing line between these two types of discrimination remains of interest and is – frequently – the object of debate.[21] Other topics of ongoing controversy include positive action, more particularly when (i.e. under what conditions) this type of differential treatment would be legitimate.[22] Another related theme concerns the ambit of possible duties of differential treatment (i.e. those aimed at overcoming hurdles to the equal participation of persons that are, in some respects, different). The latter consideration is interlinked with questions about the implications of the prohibition of indirect discrimination and the scope of application of the duties of reasonable accommodation. Unsurprisingly, we return to the previously mentioned discussions in this edited volume, as it sets out to trace the achievements, flaws and future developments of EU anti-discrimination law since the landmark 2000 directives. Prior to embarking on that fascinating journey, this section takes stock of the history of EU equality law.

In outlining the evolution of EU anti-discrimination law, we broadly distinguish three phases[23] structured around the two defining moments of amendments to the founding treaties, namely the Treaty of Amsterdam (1997) and the Treaty of Lisbon (2007).

[19] Aristotle, *Nicomachean Ethics*, V.3.

[20] See, *inter alia*, K Henrard, Equal Rights versus Special Rights: Minority Protection and the Prohibition of Discrimination (Luxembourg, Office for Official Publications of the European Communities, 2007). See also S Fredman, *Discrimination Law* (Oxford, Oxford University Press, 2011); A Numhauser-Henning, Legal Perspectives on Equal Treatment and Non-discrimination (The Hague, Kluwer, 2001).

[21] See C Tobler, *Indirect Discrimination: A Case Study into the Development of the Legal Concept of Indirect Discrimination under EC Law* (Antwerpen, Intersentia, 2005).

[22] See, *inter alia*, M Bell and L Waddington, 'Exploring the Boundaries of Positive Action under EU Law: A Search for Conceptual Clarity' (2011) 48 *Common Market Law Review* 1503; D Caruso, 'Limits of the Classic Method; Positive Action in the European Union after the New Equality Directives' (2003) 44 *Harvard International Law Journal* 331; C O'Cinneide, 'Positive Action and the Limits of Existing Law' (2006) 13 *Maastricht Journal of European and Comparative Law* 351.

[23] Note that Ellis and Watson also identify three phases, while distinguishing as the second phase the period between 1987 and 1997 due to the multiple amendments of the EEC treaty during that time, as well as the significant stream of judgments produced by the CJEU (see also below on the central role of the Court in the development of EU anti-discrimination law) – see E Ellis and P Watson, *EU Anti-Discrimination Law*, 2nd edn (Oxford, Oxford University Press, 2012). For reasons that will be more fully explained later, we identify the three phases on the basis of the EEC Treaty, the Amsterdam Treaty and the Lisbon Treaty.

A. Phase 1 – Prior to the Treaty of Amsterdam (1958–1999)

Turning to the three phases that can be distinguished in the development of EU anti-discrimination law, the first phase begins with the adoption of the EEC Treaty in 1957 and its entry into force in 1958. From the start, the right to equal treatment played an instrumental role in the construction and development of the European (Economic) Community (EC).[24] The original rationale for including a prohibition of discrimination was the realisation of the single economic market.[25] This is clearly visible in the grounds of discrimination that were included in the original EEC Treaty, giving the EC competence to legislate on nationality and gender. Indeed, 'nationality' as prohibited grounds of discrimination (Article 12 EEC, now Article 18 TFEU) only concerns the citizenship of an EU Member State and is intended to eliminate the disadvantageous treatment of persons in one EU country holding the nationality of another EU country. In this respect, it has correctly been pointed out that the prohibition of discrimination on the basis of nationality was intended to support and realise the free movement rights of persons, services, goods and capital lying at the heart of the common market project.[26] Working, providing services or offering goods for sale should not be made more complicated for persons coming from another EU Member State as compared to the own nationals of a country. Otherwise, this would jeopardise the realisation of the common market, that being predicated on a free, unimpeded flow of persons, services, goods and capital (financial flows in payment for services, goods, etc.).[27] Similarly, the inclusion of an (at first sight) very limited version of gender discrimination prohibition, namely one confined to equal pay (Article 119 EEC, now Article 157 TFEU)[28] can also be understood from this 'internal market' perspective. It was simply meant to prevent competitive advantages for countries where women are not paid as well as men.[29]

Since the Treaty of Rome, notwithstanding the humble status of the equality principle therein, the prohibition of gender discrimination has experienced

[24] See also, in relation to the EU, J Shaw, *Mainstreaming Equality in European Union Law and Policy Making* (Brussels, ENAR, 2004) 2: 'in one guise or another, the concept of equality has always been central to the evolving legal order of the EU'.

[25] See also M Bell, *Anti-Discrimination Law and the European Union* (Oxford, Oxford University Press, 2002) 6–12.

[26] Ellis and Watson (n 23) 2.

[27] Art 39 EEC Treaty, now Art 45 TFEU.

[28] Also referenced in literature as Art 141 EEC Treaty in the Treaty nomenclature during the period between Maastricht (1992) and Lisbon (2007) Treaties.

[29] As Mark Bell highlights, 'the French delegation had identified differences in national legislation on equal pay for men and women as being likely to disturb the balance of trade in the common market'. This reasoning was built on the premise that countries that do not protect equal pay for women can reduce their production costs due to their reliance on cheap female labour – see Bell (n 25) 8. See also S Roth (ed), *Gender Politics in the Expanding European Union: Mobilisation, Inclusion, Exclusion* (New York, Berghahn, 2008); D Schieck, 'Broadening the Scope and the Norms of EU Gender Equality' (2005) 12 *Maastricht Journal of European and Comparative Law* 427.

an impressive expansion. Few scholars could have imagined in the 1950s that the laconic provision of Article 119 EEC would pave the way to the far-reaching ambit of the prohibition of gender discrimination we know today, covering not only labour law and social rights, but also translating into the regulation of sex work, the prohibition of domestic violence and of human trafficking.[30] All the principal EU institutions (the CJEU, the Council, the Commission and the Parliament) have at various times and to varying degrees taken part in this development.[31]

The epoch of the 1970s was crucial for anti-discrimination law, as this was the period when the CJEU, through several preliminary rulings, provided effective protection against discrimination, not only on grounds of nationality, but also on grounds of gender. Through these preliminary rulings, the Court introduced (and applied) direct effect for several Treaty articles that were clearly directed at Member States, thus allowing action against those that had not managed or did not have the political will to turn these into fully fledged legislative programmes before the end of the transitional period on 31 December 1969.[32] In the process, the Court fostered the emancipation of EU gender equality. That legal space has been successfully mobilised in the advocacy of feminist cause litigators and social movements.[33] On the basis of the direct effect of Article 119 EEC, the Court has since developed its doctrine of sex equality as a general principle of EU law.[34]

Over the last 30 years, the EU has passed nine directives on gender equality which closely reflect the CJEU's judgments on the topic.[35] The activist Luxembourg

[30] See U Belavusau, 'EU Sexual Citizenship: Sex Beyond the Internal Market' in D Kochenov (ed), *EU Citizenship and Federalism: The Role of Rights* (Cambridge, Cambridge University Press, 2017) 417–442.

[31] ibid.

[32] M Rasmussen, 'How to Enforce European law? A New History of the Battle over the Direct Effect of Directives' (2017) 23 *European Law Journal* 290.

[33] One of the earliest examples is Elaine Vogel-Polsky, the lawyer who litigated the landmark *Defrenne* cases (1971, 1976 and 1978). Case 80/70 *Defrenne I* EU:C:1971:55; Case 43/75 *Defrenne II* EU:C:1976:56; Case 149/77 *Defrenne III* EU:C:1978:130. The first equality case was adjudicated in Luxembourg in the 1970s – Case 43/75 *Defrenne II*, while primary law did not offer any anti-discrimination provisions apart from Art 141 EEC which maintained that men and women should enjoy equal pay for equal work. Vogel-Polsky, who used the Defrenne saga to mainstream gender non-discrimination in EU law, supported Ms Defrenne, the plaintiff employed as a flight attendant. She was essentially the first to question whether Art 119 EEC had direct effect. See E Vogel-Polsky, 'L'article 119 du traité de Rome peut-il être considéré comme self-exécutant?' [1967] *Journal des tribunaux* 233. About Vogel-Polsky, see the book by E Gubin and C Jacques, Eliane Vogel-Polsky (Brussels, Institute for the Equality of Women and Men, 2007).

[34] In this respect, the jurisprudence of the Court in the follow-up phases described below is different, since it could not rely on the direct effect of Article 19 TFEU (Art 13 TEC), which was designed by the Amsterdam Treaty as clearly requiring the adoption of secondary legislation to be effective. Thus, the Equality Directives 2000 are central in understanding the structure and development of EU anti-discrimination law beyond gender.

[35] Of particular relevance (and in part inspirational for 2000 Equality Directives) are: Council Directive 75/117/EEC on the approximation of the laws of the Member States relating to the application of the principle of equal pay for men and women [1975] OJ L45/19; Council Directive 76/207/EEC on the implementation of the principle of equal treatment for men and women as regards access

Court has extended the primary law provision by interpreting the gender aspects of equal pay to include pension and social guarantees for men and women, as well as regulations regarding pregnancy and child-raising.[36] Arguably, the Court's activist interpretation in this period culminated in its rulings on transsexuals. Indeed, in the 1996 judgment *P v S*,[37] the Court interpreted the provision on the equality of men and women as applying to cases of gender reassignment.[38]

to employment, vocational training and promotion, and working conditions [1976] OJ L39/40; Council Directive on the progressive implementation of the principle of equal treatment for men and women in matters of social security [1978] OJ L6/24; Council Directive 86/378/EEC on the implementation of the principle of equal treatment for men and women in occupational social security schemes [1986] OJ L225/40; Council Directive 86/613/EEC on the application of the principle of equal treatment between men and women engaged in an activity, including agriculture, in a self-employed capacity, and on the protection of self-employed women during pregnancy and motherhood [1986] OJ L359/56; Council Directive 92/85/EEC on the introduction of measures to encourage improvements in the safety and health at work of pregnant workers and workers who have recently given birth or are breastfeeding (tenth individual Directive within the meaning of Article 16(1) of Directive 89/391/EEC) [1992] OJ L348/1; Council Directive 96/34/EC on the framework agreement on parental leave concluded by UNICE, CEEP and the ETUC [1996] OJ L145/4; Council Directive 97/80/EC on the burden of proof in cases of discrimination based on sex [1997] OJ L14/6; Directive 2002/73/EC of the European Parliament and of the Council amending Council Directive 76/207/EEC on the implementation of the principle of equal treatment for men and women as regards access to employment, vocational training and promotion, and working conditions (Text with EEA relevance) [2002] OJ L269/15 (substantially amending the 1976 Equal Treatment Directive adding definitions of indirect discrimination, harassment and sexual harassment and requiring Member States to set up equality bodies to promote, analyse, monitor and support equal treatment between women and men); Council Directive 2004/113/EC implementing the principle of equal treatment between men and women in the access to and supply of goods and services [2004] OJ L373/37; Directive 2006/54/EC of the European Parliament and of the Council on the implementation of the principle of equal opportunities and equal treatment of men and women in matters of employment and occupation (recast) [2006] OJ L204/23 (Equal Treatment Directive) (to enhance the transparency, clarity and coherence of the law, this directive was adopted in 2006, putting the existing provisions on equal pay, occupational schemes and 'the burden of proof' into a single text).

[36] About case law regarding pregnancy and child-raising, see U Belavusau, 'From Lëtzebuerg to Luxembourg: EU Law, Non-Discrimination and Pregnancy' (2010) 2 *European Law Reporter* 45. The CJEU's progressive stance on gender equality during this phase seems to echo a corresponding liberalisation at the European Court of Human Rights, making European law an important arena for the refinement of gender citizenship: S Besson, 'Gender Discrimination under EU and ECHR Law' (2008) 8 *Human Rights Law Review* 647; D Martin, 'Strasbourg, Luxembourg et la discrimination: influences croisées ou jurisprudences sous influence?' (2007) 69 *Revue Trimestrielle des Droits de l'Homme* 132.

[37] Case C-13/94 *P v S* EU:C:1996:170. Also pertinent in this context is Case C-117/01 *KB* EU:C:2004:7.

[38] Discrimination of transsexuals since then has been treated as an aspect of gender equality, as incorporated into Directive 2006/54/EC, Recital 3 Preamble: 'The Court of Justice has held that the scope of the principle of equal treatment for men and women cannot be confined to the prohibition of discrimination based on the fact that a person is of one or other sex. In view of its purpose and the nature of rights which it seeks to safeguard, it also applies to discrimination arising from the gender reassignment of a person.' In June 2010, the European Parliament adopted a resolution (the 'Figueiredo Report') calling for an inclusive EU gender equality strategy, specifically addressing issues linked to gender identity – I Figueiredo, European Parliament, 'Report on the assessment of the results of the 2006–2010 Roadmap for equality between women and men, and forward-looking recommendations' (2009/2242 (INI)).

B. Phase Two: The Treaty of Amsterdam until Lisbon (1999–2009)

The second phase was kick-started with the Treaty of Amsterdam (signed in 1997, entered into force in 1999). This was, in at least two ways, extremely important for the development of EU anti-discrimination law. First of all, gender equality was mainstreamed, with Article 3(2) TEC (now Article 8 TFEU) stipulating that in all of its activities, the European Community 'shall aim to eliminate inequalities, and to promote equality, between men and women'.[39] This significantly strengthened the prohibition of discrimination on the basis of gender as it raised constant awareness of potential discriminatory effects policies and legislation may have for women.

Secondly, the Treaty finally multiplied the protected grounds of discrimination, while establishing EU legislative competence in relation to five new grounds – race and ethnicity, religion, disability, age and sexual orientation.[40] This extension in protected grounds clearly implied a move for EU anti-discrimination law beyond the common market rationale towards a more social ethos.[41] In fact, the extension of grounds covering prohibited discrimination also signifies the importance of the right to equal treatment in securing human dignity.[42] This shift, in turn, linked perfectly with the more central role of human rights in the EU, clearly articulated previously by the Treaty of Maastricht (1992) and figuring as a true core of the EU in the Treaty of Amsterdam (1997), thus building on the CJEU's

[39] Cf. Original Art 119 EEC: 'Men and women should enjoy equal pay for equal work.' Art 157 TFEU (original Art 119 EEC) is now incomparably broader than Art 19 TFEU which has given rise to the 2000 Equality Directives. Art 157 TFEU states:

1. Each Member State shall ensure that the principle of equal pay for male and female workers for equal work or work of equal value is applied.
2. For the purpose of this article, 'pay' means the ordinary basic or minimum wage or salary and any other consideration, whether in cash or in kind, which the worker receives, directly or indirectly, in respect of his employment, from his employer.

Equal pay without discrimination based on sex means:

(a) that pay for the same work at piece rates shall be calculated on the basis of the same unit of measurement;
(b) that pay for work at time rates shall be the same for the same job.

3. The Council, acting in accordance with the procedure referred to in Article 251, and after consulting the Economic and Social Committee, shall adopt measures to ensure the application of the principle of equal opportunities and equal treatment of men and women in matters of employment and occupation, including the principle of equal pay for equal work or work of equal value.

[40] Art 13 TEC, now Art 19 TFEU.

[41] This is one of the central themes in the monograph by Bell, *Anti-Discrimination Law* (n 25).

[42] In this period, the CJEU only rarely referred to human dignity as underlying the right to equal treatment, e.g. in Case C-13/94 *P v S* (n 37) para 22.

recognition that respect for human rights amounted to a general principle of EU law.[43] Furthermore, Article 19 TFEU (introducing new grounds of equality beyond gender) found its domicile in Part Two of the Treaty, entitled 'Non-Discrimination and Citizenship of the Union'. In this respect, the project of EU anti-discrimination law is joined with the wider vision of citizenship formation in the Union, with equality becoming a distinctive feature of EU citizenship not only horizontally amongst nationals of Member States but also vertically amongst different groups of citizens inside Member States.[44]

The coming into force of the Treaty of Amsterdam in 1999 was quickly followed by the adoption of two watershed directives, the first focusing on race (Race Equality Directive, RED), the second on the other four new grounds (Framework Equality Directive, FED) introduced in Article 13 TEC (now Article 19 TFEU). The impressively speedy and smooth adoption of these instruments has been hailed in the literature.[45] It can be attributed to the combination of a certain post-Amsterdam optimism regarding equality matters in the Union amongst then centre-left elites, on the one hand, and the willingness to counteract xenophobia following the rise of radical right in the Austrian elections, on the other.[46] This is also the epoch when a separate mechanism was introduced in Article 7 TEU, aimed at ensuring, through early warning and sanctioning, that Member States respect the fundamental values of the EU, including the rule of law.[47] The speedy adoption of these Equality Directives was equally a pragmatic necessity in light of the impending Eastern enlargement. On the one hand, the adoption of these directives was expected to become more difficult in a Council of Ministers comprising many more Member States, several of which with post-communist baggage (e.g. CEE countries) or conservative elites (e.g. Cyprus or Malta). On the other hand, the swift adoption of these directives would make them part of the Union equality *acquis*, with which the acceding states would have to comply by virtue of the Copenhagen conditionality.[48] Nonetheless, Eastern European States were not

[43] About the principle of equality, see B de Witte, 'From a Common Principle of Equality to European Antidiscrimination Law' (2010) 53 *American Behavioral Scientist* 1715. Interestingly, the follow-up Equality Directives of 2000 refer to Art 6 TEU as inspiration in their Preambles, see eg Recital (2) in the Preamble to Race Equality Directive.

[44] See also B de Witte, 'The Crumbling Public/Private Divide: Horizontality in European Anti-Discrimination Law' (2009) 13 *Citizenship Studies* 515.

[45] See e.g. B de Witte, 'National Equality Institutions and the Domestication of EU Non-Discrimination Law' (2011) 18 *Maastricht Journal of European and Comparative Law* 157, 161; R Evans Case and TE Givens, 'Re-Engineering Legal Opportunity Structures in the European Union? The Starting Line Group and the Politics of the Racial Equality Directive' (2010) 48 *Journal of Common Market Studies* 221; Bell (n 25).

[46] In 2000, Jörg Haider's Freedom Party unexpectedly became second after the Social Democrats (SPÖ) in the Austrian parliamentary elections.

[47] W Sadurski, 'Adding Bite to a Bark: The Story of Article 7, EU Enlargement and Jörg Haider' (2010) 16 *Columbia Journal of European Law* 385.

[48] The correctness of this political prediction was later confirmed by the vivid resistance of a number of new Member States, many of whom have delayed transposition or have faced significant criticism regarding the way they have transposed Equality Directives. See Havelková (n 9).

the only ones delaying and resisting the new machinery of EU anti-discrimination law.[49] German legal elites, often a driving force behind EU federalism, gradually became sceptical too, especially in the wake of the CJEU's jurisprudence on age discrimination.[50]

The ensuing case law during this second phase was not as abundant as expected for several of the five additional grounds. Nevertheless, this phase did generate some landmark judgments,[51] such as *Mangold* (2005),[52] recognising the principle of non-discrimination on grounds of age as a general principle of Community law and *Coleman* (2008),[53] establishing 'discrimination by association', thus further extending the reach of EU anti-discrimination law. The first – for many years also the only – race equality judgment of the Court of Justice, *Feryn* (2008),[54] was also decided at the very end of this period along with *Maruko* (2008),[55] concerning the grounds of sexuality in the Framework Equality Directive.

C. Phase 3: Lisbon and Beyond (2009 to Present)

The Lisbon Treaty (signed in 2007, entered into force in 2009) unfolded the third phase of EU anti-discrimination law, giving an even stronger central position to the principles of equality and non-discrimination.[56] In addition to several other prominent references to equality in the core Treaty provisions,[57] Article 10 TFEU enshrines a general obligation to mainstream the right to equal treatment in relation to all grounds.[58] Albeit programmatic, this central and outspoken position for the right to equal treatment within EU law goes hand-in-hand with a stronger

[49] In 2007, the Commission was pursuing legal proceedings against no fewer than 14 Member States for belated or incomplete implementation of RED and against 11 Member States related to the transposition of FED.

[50] In this regard, scholars cite an emblematic statement by H Ladeur, the Dean of Law Faculty at Hamburg University, who suggested '[t]hat [the Anti-Discrimination Law] shall be integrated into the [German Civil Code] with its dear systematic liberal approach, one of the masterpieces of European legal culture, has to be regarded as an act of legal vandalism' (see TE Givens and R Evans *Case, Legislating Equality* (n 10) 92). See also below on Germany's resistance to the Commission proposal for a new equality directive on the same grounds as Directive 2000/78.

[51] Sometimes these pioneering judgments were even called 'explosive' (see T Uyen Do, 'A Case Odyssey into 10 Years of Anti-Discrimination Law' (2011) 12 *European Anti-Discrimination Law Review* 12).

[52] Case C-144/04 *Werner Mangold v Rudiger Helm* EU:C:2005:709.

[53] Case C-303/06 *Coleman v Attridge Law and Steve Law* EU:C:2008:415.

[54] Case C-54/07 *Centrum voor de Gelijkheid van Kansen en Racismebestrijding v firma Feryn BV* EU:C:2008:397.

[55] Case C-267/06 *Maruko v Versorgungsanstalt der deutschen buhnen* EU:C:2008:179.

[56] Ellis and Watson (n 23) 13.

[57] Arts 2, 3, 4, 9 and 21 TEU and Arts 8, 153(1) and 157(4) TFEU. See also R Zahn, *The EU Lisbon Treaty: What Implications for Anti-Racism?* (Brussels, ENAR, 2009) 11.

[58] Art 10 TFEU has been called 'the most significant commitment to promoting equality outside the framework of the rights-based model': D Chalmers, G Davies and G Monti, *European Union Law: Texts and Materials*, (Cambridge, Cambridge University Press, 2014) 618.

position for human rights within the EU. Indeed, the Lisbon Treaty made the EU Charter of Fundamental Rights (Charter, CFR)[59] part of primary EU law and thus legally binding.[60]

It should be acknowledged, however, that the Charter already had a certain influence on the development of EU law prior to the Lisbon Treaty,[61] even though it was initially merely invoked as additional support, affirming rights already enshrined in EU law through general principles.[62] While the influence of the Charter on the development of EU (human rights) law increased steadily over time,[63] since Lisbon, the instrument has been exponentially relied upon by the CJEU, also in more bold ways.[64] Even if Article 6(1) TEU underscores that the Charter's status as primary law will not imply an extension of the competences of the Union as defined in the treaties, it has aptly been pointed out that the Charter's status will breathe new life into the EU competences by focusing on the rights of the individual with regard to all EU policies.[65] An entire chapter (III) of the Charter is, in fact, dedicated to 'equality' and covers broader anti-discrimination law, including a general provision on equality before the law (Article 20 CFR) as well as a provision obliging the Union to respect cultural, religious and linguistic diversity (Article 22 CFR).

It remains to be seen how the CJEU will use the non-discrimination clause enshrined in Article 21 CFR, since this prohibits 'any discrimination based on *any ground, such as* sex, race, colour, ethnic or social origin, genetic features, language,

[59] Charter of Fundamental Rights of the European Union [2016] OJ C202/2.

[60] Art 6(1) TEU.

[61] It was indeed almost immediately picked up by Advocates General in their opinions (e.g. Case C-173/99 *BECTU v Secretary of State for Trade and Industry* EU:C:2001:81, *Opinion of AG Tizzano*, paras 27–28), swiftly followed by the Court of First Instance (Case T-54/99 *Max Mobil Telekommunkation Service GmbH v Commission* EU:T:2002:20, paras 48 and 57) and, from 2006 onwards, also by the CJEU, more particularly since Case C-540/03 *European Parliament v Council* EU:C:2006:429. See also Case C-432/05 *Unibet* EU:C:2007:163, para 37; Case C-438/05 *Viking Line* EU:C:2007:772 and the discussion in S Peers, 'The EU Charter of Rights and the Right to Equality' (2011) 11 *ERA Forum* 571. The fact that the Community legislator itself had referred to the Charter in the Directive at issue in the latter case presumably helped persuade the Court to similarly acknowledge the Charter's existence. Indeed, the Court highlighted that 'while the Charter is not a legally binding instrument, the Community legislator did, however, acknowledge its importance by stating, in the second recital in the preamble to the Directive, that the Directive observes the principles recognised not only by Article 8 of the ECHR but also in the Charter' – Case C-540/03 *European Parliament v Council*, para 38.

[62] Peers (n 61) 572. See also EF Defeis, 'The Treaty of Lisbon and Human Rights' (2010) 16 *ILSA Journal of International & Comparative Law* 416.

[63] Defeis (n 62) 416.

[64] Judge Safjan notes that the Charter is relied upon to 'influence the process of interpretation, of determination of the very content of particular norms, their extent and legal consequences, and thus they provide for the enlargement of the field of application of the European rules in the national legal orders'. See M Safjan, 'Fields of Application of the Charter of Fundamental Rights and Constitutional Dialogues in the European Union', *EUI LAW*, Centre for Judicial Cooperation, DL, 2014/2, 2.

[65] F Ferraro and J Carmona, *Fundamental Rights in the EU: The Role of the Charter after the Lisbon Treaty* (European Parliamentary Research Service, 2015) 3.

religion or belief, political or any other opinion, membership of a national minority, property, birth, disability, age or sexual orientation'. While this opens the door for any ground of discrimination, several grounds of interest are explicitly added in Article 21 of the Charter (in comparison to the already-existing palette of grounds outlined in TEU and TFEU), such as 'language', 'membership of a national minority', and 'genetic features'. While the treaties may not contain provisions for legislating over these additional grounds, Article 51 CFR does stipulate that the principles set out in the Charter should guide the development of EU policies and the implementation of these policies by national authorities.[66] Hence, difficult questions may arise before the CJEU when EU legislation and policies (and/or the national implementation thereof) have disproportionate effects on groups defined on these additional grounds of discrimination. In this respect, questions surrounding the status of third country nationals may (re)surface.

At the level of secondary equality legislation, the Union in this third phase has so far failed to adopt an updated directive proposed by the Commission in 2008 – the Council Directive Implementing the Principle of Equal Treatment between Persons Irrespective of Religion or Belief, Disability, Age or Sexual Orientation.[67] This proposal aims to extend the material scope of application of the prohibition of discrimination to the fields of education, social protection (including healthcare and social security), social advantages and access to goods and services (including housing), thus remedying the disparities in scope of application of the prohibition of discrimination on grounds of race (and gender). The envisaged directive also for the first time attempted to introduce specific provisions about multiple discrimination and to extend the prohibition of discrimination to transport.

Strikingly, and unlike the smoothly adopted 2000 Directives, this Commission proposal has been burdened by several unsuccessful negotiation rounds, reflecting a changed political climate. The changing wind has brought vivid resistance from several Member States with a range of concerns.[68] In comparison with the 2000 Directives, the negotiating parties have grown exponentially in numbers, proportionately augmenting the potential for disagreement. The rise

[66] For an analysis of what the phrase 'implementing Union law' in Art 51 CFR means, see eg G de Búrca, 'The Drafting of the European Union Charter of Fundamental Rights' (2001) 26 *European Law Review* 136.

[67] Commission of the European Communities, Proposal for a Council Directive Implementing the Principle of Equal Treatment between Persons Irrespective of Religion or Belief, Disability, Age or Sexual Orientation, COM(2008) 426 final; Commission staff working document accompanying the proposal for a Council directive on implementing the principle of equal treatment between persons irrespective of religion or belief, disability, age or sexual orientation – Summary of the impact assessment (COM(2008) 426 final), SEC(2008) 2180.

[68] M Bell, 'The Principle of Equal Treatment: Widening and Deepening' in P Craig and G de Búrca (eds), *The Evolution of EU Law* (Oxford, Oxford University Press, 2011) 620.

in right-wing governments,[69] as opposed to the predominance of central-left political forces at the turn of the century, further explains the increased resistance against progressive expansions of the anti-discrimination norm. Some Member States, including such influential players as Germany, view the proposed directive as an encroachment on national competences, also with a view to subsidiarity considerations.[70] Particular resistance is noted among certain Member States regarding the inclusion of social protection and education in the scope *ratione materiae* of the proposed directive.[71] Given the requirement of unanimity in the Council for the adoption of this directive under Article 19 TFEU, actual progress in this respect seems indiscernible at the moment.

Grounds	**Phase One (1958–1999)**	**Phase Two (1999–2009)**	**Phase Three (2009–...)**
Gender Equality	(a) Art 119 EEC (a fairly general single provision)	(a) Art 141 TEC (expansion of the provision)	(a) Art 157 TFEU (Parliament receives a role in adoption of the secondary legislation)
	(b) Secondary legislation (examples of directives)	(b) Secondary legislation (examples of directives)	(b) Charter of Fundamental Rights receiving status of primarily law (Art 23 equality between men and women)
	(c) Active jurisprudence of the Court of Justice on gender equality, based on the extensive interpretation of the general principle of equality	(c) CJEU jurisprudence	(c) Secondary legislation (examples of directives and regulations currently at place)
			(d) CJEU jurisprudence

[69] See, *inter alia*, A Chakelian, 'Rise of the Nationalists: A Guide to Europe's Far-right Parties' (New Statesman, 8 March 2017). Available at: www.newstatesman.com/world/europe/2017/03/rise-nationalists-guide-europe-s-far-right-parties.

[70] Presidency of the Council of the EU, Proposal for a Council Directive on implementing the principle of equal treatment between persons irrespective of religion or belief, disability, age or sexual orientation – Progress Report, 14867/17 (24 November 2017) 2–4. Some of the states raising concerns have good track records in terms of anti-discrimination law (and human rights more generally), such as Germany. See also above about initial optimism and subsequent disillusions of such states with regard to the 2000 Directives.

[71] See also M Bell, 'Advancing EU Anti-Discrimination Law: the European Commission's 2008 Proposal for a New Directive' (2009) 3 *Equal Rights Review* 7, 11–13.

Grounds	Phase One (1958–1999)	Phase Two (1999–2009)	Phase Three (2009–...)
Race and ethnicity, religion, sexual orientation, age, disability	(a) No provisions in primary law	(a) Art 13 TEC	(a) Art 19 TFEU
	(b) CJEU case law on transsexuals	(b) Adoption of the two key Equality Directives in 2000	(b) Charter of Fundamental Rights receiving status of primarily law (Chapter III on equality and other relevant provisions)
	(c) Failure to frame sexual orientation as a part of gender equality	(c) First jurisprudence of the Court regarding 2000 Directives (C-144/04 *Mangold* 2005, C-54/07 *Feryn* 2008, etc.)	(c) EU becomes party to the UN Convention on the Rights of Persons with Disabilities
	(d) Episodic reference to race, religion and other grounds		(d) Intensification of the Court's jurisprudence on Equality Directives 2000
Other grounds (eg linguistic rights, intersection between anti-discrimination law and rights of EU citizens, multiple discrimination)	(a) CJEU jurisprudence regarding right to a name (C-168/91 *Konstantinidis* 1992)	(a) Permissive stage in CJEU jurisprudence regarding right to a name (C-148/02 *Garcia Avello* 2003)	(a) Charter of Fundamental Rights receiving status of primarily law (Art 1 on dignity and several other grounds added, eg 'language', 'membership of a national minority', 'property' and 'political or any other opinion' and 'genetic features)
	(b) Language rights of EU citizens	(b) Language rights of EU citizens	(b) Restrictive stage in CJEU jurisprudence regarding right to a name (C-208/09 *Von Wittgenstein* 2010, C-391/09 *Wardyn* 2011)[72]

[72] About 'permissive' and 'restrictive' stages in the Court's jurisprudence about right to name, see chapter by D Kochenov in the present volume.

D. Overarching Development Trends

Throughout the three outlined phases, a steady growth of commitment to the principle of equality can be detected.[73] As highlighted above, a constant feature underpinning these three phases reveals the central influence of the CJEU's jurisprudence on the development of EU non-discrimination law. Indeed, Treaty provisions and secondary legislation are often vague, and contain ill-defined concepts, thus requiring clarification through jurisprudence. In this respect, it is important to acknowledge that EU anti-discrimination law projects a somewhat thin line between interpretation and application, on the one hand, and law-making, on the other.[74]

In the end, it is jurisprudence, and ultimately the CJEU's case law, that demarcates the reach of these concepts and rules, and also the level of protection that is provided against unjustified differential treatment.[75] The CJEU is known for its teleological interpretation, aimed at effective protection against discrimination.[76] The CJEU's determined and sustained approach in this respect is, *inter alia*, visible in its jurisprudence on non-discrimination concepts, its move towards substantive equality (beyond mere formal equality), particularly through the development of the notion of indirect discrimination and its softening approach as regards positive action measures.[77] Similarly, the Court's recognition of the right to equal treatment and the prohibition of discrimination as general principled of EU law,[78] and – last but not least – its case law on procedural requirements and remedies merit highlighting here.[79]

The Court has often underscored that since equality of treatment is a fundamental objective of both Treaty provisions and implementing legislation, a broad purposeful approach is required.[80] A prominent example of the Court's embrace

[73] Ellis and Watson (n 23) 495.

[74] See, *inter alia*, A Van Bogdandy and I Venzke, 'On the Functions of International Courts: An Appraisal in Light of their Burgeoning Public Authority' ACIL Research Paper 2012/10, 9 and 19; A Guzman, 'The Consent Problem in International Law', Berkeley Program in Law and Economics Working Paper Series 2011, 55. See also V Tzevelekos, 'Juris Dicere: Custom as a Matrix, Custom as a Norm and the Role of Judges and their Ideology in Custom Making' in NM Rajkovic, T Aalberts and T Gammeltoft-Hansen (eds), *Power of Legality: Practices of International Law and their Politics* (Cambridge, Cambridge University Press, 2011) 191, 206.

[75] See, *inter alia*, Ellis and Watson (n 23) 501–2.

[76] ibid, 498.

[77] Case C-96/80 *JP Jenkins v Kingsgate (Clothing Productions) Ltd* EU:C:1981:80; Case C-170/84 *Bilka – Kaufhaus GmbH v Karin Weber von Hartz* EU:C:1986:204; Case C-127/92 *Enderby v Frenchay Health Authority and Secretary of State for Health* EU:C:1993:859. Regarding the CJEU's softening approach towards positive action see, *inter alia*, Case C-476/99 *H Lommers v Minister van Landbouw Natuurbeheer en Visserij* EU:C:2002:183.

[78] Joined cases 117/76 and 16/77 *Albert Ruckdeschel & Co. and Hansa-Lagerhaus Ströh & Co v Hauptzollamt Hamburg-St Annen; Diamalt AG v Hauptzollamt Itzehoe* EU:C:1977:160; Case C-283/83 *Firma A Racke v Hauptzollamt Mainz* EU:C:1984:344; Case C-15/95 *EARL de Kerlast v Union régionale de coopératives agricoles (Unicopa) and Coopérative du Trieux* EU:C:1997:196; Case C-292/97 *Kjell Karlson and Others* EU:C:2000:202.

[79] See, *inter alia*, Joined cases C-231/06 to C-233/06 *Office nationale des pensions* EU:C:2007:373; Case C-81/12 *Asociaţia Accept v Consiliul Naţional pentru Combaterea Discriminării* EU:C:2013:275, para 61.

[80] See, *inter alia*, Joined cases C-75/82 and C-117/82 *Razzouk and Beydoun v Commission* EU:C:1984:116, para 16. See also Case C-147/80 *Römer v Freie und Hansestadt Hamburg* EU:C:2011:286;

of substantive equality is its development of the concept of *indirect discrimination*, thus significantly enlarging the reach of the prohibition of discrimination.[81] The Court's judgments in *Mangold* (2005)[82] that has sparked controversy in certain circles in Germany,[83] and more recently in *Test-Achats* (2011),[84] as well as the daring way in which it employs the right to equal treatment as a general principle of EU law, shows a judiciary set on protecting the right to equal treatment as best it can.[85] This approach is similarly confirmed by the consistent jurisprudence on a restrictive, rigorous interpretation of (provisions concerning) exceptions and derogations to the non-discrimination principle. Equally essential is how the Court clarifies the sharing of the burden of proof in discrimination cases, thus effectuating the reduction of the (traditionally often insurmountable) burden of proof on behalf of the victim.[86] Importantly, also in light of the development of a coherent body of EU anti-discrimination law, the CJEU has taken care to use common interpretation techniques and to treat common issues consistently across the distinctive grounds of discrimination.[87] The following section will elaborate upon several of the related 'major trends and themes'.

III. Major Trends and Themes since the Adoption of the 2000 Equality Directives

A. Disproportionality amongst Grounds of Discrimination in CJEU Jurisprudence

Our assessment of the major trends and themes emerging since the adoption of the 2000 Equality Directives is based foremost on the activities of the Court of

Case C-150/85 *Jacqueline Drake v Chief Adjudication Officer* EU:C:1986:257; Case C-303/06 *Coleman* (n 53). See also C O'Cinneide, 'The Constitutionalization of Equality within the EU Legal Order: Sexual Orientation as a Testing Ground'. (2015) 22 *Maastricht Journal of European and Comparative Law* 370, 371.

[81] See, *inter alia*, Case C-237/94 *O' Flynn v Adjudication Officer* EU:C:1996:206; Case C-96/80 *Jenkins* (n 77).

[82] Case C-144/04 *Mangold* (n 52). See also the chapters by R Horton and B ter Haar in the present volume.

[83] See, *inter alia*, IP Berlin, 'Mangold v Helm – ECJ Case C-144/04: Did the Court Gets it Wrong?', presentation at the 9th ECLN-Conference, EUI Florence, 18–19 November 2013; L Waddington, 'Recent Developments and the Non-Discrimination Directives: Mangold and More' (2006) 13 *Maastricht Journal of European and Comparative Law* 365. See also T Ćapeta, 'The Advocate General: Bringing Clarity to CJEU Decisions? A Case-Study of Mangold and Kücükdeveci' (2012) 14 *Cambridge Yearbook of European Legal Studies* 563.

[84] Case C-236/09 *Association Belge des Consommateurs Test-Achats ASBL and Others v Conseil des ministers* EU:C:2011:100.

[85] Ellis and Watson (n 23) 508.

[86] See the chapter by K Henrard in the present volume.

[87] This commonality in approach across the distinctive grounds of discrimination allows for the identification and discussion of 'key concepts in EU anti-discrimination law', such as direct and indirect discrimination or burden of proof, as is reflected in textbooks on EU anti-discrimination law, eg Ellis and Watson (n 23) Chapter 4.

Justice, which – as has been shown in the historical exploration above – has traditionally played a most activist role in sustaining the rise of its anti-discrimination law. Yet such a court-centric perspective suffers from a natural limitation. Before drawing a wider picture of the post-2000 EU anti-discrimination law, we have to keep this limitation in mind: namely that the number of judgments delivered by the CJEU with regard to the five 'new' equality grounds – added by Article 19 TFEU and the 2000 Equality Directives – has been anything but equal. Gender equality still remains the most *judicialised* aspect of equality in Luxembourg, often setting a comparative paradigm for dealing with the other five non-discrimination grounds. In contrast, from 2000 until 2017, the Court of Justice produced a substantive number of decisions regarding discrimination on the grounds of age and disability, much less so with regard to sexual orientation, and little with regard to race and religion.[88]

Summing up this account of the Court's jurisprudence by the beginning of 2018, we can herald only two fully fledged judgments of the CJEU concerning the grounds of race and ethnicity,[89] and two parallel judgments decided on the grounds of religion.[90] Apart from the sensitive nature of these areas for Member States, the scarce number of judgments can be attributed to an array of factors, including the low awareness of discriminated plaintiffs belonging to ethnic and religious minorities about their material and procedural rights under EU law, as well as an often multiple nature of experienced discrimination (e.g. combination of gender and race).[91] Furthermore, the distinction between ethnic and religious discrimination is not always crystal clear, while the material scope of the former prohibition is much wider than simply the field of employment which the Framework Equality Directive prescribes for the latter. Finally, more litigation could be expected with the rise and empowerment of equality bodies to support race and religion cases in the future, as will be explained below.

B. Material and Personal Scope of Equality Directives

While the 2000 Directives contain several common provisions, they differ markedly in terms of their scope *ratione materiae*. The Framework Equality Directive is

[88] On the alleged hierarchy embedded in the set-up of the EU Equality Directive, see also E Howard, 'The Case for a Considered Hierarchy of Discrimination Grounds in EU law' (2006) 13 *Maastricht Journal of European and Comparative Law* 420. See also L Waddington and M Bell, 'More Equal than Others: Distinguishing European Union Equality Directives' (2011) 38 *Common Market Law Review* 587.

[89] Case C-54/07 *Feryn* (n 54) and Case C-83/14 *CHEZ Razpredelenie Bulgaria AD v Komisia za zashtita ot diskriminatsia* EU:C:2015:480.

[90] Case C-157/15 *Samira Achbita and Centrum voor gelijkheid van kansen en voor racismebestrijding v G4S Secure Solutions NV* EU:C:2017:203 and Case C-188/15 *Asma Bougnaoui and Association de défense des droits de l'homme (ADDH) v Micropole SA* EU:C:2017:204.

[91] On this point, see more generally the chapter by R Xenidis in the present volume.

confined to the employment sphere, while the Race Equality Directive also covers social protection, including social security and healthcare, education and access to goods and services which are available to the public, such as housing.[92] The directives are further constrained as they do not cover the prohibition of discrimination on the basis of nationality.[93] The FED furthermore includes an exception regarding religious occupational requirements for religious bodies.[94]

On the one hand, it remains an enigma that RED, while enjoying such a rich material scope, has eventually led to only two cases decided by the Court of Justice in seventeen years.[95] On the other hand, the limited scope of FED partially explains the failure of the Court to extend the application of EU anti-discrimination law to its case law on name-spelling as part of the language rights of ethnic minorities. This jurisprudence was regarded by the CJEU as exclusively part and parcel of discrimination based on nationality (tantamount to citizenship of EU Member States), instead of as ethnic discrimination. In the absence of a formal possibility to advance RED in the 'nationality' context, the Court took an unfortunate restrictive turn in its interpretation of language rights,[96] satisfying the political appetites of local nationalism, and shielded by the esoteric protection of national identity embedded in post-Lisbon primary EU law.[97] Likewise, the Court has delivered a highly disputable judgment with regard to blood donation by gay individuals, which justified its restriction in a number of Member States,[98] without a *de jure* possibility to advance FED in this medical context.[99]

[92] For the scope of application, see Art 3 of the Race Equality Directive (compare to the modest scope embedded in Art 3 of the Framework Equality Directive).

[93] Art 3(2) RED stipulates that it does not cover difference of treatment based on nationality.

[94] Art 4(2) FED stipulates that '[…] this Directive shall thus not prejudice the right of churches and other public or private organisations, the ethos of which is based on religion or belief, acting in conformity with national constitutions and laws, to require individuals working for them to act in good faith and with loyalty to the organisation's ethos'.

[95] In part, this might be attributed to the procedural path-dependence. On the continent, race discrimination traditionally pertains to the field of criminal law rather than civil or anti-discrimination regulation as in the USA. For this point, in the context of the comparative study on US-French law, see JC Suk, 'Procedural Path Dependence: Discrimination and the Civil-Criminal Divide' (2008) 85 *Washington University Law Review* 1315.

[96] Case C-208/09 *Ilonka Sayn-Wittgenstein v Landeshauptmann von Wien* EU:C:2010:806; Case C-391/09 *Malgožata Runevič-Vardyn and Łukasz Paweł Wardyn v Vilniaus miesto savivaldybės administracija and Others* EU:C:2011:29. For a detailed analysis of this stream of cases, critiquing the Court for playing the tune of nationalism, see chapter by D Kochenov in the present volume.

[97] Art 4(2) TEU obliges EU to respect Member States' 'national identities, inherited in their fundamental structures'. For a comment on this inconsistent CJEU jurisprudence on the right to a name, see A Lazowski, E Dagilyte, P Stasinopoulos, 'The Importance of Being Earnest: Spelling of Names, EU Citizenship and Fundamental Rights' (2015) 11 *Croatian Yearbook of European Law and Policy* 1.

[98] Case C-528/13 *Geoffrey Léger v Ministre des Affaires sociales, de la Santé et des Droits des femmes and Etablissement français du sang* EU:C:2015:288.

[99] Not only does the FED not cover healthcare, Art 168(7) TFEU provides that 'Union action shall respect the responsibilities of the Member States for the definition of their health policy and for the organisation and delivery of health services and medical care'. For critique of the judgment, see U Belavusau, 'Towards EU Sexual Risk Regulation: Restrictions on Blood Donation as Infringement of Active Citizenship' (2016) 4 *European Journal of Risk Regulation* 802.

In contrast to the material scope, the *ratione personae* is similar between RED and FED, and covers both public and private sectors, including individuals and public bodies, such as state authorities, companies and social partners.[100] More specifically, EU anti-discrimination law envisages an implementation possibility through social partners, provided they take the necessary steps to ensure that they are at all times able to guarantee the result required by the FED.[101] Accordingly, EU legislation forces some states to reconsider their traditional view that fundamental rights should be binding and enforceable only against state authorities and not against private bodies.[102]

Geographically, the Equality Directives cover all current (pre-Brexit) 28 Member States of the Union.[103] Depending on the country concerned, RED and FED may be indirectly relevant beyond the EU, in the EFTA zone.[104] Although the 2000 Directives are not formally incorporated into the EEA Agreement due to the lack of a legal basis, there are signs that those states are often willing to adopt similar legislation so as to be in line with the EU mainstream.[105] In the future, these Equality Directives will also remain as a guiding force for the acceding Member States in satisfying the Copenhagen criteria of observing fundamental rights and equality.

C. Proceduralisation of EU Equality Law

One way in which the 2000 Equality Directives have undoubtedly advanced EU anti-discrimination law pertains to the new procedural set-up of this field. This is the area where one can observe a rise in cause lawyering, learning from the experience of the US Civil Rights Act 1964 and its advancement by the Equal Employment Opportunity Commission in the United States.[106] In a somewhat similar mode, the Equality Directives gave *locus standi* for organisations to

[100] See e.g. Art 3(1) FED.

[101] See Preamble (36) FED. The Court has delivered important and ardently discussed jurisprudence regarding the rights of trade unions in advancing their claims in Case C-341/05 *Laval un Partneri* EU:C:2007:809 and Case C-438/05 *Viking* (n 61). For analysis, see U Belavusau, 'The Case of Laval in the Context of the Post-Enlargement EC Law Development' (2008) 9 *German Law Journal* 2279.

[102] See B de Witte, 'The Crumbling Public/Private Divide: Horizontality in European Anti-Discrimination Law' (2009) 13 *Citizenship Studies* 515. According to De Witte, the European-driven 'horizontalisation' of anti-discrimination law is a major challenge for many national legal systems and contributes to the emergence of new, but not uncontroversial, conceptions of inclusive citizenship.

[103] However, Art 15 FED makes a reservation for Northern Ireland, where positive discrimination is allowed to tackle the under-representation of one of the main religious communities in the police service and education.

[104] Iceland, Liechtenstein, Norway and Switzerland.

[105] See, in particular, D Gudmundsdóttir, 'The Framework Directive and Icelandic Law: Sexual Orientation Discrimination' in E Ellis and K Benediktsdóttir (eds), *Equality into Reality: Action for Diversity and Non-Discrimination in Iceland* (Reykjavik, University of Iceland Press, 2011) 333.

[106] See B de Witte, 'New Institutions for Promoting Equality in Europe: Legal Transfers, National Bricolage and European Governance' (2012) 60 *American Journal of Comparative Law* 49.

represent disadvantaged groups either in the absence or on behalf of the individual plaintiffs, and also enabled these organisations to collect information and provide advice. According to Articles 7(2) RED and 9(2) FED:

> Member States shall ensure that associations, organizations or other legal entities that have, in accordance with the criteria laid down by their national law, a legitimate interest in ensuring that the provisions of this Directive are complied with, may engage, either on behalf or in support of that complainant, with his or her approval, in any judicial and/or administrative procedure provided for the enforcement of obligations under this Directive.

Likewise, earlier developments with similar national bodies in the United Kingdom and the Netherlands – borrowing from the American model – have inspired the institutionalisation of equality bodies on the EU level.[107] However, so far, this is only required under RED, not under FED. Put differently, RED stipulates:

> Member States shall designate a body or bodies for the promotion of equal treatment of all persons without discrimination on the grounds of racial or ethnic origin. These bodies may form part of agencies charged at national level with the defence of human rights or the safeguard of individual rights.[108]

In practice, however, such bodies tend to cover all grounds of discrimination from Article 19 TFEU.

As a result of these incorporations into EU anti-discrimination law, two major cases reached the CJEU via preliminary rulings from national jurisdictions notwithstanding the absence of actual individual plaintiffs complaining about discriminatory hiring practices: in the case of *Feryn*, regarding a statement by an employer in media about his reluctance to hire Moroccans,[109] and in the case of *Asociatia ACCEPT* (2013), where a club patron stated that he would never hire a homosexual football player for his team.[110] Both cases reached the Court from Belgium and Romania in the virtual absence of a single plaintiff pertaining to the disadvantaged groups at stake: Moroccan people in *Feryn* and gay individuals in *Asociatia ACCEPT*. In *Feryn*, it is furthermore striking that the plaintiff organisation (anti-racist centre) was an 'equality body' established under the RED's mechanism. That organisation launched a claim before a national labour Court against the firm *Feryn* which then wound up at the Luxembourg Court through a preliminary reference. In *ACCEPT*, an LGBT organisation brought a case against

[107] According to De Witte, we have witnessed 'a neat migration sequence US → UK → NL → EU → all individual EU states' – B de Witte, 'National Equality Institutions and the Domestication of EU Non-Discrimination Law' (2011) 18 *Maastricht Journal of European and Comparative Law* 159, 160.

[108] Art 13 RED.

[109] Case C-54/07 *Feryn* (n 54). For an overview of the case, see K Henrard, 'The First Substantive ECJ Judgment on the Racial Equality Directive' NYU Jean Monnet Working Paper Series, 2009, 1; U Belavusau, 'Fighting Hate Speech through EU Law' (2012) 4 *Amsterdam Law Forum* 20.

[110] Case C-81/12 *Asociatia Accept* (n 79). For an extensive commentary, see U Belavusau, 'A Penalty Card for Homophobia from EU Non-Discrimination Law' (2015) 21 *Columbia Journal of European Law* 353.

the national equality body under the FED for having failed to offer an accurate interpretation of EU anti-discrimination law.

These scenarios for strategic litigation by either a strong and genuinely independent equality body (as in the Belgian case) or by an autonomous human rights organisation (as in the Romanian case) essentially revolutionises future development of anti-discrimination law in Europe. Such a litigation option provides a veritable boost to otherwise 'desperate' cases with no individual plaintiffs available.

There are a number of factors that potentially prevent individual plaintiffs from launching a case, including, *inter alia*:

(a) low awareness of legal possibilities to seek judicial redress, frequently combined with imperfect knowledge of the official language of procedures (very often affecting migrants);
(b) serious physical or mental impairments (in the case of disabled people);
(c) age of affected victims (in the cases of both the youth and the elderly);
(d) religious considerations or subordinated status (e.g. women in some traditional Islamic families); and
(e) fear of public disgrace, considerations of privacy and safety (e.g. LGBT plaintiffs).

The 2000 mechanism, thus, for the first time facilitates access to national courts and, depending on the willingness of these national courts to request preliminary rulings, to the CJEU on behalf of collective actors, an aspect which – in contrast – remains a weak spot in the Strasbourg mechanism with its accent on individual claims. Hence, advocacy groups get access to courts on equality matters, albeit to a different extent in various Member States. In this respect, EU law offers an easier procedural track for collective claims pertaining to group minority interests than individual and often timely and lengthy claims at the European Court of Human Rights. Apart from preliminary rulings in the CJEU, other EU opportunities include infringement procedures and annulment actions by the institutions.[111]

If facilitated through sufficient financial and informational resources (a task that should be duly understood as an objective of the EU anti-discrimination scheme), this focus on NGOs is capable of strengthening equal opportunities in Europe under the double vigilance of EU institutions and civil society.[112] As has been highlighted in literature, EU equality bodies, however, face significant challenges, including a reduction of resources, restructuring, threats to

[111] For current EU legal opportunities specifically mapped for LGBT litigants, see U Belavusau and D Kochenov, 'Federalizing Legal Opportunities for LGBT Plaintiffs in Europe' in K Slootmaeckers et al (eds), *The EU Enlargement and Gay Politics* (London, Palgrave, 2016) 69–96.

[112] For the concept of double vigilance in EU law within the context of Rome protection, see M Dawson and E Muir, 'Individual, Institutional and Collective Vigilance in Protecting Fundamental Rights in the EU: Lessons from the Roma' (2011) 48 *Common Market Law Review* 751–55.

independence, lack of expertise, etc.[113] Nonetheless, where the national parliament and government endowed such bodies with substantial functions, these new organisations appear to fulfill an active role.[114]

D. Forms of Discrimination in EU Anti-Discrimination Law

Following a formal interpretation of the 2000 Equality Directives, we can deduce four forms of discrimination, underpinning EU anti-discrimination law for the time being.[115] The four forms of discrimination cover *direct* and *indirect discrimination*, *harassment* and *instruction to discriminate*. In addition, all the directives outlaw *victimisation* of those complaining of discrimination. Both RED and FED require Member States to:

> [I]ntroduce into their national legal systems such measures as are necessary to protect individuals from any adverse treatment or adverse consequence as a reaction to a complaint or to proceedings aimed at enforcing compliance with the principle of equal treatment.[116]

As new grounds of prohibited discrimination are added to the palate of EU anti-discrimination law, old debates are bound to be rekindled, such as the dividing line between *direct* and *indirect* discrimination.[117] These two forms of discrimination remain central in the Court's analysis, leaving harassment and instruction to discriminate in a rather more obscure role for the time being. The stark distinction in EU law between possible justifications for direct versus indirect discrimination has elicited several discussions on the scope of this dichotomy, highlighting the considerable grey zone in this regard.[118] As Henrard underscores in her contribution to this volume, this grey zone is particularly acute in cases of so-called systemic discrimination, where ingrained prejudice in society plays a considerable role. In instances of deep-seated prejudice, are neutral rules really 'neutral' notwithstanding their disparate impact maintained over decades? This line of thinking has

[113] See TE Givens and R Evans Case, *Legislating Equality* (n 10) 128.

[114] B de Witte, 'National Equality Institutions' (n 106) 178.

[115] Art 2(2) FED maintains that: '(a) direct discrimination shall be taken to occur where one person is treated less favourably than another is, has been or would be treated in a comparable situation, on any of the grounds referred to in Article 1; (b) indirect discrimination shall be taken to occur where an apparently neutral provision, criterion or practice would put persons having a particular religion or belief, a particular disability, a particular age, or a particular sexual orientation at a particular disadvantage compared with other persons'. Art 2(3)FED defines harassment, while Art 2(4) generally describes instruction to discriminate against persons on any of the grounds referred to in Article 1 as discrimination.

[116] Art 9 RED. A similar measure is contained in Art 11 FED.

[117] For a summary of distinctions between direct and indirect discrimination in EU law, see C Tobler, *Indirect Discrimination: A Case Study into the Development of the Legal Concept of Indirect Discrimination under EU Law* (Antwerpen, Intersentia, 2005).

[118] See also MJ Busstra, *The Implications of the Racial Equality Directive for Minority Protection within the European Union* (The Hague, Eleven, 2010) 148–156.

been developed in relation to the Roma people, studied as a paradigmatic example of victims of systemic discrimination, but this reasoning is arguably equally valid for several other discriminated groups regarding grounds of discrimination in the EU's palate. Put differently, a more nuanced, holistic approach is needed when qualifying particular instances of discrimination as amounting to direct or indirect discrimination.

As is reflected in the coverage of this edited volume,[119] there has not yet been case law focusing on the definition and scope of the prohibition of harassment,[120] sexual harassment, instruction to discrimination, and victimisation as instances of prohibited discrimination. The related interpretative questions remain to be resolved in the future.

The terminology of harassment is definitely a transatlantic legal transplant, protected in the United States by virtue of Title VII of the Civil Rights Act 1964. In the US, this provision was primarily meant to address discriminatory practices against racial minorities, which makes particular sense in the American employment context, whereas hate speech has been systematically justified by the Supreme Court under the First Amendment.[121] The Civil Rights Act covers the grounds of race, colour, religion, sex and national origin. By the 1980s, the US Equal Employment Opportunity Commission had issued guidelines on sexual harassment as a breach of section 703(a)(1) of Title VII of the Civil Rights Act 1964.[122] Since the 1990s, a number of European countries have been targeting hateful expressions in the employment context as a part of workplace harassment (eg *intimidatie* in Dutch, *harcèlement moral* in French and *trakasserier* in Swedish). Sweden and France were particularly active in fostering various anti-harassment practices in labour law, linking them to a worker's dignity.[123]

Article 2(3) RED stipulates that 'h]arrasment shall be deemed to be discrimination [...], when an unwanted conduct related to racial or ethnic origin takes

[119] Several chapters enumerate these concepts, as they feature in the relevant Treaty provisions, but none of them really engages with these concepts.

[120] Do note the section on harassment in the chapter by M Möschel in the present volume, where he discusses national case law, confirming that, so far, no CJEU case law on this concept exists.

[121] Unlike in continental Europe, the approach of the US Supreme Court has enfolded hate speech into the protective scope of the First Amendment. This constitutes, perhaps, the most striking discrepancy between the two principal Western free-speech models. For a broad comparative study, see U Belavusau, *Freedom of Speech: Importing European and US Constitutional Models in Transitional Democracies* (Abingdon, Routledge, 2013).

[122] For a comparative outlook, see K Zippel, *The Politics of Sexual Harassment: A Comparative Study of the United States, the European Union, and Germany* (Cambridge, Cambridge University Press, 2006); R Holtmaat, *Seksuele intimidatie: de juridische gids* (Ars Aequi Libri, 2009). See also A Numhauser-Henning and S Laulom, 'Harassment related to Sex and Sexual Harassment Law in 33 European Countries. Discrimination versus Dignity, European Network of Legal Experts in the Field of Gender Equality', 2011. The authors of the report claim that unlike in the US, where harassment is semantically constructed as discrimination, in Europe it is primarily articulated as a concern over dignity.

[123] MIS Guerrero, 'The Development of Moral Harassment (or Mobbing) Law in Sweden and France as a Step towards EU Legislation' (2004) 27 *Boston College International and Comparative Law Review* 477.

place with the purpose or effect of violating the dignity of a person and of creating an intimidating, hostile, degrading, humiliating or offensive environment'.[124] Both RED and FED permit Member States to define harassment 'in accordance with the national laws and practice of the Member States'.[125] The Court of Justice had an opportunity to define harassment twice, but in both cases limited its dictum to fairly general phrasing that does not shed much light on the position of harassment vis-à-vis direct and indirect discrimination. In the case of *Coleman* (2008), the Court held that the prohibition of harassment is not limited to the harassment of people who are themselves disabled.[126] In the case of *Asociatia ACCEPT*, the Court requalified harassment (there, an instance of homophobic speech) as established by the national Court into an instance of direct discrimination.[127]

Thus, it currently remains unclear what precisely constitutes harassment as a separate form of discrimination and how national authorities should redress it. Even in cases that resemble the definition of harassment rather than direct or indirect discrimination *sensu stricto*, the Court appears to construct harassment as a sort of direct discrimination for the maximum benefit of plaintiffs.[128] The texts of the directives implies that harassment 'shall be deemed to be a form of discrimination',[129] when unwanted conduct related to a certain ground takes place with the purpose or effect of violating the dignity of a person and of creating an intimidating, hostile, degrading, humiliating or offensive environment. However, the FED leaves further definition of the concept of harassment to the laws and practice of the Member States. The way that this harassment clause was implemented in many EU countries suggests that Member States view it as a somewhat minor form of discrimination.[130] As reflected in the Romanian case discussed below, the Court missed the opportunity to take a position about this fairly debatable assumption and to clarify subtle distinctions in categories.

[124] Art 2(3) FED gives a similar definition with regard to the respective four grounds. The Equal Treatment Directive 2006/54 gives an almost identical definition of harassment with regard to gender, but also adds one more form of discrimination, 'sexual harassment', consisting of 'any form of unwanted verbal, non-verbal or physical conduct of a sexual nature [which] occurs, with the purpose or effect of violating the dignity of a person, in particular when creating an intimidating, hostile, degrading, humiliating or offensive environment' – Art 2(1)(d) Equal Treatment Directive.

[125] Art 2(3) in both RED and FED.

[126] Case C-303/06 *Coleman* (n 53). The plaintiff was the primary caretaker of a disabled child. She was harassed and discriminated on the grounds of her child's disability. Although it was not the plaintiff herself who was disabled, the Court established direct discrimination in that case.

[127] Case C-81/12 *Asociatia Accept* (n 79).

[128] In both Case C-54/07 *Feryn* (n 54) and Case C-81/12 *Asociatia Accept* (n 79), the utterances of the employer are essentially offensive claims that could have been easily interpreted under the clauses of harassment in the secondary EU law of non-discrimination. Perhaps the only clear element that separates these two cases from incidents of harassment is that, in both cases, individuals did not experience that type of racist and homophobic bullying during employment, but were prevented from employment by virtue of a speech act.

[129] Above n 125.

[130] See Belavusau and Kochenov, above n. 111.

E. Positive Discrimination or Affirmative Action *à la Européenne*

The arrival of five 'new' grounds of discrimination with Article 19 TFEU and the 2000 Equality Directives has also put a new spotlight on so-called *positive discrimination*, often referred to in the American context as *affirmative action*. The directives in fact merged the European and American terminologies under the heading of 'positive action'. The big question, however, is whether positive action is restricted exclusively to the confines of gender equality or if it is also applicable with regard to groups of people disadvantaged for reasons related to ethnic origin, religion, sexual orientation or disability. Positive discrimination certainly aligns with the invigorated focus on substantive or real equality, but it is well known that not all its manifestations are equally well received. Indeed, as soon as a positive action measure implies preferential treatment for one category or individual and thus disadvantageous treatment for another, positive action is in tension with the right not to be discriminated against (ie not to be treated unfavourably without justification).[131] Consequently, in the cases discussed below, assessing the legitimacy of positive action concerns a controversial balancing act – not so much regarding the question of whether positive action measures have a legitimate aim, but rather whether these measures are proportionate.[132]

It has long been recognised that EU law does not wholly exclude positive action measures. Indeed, in the main anti-discrimination directives, a similar provision can be found which indicates that the principle of equal treatment shall not prevent a Member State from taking specific measures 'to prevent or compensate for disadvantages linked to [the grounds covered by the Directives]'.[133] Since these provisions are very open-ended, the case law of the CJEU and the interpretations and applications of the underlying proportionality principle provide further guidance to Member States as to what amounts to permissible action.

As highlighted by Christopher McCrudden and Sacha Prechal in their 2009 report for the EU Commission:

> [T]he ECJ has also recognized that to achieve equality of opportunity between women and men it will be necessary on occasion to go beyond the eradication of discrimination, and that positive action may be appropriate even where it results in the preferential treatment of the formerly disadvantaged group.[134]

However, as the authors acknowledge, the CJEU has traditionally adopted a very restrictive approach in its case law on gender equality, construing positive action

[131] See, *inter alia*, K Henrard, 'Boosting Positive Action: the Asymmetrical Approach towards Non-discrimination and Special Minority Rights' (2011) *Heidelberg Journal of International Law* 379, 388–389.

[132] ibid.

[133] See Art 3 Equal Treatment Directive, Art 5 RED, Art 7 FED and Art 6 Directive 2004/113.

[134] C McCrudden and S Prechal, 'The Concepts of Equality and Non-Discrimination in Europe: A Practical Approach', European Commission, 2009, 38.

as an exception to the right to equal treatment.[135] Gradually, however, the CJEU softened its position. In *Lommers* (2002), for instance, the Court did not refer to the principle that derogations from an individual right should be interpreted strictly. Instead, it held that:

> in determining the scope of any derogation from an individual right … due regard must be had to the principle of proportionality, which requires that derogations must remain within the limits of what is appropriate and necessary in order to achieve the aim in view and that the principle of equal treatment be reconciled as far as possible with the requirements of the aim thus pursued.[136]

This shift towards a more 'open' proportionality analysis remains visible in the subsequent case law, in which the Court further defines in a gradual, case-by-case, process the exact parameters of what is permissible and to what extent.[137]

Since the CJEU's case law on positive action has so far only concerned the grounds of 'gender', it remains to be seen whether the Court's reasoning, and more particularly its proportionality assessment, will vary for the other grounds. When looking at the additional grounds of prohibited discrimination and having regard to documented histories of prejudice and discrimination, race, religion and sexual orientation are obvious contenders for positive action measures aimed at compensating for the resulting, ongoing disadvantages. Age and disability[138], on the other hand, could lead to interesting case law on positive action of the 'preventive', prophylactic kind.

F. Duties of Reasonable Accommodation

The Framework Equality Directive was the first piece of legislation to enshrine duties of reasonable accommodation in EU law, yet only in relation to the grounds of 'disability'. In order to discuss duties of reasonable accommodation as a mechanism to counter discrimination, it is important to identify the underlying rationale and further define the concept. Admittedly, this notion does not have the same long pedigree as the prohibition of discrimination.[139] Nevertheless, since its emergence

[135] See Case C-450/93 *Eckhard Kalanke v Freie Hansestadt Bremen* EU:C:1995:322; Case C-409/95 *Hellmut Marschall v Land Nordrhein-Westfalen* EU:C:1997:533; Case C-158/97 *Georg Badeck and Others, interveners: Hessische Ministerpräsident and Landesanwalt beim Staatsgerichtshof des Landes Hessen* EU:C:2000:163; Case C-407/98 *Katarina Abrahamsson and Leif Anderson v Elisabet Fogelqvist* EU:C:2000:367.

[136] Case C-476/99 *Lommers* (n 76) para 39.

[137] See also Case C-319/03 *Serge Briheche v Ministre de l'Intérieur, Ministre de l'Éducation nationale and Ministre de la Justice* EU:C:2004:574; Case C-366/99 *Joseph Griesmar v Ministre de l'Economie, des Finances et de l'Industrie and Ministre de la Fonction publique, de la Réforme de l'Etat et de la Décentralisation* EU:C:2001:648.

[138] As regards disability, there is a fascinating perspective for future discussion about the relation between positive action, on the one hand, and duties of reasonable accommodation, on the other.

[139] L Waddington, 'Reasonable Accommodation' in D Schiek, L Waddington and M Bell (eds), *Cases, Materials and Texts on National, Supranational and International Non-Discrimination Law* (Oxford, Hart Publishing, 2007) 630.

in Canada and the US in the 1960s,[140] it has migrated to several other jurisdictions, including South Africa, Israel and New Zealand, as well as to the level of international and regional organisations.[141] Duties of reasonable accommodation 'fit' with the broader development towards a quest for equality, in particular as regards substantive equality. In the end, duties of reasonable accommodation aim at securing equal opportunities, by evening out barriers to full participation due to the interaction amongst personal characteristics and the way the society is structured.[142] Since reasonable accommodation measures overcome these hurdles to participation, they ensure substantively equal access to employment, to public services, to education, etc.[143]

Duties of reasonable accommodation can be framed as applications of generally accepted dimensions of the right to equal treatment – particularly the duties of differential treatment and the prohibition of indirect discrimination. In short, duties of reasonable accommodation can be seen as a particular kind of duties of differential treatment, aimed at substantive equality, while accommodation measures can be considered as important tools to prevent or remedy instances of indirect discrimination.[144]

[140] The US was the first country to identify duties of reasonable accommodation, at first through interpretation of the 1964 Civil Rights Act, and in 1972, an explicit provision on reasonable accommodation duties was added to the 1964 Act. In Canada, duties of reasonable accommodation were introduced by jurisprudence as well (more particularly, the 1985 Supreme Court judgment in *O'Malley v Simpsons Sears*). Subsequently, duties of reasonable accommodation were judicially recognised in relation to all 14 enumerated grounds of prohibited discrimination in Section 15 of the Canadian Charter of Rights and Freedoms. See also P Bosset and MC Foblets, 'Accommodating Diversity in Québec and Europe: Different Legal Concepts, Similar Results?' in Council of Europe (ed), *Institutional Accommodation and the Citizen: Legal and Political Interaction in a Pluralist Society* (Strasbourg, Council of Europe Publishing, 2010) 43–50.

[141] United Nations General Assembly, Ad Hoc Committee on a Comprehensive and Integral International Convention on the Protection and Promotion of the Rights and Dignity of Persons with Disabilities, The Concept of Reasonable Accommodation in Selected National Disability Legislation, A/AC.265/2006/CRP.1, 7 December 2005.

[142] As Bouchard and Taylor emphasise, reasonable accommodations do not amount to privileges but are meant to engage in a reasonable adaptation to counteract the rigidity of certain rules or their uniform application, which would not regard the specific traits of individuals: G Bouchard and C Taylor, *Building the Future: A Time for Reconciliation*. Abridged Report, (Gouvernement du Quebec, 2008) 68.

[143] Bosset and Foblets argue that 'the main idea underlying reasonable accommodation is that democratic states must allow everyone to participate fully in society on an equal footing as far as possible'. See Bosset and Foblets (n 140) 37.

[144] For a more extensive comment on this, see K Henrard, 'Duties of Reasonable Accommodation in Relation to Religion and the European Court of Human Rights: A Closer Look at the Prohibition of Discrimination, the Freedom of Religion and Related Duties of State Neutrality' (2012) 5 *Erasmus Law Review* 67. As Frederique Ast correctly underscores, the right to reasonable accommodation can be portrayed as the corollary of the prohibition of indirect discrimination, but there are various ways to address the disproportionate impact inherent in indirect discrimination, not all of which qualify as reasonable accommodation: Frederique Ast, 'Indirect Discrimination as a Means of Protecting Pluralism: Challenges and Limits', in Council of Europe (ed), *Institutional Accommodation and the Citizen: Legal and Political Interaction in a Pluralist Society* (Strasbourg, Council of Europe Publishing, 2010) 97.

While the underlying rationale for duties of reasonable accommodation remains the same throughout, there are striking differences in their scope of application, including the grounds of discrimination 'covered'. In some countries, duties of reasonable accommodation are identified for a broad range – or even all – grounds of discrimination, whereas for others these duties are only acknowledged in relation to particular grounds, generally disability, and often also religion.[145] When considering UN treaties and EU secondary legislation, duties of reasonable accommodation are so far only explicitly recognised in relation to disability.[146] Yet it merits underscoring that in the US and Canada, the duties were originally conceptualised in order to deal with religious diversity resulting from immigration.[147] Hence, duties of reasonable accommodation could certainly be extended to religion. More generally, as these duties are an inherent dimension of the right to equal treatment, being intrinsically related to duties of differential treatment and the prohibition of indirect discrimination, there is no reason in principle not to grant duties of reasonable accommodation a broader scope of application.[148]

In terms of possible contestations with regard to measures of reasonable accommodation, it is important to note that these duties to provide accommodation are not absolute. As for any dimension of the right to equal treatment, and as expressed in the adjective 'reasonable', proportionality considerations provide intrinsic demarcations for these duties. Relevant factors to measure reasonableness and prevent undue burdens, undue hardship or a disproportionate burden[149] on the person/institution that need to accommodate include the actual cost of the accommodation, sources of outside (e.g. government) funding, the size of the business or institution, and the duration and scope of the accommodation.[150]

While this may seem straightforward in principle, in its actual application to concrete cases, the identification of relevant factors and their relative weight often

[145] See also United Nations General Assembly, The Concept of Reasonable Accommodation (n 141).

[146] Art 5 FED; Art 5(3) GRDP.

[147] See also E Bribiosa, J Ringelheim and I Rorive, 'Reasonable Accommodation for Religious Minorities: A Promising Concept for European Anti-Discrimination Law' (2010) 17 *Maastricht Journal of European and Comparative Law* 143.

[148] See also Jennifer Jackson-Preece who considers that duties of reasonable accommodation should be available for members of all structurally disadvantaged groups: J Jackson-Preece, 'Emerging Standards of Reasonable Accommodation Towards Minorities in Europe?' in *Council of Europe, Trends in Social Cohesion No 21, Institutional Accommodation and the Citizen: Legal and Political Interaction in a Pluralist Society* (Strasbourg, Council of Europe Publishing, 2009) 120. See also Waddington and Bell who argue that duties of reasonable accommodation would similarly be justified on grounds of race or religion: M Bell and L Waddington, 'Reflecting on Inequalities in European Equality Law' (2003) 28 *European Law Review* 362. For an argument that duties of reasonable accommodation do not fall foul of the prohibition of discrimination notwithstanding their implication of differential treatment, see Henrard, 'Duties of Reasonable Accommodation' (n 144) 70–6.

[149] Art 5 FED refers to 'disproportionate burden'. Other legislations and/or lines of jurisprudence also refer to 'undue hardship' or 'undue burden'.

[150] Bosset and Foblets (n 140) 49–53; C Brunelle, *Discrimination et obligation d'accommodement en milieu de travail syndiqué* (Cowansville (Quebec), Yvon Blais, 2001) 248–251.

proves controversial. Furthermore, it may be obvious that in relation to some grounds, the controversies will, by definition, be higher (e.g. when pertaining to religious accommodation in the public space or regarding different ways of life of ethnic minorities). This varying degree of inherent controversy may explain why the EU legislator has only been willing to engage with duties of reasonable accommodation in relation to 'disability'.[151] It is clear that in the lengthy negotiations (since 2008) of the Commission proposal for a new Equality Directive,[152] duties of reasonable accommodation remain reserved for the grounds of disability.[153]

The chapter in this volume by Louisa Lourenço and Pekka Pohjankoski, focusing on the CJEU case law regarding duties of reasonable accommodation on grounds of disability, highlights that the jurisprudence presents thorny issues concerning judicial interpretation. The authors analyse the clarifications in the text of the Directive in terms of the relevant forms of reasonable accommodation and reasonability factors. While there has been some case law on the former,[154] so far there is scant case law that assists in demarcating reasonable from unreasonable accommodations. The underlying proportionality considerations may indeed require a case-by-case analysis, and hopefully, future case law of the CJEU will provide some more generalisable markers. This case law on duties of reasonable accommodation is bound to sharpen the view on duties of differential treatment, the second leg of the principle of EU law on equal treatment.[155] As the latter concept is generally applicable across the EU grounds of discrimination, it remains to be seen to what extent the CJEU might steer towards *de facto* duties of reasonable accommodation on the other grounds. As Eugenia Pastor highlights in her chapter in this volume, the Court has thus far not been forthcoming in this respect, particularly as concerns the grounds of religion.

IV. Overview of chapters

This section offers a brief overview of the chapters in this volume, which is structured into two main blocks. The first, theoretical, block will highlight academic discussion regarding contemporary EU anti-discrimination law which transcends

[151] See earlier references to the chapter by Waddington in the present volume and Jackson-Preece (n 148). See also the chapter by ER Pastor in the present volume.

[152] Proposal for a Council Directive on Implementing the Principle of Equal Treatment Between Persons Irrespective of Religion or Belief, Disability, Age or Sexual Orientation, Brussels, 2 July 2008, COM(2008) 426 final.

[153] See the chapter by L Waddington in this volume for further details.

[154] For cases that clarify that adaptations in terms of working hours could be a reasonable accommodation, see Joined cases C-335/11 and C-337/11 *HK Danmark, acting on behalf of Jette Ring v Dansk almennyttigt Boligselskab and HK Danmark, acting on behalf of Lone Skouboe Werge v Dansk Arbejdsgiverforening, acting on behalf of Pro Display* A/S EU:C:2013:222.

[155] For now, Lourenço and Pohjankoski point to possible guidance from the supervisory practice of the UN Committee on the Rights of Persons with Disabilities and ECtHR.

the boundaries of specific grounds of discrimination, unpacking themes such as multiple discrimination in EU law which embraces several grounds for complete protection, the intricacies of the burden of proof formulated in 2000 Equality Directives, atypical contracts and their problematic fit into current EU anti-discrimination law, as well as a bird's eye view of the entire Union garden of minority protection and the gap between EU Equality Directives on the federal level and implementation. Part 2 will be composed of five sections, covering all the grounds of discrimination introduced by Article 19 TFEU and codified in the 2000 Equality Directives: (1) race and ethnicity, (2) religion, (3) sexual orientation, (4) age, and (5) disability.

A. Chapters Covering Theoretical and Procedural Aspects

Since this part of the volume looks beyond specific grounds of discrimination, it opens with a chapter by **Raphaële Xenidis** focusing on by far the most challenging case – the so-called 'multiple discrimination' which refers to discrimination that transcends a single ground. Xenidis first explains how the discourse on multiple discrimination has been an essentially transatlantic transplant borrowed from US anti-discrimination theory and practice, an account which is popular in the emerging EU literature on the subject. She proceeds with a detailed analysis of practically all the cases of the Court of Justice relevant for the discussion on multiple discrimination thus exploring the apparent limits of EU anti-discrimination law. Although Xenidis notes sporadic traces of positive change in the Court's jurisprudence, practice and discussion on secondary law, she contends that the most important step, the recognition of multiple discrimination in the EU legal system, has not yet been taken.

Likewise, **Mark Bell** offers an elaborate analysis of an issue that goes beyond discussing specific grounds of discrimination, and raises a question of great pertinence related to atypical contracts. While the 2000 Equality Directives, especially FED, focus mainly on the employment sector, much of the labour relations they cover or rather would fail to cover affect non-standard types of employment (e.g. non-full time or physically remote from the employer) starting from the most common case of part-time employment and ending with the emerging phenomenon of work via digital platforms (the 'gig' economy). Bell examines whether the interaction between EU equality law and legislation regarding non-standard forms of work enhances legal protection in a harmonious and complementary fashion or whether internal differences lead to a divergence in how each is integrated and applied. He draws on two central examples: gender equality and age, offering a valuable paradigm of comparison for our volume that in its analysis specifically aspires to go beyond gender, leaving it behind as a 'seminal' comparative ground. A common feature of both gender and age discrimination, as identified by Bell, is that litigants in the most precarious forms of employment, such as casual work, encounter greater obstacles in relying on the EU equality framework.

Kristin Henrard focuses on a complicated procedural issue that is at the same time crucial for the realisation of effective protection against discrimination: the distribution of the burden of proof between the applicant/alleged victim and the defendant/alleged perpetrator. In view of the difficulties for victims to produce full proof of discrimination, a 'special' allocation of proof has been devised for discrimination cases, following which the victim merely needs to establish a presumption of discrimination. Subsequently, the burden of proof shifts to the respondent who needs to prove that no discrimination occurred. This special allocation of the burden of proof is taken up in Article 8 RED. The ongoing uncertainties of national courts in this regard translate into preliminary references to the CJEU, inviting the Court to adduce further clarifications. Henrard critically analyses several major preliminary rulings in this context. She acknowledges that in several respects, the CJEU is becoming more generous in the (often rather concrete) guidance it is willing to provide to national courts. Nevertheless, Henrard identifies two shortcomings, thus offering two recommendations to the CJEU: (1) more consistency in the identification of a speech instance of discrimination, as distinct from the instance of discrimination emerging from actual practice, and (2) a more developed understanding of the distinction between direct and indirect discrimination, and its repercussions for the shared burden of proof.

This theoretical section is rounded off by a chapter by **Dimitry Kochenov** who, due to his focus on minority protection, takes a notable step away from case law based on the Equality Directives and criticises the Luxembourg jurisprudence for having missed the chance to apply the 2000 Equality Directives on numerous occasions. As Kochenov reminds us, *de facto* minority protection is closely intertwined with the right to equal treatment and anti-discrimination. Unfortunately, the obvious potential of the Equality Directives in this respect remains largely untapped, partly because the CJEU has not risen to the occasion. According to the author, a lack of federal thinking by the EU weakens this minority framework in the Union. He therefore puts minority protection into federal settings, zooming in on migrant EU citizens and their undermined equality. This outlook makes him conclude that the Equality Directives remain somewhat inadequate in fulfilling the promise of empowering disadvantaged groups, whereas the current division of competences between the EU and Member States is still chiefly based on a market-driven approach.

B. Chapters Covering Specific Grounds of Discrimination

The next part of the volume covers five more chapters on each of the discrimination grounds introduced by Article 19 TFEU and the 2000 Equality Directives, which receive a detailed commentary by experts specialising in these respective fields. In order to ensure a consistent and coherent outcome, each author reflects on the underlying rationale of anti-discrimination law, the major developments in the CJEU jurisprudence in the last 18 years (2000–2018), the themes that require further elucidation by the Court and suggestions for improvements. In regard to certain grounds, some more particular themes are also elaborated upon, such as the Roma, veil bans, and young people.

This part begins with a section on race and ethnicity, covering one of the two 2000 Equality Directives analysed in this volume. Despite a scarce number of cases, the Race Equality Directive has been the subject of lively academic debate and of ardent transposition battles at the local level, especially with regard to a number of ethnic minorities such as Roma people.

The chapter by **Mathias Möschel** provides a detailed overview regarding the various trajectories of the Race Equality Directive, its actual and future potential impact. The author starts by highlighting the momentous and smooth adoption of the RED which was contrasted by the slow and often incorrect national implementation, and the very scarce case law before the CJEU. He maps both the success and failures in three steps, having regard to the text of the Directive, the case law of the CJEU and the interpretations by the national authorities. He concludes his overview of successes by arguing that, in certain areas, the RED has improved access to justice through its generous interpretation by the Court. However, the subsequent discussion on failures or shortcomings signals several ways in which the CJEU has actually opted for a restrictive interpretation (e.g. whether equality bodies can make a preliminary ruling to the CJEU), or has omitted to recognise the relevance of the RED in relation to the interpretation of other EU legislation, more particularly the Family Reunification Directive and the Third Country Nationals Directive. In terms of future potential for the RED, Möschel identifies both promising trends, such as increasing invocation of RED in litigation concerning employment by the EU institutions, actual infringement proceedings against several Member States regarding Roma segregation in education and a worrying lack of RED-based arguments in other cases (e.g. pertaining to the headscarf). Möschel concludes by finding a mitigated balance. While the RED has certainly changed the landscape of EU anti-discrimination law, there is still a long way to go before it will fully reach its potential, which is dependent on the interplay of various actors, including institutions at the national and EU levels as well as civil society.

Morag Goodwin's chapter discusses Romani marginalisation after the Race Equality Directive took force. She documents the limited way in which the RED has been used to tackle anti-Romani hatred and intolerance, and highlights the virtually non-existent impact in terms of an actual decline in racial discrimination against Roma. She argues that in addition to widespread anti-Romani sentiment, actual discrimination against Roma – in education, housing, the workplace and in access to services – remains an equal constant. In several respects, Goodwin welcomes the CJEU's judgment in *CHEZ*, the first substantive case about discrimination against Roma decided by the Court, particularly because the CJEU recognised the destructive psychological impact of racial discrimination. However,

Goodwin's main criticism is that the Directive fails to facilitate Roma's social inclusion because the EU legislator is not interested in actual, substantive difference. According to Goodwin, the Directive is interested only in protecting difference that is 'surface' or 'skin' deep … it focuses on the difference that is visual and not substantive. In order to begin the process of addressing anti-Romani sentiment and discrimination and to truly tackle Romani exclusion and marginalisation, the celebration of Romani difference and European diversity and compulsory group-based positive measures to rectify historical wrongs and provide genuine equal opportunities are needed. The Race Equality Directive, as it stands, only manages to scratch the surface.

From the Race Equality Directive, we transit to the Framework Equality Directive through the section about religious discrimination, as the latter often incorporates features of ethnic discrimination. Unsurprisingly, both chapters in this section on religion focus extensively on the two passionately discussed headscarf cases decided by the CJEU in 2017, pertaining to restrictions on wearing religious symbols like a headscarf at work. In fact, those are the only two cases ever decided by the Court of Justice on the grounds of religion during the 17 years the Framework Equality Directive has existed. **Eugenia Relaño Pastor** starts her chapter with a discussion of the opinions of the Advocates General in these two cases, critically analysing their underlying premise and conceptual presuppositions, which are in opposition to one another. She extends her critical analysis to the CJEU judgments, highlighting missed opportunities, also in terms of duties of reasonable accommodation, and concludes with recommendations for improvements of EU anti-discrimination law. **Anna Śledzińska-Simon** discusses the reasoning of the Court in more depth, similarly putting forward critical remarks about how it has conducted its proportionality review. Śledzińska-Simon unpacks the CJEU cases in light of a broader analysis of case law of European courts on 'laws, policies or practices that either directly target religious groups or have deleterious effects on their members'. She notes that the CJEU judgments fit the broader trend of courts deferring the veil controversy to the national decision-making authority, thus not ensuring the effective protection of freedom of religion and the freedom from discrimination in private employment, and beyond. Consequently, Śledzinska-Simon calls for a stronger stance by the courts to more resolutely address structural religious discrimination and endorse religious diversity as a legal value.

The section covering sexual orientation as a ground singled out in the Framework Equality Directive offers a certain interdisciplinary dialogue between a legal scholar and a political scientist. While **Alina Tryfonidou** offers a chapter with an almost encyclopaedically precise summary of the key legal instruments and case law in the field of EU sexual orientation law, **Phillip M Ayoub** zooms in on the factors that led to the transposition of LGB protection from EU law into national legislations, offering its empirical measurements. Tryfonidou provides a three-step account. She first assesses the FED's impact on the protection of LGB individuals and same sex-couples against discrimination, excluding transsexuals from her analysis, since – as has also been shown earlier in this introductory chapter – the rights of transgender people were initially addressed by the Court of Justice as a matter of sex equality. She then considers whether the gaps left by the FED in its fragmented protection of gays and lesbians can sufficiently be filled by other instruments, such as the Charter. Summarising the main jurisprudence in the field, Tryfonidou completes her account by discussing the prospects for the EU anti-discrimination law framework.

Ayoub complements this sketch of LGB rights in EU law by looking into the vertical and horizontal distribution of protection amongst Member States. He wonders why the legislation on LGBT rights is introduced at higher levels in some cases and less so in others. To address this puzzle, his chapter analyses changes in LGBT legislation across EU Member States between 1970 and 2009. Ayoub identifies five categories for his analysis: anti-discrimination, criminal law, partnerships, parenting rights, and equal sexual offences provisions, with regard to 'new' EU Member States in Central and Eastern Europe. He further compares these diffusion patterns with their counterparts in older Member States. This comparison leads him to argue that new-adopter States are more dependent on international resources for making novel issues visible and are more inclined to see adoption as a means to gain external legitimacy and improve their reputation. In this respect, the external mechanism introduced by the FED was paramount to the diffusion of rights. Likewise, he looks into the EU conditionality mechanism regarding the Equality Directives in the context of enlargements and criticises it from the perspective of transnational social movements.

The age-discrimination section also consists of two chapters unpacking different facets of the same phenomenon – discrimination of the 'old' and the 'young'. **Rachel Horton** explores the boundaries of the justification afforded to age discrimination under FED as interpreted by the CJEU. These justifications, listed in Article 6 FED, are remarkably wide and often accepted without criticism. Horton views as missing a coherent account of why age should be accepted as different from other characteristics. As with gender, it may be possible to see age discrimination being simply at an early journey towards a more robust rejection by society. A systemic approach to justifying age discrimination requires a clear account of all harms brought by age imbalance. The Court has arguably left too much discretion in this area to Member States, which tend to interpret those harms narrowly – a prospect that would need to be reversed in the future, according to the author.

Beryl P ter Haar completes this account of age discrimination by looking into policies which foster the widely pronounced youth protection in the European Union (EU). She offers her reader an eloquent question of whether EU age discrimination law has been a curse or a blessing from the standpoint of youth policy, which she categorises as a broad field with nine sub-fields. After analysing case law of the CJEU, ter Haar concludes on a positive note – almost exceptional amongst the much gloomier analyses of the Court's rulings in other sections of this book – suggesting that FED has supported, rather than hindered, fostering the rights of young people in the EU.

Following an overview section about EU disability law, which mostly consists of anti-discrimination provisions, **Luísa Lourenço** and **Pekka Pohjankoski** in their chapter explore the judicial interpretation of 'disability' and 'reasonable accommodation' by the CJEU. Regarding the definition of 'disability', the authors welcome the CJEU's acknowledgment of the paradigm shift from the medical to the social model, in accordance with the UN Convention on the Rights of Persons with Disabilities (CRPD). They do note the problem with the judicial application of a definition based on the social model of disability (i.e. that it may become so vast as to cover nearly all situations in human life, which would render its protective dimension meaningless). Similarly, the CJEU has held that the duty of reasonable accommodation must be interpreted broadly in light of the UN Disability Convention. However, this still leaves a critical question, namely when an accommodation is (un)reasonable, to be decided on a case-by-case basis, having regard to the relevant factors (enumerated in Article 5 of the FED). Due to the scarcity of the CJEU's case law on the concept of reasonable accommodation, the authors refer to the practice of the UN Committee on the Rights of Persons with Disabilities and the European Court of Human Rights as potentially providing guidelines for assessing the proportionality of the burden of the duty bearer.

Lisa Waddington turns to the more explicit influence of the UN Convention on the Rights of Persons with Disabilities on EU anti-discrimination law. As the EU has become a party to this Convention, EU law needs to be interpreted, as far as possible, in a manner consistent with its provisions and *telos*. Her chapter firstly explores the extent to which the CJEU has indeed relied on the CRPD when interpreting the Employment Equality Directive's prohibition of discrimination on grounds of disability. This influence is particularly visible in the definition of 'disability'. Secondly, Waddington reviews how the revisions to the Commission proposal for a new Equality Directive covering a number of grounds, including disability, were influenced by the CRPD. Lastly, her chapter reflects on the significance of the periodic review under the CRPD, and the resulting Concluding Observations by the UN Committee on the Rights of Persons with Disabilities. While the CRPD has indeed influenced EU anti-discrimination law in several respects, Waddington also flags up many lingering shortcomings.

Finally, a short concluding Epilogue written by one of the leading scholars of EU law, **Bruno de Witte**, discusses the problematic aspects of the current equality framework, and draws conclusions on those elements still in need of substantial improvements. The strong potential of EU anti-discrimination law can be unlocked by sufficient political will from EU institutions, coupled with more activism from the Court of Justice and the mobilisation of the twin directives by social movements in those Member States, which have – surprisingly – not made preliminary references to the Luxembourg Court on the newer grounds of equal treatment.

V. Conclusions

The density of instruments dedicated to the prohibition of discrimination at both a global and a regional level, and their increasing detail, have made this norm one of the most developed and refined human rights. In this respect, the 2000 EU Equality Directives mark the birth of EU anti-discrimination law as a self-standing area. Despite all the pitfalls, this EU law offers one of the highest ceilings of protection in comparative anti-discrimination law. In this volume, we have tried to identify the major themes in the recent discussion on the EU equality framework and to summarise how various grounds of equality 'beyond gender' have been interpreted at the level of the Court of Justice. Through this exploration, we aspire to show the modes in which social movements and individuals can further capitalise on the available resources of EU anti-discrimination law. If anything, an effective protection against discrimination has only become more pressing during multiple ongoing crises, namely, the economic crisis, the 'refugee' crisis, and backsliding on the rule of law. EU anti-discrimination law has, thus, reached its age of maturity – its eighteenth birthday – in confusing times, which nonetheless carry huge potential. This area of law remains a vivid justification for viewing the EU today as not only concerned with economic interests, but also embracing a wider ethos of equality emanating from EU law to Member States, even in wholly internal situations.

PART I

Theoretical and Procedural Aspects

2

Multiple Discrimination in EU Anti-Discrimination Law

Towards Redressing Complex Inequality?

RAPHAËLE XENIDIS*

I. Introduction

The complete overhaul of EU anti-discrimination law at the beginning of the 2000s triggered discussions on the necessity to tackle an issue which had been gaining attention since the end of the 1990s in Europe – multiple discrimination. Multiple discrimination pertains to situations in which a person is discriminated against on more than one ground. Let us take as an example a case of workplace discrimination against an EU citizen – a Muslim woman wearing an Islamic headscarf. Such a case might involve harmful stereotypes based on religion, but also on race and gender.[1] Do litigators and courts need to pick and choose a ground? Would a claim of multiple discrimination make a difference in terms of protection of rights or legal reasoning?

Intersectionality theory postulates that certain experiences of multiple discrimination cannot be adequately grasped and remedied by the law unless

* I am grateful to my PhD supervisor Claire Kilpatrick, to Bruno De Witte, to my friends and colleagues at the EUI Shreya Atrey, Lilla Farkas and Liiri Oja, to the editors of this book Uladzislau Belavusau and Kristin Henrard for their invaluable comments on this piece and to Marguerite Bolger, Mary Collins, David Fennelly, Joanna Maycock, David Parris, Jyostna Patel and Jean Tomkin for sharing their knowledge, insights and stories.

[1] On religious discrimination, see the chapters by E Relaño Pastor and A Śledzińska-Simon in this volume. On the construction of race in Europe, see M Möschel, *Law, Lawyers and Race: Critical Race Theory from the United States to Europe* (New York, Routledge, 2014) and on the racialisation of religious groups, see, eg N Meer (ed), *Racialization and Religion: Race, Culture and Difference in the Study of Antisemitism and Islamophobia* (New York, Routledge, 2014).

examined from the angle of the 'synergies' of the different grounds involved.[2] In our example, the experience of discrimination could arguably involve islamophobia, where racist prejudices blend with religious and cultural animosity. It would, however, also imply a gendered dimension, since the Islamic headscarf only pertains to women.[3] Consider the concrete case of an employer who adopts rules requiring religious neutrality in the employees' dress code. This situation would mean very different experiences for, say, a Muslim man or a Christian woman. Albeit presented as 'neutral', this measure would disproportionately affect Muslim women who consider the headscarf as a religious requirement, compared with employees whose religious commitment is not expressed through their garments.[4] Ignoring the intersections of religion, gender and race and how they shape particular situations could thus result in the invisibility of the specific prejudice experienced by Muslim women. Hence, the choice of grounds and comparisons in assessing multiple discrimination is important, as it can either conceal or reveal disadvantage.

With a view to protecting substantive equality, addressing multiple discrimination in EU law is important because it is a widespread problem. The 2015 Eurobarometer on discrimination in the EU revealed that around one-fourth of all discrimination experienced by respondents are of a multiple nature.[5] This share is even higher among the minority groups of a population. The respondents of a survey conducted by the Fundamental Rights Agency in 2008 and focused on ethnic minorities and immigrants indicated that around 38% of experiences of discrimination pertained to multiple grounds.[6] Some scholars even argue that multidimensional discrimination should be seen as the norm rather than the exception.[7] As German constitutional Judge Susanne Baer puts it, the 'social divisions [at the roots of inequality] are multidimensional, complicated and affected by intersectional identities'.[8] Every individual is, in fact, embedded into a complex

[2] On the theorisation of intersectionality, see K Crenshaw, 'Mapping the Margins: Intersectionality, Identity Politics, and Violence against Women of Color' (1991) 43 *Stanford Law Review* 1241; K Crenshaw, 'Demarginalizing the Intersection of Race and Sex: A Black Feminist Critique of Antidiscrimination Doctrine, Feminist Theory, and Antiracist Politics' (1989) 1 *The University of Chicago Legal Forum* 139; I Solanke, *Discrimination as Stigma: A Theory of Anti-discrimination Law* (Oxford, Hart, 2017) 133–159.

[3] See, eg A Vakulenko, '"Islamic Headscarves" and the European Convention on Human Rights: An Intersectional Perspective' (2016) 16 *Social & Legal Studies* 2.

[4] This was precisely the subject of CJEU's decisions C-157/15 *Samira Achbita and Centrum voor gelijkheid van kansen en voor racismebestrijding v G4S Secure Solutions NV* EU:C:2017:203 and C-188/15 *Asma Bougnaoui and Association de défense des droits de l'homme (ADDH) v Micropole SA* EU:C:2017:204.

[5] European Commission, *Special Eurobarometer 437: Discrimination in the EU in 2015* (European Union, 2015) 8.

[6] Calculation based on data from EU Fundamental Rights Agency, 'Data in Focus Report Multiple Discrimination' *EU-MIDIS: European Union Minorities and Discrimination Survey* (2010) 4, 10.

[7] S Elsuni and AL Göttsche, 'Multidimensional Discrimination and the Law: Views and Experiences from a German Perspective' (2016) *Sociologia del Diritto* 2.

[8] S Baer, 'Speaking Law: Towards a Nuanced Analysis of "Cases"' (2017) 18 *German Law Journal* 281.

network of social memberships and identity groups, which potentially cumulates disadvantage. Hence, inequality is a complex and multi-layered phenomenon. Grounds of discrimination cannot be understood in isolation from this broader social context.

In 2000, recitals (14) and (3) of the Race Equality Directive (RED) and the Framework Equality Directive (FED) recognised for the first time the problem posed by multiple discrimination stating that 'especially [...] women are often the victims of multiple discrimination'.[9] However, so far, no legislative reform has clarified the definition and place of 'multiple discrimination' in EU anti-discrimination law, despite ongoing discussions in the Council. Even though recent engagement with intersectionality theory at the Court of Justice of the European Union (CJEU) also shows awareness of the specific issues posed by certain forms of multiple discrimination, no fully fledged jurisprudential clarification seems to be forthcoming.[10] Acknowledging this shortcoming, the GendeRace project, the largest empirical research on multiple discrimination conducted so far in the EU, called for '[a] specific legal methodological framework'.[11] The gaps of EU anti-discrimination law with regard to the pervasive problem of multiple discrimination raise broader questions about the role of the EU as a promoter of equality.

This chapter, therefore, unpacks the degree of engagement of EU law with the problem of multiple discrimination. To this end, it investigates the issue of multiple discrimination in the EU from three angles. The first shows how scholars and activists in the EU mainly framed multiple discrimination as a feminist issue and how this shaped EU law, prevailing over a transversal understanding pertaining to the whole range of protected grounds. The second reviews how multiple discrimination served as a rationale justifying the multi-ground approach that transformed EU anti-discrimination law in 2000. This section uncovers the gaps between legislation and policy and analyses the ongoing discussions of legal reform. Finally, the third takes a closer look at the CJEU jurisprudence and reveals some sensibility for the concerns raised by intersectionality theory, despite the absence of a targeted doctrinal framework to address claims of multiple discrimination. Throughout these three sections, it is shown that even though the legal framework addressing multiple discrimination in the EU is at best patchy, awareness of the problem has increased since the anti-discrimination reforms in 2000 and growing discussions invoke the need for a legal remedy.

[9] Council Directive 2000/43/EC implementing the principle of equal treatment between persons irrespective of racial or ethnic origin [2000] OJ L180/22 (Race Equality Directive); Council Directive 2000/78/EC establishing a general framework for equal treatment in employment and occupation [2000] OJ L303/16 (Framework Equality Directive).

[10] Case C-443/15 *David L Parris v Trinity College Dublin and Others* EU:C:2016:897, Opinion of AG Kokott, paras 149–151.

[11] I Carles and O Jubany-Baucells, *GendeRace. The Use of Racial Antidiscrimination Laws: Gender and Citizenship in a Multicultural Context* (2010) 270–271. Available at: http://genderace.ulb.ac.be/rapports/GENDERACE%20FINAL%20REPORT%20sent.pdf.

II. The Emergence of the Issue of Multiple Discrimination in the EU

Historically, only nationality and sex were protected under EU equality law.[12] In 1997, however, Article 13 TEC (now Article 19 TFEU) enabled the adoption of a multi-ground framework. The multiplication of protected grounds from two to seven constituted a window of opportunity to raise public awareness about the issue of multiple discrimination.[13] Tracing these debates shows how the problem gained attention at institutional level, how it was understood and thus what demands it generated *vis-à-vis* EU law.

A. Global and European Developments of Intersectionality Theory

To understand how awareness of the issue of multiple discrimination emerged in the EU, we need to turn to the roots of the debate. From the end of the 1960s throughout the 1970s and the 1980s, feminists of colour in the US denounced the co-production of inequality and exclusion through several distinctive but interdependent social axes of power. Most prominently, they highlighted the double jeopardy caused by racism and patriarchy, but also classism, heteronormativity, imperialism and colonialism.[14] At the end of the 1980s, Crenshaw and Hill Collins' foundational pieces theorised the 'interlocking systems of oppression' and the 'matrix of domination' ensuing from the simultaneous membership in multiple marginalised social groups. Since then, a large spectrum of critical scholarship has blossomed under the unifying banner of 'intersectionality theory'.[15]

The concerns conveyed by intersectionality theorists and black feminists subsequently gained visibility in women's and human rights international fora, mainly framed as 'women's issues'.[16] With the Fourth World Conference on Women in 1995 and the ensuing Beijing Declaration, the question of multiple

[12] Art 18 TFEU (ex-Art 12 TEC) and Art 157 TFEU (ex-Art 141 TEC), originally Art 7 and Art 119 of the EEC Treaty.

[13] The anti-discrimination directives currently protect sex, racial and ethnic origin, religion or belief, disability, sexual orientation and age and nationality remains protected by the Treaty.

[14] See P Hill Collins and S Bilge, *Intersectionality* (Cambridge, Polity Press, 2016) 63–113 and A-M Hancock, *Intersectionality: An Intellectual History* (New York, Oxford University Press, 2016) 37–71.

[15] Hill Collins and Bilge (n 14) 77, 221–238. See Crenshaw (n 2) (1989), (1991); P Hill Collins, *Black Feminist Thought: Knowledge, Consciousness and the Politics of Empowerment* (Boston, Hyman, 1990). Throughout this piece I use 'intersectionality theory' as a label encompassing a large spectrum of scholarship that has either used the specific label 'intersectionality' or has developed similar theories.

[16] Hancock (n 14) 66.

discrimination against women emerged as a pressing issue.[17] As illustrated by the discussions at the UN World Conference on Racism held in Durban in 2001 and during its preparation phase,[18] '[t]he year 2000 marked an important milestone for the global dispersal of intersectionality'.[19] By 2000, intersectionality theory was both internationalised and institutionalised in the 'international diplomacy and human rights governance'.[20] As the discussion below shows, no unified terminology prevailed in this context. The terms 'intersectional discrimination', 'some other terms captur[ing] its essence' and the concept of 'multiple discrimination' have often been used interchangeably.[21]

In the mid-1990s, as the EU's mandate progressively expanded to include the defence of fundamental rights in the context of the Treaty of Amsterdam and the EU Charter of Fundamental Rights (CFR),[22] debates about multiple discrimination found an echo in the EU's preoccupation with equality. As the next sections show, some equality advocates, scholars and institutions saw in the preparation of the new anti-discrimination directives a window of opportunity to tackle multidimensional forms of discrimination. While 'intersectionality' is the label under which the issue made its way into legal debates in the US, the term 'multiple discrimination' prevailed in EU law, following the pattern sketched by international discussions. EU institutional debates did not refer to intersectionality until recently and legislation only makes mention of 'multiple discrimination'.[23] However, while the term 'multiple discrimination' remains the only one anchored in EU law, a recent linguistic shift towards the intersectionality lexicon can be observed both at international and European level.[24]

[17] 'Beijing Declaration and Platform for Action', United Nations Fourth World Conference on Women (15 September 1995) UN Doc A/CONF.177/20, para 32.

[18] Crenshaw was, for instance, invited to the first UN preparatory committee on gender and racial discrimination in 2000 to present a position paper on intersectional discrimination. See K Crenshaw, 'Gender-related aspects of race discrimination' (2000) UN Doc EGM/GRD/2000/WP.1.

[19] Hill Collins and Bilge (n 14) 88, 91.

[20] ibid. See, eg UN Committee on the Elimination of Racial Discrimination, 'General recommendation 25 on gender-related dimensions of racial discrimination' (12 May 2003) UN Doc HRI\GEN\1\Rev.6; UNCEDAW, 'General Recommendation No 28 on the Core Obligations of States Parties under Article 2 of the Convention on the Elimination of All Forms of Discrimination against Women' (19 October 2010) UN Doc CEDAW/C/2010/47/GC.2.

[21] Hill Collins and Bilge (n 14) 90.

[22] Charter of Fundamental Rights of the European Union [2016] OJ L202/2 (CFR).

[23] One of the first reports commissioned by the European Commission on the topic articulates the link between multiple discrimination and 'the intersectional methodological approach' and 'analysis' needed to deal with it. See Hanne Bielefeldt, *Tackling Multiple Discrimination: Practices, Policies and Laws* (Copenhagen, Danish Institute for Human Rights and European Commission, 2007) 17.

[24] From 2007 onwards, more and more institutional research has used the term 'intersectionality'. See, eg European Commission, *Green Paper on Equality and Non-Discrimination in an Enlarged European Union* COM (2004) 379 final; Bielefeldt (2007) (n 23); M Verloo, 'Multiple Inequalities, Intersectionality and the European Union' (2006) 13 *European Journal of Women's Studies* 211; S Burri and D Schiek, *Multiple Discrimination in EU Law: Opportunities for Legal Responses to Intersectional Gender Discrimination?* (Brussels, European Commission, 2009); A Lawson and D Schiek (eds), *EU Non-Discrimination Law and Intersectionality* (Farnham, Ashgate Publishing, 2011); L Rolandsen Agustín (ed) *Gender Equality, Intersectionality, and Diversity in Europe* (New York,

B. Terminological Controversies: A Lexical Battlefield

Controversies have arisen because of this terminological inconsistency. For instance, AG Kokott describes the term 'multiple discrimination' as 'misleading as it suggests the presence of two differences of treatment each of which would in its own right – completely independently of the other – have to be regarded as discrimination and would at most be aggravated by the existence of further grounds for a difference of treatment'.[25] A majority of scholars seems to understand multiple discrimination as an umbrella term covering intersectional but also other multidimensional forms of discrimination, such as 'sequential', 'compound' or 'additive' discrimination.[26] By contrast, other commentators claim that multiple discrimination is distinct from, and does not encompass, intersectional discrimination.[27]

The label 'intersectional' characterises instances of discrimination that are produced by the synergies of co-constitutive status-based systems of disadvantage.[28] Conversely, the words 'sequential' and 'additive' or 'compound' have been said to refer to situations in which multiple grounds are involved in instances of discrimination that can be assessed separately.[29] Concretely, 'sequential' discrimination corresponds to situations where several occurrences of discrimination take place at different times based on different grounds.[30] An example would be the case of an older worker being first harassed in his workplace based on racist motives, and later on discriminated against based on ageist stereotypes, leading to him being refused a promotion. Additive discrimination is said to refer to situations in which discrimination is produced through independent motives related to different grounds but in the same instance.[31] For example, if a job seeker is

Palgrave Macmillan, 2013); S Fredman, *Intersectional Discrimination in EU Gender Equality and Non-discrimination Law* (Luxembourg, European Commission, 2016); N Crowley, *Innovating at the Intersections: Equality Bodies Tackling Intersectional Discrimination* (Brussels, Equinet, 2016); S Carrera et al (ed), *Towards a Comprehensive EU Protection System for Minorities* (Brussels, European Union, 2017). See also the linguistic evolution at UN level, from CEDAW 20014 general recommendation 25 tackling 'multiple discrimination' and 2010 general recommendation 28 on 'intersectionality' six years later (n 20).

[25] Case C-443/15 *Parris* (AG Opinion) (n 10).

[26] See, eg M Bell, *Racism and Equality in the European Union* (Oxford, Oxford University Press, 2009) 21–22; Fredman (n 24) 27–28; D Schiek, 'From EU Non-Discrimination Law towards Multidimensional Equality Law for Europe' in D Schiek and V Chege (eds), *European Union Non-discrimination Law: Comparative Perspectives on Multidimensional Equality Law* (London, Routledge-Cavendish, 2009); R Nielsen, 'Is EU Equality Law Capable of Addressing Multiple and Intersectional Discrimination Yet?' in ibid; I Solanke, 'Putting Race and Gender Together: A New Approach to Intersectionality' (2009) 72 *Modern Law Review* 723, 727–728.

[27] T Makkonen, *Multiple, Compound and Intersectional Discrimination: Bringing the Experiences of the Most Marginalized to the Fore* (Turku, Institute For Human Rights, Äbo Akademi University, 2002) 10–11.

[28] See Solanke (2017) (n 2) 133–159.

[29] See Fredman (n 24); Burri and Schiek (n 24); Makkonen (n 27).

[30] See Fredman (n 24) 27–28.

[31] See Burri and Schiek (n 24).

denied employment both because the firm applies a said 'neutral' clothing policy that prohibits the wearing of Islamic headscarves at work and refuses to reasonably accommodate her wheelchair, this could be described as additive discrimination.

Perhaps most importantly, the term 'intersectionality' refers to a particular history, intellectual heritage and context of emergence. By using the language of intersectionality, one must acknowledge its anchoring within black feminism and critical race studies, its function as a response to the US civil rights movement and its reference to the total oppression of black women in the context of slavery. Debates have emerged in this regard about the de-politicisation and 'whitening' of intersectionality discussions.[32] By contrast, the term multiple discrimination emerged in a more international and institutional context. Some commentators have suggested that the conversation in the EU developed around the latter notion because it provides the most 'neutral' and 'overarching' terminology.[33] Nevertheless, discussing multiple discrimination necessarily takes place within the frame set by intersectionality scholarship.

The commonality of these two concepts lies in the question at the core of the present chapter: what challenge do they pose to EU law? How to assess a claim in which the grounds invoked are inseparably involved in the production of discrimination? This question arises because EU anti-discrimination law and doctrine have been described as 'single-axis' systems, in which claims of discrimination are only investigated on the basis of a single ground at a time, thus missing their synergies.[34] Thus, only those discriminations that involve synergies of status-based structures of disadvantage actually challenge this system. Additive and sequential discrimination can be dealt with by the prevailing single-axis framework. By contrast, intersectionality theorists underline the need to 'addres[s] inequalities at a structural level and explor[e] the dynamics between [them…], recognising that the experiences of individuals cannot be fully appreciated by separating the oppressions they are subject to'.[35] Thus, the single-axis framework prevailing in EU law is not appropriate where grounds cannot be disentangled in their co-constitutive dynamics of inequality production.

Despite these clarifications, the relationship between multiple discrimination and intersectionality remains inconsistently – sometimes even contradictorily – accounted for, and the terminology varies among authors. This chapter does not aspire to settle a decades-long debate about the degree of overlap and difference between intersectional and multiple discrimination. Rather, by laying out the

[32] S Bilge, 'Le Banchiment de l'Intersectionnalité' (2015) 28 *Recherches féministes* 2; I Solanke, 'Intersectionality in the UK: Between the American Paradigm and the European Paradox' (2016) *Sociologia del Diritto* 2.

[33] Burri and Schiek (n 24) 4. It also presented the advantage of being a global reference, following its earlier endorsement by the UN (n 19).

[34] See Fredman (n 24) 30; (n 26).

[35] A Bach, L Barrington-Leach and R Minto (eds), 'Protecting All Women from Discrimination: Steps to Take at European and National Level' (Brussels, European Women's Lobby, February 2010), 32.

terminological indeterminacy and controversy, it shows how language crystallises power relations and embodies knowledge politics. To do justice to the language enshrined in EU law, the term multiple discrimination is used throughout this chapter. However, this chapter also reflects the existing lexical inconsistency across regulatory fields, institutions, social entrepreneurs and scholarly authorities in the EU, as well as the recent linguistic shift from 'multiple' to 'intersectional' discrimination observable since the beginning of the 2010s.

The next section refines the understanding of the issue of multiple discrimination in the EU context by investigating the emergence, mobilisations and usages of the notion. Shedding light on the actors that pushed for the recognition of multiple discrimination in EU law, their interests and their agenda ultimately uncovers the meaning they intended to give to the term as well as the legal effect they expected from its introduction into EU legislation.

C. Strategic Mobilisations of the Multiple Discrimination Issue: A Predominantly Feminist Agenda

The meaning of multiple discrimination in the EU has been deeply affected by its context of mobilisation and the history of the construction of EU anti-discrimination law, that have both featured gender equality as a political priority. Since gender equality has been already protected from discrimination since the Rome Treaty in 1957, feminist activists were in a privileged position to influence the content of the legal reform broadening the EU equality protection system. The progressive development of anti-racist advocacy movements at national and transnational level and their demands for legislative reforms to combat racism in the EU from the 1990s onwards, notably through the Starting Line, contributed to the emergence of the issue of multiple discrimination on the feminist agenda.[36]

From the end of the 1980s and the beginning of the 1990s onwards, a number of feminist groups at national level became concerned by the rise of xenophobia and racism in the EU, and by the lack of voice given to migrant and ethnic minority women.[37] In 1995, a report drafted by the European Forum of Socialist-Feminists

[36] See, eg I Chopin and J Niessen, *Proposals for Legislative Measures to Combat Racism and Promote Equal Rights in the European Union* (London, Commission for Racial Equality, 1998).

[37] See A Subhan, *Confronting the Fortress: Black and Migrant Women in the European Union* (Brussels, European Parliament, 1995); S Lees and M McIntosh, 'European Forum of Socialist-Feminists' (1986) 23 *Feminist Review* 139; J Patel, *Overcoming Discrimination: Selected Strategies Empowering Black, Ethnic Minority and Migrant Women* (European Women's Lobby, 1999). Available at: www.womenlobby.org/Overcoming-Discrimination-Selected-Strategies-Empowering-Black-Ethnic-Minority?lang=en 5, 21, 23; European Women's Lobby, (EWL) Position Paper on integration a gender dimension in the proposed measures to implement the anti-discrimination clause (art. 13 of the EC Treaty) (August 2000). Available at: www.womenlobby.org/-Position-Papers-?lang=en&debut_rubrique_articles=10#pagination_rubrique_articles.

(EFSF), commissioned by the European Women's Lobby (EWL) and published by the European Parliament notably addressed 'the multiple ways in which black and migrant women are discriminated against in the labour market, in immigration processes and as a result of racism'.[38] In warning that '[i]f nothing is done to counter this, the development of the Single Market is likely only to enhance this disadvantage', EFSF was already pointing at the gaps in EU law with regard to the problem of multiple discrimination based on sex and race.[39] This brief historical account reveals that early conceptualisations of the multiple discrimination problem were mainly channelled onto the EU policy and legislative agenda through feminist groups. From the outset, the question of multiple discrimination was thus posed, both in international fora and at EU level, from the angle of women's rights.

Multiple discrimination was also on the agenda of advocacy groups engaged in anti-racist legislative lobbing from the 1980s to 2000, albeit in implicit terms. In fact, they had initially pushed for a directive prohibiting discrimination both on the basis of race and religion, to tackle the dangers posed by the racialisation of certain religious groups in Europe.[40] However, the two issues were finally separated in the 2000 Directives (RED and FED). Hence, the multiple discrimination problem materialised on the EU agenda as a feminist issue.

At the legislative level, this women's rights based understanding of multiple discrimination shows in the framing of the issue. The EU is under a duty to promote gender equality, '*especially since women are often the victims of multiple discrimination*'.[41] This formulation reflects the legislative lobbying of feminist advocacy groups like EWL on the Commission and the Parliament. Gender activists in fact had a double interest in bringing the issue of multiple discrimination to the fore.

First, they aimed to avoid a dilution of the resources dedicated by the EU to anti-discrimination policies across the new spectrum of protected grounds, and to ensure the continuity of the political attention granted to feminist issues.[42] The publicity given to the issue of multiple discrimination against women was therefore a strategic way to uphold the protection of gender equality as a priority on the Union's agenda. Indeed, the explanatory memorandum accompanying the FED states that:

> Although equal treatment on the grounds of sex is not covered as such by this Directive, it is nevertheless recognised that discrimination on the grounds of either race/ethnic origin, disability, age, religion/belief or sexual orientation may affect women and men differently. The structural inequalities linked to sex and gender roles of women and

[38] Subhan (n 37) 25.

[39] ibid.

[40] Chopin and Niessen (n 36).

[41] Recitals (14) and (3) of the Race Equality and the Framework Equality Directives (emphasis added).

[42] G Vara Arribas and L Carrasco, 'Gender Equality and the EU: An Assessment of the Current Issues' (2003) 1 *Eipascope* 24.

> men are frequently even more important in the context of dual, triple or multiple discrimination […]. The necessity to apply a gender mainstreaming approach is a logical consequence […].[43]

In the same vein, the Commission's explanatory memorandum accompanying its proposal for the RED makes the case for 'double discrimination' and the 'mainstreaming' of sex equality into the race equality protection.

EWL framed the 'integration of the principle of gender mainstreaming in the draft directive[s]' as a consequence of the need 'to tackle the issue of double/multiple discrimination that many women face'.[44] The rationale put forward was that sex discrimination is 'of a particular structural nature' and concerns 'half of the population'.[45] By contrast, multiple discrimination is absent from the directives protecting gender equality, which confirms its primary conceptualisation as a women's rights issue. The downside of this development is that multiple discrimination has not (yet) been defined in EU law as a transversal problem that could lead to other forms of structural discrimination beyond gender-plus configurations.[46]

Second, the broadening of the protection against discrimination constituted an opportunity for the advocates of gender equality to build alliances with other groups. Because equality advocacy in Europe is mostly structured around salient social identities (race, sexual orientation, etc.), it often leads to what Crenshaw calls 'political intersectionality', a situation in which identity politics is detrimental to the participation and representation of groups at the intersection of several axes of disadvantage.[47] Hence, multiple discrimination can be used as a strategic argument to build coalitions across groups, thus bridging ground-based advocacy.

For feminist activists, 'acknowledging multiplicity and intersectionality ha[d] the potential to strengthen the issue of gender equality'.[48] However, the mobilisation of the multiple discrimination issue as a political mainstreaming strategy and a coalitional tool by feminists partially failed to avoid competition. Cullen explains that tensions arose at the time of the preparation of the 2000 directives because

[43] Explanatory memorandum accompanying the Proposal for a Council Directive COM/2008/0426 final on implementing the principle of equal treatment between persons irrespective of religion or belief, disability, age or sexual orientation [2008] C303/8.

[44] See European Women's Lobby n 37). See also the amendments proposed by the European Parliament, 'Report on the proposal for a Council directive on implementing the principle of equal treatment between persons irrespective of racial or ethnic origin' A5 (2000) 136 final, 16 May 2000 and 'Report on the proposal for a Council directive on the proposal for a Council directive establishing a general framework for equal treatment in employment and occupation' A5 (2000) 264, 21 September 2000.

[45] EWL(n 37).

[46] See P Cullen, 'The Platform of European Social NGOs: Ideology, Division and Coalition' (2010) 15 *Journal of Political Ideologies* 317, 331.

[47] Crenshaw (1991) (n 2).

[48] Burri and Schiek (n 24) 5.

EWL understood multiple discrimination as 'a hierarchical phenomenon defined as different forms of discrimination added to structural discrimination based on sex', putting forward that 'most people disadvantaged by intersectional discrimination are female', a position not necessarily shared by other NGOs.[49]

At the legislative level, the issue of intersectionality has not yet given rise to a transversal framework applicable to multidimensional discrimination across all protected grounds.[50] This shortcoming could explain why multiple discrimination as a legal concept has not had more bite in EU law so far.

III. Differentiated Protection Against Multiple Discrimination

The reforms introduced by the 2000 directives anchored the notion of multiple discrimination in EU law. However, its underdevelopment entertains uncertainties and confusion around its meaning, legal relevance, and utility for the fight against discrimination in the EU. The consequence is a gap between the empirically demonstrated problems posed by multiple discrimination and the patchy protection offered by EU law.

A. Legislation: Very Limited Protection

The attention given to multiple discrimination in EU law is an important, but limited, achievement. Firstly, the discussions about multiple discrimination have not translated into a full prohibitive apparatus. Only enshrined in the recitals (14) and (3) of the RED and FED, this issue is currently not addressed through a binding legal provision. Nonetheless, it has political value as a guideline in making and interpreting EU anti-discrimination law. This lack of directly binding force is paired with a silence on content, as the notion is not defined. The situation raises questions as to the meaning and purpose of this relatively new concept in EU anti-discrimination law that have still not been clarified today.

The Commission, however, highlighted the 'need to tackle', 'defin[e]' and 'provide effective remedies' for multiple discrimination on the occasion of its proposal for a Horizontal Directive in 2008.[51] Despite these acknowledgments, the

[49] ibid and Cullen (n 46).

[50] However, a recent institutional report on minority rights indicates a re-mobilisation of intersectionality theory to understand the grounds of race, ethnicity, nationality, culture, religion and language as co-constitutive, i.e. 'closely linked and interrelated'. See Carrera et al (n 24).

[51] Proposal for a Council Directive COM/2008/0426 final on implementing the principle of equal treatment between persons irrespective of religion or belief, disability, age or sexual orientation [2008]

Commission ultimately opted for a non-binding provision modelled on the recitals of the RED and FED.[52]

The Parliament, consulted in the framework of what was originally the consultation procedure,[53] proposed a systematic prohibition of multiple discrimination through comprehensive amendments, including a transversal definition in Article 1 of the envisaged directive:

> 1. This Directive lays down a framework for combating discrimination, including multiple discrimination […].
>
> 2. Multiple discrimination occurs when discrimination is based:
>
> (a) on any combination of the grounds of religion or belief, disability, age, or sexual orientation, or
>
> (b) on any one or more of the grounds set out in paragraph 1, and also on the ground of any one or more of
>
> (i) sex […],
>
> (ii) racial or ethnic origin […], or
>
> (iii) nationality[…].
>
> 3. In this Directive, multiple discrimination and multiple grounds shall be construed accordingly.[54]

It also proposed to modify recital (13) by amendments 10 and 23 as follows:

> This Directive also takes into account multiple discrimination. As discrimination can occur on two or more […] grounds […], the Community should […] promote equality, whatever combination of characteristics […] a person may have. Effective legal procedures should be available to deal with situations of multiple discrimination. In particular national legal procedures should ensure that a complainant can raise all aspects of a multiple-discrimination claim in a single procedure.[55]

The Parliament also proposed to systematically include multiple discrimination as a concept in its own right, along with indirect and direct discrimination and discrimination by association.[56]

OJ C303/8. See E Howard, 'The Case for a Considered Hierarchy of Discrimination Grounds in EU Law' (2006) 13 *Maastricht Journal of European and Comparative Law* 445. The Commission cites expert reports to justify this innovation.

[52] See European Commission, Explanatory Memorandum COM (2008) 426 final.

[53] However, after the Lisbon Treaty came into force, the special legislative procedure for legislation on discrimination followed the consent procedure delineated in Art 289(2) TFEU. The approval of the European Parliament therefore became binding.

[54] See European Parliament Legislative Resolution of 2 April 2009 on the Proposal COM(2008)0426, Amendment 37 of the EP, 2009, Art 1.

[55] Amendments 10 and 23, see (n 54).

[56] See (n 54): amendments 7, 12, 16 on the recitals citing the different existing forms of discrimination and 80 on reporting obligations.

B. Latest Developments: Towards Legislative Clarifications on Multiple Discrimination?

Until recently, the Council had retained none of the Parliament's proposed legislative changes concerning multiple discrimination.[57] Discussions of the legislative proposal since 2008 have not yielded unanimity so far, curtailing the perspective of an upcoming change. All in all, even though EU civil society, anti-discrimination experts and the European Parliament have pushed for reforms towards a comprehensive framework of protection against multiple discrimination beyond the current gender-plus understanding, these attempts have not been successful. Multiple discrimination thus remains a grey zone, officially depicted as a problematic issue, but still outside of the binding scope of the anti-discrimination directives.

Recent Council discussions on the Commission's 2008 Proposal, held in June 2017, nevertheless point towards a clearer and stronger stance on multiple discrimination. This could potentially translate into a legislative prohibition if the new anti-discrimination directive was adopted, especially because of the Commission's support. A report reveals that the 2017 Maltese presidency aimed to 'clarify the issue of multiple discrimination', recognising that 'discrimination on the grounds covered in the proposal could also intersect with discrimination on the grounds of racial or ethnic origin and nationality, as well as sex or gender identity'.[58] The new text under discussion also understands 'multiple discrimination in general terms instead of singling out a specific combination of grounds' as is currently the case with 'multiple discrimination against women'. Hence, the current women's rights based understanding of the problem of multiple discrimination could evolve towards a more transversal one.

Concretely, recital (12) of the new text clarifies that direct discrimination includes multiple discrimination.[59] While recital (13) still specifies that 'women are often the victims of multiple discrimination', new recital (12)(ab) acknowledges that '[d]iscrimination on the basis of religion or belief, disability, age or sexual orientation may *be compounded by or intersect with* discrimination on grounds of sex or gender identity, racial or ethnic origin, and nationality'.[60] Recital (21) authorises Member States to take positive action measures to support 'group[s] of

[57] See Council, 'Proposal for a Council Directive on implementing the principle of equal treatment between persons irrespective of religion or belief, disability, age or sexual orientation (consolidated text)' ST 14500/16, 14 December 2016.

[58] Council, 'Proposal for a Council Directive on implementing the principle of equal treatment between persons irrespective of religion or belief, disability, age or sexual orientation (consolidated text)' ST 9481/17, 1 June 2017.

[59] ibid.

[60] ibid.

persons [...] *having a combination of characteristics*'.[61] The proposal also prohibits multiple discrimination in its binding provisions Articles 2(2)(a) and (b) 'on one or more [...] grounds' and for 'indirect discrimination on one or *multiple grounds*'.[62] At the definitional level, however, the use of both the terms 'compounded by' and 'intersect' generates confusion as regards the difference between the two terms and the challenges they pose to EU law.

As it stands, the proposal bears witness to a growing awareness of the harms created by multiple discrimination and indicates a willingness to close the legal gap. That said, the Council discussions reveal disagreements as to the place of multiple discrimination in the directive, the grounds covered and the attached sanctions.[63] More generally, currently all member states do not unanimously support the inclusion of multiple discrimination in the directive.[64] Hence, the perspective of a full legislative ban is still distant and multiple discrimination remains a grey zone in EU legislation at present.

C. The Policy Path: Recommendations, Enforcement, Monitoring, Funding

By contrast to fragmentary legislation, intersectionality has been a blossoming concept in policy and academic debates at the EU level. The problem of multiple discrimination has gained visibility through the Commission's efforts to push the EU's equality programme forward, in a time of legitimacy crisis and legislative deadlock, supported by a growing body of research. As a political rhetoric, multiple discrimination has become a rationale for further reform and better enforcement of anti-discrimination law. Diverse policy tools aim to fill the gap between a declared necessity to fight against multiple discrimination and the absence of clear legislative guidelines.

At the political and institutional level, the Commission, national equality bodies and experts have contributed to the production of an important body of research, reports, and programs for action addressing multiple discrimination.[65] From 2000 onwards, EU institutions regularly noted the existence of, and the

[61] ibid.

[62] ibid.

[63] See Council, 'Proposal for a Council Directive on implementing the principle of equal treatment between persons irrespective of religion or belief, disability, age or sexual orientation (consolidated text)' ST 10779/17, 29 June 2017, 9.

[64] ibid at 8.

[65] See, eg Council, Decision 2000/750/EC establishing a Community action programme to combat discrimination (2001 to 2006) [2000] OJ L303/23; Council, Decision No 1554/2005/EC establishing a programme relating to the Community framework strategy on gender equality [2005] OJ L255/9 and Council, 'Resolution on the situation of persons with disabilities in the European Union' [2008] OJ C75/1; European Parliament, 'Resolution on the situation of women from minority groups in the European Union' 2003/2109(INI), 9 March 2004; European Parliament, 'Resolution on the situation of Roma women in the European Union' 2005/2164(INI), 1 June 2006; Commission, 'Non-discrimination

need to tackle, multiple discrimination.[66] In 2004, the Commission stated in a Green Paper that '[t]he development of an integrated approach [wa]s intended, in particular, to respond to situations of multiple discrimination'.[67] In 2007 and 2009, two major research reports were financed and published by the European Commission on the topic, followed by more recent reports on 'intersectional discrimination'.[68]

The issue has thus progressively gained relevance in policy discussions and scientific research, despite its limited anchoring in legislation. This is especially visible in the areas of enforcement, monitoring and funding. For example the 'Community action programme to combat discrimination 2001–2006' recommended effective monitoring of multiple discrimination, while the European Year for Equal Opportunities in 2007 promoted a 'balanced treatment of grounds with the focus on multiple discrimination and an obligation to mainstream gender across all activities'.[69] The Commission also dedicated special funding to improve the situation of Roma women as a group facing multiple discrimination.[70]

In practice, the conceptualisation of multiple discrimination in EU policy retains a predominant gender dimension. Even though signs of diversification are visible, a transversal policy strategy to combat all kinds of multiple discrimination has not yet been elaborated. At the same time, the production of a political discussion on intersectional discrimination by the EU Commission might be perceived as part of a new mode of governance aiming to create consensus within the EU political space, and thus encourage reforms at the national level. This form of top-down acculturation could potentially lead to consensus building over time, and to overcoming the current Member State opposition to reform.

At the discursive level, one observes that the conceptualisation of multiple discrimination shifted over time, translating into a progressive change of linguistic paradigm. Two stages appear in the conversations about multiple discrimination. From debates on a multi-ground equality framework, discussions on multiple discrimination emerged. In a second moment, the term intersectionality surged in recent analyses and progressively competed with framing in terms of multiple

and equal opportunities for all – A framework strategy' COM(2005) 224 final (Brussels, 2005); Commission, 'Strategy for equality between women and men' (2010); Commission, 'Report on the implementation of the UN Convention on the Rights of Persons with Disabilities (CRPD) by the European Union 2010–2015' SWD(2014) 182 final (Brussels, 2014). See also Carles and Jubany-Baucells (n 11); D Schiek and J Mulder, 'Intersectionality in EU Law: a Critical Re-appraisal' in Lawson and Schiek (n 22) 27, 3; BG Bello, 'Discriminazione multiple e intersezionalità: queste sconosciute!' (ASGI, 2015). Available at: www.asgi.it/wp-content/uploads/2015/05/Approfondimento-Barbara-Giovanna-Bello_-Maggio-2015.pdf.

[66] See ibid.

[67] European Commission (n 22) 28.

[68] See Bielefeldt (n 23); Burri and Schiek (n 24) and eg Crowley (n 24); Fredman (n 24).

[69] See Commission, 'Implementation, results and overall assessment of the 2007 European Year of Equal Opportunities for All' COM (2009) 269 final, 19 June 2009. Decision 2000/750/EC (61), recital 5, Art 2 and annex (I)(e).

[70] ibid.

discrimination.[71] This evolution reflects a change in the political demands associated with the notion of multiple discrimination.

Originally serving as a rhetorical keystone giving seeming coherence and unity to a fragmented body of anti-discrimination norms, the discourse on the necessity to combat multiple discrimination was pushed forward as a leitmotiv for a comprehensive equality protection.[72] Following a similar logic of coherence, the problem of multiple discrimination has also been instrumentalised as a tool of resource management. The majority of Member States have, for instance, re-arranged their anti-discrimination institutions following an integrated approach with single equality bodies or integrated human rights institutions.[73] This has caused some concern about the redistribution of constant (or shrinking) resources across more grounds, and the dilution of ground-specific expertise along a broader spectrum.[74] In this first stage, however, the real problems caused by multiple discrimination were not soundly addressed. In 2006, Verloo regretted that 'studies do not use (structural) intersectionality as a concept to help understand the nature of the relationship between different inequalities'.[75]

In the second stage, the instrumental use of the issue of multiple discrimination as a political leitmotiv gave way to deeper reflections on the problem itself and how it challenges EU law in its current state. For instance, the GendeRace report calls for 'an explicit reference to multiple discrimination as an especially vulnerable form of discrimination within the new European Directive enlarging the scope of protection against discrimination' and '[a]n operational definition of multiple and intersectional discrimination meet[ing] the standards set out in Article 21 […ECFR…] that could render it possible to offer protection from multiple discrimination'.[76] Similarly, the Fundamental Rights Agency calls for policies, data collection, equality bodies and complaint procedures that facilitate the identification and treatment of multiple discrimination, as well as for a legislative definition and prohibition.[77] In parallel, growing academic interest in the field has revived and shifted the debate on multiple discrimination towards intersectionality.[78] By underlining the specific nature of intersectional discrimination, these discussions seem to push for legislative and doctrinal reforms to improve equality protection beyond the predominant gender-plus understanding of multiple discrimination.

[71] See (n 22).

[72] See Decision 2000/750/EC (n 61).

[73] Art 13 of the RED and Arts 12 and 20 of the Gender Directives 2004/113/EC and 2006/54/EC have rendered compulsory the creation of national equality bodies dealing with assistance to victims, reporting and recommendations in the fields of sex and race equality.

[74] See S Walby, J Armstrong and S Strid, 'Intersectionality and the Quality of the Gender Equality Architecture' (2012) 19 *Social Politics: International Studies in Gender, State & Society* 446.

[75] Verloo (n 24) 215.

[76] Carles and Jubany-Baucells (n 10) 270–271.

[77] EU-MIDIS, 17. See (n 6).

[78] See Schiek and Chege (n 24); Lawson and Schiek (n 11). See also Carles and Jubany-Baucells (n 10); Fredman (n 22).

While the solutions offered to the problem of multiple discrimination suffer from a discrepancy between political ambitions and legal means, questions remain as to whether and how the problem could be tackled within the current EU anti-discrimination apparatus. Although a legislative ban would bring much-needed clarity, the references to multiple discrimination in the RED and FED suggest that the problem could be addressed through judicial interpretation. However, so far the Court of Justice has not played its part in addressing intersectional discrimination.

IV. Remedying Multiple Discrimination: Obstacles and Resistance

Despite its historical role in advancing equality in the early age of the EU, the Court of Justice has not taken the lead on new anti-discrimination innovations to tackle multiple discrimination. Even though similar issues have been brought to the attention of the Court before, the question was only posed explicitly for the first time in 2016. However, to this day, the CJEU has neither proposed a doctrinal framework nor appropriate remedies to deal with multiple discrimination. This deficit is problematic as important strands of inequality risk remaining under the Court's radar. It is especially disconcerting considering the general lack of minimum standards dealing with intersectional discrimination in Member States. The absence of explicit jurisprudential guidelines to recognise and remedy multiple discrimination thus contributes to the invisibility of the harms it causes.

A. Obstacles to the Recognition of Multiple Discrimination

The barriers preventing the doctrinal recognition of synergistic discrimination based on multiple grounds are numerous and diverse. Firstly, the absence of an explicit and binding prohibition of multiple discrimination in EU legislation is problematic. It does not provide the Court with a clear mandate in redressing complex forms of inequality or in conducting combined analyses of discrimination.[79] However, national examples show that multiple discrimination has been recognised through judicial interpretation in jurisdictions which did not necessarily have a specific legislative provision.[80]

Secondly, the current legislative architecture encourages a fragmented approach. The anti-discrimination apparatus, composed of different legislative instruments,

[79] See Case C-443/15 *Parris* EU:C:2016:897.

[80] Only eight EU Member States have references to multiple discrimination in their legislation. See Fredman (n 22) 51–53.

the Treaties and the ECFR, apply different regimes of exceptions, justifications, remedies and scopes of application *ratione materiae* to different grounds. This poses questions about the relevant legal regime and standard of review in case of multiple discrimination. Hence, the harmonisation of the material scopes of the different directives through a Horizontal Directive would be an important step towards the facilitation of an integrated approach to multiple discrimination.

Thirdly, even though nothing prevents applicants from bringing claims of multiple discrimination to the Court of Justice, the complexities highlighted above contribute to deter them. It encourages litigators to strategically select the most 'intuitive' (or perhaps 'favourable') ground, thus limiting access to justice for the victims of multiple discrimination.

The prevailing single-ground approach is a fourth obstacle to efficient redress because it heightens the evidence threshold by requiring proof for each ground taken in isolation, which is at odds with the reality of co-constitutive forms of multiple discrimination. This links to the difficulties of selecting appropriate comparators for multiple discrimination cases:[81] should the comparator be someone who shares one, all or none of the characteristics claimed? To render situations of intersectional discrimination visible, the comparison should arguably be made with the most privileged individual in all concerned groups, be it real or hypothetical.[82] However, even such inclusive comparisons often lead to truncated visions of the reality of inequality.[83]

Because 'inequalities are not independent' but rather the product of 'many historical, political, social and cultural intersections',[84] a contextual and situated analysis informed by an interdisciplinary methodology relying on social science could better inform the analyses of discrimination by courts.[85] As some pregnancy discrimination case law proves, the Court of Justice punctually abandoned the comparator-based framework in favour of a more contextual analysis.[86] A victim's perspective approach focusing on harmful effects – as already used in cases of harassment and stereotyping in the US – as opposed to a perpetrator's perspective focusing on differential treatment and the use of grounds as 'vehicles'

[81] See S Goldberg, 'Discrimination by Comparison' (2011) 120 *Yale Law Journal* 690; M Kotkin, 'Diversity and Discrimination: A Look at Complex Bias' (2009) 50 *William and Mary Law Review* 1439.

[82] See UK Equality Act 2010 and its pending provision on double discrimination, which recommends comparing with the most privileged categories.

[83] See Goldberg; Kotkin (n 81).

[84] Verloo (n 24) 222.

[85] Canadian courts have acknowledged this necessity: 'In Canada, as the understanding of human rights evolves, the focus is increasingly on a contextualized approach to discrimination' in Ontario Human Rights Commission, 'An intersectional approach to discrimination: Addressing multiple grounds in human rights claims' (2001). See also the socio-legal framework proposed in I Solanke, 'A method for intersectional discrimination in EU Labour Law' in A Bogg, C Costello and ACL Davies (eds), *Research Handbook of European Labour Law* (Cheltenham, Edward Elgar Publishing, 2016).

[86] See Case C-177/88 *Elisabeth Johanna Pacifica Dekker v Stichting Vormingscentrum voor Jong Volwassenen (VJV-Centrum) Plus* EU:C:1990:383.

to think about stigmatisation and disadvantage, would certainly lead to better recognition of co-constitutive forms of multiple discrimination.[87] As Kotkin puts it, 'nothing in discrimination law doctrine [...] necessarily prevents some expansion of the evidentiary pool in this manner'.[88] However, courts in general, and the CJEU in particular, are reluctant to abandon the comparator-based test, probably because of the scientific appearance and the colour of neutrality it confers to anti-discrimination analysis.[89]

Despite this reticence, landmark cases like *Roca Álvarez* (2010),[90] *Coleman* (2008),[91] and *CHEZ* (2015)[92] show that the Court's jurisprudence can prove well informed by assessments of social power relations, stereotyping and inequality structures. Therefore, this kind of contextual analysis already developed in some other fields of the Court's equality jurisprudence could be a useful complement to the hypothetical comparators already in use. However, it poses questions pertaining to resources and expertise, where national equality bodies could play an important role.

These obstacles make the recognition of co-constitutive forms of multiple discrimination difficult, yet the next section shows that the CJEU has more and more explicitly grappled with the problem of multiple discrimination in recent times.

B. Multiple Discrimination at the CJEU: An Issue Too Long Overlooked

So far, preliminary references have not given the Court many occasions to become aware of the magnitude of the issue of multiple discrimination. Besides, even when judges have been exposed to this reality, a single-ground approach has mostly prevailed. Nonetheless, some signs in the CJEU discrimination jurisprudence show sensibilities for the problem of complex inequality and co-constitutive discrimination, even where the language of multiple discrimination is absent.

[87] See Justice L'Heureux Dubé's dissent in *Egan v Canada*, [1995] 2 SCR 513 and *Price Waterhouse v Hopkins*, 490 US 228 (1989), 109 S Ct 1775. On the perspective discussion, see AD Freeman, 'Legitimizing Racial Discrimination through Antidiscrimination Law: A Critical Review of Supreme Court Doctrine' (1978) 62 *Minnesota Law Review* 1049. On stereotyping, see A Timmer, 'Judging Stereotypes: What the European Court of Human Rights Can Borrow from American and Canadian Equal Protection Law' (2015) 63 *The American Journal of Comparative Law* 239.

[88] Kotkin (n 81).

[89] See Goldberg (n 81) 728.

[90] Case C-104/09 *Pedro Manuel Roca Álvarez v Sesa Start España ETT SA* EU:C:2010:561.

[91] Case C-303/06 *S Coleman v Attridge Law and Steve Law* EU:C:2008:415.

[92] Case C-83/14 *CHEZ Razpredelenie Bulgaria AD contre Komisia za zashtita ot diskriminatsia* EU:C:2015:480.

i. Overview of the Cases brought on Multiple Grounds

Table 2.1 below tracks all cases so-far decided by the CJEU in which claims of discrimination invoking multiple grounds have been put forward.[93] It helps to understand how multiple discrimination claims reach the CJEU and how they are dealt with by the Court.

Eliminating the cases that have been either rejected or dismissed by the Court (in grey), we are left with a pool of seven multiple discrimination cases since 2007. Among these six preliminary references and one staff (appeal) case where discrimination has been scrutinised, five cases have been formally examined through a single-ground lens, namely *Lindorfer* (2007), *Kleist* (2010), *Odar* (2012), *Z.* (2014) and *Parris* (2016). *Meister* (2012) and *Milkova* (2017) are the only cases in which the Court has formally adopted a combined approach.[94] In *Lindorfer* and *Kleist*, which involved combined claims of sex and age discrimination, only the sex discrimination claim was examined.[95] Age was not examined because it was not a protected ground at the time of the facts in *Lindorfer*, and it was not referred by the national Court in *Kleist*.

Hence, the only claims where multiple grounds were really taken into account were *Meister*, *Odar*, *Z.*, *Parris* and *Milkova*.[96] In these cases, the Court either did not examine the multiple discrimination claim on substance (*Meister* and *Milkova*) or formally declined to construct a targeted doctrinal framework to assess multiple discrimination.[97] These decisions, albeit revealing fundamental gaps in the Court's ability to redress multiple discrimination, are nonetheless important because they show some signs of intersectional sensibility at the CJEU even where the language of multiple discrimination is absent.[98] From the above-mentioned case law, we can trace three ways in which the CJEU has, to varying extents, displayed sensibility for the question of co-constitutive inequalities in multiple discrimination cases.[99]

[93] Last updated in March 2017. The present analysis only considers cases that have explicitly invoked multiple grounds but some cases that have been brought under a sole protected ground could be analysed as multiple discrimination cases. See for instance the analysis in J Fudge and A Zbyszewska, 'An Intersectional Approach to Age Discrimination in the European Union: Bridging Dignity and Distribution?' in A Numhauser-Henning and M Rönnmar (eds), *Age Discrimination and Labour Law: Comparative and Conceptual Perspectives in the EU and Beyond* (Alphen aan den Rijn, Kluwer, 2015).

[94] See Table 2.1

[95] ibid.

[96] ibid.

[97] ibid.

[98] The expression 'intersectional sensibility' refers to the fact that the Court, despite never using a fully fledged intersectional method, has shown signs of engagement with the problems raised by multiple discrimination and the recommendations of intersectionality theory. See Fredman (n 24) 71–79.

[99] These labels are based on McCall's delineation of inter-, intra- and anti-categorical complexity in L McCall, 'The Complexity of Intersectionality' (Spring 2005) 30 *Signs* 1771.

Table 2.1 Cases decided by the CJEU involving multiple grounds of discrimination

CASE	GROUNDS CLAIMED	TYPE OF CLAIM	DECISION
C-227/04 P *Maria-Luise Lindorfer v. Council of the European Union* EU:C:2007:490, [2007] ECR I-6767 (Appeal following decision T-204/01 (2004) of the General Court) Facts: An EU worker claimed that the use of gender-based actuarial factors in the calculation of her pension benefits and their conversion in national currency put her at a disadvantage.	• Sex • Age • Nationality	**Combined** claim of breach of the principle of equal treatment based on age and sex (T-204/01, [44]) **Separate** claim of discrimination based on nationality (T-204/01, [39])	**Separate examination:** discrimination based on sex but no discrimination based on age; nationality-based claim dismissed
C-356/09 *Pensionsversicherungsanstalt v Christine Kleist* EU:C:2010:703, [2010] ECR I-11939 Facts: the company employing Ms. Kleist decided to terminate the contracts of all employees satisfying the conditions for retirement. The qualifying was 60 for women and later for men. Ms. Kleist wished to continue working and claimed age and sex discrimination.	• Sex • Age (only in Kleist's submitted observations, not in the preliminary reference questions)	Question **only based on** • **Sex:** Article 3(1)(c) of Directive 76/207 NB: in the preliminary reference, there was no question regarding age discrimination, and thus the CJEU did not examine Directive 2000/78/EC. However, the applicant claimed both sex and age discrimination based on both directives. The CJEU only examined sex discrimination but age entered into the analysis through the question of pension rules.	**Single-ground examination:** • Direct discrimination based on sex • No question about age discrimination, hence no finding on this issue.

(continued)

Table 2.1 ***(Continued)***

CASE	GROUNDS CLAIMED	TYPE OF CLAIM	DECISION
C-310/10 *Ministerul Justiției și Libertăților Cetățenești v Ștefan Agafiței and Others* EU:C:2011:467, [2011] ECR I-05989 Facts: Romanian judges claimed discrimination as regards pay, based on social class or socio- professional membership and place of work.	• Place of work (not protected under EU law) • Membership in a socio-professional category (not protected under EU law)	**Combined** question based on • Article 15 of Council Directive 2000/43 • Article 17 of Council Directive 2000/78	**Inadmissibility of** the preliminary reference: the grounds cited are not protected under the Directives 2000/43/EC and 2000/78/EC
C-415/10 *Galina Meister v Speech Design Carrier Systems GmbH* EU:C:2012:217 [2012] Facts: after her application to an advertised job position had been dismissed twice without her being invited to an interview although her profile matched the job description, Ms Meister asked the employer to provide information on her rejection, which the employer refused to do. She claimed discrimination based on sex, ethnic origin and age.	• Sex • Ethnic origin • Age	**Combined** question based on • Sex: Article 19(1) of Directive 2006/54 • Ethnic origin: Article 8(1) of Directive 2000/43 • Age: Article 10(1) of Directive 2000/78 (NB: the articles claimed cover the exact same provision)	**No examination on the substance of the grounds (taken as combined)** Direct or indirect discrimination might exist – it is for the national Court to decide. There is no right to information for the rejected applicant vis a vis the employer.

C-152/11 *Johann Odar v Baxter Deutschland GmbH* EU:C:2012:772 [2012] Facts: In calculating the compensation of the applicant, the employer applied a formula that automatically reduced the entitlement for workers over 54 years of age. In addition, the calculation formula took into account an earliest possible retirement age of 60 based on the applicant's severe disability, instead of 65 for non-disabled workers. This further reduced the applicant's compensation, who claimed discrimination on grounds of both age and disability.	• Age • Disability	**Separate** questions on grounds of age and disability based on • Age: Articles 1 and 16 of Directive 2000/78 or justified under Article 6(1)(a) Disability: Articles 1 and 16 of Directive 2000/78	**Separate examination but combination considered.** Discrimination on grounds of disability (age taken into account in the proportionality analysis)
C-363/12 *Z. v A Government department e The Board of management of a community school* EU:C:2014:159 [2014] Facts: a woman born without a uterus but with an otherwise functioning reproductive system resorted to surrogacy to give birth to her biological child. She requested maternity leave but was refused the leave on grounds that she had not been pregnant. She claimed on grounds of sex and disability discrimination. NB: intersectional discrimination argument brought at oral proceedings	• Sex • Disability	**Separate** questions on grounds of sex and disability based on: • Sex: Article 3 TEU, Articles 8 TFEU and 157 TFEU, and/or Articles 21, 23, 33 and 34 of the Charter of Fundamental Rights of the European Union and Art 4 and 14 of Directive 2006/54 • Disability: Article 10 TFEU, and/or Articles 21, 26 and 34 of the Charter and Articles 3(1) and 5 of Directive 2000/78	**Separate examination:** no discrimination – outside the scope of EU law

(continued)

Table 2.1 ***(Continued)***

CASE	GROUNDS CLAIMED	TYPE OF CLAIM	DECISION
C-423/15 *Nils-Johannes Kratzer v R+V Allgemeine Versicherung AG* EU:C:2016:604 [2016] Facts: The application of Mr Kratzer to a trainee position was rejected. He sent the employer a demand for compensation against age discrimination. The employer asserted that it was not its intention and invited him for an interview. Mr Kratzer refused to go to the interview and brought a claim of sex discrimination to courts. He later added a claim of sex discrimination when he realised that only female interns had been selected.	• Sex • Age	**Combined** question based on • Age: Article 3(1)(a) of Directive 2000/78 • Sex: Article 14(1)(a) of Directive 2006/54	Cannot be considered as a case of discrimination: **abuse of rights.**
C-443/15 *David L. Parris v Trinity College Dublin and Others* EU:C:2016:897 [2016] Facts: Mr Parris was refused access to a scheme for survivor's benefits by his employer on grounds that he had entered partnership with his same-sex partner past the age of 60. In fact, the reform authorising same-sex partnerships in Ireland was passed after Mr Parris was already 60, excluding any earlier application to the survivor's benefits scheme. Mr Parris brought a claim of discrimination on grounds of age and sexual orientation.	• Sexual orientation • Age	**Separate and combined** questions based on • Sexual orientation: Article 2 of Directive 2000/78 *If not:* • Age: Article 2, in conjunction with Article 6(2) of Directive 2000/78 *If not:* • Combination of sexual orientation and age: Article 2 in conjunction with Article 6(2) of Directive 2000/78	**Separate examination:** no discrimination neither separately nor in combination

C-27/16 *Angel Marinkov contre Predsedatel na Darzhavna agentsia za balgarite v chuzhbina* EU:C:2016:943 [2016] Facts: Mr Marinkov's employment relationship was terminated because of a restructuration. His position was suppressed while two other similar positions were created to replace his two female colleagues' former positions. No precise criteria were defined to decide who would be maintained or not. Mr Marinkov thus claimed sex discrimination in combination with directive 2000/78/EC.	• Sex • Unknown ground under Directive 2000/78/EC (the preliminary reference does not mention on which ground)	**Combined** questions based on: • Article 3(1)(c) of directive 2000/78 • Article 14(1)(c), 18 and 25 of directive 2006/54	**Incompetence of** the Court
C-406/15 *Petya Milkova v Izpalnitelen direktor na Agentsiata za privatizatsia i sledprivatizatsionen kontrol* EU:C:2017:198 [2017]	• Disability • Civil servant status (not protected under EU law)	**Combined** questions based on: • Article 4 and 7 of directive 2000/78 • Article 5(2) of UNCRPD	**No examination on the substance of the grounds (taken as combined)**

(continued)

Table 2.1 *(Continued)*

CASE	GROUNDS CLAIMED	TYPE OF CLAIM	DECISION
Facts: Ms Milkova's worked as a civil servant in an Agency employing both employees and civil servants. When her work contract was terminated, no authorisation was asked to the labour inspectorate, although this is required for employees living with disabilities. Although Ms Milkova's disability should have obliged her employer to ask for such an authorisation, would she have been an employee, such an authorisation was not mandatory because of her civil servant status. Ms Milkova thus claimed discrimination involving her professional status and her disability.		(although the national Court clarified that it understood the differential treatment to be based on the applicant's professional status, it expressed doubts as regards the respect of the principle of equal treatment based on disability)	It is for the national Court to determine whether there is discrimination based on civil servant status within the category of disabled employees: • Civil servant status is not a ground covered by EU law • Disability is not the ground on which differential treatment arose • If the national Court finds discrimination, the positive action measures afforded to disabled employees must be extended to civil servants.

ii. The Contextual Route

The first indication as to how to assess multiple discrimination cases can be read in *Meister*.[100] In this case, the applicant complained because the employer, who had twice rejected her application without hiring any other candidate, refused to disclose information on the reasons for her rejection. Without this information, she could not attempt to establish a *prima facie* case of discrimination and was thus deprived of a legal remedy, although she alleged multiple discrimination based on sex, age and ethnic origin. Albeit leaving the examination of the issue of discrimination on substance to the national Court, the Court opened the door for contextual assessment in discrimination cases. The decision upheld AG Mengozzi's recommendation to 'take[e] into account the wider factual context' when establishing a comparator is impossible.[101] Because the establishment of a comparator proves difficult in co-constitutive forms of multiple discrimination, the contextual methodology could prove useful, and would also allow to take into account the role of negative ascriptions, harmful stereotypes, stigmatisation and specific kinds of vulnerability. In *Meister*, however, such a contextual assessment with a view of establishing a *prima facie* case of discrimination was left to the national Court. Hence, the CJEU's insight in the ways the assessment could be conducted remains limited.

iii. The Intra-categorical Route: Looking for Modifying Factors of Disadvantage

Ground-based analyses of discrimination that take into account modifying vectors of disadvantage have been elsewhere called 'capacious interpretation of grounds'.[102] This approach addresses the relevant 'multiple intersecting power relations' by taking into account 'all aspects of an individual's identity [...] even within one identity ground', '[r]ather than focusing on only one axis of disadvantage and assuming the remaining characteristics are privileged'.[103] In *Odar*, a worker resigned after reaching an agreement with his company that it would not affect his compensation rights.[104] As he was older than 54 at the time of his contract termination, the compensation was calculated based on the earliest retirement date possible. Because of his severe disability, Mr. Odar could retire at age 60, instead of the standard retirement age of 65. Consequently, his compensation was calculated based on a shorter length of service and was reduced. The earlier retirement date meant that a compensatory measure to accommodate his disability was

[100] See Table 2.1.
[101] See ibid: AG Opinion in Case C-415/10 *Meister* EU:C:2012:217, paras 31, 37, 38.
[102] Fredman (n 24) 10.
[103] ibid. See CEDAW and CERD (n 20). 'Convention on the Rights of Persons with Disabilities' (adopted 13 December 2006, entered into force 3 May 2008) UNGA Res 61/106.
[104] See Table 2.1.

thus turned into a financial disadvantage. As a result, Mr Odar claimed discrimination based both on age and disability.

The question of discrimination was split on each ground. Despite this separation, the Court implicitly acknowledged the synergistic effects of age and disability, albeit not using the language of multiple discrimination. It, in fact, introduced age as a modifying factor of disadvantage in the proportionality analysis of the disability-based discrimination question. By considering the effects of old age on disability, the Court acknowledged 'the risks faced by severely disabled people, who generally face greater difficulties in finding new employment, as well as *the fact that those risks tend to become exacerbated as they approach retirement age*'.[105] In the weighted (or infringed) proportionality test that followed, the CJEU also stated that '[s]everely disabled people have *specific needs, stemming* both from the protection their condition requires and *from the need to anticipate possible worsening of their condition* [because] *with advancing age, those financial needs may increase*'.[106] In so doing, the Court shed light on the reinforcing dynamics of the discriminatory effects. Even if age discrimination was not acknowledged *per se*, it influenced the assessment of the effects of the policy on ageing disabled people.

The intra-ground approach thus allows for a more flexible analysis, taking into account modifiers and synergistic factors within a less rigid comparator-based approach to discrimination.[107] Similar approaches can be fragmentarily detected in the Court's approach to claims that have been brought on single grounds but involve more factors, even though no mention of either 'multiple discrimination' or 'intersectionality' is made.[108] This has notably been the case regarding discrimination concerning combinations of gender and age, for instance with questions of earlier retirement age limits imposed on women with respect to men or disadvantages in pension benefits due to interrupted labour periods linked to maternity leave.[109] Cases concerning the survivor's pension benefits in same-sex partnerships similarly showed sensibility in respect of the interactions of sexual orientation and age.[110] Finally, the famous *P v S* (1996) case shows how an intersectional appreciation of the different implications of gender status led the Court to acknowledge that gender identity is covered by the protection against sex discrimination.[111]

iv. The Inter-categorical Route: Focus on the Intersections

If the intra-ground approach has been already hinted at by the Court and could be a doctrinal avenue to assess multiple discrimination, other claims have

[105] See ibid, Case C-152/11 *Odar* EU:C:2012:772, para 69 (emphasis added).

[106] ibid.

[107] Fredman (n 24) 69.

[108] See, eg Fredman (n 24) 71–72; Fudge and Zbyszewska1 (n 93) 159–160.

[109] ibid, 71. See, eg Case C-152/84 *Marshall v Southampton Area Health Authority* EU:C:1986:84; Case C-408/92 *Smith v Avdel Systems Ltd.* EU:C:1994:349.

[110] See Fredman (n 24) 72. See Case C-267/06 *Maruko v Versorgungsanstalt der deutschen Bühnen* EU:C:2008:179; Case C-147/08 *Römer v Freie und Hansestadt Hamburg* EU:C:2011:286.

[111] See Fredman (n 24) 75. See Case C-13/94 *P v S and Cornwall County Council* EU:C:1996:170.

explicitly asked the Court to analyse the intersections of different grounds. *Z.* and *Parris* follow this model and will be the object of this and the next section.[112] In the *Z.* case, the litigators emphasised the synergistic nature of the multiple discrimination arising from a decision to refuse maternity leave to a worker who could not bear a child because of a disability, but who had become a mother via a surrogacy arrangement. While the preliminary reference split the claim of discrimination on grounds of gender and disability, the litigators introduced an intersectional argument at the oral stage.[113]

The Court, however, dissected the question based on each ground and missed the synergistic discriminatory effects produced by the interaction of sex and disability, hence erasing the specific disadvantage of the applicant. In its sex discrimination test, the Court compared the applicant to commissioning fathers, and did not find sex discrimination. This comparison is surprising, as fathers do not benefit from paternity leave in EU law, be they commissioning or not.[114] Second, in its disability discrimination test, the CJEU compared the applicant to non-disabled workers and gave disability a restrictive interpretation as a work impairment, considering that the absence of a uterus for the applicant did not impair her ability to work. Hence, despite asking for an inter-categorical approach, the litigators did not manage to have the Court abandon its strict single-axis approach. In this case, an inter-categorical approach considering the co-exclusionary effects of disability and gender on access to motherhood would have helped to overcome a strictly biological conception of maternity.

v. Parris: *A Recent Illustration of the Blind Spots of EU Equality Law*

This section focuses on *Parris*, the most recent multiple discrimination case at the CJEU and the first to explicitly ask about the combined effects of multiple grounds. In *Parris*, a rule required workers subscribing to survivor's benefits schemes to enter civil partnership before age 60. Mr Parris was, however, unable to do so, as same-sex partnerships were not recognised in Ireland until after his 60th birthday. Like Mr Parris, same-sex couples older than 60 on the date of entry into force of the Irish Civil Partnership Act in 2015 were excluded from the survivor's benefits scheme by the age limit, while younger same-sex couples could subscribe, and heterosexual couples always had this possibility (pre- as well as post-2015) before turning 60. Understanding the interplay of age and sexual orientation as vectors of the specific exclusion of older same-sex couples in this case is crucial to fully grasp the nature of the discrimination at stake.[115]

[112] See Table 2.1.

[113] This information is based on an interview with David Fennelly.

[114] Some jurisprudential precedents had excluded comparison for discrimination assessments concerning maternity. See Case C-177/88 *Dekker* (n 86).

[115] For more detailed accounts on the questions of age discrimination, precarious work and LGBT rights in Europe, see the chapters by A Trydonidou, P Ayoub, B Ter Haar, R Horton and M Bell in this volume.

The applicant brought a claim before the Irish Labour Court, which referred three questions to the CJEU. First, is the rule at stake discriminatory on grounds of sexual orientation? Second, if not, is the rule at stake discriminatory on grounds of age? Third, if not, does the rule at stake create discrimination arising 'from the combined effect of the age and sexual orientation of a member of the scheme?'[116] Asking both the either-or and the combination question is obviously a strategy to open as many avenues as possible for legal reasoning on multiple discrimination. At the same time, it risks obfuscating the co-constitutive nature of the multiple discrimination at stake. In fact, the third question is framed as a fall-back option in case none of the first two claims is recognised. While it is strategically understandable given the absence of an explicit recognition of multiple discrimination at the CJEU and the uncertainties about how to address it, this framing also opens an emergency exit for the Court to avoid confronting the problem of multiple discrimination.

AG Kokott's opinion openly recognised the problem posed by multiple discrimination:

> The Court's judgment will reflect real life only if it duly analyses the combination of those two factors, rather than [...] in isolation.[117]

First analysing each ground separately before turning to their combination is conceptually misleading, and to some extent self-contradictory, because it pictures intersectional analysis as a fall-back option in case single-ground claims are dismissed. Nonetheless, Kokott's analysis has strategic salience in that it purports to open several ways for legal reasoning on multiple discrimination. She in fact explained:

> The combination of two or more different grounds [...] is a feature which lends a new dimension to a case such as this and must be taken duly into account in its assessment under EU law [because] it would be inconsistent with the meaning of the prohibition on discrimination [...] for a situation such as that at issue here to be split and assessed exclusively from the point of view of one or [the] other [...] grounds [...] in isolation.[118]

Kokott subsequently analysed the combination of grounds from the point of view of indirect discrimination and particular disadvantage and conducted an 'infringed' proportionality test:

> The combination of two or more [...] grounds [...] may also mean that, in the context of [a] proportionality test, the interests of the disadvantaged employees carry greater weight, which increases the likelihood of undue prejudice to the persons concerned, thus infringing the requirements of proportionality *sensu stricto*.[119]

[116] Case C-443/15 *Parris* (n 79) para 29.
[117] Case C-443/15 *Parris* (AG Opinion) (n 10).
[118] See Table 2.1: Case C-443/15 *Parris* (AG Opinion) (n 10) paras 4, 153.
[119] See ibid, para 157 (emphasis added).

Kokott thus suggested a higher standard of judicial review to assess the 'new dimension' created by co-constitutive forms of multiple discrimination.[120] As cases of multiple discrimination are often less visible and more difficult to identify, this proposal sketches a valid test to assess the harm created by combinations of grounds. However, AG Kokott's opinion fails to propose a detailed method of combined analysis, leaving the practical operationalisation of her infringed proportionality test in the dark. This is problematic as the CJEU lacks guidance on how such a test should unfold. Besides, Kokott's conclusion on the existence of indirect discrimination based on sexual orientation but not age is disputable, as the community affected by the discriminatory rule only encompasses older same-sex couples.[121] Despite these shortcomings, the identification of, and confrontation with, multiple discrimination at the CJEU constitutes a step forward.[122]

In its decision, the Court, however, did not follow Kokott's recommendations. It first examined both grounds of age and sexual orientation separately, whereas the third question regarding the combination of grounds should have been examined in the first place to do justice to the multiple discrimination claim. The separate examination led to the conclusion that there was no direct discrimination based on sexual orientation because the age limit rule was neutral and did not directly target same-sex couples. The Court then avoided the question of indirect discrimination by invoking national sovereignty on the regulation of marriage and partnerships, while it should have focused on the particularly disadvantageous effects of the rule at stake for older workers and their same-sex partners. Secondly, the Court recognised that there was a differential treatment on grounds of age, however this did not constitute discrimination because it fell into the exceptions allowed by Article 6(2) FED. Thirdly, in a very brief assessment of four paragraphs, the Court dismissed the question of multiple discrimination by refusing to look at the combined effect of two grounds. It acknowledged that 'discrimination may indeed be based on several […] grounds', yet it refused to investigate their synergy by arguing that 'there is […] no new category of discrimination resulting from the combination of more than one of those grounds […] that may be found to exist where discrimination on the basis of those grounds taken in isolation has not been established'.[123] This reflects an additive thinking, where two grounds are considered to add up to each other if proven separately, and recalls the infamous *DeGraffenreid* decision in which US judges refused to create a 'super remedy'.[124]

[120] ibid.

[121] ibid, para 164.

[122] Notably, the research commanded by the European Commission has visibly influenced AG Kokott, who cites reports on multiple discrimination. Ibid, fn 76. See also (nn 23 and 24).

[123] Case C-443/15 *Parris* (n 79) para 80. The fact that both grounds claimed are protected by the same directive should have made it easier for the Court to examine their interaction.

[124] *DeGraffenreid v General Motors Assembly Division, St Louis*, 558 F2d 480, C.A.Mo. 8th Cir. (1977), para 143.

Hence, the reasoning of the CJEU obscures the reality of co-constitutive disadvantage.[125] Following the recommendations of intersectionality theory, the CJEU should have instead understood that discrimination arises from the co-constitutive effects of two systems of exclusion: the historical exclusion of same-sex partners from a large subset of civil and family rights; and the economic marginalisation of older people when retreating from the labour market. Hence it should have lowered the evidence threshold by not requiring each ground to be proven separately. Asking for separate evidence in fact is likely to erase particular disadvantage by raising the evidentiary threshold.[126] An intersectional frame of analysis has particular added value when the grounds analysed separately are not deemed to amount to discrimination. Their interaction might, in fact, yield sufficient evidence to prove the harm. Instead, the reasoning of the Court completely dismissed this possibility by stating the reverse idea, namely that intersectional discrimination should first be proven based on separate grounds and then in combination. Hence, the conclusion reached by the Court that 'where a national rule creates neither discrimination on the ground of sexual orientation nor discrimination on the ground of age, that rule cannot produce discrimination on the basis of the combination of those two factors' is flawed.[127]

Unpacking the synergistic nature of discrimination in *Parris* helps to understand the cracks in the reasoning of the CJEU. The discriminatory harm is, first, the product of historically anchored gender stereotypes. The principle of survivor's benefits is rooted in the understanding that men are the sole family's breadwinners and that upon their retirement, the (heterosexual) family needs to be sustained through the pension rights accumulated by the male worker over his working life. To ensure the stability of this model, women engaged in non-salaried household and care work are entitled to the pension rights of their male partners in the event of their early death. This risk-minimising contract, sealed though marriage, has long served to stabilise the social contract between a male breadwinner and a female caregiver.[128] Since the idea of masculinity is stereotypically paired with heteronormativity, breadwinning and waged work, the breadwinner-caregiver model does not apply to same-sex couples. Therefore, marriage as a stabiliser of heteronormative social relationships serves to exclude same-sex couples from survivor's (and marriage-related) benefits. To understand how the synergistic effects of different systems of exclusion like patriarchy, heteronormativity and ageism interact with

[125] ibid and Case C-443/15 *Parris* (n 79) para 80.

[126] This evidentiary problem has been recognised elsewhere. See *Jefferies v Harris County Community Action Assn* 615 F 2d 1025 (5th Cir 1980) and *Baylis-Flannery v DeWilde (cob. Tri Community Physiotherapy)*, [2003] OHRTD No 20.

[127] Case C-443/15 *Parris* (n 79) para 81.

[128] See C Pateman, *The Sexual Contract* (Stanford, Stanford University Press, 1988). For an analysis in the EU context, see also U Belavusaŭ, 'EU Sexual Citizenship: Sex beyond the Internal Market' in D Kochenov, *EU Citizenship and Federalism: The Role of Rights* (Cambridge, Cambridge University Press, 2017).

society's most anchored organisational structures and in so doing produce complex systems of inequality, we need to look at the historical context of production of norms. This is what an intersectional framework would have helped do in *Parris*. In refusing to engage with a contextual assessment either through an intra- or an inter-categorical analysis of the case, the CJEU erased the cumulative effect of different systems of inequality. Both its single-ground analysis and its refusal to tackle the combination of grounds were flawed because they ignored that exclusions based on sexual orientation experienced over a lifetime produce consequences which are felt particularly strongly in old age. These exclusions lock out from societal institutions, which in turn bars from economic benefits and solidarity while financial dependency increases with ageing. One thing *Parris* makes clear is that an intersectional framework as a doctrinal tool for analysing complex discriminations is not a superficial demand for theoretical refinement, but rather a practical way to deal with types of discriminations that can hardly be redressed through the current doctrine.

V. Conclusion

To conclude, even though scholarly research has shown the extent and gravity of intersectional disadvantage, the protection offered by EU anti-discrimination law through the Race Equality and the Framework Equality Directives remains patchy at best. The CJEU, albeit recently invited to fill this gap in *Parris*, has so far refused to construct an explicit doctrinal framework to deal with the problem of multiple discrimination. As the demonstration in this chapter has shown, the argument of multiple discrimination against women has so far mainly been used to reassert the structural significance of the problem of sex discrimination and the priority given to gender equality on the EU anti-discrimination agenda. Hence, both at the legislative and judicial levels, a full framework to address multiple, and a fortiori intersectional, discrimination transversally across the whole spectrum of grounds is still missing, despite sporadic signs of progressive change.

Furthermore, the lack of consistent terminology across time and space in the EU adds confusion to an already complex debate. Even though the question of multidimensional inequality emerged under the label of multiple discrimination in the EU context, it cannot be understood in isolation from the broader and older debate on intersectionality. A recent linguistic shift in European discussions shows that the issue of multiple discrimination has come to be increasingly considered in relation to intersectionality scholarship. While multiple discrimination remains the sole concept anchored in the 2000 Directives, current discussions about a possible anti-discrimination reform blur the line by referring to both terminologies. Future legislation could make a crucial contribution to this point of debate by bringing necessary clarifications.

The unclear legal status of the issue of multiple discrimination, as well as its lack of definition in the Race and Framework Equality Directives, is problematic because the EU has so far failed to give guidance to Member States on how to redress the pervasive problem of multiple discrimination. As a result, applicants and litigators are often deterred from bringing such cases to Court, hence leading to a minimisation of the problem, a lack of judicial attention, and a limited access to justice for victims.

However, awareness of the harms created by situations of multiple discrimination seems to be increasing. In the very same case in which the CJEU denied judicial recognition to the problem of multiple discrimination, AG Kokott explicitly discussed intersectionality scholarship and called for an apposite doctrinal solution. This acknowledgment may well have planted a seed which could give impetus to a renewed debate on the necessity to tackle multiple discrimination and, ultimately to adopt doctrinal and legislative reforms.

In addition, this chapter has demonstrated how the CJEU has shown sensitivity for the issue of intersectionality in its past case law, although not in formal terms. The Court's anti-discrimination jurisprudence in fact indicates some awareness of the existing synergies between the social systems that create and sustain disadvantage. This structural attention to the multidimensionality of the phenomenon of discrimination could lead to interesting developments in the future, in particular along the lines of the intra-categorical and contextual approaches delineated in this chapter.

Most importantly, current discussions in the Council suggest a turning point in the debate about multiple discrimination. In line with the growing attention granted to the problem in research and policy-making in the EU, negotiations over the horizontal anti-discrimination reform proposed by the Commission in 2008 most recently shifted to include a comprehensive discussion of the issue of multiple discrimination. Such an explicit legislative recognition would be a *première* in EU law, and would give the CJEU a clear mandate to tackle this form of neglected and complex discrimination. This change would be a welcome development of EU law given the magnitude and pervasiveness of the phenomenon of multiple discrimination. It could contribute to realising the EU's political ambitions in terms of advancing the human right to equality.

3

EU Equality Law and Precarious Work

MARK BELL

I. Introduction

One manifestation of inequality within the labour market is an over-representation of women and minorities in jobs with lower pay, greater insecurity and less protection from employment legislation. Some of these connections are well-known, such as the preponderance of women among those working part-time. Comparatively less attention has been paid to how other characteristics intersect with the type of employment relationship. For example, young, foreign-born workers are highly likely to be working in jobs with a temporary contract[1] and the risk of being underemployed for non-EU nationals is more than double that for EU citizens living in their state of nationality.[2] Research has indicated that disabled people can be over-represented amongst those working part-time,[3] while data in the UK has uncovered an over-representation of black and minority ethnic workers in areas such as temporary work, agency work, low-paid work and under-employment.[4] Other research has also drawn attention to the impact of age on labour market experience; 'very atypical' forms of work are more common amongst those aged under 29 or over 50.[5] Given evidence that precariousness in the labour market is associated with certain equality characteristics, this chapter makes a critical assessment of the role played by EU equality law in an effort to improve the quality of such forms of work.

[1] Eurofound, 'Aspects of Non-Standard Employment in Europe' (Dublin, Eurofound, 2017) 2.

[2] Eurostat, 'Underemployment and Potential Additional Labour Force Statistics' (2017). Available at: http://ec.europa.eu/eurostat/statistics-explained/index.php/Underemployment_and_potential_additional_labour_force_statistics.

[3] T Shakespeare, *Disability Rights and Wrongs Revisited* 2nd edn (Abingdon, Routledge, 2014) 32.

[4] TUC, 'Living on the Margins: Black Workers and Casualisation' (2015). Available at: www.tuc.org.uk/sites/default/files/LivingontheMargins.pdf. See also TUC, 'Insecure Work and Ethnicity' (2017). Available at: www.tuc.org.uk/sites/default/files/Insecure%20work%20and%20ethnicity_0.pdf.

[5] Eurofound, 'Very Atypical Work: Exploratory Analysis of Fourth European Working Conditions Survey' (Dublin, Eurofound, 2010) 28.

The economic crisis accentuated the debate around precariousness in the labour market. This is connected to a longer-term trajectory of growth in jobs that diverge from the characteristics of the 'standard employment relationship' (SER);[6] in other words, the traditional image of a full-time, permanent worker who was directly employed by the provider of work. Precarity is a contested concept that is open to a range of interpretations, but it is often linked to concerns around a decline in job security and an increase in low quality, low paid forms of employment.[7] Some readings of precarious work view this as synonymous with specific types of employment relationship, such as part-time, fixed-term, agency or casual work.[8] In contrast, other interpretations focus on identifying the characteristics of precariousness in the labour market, which may arise in any form of employment.[9] One of the most commonly cited approaches is that of Rodgers, who connected the precariousness of work to variables such as: the degree of certainty of continuing work; the control enjoyed by workers (for example over working conditions); the extent of protection of workers; and the level of income.[10] He argued that 'it is some combination of these factors which identifies precarious jobs, and the boundaries around the concept are inevitably to some extent arbitrary'.[11]

EU employment law and policy since the 1990s has sought to encourage labour market flexibility within the Member States, including diversity in the range of employment relationships.[12] This prompted fears that the pursuit of flexibility may lead to precariousness through a deterioration in the protections associated with the SER. The EU has tried to counter such worries through the notion of 'flexicurity', which entails a trade-off between reduced security in one's current job in exchange for a stronger safety net of social protection and an active labour market policy to enable individuals to transition between jobs throughout their working lives.[13] One ingredient in this policy recipe has been improving the quality of diverse forms of employment relationship in an effort to make these

[6] S McKay, 'Disturbing Equilibrium and Transferring Risk: Confronting Precarious Work' in N Countouris and M Freedland (eds), *Resocialising Europe in a Time of Crisis* (Cambridge, Cambridge University Press, 2013) 191, 203.

[7] L Rodgers, *Labour Law, Vulnerability and the Regulation of Precarious Work* (Cheltenham, Edward Elgar, 2016) 5.

[8] L Vosko, M MacDonald and I Campbell, 'Gender and the Concept of Precarious Employment' in L Vosko, M MacDonald and I Campbell (eds), *Gender and the Contours of Precarious Employment* (Abingdon, Routledge, 2009) 1, 6.

[9] ibid. See also, A Kalleberg, 'Precarious Work, Insecure Workers: Employment Relations in Transition' (2009) 74 *American Sociological Review* 1; J Fudge and R Owens, 'Precarious Work, Women, and the New Economy: the Challenge to Legal Norms' in J Fudge and R Owens (eds), *Precarious Work, Women, and the New Economy: the Challenge to Legal Norms* (Oxford, Hart Publishing, 2006) 3, 11.

[10] G Rodgers, 'Precarious Work in Western Europe: the State of the Debate' in G Rodgers and J Rodgers (eds), *Precarious Jobs in Labour Market Regulation: the Growth of Atypical Employment in Western Europe* (Geneva, International Institute for Labour Studies, 1989) 1, 3.

[11] ibid.

[12] N Kountouris, 'The Legal Determinants of Precariousness in Personal Work Relations: A European Perspective' (2012) 34 *Comparative Labor Law & Policy Journal* 21, 38.

[13] ibid 39; L Rodgers (n 7) 111.

seem more palatable and less precarious, for workers who are no longer able to secure work under SER conditions. In legislative terms, this has taken the form of several directives on 'atypical' work, most notably those on part-time, fixed-term and agency work.[14] The subsequent case law on part-time and fixed-term work has demonstrated the potential of the legislation to be used as an instrument for combating precariousness, albeit imperfect and constrained in its effects. For example, the Court of Justice of the EU (CJEU) has rejected the idea that employers can, without rigorous justification, exclude part-time and fixed-term workers from important benefits such as length-of-service pay increments or access to occupational pensions.[15]

While the Atypical Work Directives[16] are an obvious point of reference when thinking about how labour market precariousness can be tackled, it is important to recognise the complementary role of EU equality law. The marginalisation of part-time workers has been a recurrent theme of gender equality case law since the seminal decision in 1986 in *Bilka-Kaufhaus*.[17] In that case, the CJEU held that excluding part-time workers from an occupational pension scheme could constitute indirect sex discrimination where the exclusion affected 'a far greater number of women than men'.[18]

This chapter explores developments since 2000 to consider the role of EU equality law in relation to precarious work. The Part-time Work Directive was adopted in 1997 and the Fixed-term Work Directive in 1999. These instruments arrived just as the EU was expanding and updating its equality legislation. The chapter begins by examining the example of gender equality; this is the area where equality law has been most extensively used to tackle poor working conditions for those in 'atypical' forms of employment. The second part of this chapter considers whether the Equality Directives adopted in 2000 have been used in a similar fashion. To this end, it takes the example of age, as there is a growing body of data at EU level that identifies connections between age and type of employment relationship. A number of cases brought under the Framework Equality Directive[19] have already touched upon the precarious working conditions that affect younger and older workers, so these provide an opportunity to consider whether the CJEU is following a similar path to that already established in its gender equality case law.

[14] Council Directive 97/81/EC concerning the Framework Agreement on part-time work concluded by UNICE, CEEP and the ETUC [1998] OJ L14/9 (Part-time Work Directive); Council Directive 1999/70/EC concerning the framework agreement on fixed-term work concluded by ETUC, UNICE and CEEP [1999] OJ L175/43 (Fixed-term Work Directive); Directive 2008/104/EC of the European Parliament and of the Council on temporary agency work [2009] OJ L327/9 (Agency Work Directive).

[15] See, eg Case C-307/05 *Del Cerro Alonso v Osakidetza-Servicio Vasco de Salud* EU:C:2007:509; Case C-268/06 *IMPACT v Minister for Agriculture and Food and others* EU:C:2008:223; Case C-177/14 *Regojo Dans v Consejo de Estado* EU:C:2015:450.

[16] For example the Part-Time, Fixed-Term and Agency Work Directives (n 14).

[17] Case 170/84 *Bilka-Kaufhaus GmbH v Weber Von Hartz* EU:C:1986:204.

[18] ibid para 31.

[19] Council Directive 2000/78/EC establishing a general framework for equal treatment in employment and occupation [2000] OJ L303/16 (Framework Equality Directive).

II. Gender Equality Directives and Precarious Work

The gendered nature of precarious work is most visible in relation to part-time work. In 2015, 19.6 per cent of those working in the EU were part-time.[20] Thirty-two per cent of women work part-time, while the figure for men is 8.9 per cent.[21] At first glance, it might not seem evident why part-time work is connected with precarious work. Unlike fixed-term work, part-time work is not necessarily insecure in terms of its duration. In contrast to agency work, part-time workers will often have a clear contractual relationship with the provider of employment. Moreover, workers do report benefits from part-time work; for example, the 2015 European Working Conditions Survey found that part-time workers were more likely than full-time workers to state that there was a good fit between their work and their family or social commitments.[22] Nevertheless, the precariousness of part-time work stems from its association with low occupational status, low pay and low protection in terms of employment law and social security. The ILO's 2007 global report concluded that:

> in most countries part-time work remains women's work and is synonymous with low status, low training and limited career opportunities, despite its being often presented as available to both working mothers and fathers. Moreover, part-time may often be involuntary, in the sense that it is a second-best option to a full-time job.[23]

Involuntary part-time work is connected to under-employment, where the worker would prefer longer working hours. Sixty-seven per cent of part-time workers in the EU are under-employed, of which sixt-seven per cent are women.[24] In some Member States, involuntary part-time work has become a striking feature of the labour market during the economic crisis. In Greece, for example, 72.1 per cent of those working part-time were under-employed; in Spain, this was 57.3 per cent.[25] The high rate of female part-time workers who are under-employed may disclose a covert phenomenon of casual work. This is connected to the growth, in some states, of part-time work with a low number of guaranteed weekly hours.[26] The worker is often willing to accept any additional work that is offered by the employer (in order to raise their income). Therefore, she

[20] European Commission, 'Employment and Social Developments in Europe. Annual Review 2016' (Luxembourg, Publications Office of the European Union, 2016) 215.

[21] ibid 216.

[22] Eurofound, 'Sixth European Working Conditions Survey – Overview report' (Luxembourg, Publications Office of the European Union, 2016) 115.

[23] ILO, 'Equality at Work: Tackling the Challenges. Global Report Under the Follow-Up to the ILO Declaration on Fundamental Principles and Rights at Work' International Labour Conference 96th session 2007, report I(B), 78.

[24] Eurostat, 'Almost 10 million part-time workers in the EU would have preferred to work more' (2015). Available at: http://ec.europa.eu/eurostat/fr/web/products-press-releases/-/3-27042015-AP. See also, Eurofound, 'Sixth European Working Conditions Survey' (n 22) 116.

[25] ibid.

[26] Vosko et al (n 8) 16.

needs to keep herself available in case extra work arises. This psychological uncertainty exacerbates the dependency on the employer.[27] Rodgers suggests that the most precarious forms of part-time work, such as those with a high variability in working time, often blend with other categories of atypical work, such as temporary or casual work.[28] This is supported by research on 'very atypical' work in Europe, which found that those working fewer than 10 hours per week were less likely to have an indefinite contract than those with longer working hours.[29] Women were, in general, over-represented amongst those in 'very atypical' work, which may also reflect its concentration in certain sectors, such as hotels and restaurants.[30]

Gender differences in relation to other forms of work associated with precariousness are less pronounced. In the EU, women are slightly over-represented amongst those engaging in fixed-term work: 12.8 per cent compared to 11.2 per cent for men.[31] In contrast, men have a higher rate of self-employment:[32] 18.8 per cent as opposed to 10.4 per cent among women.[33] Even where participation rates are similar, it must be recognised that the impact of precarious work on women may differ from that experienced by men. Research has highlighted the difficulty of combining unpredictable working hours with caring responsibilities.[34] This is especially acute for those workers with no guaranteed working hours, often summarised in the label 'zero-hours contract'. In the UK, 54 per cent of these workers are women and their typical weekly working hours are less than those of male zero-hours contract workers: 37.4 per cent of women worked less than 15 hours per week compared to 29.4 per cent of men.[35]

A. Gender Equality after the Part-time Work Directive

By the time of the adoption of the Part-time Work Directive in 1997, there had already been a significant body of case law from the CJEU recognising that less favourable treatment of part-time workers could constitute indirect sex

[27] JJ Votinius, 'On the Gendered Norm of Standard Employment in a Changing Labour Market' in Fudge and Owens (n 9) 268.

[28] G Rodgers (n 10) 4.

[29] Eurofound, 'Very Atypical Work' (n 5) 10.

[30] ibid 19.

[31] European Commission, 'Employment and Social Developments in Europe' (n 20) 216.

[32] Some forms of self-employment share features of precariousness, in particular those characterised by strong economic dependence on a single provider of work and/or where self-employment is a mechanism to circumvent employment law and social security protections: G Rodgers (n 10) 5.

[33] European Commission (n 20) 216.

[34] M Clarke, W Lewchuk, A de Wolff and A King, '"This just isn't sustainable": Precarious Employment, Stress and Workers' Health' (2007) 30 *International Journal of Law and Psychiatry* 311, 322.

[35] TUC, 'The Decent Jobs Deficit – The Human Cost of Zero-Hours Working in the UK' (2014) 29–30. Available at: www.tuc.org.uk/research-analysis/reports/decent-jobs-deficit-human-cost-zero-hours-working-uk.

discrimination, where women were over-represented amongst those working part-time.[36] This case law often related to threshold requirements in terms of weekly working hours, below which the worker was excluded from benefits such as sick pay,[37] bonuses[38] or severance payments.[39] The Framework Agreement on Part-time Work prohibited less favourable treatment in employment conditions of part-time workers compared to full-time workers, subject to the possibility of objective justification.[40] After the creation of a specialised legal remedy for part-time workers, the question arose as to its relationship with the pre-existing route of indirect sex discrimination.

The initial response from the CJEU appeared to indicate a preference for regulation via gender equality legislation. In *Steinicke* (2003),[41] a part-time worker challenged a national rule that limited access to a special scheme of pre-retirement part-time work to those who had worked full-time for three out of the previous five years. While the referring court queried the compatibility of this requirement with both the Framework Agreement on Part-time Work and gender equality legislation, the Court tersely determined that, as the facts fell within the scope of the Equal Treatment Directive,[42] there was no need to consider the applicability of the Framework Agreement.[43] However, subsequent case law has recognised the possibility of combining both instruments within a single case and Advocates-General have taken the view that there is no particular hierarchy between them.[44] With this in mind, female litigants would appear best advised to invoke both if possible.[45] The shortcomings of relying only on the Framework Agreement were exposed in *Mascellani* (2014).[46] This case concerned an Italian court official who had been working part-time (three days a week) since 2000. She used the remainder of her time to care for her family, including a 90-year-old parent who lived with her, as well as pursuing a university degree.[47] In 2011, she was unilaterally

[36] For an overview, see D McCann, *Regulating Flexible Work* (Oxford, Oxford University Press, 2008) 61; E Ellis and P Watson, *EU Anti-Discrimination Law* 2nd edn (Oxford, Oxford University Press, 2012) 148.

[37] Case 171/88 *Rinner-Kuhn v FWW Spezial-Gebaudereinigung GmbH & Co KG* EU:C:1989:328.

[38] Case C-281/97 *Krüger v Kreiskrankenhaus Ebersberg* EU:C:1999:396.

[39] Case C-33/89 *Kowalska v Freie und Hansestadt Hamburg* EU:C:1990:265.

[40] Clause 4(1).

[41] Case C-77/02 *Steinicke v Bundesanstalt für Arbeit* EU:C:2003:458.

[42] Directive 2006/54/EC of the European Parliament and of the Council on the implementation of the principle of equal opportunities and equal treatment of men and women in matters of employment and occupation (Recast) [2006] OJ L204/23 (Equal Treatment Directive).

[43] ibid para 52.

[44] Case C-313/02 *Wippel v Peek & Cloppenburg GmbH & Co KG* EU:C:2004:308, Opinion of AG Kokott, para 67; Joined Cases C-55/07 and C-56/07 *Michaeler, Subito GmbH, and Volgger v Amt für sozialen Arbeitsschutz, Autonome Provinz Bozen* EU:C:2008:42, Opinion of AG Ruiz-Jarabo Colomer, para 28.

[45] A male part-time worker could, of course, raise the indirect sex discrimination argument, but this would require evidence that men were over-represented amongst the part-time workers affected by the treatment in question.

[46] Case C-221/13 *Mascellani v Ministero della Giustizia* EU:C:2014:2286.

[47] Case C-221/13 *Mascellani v Ministero della Giustizia* EU:C:2014:479, Opinion of AG Wahl, para 18.

informed that she would have to work full-time over six days per week. The CJEU held that the Framework Agreement on Part-time Work did not preclude an employer requiring a part-time worker to change to full-time work, even without the worker's consent.[48] It rejected the idea that this constituted less favourable treatment on the basis that no comparable situation for a full-time worker could be identified.[49]

The reasoning in *Mascellani* placed considerable emphasis on the role played by part-time work in furthering labour market flexibility.[50] In 1996, Italian law had granted a right to public-sector employees to change from full-time to part-time employment, yet in 2008, this was qualified by the addition of a requirement that such a change would not prejudice the smooth running of the organisation.[51] A further reform in 2010 provided the state with a 180-day period to review the working time of those granted part-time work under the 1996 law, such as Ms Mascellani.[52] These legislative reforms were linked by the state to the sustainability of public finances,[53] and Advocate-General Wahl accepted the premise that the Framework Agreement on Part-time Work permits Member States to 'reduce the level of protection afforded under their rules on part-time work in times of turmoil'.[54] The effect on the individual part-time worker appeared to be a lower priority: 'a worker is always at liberty to end the employment relationship if he or she does not wish to work full-time'.[55]

This is a remarkably thin concept of liberty, which pays little regard to the reality of choice for those with caring responsibilities. It is often the lack of accessible or affordable care services that actually compels the worker to work part-time.[56] Mascellani exposed one dimension to the precariousness of part-time work; if the employer retains the unilateral prerogative of revoking part-time working, even after a period of over ten years as in this case, the worker is left with considerable insecurity. It is, therefore, worth reflecting on whether gender equality legislation could have provided a different outcome.

Article 2(1)(b) of the Equal Treatment Directive 2006 provides the following definition of indirect discrimination:

> Where an apparently neutral provision, criterion or practice would put persons of one sex at a particular disadvantage compared with persons of the other sex, unless that provision, criterion or practice is objectively justified by a legitimate aim, and the means of achieving that aim are appropriate and necessary.

[48] Case C-221/13 *Mascellani* (n 46) para 24.
[49] ibid para 27.
[50] ibid para 25.
[51] ibid para 3.1; Sentenza n.224/2013, Corte Costituzionale.
[52] ibid.
[53] ibid para 2.3.2.
[54] Case C-221/13 *Mascellani* (AG Opinion) (n 46) para 54.
[55] ibid para 53.
[56] European Commission, 'Report on Equality between Women and Men – 2010' (Luxembourg: Publications Office of the European Union 2010) 40.

Given the over-representation of women in part-time work, if an employer requires part-time workers to change their hours to full-time work, this will often place women at a particular disadvantage when compared to men. While being offered longer working hours might be viewed as a benefit by some workers (most obviously those who are under-employed and seeking additional work), the data cited earlier indicated that in most Member States this was a minority of those in part-time work. More specifically, the sub-group of those working part-time and combining this with caring responsibilities will be disadvantaged by a unilateral change in their working hours given the potential disruption to their ability to combine work and family life; women are commonly over-represented in this sub-group. Mascellani exposed the shortcomings of the comparator test within the Framework Agreement on Part-time Work, more particularly for the situation of a part-time worker required to become a full-time worker. According to the CJEU, there was no comparable full-time worker in those circumstances.

Proceeding via the indirect sex discrimination route should shift the focus of the inquiry away from a strict comparator test and onto the potential justification for the employer's practice.[57] This should demand a more searching and rigorous analysis than the loose references to labour market flexibility in Mascellani. It was unclear from the proceedings why compelling some workers to increase their working time would make a significant contribution to improving public finances. It must also be borne in mind that the CJEU has held that 'budgetary considerations cannot justify discrimination against one of the sexes'.[58] At a minimum, invoking gender equality legislation would have ensured a more balanced weighing of the interests of the employer and the worker, as well as rendering visible the gendered consequences of prioritising labour market flexibility in this fashion.

B. Gender Equality and Other Forms of Precarious Work

While part-time work provides the most frequent examples of gender equality law interacting with precarious work, there are other instances of intersection. Notably, legislation and case-law aim to secure rights relating to pregnancy, maternity and parental leave for non-standard workers. With regard to the protection of pregnant workers, the CJEU has held that it is unlawful to dismiss a fixed-term worker who cannot complete the full duration of the contract due to pregnancy.[59]

[57] Although the CJEU has, at times, also imposed a comparator test within indirect sex discrimination, as discussed in the next section of this chapter.

[58] Joined Cases C-4/02 and C-5/02 *Schönheit v Stadt Frankfurt a.M., Becker v Land Hessen* EU:C:2003:583, para 85.

[59] Case C-109/00 *Tele Danmark A/S v Handels- og Kontorfunktionærernes Forbund I Danmark (HK)* EU:C:2001:513, para 31.

In addition, it constitutes unlawful sex discrimination if an employer's reason for failing to renew a fixed-term contract is the worker's pregnancy.[60]

The Court has also sought to ensure that those persons whose working arrangements lie on the boundary between employment and self-employment are not deprived of protection. In *Danosa* (2010),[61] the complainant was appointed to be the sole member of a board of directors for a limited liability company. Seven months later, the general meeting of the shareholders of the company decided to remove her from this position. At the time, she was eleven weeks pregnant and she brought a case challenging her dismissal. The company argued that this was a commercial contract rather than one of employment. In contrast, the CJEU felt that the core elements of its concept of 'worker' were present: remuneration was provided for services performed and she was carrying out services under direction or control, even if the latter was quite limited.[62] Accordingly, she enjoyed protection from dismissal due to pregnancy.[63] As mentioned earlier, not all forms of self-employment have characteristics of precariousness. *Danosa* provides an illustration of circumstances where the relationship may be treated by national law as self-employment, yet the individual appears to be dependent upon a sole organisation for her principal source of income. Depriving such individuals of the benefit of employment protection legislation heightens their precariousness, so the wide reading of 'worker' adopted by the CJEU in this case helps to guarantee a floor of protection. Recent legislation strikes a similar chord. The Revised Parental Leave Directive expressly applies to part-time, fixed-term and agency workers,[64] while Directive 2010/41 applies the principle of equal treatment between women and men to those pursuing 'an activity in a self-employed capacity'.[65]

These examples of gender equality law and instruments on the reconciliation of work and family life being applied to non-standard work must, however, be balanced by instances that expose shortcomings in the response to precariousness. Specifically, the comparator test applied by the Court when identifying the possibility of sex discrimination can rebound upon the complainant where, due to precariousness, her circumstances are deemed to be incomparable to those in a standard employment relationship. This can be witnessed in two examples.

[60] Case C-438/99 *Jiménez Melgar v Ayuntamiento de Los Barrios* EU:C:2001:509, para 46.

[61] Case C-232/09 *Danosa v LKB Līzings SIA* EU:C:2010:674.

[62] ibid para 51.

[63] ibid para 74.

[64] Clause I(3), Council Directive 2010/18/EU implementing the revised Framework Agreement on parental leave concluded by BUSINESSEUROPE, UEAPME, CEEP and ETUC and repealing Directive 96/34/EC [2010] OJ L68/13 (Revised Parental Leave Directive).

[65] Directive 2010/41/EU of the European Parliament and of the Council on the application of the principle of equal treatment between men and women engaged in an activity in a self-employed capacity and repealing Council Directive 86/613/EEC [2010] OJ L180/1, Art 1(1). The Court has also held that men should not be deprived of parental leave rights by virtue of their female partner being self-employed rather than employed: Case C-104/09 *Roca Álvarez v Sesa Start España ETT SA* EU:C:2010:561; Case C-5/12 *Betriu Montull v INSS* EU:C:2013:571.

The case of *Allonby* (2004)[66] concerned a part-time lecturer who had been working for six years on a succession of one-year contracts and who was paid on an hourly basis. For financial reasons, her college decided to cease direct employment of part-time lecturers and instead to recruit them via a temporary employment agency, where they were treated as being self-employed. Ms Allonby was dismissed, but then continued to work for the college via the agency. This had the effect, however, of reducing her salary and depriving her of certain employment benefits, such as the occupational pension scheme for teachers. The issue of sex discrimination arose as a significantly higher number of female teachers were affected by this reorganisation.[67] While the CJEU held that she was a worker for the purposes of EU gender equality law, it rejected the possibility for her to compare her salary with that of the teachers who remained directly employed by the college.[68] The Court took the view that comparators, for the purposes of equal pay law, had to have a single source of income. As she was paid by the agency, she could not compare herself to those paid directly by the college. From any standpoint, Ms Allonby's situation as a part-time, temporary worker has all the hallmarks of precariousness. Yet the employer succeeded in evading the application of equal pay law through its efforts to accentuate her precariousness by inserting an employment agency into their pre-existing relationship.

Another example of the significance of how the comparator test is deployed can be found in *Wippel* (2004).[69] This case involved a retail worker who was hired on a 'work on demand' contract. She had no guaranteed hours and these were determined on a case-by-case basis, with the possibility for her to decline hours that the company offered to her. She argued that this was both less favourable treatment of part-time workers and indirect sex discrimination on the basis that, unlike other full-time and part-time workers, she had no pre-determined salary based on a guaranteed level of weekly hours.[70] The Court rejected her actions under both the Framework Agreement on Part-time Work and the Equal Treatment Directive. It held that she was not in a comparable situation to other workers whose contracts provided for fixed working hours because workers in her situation had the choice of accepting or refusing the hours offered.[71]

The significance of this case has, if anything, grown over time. Research by Eurofound indicates that the economic crisis did not lead to significant overall growth in non-standard employment across the EU (although the experience of individual states differed). There is evidence, however, that the character of

[66] Case C-256/01 *Allonby v Accrington & Rossendale College* EU:C:2004:18.

[67] Of those made redundant and then re-employed via the agency, 231 were women and 110 were men. Of those retained as directly employed lecturers by the college, the majority were men (Case C-256/01 *Allonby v Accrington & Rossendale College* EU:C:2003:190, Opinion of AG Geelhoed, para 11).

[68] Case C-256/01 *Allonby* (n 66) para 50.

[69] Case C-313/02 *Wippel v Peek & Cloppenburg GmbH & Co KG* EU:C:2004:607.

[70] ibid para 52.

[71] ibid paras 59–64.

non-standard employment has changed, with a growth in casual work, workers with very short weekly working hours, as well as involuntary part-time work (which is often linked to casualisation).[72] Casual work is a species of part-time work, yet its flexibility means that average weekly working hours can vary greatly; in some cases, the volume of work performed is more similar to full-time work. Moreover, the duration of some casual relationships can become extended; even Ms Wippel had been employed for 21 months by the time she started legal proceedings. The decision in *Wippel* is problematic, because it implies that differences in contractual terms can render a particular group of workers incomparable to all others, thereby excluding any recourse to the protections available under either the Atypical Work Directives or those on equality. Arguably, this needs to be reconsidered.

In *Wippel*, the claim was one of indirect sex discrimination. While the legislative definition of direct discrimination refers to the identification of another person 'in a comparable situation',[73] this is absent from the definition of indirect discrimination.[74] It is, therefore, a conflation of the two concepts for the Court to preclude an analysis of possible indirect discrimination on the basis that the two groups of workers being compared are dissimilar. If, in a given workplace, those working under zero-hours contracts are disproportionately women,[75] then practices that treat such workers less favourably place women at a particular disadvantage in comparison to men. Indirect discrimination is, of course, balanced by the possibility of objective justification of the practice in question. This provides the juncture at which the employer may be able to bring forward sufficient reasons for why zero-hours contract workers are treated differently to their fixed-hours counterparts. For example, in *Wippel*, Advocate-General Kokott expressed the view that work-on-demand contracts were not inherently disadvantageous to workers, but if the manner in which these were used gave rise to abuse, then indirect sex discrimination could occur.[76] This approach might not have resulted in a positive outcome for Ms Wippel, but it would be a better foundation for analysing future indirect discrimination claims from those engaged in types of casual work.

III. Age Equality and Precarious Work

The second part of this chapter considers the relationship between age and precarious work. This is a more recent evolution as the prohibition on age discrimination

[72] Eurofound, 'Aspects of Non-Standard Employment in Europe' (n 1) 9 and 20.

[73] Equal Treatment Directive, Art 2(1)(a).

[74] ibid Art 2(1)(b).

[75] Notably, AG Kokott did not approach the question of indirect sex discrimination in the same manner as that of the Court. She focused on the relative proportions of women and men employed via on-demand contracts (84.84% women) and those employed on fixed-hours contracts (75.82% women). She felt that the difference in the proportion of women working on demand or with fixed hours was not sufficient to establish indirect discrimination – Case C-313/02 *Wippel* (AG Opinion) (n 41) para 121.

[76] ibid para 125.

in the Framework Equality Directive dates from 2000 and some Member States availed of the extended implementation period that ran until 2006.[77] While the volume of case law tackling these issues is more limited, there are clear signs of how age and precarious work intersect.

A. Age, Precarity and the Labour Market

While precarious work can affect persons of all ages, there is some evidence that it impacts particularly heavily on both younger and older workers. Certainly, these groups are over-represented in non-standard forms of employment. As mentioned earlier, 19.6 per cent of employment in the EU is part-time,[78] but this figure rises to 32 per cent for 15–24 year olds[79] and 38 per cent for those over 65.[80] Younger people often engage in part-time working in conjunction with studying, while older people may have recourse to part-time working as a type of partial retirement. Insofar as these forms of work are freely chosen, this may be beneficial for all parties. Yet young people in particular frequently encounter involuntary part-time work. This phenomenon has grown during the economic crisis with 30 per cent of 15–24 year olds in the EU citing the impossibility of finding a full-time job as the reason for working part-time.[81] In some states, involuntary part-time work amongst young people is strikingly high; it constitutes more than two-thirds of young people working part-time in Italy, Romania, Greece and Spain.[82]

Young people are also over-represented amongst those in temporary employment. While 13.8 per cent of employees in the EU have fixed-term contracts,[83] this figure rises to 22 per cent of those aged 25–29, and 43 per cent of 15–24 year olds.[84] Research by the European Foundation found evidence that one in five workers aged 15–29 were engaged in 'very atypical' forms of work, such as having no employment contract, working less than 10 hours per week or having a temporary contract with a duration of less than six months.[85] This data preceded the economic crisis and, in some states, this has resulted in a growth in precarious

[77] On age discrimination and EU law, see, *inter alia*, the chapters by R Horton and B ter Haar in the present volume, and C Tobler, 'The EU Age Discrimination Law and Older and Younger Workers: Court of Justice of the European Union Case Law Development' in Ann Numhauser-Henning and Mia Rönnmar (eds), *Age Discrimination and Labour Law – Comparative and Conceptual Perspectives in the EU and Beyond* (Alphen aan den Rijn, Wolters Kluwer, 2015).

[78] European Commission, 'Employment and Social Developments in Europe' (n 20) 215.

[79] Eurostat Statistical Books, 'Being Young in Europe Today' (Luxembourg, Publications Office of the EU, 2015) 154.

[80] Eurofound, 'Work Preferences after 50' (Dublin, Eurofound, 2014) 9.

[81] Eurostat Statistical Books (n 80) 157.

[82] ibid 156.

[83] European Commission (n 20) 257.

[84] Eurostat Statistical Books (n 79) 153.

[85] Eurofound, 'Very Atypical Work' (n 5) 14.

working by young people. In the UK, for example, 39.6 per cent of those employed under zero-hours contracts are aged 16–24, while the same age cohort represents 23.4 per cent of agency workers.[86] While there is strong evidence of precarious forms of working affecting young people, data also indicates that 'very atypical' work increases amongst those over 50.[87] People aged over 55 are also strongly over-represented amongst those in self-employment.[88] More generally, older workers are affected by the insecurity of employment. This is particularly true where national law permits mandatory retirement, which places workers on any type of contract at risk of dismissal once they have exceeded the age threshold.[89]

B. Older Workers and Recourse to Fixed-term Contracts

Several cases have shone a light on practices that expose older workers to an elevated risk of being employed via a fixed-term contract. This lay at the heart of the Court's first engagement with age discrimination in *Mangold v Helm* (2005).[90] In this famous decision, the Court held that a provision of German law which permitted recourse to fixed-term contracts without the need for objective justification for those over the age of 52 constituted direct age discrimination that lacked sufficient justification.[91] This signalled the potential for the Framework Equality Directive to fill some of the gaps in protection found in the Framework Agreement on Fixed-Term Work. *Mangold* concerned the conditions under which an employee could be initially hired under a fixed-term contract. While the Framework Agreement regulates the successive use and renewal of such contracts, it does not, according to the CJEU, impose restrictions on the first occasion when a fixed-term contract is issued to a worker.[92]

Mangold indicated the potential of the Framework Equality Directive to challenge the idea that retaining older workers in the labour market provides a blanket justification for any form of reduction in employment protection standards. However, subsequent cases have demonstrated more caution on the part of the Court. In *Georgiev* (2010),[93] Bulgarian law required professors to retire at 65, but permitted the extension of their employment through recourse to fixed-term contracts valid for 12 months, with a ceiling of three additional years of

[86] 16–24 year olds form 13 per cent of the working age population: TUC (n 35) 20.

[87] Eurofound (n 5) 14.

[88] S Bisom-Rapp, A Frazer and M Sargeant, 'Decent Work, Older Workers and Vulnerability in the Economic Recession: A Comparative Study of Australia, the United Kingdom and the United States' (2011) 15 *Employee Rights and Employment Policy Journal* 43, 85.

[89] ibid 81.

[90] Case C-144/04 *Mangold v Helm* EU:C:2005:709.

[91] ibid para 65.

[92] ibid paras 40–43.

[93] Joined Cases C-250/09 and C-268/09 *Georgiev v Tehnicheski universitet – Sofia, filial Plovdiv* EU:C:2010:699.

employment. The CJEU accepted that this was a difference of treatment based on age because the employment conditions of such professors became 'more precarious' than those under 65 who were employed on contracts of indefinite duration.[94] It concluded, however, that using fixed-term contracts in this manner was capable of justification. To this end, the Court argued that:

(a) this reflected 'an employment policy which seeks, *inter alia*, to encourage the promotion of younger teaching staff to posts as university professors';[95]
(b) the professors would be entitled to a retirement pension by this age; and
(c) the maximum number and duration of fixed-term contracts were compatible with the requirements on preventing abuse within the Framework Agreement on Fixed-Term Work.

Focusing on the question of precarious work, it is important to disentangle the general justifications for mandatory retirement and the specific justifications for the recourse to fixed-term contracts witnessed in this case. The Court cited the need to encourage the recruitment of younger teaching staff. Setting to one side the doubts over whether mandatory retirement necessarily leads to more posts for younger staff,[96] it is difficult to identify how the policy of permitting extension via fixed-term contracts pursues that aim. Indeed, it could be argued that this runs counter to the stated aim insofar as it might lead to a delay in the appointment of a younger replacement. It is also difficult to see how the fact that the professor was entitled to a pension provides a justification for the use of a fixed-term contract. Again, this seems to be a justification for mandatory retirement rather than extended working under temporary contracts. Finally, while the Court is correct that limiting the use of fixed-term contracts to a maximum period of three years, including two renewals, is not, on the face of it, contrary to the Framework Agreement, this misses the context of the employment relationship. The case did not concern the first hiring of a worker, but rather the continuation of a prior contract of indefinite duration. Arguably, the Framework Agreement is premised on a transition towards a contract of indefinite duration, rather than contractual changes in the opposite direction. Overall, the justifications advanced by the Court do not seem tailored to the specific practice of extending employment via fixed-term contracts, rather than permitting the worker to retain their pre-existing contractual terms.

The case of *Kumpan* (2011)[97] also concerned the use of fixed-term contracts following mandatory retirement. Ms Kumpan was a flight attendant for Lufthansa and, in accordance with the applicable collective agreement, her indefinite contract

[94] ibid para 34.
[95] ibid para 61.
[96] For example, the posts might not be replaced if there is a need for financial savings, or they might be replaced at a lower grade.
[97] Case C-109/09 *Deutsche Lufthansa AG v Kumpan* EU:C:2011:129.

of employment ended when she turned 55. There was, however, a provision for multiple 12-month renewals of the employment contract, which could continue until the age of 60. As she was approaching 60, she challenged the limitation on her fixed-term contract. Her situation was compounded by a provision of German law providing that objective justification for the conclusion of a fixed-term employment contract was not required for those over the age of 58.[98] Although the referring court queried the compatibility of this practice with both the Framework Equality Directive and the Framework Agreement on Fixed-term Work, the Court chose to focus on the latter. Clause 5(1) of the Framework Agreement requires Member States to make a choice concerning the measures to be put in place to prevent the abusive recourse by employers to successive fixed-term contracts. In this case, national law did not apply any conditions relating to the successive use of fixed-term contracts for workers who exceeded the age of 58. The CJEU held that this failed to comply with the obligations arising in the Framework Agreement.[99] In the light of this conclusion, the Court held, without elaboration, that it was unnecessary to address the potential conflict with the Framework Equality Directive.[100]

The decisions in *Mangold*, *Georgiev* and *Kumpan* indicate that the Court will apply a strict level of scrutiny to legislative measures that exclude older workers from laws regulating fixed-term work, especially if these apply in an abstract fashion to all workers over a given age. It may also be an influential factor that *Mangold* and *Kumpan* concerned workers in their 50s, an age when eligibility for a pension may be limited. In contrast, the Court seems more disposed to permit departures from the normal standards on fixed-term work in respect of workers who are already entitled to a pension and where the use of such contracts is for a limited period. Yet pension entitlement is a problematic criterion because mere qualification for a pension does not determine the level of that pension. Some workers wish to continue working to enhance the level of their pension. Given that women more frequently interrupt their careers for caring responsibilities, combined with periods of part-time work, they may have a particular motivation for continuing to work irrespective of pension eligibility.[101] Moreover, clause 5(1) of the Framework Agreement does not specify any upper threshold on the number of renewals of fixed-term contracts to be permitted, nor their maximum duration. While the Court in *Georgiev* viewed the Bulgarian practice of two renewals within three years as complying with clause 5(1), it remains unclear whether Lufthansa's practice of four renewals within five years was also acceptable. In *Kumpan*, the Court focused on the age limit in the national legislation on fixed-term work, rather than the approach taken in the collective agreement.

[98] ibid para 10.
[99] ibid para 43.
[100] ibid para 58.
[101] D Schiek, 'Age Discrimination before the ECJ – Conceptual and Theoretical Issues' (2011) 48 *Common Market Law Review* 777, 795.

C. Precarity and Younger Workers

Given the very high levels of youth unemployment in some Member States, there is a difficult balance to be struck between incentivising employers to recruit young people and avoiding measures that exacerbate their precarious position. Kountouris draws attention to the role that legislation can play in creating precariousness in the labour market;[102] this can be the case where the law reduces the normal level of employment protection based on age, such as lower minimum wage entitlements. The Framework Equality Directive accepts the principle that there can be justifications for treating young workers differently on grounds of age. Article 6(1)(a) refers to:

> the setting of special conditions on access to employment and vocational training, employment and occupation, including dismissal and remuneration conditions, for young people, older workers and persons with caring responsibilities in order to promote their vocational integration or ensure their protection.

Although the directive incorporates a degree of flexibility, it is still necessary to show that such measures are 'objectively and reasonably justified'.[103] A number of early cases suggested that the Court would subject laws that treated young workers differently to careful scrutiny.[104]

The case of *Hütter* (2009)[105] related to an Austrian provision excluding periods of employment under the age of 18 from counting towards length of service entitlements. This delayed progress through salary scales, with effects on pay that would endure over time. The Court found the justifications advanced for this provision were not appropriate and even contradictory to the objective of promoting young people's access to the labour market.[106] In *Kücükdeveci* (2010),[107] the notice to which an employee was entitled prior to dismissal accrued with length of service, but to the exclusion of periods of service under the age of 26. The complainant received one month's notice, whereas she would have been entitled to four months if her service when she was younger than 26 had been taken into account. The referring court stated that this measure aimed 'to afford employers greater flexibility in personnel management by alleviating the burden on them in respect of the dismissal of young workers, from whom it is reasonable to expect a greater degree of personal or occupational mobility'.[108] As in *Hütter*, the CJEU was not persuaded

[102] See Kountouris (n 12).

[103] Framework Equality Directive, Art 6(1). An example of a measure designed to promote access to training for young people is found in Case C-548/15 *JJ de Lange v Staatssecretaris van Financiën* EU:C:2016:850.

[104] For a more detailed discussion of these cases, see the chapter by ter Haar in the present volume.

[105] Case C-88/08 *Hütter v Technische Universität Graz* EU:C:2009:381.

[106] ibid para 49.

[107] Case C-555/07 *Kücükdeveci v Swedex GmbH & Co KG* EU:C:2010:21.

[108] ibid para 39.

by this reasoning, especially given that the effects of discounting service before 26 applied irrespective of the employee's actual age at the time of dismissal.[109]

If the above cases indicated a relatively strict level of scrutiny for differences of treatment that adversely affected young workers, they are contradicted by other judgments, where the Court adopted a more permissive approach to the choices of national labour law. In *O*,[110] French law provided for a payment of 10 per cent of total gross remuneration upon the expiry of a fixed-term contract. This did not, however, apply to contracts with young people during school holidays and university vacations. A challenge to this exception was rejected by the Court on the basis that young people performing such work are not in a comparable position to other types of fixed-term contract workers.[111] It is difficult to sustain this analysis because the nature of the work performed may be the same as that of other temporary workers or workers with a contract of indefinite duration. The Court relied upon the intention of the worker as the basis for distinguishing the comparators; as students did not intend to continue in the labour market after the fixed-term contract expired, they were different from other temporary workers.[112] Yet fixed-term contract workers will have a variety of intentions in relation to their further pursuits, so this is a tenuous basis for deeming student workers not to be in a comparable situation. As discussed earlier in relation to *Allonby* and *Wippel*, this is another instance of the Court using the comparator test as a preliminary hurdle that filters out claims from those in non-standard employment.

Admittedly, the facts of *O* were not compelling as the work had only been performed for four days and it was done with the sole purpose of engineering a challenge to the relevant legal provision.[113] In contrast, *Abercrombie & Fitch v Bordonaro* (2017)[114] starkly exposed the precarious position of young workers in casual forms of employment. At the time that Mr Bordonaro was hired, Italian legislation permitted the use of 'on-call' employment contracts in any circumstance where the worker was either under 25 or over 45 (an age limit later raised to 55). For around 18 months, Bordonaro worked several nights per week in the company's warehouse, but no further work was offered after he reached the age of 25. He challenged the termination of his employment as age discrimination and the compatibility of his treatment with the FED was referred to the CJEU. The Court accepted that he fell within the concept of 'worker' for the purposes of the Directive and that he could compare his situation to that of a worker aged between 25 and 45. For the latter, on-call contracts could only be used to perform services of 'a discontinuous or intermitted nature' and for limited periods of

[109] ibid para 40.
[110] Case C-432/14 *O v Bio Philippe Auguste SARL* EU:C:2015:643. See further the chapter by ter Haar in the present volume.
[111] ibid para 37.
[112] ibid para 36.
[113] ibid para 15.
[114] Case C-143/16 *Abercrombie & Fitch Italia Srl v Bordonaro* EU:C:2017:566.

time.[115] The CJEU recognised that Italian law permitted, in effect, his dismissal on grounds of age, but it held that the relevant legislation was objectively justified:

> a measure which authorises employers to conclude less rigid employment contracts may, having regard to the broad discretion enjoyed by the Member States in that area, be considered as being appropriate to achieve a degree of flexibility on the labour market. The view may be taken that undertakings may be encouraged by the existence of an instrument less onerous and costly than the usual contract and thus be prompted to respond more to job applications from young workers.[116]

A striking feature of this decision is the broad deference given by the Court to the choice of the Member State. As Horton observes, it is improbable that the Court would view a reduction in legal protection as a legitimate means of combating labour market under-representation in relation to other discrimination grounds.[117] Fundamentally, the judgment failed to interrogate whether there was evidence to support the proposition that recourse to casual employment contracts for younger (and older) workers had the desired effect of improving their position in the labour market. The Court mentioned the low employment participation rate of those under 25 in Italy and the argument of the Italian Government that this measure was designed to give young people an 'initial opportunity' of gaining labour market experience.[118] Yet that rationale is contradicted by the simultaneous application of this measure to older workers who almost certainly already had work experience. Moreover, the law applied to all those under 25 irrespective of whether or not this was their first job. In contrast, in *Mangold*, the Court rejected the idea that employment protection should be lower for all older workers in order to combat higher rates of unemployment because such measures would affect all those in the relevant age category whether or not they had been affected by unemployment.[119] The Court's judgment is in stark contrast to the approach recommended by Advocate-General Bobek.[120] His opinion identified the risk that such measures led to 'younger workers being pigeonholed in the more precarious clusters of the labour market'.[121]

IV. Conclusion

Although the late 1990s witnessed both the adoption of the Atypical Work Directives and the expansion of EU equality legislation, there was relatively little cross-fertilisation between these instruments at their inception, with the notable exception of part-time work and gender equality. Changes in the labour

[115] ibid para 26.
[116] ibid para 41.
[117] See the chapter by Horton in the present volume.
[118] Case C-143/16 *Abercrombie* (n 114) paras 34–35.
[119] Case C-144/04 *Mangold* (n 90) para 64.
[120] Case C-144/04 *Mangold v Helm* EU:C:2005:420, Opinion of Advocate General Bobek.
[121] ibid para 90.

market since then, and especially during the economic crisis, have seen greater focus on non-standard forms of employment. The empirical data discussed in this chapter indicate that some groups are more affected by labour market precarity than others. It is, therefore, relevant to consider the role that EU equality law can play in combating precariousness.

The examples considered in this chapter show that the Atypical Work Directives and the Equality Directives often intersect in their application. At times, the issue is framed by courts (and presumably also by litigators) as one or the other; for example, in *Mascellani*, the referring court did not raise the possibility of indirect sex discrimination, while in *Kumpan*, the CJEU decided that it did not need to address separately the question of age discrimination. This is unhelpful, because it overlooks the substantive differences between the directives; arguably, the Equality Directives impose a more rigorous standard of protection than that found in the legislation on atypical work. Moreover, sidelining the equality dimension to such cases obscures the disparate impact of precariousness on certain groups in the labour market, such as women and younger or older workers. To be clear, this chapter is not arguing that the Equality Directives should displace the role of the Atypical Work Directives; instead, there is a need to ensure that the potential application of both sources of law are considered in litigation.

The experience of gender equality legislation provides the clearest evidence of how equality law can assist in tackling precarious working conditions. The CJEU case law has undoubtedly made a contribution to ensuring that part-time workers have access to the same range of benefits and protections as full-time workers. Such litigation has been aided by the accumulation of data that frequently establishes a strong over-representation of women amongst part-time workers. Data is often less available in relation to other equality characteristics. For example, there seems to be less data on the experience of disabled workers in terms of their types of employment relationship and data on casual forms of employment is sparser. These gaps in information may hinder efforts to identify patterns of indirect discrimination. Better data could also help illuminate the extent to which there may be intersectional inequalities in non-standard forms of employment, such as the position of women of ethnic minority origin.

The case law on age discrimination indicated that the Equality Directives of 2000 can also be relevant to precarious work. In a similar fashion to gender equality law and part-time work, there have been some instances of litigation on age discrimination tackling less favourable working conditions for those in non-standard employment. The approach of the CJEU to such cases appears inconsistent, specifically with regard to the intensity of judicial scrutiny of justifications for age discrimination.[122] In cases such as *Mangold*, *Hütter* and *Kücükdeveci*, the Court carefully scrutinised the justifications advanced by Member States and it was willing to question the coherence of national policies. Elsewhere, the CJEU has been more deferential to national law and public policy. For example,

[122] For a more detailed analysis of consistency within age discrimination case-law, see Tobler (n 78).

Georgiev conforms to a general pattern of the Court applying a wide margin of discretion in relation to mandatory retirement.[123]

A common feature of case law on both gender and age discrimination is that litigants in the most precarious forms of employment, such as casual work, encounter greater obstacles to relying on equality law. Rigid applications of the comparator test, such as those seen in *Allonby* or *Wippel*, threaten to compound precariousness by rendering it very difficult for some workers to invoke equality law protections.[124] The cases stumble at the initial hurdle of comparability, thereby preventing any analysis of the justification for the difference in their treatment. The decision in *Bordonaro* illustrates the other side of the coin. While the claimant was able to identify an appropriate comparator, his case foundered in the face of the 'light touch' scrutiny of justifications based on labour market flexibility. This may reflect the weaker norms that apply to the treatment of casual workers. There is some evidence that such forms of work increased during the economic crisis.[125] Moreover, the emerging phenomenon of work via digital platforms (the 'gig' economy) represents another form of non-standard employment beyond those categories already protected in the Atypical Work Directives.[126] Equality law offers a prism through which to recognise that such evolutions in labour market behaviour can have a disparate impact on women and minorities. The challenge facing the courts is to ensure that equality law is interpreted in a manner that does not reinforce the marginalisation of such workers.

This task would be helped if there were a firmer normative foundation for applying the principle of equal treatment to all types of non-standard work rather than just those categories found in the Atypical Work Directives. At the time of writing, an evolution in this direction may be emerging. The European Commission has proposed the adoption of the 'European Pillar of Social Rights'.[127] Although this is not intended to be a legally binding instrument, it proclaims principles and rights that are designed for implementation by the EU and participating Member States. As proposed, paragraph 5(a) states that 'regardless of the type and duration of the employment relationship, workers shall have the right to fair and equal treatment regarding working conditions, access to social protection and training'.[128] When coupled with the Pillar's guarantees of gender equality and equal opportunities, this initiative might contain the seeds of a more comprehensive approach to addressing equality and precariousness in the labour market.

[123] E Dewhurst, 'The Development of EU Case-Law on Age Discrimination in Employment: "Will You Still Need Me? Will You Still Feed Me? When I'm Sixty-Four?"' (2013) 19 *European Law Journal* 517, 534.

[124] L Vosko, *Managing the Margins – Gender, Citizenship and the International Regulation of Precarious Employment* (Oxford, Oxford University Press, 2010) 101.

[125] Eurofound, 'Aspects of Non-Standard Employment in Europe' (n 1) 9 and 20.

[126] ibid 21.

[127] European Commission, 'Establishing a European Pillar of Social Rights' COM (2017) 250 final.

[128] European Commission, 'Proposal for a Interinstitutional Proclamation on the European Pillar of Social Rights' COM (2017) 251 final.

4

The Effective Protection against Discrimination and the Burden of Proof

Evaluating the CJEU's Guidance Through the Lens of Race

KRISTIN HENRARD

I. Introduction

Too often we are confronted with the harsh reality that having rights does not always translate into enjoying them.[1] In liberal democracies under the rule of law, when one's rights are not respected, ultimate redress can be sought through a court of law. However, one's success crucially depends on what one needs to prove for a favourable ruling from the courts. Put differently, the effective protection of (fundamental) rights, including the prohibition of discrimination, hinges on questions of proof, particularly the determination of the standard of proof and the allocation thereof between the parties. Accordingly, within this volume about the 2000 EU Equality Directives it is indispensable to focus on the burden of proof and its division between applicant and defendant.

Victims of discrimination tend to face tremendous difficulties in producing proof,[2] since the required information is often only accessible to the perpetrator. These evidential difficulties for the victim in turn carry the risk of undermining the effective enforcement of the prohibition of discrimination, and thus the effective protection against discrimination.[3] The development of the special

[1] We are reminded of the occurrence of human rights violations on a daily basis, at times on a massive scale, at times on a smaller but nevertheless disconcerting scale, also in the EU countries. See, e.g. S Cardenas, *Human Rights in Latin America: A Politics of Terror and Hope* (Philadelphia, University of Pennsylvania Press, 2012); European Union Agency for Fundamental Rights, *Fundamental Rights Report 2017 – FRA Opinions* (Vienna, Publications Office of the European Union, 2017).

[2] See also R Belton, 'Burdens of Pleading and Proof in Discrimination Cases: Towards a Theory of Procedural Justice' (1981) *Vanderbilt Law Review* 1205.

[3] See, e.g. I Higgins, 'Enforcement and the New Equality Directives' in C Costello and E Barry (eds), *Equality in Diversity: The New Equality Directives* (Dublin, Irish Centre for Equality Law, 2003) 397.

allocation of the burden of proof or the shared burden of proof, is meant to counter this risk.

In Europe, the Court of Justice of the European Union (CJEU) actually took the lead in adopting the shared burden of proof and developed a steady line of jurisprudence from the *Danfoss* case (1989) onwards.[4] Subsequently, this case law was enshrined in the Burden of Proof Directive focused on discrimination on the basis of sex (1997)[5] and confirmed in all subsequent non-discrimination directives,[6] thus extending the concept to the 'new' protected grounds, including race.

The clarification of the shared burden of proof in the Court's case law is gradual,[7] as it occurs on a case-by-case basis.[8] Hence, it comes as no surprise that the CJEU still receives several requests for preliminary ruling inviting further clarifications in this respect. Since the wording of the provision on the special allocation of the burden of proof is similar across the protected grounds, the Court is bound to develop parallel lines of jurisprudence. This chapter focuses on the CJEU's case law on the shared burden of proof in the context of the Race Equality Directive (Article 8 RED)[9] because both the directive itself and the relevant case law have been hailed as vigorously pursuing the effective protection against the prohibition of racial discrimination. The directive has been argued to put 'race' at the top of the equality hierarchy in EU law,[10] not only because of its unparalleled broad scope of application, but also because of the very high level of protection against

[4] Case C-109/88 *Handels-og Kontorfunktionerernes Forbund I Danmark v Danks Arbejdsgiverforening* EU:C:1989:383.

[5] Council Directive 87/80/EC on the burden of proof in cases of discrimination based on sex [1997] OJ L14/6 (Burden of Proof Directive).

[6] Council Directive 2000/43/EC implementing the principle of equal treatment between persons irrespective of racial or ethnic origin [2000] OJ L180/22 (Race Equality Directive), Art 8; Council Directive 2000/78/EC establishing a general framework for equal treatment in employment and occupation [2000] OJ L303/16 (Framework Equality Directive), Art 10.

[7] See the more elaborate argumentation in favour of 'system reasoning' by the CJEU in K Henrard, 'The First Substantive ECJ Judgement on the Racial Equality Directive: A Strong Message in a Conceptually Flawed, and Responsively Weak Bottle', Jean Monnet Working Paper 09/09.

[8] See, e.g. Case C-127/92 *Enderby v Frenchay Health Authority* EU:C:1993:859, Case C-167/97 *R v Secretary of State for Employment, ex parte Seymour Smith and Perez* EU:C:1999:60; and see the cases discussed below. See also the extensive report by L Farkas and O O'Farrel for the European Commission, *Reversing the Burden of Proof: Practical Dilemmas at the European and National Level* (Luxembourg, Publications Office of the EU, 2015).

[9] See, e.g. C Hermanin, 'Europeanization through Judicial Enforcement? The Case of Race Equality', (2012) PhD Thesis, Department of Political and Social Sciences, European University Institute, 23; M Ambrus, M Busstra and K Henrard, 'The Racial Equality Directive and Effective Protection against Discrimination: Mismatches between Substantive law and Its Application' (2010) 3 *Erasmus Law Review* 165, 165–166. See also the practice of the Advisory Committee on the Framework Convention for the Protection of National Minorities, which in regard to the effective protection against racial discrimination focuses strongly on sharing the burden of proof, often explicitly referring to the Race Equality Directive in this respect: *inter alia* ACFC/OP/III(2011)0008, para 41; ACFC/OP/IV(2014), para 25; ACFC/OP/II(2013)001, para 32.

[10] M Bell, 'EU Anti-racism Policy: The Leader of the Pack?' in H Meenan (ed), *Equality Law in an Enlarged European Union: Understanding the Article 13 Directives* (Cambridge, Cambridge University Press, 2007) 178–180.

racial differentiations it provides.[11] Indeed, in comparison with the other grounds, it is striking that the Race Equality Directive contains very limited exceptions to the prohibition of *direct* racial discrimination – only genuine and determining occupational requirements (Article 4) and positive action (Article 5).[12] In terms of the CJEU's case law, two of the three substantive preliminary rulings on the Race Equality Directive so far contain significant sections on the shared burden of proof, even when the national Court itself does not ask explicit questions about it.[13] Clearly, this is an area which the CJEU considers crucial for the proper implementation of the Race Equality Directive and its promise of effective protection against racial discrimination.

Following the special allocation of the burden of proof, persons who claim violations of the principle of equal treatment only have to establish a *prima facie* case of discrimination,[14] after which it is for the respondent to prove that no discrimination has occurred. In other words, the burden of proof is divided over both parties and requires two assessments:

(a) Did the claimant establish a *prima facie* case?

(b) Did the defendant then rebut the presumption of discrimination?

How much this shared burden of proof contributes to the effective protection against discrimination depends on the exact criteria for what amounts to a *prima facie* case on the one hand and what needs to be satisfied to rebut the

[11] GN Toggenburg, 'The Race Directive: A New Dimension in the Fight against Ethnic Discrimination in Europe' (2001/2) 1 *European Yearbook on Minority Issues* 231, 234.

[12] Cf Framework Equality Directive contains a general exception in Art 2(5) as well as ground-specific exceptions in Arts 4(2), 5, 6 and 15. For a more extensive discussion, see E Howard, 'The Case for a Considered Hierarchy of Discrimination in EU Law' (2006) 13 *Maastricht Journal of European and Comparative Law* 445, 447–448.

[13] In addition to the two preliminary rulings that will be discussed at length below, the CJEU also pronounced itself in Case C-668/15 *Jyske Finans A/S v Ligebehandlinksnaevnet* EU:C:2017:278 (widely known as *Huskic*) concerning the practice of a credit institution to require additional identification from a customer whose driving licence indicates a country of birth other than a Member State of the EU or of the EFTA. The case invites criticism for defining 'race or ethnic origin' by reference to a particular ethnic origin, thus excluding xenophobic practices against foreigners at large (paras 20, 31, 33). However, the reference in para 20 to 'presumption' indicates that the facts do not establish a *prima facie* case of discrimination because the causal link cannot be presumed: 'a person's country of birth cannot, in itself, justify a general presumption that that person is a member of a given ethnic group such as to establish the existence of a direct of inextricable link between those two concepts'.

In addition, the Court of First Instance has dealt with two cases concerning the Race Equality Directive: Case T-11/03 *Afari v ECB* EU:T:2004:77; Joined Cases F-106/13 and F-25/14 *DD v EU Agency for Fundamental Rights* EU:F:2016:205. Afari challenged a disciplinary measure imposed on her, claiming racist discrimination and racist harassment. Her challenge under Article 8 RED that she had not benefited from the special allocation of the burden of proof was given short shrift by the CFI, because she had not 'adduced evidence from which it might be presumed that' direct or indirect racial discrimination had occurred (para 162). Unfortunately, the CFI reasoning is not very explicit and thus allows deductions about the requisites for establishing a *prima facie* discrimination case. For a brief discussion of the second case, see the chapter by M Moschel in this volume.

[14] Art 8 RED: 'establish facts from which it may be presumed that there has been direct or indirect discrimination'.

presumption on the other. Furthermore, as the shared burden of proof applies to direct and indirect discrimination, the criteria should be attuned to reflect the different nature of those forms of discrimination. Put differently, the identification of the criteria for establishing a *prima facie* case is intrinsically related to the ongoing discussion about the exact borderline between direct and indirect discrimination.

The first two preliminary rulings based on the Race Equality Directive, *Feryn* (2008) and *CHEZ* (2015), have both been praised for the generous, teleological interpretations of 'who' can bring complaints about 'what'.[15] *Feryn*[16] raised the question whether a public announcement by a director that his company would not hire Moroccans (because of the alleged concerns of clients) amounts to racial discrimination even without an actual victim. *CHEZ*[17] confronted the CJEU with the practice of an electricity company of placing their meters at inaccessible heights in town districts predominantly inhabited by Roma. The Court had to clarify not only whether this practice is discriminatory, but also whether a non-Roma living in such a district and thus (negatively) affected by the measure, can complain about its discriminatory nature.

In both cases, and especially in *CHEZ*, the CJEU provided guidance to the national courts about the shared burden of proof. However, as will be discussed below, in neither case did the Court use all the opportunities it was given to address the uncertainties of the national courts regarding the shared burden of proof.

This chapter sets out to analyse the clarifications by the CJEU since 2000 about sharing the burden of proof in racial discrimination cases, which thus contribute to the effective protection against racial discrimination. Furthermore, the chapter highlights the interrelation between the shared burden of proof and several other conceptual aspects, namely the recognition of a 'speech' instance of discrimination and the distinction between direct and indirect discrimination. The preliminary rulings in *Feryn* and *CHEZ* will be discussed, highlighting both the positive aspects and any flaws in the Court's reasoning. The analysis of *Feryn* will be complemented by an exploration of a preliminary ruling on very similar facts albeit concerning the grounds of sexual orientation, namely *Accept* (2013).[18]

[15] See, e.g. A Eriksson, 'European Court of Justice: Broadening the Scope of European Nondiscrimination Law' (2009) 7 *International Journal of Constitutional Law* 744. Cf footnote 13 above on criticism regarding the *Huskic* preliminary ruling.

[16] Case C-54/07 *Centrum voor gelijkheid van kansen en voor racisme bestrijding v Firma Feryn NV* EU:C:2008:397. For a detailed account of *Feryn*, see K Henrard, Jean Monnet Paper 09/09 (n 7); U Belavusau, 'Fighting Hate Speech through EU Law' (2012) 4 *Amsterdam Law Forum* 20.

[17] Case C-83/14 *CHEZ Razpredelenie Bulgaria AD v Komisia za zashtita ot diskriminatsia (CHEZ and another, third parties)* EU:C:2015:480. For a detailed account of *CHEZ*, see the chapters by M Goodwin and M Möschel in the present volume.

[18] Case C-81/12 *Asociația v Consiliul Național pentru Combaterea Discriminării* EU:C:2013:275. While *Accept* concerned sexual orientation and was thus decided not on the basis of the RED but the FED, the factual settings are so similar to *Feryn* that it merits to be reviewed whether and how *Accept* builds on the Court's reasoning in *Feryn*. See also U Belavusau, 'A Penalty Card for Homophobia from EU Non-Discrimination Law: Comment on Asociația Accept' (C-81/12)' (2015) 21 *Columbia Journal of European Law* 237, 241–243.

While the Court seems gradually more willing to provide more detailed and concrete guidance to national courts, ample scope remains for further clarification, also in light of the particularly broad scope *ratione materiae* of the Race Equality Directive.

II. *Feryn* and *Chez*: Clarifications about the Scope of Application of the Racial Discrimination Prohibition

In *Feryn*,[19] the Court clarified that when an employer declares publicly that (s)he will not recruit employees of a particular ethnic origin, this is bound to dissuade certain candidates from applying and therefore hinders their access to the labour market. The lack of an identifiable victim that complains about not being hired because of his/her ethnicity is immaterial in this respect.[20] The Court thus at least implicitly acknowledges that this public statement in itself constitutes 'less favourable treatment on grounds of racial or ethnic origin' and is therefore tantamount to direct racial discrimination (Article 2(2)(a) RED). This message carries a tremendous credibility and dissuasive force, when coming from a firm's director. Withholding the finding of discrimination because no specific person of that ethnic origin has actually been turned down in the circumstances is incongruous as the lack of rejections may go hand-in-hand with the absence of applications, reflecting the actual dissuasive force – and harm – of the employer's message.[21]

Interestingly, the Court had an opportunity to refine its view on discriminatory statements regarding recruitment in a case concerning homophobic utterances by a patron of a football club.[22] As this case is closely related to *Feryn*, it seems only appropriate to compare the Court's reasoning, even if the Race Equality Directive is not concerned. In *Accept*, the CJEU in several respects confirmed its reasoning in the earlier *Feryn* case. The CJEU indeed repeated that a public statement about excluding particular groups of persons as potential recruits can amount to a prohibited discrimination, without there being the need for an identifiable victim. The facts of this case allowed the Court to clarify that discrimination occurs even when the person making the statement is actually not legally capable of binding the firm in recruitment matters, as long as that person appears to play an important role in the management of that employer. The Court furthermore offered two factors that the national Court – making the ultimate assessment – may take into account, namely the perception of the public or social groups, and whether or not the employer has clearly distanced themselves from the statements concerned.[23]

[19] The analysis of the *Feryn* case builds on conceptual findings developed in the Jean Monnet Working Paper 09/09 by the author (n 7).

[20] Case C-54/07 *Feryn* (n 16) para 25.

[21] ibid.

[22] Case C-81/12 *Accept* (n 18).

[23] ibid, paras 50–51.

While the Court did not explicitly note the dissuasive force of the public statement concerned, the reference to the perception of the public or social groups arguably hints at the *de facto* impact of the statement. The related *implicit* acknowledgement that a public statement as such can amount to discrimination certainly reflects a conscious choice of a teleological interpretation of the Race Equality Directive, aimed at the effective protection against discrimination.[24]

In *CHEZ*, the applicant challenged the practice of an electricity company which installed electricity meters in a town's district, which is predominantly inhabited by Roma, at an inaccessible height of 6 to 7 metres, while in other parts of the same town these were set at 1.7 metres. The company defended this practice by referring to an alleged higher frequency in tampering with meters and unlawful connections in the district concerned. In its reasoning, the CJEU acknowledged the interplay of a range of factors that culminate in the systemic discrimination against Roma communities.[25] In this regard, the Court also underscored the particularly problematic 'sweeping' nature of the discriminatory measures, also affecting persons who do not belong to the protected group. The CJEU accepted that a non-Roma can complain about a practice which is discriminatory against Roma, when the non-Roma lives in the 'Roma' district to which the measure applied and is thus similarly affected. The reason is that the prohibition of discrimination applies not to a particular category of persons but by reference to the grounds mentioned.[26] Accordingly, the Court extended the concept of *discrimination by association*[27] to indirect (racial) discrimination.[28] Actually, this expansion of the category of persons that are considered victims that can file complaints concerns – as aptly recognised by Advocate General Kokott – 'victims by way of collateral damage'.[29]

[24] In its reasoning, the Court also had to justify this finding in light of Article 7 RED which confines Member State obligation to ensure the availability of judicial or administrative procedures to instances with actual victims. Put differently, the Court had to find a way to 'fill' the lacuna in the Race Equality Directive and overcome the ensuing internal inconsistency.

[25] S Cox, 'When all the People in a District are Victims of Racial Discrimination: CJEU Ruling in *CHEZ v Nikolova*' (*EU Law Analysis*, 24 July 2015). Available at: http://eulawanalysis.blogspot.nl/2015/07/when-all-people-in-district-are-victims.html. For a more detailed appraisal of Roma discrimination in the context of EU law, see the chapter by M Goodwin in the present volume.

Cf AG Kokott in *Belov* took the opposite view regarding the standing of the national equality body: Case C-394/11 *Valeri Hariev Belov v CHEZ Elektro Balgaria AD and Others* EU:C:2012:585, Opinion of AG Kokott.

[26] Case C-83/14 *CHEZ* (n 17) para 50.

[27] ibid para 56, following the Court's earlier reasoning in Case C-303/06 *S Coleman v Attridge Law and Steve Law* EU:C:2008:415, paras 38 and 50.

[28] C Cahn, 'Court of Justice of the EU Rules Collective and Inaccessible Electrical Metres Discriminate against Roma: CHEZ Razpredelenie Bulgaria AD v Komisia za zashtita ot diskriminatsia (C-83/14)' (2016) 18 *European Journal of Migration and Law* 112, 115; R Grozev, 'A Landmark Judgment of the Court of Justice of the EU – New Conceptual Contributions to the Legal Combat against Ethnic Discrimination' (2015) 15 *Equal Rights Review* 168, 172–173.

[29] Case C-83/14 *CHEZ Razpredelenie Bulgaria AD v Komisia za zashtita ot diskriminatsia (CHEZ and another, third parties)* EU:C:2015:480, Opinion of AG Kokott, para 58.

This teleological interpretation of the relevant provisions of the Race Equality Directive provides optimal possibilities to challenge alleged discriminatory measures and can certainly be seen to fortify the effective protection against racial discrimination. As will be corroborated by the analysis below, the Court in *CHEZ* fully took the opportunity to pronounce itself on the particularly problematic nature of systemic discrimination, and sent strong signals about the high level of scrutiny to be adopted in this regard.[30]

III. Sharing the Burden of Proof: Setting the Scene

As argued above, effective protection against discrimination hinges, in many important respects, on the special allocation of the burden of proof reducing such burden for the alleged victim. Article 8 RED reflects a special two-phase allocation of the burden of proof between the applicant and respondent. In the first phase, the applicant has to 'establish … facts from which it may be presumed that there has been direct or indirect discrimination'. Once this *prima facie* case of discrimination case is established, a second 'rebuttal' phase begins in which the respondent needs to 'prove that there has been no breach of the principle of equal treatment'. The CJEU case law reveals that national courts are often uncertain about what amounts to a *prima facie* case of discrimination and what would amount to a successful rebuttal of this presumption. Some of these uncertainties are due to the relationship between speech announcing discriminatory recruitment practice on the one hand and actual discriminatory recruitment practice on the other; others flow from the distinction between direct and indirect discrimination. These two areas of uncertainty and the concomitant need for the CJEU to provide the necessary clarification, will be elaborated upon in section 3A and 4 respectively, while critically analysing the CJEU's reasoning in *Feryn* (on both points) and *CHEZ* (on the latter point only). First, some preliminary remarks are made on the two phases established by the shared burden of proof.

The exact requirements for establishing a *prima facie* case of discrimination are not immediately obvious. Nevertheless, when identifying the markers relevant for a presumption of discrimination, there should be some relation to the substantive elements of discrimination, such as a harm (less favourable treatment or disadvantage, with a comparative/comparable element) and a causal relationship between that harm and the protected grounds (racial or ethnic origin in case of

[30] Earlier in Case C-394/11 *Valeri Hariev Belov v CHEZ Elektro Balgaria AD and Others* EU:C:2013:48, concerning very similar facts, the CJEU had adopted a rather restrictive definition of 'Court' in Art 267 TFEU, denying this status to the national equality body concerned, which had precluded it from ruling on the substance of the case. See, e.g. M Möschel, 'Race Discrimination and Access to the European Court of Justice: *Belov*' (2013) 50 *Common Market Law Review* 1433. In *CHEZ*, the referring instance was a national court, so it remains to be seen whether the CJEU would accept a reference by a national equality body in the future.

the Race Equality Directive). While the substantive elements of discrimination are to a significant extent entangled, the inferences to be made will fundamentally be about the causal relationship between the harm and the protected grounds.

In the second phase, the respondent can try to rebut the presumption of discrimination that was established. In fact, this second phase encompasses two possibilities.[31] The respondent can first of all try to negate the presumption, by negating the 'harm' or – more often – the causal relationship between the harm and the protected grounds. Indeed, at the end of the *prima facie* phase this causal link is only established at the level of a presumption. Second, if the *negation* is not successful, the respondent can try to put forward a *justification* for the presumed discrimination. These two possibilities concern two different aspects: the former sees to the question of whether a distinction is made on grounds of ethnic origin, whereas the latter concerns the possible lawfulness of a distinction on ethnic origin grounds.

It merits underscoring that in EU law, justification is rather restricted for instances of direct discrimination since the legitimate aims that can be invoked are exhaustively enumerated. For indirect discrimination, this is fundamentally different as EU law uses an open justification test similar to the 'reasonable and objective justification' developed in general international law.[32]

A. Sharing the Burden of Proof: Discriminatory Public Speech vs Discriminatory Recruitment Practice

i. Feryn

The preliminary reference in *Feryn* included many questions pertaining to the shared burden of proof and, more particularly, its application to statements about current and future recruitment policies, the ensuing recruitment decisions and the impact on the workforce composition. Regrettably, the Court's reasoning is far from precise and accurate, which leads to confusing statements that fail to provide guidance to the national court(s). The Court qualifies the public statement both as constituting direct discrimination[33] and as potentially amounting to a *prima facie*

[31] See also Ambrus, Busstra and Henrard (n 9) 177–178.

[32] On the 'reasonable and objective justification' test developed in general international law, see e.g. K Henrard, The Impact of International Non-discrimination Norms in Combination with General Human Rights for the Protection of National Minorities: The European Convention on Human Rights, DH-MIN(2006)020; K Henrard, The Impact of International Non-discrimination Norms in combination with General Human Rights for the Protection of National Minorities: Several United Nations Human Rights Conventions, DH-MIN (2006)021. See also W Vandenhole, *Non-Discrimination and Equality in the View of the UN Human Rights Treaty Bodies* (Antwerpen, Intersentia, 2005). Compare with the formulation used in the definition of indirect discrimination, e.g. in Art 2(2)(b) RED.

[33] Case C-54/07 *Feryn* (n 16) para 28: 'the fact that an employer states publicly that it will not recruit employees of a certain ethnic or racial origin *constitutes direct discrimination* in respect of recruitment within the meaning of Article 2(2)(a) of Directive 2000/43, such statements being likely strongly

case of direct discrimination,[34] without clarifying that in the former statement it is rather concerned with questions of definition, while in the latter it turns to the shared burden of proof. Unfortunately, instead of providing clarification, this sloppy reasoning risks perpetuating the uncertainty of national courts about the respective meaning of 'discrimination' and 'a prima facie case of discrimination'.

Similarly, in its application of Article 8 RED, the Court argues as follows:

> *[s]tatements* by which an employer publicly lets it be known that, under its *recruitment policy*, it will not recruit any employees of a certain ethnic or racial origin may constitute facts of such a nature as to give rise to a presumption of a discriminatory policy.
>
> It is thus for that employer to adduce evidence that it has not breached the principle of equal treatment, which it can do, *inter alia*, by showing that the *actual recruitment practice* of the undertaking does not correspond to those statements.[35]

The Court's reasoning ultimately denies that a director's public statement about the firm's recruitment policy can amount to discrimination in and of itself, irrespective of the actual practice. Instead, the reasoning implies that an announcement of a discriminatory recruitment policy merely leads to a presumption of discrimination, more particularly of discriminatory recruitment practices.

The Court's reasoning could have been much clearer and informative, had it distinguished between the *speech* of the firm's director as one potential case of discrimination and the *actual recruitment practice* of the firm as a second. The concomitant separate allocations of the burden of proof would have been sounder conceptually.[36]

Arguably, the public statement made in *Feryn* by one of the directors amounts to conclusive, direct proof of the *speech instance of discrimination*, which does not leave room for negation. Thus, the Court would not need to share the burden of proof to establish racial discrimination.[37] In addition, a public statement such as the one in *Feryn* could be considered as raising a presumption of directly *discriminatory recruitment practice*. In the end, the Court's statement in this respect is correct, but only when the two possible instances of discrimination are neatly separated.

to dissuade certain candidates from submitting their candidature and, accordingly, to hinder their access to the labour market' (emphasis added).

[34] ibid para 31.

[35] See paras 31–32 (emphasis added).

[36] There actually exists best practice of some of the national equality bodies in this respect, demonstrating that it makes indeed for clear and convincing reasoning when these two instances of discrimination are consistently distinguished in the related reasoning. For a more detailed analysis with references to examples from the Opinions of the Dutch Equal Treatment Commission (now the Netherlands Institute for Human Rights), see Henrard, Jean Monnet Working Paper 09/09 (n 7) 14–16 and footnotes 45–47.

[37] However, it would be possible for the board of directors to make a public statement that henceforth discriminatory selection criteria will no longer be used. This speech could be accepted as a cessation (from that moment onwards) of the 'speech' act of discrimination, when made in a credible context, thus balancing out the dissuasive force of the earlier public statement by one of the directors. In the *Feryn* case, such a public statement was actually made, together with the Belgian Equality Body in charge of supervising the recruitment practice of the company concerned.

Moreover, the Court's reasoning regarding the second phase provides a suboptimal clarification for national courts, since it does not explain the two (theoretical) possibilities for a rebuttal, namely *negation* and *justification*. Since the limited exceptions to the prohibition of direct discrimination on racial grounds are clearly not applicable, Feryn's director cannot avail itself of a justification. In other words, Feryn could only try to rebut the presumption of discrimination by negation.

The Court indicates that the 'employer [should] adduce evidence that it has not breached the principle of equal treatment, which it can do, *inter alia*, by showing that the *actual recruitment practice* of the undertaking does not correspond to those statements.[38] The Court thus suggests that the employer is not restricted to proof about the actual recruitment practice to show that he did not breach the principle of equal treatment. However, no further indications were given on what these other ways would be.

Recognising the strong dissuasive force of a public speech by a company's director arguably precludes any type of evidence about the actual recruitment practice from being considered sufficient to negate the presumption of discriminatory recruitment practice. Defining what amounts to actual recruitment practices that are not racially discriminatory requires further demarcation. It would seem unreasonable to demand a review of all recruitment decisions ever taken. Even then it is unclear what would constitute sufficient proof (i.e. evidence that racial prejudice did not have any role to play in any of these decisions). Similarly, proving that a segment of the personnel has a particular ethnic background would not suffice, as the impact of racial prejudice in at least some instances could not be ruled out. Moreover, a credible public statement denouncing the discriminatory statement, explicitly distancing the firm concerned from this type of policy and practice would appear essential to negate the presumption. Contextual elements regarding the way in which this statement is made and by whom (in the hierarchy of the firm) would need to be considered as well.

In other words, while some inferences are possible between statements about discriminatory recruitment practice and actual recruitment practice, for a sound allocation of the burden of proof it remains crucially important to distinguish between two possible instances of discrimination (i.e. speech and actual practice) and not to inappropriately include proof of actual recruitment practice in the assessment of discriminatory statements about this practice.

ii. ACCEPT

The *Accept* judgment is welcomed as further clarifying the shared burden of proof and the two phases it encompasses. The CJEU builds on the idea of the dissuasive force of public speech, while seemingly veering towards a more explicit recognition of speech as an instance of discrimination. Nevertheless, on closer

[38] Case C-54/07 *Feryn* (n 16) para 32.

scrutiny the Court still qualifies discriminatory public speech as a mere presumption of discrimination, and thus not an act of discrimination, as suggested above. Therefore, the Court's judgment in *Accept* clearly merits closer examination.

It is certainly commendable that the CJEU maintains a teleological interpretation, acknowledging the potentially exclusionary power of mere speech, particularly about discriminatory recruitment policy. The Court clarified in *Accept* that the dissuasive force of such a statement is equally strong when it comes from a person that may not be able to legally bind the club, but is nevertheless perceived to play a leading role in the club. However, the Court still fails to explicitly distinguish between two possible instances of discrimination – public speech about recruitment policy on the one hand and actual recruitment practice on the other. Indeed, the former public speech should be seen as discriminatory in itself, separate from and irrespective of the actual recruitment practice. Similarly, the Court is still ambiguous about the 'status' of the public speech concerned, seemingly only considering it a *prima facie* case of discrimination.

The specific facts of *Accept* also raise additional questions. It is possible that the Court in *Accept* considered the public speech merely a *prima facie* case of discrimination, because it was made by a person not actually able to legally bind the club, so as to allow for a counter-statement by the actual 'employer' to influence the assessment. Yet, the CJEU's reasoning reveals its struggle with the role of such a counter-statement, as either influencing the finding of a *prima facie* case (first phase)[39] or constituting one of the possible elements in the (second) rebuttal phase for negating the presumption of discrimination.[40]

Regarding the rebuttal of the *prima facie* case, the Court first clarifies that disproving the presumption would not require proof that the relevant protected group had been recruited in the past.[41] Two comments need to be made here. First of all, the Court refers to the problem that such proof would conflict with the right to privacy of the players concerned, which leaves open the possibility that proof of past recruitment of particular groups could be required when this can be done without interfering with privacy rights. Second, it remains unclear whether (and under what conditions) proof of past recruitment could be sufficient to rebut the presumption. The Court then goes on to indicate that the *prima facie* case 'may be refuted with a body of consistent evidence'.[42] In a case triggered by a public statement, it is certainly to be welcomed that the Court focuses on counter-speech and express provisions of recruitment policy aimed at ensuring equal treatment as possible elements for refuting the presumption of discrimination. This could

[39] Case C-81/12 *Accept* (n 18) para 50: 'the fact that such an employer might not have clearly distanced itself from the statements concerned is a factor which the Court hearing the case may take into account in the context of the overall appraisal of the facts'.

[40] ibid para 58: 'a *prima facie* case of discrimination on grounds of sexual orientation may be refuted with a body of consistent evidence … might include, for example, a reaction by the defendant concerned clearly distancing itself from public statements on which the appearance of discrimination is based'.

[41] ibid para 57.

[42] ibid para 58.

indeed be understood as implying a more pronounced recognition of a speech instance of discrimination.

The Court is applauded for recognising both in *Feryn* and *Accept* the strong dissuasive force of statements about discriminatory recruitment policy. *Accept* extends this focus on *de facto* dissuasive impact, by acknowledging that a statement by a person with merely perceived power in a sports club can be similarly dissuasive. Nevertheless, the Court never fully recognises discriminatory public speech as a separate instance of discrimination, distinct from any discriminatory action. Consequently, the CJEU does not develop two distinct allocations of the burden of proof and fails to give proper guidance to the national courts about the special allocation of the burden of proof. Similarly, the Court does not properly explain the rebuttal phase, which requires distinguishing the two theoretical options for rebuttal (i.e. negation and justification).[43]

IV. The Sharing of the Burden of Proof and the Distinction between Direct and Indirect Discrimination

This part starts with a theoretical consideration of how the proper sharing of the burden of proof in discrimination cases in EU law requires a clear conceptualisation of the dividing line between direct and indirect discrimination. Subsequently, the CJEU's reasoning in the *Feryn* and *CHEZ* cases is discussed in this respect.

The different 'nature' of direct and indirect discrimination necessarily impacts sharing the burden of proof, since the first phase concerns establishing a presumption of either direct or indirect discrimination.[44] When comparing the respective definitions of direct and indirect discrimination in the Race Equality Directive,[45] certain common elements emerge as inherent in the concept of discrimination, including a harm (less favourable treatment or disadvantage, with an element of comparison or comparability), and a causal relationship between that harm and the protected grounds (racial or ethnic origin in the RED). The main differences between these definitions of direct and indirect discrimination point to their difference in nature, and are, on the hand, the individual *versus* group focus, and on the other, the degree of directness of the causal relationship between the harm and the protected ground. Regarding the individual *versus* group focus, direct

[43] It can nevertheless be noted that the Court correctly establishes 'refutation' (synonymous to 'negation') in relation to the burden of proof of the defendant (Case C-81/12 *Accept* (n 18) para 56), which is *in casu* the only real option to rebut the presumption.

[44] See Art 8(1) RED.

[45] Art 2(2)(a) and (b) respectively read 'direct discrimination shall be taken to occur where *one person* is treated *less favourable* than another is, has been or would be treated in a *comparable situation* on grounds of racial or ethnic origin' and 'indirect discrimination shall be taken to occur where an apparently neutral provision, criterion or practice would put *persons* of a racial or ethnic origin at a *particular disadvantage, compared to* other persons, unless [reasonable and objective justification].

racial discrimination entails *one* person being treated less favourably than another (on grounds of ethnicity), whereas indirect discrimination concerns measures that put *persons of a particular racial or ethnic origin* at a disadvantage compared to other persons.

This chapter focuses on the difference in directness of the causal relationship between harm and the protected grounds, since the inferences for establishing a *prima facie* case fundamentally concern this causal relationship. Direct discrimination occurs when there is a direct causal link between a person's ethnic origin and the (less favourable) treatment complained about (i.e. the differentiation is explicitly based on the protected grounds). For indirect discrimination, the causal link is less direct and requires additional considerations, having regard to the effects of the measures (e.g. the measure disproportionately affects persons characterised by the protected grounds). However, the difference between direct and indirect discrimination is not always that clear, especially when the contested measure makes a differentiation based on a characteristic which is closely related to the protected grounds. It could be argued that a differentiation based on a characteristic inextricably linked with a protected ground should automatically be categorised as direct discrimination on such grounds.[46] Nevertheless, this approach raises tricky questions about the tipping point on the sliding scale between characteristics that are inextricably linked and those that are less obviously but still closely connected to the protected grounds.[47]

It is in any event striking that in both *Feryn* and *CHEZ*, the questions asked by the national courts showed a strong uncertainty about qualifying the cases as either direct or indirect discrimination. Both references arguably concerned cases of systemic discrimination, in *Feryn* against certain migrant communities, and in *CHEZ* against the Roma. Especially in such instances of systemic discrimination and the related deep-seated prejudices, it becomes evident that the dividing line between direct and indirect discrimination is not as neat as one might want to believe, given the importance in EU law of that distinction, since it translates into radically different justification mechanisms. Hence, further thought needs to go into where and how to draw the line: when is the causality strong enough to denote direct discrimination, and when is it so weak that one is faced with indirect discrimination? What exactly makes a causal relationship strong (or weak)? How is this related to the underlying motive for a particular measure – differentiation? Where on the scale of strong/weak causality are unconscious biases and prejudices situated?

The language of 'purpose or effect' (impairing the equal enjoyment of human rights) in the UN Convention on the Elimination of all Forms of Racial Discrimination (CERD) seems to oppose intent with effect. Intent to differentiate

[46] For reasoning in this direction see Case C-83/14 *CHEZ* (Opinion of AG Kokott) (n 29) para 86.

[47] See also C McCrudden, 'The New Architecture of EU Equality Law after CHEZ: Did the Court of Justice Reconceptualise Direct and Indirect Discrimination?' (2016) *European Equality Law Review* 1, 6–7.

and to disadvantage on particular grounds does reflect a strong causality and seems more problematic than disadvantages which are merely an unintended side-effect, a result of how majority society is organised. This understanding of the underlying difference in 'intent' between direct and indirect discrimination, and of the related difference in the degree of 'heinousness', could actually explain the divergent justification schemes for direct versus indirect discrimination in EU law.[48] Arguably, when a bias or ingrained prejudice against a particular ethnic group is at the root of disadvantageous treatment, the latter can still be seen as 'on grounds of' ethnicity, even if it does not feature explicitly. In other words, as long as the protected grounds play a causal role, be that consciously or unconsciously, the causality would be strong, pointing to direct discrimination. Indeed, the presence of prejudice and bias is arguably closer to 'intent', going beyond mere 'effect'.[49]

How to understand, then, the case law of the CJEU in which it underscores, in line with general anti-discrimination theory, that establishing an instance of direct discrimination does not require proof of intent?[50] Arguably this approach merely reflects common knowledge that proving 'intent' is extremely difficult, especially when it has not been made explicit or is even 'hidden', as may happen more often than not. 'Intent' (to disadvantage), including bias and prejudice, is arguably still what direct discrimination intends to capture, but difficulties in proving the requisite state of mind make courts turn to actual practice and its effects in order to infer intent (including bias).[51] However, this also causes confusion because looking at the effects and impact of a measure is supposedly typical for indirect discrimination. Nevertheless, a distinction between direct and indirect discrimination can still be made in terms of the strength of the causality that can be inferred from the practice concerned.

In this respect, it can be argued that when the disproportionately disadvantageous impact of a measure on a particular group is known for a long time, and the measure is nevertheless maintained without modifications (exceptions) for preventing the disproportionate impact, retaining such a measure can actually be considered as reflecting intent of the disadvantageous impact which points to direct discrimination.[52] This understanding can arguably be detected (at least implicitly) in the CJEU's case law, where the Court recognises that if a measure only impacts one particular group, this constitutes direct discrimination based on the grounds that identify the group concerned.[53] The cases in which this line of reasoning was

[48] See also Case C-83/14 *CHEZ* (Opinion of AG Kokott) (n 29) para 71.

[49] See also L Quillian, 'New Approaches to Understanding Racial Prejudice and Discrimination' (2006) 32 *Annual Review of Sociology* 299, 300.

[50] E Ellis, *EU Anti-discrimination Law* (Oxford, Oxford University Press, 2005) 103.

[51] Quillian (n 49) 302–303, 309.

[52] See, e.g. in relation to the disproportionate side-lining of Roma children to special schools for mentally retarded children through the use of (arguably biased) tests, K Henrard, 'Noot bij EHRM, 29 January 2013, Horvath en Kiss t. Hongarije' (2013) *EHRC* 1453.

[53] See, e.g. Case C-177/88 *Dekker v Stichting Vormingscentrum voor Jong Volwassenen (VJV Centrum)* EU:C:1990383; Case C–196/02 *Nikoloudi v Organismos Tilepikinonion Ellados AE* EU:C:2005:141;

followed, such as *Nikoloudi* (2005) and *Maruko* (2008),[54] all concern measures with all-too-well-known disproportionate negative impacts on a protected group. A similar line of reasoning seems to explain why the CJEU at times identifies a case of direct discrimination in instances where there is a lack of accommodation for the special needs of particular vulnerable groups. Likewise, there is supposedly awareness that not making the necessary adaptations has a disproportionate negative impact on the groups concerned. Hence, not making the effort to adapt the rules can then be understood as intentionally excluding groups from a particular benefit, pointing to a 'reversed' bias.[55]

Admittedly, difficult questions still remain about the exact dividing line between direct and indirect discrimination, *inter alia*, concerning the degree of disproportionate impact that would be considered sufficient to reveal a strong causality between harm and protected grounds so as to infer actual intent to discriminate. A linking issue is determining the time frame for imputing intent to discriminate from the continued use of measures notwithstanding their disproportionate impact.[56]

Upon a closer look at the shared burden of proof, the often-blurry distinctions between direct and indirect discrimination become apparent. The preceding analysis has clarified that a *prima facie* case mostly concerns inferences about the causal relationship between harm and protected grounds. Interestingly, both for direct and indirect discrimination, courts make inferences from the actual practice and the effects of this practice. However, such regard for the practice/effects of a measure when establishing a *prima facie* case of discrimination, and to some extent also in the negation of this presumption, complicates and confuses the distinction between the two types of discrimination, and also the related sharing of the burden of proof. In this respect, further clarifications by the CJEU about the role of the practice and effects elements in sharing the burden of proof for discrimination cases are obviously welcome.

Moreover, one can identify striking differences not only in the way in which practice is used to establish a *prima facie* case of direct or indirect discrimination, but also in considering the possibilities to rebut the presumption, and the place for the practice/effects elements in this respect. For a *prima facie* case of direct discrimination, practice is utilised to establish a presumption that the underlying reason or motive for (or prejudice informing) the disadvantageous

Case C-267/06 *Tadao Maruko v Versorgungsanstalt der deutschen Bühnen* EU:C:2008:179. See also RC Tobler, 'Limits and Potential of the Concept of Indirect Discrimination' (Brussels, European Commission, 2008) 48–51.

[54] Case C-196/02 *Nikoloudi* (n 53); Case C-267/06 *Maruko* (n 53).

[55] See, e.g. Ambrus, Busstra and Henrard (n 9) 173–74 where the cases C-116/06 *Sari Kiiski v Tampereen kaupunki* EU:C:2007:536 and C-423/04 *Richards v Secretary of State for Work and Pensions* EU:C:2006:256 are discussed.

[56] See also below the argument that especially in case of systemic, ingrained discrimination against a particular group, the dividing line between direct and indirect discrimination becomes blurry. A proper theoretical paradigm on the exact delineation of these two types of discrimination would thus be especially relevant for such cases.

treatment is the protected ground. One can try to establish a presumption of a direct causal link between disadvantageous treatment and protected grounds, for example through situation testing. It requires well thought through settings so as to isolate the protected grounds as the only variable. In this respect, further clarifications by the CJEU are eagerly awaited in subsequent cases. In relation to indirect discrimination, the disproportionate impact of a measure on a group is a question of fact that establishes as such a strong indirect causal link between the measure and the protected grounds. In terms of rebuttal, for indirect discrimination it is virtually impossible to negate the indirect causal link between measure and protected grounds, while there is certainly scope for an objective justification for the disparate impact concerned.

The primary focus may turn out not to be on practice/effects elements in the construction of the objective justification; this will be shown by further case law might. In EU law, there is virtually no possibility to justify direct discrimination considering the narrow and exhaustive list of exceptions. However, the defendant can try to negate the causal link by showing that the actual reason or motive for the disadvantageous treatment was not the protected grounds. In this respect, one would expect proof through 'counter' practice (possibly of a speech-nature, see above) – another line of enquiry on which additional guidance from the CJEU is welcomed.

A. Shared Burden of Proof and Direct vs Indirect Discrimination: *Feryn* and *CHEZ*

The following analysis of the two preliminary rulings under the Race Equality Directive will investigate whether and to what extent the CJEU has clarified the two phases of the shared burden of proof and the related questions about the dividing line between direct and indirect discrimination.

i. Feryn

The Court in *Feryn* refrained from clarifying the fundamental distinction between direct and indirect discrimination, notwithstanding the uncertainties expressed by the national Court in its preliminary reference questions. The Court did qualify the director's speech as a potential instance of direct discrimination but failed to tie the facts of the case *explicitly* to the definitions of the Race Equality Directive. In this respect, the Court could have built on its assessment of the strong dissuasive force of a public statement by a firm's director to establish 'less favourable treatment'. Furthermore, the explicit statement that persons with a particular ethnic origin would not be employed arguably establishes a direct causal link with the protected grounds. Consequently, the statement concerned fits the definition of direct discrimination in Article 2(2)(a) RED. The Court could have explicitly responded to the question from the national Court about the components of the indirect discrimination definition in the Race Equality Directive. Maybe even more importantly, it could have tied its reply to the more conceptual discussion about the different degree of directness of the causal link (between differentiation/disadvantageous treatment and grounds) for direct and indirect discrimination respectively. Relatedly, the CJEU could have delved into the challenges and related minimum requirements involved in trying to establish questions of intent/motive/prejudice through the practice/effects of particular measures. This would have undoubtedly resulted in a more principled incorporation of practice/effects elements in the application of the shared burden of proof in the case of direct discrimination.

The *Feryn* case was particularly challenging due to the fact that the complaint targeted the speech of the firm's director publicly announcing a discriminatory hiring policy, and not particular instances of discriminatory hiring practices. This entailed difficult questions on top of the uncertainty pertaining to the dividing line between direct and indirect discrimination. The latter requires a consideration of the possible relation between intent/motive/prejudice – a conscious or unconscious state of mind on the one hand, and the disadvantageous practice/effects on the other. The identification of a speech instance of discrimination, as separate from a practice, concerns a further distinction within the practice/effects 'materialisation' phase. Initially, the Court appears to qualify a particular public speech as an (potential) instance of direct discrimination in and of itself, irrespective of its actual implementation, acknowledging the strong dissuasive force for a certain ethnic group.[57] However, in its subsequent reasoning, it does not identify two separate (potential) instances of discrimination – one pertaining to the public speech (the speech instance), and one to the actual recruitment practice of the firm (the practice instance), each with its own sharing of the burden of proof. By an unprincipled mingling of the practice elements in how the burden of proof is shared in relation to the public speech instance of discrimination, the Court actually seems to question whether mere speech can amount to an instance of prohibited discrimination.[58]

ii. CHEZ

In *CHEZ*, the national courts were not confronted with difficult questions pertaining to a speech instance of discrimination and its relation to actual practice, yet there were similar uncertainties about the dividing line between direct and indirect discrimination as in *Feryn*.

A few preliminary remarks are in order about the Court's reasoning in *CHEZ*. First, the way in which the questions by the national Court were answered strongly

[57] Case C-54/07 *Feryn* (n 16) para 25.

[58] For a more elaborate argumentation see Henrard, Jean Monnet Paper 09/09 (n 7) 14–16.

confirms the extent to which a distinction between direct and indirect discrimination has implications for the (correct) application of the sharing of the burden of proof. Indeed, while most of the questions by national Courts pertained to the distinction between direct and indirect discrimination, the CJEU consistently added in its answers the implications for the sharing of the burden of proof.[59] Adding this information *proprio motu* can also be interpreted as a manifestation of the Court's resolve to avail of the opportunity to clarify the sharing of the burden of proof as a central component of the 2000 EU Equality Directives aiming to enhance the effectiveness of the protection against discrimination.

Furthermore, it is striking that the Court provided – in several respects – very concrete guidance on the sharing of the burden of proof. Notwithstanding the repetition of the mantra regarding preliminary rulings that the ultimate application to the facts of the case needs to be done by the national Courts, it is often hard to miss what the CJEU considered the national Court should decide *in concreto*. Indeed, the Court provided strong guidance that a *prima facie* case of direct racial discrimination could be established. Second, the CJEU pointed out that if the national Court would not find a *prima facie* case of direct discrimination, then it should be considered a *prima facie* case of indirect discrimination.[60] Third, the Court also provided several strong hints to the national Court that there would be no room for finding a reasonable, objective justification *in casu*.[61] Notwithstanding the Court's very concrete reasoning, often closely tied to the facts of the case, the following more in-depth analysis will demonstrate that clarifications of a more general nature were also provided.

As regards *direct discrimination* in *CHEZ*, the Court's reasoning centred around the question of whether race was the direct cause, i.e. the actual reason for the challenged practice.[62] While the Court did not use the word 'intent', it clearly sought to determine whether ethnic origin is the direct causal factor for the challenged practice, i.e. if the practice was adopted because of the Roma ethnicity and related prejudices towards the group predominantly living there. In this respect, the Court underscored that:

> it is sufficient, in order for there to be direct discrimination within the meaning of Article 2(2)(a) of Directive 2000/43, that ethnic origin determined the decision to impose the treatment'. In the preceding paragraph the Court had already highlighted that 'the mere fact that the district at issue … is also lived in by inhabitants who are

[59] Case C-83/14 *CHEZ* (n 17) paras 77–85.

[60] ibid para 105: 'assuming that the referring court comes to the conclusion that it is not established that the practice at issue amounts to direct discrimination on the grounds of ethnic origin, *it must be stated that the facts as found by that Court permit the view to be taken that* such a practice displays the characteristics required to constitute indirect discrimination' (emphasis added).

[61] See Case C-83/14 *CHEZ* (n 17) paras 121, 124–127.

[62] The CJEU did not address AG Kokott's suggestion about identifying direct discrimination when an apparently neutral measure affects of is capable of affecting persons possessing the protected characteristic, while the measure is inextricably linked to the protected characteristic: see also McCrudden (n 47) 6.

> not of Roma origin, does not rule out that such a practice was imposed in view of the Roma ethnic origin shared by most of that district's inhabitants.[63]

The CJEU actually gave the national Court no less than four hints indicating that the facts are deemed to point towards a *prima facie* case of direct racial discrimination.[64] First, the Court highlighted that high meters were only placed in urban districts where the majority of the inhabitants are Roma. Second, the CJEU opined that the company's assertion that 'damage and unlawful connections are perpetrated mainly by Bulgarian nationals of Roma origin … could, in fact, suggest that the practice at issue is based on ethnic stereotypes or prejudices'.[65] Third, the CJEU considered it significant that no proof was adduced about the actual damage and tampering in the district concerned. Fourth, the Court implicitly argued that the lack of individualised measures and the lasting nature of the practice again points to deep-seated prejudices against the group that makes up the overwhelming majority in the district concerned. While the Court's reasoning is indeed very much tied to the facts of this case, some general pointers for a *prima facie* case of racial discrimination can be distilled, such as indications that measures are taken based on prejudice instead of actual facts (and proof thereof) and (related) indications that measures are not really tailored but target a group as a whole.

The Court chose to discuss the *rebuttal* of the possible finding of a *prima facie* case of racial discrimination immediately after the discussion of the causal factor, and prior to the other elements of a *prima facie* case of direct discrimination, while limiting the rebuttal to the causality factor. This shows that it considered causality to constitute the central question in the case. Moreover, it easily identified a 'less favourable treatment' considering both the difficulties in checking one's electricity meter and the stigmatising effect of the practice, while pointing out that all final consumers supplied by the same distributor in the same urban region are in a comparable situation.[66]

Unfortunately, the Court limits its discussion of the rebuttal phase to highlighting that the respondent would have to prove that the practice is exclusively based on objective factors, not to do with ethnicity.[67] It could have clarified that of the two possibilities for rebuttal, only negation would be possible *in casu*, since none of the limited exceptions to the prohibition of direct racial discrimination apply. Given the preceding pointers of the CJEU about the *prima facie* case of direct discrimination, a successful refutation by the respondent seems highly unlikely. In other words, were the national Court to follow the CJEU's hints and opt for the direct discrimination track, the CJEU's reasoning points towards a conclusion of prohibited direct discrimination.

[63] Case C-83/14 *CHEZ* (n 17) paras 75–76.
[64] Consecutively addressed in Case C-83/14 *CHEZ* (n 17) paras 81–84.
[65] ibid para 82.
[66] Case C-81/12 *Accept* (n 18) paras 87–88 respectively.
[67] ibid para 85.

The Court's approach to the questions about *indirect discrimination* sought to explain the concept by differentiating it from direct discrimination. In line with the *effect-intent* distinction that is explicitly used in CERD, the Court highlights that it is the disparate negative impact on a particular group, not intent, that matters in relation to indirect discrimination. However, direct discrimination presupposes that a measure 'has been introduced for reasons relating to racial or ethnic origin'.[68] The Court went on to show that the facts of the case can also be perceived in terms of an apparently neutral measure (adapting the height of meters to counter tampering and damage) that has a disproportionate impact on Roma, since the high meters are only installed in districts mainly inhabited by Roma.[69]

Interestingly, the CJEU thus portrayed both direct and indirect discrimination as plausible options. Keeping open the possibility of both 'tracks' can be seen as reflecting an understanding and acknowledgement by the Court that the dividing line between direct and indirect discrimination is indeed not always crystal clear. Especially in case of systemic discrimination, and deep-seated prejudices against a group, the dividing line becomes murky. The Court's reasoning appears to favour a two-step model in these circumstances: first, direct discrimination should be assessed, and if that fails, the indirect discrimination track can be proceeded with.[70] Nevertheless, further judgments on cases of systemic discrimination are needed to reveal whether this two-step model is tied to the specificities of the particular case or is applicable more generally.

Likewise, the Court could have clarified the rebuttal phase better by indicating that it could only concern a justification of the disparate impact, not a refutation. Strikingly, the guidance given to the national Court was again rather strong and concrete, indicating that an objective justification would be virtually impossible. The Court underscored that the company cannot simply hide behind the so-called 'common knowledge' but instead not only has to specify the actual damage it has sustained in the district, but also has to demonstrate that after twenty-five years there would still be a need for this practice.[71] The CJEU furthermore handed to the national courts all the factors they *should* consider in their assessment. The practice may be considered suitable for reaching the legitimate aim, but the national Court should consider the possibility of other suitable, less restrictive means (e.g. different types of meters) in line with the techniques used by other electricity companies to combat damage and tampering.[72] Regarding the national Court's proportionality review, the Court highlighted not only the widespread and long-standing nature of the practice at issue, but also its offensive and stigmatising effect.[73] The Court actually translated these hints

[68] Case C-83/14 *CHEZ* (n 17) para 95.
[69] ibid paras 106–107 respectively.
[70] ibid para 105.
[71] ibid paras 116–117.
[72] ibid paras 113–114, 120–122.
[73] ibid paras 124–125.

into a more outspoken overarching conclusion that 'the disadvantages … appear disproportionate to the objectives pursued'.[74] Moreover, as regards the rebuttal phase, the very concrete factors put forward by the Court can be considered as pointing to elements that are more generally relevant when evaluating attempts to rebut a presumption of racial discrimination. Such factors would include the inherent suspect nature of widespread and long-standing measures, particularly where these are not sufficiently tailored nor preceded by a search for less restrictive measures to attain a particular legitimate aim.

Clearly, the CJEU in *CHEZ* (in contrast to its reasoning in *Belov*) went out of its way to provide sufficient guidance to the national Court, to the point of de facto making the assessment *in concreto*. In relation to the sharing of the burden of proof, this is particularly visible regarding the establishment of a *prima facie* case of direct racial discrimination, and the justification of a *prima facie* case of indirect racial discrimination. It was already argued that it is possible to deduce factors of more general relevance. The Court could still improve its reasoning, and the guidance for national courts, if it were more explicit about the two possibilities to rebut a presumption – negation and justification.

V. Conclusion

This chapter began with highlighting the high practical importance of the matter of proof. The success of vindicating one's right to protection against racial discrimination greatly depends on what must be proven before a Court of law and to what extent. The special allocation of the burden of proof between the applicant and defendant is a response to the evidential difficulties for victims of (racial) discrimination. However, this shared burden of proof can only have the intended effect of enhancing the protection against racial discrimination, if the courts know how to apply it. The inclusion of this principle into EU anti-discrimination law thus requires jurisprudence clarifying the criteria of what constitutes a *prima facie* case and what is required to rebut that presumption. Relatedly, the CJEU's case law should not contain confusing reasoning which may further increase the uncertainties of national courts about the difference between a presumption of discrimination on the one hand, and discrimination on the other.

The preceding analysis showed that the CJEU is increasingly more generous in the level of clarification it is willing to give regarding the shared burden of proof in racial discrimination cases, thus contributing to the effective protection against such discrimination. In *Feryn, Accept* and especially in *CHEZ*, the CJEU provided guidance to the national courts about the shared burden of proof; yet it did not use all the opportunities it was given to address the uncertainties of the national courts.

[74] ibid para 127.

First, the analysed case law highlighted the importance of precision when identifying distinctive instances of discrimination, also as regards the different types of acts that could qualify as 'less favourable treatment' in terms of direct discrimination. The *Feryn* and *Accept* cases show the importance of consistently distinguishing between a speech (policy announcement) and a practice (policy implementation) instance of discrimination, translating into two separate allocations of the burden of proof. In *Feryn* and *Accept*, the Court seemed to acknowledge that a public speech with a discriminatory message could in itself amount to a prohibited instance of direct racial discrimination. However, a closer investigation of the reasoning in *Feryn* pertaining to the shared burden of proof reveals that the Court did not actually distinguish between a speech and a practice instance of discrimination, but rather considered proof of 'actual practice' as a possible rebuttal of the presumption of direct racial discrimination raised by the public speech. This would seem to deny that speech in itself, irrespective of actual practice, can constitute an instance of prohibited discrimination. The reasoning of the Court was somewhat better in *Accept* because of the focus on counterstatements and recruitment policy documents for the rebuttal phase. However, in the end it still did not identify and analyse two possible cases of discrimination separately (one related to speech, the other to recruitment practice). Indeed, the differences between the judgments appear informed by the specific facts of the case, more particularly its recognition that proof of actual recruitment of persons with a particular sexual orientation would conflict with their right to privacy.

Second, both *Feryn* and *CHEZ* reveal the persisting uncertainties (also among national courts) about the exact borderline between direct and indirect discrimination – a distinction that has implications for the determination of a *prima facie* case. Regrettably, the CJEU did not develop more of a theoretical frame to distinguish between *direct* and *indirect* discrimination, and hence did not optimally clarify the shared burden of proof. Its apparent reluctance was already visible in *Feryn*, where the national Court's question about indirect discrimination was not answered. The preceding analysis of *CHEZ* has revealed that the Court's reasoning seems to embrace the 'intent *versus* effect' paradigm visible in CERD. Nevertheless, it still has not adopted a clear theoretical paradigm about the exact dividing line, which has negative repercussions when the Court develops its reasoning in relation to the sharing of the burden of proof.

The Court's identification of the factors relevant for establishing a *prima facie* case for direct as well as indirect discrimination makes either qualification plausible in *CHEZ*. Nevertheless, a preference for a finding of direct discrimination can be detected, illustrated by the numerous hints about a *prima facie* case of direct discrimination. Since direct discrimination is virtually impossible to refute and the Court, in its exploration of the indirect discrimination route provides several indications about the lack of justification, it becomes obvious that it strongly favours a finding of a prohibited instance of discrimination. Simultaneously, the CJEU acknowledges that the distinction between direct and indirect discrimination is not always crystal clear. The latter approach seems particularly relevant for cases of systemic discrimination, where the dividing line between direct and indirect discrimination for one particular instance of discrimination is, by definition, fluid.

In light of the focus of this chapter, it is important to note that the Court in *CHEZ* (unlike in *Belov*)[75] took the opportunity for clarification, and was strikingly elaborate and concrete in its guidance, also concerning the shared burden of proof. The Court was particularly informative and specific about the establishment of a *prima facie* case of direct discrimination and the justification of a presumption of indirect discrimination for rebuttal. As the preceding analysis revealed, more generally valid factors (for the establishment of a *prima facie* case and its rebuttal) can still be deduced from its very concrete reasoning.

Finally, as was underscored in the preceding analysis, in all the explored cases, the Court failed to engage in a more explicit discussion of the two rebuttal possibilities of a *prima facie* case of discrimination (i.e. negation and justification).

Overall, further guidance from the CJEU is welcome in at least two respects.[76] First, the Court needs to adopt a consistent identification of a speech instance of discrimination and the related sharing of the burden of proof. Second, a theoretical paradigm for distinguishing between direct and indirect discrimination must be developed, which would result in clearer reasoning regarding the shared burden of proof. In relation to the matter of proof, further preliminary rulings on cases of systemic discrimination could clarify whether and to what extent the Court envisages a two-step model for the analysis of alleged discrimination, evaluating first direct, then indirect discrimination. Regarding the ways in which further guidance from the CJEU can be obtained, it is unfortunately beyond the scope of this chapter to elaborate on the recommendation voiced elsewhere for more system reasoning by the CJEU,[77] and to dwell on ways in which the number of preliminary rulings on the Race Equality Directive can be optimised. Clearly, there is a multitude of options for advancing the academic literature on EU anti-discrimination law after this edited volume sees the light.

[75] In Case C-394/11 *Belov* (n 30), the Court clearly missed the opportunity to assess a complex but rather typical case of alleged racial discrimination against Roma, certainly one of the target groups of the Race Equality Directive. The reasoning of AG Kokott in that case revealed that the Court could have just as easily accepted the preliminary reference as admissible. See also chapters by M Möschel and M Goodwin in the present volume.

[76] Also, considering the broad scope of application *ratione materiae* of the RED, several matters, each yielding their own context specific problems, have not yet been explored.

[77] See Henrard, Jean Monnet Working Paper 09/09 (n 7) 29–34.

5

When Equality Directives Are Not Enough

Taking an Issue with the Missing Minority Rights Policy in the EU

DIMITRY KOCHENOV*

I. Introduction: Minority Groups beyond the Directives

Besides the relevant secondary legislation, minority protection is one of the fundamental values of the European Union (EU)[1] and the Charter of Fundamental Rights of the European Union (CFR) makes a clear reference to minority protection.[2] This seeming richness of instruments notwithstanding, even following the adoption of the EU Equality Directives in 2000, a well-articulated over-arching minority protection policy in EU law is missing.[3]

The current situation could be explained by the specificity of minority protection in the EU's federal setting.[4] In this chapter, the emphasis will be put

* Professor of EU Constitutional Law, University of Groningen. I wish to thank Timofey Agarin Uladzislau Belavusau and Kristin Henrard for their help with this piece.

[1] Treaty on European Union [2016] OJ C202/1 (TEU), Art 2. On values in EU law see, e.g. A Williams, 'Taking Values Seriously: Towards a Philosophy of EU Law' (2009) 29 *Oxford Journal of Legal Studies* 549; D Kochenov, 'The *Acquis* and Its Principles: The Enforcement of the "Law" versus the Enforcement of the "Values" in the European Union' in A Jakab and D Kochenov (eds), *The Enforcement of EU Law and Values* (Oxford, Oxford University Press, 2017).

[2] Charter of Fundamental Rights of the European Union [2016] OJ C202/2, Art 21(1).

[3] See, e.g. A Van Bossuyt, 'L'Union européenne et la protection des minorités: Une question de volonté politique' (2010) *Cahiers de droit européen* 425, 427–439. The same equally applies to the definitions of minorities, as Kristin Henrard reports: 'it seems wiser to conclude that there is indeed no set definition of the concept of 'minority' within the EU' – K Henrard, 'An EU Perspective on New Versus Traditional Minorities: On Semi-Inclusive Socio-Economic Integration and Expanding Visions of "European" Culture and Identity' (2010) 17 *Columbia Journal of European Law* 57, 68. Neither FED nor RED defines a concept of "minority".

[4] It has been rightly argued that 'the fixture of the 'federal' label to the European construct may not be as disputed as it once was' – K Lenaerts and K Gutman, '"Federal Common Law" in the European

on the need to draw a clear dividing line between Member State level minority protection and EU-level minority protection, with important consequences for the definition of minorities, as well as approaches to the regulation of the whole sphere of minority protection and the assessment of its successes in light of EU Equality Directives 2000. The argument evolves around the scrutiny of the position of the migrant EU citizens in the EU, presenting the usual focus on EU minority protection in a somewhat unusual light to demonstrate how the federal element in the division of competences between the EU and its Member States affects the operation of minority protection and non-discrimination. This chapter takes a broader view and is simultaneously more focused on the internal market than the literature on minority protection in the EU normally suggests. Adopting this perspective highlights that the Equality Directives are clearly inadequate. The current division of competences in the EU explains the reigning market-driven approach to the issue,[5] as well as the weakness of regulation in those fields, which are – at least partly – in the EU's hands, and further problems with the scope of EU law and the enforcement of EU rules. A serious gap exists between the external and the internal approaches to the EU's minority protection.[6] Moreover, the EU has failed to formulate a coherent (or, indeed, any) minority protection policy which could be detached from internal market considerations.[7]

II. General Context of Minority Protection in the EU

Minority protection is one of the most sensitive areas of EU law, since any consensus on this issue among the Member States is missing. Many of them do not recognise the idea of minority protection as such[8] and have not even ratified the Framework Convention[9] – the main international law instrument on the matter in Europe[10] – or did so with extremely far-reaching derogations. Furthermore,

Union: A Comparative Perspective from the United States' (2006) 54 *American Journal of Comparative Law* 1. See also R Schütze, *From Dual to Cooperative Federalism* (Oxford, Oxford University Press, 2009); R Schütze, 'On 'Federal' Ground: The European Union as an (Inter)National Phenomenon' (2009) 46 *Common Market Law Review* 1069; D Kochenov (ed), *EU Citizenship and Federalism: The Role of Rights* (Cambridge, Cambridge University Press, 2017).

[5] D Kochenov, 'On Tiles and Pillars: EU Citizenship as a Federal Denominator' in Kochenov, *EU Citizenship and Federalism* (n 4).

[6] D Kochenov, 'A Summary of Contradictions: An Outline of the EU's Main Internal and External Approaches to Ethnic Minority Protection' (2008) 31 *Boston College International & Comparative Law Review* 1.

[7] Treaty on the Functioning of the European Union [2016] OJ C202/1 (TFEU), Art 26(2).

[8] These include, most notably, France and Greece.

[9] Framework Convention for the Protection of National Minorities (adopted 1 February 1995, in force 1 February 1998). The Member States of the Union who have not ratified the Convention include Belgium, France, Greece, and Luxembourg. For commentary on the Framework Convention, see, e.g. M Weller (ed), *The Rights of Minorities: A Commentary on the European Framework Convention for the Protection of National Minorities* (Oxford, Oxford University Press, 2006); A Verstichel, A Alen, B de Witte, P Lemmens (eds), *The Framework Convention for the Protection of National Minorities: A Useful Pan-European Instrument?* (Antwerp, Intersentia, 2008).

[10] The European Court of Human Rights (ECtHR) has not only recognised the 'minority way of life' within the context of Art 8 of the European Convention on Human Rights (ECHR), but also

harmonisation of national legislation in line with the 2000 EU Equality Directives has been equally problematic.[11]

As per Article 5(3) of the Treaty of European Union (TEU), the powers not conferred on the EU unquestionably remain with the Member States, which is fundamentally important as any unequivocal general legal basis for minority protection is missing notwithstanding the obvious relevance of EU Equality Directives. Naturally, the Court of Justice of the European Union (CJEU) would normally intervene to ensure that Member States' own competences are not used to the detriment of achieving the objectives of integration as stated in the Treaties,[12] as well as to ensure that EU law and national implementing measures are all interpreted in the light of the values on which the Union is built and the objectives[13] which the EU is striving to achieve – even if such actions fall outside the scope of EU law *sensu stricto*.[14] Such negative integration does not open the door to regulating the areas which are not perceived as lying within the scope of the Union's competences. In other words, the breadth of the formulation of the integration goals, as well as the values on which the EU is based, 'including the [protection of the] rights of persons belonging to minorities',[15] do not guarantee that the EU will be able to regulate for, let alone enforce, the far-reaching promises the Treaties contain.[16]

Thus, even from a federal perspective, the EU fails to build on clearly articulated and enforceable values which help to distil an idea of justice underlying its law. It is more-or-less powerless in the face of a defiant Member State refusing to take the values of Article 2 TEU seriously.[17] In the context of minority protection, it is unquestionable that the relevant provisions of the Charter of

found that the Framework Convention is a product of the general consensus on the issue of minority protection among the Member States of the Council of Europe, which has a clear potential to move the Framework Convention within the context of EU law. See, e.g. *Chapman v UK* App no 27238/95 (ECtHR, 18 January 2001), para 93; *Muñoz Diaz v Spain* App no 49151/07 (ECtHR, 8 December 2009). For analysis see Henrard, 'An EU Perspective' (n 3) 85–87; A Van Bossuyt, 'Fit for Purpose or Faulty Design? Analysis of the Jurisprudence of the European Court of Human Rights and the European Court of Justice on the Legal Protection of Minorities' (2007) *Journal on Ethnopolitics and Minority Issues in Europe* 1.

[11] See, e.g. B Havelková, 'Resistance to Anti-Discrimination Law in Central and Eastern Europe' (2016) 17 *German Law Journal* 627.

[12] Art 4(3) TEU.

[13] The values are outlined in Art 2 TEU and the objectives in Art 3 TEU. See also, CJ Bickerton, *European Integration: From Nation-states to Member States* (Oxford, Oxford University Press, 2012); Kochenov, 'The *Acquis* and Its Principles' (n 1).

[14] For a discussion, see JHH Weiler, 'Epilogue: Living in a Glass House: Europe, Democracy and the Rule of Law' in C Closa and D Kochenov (eds), *Reinforcing Rule of Law Oversight in the European Union* (Cambridge, Cambridge University Press, 2016).

[15] Art 2 TEU.

[16] For a compelling analysis of the limitations of the reference to minorities, see Van Bossuyt, 'L'Union européenne' (n 3) 440–444. For more on EU values and their legal effects, see, e.g. C Hillion, 'Overseeing the Rule of Law in the EU: Legal Mandate and Means' in Closa and Kochenov, *Reinforcing Rule of Law Oversight* (n 14).

[17] J-W Müller, 'Should the European Union Protect Democracy and the Rule of Law in Its Member States' (2015) 21 *European Law Journal* 141; D Kochenov, 'EU Law without the Rule of Law: Is the Veneration of Autonomy Worth It?' (2015) 34 *Yearbook of European Law* 74.

Fundamental Rights aimed at the respect of minorities[18] have the same limitations and can merely serve as interpretative aids,[19] not as a legal basis for action.[20] Should regulation of a field of shared competence be required at EU level, rather than at the level of the Member States, two options are open to the Union. The first consists of trying to secure a Treaty amendment enlarging the scope of its powers;[21] the second in attaching the regulation of the field concerned to a broader context of the internal market *acquis*, without emphasising a potentially sore issue.[22]

The former is currently not a real option. Lacking clear specific legal bases beyond Articles 19 and 157 TFEU, lacking Member State consensus and without a clear minority protection policy, the EU's ability to act in this field are far from clearly articulated. Consequently, the expectations of the citizens, minority groups and the Member States almost never overlap as regards minority protection, making the EU's intervention at times terribly contested. This is amplified by the fact that supranational EU regulation has a clear potential to dilute national minority-sensitive policies, as they come to be regarded as incompatible with the internal market. Although the CJEU recognised in its case law from *Groener* (1989)[23] to *Angonese* (2000)[24] that minority protection could be a legitimate objective for the Member States to pursue even in deviation from the EU's *acquis*, the strict proportionality test applies meaning that

[18] Art 21(1) CFR. For a general analysis, see Henrard, 'An EU Perspective' (n 3) 85–88; G von Toggenburg, 'The EU's Evolving Policies *vis-à-vis* Minorities: A Play in Four Parts and an Open End' (2008) EURAC Research Paper (Bolzano).

[19] Henrard, 'An EU Perspective' (n 3) 86–87. Henrard puts an emphasis on the role to be played by the Charter at the pre-legislative stage, when the Commission screens the legislative proposals against the provisions of the Charter. Yet, the actual contribution of such screenings can be put in doubt, since its effectiveness in other fields has been abundantly criticised. See, e.g. G Davies, 'Subsidiarity: The Wrong Idea, in the Wrong Place, at the Wrong Time' (2006) 43 *Common Market Law Review* 63, demonstrating that such pre-screening in the context of the principle of subsidiarity does not work.

[20] Van Bossuyt, 'L'Union européenne' (n 3) 447.

[21] According to Art 48 TEU, two types of amendment procedures are possible, but both of them require national ratifications. The third possibility would be to try to use the flexibility clause of Art 352 TFEU, but it seems to be hardly applicable in this context, given that it is tied to the internal market and the protection of minorities will likely be a departure from the general economic rationale of European integration.

[22] As an example, although the EU does not have competences in the area of family law, its internal market rules potentially have a far-reaching effect on the spread and *de facto* recognition of same-sex unions and families around the Union. For analysis, see D Kochenov, 'On Options of Citizens and Moral Choices of States: Gays and European Federalism' (2009) 33 *Fordham International Law Journal* 156; U Belavusau and D Kochenov, 'Federalizing Legal Opportunities for LGBT Movement in the Growing EU' in K Slootmaeckers, H Touquet and P Vermeersch (eds), *EU Enlargement and Gay Politics, The: The Impact of Eastern Enlargement on Rights, Activism and Prejudice* (Basingstoke, Palgrave Macmillan, 2016). Poland, disappointed with the perceived current developments, even appended a special Declaration to the Treaties, trying to shield its family law from liberal influences and the Charter (Declaration No. 61).

[23] Case C-379/87 *Anita Groener v Minister for Education and the City of Dublin Vocational Educational Committee* ECLI:EU:C:1989:599.

[24] Case C-281/98 *Roman Angonese v Cassa di Risparmio di Bolzano SpA* ECLI:EU:C:2000:296; Case C-274/96 *Horst Otto Bickel and Ulrich Franz* ECLI:EU:C:1998:563.

there is no guarantee that minority protection, however highly cherished, will actually prevail.[25]

The situation is further complicated by the simple fact that, taken as whole, the EU is remarkably diverse, boasting numerous categories of recognised (as well as *de facto* clandestine) majorities, which makes it almost impossible to come up with any tenable and shared concept of *minorities* in the Union. Majorities thus only exist at the Member State level. This gap does not mean, however, that the same applies to minorities. Indeed, in the absence of a dominant culture, language, historical tradition and other such factors, anyone and indeed, everyone, in the EU belongs to a minority of some kind. Moreover, the vulnerability of numerous minority groups can even be seen as being augmented by EU integration. Perhaps we could assume that Germans in France will inevitably fall into the category of a minority (although not necessarily vulnerable), while Turks will be generally considered a minority in both France and Germany. Although in certain situations (e.g. during employment discrimination) Turks in Germany would fall into the material scope of RED, Germans in France will be hardly covered by RED, as the recent approach of the CJEU revealed with regard to the case law on the name-spelling of minorities in Lithuania.[26] This is one of the vivid paradoxes of the current disregard for the fully fledged and clearly defined minority protection at EU level, with confusing borderlines between EU anti-discrimination law on the grounds of race and ethnicity and discrimination on the grounds of nationality, safeguarding EU citizenship and the free movement of EU nationals.

The EU's commitment to facilitating the freedom of movement of its citizens[27] and long-term resident third-country nationals[28] within its territory can only lead to the growth of cultural, religious and any other possible kinds of diversity. If anything, this calls for a synergetic approach to tackling minority protection. While regrettably, 'minorities are not determined at the EU level with reference to the entire [Union]',[29] there is no reason why this approach should prevail in the future, at least in the context of the vulnerable groups *created* by EU law. In fact, EU law generates markedly different outcomes in the sphere of the minority

[25] The literature on the limiting effects of the internal market on regional specificity, including regional powers and minority protection is voluminous. See, e.g. G von Toggenburg, 'A Remaining Share or a New Part? The EU's Role *vis-à-vis* Minorities after the Enlargement Decade' in M Weller, D Blacklock and K Nobbs (eds), *The Protection of Minorities in the Wider Europe* (Basingstoke, Palgrave Macmillan, 2008) 95, 111; RF Weber, 'Individual Rights and Group Rights in the European Community's Approach to Minority Languages' (2007) 17 *Duke Journal of Comparative & International Law* 361; D Kochenov, 'Regional Citizenships in the EU' (2010) 35 *European Law Review* 307.

[26] Case C-391/09 *Runevič-Vardyn and Wardyn* EU:C:2011:291. For more about the critique of this linguistic line of cases, see *infra*.

[27] Art. 21 TFEU. D Kochenov and R Plender, 'EU Citizenship: From an Incipient Form to an Incipient Substance? The Discovery of the Treaty Text' (2012) 37 *European Law Review* 369.

[28] This category probably benefits from free movement law more fictitiously than in reality. Directive 2003/109 concerning the status of third-country nationals who are long-term residents [2004] OJ L16/44, Art 11. For analysis, see D Acosta Arcarazo, 'Civic Citizenship Reintroduced? The Long-term Residence Directive as a Post-National Form of Membership' (2015) 21 *European Law Journal* 200.

[29] Henrard, 'An EU Perspective' (n 3) 64.

(or 'local interest') protection, depending on the framing of the issue. Where the issue is presented in economic terms (e.g. when minority protection is part of the forging of the internal market narrative focusing primarily on economic activities), EU law is bound to intervene, striking down the measure.[30] However, if minority protection is taken outside the economic context – and the boundary between 'economic' and 'non-economic' is by definition blurred, ambiguous and unclear – the issue remains *de facto* mute without any protection ensued.[31] This is due to the fact that the whole EU legal system is based on (mostly undisclosed) market-focused assumptions,[32] such as the (economic) objectives of the integration process, which are both presumed to be good for all Europeans as outlined and are not contestable by democratic means.[33] This is not good news for the vulnerable groups in need of protection, particularly given how blurred the line is between 'market-related' and 'non-market-related' issues. Furthermore, both FED and RED target primarily employment discrimination, thus revealing an established economic rationale behind their adoption, while only RED spreads its material scope a bit further to cover social protection, education and access to goods and services.

It is submitted that the literature has not paid sufficient attention to the need for and the vistas of a necessary adaptation to the supranational reality, which is officially tongue-in-cheek 'apolitical'.[34] Yet the restriction on buying a home to protect the local interest (which could be legitimate) is a violation of EU law,[35] while having a name misspelled in a state-orchestrated campaign to eradicate the public presence and visibility of minority cultures is permissible, unless such humiliation concerns an EU citizen using Treaty rights which might potentially affect his business, as seen in *Konstantinidis*.[36] The level of scholarly complacency with this state of affairs in minority protection (just as in other spheres) is, regrettably, extremely high.[37]

[30] Virtually all of the non-discrimination on the basis of nationality case-law is a testimony to this approach, which is at the core of the nature of the EU.

[31] See, e.g. Case C-391/09 *Runevič-Vardyn and Wardyn* EU:C:2011:291. The CJEU remarkably missed an opportunity to bring RED into the scope of protection for linguistic minorities within the EU. On the evolution of the approaches to the boundary between 'economic' and 'non-economic' in EU law see, e.g. Kochenov and Plender, 'From an Incipient Form' (n 27).

[32] MA Wilkinson, 'Politicising Europe's Justice Deficit: Some Preliminaries' in D Kochenov, G de Búrca and A Williams (eds), *Europe's Justice Deficit?* (Oxford, Hart, 2015); G Peebles, '"A Very Eden of the Innate Rights of Man"? A Marxist Look at the European Union Treaties and Case Law' (1998) 22 *Law and Social Inquiry* 581; D Kochenov, 'Introduction: On Tiles and Pillars' (n 5).

[33] G Davies, 'Social Legitimacy and Purposive Power: The End, the Means and the Consent of the People' in Kochenov et al, *Europe's Justice Deficit?* (n 32) 259.

[34] A José Menéndez, 'Whose Justice? Which Europe?' in Kochenov et al (ed) (n 32) 137.

[35] Joined cases C-197/11 & C-203/11 *Libert ea v Gouvernement flamande* and *All Projects & Developments NV ea v Vlaamse Regering* ECLI:EU:C:2013:288.

[36] Case C-391/09 *Runevič-Vardyn and Wardyn* (n 31); Case C-168/91 *Christos Konstantinidis v Stadt Altensteig* ECLI:EU:C:1993:115.

[37] But see Peebles, '"A Very Eden of the Innate Rights of Man?"' (n 32); M Bartl, 'Internal Market Rationality, Private Law and the Direction of the Union: Resuscitating the Market as the Object of the

The progress of EU integration necessarily limits the Member States' ability to regulate a number of vital issues related to minority protection, including, in particular, granting minorities special rights[38] and affirmative action policies.[39] These sit uneasily with the *acquis* for the simple reason that minority protection is not among the policies implemented by the EU. Thus, for the biggest part, EU law is, to agree with Henrard, 'minority agnostic'.[40] This has obvious negative consequences for the development of the law and policy at the EU as well as the Member State levels, since it undermines the ability of both legal orders to introduce any minority protection measures, particularly with regard to the Member States.

Given that the powers of the EU are interpreted teleologically and in a goal-orientated manner,[41] EU law does not allow for reserved domains where it would not be able to intervene. In practice, this means that even in the areas where the Member States have a sole power to regulate, EU law demands that the regulation of minority protection be in line with the principles and objectives of EU integration as interpreted by the CJEU.[42] Deferring to the regulatory approaches of Member States is a great pretext for the Court to project itself as an institution sensitive to Member States' concerns.[43] Yet, in this same context, the EU can equally be viewed as accommodating the practices of the Member States designed to humiliate and oppress their minority citizens. Consequently, effective minority protection is highly unlikely in light of Member States' growing concerns for the perceived protection of the cultural specificity of their majority populations within the broader context of the EU as a whole, despite the sporadic topicality of the EU Equality Directives.

Moreover, the application of any minority protection measures is necessarily tainted with the internal market bias, as long as the safeguarding and development of the EU's internal market in treated as *the* measure of EU's success. This introduces a systemic disregard of other potentially vital interests, thus manifesting the

Political' (2015) 21 *European Law Journal* 572; D Kukovec, 'Law and the Periphery' (2014) 21 *European Law Journal* 406.

[38] This is usually done via local citizenships or special statuses, which are severely undermined by EU law, since they cannot be in conflict with the law of the Union (i.e. cannot actually be consequential in promoting difference in treatment between EU citizens). See von Toggenburg, 'A Remaining Share' (n 25) 111; Weber, 'Individual Rights' (n 25) 361; Kochenov, 'Regional Citizenships' (n 25).

[39] For an analysis see, e.g. D Pager, 'Strictness and Subsidiarity: An Institutional Perspective on Affirmative Action at the European Court of Justice' (2003) 26 *Boston College International & Comparative Law Review* 35; D Caruso, 'Limits of the Classical Method: Positive Action in the European Union after the New Equality Directives' (2003) 44 *Harvard International Law Journal* 331.

[40] Henrard, 'An EU Perspective' (n 3) 58.

[41] A von Bogdandy and J Bast, 'The European Union's Vertical Order of Competences: The Current Law and Proposals for Reform' (2002) 39 *Common Market Law Review* 227.

[42] See, e.g. Case C-135/08 *Janko Rottman v Freistaat Bayern* ECLI:EU:C:2010:104, para. 55; Case C-369/90 *Mario Vicente Micheletti and others v Delegación del Gobierno en Cantabria* ECLI:EU:C:1992:295, para. 10. This is fully in line with the principle of sincere cooperation expressed in Art 4(3) TEU.

[43] K Lenaerts, 'The Court of Justice of the European Union and the Protection of Fundamental Rights' (2011) 31 *Polish Yearbook of International Law* 79.

EU's justice deficit.[44] At the same time, since minority protection is not working as a fully fledged objective of the EU, the CJEU's self-restraint often implies that the Member States are free to engage in direct ethnic discrimination.[45] In this context, it is not surprising that minority-related laws and policies introduced by the Member States are very likely to either fail the test of compliance with the EU's internal market rationale or turn into an anti-minority measure. Moreover, it seems that the Member States willing to protect minorities end up being hostages of states, such as Greece or France, which are hostile to the idea. EU law, which is insensitive to minority protection issues due to the labours of such Member States, can also negatively affect the minority protection in all other states. Consequently, at this stage the relevant national regulation will benefit from a refinement of the objective of minority protection at the EU level, possibly including an introduction of a specific legal basis to this end, rather than merely a mention in Article 2 TEU.

This being said, the rhetoric of cultural diversity between the Member States has so far encouraged the quashing of minorities and their rights. This practice needs to be put into reverse: culture is a coin with two sides and focusing uniquely on the side which is state-endorsed and state-mandated – the approach of the EU – neglects and harms the 'other' culture of the Member States, as lived and perceived by all the inhabitants of the state in question, including those who are excluded from the official narrative. For a Pole in Vilnius to hear that the Lithuanian language is the most cherished heritage of the tiny nation and hence justifies the misspelling of her name – as there is simply no 'w' in the language, never mind a **w**hiskey bottle in every bar – is untenable reasoning in a city gifted to the Lithuanian SSR by Stalin, where Polish culture is historically omnipresent.[46] Naturally, history is complex, and that is the crux of the matter. There is no Lithuania without a 'w' in the past, just as there is no Lithuania without a 'w' in the present – official position of the state (which is abusive to minorities) – notwithstanding. Similarly, refusing a Latvian Jew the right to have a real name which is not misspelled by Latvian authorities to hide his Jewish identity has nothing to do with the protection of Latvian culture, as the UN Human Rights Committee rightly found in a decision never followed by the CJEU.[47] The whole new line of CJEU cases on name spelling after 2000 takes a very restrictive turn in comparison to the 1990s, and is steeply antagonistic to the idea of minority

[44] For the analysis of this problem see Kochenov et al (eds), *Europe's Justice Deficit* (n 32).

[45] On a broad range of examples relating to ethnic discrimination connected to language see, e.g. D Kochenov, V Poleshchuk and A Dimitrovs, 'Do Professional Linguistic Requirements Discriminate? A Legal Analysis: Estonia and Latvia in the Spotlight' (2013) 10 *European Yearbook of Minority Issues* 137.

[46] On the experiences of Wilno by two leading poets, both natives of the city, see T Venclova, *The Winter Dialogue (with a dialogue between the author and Czesław Miłosz)* (Northwestern University Press, Chicago, IL 1999) illustrating how untenable the Court-endorsed 'culture' is. Until 1939, the majority of the Vilnius-dwellers (Wilno, Vilna in various languages) were Jews, Poles and Belarusians, with ethnic Lithuanians comprising only a tiny percentage of its population.

[47] UN CHR, *Raihman v Latvia* (Communication No 1621/2007).

protection.[48] It would appear logical to expect that with the arrival of RED and FED in the same period, the Court would be more willing to support the linguistic rights of minorities. Yet the CJEU has erroneously chosen to exclude RED from applicability in such cases, which is clearly contrary to the logic of minority protection. It has instead permitted the rise of the dubious shield of 'national identity' as a value standing higher than minority protection and functioning, as is clear from the examples above, as an EU-endorsed assault on minority cultures aimed at humiliating Lithuanian Poles and rendering Jews and other minorities in Latvia invisible by refusing them a right to a name.[49] The fact that the Court ends up endorsing light-hearted tinkering with history at the expense of the minority cultures is most alarming, particularly given that purely economic arguments suddenly *do* bring about a result which involves the protection of a name and identity.[50] Such cases undermine the coherence and consistency of the EU's engagement with minority protection.

III. Migrant EU Citizens

EU citizens moving across the internal borders within the Union are protected from any attempts of the Member States to 'integrate' them into their society by repressive means.[51] Their situation stands out as a rare example of a liberal *laissez-faire* approach in the problematic reality of opposition to immigration in Europe.[52] Non-discrimination on the basis of nationality within the scope of application of EU law creates a very special legal context for migrant EU citizens. They are shielded from the practice of testing knowledge of the local 'culture', language and 'history', which has gained in popularity in the Member States over years,[53] and is applied exclusively to third-country nationals.[54] This highly problematic practice, which technically contradicts the spirit of RED, allegedly improves social cohesion, yet is *de facto* employed solely to discourage immigration, thus amounting to the

[48] A Łazowski, E Dagilytė, P Stasinopoulos, 'The Importance of Being Earnest: Spelling of Names, EU Citizenship and Fundamental Rights' (2015) 11 *Croatian Yearbook of European Law & Policy* 1.

[49] Art 4(2) TEU.

[50] Case C-168/91 *Christos Konstantinidis* (n 36).

[51] T Triadafilopoulos, 'Illiberal Means to Liberal Ends? Understanding Recent Immigrant Integration Policies in Europe' (2011) 37 *Journal of Ethnic and Migration Studies* 861. C Joppke, 'Double Standards? Veils and Crucifixes in the European Legal Order' (2013) 54 *European Journal of Sociology* 97.

[52] L Orgad, '"Cultural Defence" of Nations: Cultural Citizenship in France, Germany and the Netherlands' (2009) 15 *European Law Journal* 719.

[53] R Bauböck and C Joppke (eds), 'How Liberal Are Citizenship Tests?' (2010) EUI Working Paper, RSCAS 2010/41; C Joppke, 'Beyond National Models: Civic Integration Policies for Immigrants in Western Europe' (2007) 30 *West European Politics* 1.

[54] For the analysis of the whole context of the use of culture as a method of exclusion in Europe see, e.g. C Joppke, *Citizenship and Immigration* (Oxford, Polity Press, 2010) 111–44. See also L Orgad, 'Illiberal Liberalism: Cultural Restrictions on Migration and Access to Citizenship in Europe' (2010) 58 *American Journal of Comparative Law* 53.

ultimate example of intolerance in the wise words of Joseph Weiler.[55] 'Come, be one of us'[56] becomes an insistent invitation to cease being oneself at the same time.[57] Most worryingly, such repressive approaches have been endorsed by the Court of Justice as unproblematic in the cases where EU citizens belonging to minorities are denied rights at home, including non-discrimination on the basis of nationality, upon a temporary return from a different Member State, as was the case in *Runevič-Vardyn* (2011). Crucially, the time-tested cross-border logic of embedding a case in internal market discourse, well-known since *Singh*[58] and reconfirmed countless times including in *D'Hoop* and other decisions,[59] is ignored by the CJEU when minorities need protection from the embedded discriminatory design of the constitutional system in their home Member State. If an EU worker returning to the Member State of nationality belongs to an ethnic minority, the principle of non-discrimination on the basis of nationality thus simply does not apply.

There is no doubt that, should EU law not prohibit nationality discrimination – again with a remarkably short-sighted exception granted to the states where the suppression of minority cultures is among the core features of constitutionalism – Member States would eagerly subject all EU citizens to the same humiliating treatment, which is now reserved uniquely for third country nationals. This puts citizens on an entirely different footing compared with third country nationals, because migrant EU citizens must be treated in the same manner as the locals.[60] Moreover, should the national regulation create any actual[61] or potential[62] obstacles to free movement (whether or not directly based on nationality)[63] – or obstacles to the enjoyment of the essence of other EU citizenship rights,[64] it will

[55] JHH Weiler, 'In Defence of the *Status Quo*: Europe's Constitutional *Sonderweg*' in JHH Weiler and M Wind (eds), *European Constitutionalism beyond the State* (Cambridge, Cambridge University Press, 2003) 7.

[56] ibid, 19.

[57] I Michalowski, 'Required to Assimilate? The Content of Citizenship Tests in Five Countries' (2011) 15 *Citizenship Studies* 749. G Sasse, 'Securitization or Securing Rights? Exploring the Conceptual Foundations of Policies Towards Minorities and Migrants in Europe' (2005) 43 *Journal of Common Market Studies* 673.

[58] Case C-370/90 *Surinder Singh* EU:C:1992:296.

[59] Case C-224/98 *D'Hoop* EU:C:2002:432.

[60] See, e.g. G Davies, '"Any Place I Hang My Hat?" or: Residence is the New Nationality' (2005) 11 *European Law Journal* 43. For the general context, see D Kochenov, 'Beyond the Cherry Blossoms and the Moon' (2013) 62 *International & Comparative Law Quarterly* 97.

[61] Case C-192/05 *Tas-Hagen en Tas and R.A. Tas v Raadskamer WUBO van de Pensioen- en Uitkeringsraad* ECLI:EU:C:2006:223.

[62] Case C-148/02 *Carlos Garcia Avello v Belgian State* ECLI:EU:C:2003:539.

[63] F Jacobs, 'Citizenship of the European Union – A Legal Analysis' (2007) 13 *European Law Journal* 591.

[64] See, e.g. Case C–34/09 *Gerardo Ruiz Zambrano v Office national de l'emploi* ECLI:EU:C:2011:124. D Kochenov, 'A Real European Citizenship; A New Jurisdiction Test; A Novel Chapter in the Development of the Union in Europe' (2011) 18 *Columbia Journal of European Law* 55; K Lenaerts and J Gutiérrez-Fons, 'Epilogue: EU Citizenship. Hopes and Fears' in Kochenov, *EU Citizenship and Federalism* (n 4).

not be tolerated by the Union, as long as a link with EU law – the weakest and the most esoteric part of the current construct – is demonstrated and recognised.[65] Hence, Member States' policies aiming at the 'integration' of migrants,[66] which is arguably the main goal behind the assimilationist policies targeting third country nationals in a huge number of the Member States, generally do not apply to EU citizens.

The protection of EU citizens from the possible intervention with their lives by the authorities of their new Member State of residence is directly connected with the obligation on the EU to respect the identities of the Member States.[67] This clearly applies not only to the Member States as such, but also to their nationals, who are entitled to live anywhere in the Union without being forced to relinquish their cultural, political and socio-economic ties with their Member State of nationality.[68] This has two important consequences for minority protection in the EU in general – both positive and negative.

First, EU citizens moving to other Member States put national integration policies in doubt, since such citizens seem to be able to function pretty well in the host societies, hinting at the fact that instead of tests, suspicion and political rituals establishing the right of passage,[69] basic equal treatment can be the key to actual, not theoretical, social integration. The role that EU citizens come to play in the context of the migrants' 'integration' policies is therefore pivotal in showcasing that integration policies are unnecessary; their only possible function being to discriminate against third country nationals on the wrong premises, which do not apply to EU citizens.

The negative aspect is directly related to the special position enjoyed by the migrant EU citizens in any host Member State. Should the host Member State have a special minority protection policy in place, which would provide for special rights for a certain group of local citizens, the newcomers from other Member States cannot be excluded from benefitting from those rights. Such extension[70] can undermine the policy behind establishing the special treatment in the first place.[71] Only the minority protection initiatives put into the primary law of the EU in the pre-accession context[72] (e.g. the provisions on

[65] On the problematic nature of such 'links with EU law' as currently construed, see E Spaventa, 'Earned Citizenship – Understanding Citizenship through Its Scope' in Kochenov, *EU Citizenship and Federalism* (n 4).

[66] For a general overview see, e.g. R Cholewinski, 'Migrants and Minorities: Integration and Inclusion in the Enlarged European Union' (2005) 43 *Journal of Common Market Studies* 695.

[67] For analysis, see E Cloots, *National Identity in the EU* (Oxford, Oxford University Press, 2015).

[68] The requirement to give up one's previous EU nationality upon naturalising in the Member State of residence following the exercise of EU free movement rights (which is still the law in almost one-third of Member States) is obviously in conflict with this logic and represents an important problem: D Kochenov, 'Double Nationality in the EU: An Argument for Tolerance' (2011) 17 *European Law Journal* 323.

[69] S Lukes, 'Political Ritual and Social Integration' (1975) 9 *Sociology* 289.

[70] Case C-274/96 *Criminal Proceedings against Bickel and Franz* EU:C:1998:563.

[71] Kochenov, 'Regional Citizenships' (n 25); Henrard, 'An EU Perspective' (n 3) 88.

[72] Kochenov, 'A Summary of Contradictions' (n 6).

Sami agriculture,[73] seem to be immune from the ever-penetrating effects of the principle of non-discrimination on the basis of nationality. An argument can be made that even the residents of highly legally specific minority-inhabited territories which are not entirely within the scope of EU law could not benefit from preferential treatment in all cases.[74]

This reality, however problematic for the Member States with strong minority protection regimes, is not easy to deal with from a legal perspective. The conflict between the desire to grant special rights to minorities and the fundamental importance of the status of EU citizenship, which is intended, in the words of the Court, to be 'the fundamental status of the nationals of the Member States',[75] is too pronounced in this context to be easily downplayed. Should any stable consensus that this issue represents a problem arise among the Member States (which is unlikely, given the firm doctrinal vision of Member States such as France and Greece), the only resolution seems to be a better incorporation of minority protection issues. For instance, a particular emphasis could be placed on special rights corresponding to the second part of the *Albanian Schools* test in EU primary law.[76] In this case, the Permanent Court of International Justice (PCIJ) insisted on two elements of minority protection, stating that simple non-discrimination is not enough if it is not accompanied by special rights. Such reflection missing, there is no valid reason in the context of EU law for discriminating between migrant EU citizens and the locals, even if they belong to a minority, in terms of access to special rights provided by the Member States.[77] This clearly demonstrates that EU citizens remain the most, if not the only, truly privileged group in EU law, exemplifying the tension with regard to minority protection and special rights inherent in the system of EU law.

IV. Indirect Minority Protection: An Almost Pessimistic Balance Sheet

It is thus hardly possible to speak about the EU's engagement with minority issues at both levels of the *Albanian Schools* test, including non-discrimination

[73] D Perrot and F Miatti, 'Les lapons et les îles Åland dans le quatrième élargissement: Contribution à l'étude de la différenciation juridique au sein de la Communauté européenne' (1997) 413 *Revue du marché commun et de l'Union européenne* 670.

[74] D Kochenov, 'EU Citizenship in the Overseas' in D Kochenov (ed), *EU Law of the Overseas: Outermost Regions, Associated Overseas Countries and Territories, Terriories Sui Generis* (The Hague, Kluwer Law International, 2011).

[75] Case C-34/09 *Ruiz Zambrano* (n 64) para 41.

[76] PCIJ Advisory Opinion on *Minority Schools in Albania* [1935] PCIJ Rep 17.

[77] Although the CJEU recognises, as has been stated above, that minority protection can form a legitimate ground for deviating from the provisions of the *acquis*, it is impossible to predict how far it would be willing to go in allowing for such deviations to happen. So far, Case C-379/87 *Anita Groener v Minister of Education* ECLI:EU:C:1989:599 remains probably the only, albeit somewhat dubious, example of the Court's permissiveness in this field.

and special minority protection measures. Indirectly, however, a number of important possibilities are open for the Union to regulate the legal situation of vulnerable minority groups. Two lines of development come to mind in this regard. The first is confined to the evolution of the non-discrimination requirements, not minority protection measures *sensu stricto*.[78] The second theoretically concerns fully fledged minority protection, but is only limited to the external action of the EU and has only an indirect bearing on the legal situation of minorities *inside* it. All in all, the fundamental question of whether minorities should be awarded special protection seems to remain unresolved in the context of primary EU law and 2000 Equality Directives, reflecting the divisions among the Member States over the issue.

Non-discrimination requirements were viewed as an integral part of, first, the internal market – including non-discrimination on the basis of sex[79] and nationality[80] – and, later, as belonging to the fundamental principles of European integration.[81] Moreover, the Court also recognised an unwritten general principle of equality to be part of EU law.[82] The broadening of the range of the prohibited grounds of discrimination in the EU is a painful story.[83] As any other polity, probably, the Union has always been much better on paper and in its own eyes than in practice.[84] In fact, moving beyond the prohibition of sex discrimination and discrimination on the basis of nationality, the EU's role in fighting discrimination was very limited until the most recent amendments of the Treaties. In one example,[85] the Court only safely disregarded international practice[86] *not* to end

[78] Kochenov, 'A Summary of Contradictions' (n 6) 12–15; B de Witte, 'The Constitutional Resources for an EU Minority Protection Policy' in G von Toggenburg (ed), *Minority Protection and the Enlarged European Union* (Budapest, OSI, 2004) 107, 118–123; K Henrard, *Devising an Adequate System of Minority Protection: Individual Human Rights, Minority Rights and the Right to Self-Determination* (The Hague, Kluwer Law International, 2000).

[79] See, e.g. E Ellis, *EU Anti-Discrimination Law* (Oxford, Oxford University Press, 2005).

[80] G Davies, *Nationality Discrimination in the European Internal Market* (The Hague, Kluwer Law International, 2003). On the possibility of including non-EU nationalities, see P Boeles, 'Europese burgers en derdelanders: Wat betekent het verbod van discriminatie naar nationaliteit sinds Amsterdam?' (2005) *Sociaal-economische wetgeving* No 502, 12.

[81] T Tridimas, *The General Principles of EU Law* 2nd edn (Oxford, Oxford University Press, 2006) 59; G de Búrca, 'The Role of Equality in European Community Law' in A Dashwood and S O'Leary (eds), *The Principle of Equal Treatment in EC Law* (London, Sweet and Maxwell, 1997) 13, 14.

[82] See, e.g. C-292/97 *Kjell Karlsson and Others* ECLI:EU:C:2000:202, para 39; Joined cases C-27 and 122/00 *The Queen v Secretary of State for the Environment, Transport and the Regions, ex parte Omega Air Ltd and Omega Air Ltd, Aero Engines Ireland Ltd and Omega Aviation Services Ltd v Irish Aviation Authority* ECLI:EU:C:2002:161, para 79; Case C-300/04 *MG Eman and OB Sevinger v College van burgemeester en wethouders van Den Haag* ECLI:EU:C:2006:545, para 57. This principle allows for some accommodation of minorities' needs: Case C-130/75 *Vivien Prais v Council of the European Communities* ECLI:EU:C:1976:142.

[83] See, e.g. M Bell, 'The Principle of Equal Treatment: Widening and Deepening' in P Craig and G de Búrca (eds), *The Evolution of EU Law* 2nd edn (Oxford, Oxford University Press, 2011) 611.

[84] B Carolan, 'Rights of Sexual Minorities in Ireland and Europe: Rhetoric versus Reality' (2001) 19 *Dickinson Journal of International Law* 387. See generally Kochenov, *Europe's Justice Deficit?* (n 32).

[85] Case C-249/96 *Lisa Jacqueline Grant v South-West Trains* ECLI:EU:C:1998:63.

[86] UN Human Rights Committee Communication No 941/2000 *Young v Australia* [2003] paras 10.2–13; UN Human Rights Committee Communication No 488/1992 *Toonen v Australia* [1994]

discrimination based on sexual orientation.[87] With the likes of *Grant* (1998) and *Runevič* among its achievements – which are merely the tip of the iceberg – the CJEU cannot generally boast a really distinguished human rights record.[88]

The introduction of Article 13 EC by the Treaty of Amsterdam (now Article 19 TFEU) was partly a response to the Court's embarrassing reactionism in this field[89] and ultimately resulted in two directives[90] prohibiting discrimination on a number of important grounds. These instruments, however, are far from perfect[91] and are not applied by the Court in the clearest possible way.[92] The lobby of the Member States who see a problem in the prohibition of discrimination ensures that the improvement of the current situation via law-making is virtually impossible: to move forward, unanimity is required.[93] All in all, following the entry into force of the directives and the CJEU's (however much criticised) decisions in *Asociația ACCEPT* (2013),[94] *Maruko* (2008)[95] and *Feryn* (2008),[96] the EU has managed to build up an anti-discrimination framework which is starting to bear fruit[97] – a huge step forward compared with the significant vacuum of the preceding decade. The sweetness of this fruit is still unclear, however.

The story is somewhat more pessimistic in the area of minority protection *sensu stricto*. Minority protection, as any other human rights issue, was not in the treaties at the very beginning and has gradually developed over the years. In the course of its evolution, a seemingly natural divide emerged between internal and

paras 6.9–7.6. For analysis of their dismissal by the CJEU, see e.g. Kochenov, 'On Options of Citizens' (n 22) 176–180 (and the literature cited therein).

[87] See also A Koppelman, 'The Miscegenation Analogy in Europe, or, Lisa Grant Meets Adolf Hitler' in R Wintermute and M Andenæs (eds), *Legal Recognition of Same-sex Partnerships: A Study of National, European, and International Law* (Oxford, Hart, 2001) 623.

[88] See, e.g. A Williams, *Ethos of Europe* (Cambridge, Cambridge University Press, 2010).

[89] For analysis see, e.g. B Carolan, 'Judicial Impediments to Legislating Equality for Same-sex Couples in the European Union' (2005) 40 *Tulsa Law Review* 527.

[90] Directive 2000/43/EC implementing the principle of equal treatment between persons irrespective of racial and ethnic origin [2000] OJ L180/22; Directive 2000/78/EC establishing a general framework for equal treatment in employment and occupation [2000] OJ L303/16. Cf. L Waddington and M Bell, 'More Equal than Others: Distinguishing European Union Equality Directives' (2001) 38 *Common Market Law Review* 587.

[91] Waddington and Bell (n 90).

[92] See Introduction by Belavusau and Henrard in the present volume.

[93] Art 19(1) TFEU.

[94] Case C-81/12 *Asociația ACCEPT v Consiliul Național pentru Combaterea Discriminării* ECLI:EU:C:2013:275. For a wonderful discussion, see U Belavusau, 'A Penalty Card for Homophobia from EU Non-Discrimination Law' (2015) 21 *Columbia Journal of European Law* 237. Cf Belavusau and Kochenov, 'Federalizing Legal Opportunities for LGBT Movement' (n 22).

[95] Case C-267/06 *Tadao Maruko v Versorgunsanstalt der Deutschen Bühnen* ECLI:EU:C:2008:179. For analysis, see G von Toggenburg, '"LGBT" Go Luxembourg: On the Stance of Lesbian Gay Bisexual and Transgender Rights before the European Court of Justice' (2008) *European Law Review* 174; Kochenov, 'On Options of Citizens' (n 22) 179 *et seq*.

[96] Case C-54/07 *Centrum voor gelijkheid van kansen en voor racismebestrijding v Firma Feryn NV* ECLI:EU:C:2008:397. For analysis, see K Henrard, 'The First Substantive ECJ Judgment on the Racial Equality Directive: A Strong message in a Conceptually Flawed, and Responsively Weak Bottle' (2009) Jean Monnet Working Paper No 09/09.

[97] See, e.g. Ellis (n 9); V Chege, *Multidimensional Discrimination in EU Law: Sex, Race and Ethnicity* (Baden-Baden, Nomos, 2011).

external aspects of minority protection. This is due to the fact that minority issues first appeared on the EU's agenda when new Member States were being incorporated (i.e. in the context of enlargement).[98]

We observe an interesting evolution in this context. The exclusionary logic of the first enlargement round meant that the inhabitants of the Isle of Man, the Channel Islands and the Færœ Islands were (partly) omitted from the application of the provisions of the Treaties,[99] with the aim of safeguarding their local identities. However, the EU moved towards promoting somewhat more subtle measures during the enlargement rounds that followed.[100] Yet, the real boost of interest in minority protection issues only happened during the last two enlargement rounds,[101] which incorporated the former socialist states of Central and Eastern Europe. While the enlargements that preceded the latest rounds allocated only a very limited role to minority protection and were driven by the considerations of preserving minority cultures via exclusion from the scope of EU law,[102] the last three rounds, coinciding with the adoption of the 2000 EU Equality Directives, saw an overwhelming securitization of minority protection issues. Faced with the war in Yugoslavia and later problems in Kosovo and Macedonia, the EU acknowledged the potential threat to the stability of the continent posed by minority-related issues, if these were not properly resolved.[103] It is notable that although the general trend of the EU's minority-sensitive approach to the regulation of its own enlargements has remained on the agenda, the main motivation behind minority protection has shifted considerably, as did the means. The last three rounds of enlargements did not approach minority protection issues via exclusion, but rather via a non-discrimination approach to be found in the Treaties in force. Likewise, the remarkably speedy adoption of Equality Directives in 2000 can be partially explained by the motivation to progress quickly before the eastward enlargement which could eventually jeopardise the smooth adoption of these instruments as a unanimous vote in Council is required.[104]

[98] For analysis, see Kochenov 'A Summary of Contradictions' (n 6) 2 *et seq* (and the literature cited therein).

[99] ibid 15–17. See also G von Toggenburg, 'Minority Protection in a Supranational Context: Limits and Opportunities' in von Toggenburg, *Minority Protection* (n 24).

[100] Kochenov 'A Summary of Contradictions' (n 6) 17–18; Perrot and Miatti, 'Les lapons et les îles Åland dans le quatrième élargissement' (n 73).

[101] For the analysis of this process, see Kochenov 'A Summary of Contradictions' (n 6); C Hillion, 'Enlargement of the EU – The Discrepancy between Membership Obligations and Accession Conditions G Regards the Protection of Minorities' (2003) 27 *Fordham International Law Journal* 715; J Hughes and G Sasse, 'Monitoring the Monitors: EU Enlargement Conditionality and Minority Protection in the CEECs' (2003) 1 *Journal on Ethnopolitics and Minority Issues in Europe* 1; K Henrard, 'The Impact of the Enlargement Process on the Development of a Minority Protection Policy within the EU: Another Aspect of Responsibility / Burden Sharing?' (2002) 9 *Maastricht Journal of European and Comparative Law* 357.

[102] A direct alternative to such approach is sketched by J Waldron 'Minority Cultures and the Cosmopolitan Alternative' in W Kymlicka (ed), *The Rights of Minority Cultures* (Oxford, Oxford University Press, 1995) 93.

[103] Van Bossuyt, 'L'Union européenne et la protection des minorités' (n 3).

[104] See, e.g. the introduction by U Belavusau and K Henrard in this volume.

Given the discrepancy between the internal and external competences of the Union, which is especially pronounced in the context of the preparation of enlargements, the EU institutions were free to impose any conditions on the candidate countries, including those which would not be backed by corresponding internal competences of the Union.[105] Minority protection became one such condition.[106] First, established by the European Council as part of the Copenhagen political criteria in 1993,[107] the duty to ensure the 'respect for and the protection of minorities' became a direct condition addressed to all the countries seeking to join the Union. This same line was reinforced in the context of the ongoing Balkan pre-accession process through the formulation of the principle of 'good neighbourly relations' to which all the acceding states now have to subscribe.[108] This requirement was built into the conditionality-based approach to enlargement,[109] which has since been criticised in the literature regarding the limits of implementation.[110] In the fields of both sexual (covered by FED) and ethnic (covered by RED) minority protection, which remained outside the scope of the EU's internal competences before the entry into force of the Treaty of Amsterdam that introduced Article 13 EC (now 19 TFEU), the EU has largely failed to formulate any coherent set of demands based on EU Equality Directives, thus demonstrating a huge variation in its approaches to different countries and different minorities.[111] Instead, the EU relied on the Council of Europe standards[112] to provide minimum requirements that were viewed by the candidate countries and the Union alike as sufficient to meet the EU's dubious minority protection test.[113] Moreover, the elaboration of any clear standards was made

[105] For analysis, see Kochenov, *EU Enlargement and the Failure of Conditionality* (The Hague, Kluwer Law International, 2008) 80–2.

[106] For a detailed analysis, see Kochenov 'A Summary of Contradictions' (n 6) 20–22; JW van der Meulen, *Bescherming van minderheden als criterium bij EU-uitbreiding: de Europese Commissie en Midden-Europa* (The Hague, Clingendael, 2003); Henrard, 'The Impact of the Enlargement Process' (n 101).

[107] Bulletin of European Communities, No 6, 1993. On the Copenhagen criteria, see C Hillion, 'The Copenhagen Criteria and Their Progeny' in C Hillion (ed), *EU Enlargement: A Legal Approach* (Oxford, Hart, 2004) 1; D Kochenov, 'Behind the Copenhagen Façade. The Meaning and Structure of the Copenhagen Political Criterion of Democracy and the Rule of Law', 8(10) *European Integration online Papers* 1.

[108] P Van Elsuwege, 'Good Neighbourliness as a Condition of Accession to the European Union: Finding Balance between Law and Politics' in D Kochenov and E Basheska (eds), *Good Neighbourliness in the European Legal Context* (Leiden, Brill, 2015). See also E Basheska, 'The Position of the Good Neighbourliness Principle in International and EU Law' in Kochenov and Basheska, *Good Neighbourliness.*

[109] Kochenov, *EU Enlargement and the Failure of Conditionality* (n 105) 65–80.

[110] ibid.

[111] Kochenov, 'A Summary of Contradictions' (n 6); Hillion, 'Enlargement of the EU' (n 101); Hughes and Sasse, 'Monitoring the Monitors' (n 101).

[112] von Toggenburg, 'A Remaining Share' (n 25); D Kochenov, 'An Argument for Closer Cooperation between the European Union and the Council of Europe' (2006) 2 *Croatian Yearbook of European Law & Policy* 311.

[113] W Kymlicka, 'The Evolving Basis of European Norms of Minority Rights: Rights to Culture, Participation and Autonomy' in M Welles, D Blacklock and K Nobbs (eds), *The Protection of Minorities in the Wider Europe* (Basingstoke, Palgrave Macmillan, 2008) 11.

particularly difficult by the veto-wielding position of some Member States hostile to the very idea of minority protection,[114] especially Greece.[115]

It is thus impossible to characterise the EU in its external action as a successful promoter of minority protection standards: there were no common standards and these were not uniformly promoted.[116] Eastern European countries entered the EU with homophobic rhetoric by the top officials,[117] ethnically segregated schools,[118] and newly built ghettos,[119] with a huge percentage of their populations deprived of citizenship on the ground of belonging to minority groups,[120] and with linguistic inspections established for the 'protection' of the state language,[121] all of which promoted societal division and intolerance. Even the correct spelling of names in minority languages was not allowed,[122] depriving individuals belonging to minority cultures of the essence of their personality.

Post-accession, the situation has not improved much. It has argubly become worse, despite a clear obligation to harmonise national legislation in line with, *inter alia*, the 2000 Equality Directives. In fact, minorities are now under threat of losing their citizenship as punishment for accepting the nationality of a kin-state.[123] The CJEU has firmly endorsed Member States' rights under cultural specificity to erase their Poles, Jews and other minorities from the records by prohibiting them from using their names.[124] Moreover, xenophobia and anti-Semitism are on the rise in a number of Member States.[125]

[114] E Basheska, '(Mis)application of the Good Neighbourliness Principle in International and EU Law: The Case of the Republic of Macedonia' in Kochenov and Basheska, *Good Neighbourliness* (n 108).

[115] E Basheska and D Kochenov, 'Thanking the Greeks: The Crisis of the Rule of Law in EU Enlargement Regulation' (2015) 39 *Southeastern Europe* 392.

[116] The picture in this area was thus not different from what could be observed in other fields: judiciaries, the rule of law, general human rights, etc. For a detailed overview, see Kochenov, *EU Enlargement and the Failure of Conditionality* (n 105).

[117] For a number of examples, see D Kochenov, 'Gay Rights in the EU: A Long Way Forward for the Union of 27' (2007) 3 *Croatian Yearbook of European Law & Policy* 479, 486.

[118] J Greenberg, '*Brown v. Board of Education*: An Axe in the Frozen Sea of Racism' (2004) 48 *Saint Louis University Law Journal* 869; *DH and Others v Czech Republic* App No 57325/00 (Grand Chamber) (ECtHR, 13 November 2007).

[119] The Commission documented the progress in the building and later in the dismantlement of one such ghetto (in Ústí nad Labem) in great detail during the pre-accession monitoring exercise: Kochenov 'A Summary of Contradictions' (n 6).

[120] P Van Elsuwege, *From Soviet Republics to EU Member States: A Legal and Political Assessment of the Baltic States' Accession to the EU* Vol. 2 (Leiden, Martinus Nijhoff, 2008) 421–449.

[121] *Podkolzina v Latvia* App No 46726/99 (ECtHR, 9 April 2002); For the general context, see F de Varennes, 'The Protection of Linguistic Minorities in Europe and Human Rights: Possible Solutions to Ethnic Conflicts?' (1996) 2 *Columbia Journal of European Law* 107, 136–142.

[122] UN Human Rights Committee Communication No 1621/2007 *Raihman v Latvia* [2010]. The views of the committee under the ICCPR thus depart from the position embraced by the ECt.HR in similar cases: *Julia Mentzen* (also known as: *Mencena) v Latvia* App No 71074/01 (ECtHR, 7 December 2004); *Kuharec* (also known as: *Kuhareca) v Latvia* App No 71557/01 (ECtHR, 7 December 2004).

[123] J-M Araiza, 'Good Neighbourliness as the Limit of Extra-territorial Citizenship: The Case of Hungary and Slovakia' in Kochenov and Basheska (eds), *Good Neighbourliness* (n 108).

[124] Case C-391/09 *Runevič-Vardyn and Wardyn* (n 31).

[125] European Union Agency for Fundamental Rights and Institute for Jewish Policy Research, 'Discrimination and Hate Crime against Jews in EU Member States: Experiences and Perceptions of Antisemitism' (Luxembourg, Publications Office of the EU, 2013).

Consequently, the key problems of minority protection in the EU remained unsolved. Even more worrisome, numerous other problems related to the Member States' adherence to the values of the Union enshrined in Article 2 TEU have recently resurfaced. It is important to note that pre-accession regulation gave the EU institutions their first taste of engaging with minority protection issues, which ultimately led to the Treaty amendments. Were it not for the practice of the last two enlargement rounds before the accession of Croatia, the reference to the protection of minorities as one of the values of the EU would hardly be included in Article 2 TEU.[126] Unlike Article 19 TFEU, Article 2 TEU does not offer any legal basis for the adoption of secondary law on EU minority protection. Even though it is true that upon the completion of enlargement, the EU lost its wholesale possibility to influence policy in the field of minority protection in the new Member States, one cannot ignore the fact that the very purpose of the creation of the EU coincides with the needs of persons belonging to vulnerable groups to improve their situation beyond mere rhetorical commitment to freedom of movement. Once the regulation of different questions, including 'moral' issues which at times lead to the suppression of the persons belonging to minority groups with a 'democratic sanction' from the majority (as regards marriage, religion, education, child adoption, etc.) remains different from jurisdiction to jurisdiction throughout the EU, new important rights can be supplied simply by introducing a legal possibility of unrestricted movement between jurisdictions with different regulation.

The openness of EU law to the enforcement of citizens' free movement has far-reaching consequences for the reinforcement of the general spirit of tolerance throughout the EU, especially because of its vertical division of powers. EU law protects its citizens from unfavourable treatment when exercising their fundamental EU citizenship right to move to a different Member State.[127] This protection is valid against any Member State of the Union, including one's own. There is potential for EU law to ensure that mutual recognition of legal acts exists even between the Member States which adopted contrarian 'moral' stances on minority-relevant issues. Although Greece does not recognise same-sex marriage, a couple married in a Member States which does, who resided in a different jurisdiction and then moved to Greece will have to be treated as a married couple notwithstanding the rules of Greek national law. In another example, spouses of migrant EU citizens who are third-country nationals are shielded by EU law from any assimilationist policies of their new Member State of residence, which would apply to citizens and third country nationals perceived as having no connection

[126] For further analysis of the influence of the last enlargement rounds on EU minority protection, see von Toggenburg, 'A Remaining Share' (n 25); Henrard, 'The Impact of the Enlargement Process' (n 101).

[127] The EU citizens are covered irrespective of whether such unfavourable treatment arises out of discriminatory treatment of those who moved (e.g. Case C-224/98 *Marie-Nathalie D'Hoop v Office national de l'emploi* ECLI:EU:C:2002:432), or without discrimination (e.g. Case C-192/05 *K Tas-Hagen and RA Tas v Raadskamer WUBO van de Pensioen- en Uitkeringsraad* ECLI:EU:C:2006:676).

with EU law[128] (e.g. language and 'culture' tests and many hours of irrelevant training).[129] The practical consequences of the legal duality of rules which apply both to locals and migrants are such that illiberal local regulation comes to be applied simultaneously alongside the more permissive EU one. This *de facto* results (or so one would hope) in the further penetration of tolerance into the national legal systems, demonstrating the incoherent nature of the claims and goals behind the policies of intolerance, stigmatisation, and the social exclusion of the other.[130]

One must, however, be clear about the limits of the freedom of movement in providing a solution for the protection of Member States' minorities in the long run. Whole ethnic and religious groups cannot migrate: the core benefit of EU membership for minority groups clearly lies elsewhere and ideally should have been covered, *inter alia*, by EU Equality Directives. Let us call this the breaking open of 'container societies'. EU-wide freedom of movement enhances the opportunity for local inhabitants of all the Member States to come into contact with the cultures they would not necessarily deem as 'their own'. Like US States, EU Member States are not empowered to 'select their citizens',[131] in the sense that no discrimination on the basis of nationality – among a number of other grounds – is allowed. *All* EU citizens, including gay families, orthodox priests, and the speakers of Luxembourgian, have a right of residence in *any* of the Member States of the European Union.

V. Conclusion

Bearing in mind the constant tension between the EU and its component parts as regards the allocation of competences,[132] it is necessary to adopt a realistic approach to assessing the failures and successes of minority protection in light of the EU Equality Directives. Furthermore, the situations described here automatically disqualify any attempts to approach the issue of defining a minority deductively. The documents of EU institutions or Member States reveal little about which minorities there are and what belonging to a minority means.[133] Likewise,

[128] On the problematic tests used by the CJEU to establish such connection, see, *inter alia*, D Kochenov, 'Citizenship without Respect: The EU's Troubled Equality Ideal' (2011) Jean Monnet Working Paper (NYU Law School) No 08/10, 34–58 (and the literature cited therein).

[129] R van Oers, E Ersbøll and D Kostakopoulou (eds), *A Re-definition of Belonging?* (The Hague, Brill, 2010) 307; C Joppke, 'Immigration and the Identity of Citizenship: The Paradox of Universalism' (2008) 12 *Citizenship Studies* 533.

[130] D Kostakopoulou, 'The Nexus of Migration and Integration in the Light of Human Rights Norms' in R Plender (ed), *International Migration Law* (The Hague, Martinus Nijhoff, 2014).

[131] US Supreme Court *Saenz v Roe*, 526 US 489, 510–511 (1999).

[132] Such tensions are inherent in any vertical arrangement of power. In this sense 'the European Union is uniquely European in the same sense that other federalisms are uniquely American, German, or Swiss' – C Schönberger, 'European Citizenship as Federal Citizenship: Some Citizenship Lessons of Comparative federalism' (2007) 19 *Revue européenne de droit public* 61, 67.

[133] For attempts to employ deductive approach see, e.g. Henrard, 'An EU Perspective' (n 3) 65–67.

EU Equality Directives rather point to a range of disadvantaged groups than define minorities, and do not offer a fully fledged mechanism of minority protection. It is most unwise to expect the EU to do what the Member States are best suited to. One's EU-related expectations should be focused on providing sufficient *flexibility* regarding the possible accommodation of the Member State-level policies in the context of the internal market and, equally importantly, on dealing with Europe-wide *non-discrimination*[134] and cultural diversity protection issues.[135] These include the situation of third-country nationals, EU citizens and trans-border minorities, such as the Roma. That Muslims are a religious minority in the eyes of the EU's Fundamental Rights Agency,[136] rather than an ethnic one,[137] does not remove an ethnic component from the identity of this minority. Adopting a classical dual approach to minority protection which goes back to the Opinion by the Permanent Court of International Justice in the *Albanian Schools* case,[138] it is clear that just as identities intertwine, so do possible grounds of discrimination, as well as the particular needs of minority groups. Consequently, the ways to deal with vulnerable groups in terms of providing for a sufficient legal framework within EU anti-discrimination law (currently based on FED and RED in addition to gender equality) and minority protection equally face mutual diffusion in the context where freedom of movement remains the core principle underpinning EU integration.

As long as the EU endorses the discriminatory practices of its Member States as expressed in their 'culture', even when this implies disregarding the spirit of the EU Equality Directives or alternatively finds the regimes of minority protection in place in the Member States to conflict with the internal market rules, a concerted revision of the EU's approach to minorities is likely to remain a task for the future. The trouble is, however, that the EU is overwhelmingly inconsistent in either quashing national minority protection (i.e. its policies pertaining to EU citizenship and anti-discrimination law) or weighing in on a discussion in the Member States wishing to punish their minorities for being different. Imperatively, it would appear that the EU does not consider minority protection as a true value despite its 2000 Equality Directives, thus depriving the matter not only of coherence, but also of any systemic importance.

[134] Art 3(3)(2) TEU: '[The Union] shall combat social exclusion and discrimination, and shall promote social justice and protection of equality between women and men [...]'.

[135] Art 3(3)(4) TEU: '[The Union] shall respect its rich cultural and linguistic diversity [...]'. See also B de Witte, 'The Cultural Dimension of Community Law' in *Collected Courses of the Academy of European Law* Volume IV, book 1 (The Hague, Kluwer Law International, 1995) 229.

[136] See generally, G von Toggenburg, 'The Role of the EU Fundamental Rights Agency: Debating the "Sex of the Angels" or Improving Europe's Human Rights Performance?' (2008) 33 *European Law Review* 385.

[137] Henrard, 'An EU Perspective' (n 3) 67.

[138] PCIJ *Minority Schools in Albania* (n 74).

PART II

Race and Ethnicity

6

Eighteen Years of Race Equality Directive

A Mitigated Balance

MATHIAS MÖSCHEL

I. Introduction

A little more than 17 years ago, European politicians decided to introduce a directive protecting against race discrimination (the 'Race Equality Directive' or 'RED')[1] as well as a directive for equal treatment in employment (the 'Framework Equality Directive' or 'FED').[2] The events, pre-conditions and the multiple actors involved in the birth of the former directive and its Anglo-Dutch concept of non-discrimination have been analysed in detail elsewhere and will not be further discussed here.[3] Rather, this contribution attempts to map and assess the successes and/or failures of the Race Equality Directive in its first eighteen years of application across Europe.

Certainly, the high expectations before the birth of the RED stand in contrast with its first years of life. Contrary to its rapid vote at the European level, implementation at the national level was slow. The eagerly awaited baby had almost immediately turned into something of a scarecrow. In a 2014 report to the European Parliament and the Council, the European Commission stated that it had launched infringement proceedings for non-conformity with both of the

[1] Directive 2000/43/EC implementing the principle of equal treatment between persons irrespective of racial or ethnic origin [2000] OJ L180/22 (Race Equality Directive).

[2] Directive 2000/78/EC establishing a general framework for equal treatment in employment and occupation [2000] OJ L303/16 (Framework Equality Directive).

[3] See, e.g. A Tyson, 'The Negotiation of the European Community Directive on Racial Discrimination' (2001) 3 *European Journal of Migration and Law* 199; A Geddes and V Guiraudon, 'Britain, France and EU Anti-Discrimination Policy: The Emergence of an EU Policy Paradigm' (2004) 27 *West European Politics* 334; I Solanke, *Making Anti-Racial Discrimination Law. A Comparative History of Social Action and Anti-Racial Discrimination Law* (Abingdon, Routledge, 2009); M Bell, *Racism and Equality in the European Union* (Oxford, Oxford University Press, 2009); E Howard, *The EU Race Directive: Developing the Protection Against Racial Discrimination Within the EU* (Abingdon, Routledge, 2010).

above mentioned directives against 25 Member States, mainly between 2005 and 2007, with the Bulgarian and Croatian transposition still being examined.[4]

Slow and incorrect implementation was not only because of 'passive' sloppy legislative techniques due to a lack of familiarity with the concept of non-discrimination in most continental European countries.[5] It was also the fruit of resistance by legal scholars, especially in Germany, who stated boldly that with the law implementing the RED, the *Allgemeines Gleichbehandlungsgesetz* (AGG),[6] Germany would turn into a 'Jacobin Republic of virtues',[7] that 'Germany becomes totalitarian again',[8] that 'political correctness is now a legal obligation',[9] and that the equality body created pursuant to the Race Equality Directive is an 'unconstitutional monster'.[10]

Little wonder that this piece of legislation has not really taken off as some might have expected, hoped or dreaded. This contribution will first look at the successes of the Race Equality Directive (Section II) before mapping its failures or shortcomings (Section III) during these 18 years. The last section (IV) will cast a look at its future adulthood which, unsurprisingly, appears as mitigated as its childhood and youth.

II. Successes

It would be an exaggeration to state that the RED was a born under the wrong sign or with an unpromising future. Indeed, a number of elements demonstrate that it has kept, at least on paper, some of its promises.

A. General Observations

Certainly, one of the main achievements of the RED is placing the issue of racial equality on the legislative agenda and into the legal consciousness of

[4] European Commission, 'Joint Report on the application of Council Directive 2000/43/EC of 29 June 2000 implementing the principle of equal treatment between persons irrespective of racial or ethnic origin ('Racial Equality Directive') and of Council Directive 2000/78/EC of 27 November establishing a general framework for equal treatment in employment and occupation ('Employment Equality Directive')' COM(2014) 2 final, 3.

[5] On such implementation in France, Germany and Italy, see C Hermanin, *Europeanization through Judicial Enforcement? The Case of Race Equality Policy*, PhD Thesis (Florence, European University Institute, 2012). For a comparison of the United Kingdom, France and Spain, see C Frank and PH Hamman, *Quelle mise en œuvre de la directive européenne contre les discriminations raciales?* (Louvain-la Neuve, De Boeck, 2014).

[6] Allgemeines Gleichbehandlungsgesetz of 14 August 2006, *BGBl.* I p 1897.

[7] F-J Säcker, '"Vernunft statt Freiheit": die Tugendrepublik der neuen Jakobiner' (2002) *Zeitschrift für Rechtspolitik* 286.

[8] J Braun, 'Übrigens – Deutschland wird wieder totalitär' (2002) *Juristische Schulung* 424.

[9] K Adomeit, 'Political correctness – jetzt Rechtspflicht!' (2006) *Neue Juristische Wochenschrift* 2169.

[10] W Phillip, 'Ein verfassungswidriges Monstrum – Die Antidiskriminierungsstelle des Bundes' (2006) *Neue Zeitschrift für Verwaltungsrecht* 1235.

many European countries. Even more importantly, it extended constitutional protection against racial discrimination from the public domain and state action into the private sphere where beforehand racism could be engaged in freely, without real sanction, in many European countries.[11] Today, however, race discrimination is prohibited, *inter alia*, in private employment, education, housing, social security and health care, as well as the provision of goods and services.[12]

A second success is the requirement that 'Member States shall designate a body or bodies for the promotion of equal treatment of all persons without discrimination on the grounds of racial or ethnic origin'.[13] This was a radical innovation given that no such body existed in most Member States. The competences of these equality bodies must at least include independent assistance to victims of discrimination, independent surveys on discrimination and independent reports and recommendations on issues relating to racial discrimination.[14] Until now, a patchwork of sometimes widely differing solutions has been adopted; in some Member States, the attributed competences and powers are quite considerable.[15]

A third success is that the RED does not prevent Member States from adopting more protective standards or measures against race discrimination than those envisaged by this instrument. For instance, Article 5 of the RED allows for the possibility of positive (or affirmative) action by providing that 'the principle of equal treatment shall not prevent any Member State from maintaining or adopting specific measures to prevent or compensate for disadvantages linked to racial or ethnic origin'.[16] While many EU Member States see affirmative action on the basis of race as highly problematic, this provision guarantees that those countries which do have certain race-based positive action programmes, such as the policy of assigning 'special places' for Roma in Romanian universities,[17] are deemed not to be infringing EU law or the principle of equality.

Procedurally, the RED has been endowed with a number of welcome attributes. On the one hand, the shift away from the model of protection from discrimination through criminal law to civil law protection has eliminated some obstacles.[18] This avoids the intervention of a third party in the form of a prosecutor who might

[11] In more detail on this see, eg B de Witte, 'The Crumbling Public/Private Divide: Horizontality in European Anti-discrimination Law' (2009) 13 *Citizenship Studies* 515.

[12] RED, Art 3(1).

[13] ibid, Art 13(1).

[14] ibid, Art 13(2).

[15] For more information on these new bodies, see B de Witte, 'New Institutions for Promoting Equality in Europe: Legal Transfers, National Bricolage and European Governance' (2012) 60 *American Journal of Comparative Law* 49.

[16] RED, Art 5.

[17] For more information on this, see MC Pantea, 'Affirmative Action in Romania's Higher Education: Roma Students' Perceived Meanings and Dilemmas' (2015) 36 *British Journal of Sociology of Education* 896.

[18] In many European countries sanctioning race discrimination via criminal law occurred as a consequence of the ratification of the United Nations Convention on the Elimination of All Forms of Racial Discrimination entered into force on 4 January 1969.

decide to drop the case, thus preventing it from reaching the highest echelons of the judicial pyramid.[19] In addition, there is no more necessity to show criminal discriminatory intent. This has paved the way for the concept *of indirect race discrimination*, as defined in Article 2 of the RED.[20] Last, but not least, this concept of indirect discrimination was eventually explicitly picked up by the European Court of Human Rights (ECtHR) in one of its most famous judgments on Roma education segregation in the Czech Republic.[21] On the other hand, the easier burden of proof on the plaintiff, which shifts to the defendant once the plaintiff has shown a *prima facie* case of discrimination, has also facilitated litigation and cleared away some obstacles to litigating non-discrimination cases.[22]

B. CJEU Case Law

These positive attributes with which the Race Equality Directive has been endowed were further shaped by the Court of Justice of the European Union (CJEU). Its first case interpreting this instrument, *Feryn*,[23] dates back to 2008 and is certainly one of the best examples of this trend. In that case, the Court held that the statements made by a Belgian company director that his company would not hire immigrants because his customers did not want immigrant fitters to install doors in their homes was direct race discrimination under the RED. In particular, the CJEU rejected the defendant's argument that cases of 'victimless discrimination' (i.e. where no identifiable victim in terms of a specific plaintiff can be found) would not fall under the definition of discrimination.

[19] See, e.g. the French case regarding a prison which had subdivided prison blocks according to racial criteria. While acknowledging the fact that such a subdivision had taken place, both the first instance Court and the Court of appeals rejected the claims by narrowly interpreting the criminal definition of race discrimination (*Tribunal de Grande Instance de Paris*, Juge d'Instruction, no 243/02/88, 17 July 2003; *Cour d'appel de Paris*, Première Chambre de l'Instruction, no 2003/05865, 10 November 2003). When *SOS Racisme*, an anti-racist NGO, decided to bring the claim to the French Supreme Court, the prosecutor decided not to pursue the claim, which ultimately led the *Cour de cassation* to reject the claim without considering the merits (*Cour de cassation*, Chambre Criminelle, no G 03-87.649, non-admissibility decision, 11 May 2004). For more details on this case, see M Möschel, *Law, Lawyers and Race: Critical Race Theory from the United States to Europe* (Abingdon, New York: Routledge, 2014) 160–162.

[20] Art 2(1)(b) RED states that 'indirect discrimination shall be taken to occur where an apparently neutral provision, criterion or practice would put person of a racial or ethnic origin at a particular disadvantage compared with other persons, unless that provision, criterion or practice is objectively justified by a legitimate aim and the means of achieving that aim are appropriate and necessary'.

[21] *DH and Others v the Czech Republic* App no 57325/00 (ECtHR, 14 November 2007), in particular paras 184 and 187.

[22] The importance of this mechanism has already been recognised earlier in Council Directive 97/80/EC on the burden of proof in cases of discrimination based on sex [1998] OJ L014/6. For a deeper insight into a complicated issue of the burden of proof in the context of the Equal Treatment Directive, see the chapter by K Henrard in the present volume.

[23] Case C-54/07 *Centrum voor gelijkheid van kansen en voor racism-bestrijding v Firma Feryn NV* EU:C:2008:397.

The second example, the *CHEZ (Nikolova)* judgment (2015),[24] is much more recent. The issue here was that in certain Romani districts of a number of Bulgarian towns, the national electricity provider CHEZ RB installed electricity meters at a height of seven metres, allegedly to prevent them being tampering with. Asked whether such a practice amounted to racial discrimination, the CJEU answered affirmatively.[25] A number of particularly interesting points should be highlighted here. First, unlike a previous CJEU judgment concerning similar circumstances,[26] this case was triggered by a non-Romani woman who was running a store in that district. Consequently, the CJEU extended the concept of discrimination by association[27] – which it had already recognised for disability discrimination in its *Coleman* judgment[28] – to the domain of race discrimination.[29] This is a prime example of cross-fertilisation from one non-discrimination directive to another. Second, *CHEZ* represents the first occasion where the interpretation of the RED concerned Roma discrimination. In spite of the Roma having become Europe's quintessential contemporary racial minority, so far the CJEU's case docket had been surprisingly empty on Roma matters.[30] Third, this is one of the few EU law discrimination cases to deal with discrimination outside of the employment domain.

A last important positive point to be drawn from the *CHEZ* judgment is that the CJEU based its reasoning and findings on the argument that the RED is an expression of the principle of equality – a general principle of EU law also enshrined in Article 21 of the EU Charter of Fundamental Rights[31] – and therefore a restrictive interpretation of the directive was not accepted. The Court had already stated as much in an earlier judgment,[32] and repeated this point three times in *CHEZ*.[33]

Such an application of the RED as the expression of the general principle of equality can be found in a subsequent CJEU judgment in *Deckmyn* (2014), in which a famous comic drawing had been reproduced but some of the characters replaced with offensive images of Muslim women and people of colour.[34]

[24] Case C-83/14 *CHEZ Razpredelenie Bulgaria AD v Komisia za zashtita ot diskriminatsia* EU:C:2015:480. The name *Nikolova* indicates the name of the original plaintiff in the case.

[25] For a more detailed comment on this case, see SB Lahuerta, 'Ethnic Discrimination, Discrimination by Association, and the Roma Community: CHEZ' (2016) 53 *Common Market Law Review* 797.

[26] Case C-394/11 *Valeri Hariev Belov v CHEZ Elektro Balgaria AD and Others* EU:C:2013:48.

[27] On this concept, see C Karagiorgi, 'The Concept of Discrimination by Association and Its Application in the EU Member States' (2014) *European Anti-Discrimination Law Review* 18, 25.

[28] Case C-303/06 *S. Coleman v Attridge Law and Steve Law* EU:C:2008:415.

[29] Case C-83/14 *CHEZ* (n 24) para 56. See also Case C-83/14 *CHEZ* EU:C:2015:170, Opinion of AG Kokott, paras 52–61.

[30] On the general marginalisation of the Roma in Europe, see the chapter by M Goodwin in the present volume.

[31] Charter of Fundamental Rights of the European Union [2016] OJ C202/393.

[32] Case C-391/09 *Malgožata Runevič-Vardyn and Łukasz Paweł Wardyn v Vilniaus mietso savivaldybės administracija and Others* EU:C:2011:291.

[33] ibid paras 42, 56 and 66.

[34] Case C-201/13 *Johan Deckmyn, Vrijheidsfonds VZW v Vandersteen et al* EU:C:2014:2132.

In interpreting whether such a reproduction would fall under the parody exception of the Copyright Directive[35] – and thus be allowed as an exercise of freedom of expression – the CJEU drew attention to the principle of racial non-discrimination enshrined in the RED. It emphasised that national courts need to take this principle into account, *inter alia*, because the plaintiffs as the original publishers of the drawings have a legitimate interest in ensuring that their copyright is not associated with discriminatory messages.[36]

Through the CJEU's case law, the RED and the principle of non-discrimination have obtained quasi-constitutional status, via the mechanism of general principles of EU law and/or Article 21 of the EU Charter of Fundamental Rights. The general principle of non-discrimination on the grounds of race can and should therefore be relevant when interpreting other EU law instruments or other forms of EU action.

C. National (Case) Law

At the national level, a number of interesting developments have also taken place. First and foremost, a number of countries have granted extensive powers to their equality bodies and broad standing rights to NGOs, which has really helped the development of national as well as European case law.[37]

Moreover, a number of cases from national jurisdictions have dealt with race discrimination and interpreted legislation implementing the RED. These cases are important because they address some of the most commonplace and structural instances of discrimination faced by racial minorities all over Europe. Specific cases from a range of jurisdictions will be described here to provide an idea of what circumstances give rise to litigation and which different forms of race discrimination are thus addressed.[38] Three particular areas are highlighted where interesting interpretations and developments are taking place.

D. Harassment

The first area concerns the notion of harassment introduced by the RED along with the other prohibitions of direct discrimination, indirect discrimination and

[35] Directive 2001/29/EC of the European Parliament and of the Council on the harmonization of certain aspects of copyright and related rights in the information society 2001 OJ L167/10.

[36] ibid paras 30–31.

[37] The best example may be Belgium where two of the most important anti-discrimination cases at the EU law level were initiated: Case C-54/07 *Feryn* (n 23) and Case C-236/09 *Association Belge des Consommateurs Test-Achats ASBL and Others v Conseil des ministres* EU:C:2011:100.

[38] For continued updates on European case law, see the websites and/or publications of various national equality bodies, anti-racist NGOs and also the *European Anti-Discrimination Law Review/European Equality Law Review*.

instruction to discriminate.[39] Certainly, the RED allows for national variations by providing that the 'concept of harassment may be defined in accordance with the national laws and practice of the Member States'.[40] Nevertheless, the advantage of racial *harassment* as opposed to the concepts of *direct* and *indirect discrimination* is that, at least in theory, there is neither the need to identify an 'Artistotelian' comparator nor the need to prove intent or its absence. Hence, it is surprising that there are no CJEU judgments directly interpreting what constitutes such racial harassment.[41] Nevertheless, at the national, level case law can be found which demonstrates how litigation on the basis of harassment may provide an effective and wide-ranging means of addressing structural aspects of race discrimination, at times even going beyond the scope of the RED.

Two examples of finding the defendant guilty of racial harassment (*molestie*) come from Italy.[42] The first case[43] concerned a training manual for aspiring Italian barristers which, for the misdemeanour of acquiring chattels of suspicious origins,[44] gave the example that the chattel, despite its high value, is offered for sale by a beggar, a gypsy or a known criminal. An Italian anti-racism NGO claimed that this association of Roma with criminal activity was contrary to the Italian legislation implementing the RED and, in particular, amounted to racial harassment. The first instance court agreed, also specifying that the harassment provision does not require intent. The publishing house was consequently ordered to take the publication containing this language off the market and to delete the discriminatory passages from any future editons.

The second case dealt with a message brimming with discriminatory language which was hanging in the offices of the *Lega Nord* in the centre of a small town in Northern Italy.[45] The first instance court held that this behaviour constituted unwanted conduct which had the purpose or effect of violating the dignity of a person and of creating an intimidating, hostile, degrading, humiliating or offensive environment. Moreover, it was not necessary that the plaintiff belong to any specific race or ethnicity; it sufficed that she was associated with the protected categories. Put differently, a case of racial harassment by association was established.[46]

[39] Art 2(3) RED defines harassment as 'when an unwanted conduct related to racial or ethnic origin takes place with the purpose or effect of violating the dignity of a person and of creating an intimidating, hostile, degrading, humiliating or offensive environment'.

[40] ibid.

[41] So far, the issue has only come up indirectly in AG Kokott's opinion to the *Belov* case dealing with a similar fact pattern as the *CHEZ* judgment discussed above. See Case C-394/11 *Belov* EU:C:2012:585, Opinion of AG Kokott, para 98.

[42] In Italy, the Race Equality Directive has been transposed by the *decreto legislativo* of 9 July 2003, no 215.

[43] *Tribunale ordinario di Roma*, Sezione I civile, 16 February 2015, no 37070/12.

[44] Italian Criminal Code Art 712.

[45] *Tribunale ordinario di Brescia*, 31 January 2012, no 3298/2011. The message was directed both against a representative of the trade union, Vittoria Romana Gandossi, and an unnamed third-country resident of Adro, called 'Bedouin', whom she was apparently protecting from being kicked out of locally subsidised housing.

[46] There are other cases involving similar 'political' and discriminatory messages by the *Lega Nord* where trial courts have found racial harassment. On such case law, see ASGI, W Citti (ed), *La tutela*

The Hungarian Supreme Court also intervened in a similar case involving discriminatory speeches and statements against the Roma by the mayor of a small town by holding that such behaviour constituted racial harassment because it violated the dignity and equality of Hungarian national minorities. In particular, that Court rejected the claim that the literal interpretation of the applicable legislation would only apply to individual as opposed to group claims.[47]

Therefore, this national case law demonstrates that the prohibition of racial harassment can actually serve as a useful instrument outside of the employment domain in cases involving racism against all sorts of racist images and/or statements. Furthermore, harassment can be invoked beyond individual claims, without needing to refer to a comparator or to discriminatory intent.

E. Housing

Another area of case law where one can see developments and inroads is in the domain of housing. In a recent Austrian case, the administrative Court of the Land Vorarlberg held that a housing advertisement on an internet page through which an apartment was offered 'preferably to Austrians (*Inländer*)' not only amounted to discrimination on the grounds of race/ethnicity but also on the grounds of gender.[48] In fact, the administrative Court held that the German word *Inländer* refers only to male Austrians and discourages women from applying. Thus, it felt the necessity to add that ground of discrimination to the original one. This is a surprising and rare example of court-triggered intersectionality analysis.[49]

In Germany, a court of appeal awarded damages to an African couple who were not allowed to visit an apartment on the grounds that the apartment would not be rented to 'Niggers … ahhhm Blacks or Turks'.[50] More recently, a first instance court held that asking people of Turkish or Arabic descent for a higher rental price for their apartments constituted direct discrimination.[51] Similarly, in Italy, there are a number of cases where courts found racial discrimination: for instance, the refusal by a real estate agency to look for housing for a woman of third country origin[52] or the creation by a housing agency of a separate channel of housing offers for

contro le discriminazioni etnico-razziali e religiose (31 August 2013) 38–39. Available at: www.asgi.it/banca-dati/tutela-civile-contro-discriminazioni-etnico-razziali-religiose-guida-normativa-giurisprudenza/.

[47] *Kúria*, 29 October 2014, no Kfv.III.37.848/2014/6. For more details on the complex litigation, see I Haller, R Iordache and A Kadar, 'Using Anti-Discrimination Remedies for Discriminatory Speech – The Hungarian and Romanian Experiences' (2016) 2 *European Equality Law Review* 1, 7–9.

[48] *Landesverwaltungsgericht Vorarlberg*, 14 July 2014, LVwG-1-388/R4-2014.

[49] For a wider perspective on intersectionality in EU anti-discrimination law, see the chapter by R Xenidis in the present volume.

[50] *Oberlandesgericht Köln*, 19 January 2010, 24 U 51/09.

[51] *Amtsgericht Berlin Tempelhof-Kreuzberg*, 19 December 2014, 25 C 357/14.

[52] *Tribunale di Milano*, ordinanza 30 March 2000 (the Italian word *extracomunitario* which corresponds roughly to third-country national has a highly negative connotation).

third country nationals on their website where no offers were posted.[53] It should be noted that both cases were decided under previously existing legislation and thus not under the RED.

F. Disc(o)rimination

Another significant area of litigation in which positive developments can be observed is access to entertainment structures, such as discothèques, nightclubs, theatres, cafés, bars and the like. Admittedly, the improvements in this context can also be observed in countries outside of the EU and predate the adoption of the RED.[54] For instance, one of the earliest Italian cases on race discrimination involved a Moroccan and a Tunisian citizen who were denied access to a place in which – ironically – there was an ongoing show of African dances.[55] The first French case allowing for 'situation testing' or simply 'testing' as a means of proof in criminal trials[56] also predates the RED and involved racially selective entry into two nightclubs.[57]

The RED follows that pre-existing litigation trend.[58] Since its entry into force, in many European countries these entrance to entertainment structure cases continue to be successfully litigated by plaintiffs who have been denied entrance to certain entertainment structures on the grounds of their race/ethnicity.[59] The RED has facilitated litigating such cases by taking them out of the criminal law domain and as a consequence, raising awareness by making them more visible.

In conclusion to Section II of this contribution, it can certainly be stated that the RED has induced some change and, in certain areas, provided access to justice where none (or very little) was offered before. However, these observations

[53] *Tribunale di Bologna*, ordinanza 22 February 2001.

[54] See, eg in the United States one of the first post-Civil War US Supreme Court decisions interpreting the new XIVth Amendment's Equal Protection Clause: *The Civil Rights Cases*, 109 US 3 (1883).

[55] *Tribunale di Torino*, Sezione I penale: 13 January 1997.

[56] This is an experimental reconstruction of a specific situation whereby different people with different racial/ethnic/national backgrounds are made to apply for a job or housing or to enter into an entertainment structure. If only those belonging to a specific racial/ethnic/national minority are rejected or denied entry, that can count as *prima facie* evidence that in an underlying discrimination dispute, race discrimination has indeed taken place.

[57] *Cour de cassation*, chambre criminelle, 11 June 2002, no 01-85559 (this decision became notorious because it admitted testing as a means of proof in discrimination cases).

[58] See, e.g. a Polish decision involving the exclusion of a Roma individual from a club. The Poznań Court of Appeals found direct discrimination and ordered the publication of an apology in local newspapers, on the bar's website as well as damages corresponding to a little more than €2,000 to be paid for a regional Roma cultural association: *Sąd Apelacyjny w Poznaniu*, 29 February 2012, I Aca 1162/11. See also the Italian Supreme Court decision confirming the conviction for race discrimination of a bar manager who repeatedly refused to serve coffee to third-country nationals (*extracomunitari*): *Corte di cassazione*, Sezione III penale, no 46783, 5 December 2005.

[59] See, e.g. for Germany, *Amtsgericht Oldenburg*, 23 July 2008, 2 C 2126/07; *Amtsgericht Bremen*, 20 January 2011, 25 C 0278/10; *Oberlandesgericht Stuttgart*, 12 December 2011, 10 U 106/11; *Amtsgericht Leipzig*, 18 May 2012, 118 C 1036/12.

are tempered if not overshadowed by the failures or shortcomings which are discussed in Section III.

III. Failures or Shortcomings

Where there is light there are necessarily also some shadows. This is no different in the case of the RED. Therefore, this contribution speaks about a mitigated balance.

A. General Observations

One of the most recent 'official' assessments of the RED by the European Union Agency of Fundamental Rights (FRA) mentions amongst the different challenges to realising the aims of the Directive: (i) absence of awareness of equality legislation, (ii) failure to recognise and reluctance to report instances of discrimination, (iii) high legal costs and limits of dispute settlements, (iv) absence of data and preventive/promotional measures in many countries.[60]

Beyond these issues that partly explain why this instrument has not taken off, a number of other points must be added. These partially overlap and add to the problems already highlighted in the literature,[61] and in an even more recent shadow report on the RED by the Open Society Justice Initiative.[62]

The discussion above demonstrated the extent of the resistance to the Directive and noted how the European Commission had to threaten several states with infringement procedures for failure to implement or the incorrect implementation of this instrument. One commonality among many Member States, especially in mainland Europe, is the reluctance to use the word 'race'. In part, this has to do with the shadow of World War II and the Holocaust; speaking about race seems to revive that period. The problematic aspects of such an attitude have been critiqued elsewhere in detail.[63] One of the consequences of this attitude is the strong resistance to introducing racial/ethnic statistics, notwithstanding its crucial assistance in combatting racial discrimination, and particularly indirect discrimination in most continental European countries.[64]

[60] European Union Agency for Fundamental Rights, 'The Racial Equality Directive: Application and Challenges' (Luxembourg, Publications Office of the European Union, 2012) 19–24.

[61] See, e.g. M Ambrus, M Busstra and K Henrard, 'The Racial Equality Directive and Effective Protection against Discrimination: Mismatches between the Substantive Law and its Application' (2010) 3 *Erasmus Law Review* 165.

[62] C Hermanin and E de Kroon, 'The Race Equality Directive: A Shadow Report. Lessons Learnt from the Implementation in Nine EU Member States' (Brussels: Open Society European Policy Institute, 2013).

[63] On these points, see, e.g. Möschel, *Law, Lawyers and Race* (n 19) 110–139.

[64] See RED Preamble Recital 15: 'The appreciation of the facts from which it may be inferred that there has been direct or indirect discrimination is a matter for national judicial or other

Additional obstacles are the disparity in strength between the national equality bodies and the limited standing for NGOs to bring non-discrimination claims. Indeed, there are vast differences as to the functioning or malfunctioning of the equality bodies that have been set up in the Member States. Where functioning equality bodies predated the RED, these are generally strong institutions with adequate tasks, powers and funding, sometimes even empowered to bring non-discrimination claims autonomously. In other Member States, however, these bodies suffer from lack of independence, underfunding, few competences and/or lack of visibility.[65] Moreover, some countries have concrete procedural obstacles for anti-racist associations or NGOs to bringing non-discrimination claims, especially in the name of collective interests and/or in the place of the actual victims of discrimination.[66] For example, in Italy, such associations and/or NGOs need to be first approved and registered by ministerial decrees.[67]

Last, but not least, race non-discrimination law more generally has also come under friendly fire from different angles. On the one hand, anti-discrimination law and EU anti-discrimination law in particular, has been critiqued for its underlying liberal ethos which (potentially) limits its capacity to trigger wide structural changes.[68] On the other hand and in a somewhat similar vein, the CJEU in *Parris* (2016)[69] seemed to follow a US trend of reticence towards intersectional claims brought by women of colour,[70] since it rejected the idea that the FED allows for intersectional claims in a case involving discrimination on the grounds of age and sexual orientation. Additionally, in the EU context, the different EU non-discrimination directives have varying material scopes which could lead to difficulties when bringing claims involving multiple and/or intersectional grounds

competent bodies, in accordance with rules of national law or practice. Such rules may provide in particular for indirect discrimination to be established by any means including on the basis of statistical evidence.'

[65] This is, for example, the case in Italy where the *UNAR* (*Ufficio nazionale antidiscriminazioni razziali*) is hierarchically organised under the Prime Minister's office or in Spain where the *Consejo para la Eliminación de la Discriminación Racial o Étnica* depends on the Health Ministry with a reduced budget. For a comparison of these different bodies see, e.g. M Ammer et al, 'Study on Equality Bodies Set Up Under Directives 2000/43/EC, 2004/113/EC and 2006/54/EC: Synthesis Report' (Vienna/Utrecht, Human European Consultancy in partnership with the Ludwig Boltzmann Institut, 2010). In academic literature, see B de Witte, 'New Institutions for Promoting Equality in Europe: Legal Transfers, National Bricolage and European Governance' (2012) 60 *American Journal of Comparative Law* 49, 60–65.

[66] On the importance of such broad standing rules, see L Farkas, 'Limited Enforcement Possibilities under European Anti-Discrimination Legislation – A Case Study of Procedural Novelties: *Actio Popularis* Action in Hungary' (2010) 3/3 *Erasmus Law Review* 181.

[67] The first decree was issued in 2005, the next in 2010 and the last one in 2013. See ASGI, W Citti (n 46).

[68] D Chalmers, 'The Mistakes of the Good European?' in S Fredman (ed), *Discrimination and Human Rights: the Case of Racism* (Oxford, Oxford University Press, 2001).

[69] Case C-443/15 *David L Parris v Trinity College Dublin and Others* EU:C:2016:897.

[70] See to that effect KW Crenshaw, 'Mapping the Margins: Intersectionality, Identity Politics, and Violence against Women of Color' (1991) 43 *Stanford Law Review* 1241. See also the chapter by R Xenidis in the present volume.

of discrimination.[71] This has raised criticism about leading to differing levels of protection and hierarchies of discrimination.[72] For instance, a claim for race and/or gender discrimination of a Muslim woman wearing a veil could also be brought outside of the employment context but if she wanted to add religious discrimination, under current EU law her claim would be limited to the employment domain.[73]

B. CJEU Case Law

First of all, an examination of the wording of the Race Equality Directive[74] shows it neither applies to the difference of treatment based on nationality nor does it have any bearing on the provisions and conditions relating to the entry into and residence of third-country nationals and stateless persons on the territory of Member States, or on the treatment which arises from the legal status of the third-country nationals and stateless persons concerned.[75] Indeed, in *Kamberaj* (2012), the CJEU rejected the application of the Race Equality Directive to the refusal by the Italian Autonomous Province of Bozen to grant a housing benefit to a long-term resident third-country national.[76] In other words, under the cloak of immigration and nationality rules or through claims that the discriminatory treatment is based on nationality rather than race or ethnicity, a range of discriminatory practices can escape the application of the RED. Similarly, in *Runevič-Vardyn* (2011),[77] despite stating that the scope of the RED should be interpreted broadly,[78] the CJEU eventually held that '[n]ational rules which provide that a person's surnames and forenames may be entered on the certificate of civil status of that State only in a form which complies with the rules governing the spelling of the official national language relate to a situation which does not come within the scope of Council Directive 2000/43/EC'.[79]

In addition, in its recent *Huskic* judgment (2017), the CJEU held that the practice of a credit institution which requires a customer whose driving licence indicates a country of birth other than a Member State of the European Union

[71] To that effect, see, e.g. S Benedí Lahuerta, 'Race Equality and TCNs, or How to Fight Discrimination with a Discriminatory Law' (2009) 15 *European Law Journal* 747; PJ Neuvonen, '"Inequality in Equality" in the European Union Equality Directives: A Friend or a Foe of More Systematized Relationships between the Protected Grounds?' (2015) *International Journal of Discrimination and the Law* 1.

[72] On this idea of hierarchies see, e.g. M Bell and L Waddington, 'More Equal Than Others? Distinguishing EU Equality Directives' (2001) 38 *Common Market Law Review* 587.

[73] On such cases, see the chapters by E Pastor and A Sledzińska in the present volume.

[74] Art 3(2) RED.

[75] On this, see one of the early comments on the Race Equality Directive by D Chalmers, 'The Mistakes of the Good European' in Fredman (n 68) 218–220.

[76] Case C-571/10 *Servet Kamberaj v Istituto per l'Edilizia sociale della Provincia autonoma di Bolzano (IPES) and Others* EU:C:2012:233, especially paras 47–50 and 64–65.

[77] Case C-391/09 *Runevič-Vardyn* (n 32).

[78] ibid para 43.

[79] ibid point 1 of the judgment.

or of the EFTA to produce additional identification in the form of a copy of the customer's passport or residence permit constitutes neither direct nor indirect race/ethnic discrimination.[80] The case is interesting because the national equal treatment body and the first instance court in Denmark had respectively found indirect and direct discrimination on the grounds of race/ethnicity. The CJEU instead 'overruled' these findings by rejecting the direct discrimination argument because 'a person's country of birth cannot, in itself, justify a general presumption that that person is a member of a given ethnic group'[81] and because the RED does not cover nationality discrimination.[82] Moreover, the Court held that indirect discrimination applies only if the measure places a person of a particular ethnic origin at a disadvantage.[83] Given that the measure here applied indistinctly to all non-EU/EFTA citizens, it cannot be presumed that a particular ethnicity was envisaged.

Second, if one looks at the CJEU's case law interpreting the RED, it quickly becomes evident how few cases have reached the European Court, especially when compared to the interpretation of its twin directive, the Framework Equality Directive, regarding which many judgments involving other grounds of discrimination (mainly age) have been handed down over the years.[84] As this chapter

[80] Case C-668/15 *Jyske Finans A/S v Ligebehandlingsnævnet* EU:C:2017:278. The name *Huskic* indicates the name of the original plaintiff.

[81] ibid para 20.

[82] ibid para 24.

[83] ibid *mutatis mutandis* paras 27 and 31.

[84] See by grounds of discrimination. **Age:** Case C-144/04 *Werner Mangold v Rüdiger Helm* EU:C:2005:709; Case C-427/06 *Birgit Bartsch v Bosch und Siemens Hausgeräte (BSH)* EU:C:2008:517; Case C-388/07 *Age Concern England v Secretary of State for Business, Enterprise and Regulatory Reform* EU:C:2009:128; Case C-555/07 *Seda Kücükdeveci v Swedex GmbH & Co KG* EU:C:2010:21; Case C-405/08 *Ingeniørforeningen i Danmark v Region Syddanmark* EU:C:2010:69; Case C-45/09 *Gisela Rosenbladt v Oellerking Gebäudereinigungs GmbH* EU:C:2010:601; Joined Cases C-159/10 and C-160/10 *Gerhard Fuchs and Peter Köhler v Land Hessen* EU:C:2011:508; Joined Cases C-297/10 and C-298/10 *Sabine Hennigs v Eisenbahn-Bundesamt. and Land Berlin v Alexander Mai* EU:C:2011:560; Case C-447/09 *Reinhard Prigge and Others v Deutsche Lufthansa AG* EU:C:2011:573; Case C-132/11 *Tyrolean Airways Tiroler Luftfahrt GmbH v Betriebsrat Bord der Tyrolean Airways Tiroler Luftfahrt GmbH* EU:C:2012:329; Case C-141/11 *Torsten Hörnfeldt v Posten Meddelande AB* EU:C:2012:421; Case C-286/12 *Commission v Hungary* EU:C:2012:687; Case C-546/11, *Dansk Jurist- og Økonomforbund v Indenrigs- og Sundhedsministeriet* EU:C:2013:603; Case C-530/13 *Leopold Schmitzer v Bundesministerin für Inneres* EU:C:2014:2359; Case C-529/13 *Georg Felber v Bundesministerin für Unterricht, Kunst und Kultur* EU:C:2015:20; Case C-417/13 *ÖBB Personenverkehr AG v Gotthard Starjakob* EU:C:2015:38; Case C-515/13 *Ingeniørforeningen i Danmark v Tekniq* EU:C:2015:115; Case C-20/13 *Daniel Unland v Land Berlin* EU:C:2015:561; Case C-441/14 *Dansk Industri (DI) v Estate of Karsten Eigil Rasmussen* EU:C:2016:278; Case C-122/15 *C.* EU:C:2016:391; Case C-159/15 *Franz Lesar v Telekom Austria AG* EU:C:2016:451; Case C-548/15 *JJ de Lange v Staatssecretaris van Financiën* EU:C:2016:850; Case C-258/15 *Gorka Salaberria Sorondo v Academia Vasca de Policía y Emergencias* EU:C:2016:873; Case C-539/15 *Daniel Bowman v Pensionsversicherungsanstalt* EU:C:2016:977. **Disability:** Case C-13/05 *Sonia Chacón Navas v Eurest Colectividades SA* EU:C:2006:456; Case C-303/06 *Coleman* EU:C:2008:415; Case C-152/11 *Johann Odar v Baxter Deutschland GmbH* EU:C:2012:772; Case C-363/12 *Z. v A Government Department and the Board of Management of a Community School* EU:C:2014:159; Case C-354/13 *Fag og Arbejde (FOA) v Kommunernes Landsforening (KL)* EU:C:2014:2463; Case C-395/15 *Mohamed Daouidi v Bootes Plus SL and Others* EU:C:2016:917; Case C-406/15 *Petya Milkova v Izpalnitelen direktor na Agentsiata za privatizatsia i sledprivatizatsionen*

has shown, since the adoption of the RED, only three judgments – *Feryn*, *CHEZ* and *Huskic* – have actually dealt with its substantive aspects. Beyond the positive features of these cases, which were highlighted above, it is striking that *Feryn* has been framed as a case of 'victimless discrimination', *CHEZ* as a case of 'indirect discrimination by association' and *Huskic* was dealing with a relatively trivial issue. With all the forms of (structural) racial discrimination taking place throughout the EU Member States, what reached the CJEU is one decision where there was no direct victim, one where the plaintiff was not Roma and one where the plaintiff was a Danish citizen of Bosnian origin. This might lead one to believe that racial discrimination is exceptional and distant and that the rules to protect against such discrimination actually only work when there is no victim or when they accessorily also protect someone belonging to the majority group, leaving all the broad structural issues of racism in Europe (e.g. racial profiling) untouched.[85]

The few other judgments concerning the Race Equality Directive have either limited its scope[86] or dealt with more procedural issues, such as whether the Bulgarian equality body is a court or tribunal which has the right to refer a preliminary ruling to the CJEU,[87] or how far access to information from a potential employer should be granted to plaintiffs claiming certain forms of discrimination.[88] This is not to dismiss the importance of such issues and interpretations. However, beyond the legal critiques concerning the two latter cases of *Belov* (2013) and *Meister* (2012),[89] one can also wonder from a more sociological perspective whether this is the kind of expected case law. The *Runevič-Vardyn* case concerned the refusal by Lithuanian authorities to transcribe Polish language names into the civil registers. The *Kamberaj* judgment was about a long-term Albanian resident in Italy. The *Meister* case involved a Russian engineer whose job application was denied by a German company. The *Huskic* judgment was about a Danish citizen with Bosnian origins. Yet another case before the CJEU was declared inadmissible because the plaintiffs were claiming discrimination on grounds of membership of a socio-professional category or place of work

kontrol EU:C:2017:198. **Sexual orientation**: Case C-267/06 *Tadao Maruko v Versorgungsanstalt der deutschen Bühnen* EU:C:2008:179; Case C-147/08 *Jürgen Römer v Freie und Hansestadt Hamburg* EU:C:2011:286; Case C-81/12 *Asociația Accept v Consiliul Național pentru Combaterea Discriminării* EU:C:2013:275; Case C-267/12 *Frédéric Hay v Crédit agricole mutuel de Charente-Maritime et des Deux-Sèvres* EU:C:2013:823; Case C-443/15 *Parris* EU:C:2016:897. **Religion:** Case C-157/15 *Samira Achbita and Centrum voor gelijkheid van kansen en voor racismebestrijding v G4S Secure Solutions NV* EU:C:2017:203; Case C-188/15 *Asma Bougnaoui, Association de défense des droits de l'homme (ADDH) v Micropole Univers SA* EU:C:2017:204.

[85] See Case C-201/13 *Deckmyn* (n 34) where the interests to be taken into account were not those of Muslim women wearing a veil or of people of colour but those of the original cartoonists who did not wish their drawings to be associated with such discriminatory messages.

[86] Case C-391/09 *Runevič-Vardyn* (n 32) and Case C-571/10 *Kamberaj* (n 76).

[87] Case C-394/11 *Belov* (n 26).

[88] Case C-415/10 *Galina Meister v Speech Design Carriers GmbH* EU:C:2012:217.

[89] M Möschel, 'Race Discrimination and Access to the European Court of Justice: *Belov*' (2013) 50 *Common Market Law Review* 1433; L Farkas, 'Getting it Right the Wrong Way? The Consequences of a Summary Judgment: The *Meister* Case' (2012) 15 *European Anti-Discrimination Law Review* 23.

either under the RED or the FED.[90] As is evident, few of these cases tackle the paradigmatic, historical issues of race discrimination that occur in all European countries, such as anti-Semitism, anti-Black racism, anti-Roma racism and/or Islamophobia.

Third, it is also questionable how far the recently acquired constitutional status of the RED will impact the interpretation of other EU legislation.[91] The main areas in which this could be done concern the cases on the interpretation of the Family Reunification Directive[92] and the Third Country Nationals Directive.[93] In this context, a number of cases have been decided over the past years by the CJEU in which the RED is not explicitly invoked. For instance, the European Parliament brought a claim against the Council regarding the Family Reunification Directive but the judgment did not mention race discrimination as one of the principles against which the Directive should be assessed. Yet, the Court, *inter alia*, referred to the principle of non-discrimination on the grounds of age (only) and Article 14 of the European Convention on Human Rights (ECHR).[94] Moreover, the CJEU held that a waiting period of up to two or even three years was not contrary to the right to family reunification or to other fundamental rights.[95] In another judgment concerning the same instrument, the CJEU also decided that national laws on family reunification may require spouses and registered partners to have reached the age of 21 by the date when they lodge the application seeking to be considered family members entitled to reunification.[96] The Court's approach does not take into account the fact that many of these rules, while being cloaked in the language of the right to family reunification, have been adopted under (political) pressure by Member States who are dealing with xenophobic and racist calls to shut down borders and make coming to Europe increasingly difficult.

Civic integration measures imposed on third country nationals and/or on the family members who intend to join them are another example of the trend to reduce the influx of third country nationals. The CJEU has adjudicated over these measures in the past years, yet the debate about their racially discriminatory impact has been largely absent.[97] Such civic integration measures have sprung up in a number of countries as a backlash against immigration and mainly target people who are from developing countries with perceived different cultures,

[90] Case C-310/10 *Ministerul Justiţiei şi Libertăţilor Cetăţeneşti v Ştefan Agafiţei and Others* EU:C:2011:467.

[91] See, eg Case C-201/13 *Deckmyn* (n 34) paras 29–31.

[92] Council Directive 2003/86/EC on the right to family reunification [2003] OJ L251/12 (Family Reunification Directive).

[93] Council Directive 2003/109/EC concerning the status of third-country nationals who are long-term residents [2004] OJ L16/44 (Third Country Nationals Directive).

[94] Case C-540/03 *European Parliament v Council of the European Union* EU:C:2006:429, para 32.

[95] ibid paras 97–107.

[96] Case C-338/13 *Noorzia v Bundesministerium fürs Innere* EU:C:2014:2092.

[97] For more detail on these integration requirements, see G Hogan-Brun, C Mar-Molinero and P Stevenson (eds), *Discourses on Language and Integration: Critical Perspectives on Language Testing Regimes in Europe* (Amsterdam, John Benjamin Publishers Co, 2009).

religions and also skin colour. Therefore, imposing such requirements, especially after one has already acquired long-term resident status, contributes to the stigmatisation of such residents and could be seen as racial harassment.

The CJEU has been called upon to interpret such measures both under the Third Country Nationals Directive and under the Family Reunification Directive in a number of cases. However, it has not obliged national courts to take into account the issue of race discrimination either via the RED or Article 21 of the EU Charter of Fundamental Rights in interpreting these instruments. Examples of this can be found in two preliminary references from the Netherlands. The first reference asked whether a Dutch civic integration examination imposed via the menace of fines on third-country nationals who had already obtained long-term resident status is compatible with the Third Country Nationals Directive.[98] The second case concerned the compatibility of imposing a national pre-departure integration exam on the spouse of a third-country national EU resident with the Family Reunification Directive.[99] Without entering into detail about these cases,[100] the CJEU held that such measures were, in principle, compatible with the two instruments but that they might be disproportionate in the former case and that they actually are in the latter.

Nevertheless, a recent ECtHR judgment demonstrates that challenging the racial underpinnings of family reunification rules and or civic integration measures is not completely implausible. In *Biao v Denmark* (2016), the Danish family reunification rules that had been altered so as to include predominantly ethnic, white Danes and to exclude non-ethnic white Danes who had acquired Danish citizenship later in life were held contrary to Article 8 ECHR (right to family life) and, more importantly, Article 14 ECHR (right to non-discrimination).[101] The ECtHR held that this constituted indirect race discrimination, thus showing that it is legally possible, albeit difficult, to challenge the racial underpinnings of such legislation.[102]

C. National (Case) Law

Naturally, problems not only emerge at the EU level, but also at the Member State level regarding the implementation of the RED. The different general observations

[98] Case C-579/13 *P and S v Commissie Sociale Zekerheid Breda and others* EU:C:2015:369.

[99] Case C-153/14 *Minister van Buitendlandse Zaken v K. and A.* EU:C:2015:453. Another preliminary reference concerning German pre-integration measures asked a similar question but was cancelled by order from the CJEU: Case C-527/14 *Ukamaka Mary Jecinta Oruche and Nzubechukwu Emmanuel Oruche v Bundesrepublik Deutschland* EU:C:2015:599.

[100] For an analysis of both cases, see M Jesse, 'Integration Measures, Integration Exams, and Immigration Control: *P and S* and *K and A*' (2016) 53 *Common Market Law Review* 1065.

[101] *Biao v Denmark* App no 38590/10 (ECtHR, 24 May 2016).

[102] For a more detailed comment on this case, see M Möschel, 'The Strasbourg Court and Indirect Race Discrimination: Going beyond the Education Domain' (2017) 80 *Modern Law Review* 121.

concerning the RED mentioned above under Section III, A. all play a role in the specific issues raised here.

An initial point is the relative dearth of case law on the RED, reflecting the situation at EU level. For example, despite increased litigation since the early 2000s, France has very little case law on race discrimination. This can be explained by the fact that, until that point, the majority of discrimination litigation relied on criminal law, limiting this notion to intentional race discrimination.[103] Since the 2000s, there has been a shift from criminal law to (mainly) employment law, resulting in more claims.[104] Nevertheless, the cases are still far from numerous. Albeit for different reasons, the RED is equally rarely invoked in Italy. However, in this country, many cases involving the discrimination of third country nationals and their exclusion from all areas of public life were mainly litigated under a previous anti-discrimination provision inserted into the Italian Immigration Code.[105] As opposed to the RED, that instrument does not exclude nationality discrimination from the prohibited grounds. Consequently, many cases in which the Italian State excluded third-country nationals from accessing public employment or social benefits were litigated under the Immigration Code.[106] To some extent, in the Italian context, the existence of a competing internal instrument can be seen as overshadowing the external European one.

Secondly, and partly reflecting the case law of the CJEU, the types of cases litigated nationally tend to not cover anti-Semitism, anti-Black racism, anti-Roma racism or Islamophobia. For example, in Germany and Austria a number of cases that were litigated as race/ethnicity discrimination actually dealt with language requirements for certain employment positions and the litigants did not necessarily belong to a racial minority, even though these requirements certainly point to hidden direct discrimination.[107] In another German lawsuit, a first instance

[103] See J Suk, 'Equal by Comparison: Unsettling Assumptions of Antidiscrimination Law' (2007) 55 *American Journal of Comparative Law* 295.

[104] On this point, see M Möschel, 'L'intersectionnalité dans le contentieux de la non-discrimination relatif au domaine de l'emploi en France' in S Hennette-Vauchez, D Roman and M Pichard (eds), *La loi & le genre* (Paris, CNRS Editions, 2014) especially 702–714.

[105] Article 43 of the *Decreto legislativo* 25 July 1998, no. 286, which contains a broad definition of discrimination in many areas of public life (political, economic, cultural, social) on the grounds of race, colour, descent, national or ethnic origins and religious practices and beliefs which extends to both direct and indirect discrimination.

[106] For an overview of some of these cases, see ASGI, W Citti (ed), (n 46).

[107] See, e.g. the judgment in Case C-415/10 *Meister* (n 88) which originated from Germany. See other cases in Germany dealing with language issues litigated as racial/ethnical discrimination: *Arbeitsgericht Berlin*, 11 February 2009, 55 Ca 16952/08 (holding that a premature rejection of an application on the grounds that the applicant was not a native German speaker was *prima facie* evidence of ethnic/racial discrimination); *Arbeitsgericht Hamburg*, 26 January 2010, 25 Ca 282/09 (holding that the German language requirement for postmen was indirect discrimination on the grounds of race/ethnicity); but see to the contrary *Arbeitsgericht Berlin*, 26 September 2009, 14 Ca 10356/07 (holding that the rejection of a job application from an applicant with a migration background due to insufficient knowledge of German does not, by itself, constitute discrimination on the grounds of race/ethnicity); also *Bundesarbeitsgericht*, 28 January 2010, 2 AZR 764/08 (holding that firing a Spanish production aide in the automobile industry because he was not able to read German was not indirect discrimination

tribunal found no race discrimination in a claim brought by a plaintiff from former Eastern Germany whose job application in a Western German company had been rejected.[108]

Lastly, lawyers and judges may simply lack knowledge of the RED (but also of other instruments to fight race discrimination). In one of the first cases on racial profiling in France, the French State was convicted and required to pay the plaintiff a total of €3,000.[109] In terms of the outcome, this was a successful claim. However, in deciding whether or not the French statute transposing a number of non-discrimination directives applies,[110] the Court of Appeals held that the scope of the statute was limited to the employment and social domain and therefore did not apply to the case at hand. Such an outcome was partly possible because the judgment even misquoted the title of the RED as applying only in the employment and social domain.[111]

IV. Future

Having discussed some of the successes and failures of the RED, it is useful to venture a look into the (near) future. As was the case for the childhood and youth of this instrument, its adulthood similarly contains both light and some shadows.

On the bright side, there are activities that touch upon some of the structural issues involving racism in Europe. Importantly, the European Commission has taken first steps in the infringement proceedings against the Czech Republic,[112] Slovakia[113] and Hungary.[114] These countries are accused of Roma education

on the grounds of race/ethnicity). In Austria: *Unabhängiger Verwaltungssenat Steiermark*, 26 August 2013, UVS 30.11. 1V 2012–4 (holding that German language requirement for petrol station employees constitutes indirect discrimination on the grounds of race/ethnicity) and *Landesverwaltungsgericht Tirol*, 14 January 2014, LVwG-2013/23//3455-2 (holding that a job notice looking for graphic designers who are exclusively German native speakers constitutes indirect discrimination on the grounds of race/ethnicity).

[108] *Arbeitsgericht Stuttgart*, 15 April 2010, 17 Ca 8907/09.

[109] *Cour d'appel de Paris*, Pôle 2, Chambre 1, 24 June 2015, no. 13/24255, p. 6.

[110] Loi n° 2008-496 of 27 May 2008.

[111] Directive 2000/43/CE du Conseil du 29 juin 2000: lutte contre les discriminations dans le domaine de l'emploi, de la protection sociale, du relèvement du niveau de la qualité de la vie, de la cohésion économique et sociale et de la solidarité.

[112] 'Brussels Takes Action against Czech Republic over Roma School Discrimination' (*Open Society Foundations*, 25 September 2014). Available at: www.opensocietyfoundations.org/press-releases/brussels-takes-action-against-czech-republic-over-roma-school-discrimination.

[113] European Commission's Decision to Initiate Infringement Proceedings against Slovakia' (*Equinet: European Network of Equality Bodies*, 30 April 2015). Available at: www.equineteurope.org/European-Commission-s-decision-to.

[114] 'European Commission Targets School Segregation of Roma Children in Hungary with Launch of Infringement Procedure' (*Equinet: European Network of Equality Bodies*, 27 May 2016). Available at: www.equineteurope.org/European-Commission-targets-school-segregation-of-Roma-children-in-Hungary-with.

segregation. Notably, it is unprecedented that the infringement not only concerns technical issues relating to the wrongful implementation of the RED (e.g. the lack of independence of an equality body). Instead, the merits of a state's policies are actually entered into. Moreover, the ECtHR already declared a violation of human rights in this area eight years ago, which highlights some failures in the implementation process of the Strasbourg Court's judgments.

The RED has also increasingly been invoked in litigation concerning employment by the EU institutions themselves, a matter scarcely discussed in the EU's anti-discrimination literature so far. An early case decided by the European Court of First Instance dealt with the claim by a Black woman working at the European Central Bank alleging racial harassment and discrimination on the grounds of race.[115] She unsuccessfully claimed the violation of a number of provisions of the RED, *inter alia,* Article 8 on shifting the burden of proof.[116] A more recent case was more successful from the plaintiff's perspective. This decision by the EU Civil Service Tribunal concerned a temporary staff member of the FRA who complained about the decision by the Director of FRA to terminate his contract of indefinite duration as a member of the temporary staff.[117] This termination had been preceded by claims that the staff member had been a victim of ethnic discrimination, because he had been passed over for certain promotions when the FRA was reorganised. Ultimately, a violation of the principle of respect for the rights of the defence was found, but the reference to the RED appears in various points of the judgment.[118] Hence, it would appear that the application of the Race Equality Directive has penetrated into the actions of EU staff as well.

On the dark side, anti-discrimination enthusiasm has waned after the adoption of the relevant EU directives. A proposal to harmonise and to an extent broaden the application of these instruments[119] has been politically stalled for almost ten years, with little hope of this situation changing anytime soon.[120]

Moreover, in terms of case law, the CJEU recently handed down two judgments concerning the Islamic headscarf and the compatibility with EU law of company bylaws or decisions prohibiting the wearing of such a garment in certain work situations. However, neither of the requests for a preliminary ruling from the Belgian and French Supreme Courts invoke the issue of race discrimination in their preliminary references. The French Supreme Court asked whether a customer's wish to have services provided by an employee who does not wear the Islamic

[115] Case T-11/03 *Afari v ECB* EU:T:2004:77.

[116] ibid paras 150–175.

[117] Joined Cases F-106/13 and F-25/14 *DD v European Union Agency for Fundamental Rights (FRA)* EU:F:2016:205.

[118] ibid paras 22 and 43.

[119] European Commission, 'Proposal for a Council Directive on implementing the principle of equal treatment between persons irrespective of religion or belief, disability, age or sexual orientation' COM(2008) 426 final.

[120] Nevertheless, some discussions are still taking place within the Council. See Procedure 2008/0140/APP. Available at: http://eur-lex.europa.eu/procedure/EN/2008_140#1218398.

headscarf could be deemed a genuine occupational requirement which might justify indirect discrimination on the grounds of religion.[121] A parallel could have been drawn with the *Feryn* judgment where the Court rejected the employer's argument that it was his clients not him who did not want immigrant or Moroccan employees. However, neither Advocate-General Kokott[122] nor Advocate-General Sharpston[123] in their almost diametrically opposed opinions, nor the CJEU in the two judgments mentioned the RED or *Feryn*.[124] It would be interesting to see the issue of racism in conjunction with Islamophobia raised more openly in future cases.

The fact that the RED is rarely invoked in preliminary reference procedures is also confirmed by a look at the cases still to be adjudicated. While there are a number of cases pending before the EU tribunals concerning the interpretation of the FED, there is currently only a single pending case invoking the RED – the staff case against the FRA mentioned above where there are remaining issues about the awarded damages.[125] Therefore, one can see a continuation of the trend that contradicts the alleged threat of European courts being flooded with cases dealing with race discrimination.

In conclusion, in its first 18 years, high hopes (but also fears) had been placed on the Race Equality Directive from its birth and indeed, to some extent, its simple fact of existence has already changed the landscape. Nevertheless, there is still a way to go for the RED to fully grow into its potential. Such potential will only flourish if and when a number of actors ranging from social movements, NGOs and various institutions at the national as well as EU level actually help it grow up toward fully fledged adulthood.

[121] Case C-188/15 *Bougnaoui* EU:C:2017:204 (n 84).

[122] Case C-157/15 *Achbita* EU:C:2016:382, Opinion of AG Kokott.

[123] Case C-188/15 *Bougnaoui* EU:C:2016:382, Opinion of AG Sharpston.

[124] Case C-157/15 *Achbita* EU:C:2017:203 (n 84) and Case C-188/15 *Bougnaoui* (n 84).

[125] Joined Cases F-106/13 and F-25/14 *DD v FRA* (n 117). For the pending cases, see the webpage of the CJEU where, on 23 April 2017, by searching for the FED and the RED under pending cases only one case showed up for the RED and eleven cases for the FED. Available at: http://curia.europa.eu/juris/recherche.jsf?cid=42405.

7

Romani Marginalisation after the Race Equality Directive

MORAG GOODWIN*

I. Introduction

The creation of Directive 2000/43/ EC implementing the principle of equal treatment between persons irrespective of racial or ethnic origin (Race Equality Directive (RED))[1] was a landmark achievement. I remember it well. I began working at the European Roma Rights Centre in Budapest in the following September and my new colleagues were still celebrating. It is important that we remember, from our current vantage point more than 15 years on, how important both equality directives[2] were – not simply in establishing an unequivocal standard on discrimination but in stating clearly what kind of Europe we want to be at a time when the far right were again coming out of the shadows. The European Court of Human Rights had failed to provide leadership on the issue of racial discrimination throughout the shocks and upheavals of the 1990s[3] and it was the European Union that stepped up. The Race Equality Directive deserved to be celebrated.

However, 15 years later, it is not so clear that we should still be celebrating – at least, not those of us concerned with Romani exclusion. This chapter considers the RED from the perspective of Romani marginalisation. Roma were then,

* Thanks to the editors for their comments and suggestions. Any remaining errors are, of course, my own.

[1] Council Directive 2000/43/EC implementing the principle of equal treatment between persons irrespective of racial or ethnic origin [2000] OJ L180/22 (Race Equality Directive).

[2] The second non-discrimination directive from the same year was Council Directive 2000/78/EC establishing a general framework for equal treatment in employment and occupation [2000] OJ L303/16. This Directive concerned discrimination based on religion or belief, disability, age or sexual orientation in relation to a much narrower area of social life than the RED.

[3] For more on the failure of the ECtHR to address racial discrimination, see M Goodwin, 'DH and Others v Czech Republic: A Major Set-Back for Non-Discrimination Norms in Europe' (2006) 7 *German Law Journal* 421.

and remain, the most marginalised European group within the Union.[4] I wish to suggest that the Directive has failed to effect change in the situation of many, if not most, Romani communities. This failure can be understood in two ways. The first, and simpler, is that 15 years after the adoption of the RED, there has been little decrease in marginalisation for the vast majority of Roma. It is important to note here that the Directive, and indeed EU action in general, make up only one part of a raft of initiatives directed towards Roma in the last two decades. The most notable is the *Decade of Roma Inclusion* (2005–2015), a collaborative project between international organizations including the World Bank, OSCE, Council of Europe, and various states, both EU and non-EU members.[5] I am thus aware of the impossibility of isolating the effect of the RED on Romani marginalisation from all these other efforts; moreover, there are all sorts of reasons for the ostensible inability of the RED to make much of a concrete difference to Romani lives within the EU that might have nothing to do with the quality of the Directive itself. Nonetheless, if life has improved very little for Romani individuals and communities over the 15-year period, it does not seem unreasonable to suggest that it has somehow failed to make much of a difference (without, of course, saying anything about why that might be the case).

The second argument is, however, more pungent. I wish to suggest that the RED has failed in relation to Romani marginalisation not because of the obvious reason that law alone cannot affect social change – a point that the Commission fully acknowledges[6] – but because the Directive has failed on a deeper, conceptual level to address questions of social inclusion.

II. Romani Margninalisation then and now

In order to understand what the RED has achieved in relation to Romani marginalisation, it is first necessary to detail that marginalisation then and now.[7] It is not possible to provide an exact comparison between 2000 and 2015, as reports on Romani living standards were not necessarily published in those years and often rely on data collected much earlier – sometimes up to eight years earlier. Moreover, the methods of calculating comparative poverty rates or living standards differ

[4] In addition to studies cited in section II of this chapter, see A McGarry, *Romophobia. The Last Acceptable Form of Racism* (London, Zed Books, 2017).

[5] The official website of the decade (www.romadecade.org) appears to have been deactivated (last checked 30 April 2017). Information on the decade is still available on sites of participating international organisations, e.g. the World Bank: www.worldbank.org/en/region/eca/brief/roma.

[6] European Commission, Report on the implementation of the EU Framework for National Roma Integration Strategies 2015, COM(2015) 299 final.

[7] Here, marginalisation refers to a combination of 'objective' marginalisation, as evidenced by socio-economic factors, and 'subjective' marginalisation (ie the feeling of being excluded from society). Where marginalisation becomes extreme, it constitutes socio-economic exclusion.

not only between countries but also by report.[8] It is also important to be aware of the significant differences as to the scope and depth of marginalisation between Romani communities and within communities: certain Romani groupings are more marginalised than others; rural communities face greater access problems than those in urban areas; and women are less likely to have a basic education or access to employment.[9] In addition, reports focus overwhelmingly on countries of Central and Eastern Europe (CEE). This is in part because this is where the majority of Roma live; in part because of the interest in how vulnerable groups were affected by the transition processes; and in part because of the political reality within the EU that sees countries such as France or Italy as being less likely to be subject to investigation for their treatment of Roma. Thus, the attempt here to give substance to Romani marginalisation is more of a broad-brush impression of the situation of Roma in Europe at either end of this 15-year period than a detailed assessment, and it is necessarily focused on CEE countries.[10] Comparisons are given to the majority non-Romani population; more importantly, to the non-Romani majority living in close proximity because this is the best indication that Romani communities are especially marginalized, and most likely on racial or ethnic grounds.

In 2000, the World Bank published a report entitled, *Roma and the Transition in Central and Eastern Europe: Trends and Challenges*.[11] In the report, its author Dena Ringold detailed the challenges facing Romani communities across the region in the wake of the fall of Communism. By 2000, it had become clear that the Roma were one of the groups hardest hit by the collapse of the socialist regimes. The overwhelming representation of the Roma in low-skilled jobs and with low educational levels meant that they were the least well prepared for the transition to a market economy which, in turn, led to what the report terms 'a spiral of impoverishment'.[12] Despite the inherent difficulty of measuring poverty along ethnic lines, the report concluded that Roma were overwhelmingly more likely to be poor in the countries of Central and Eastern Europe (CEE) and were far more likely to fall into poverty. The 1997 household survey in Bulgaria suggested that 84 per cent of Romani households lived below the poverty line set nationally as two-thirds of median income, compared to 36 per cent for ethnic Bulgarians. Similar patterns of comparative deprivation emerged from data in Romania and

[8] On the difficulty of monitoring progress of Romani inclusion due to data collection and comparison problems, see E Friedman, *Decade of Roma Inclusion Progress Report* (United Nations Development Programme, 2015) 16–17. Available at: www.eurasia.undp.org/content/rbec/en/home/library/roma/decade-of-roma-inclusion--progress-report.html.

[9] On this point, see the chapter by R Xenidis in the present volume.

[10] This is, of course, not to suggest that Roma fare better in Western Europe; see the European Roma Rights Centre website for detailed evidence to the contrary. Available at: http://errc.org.

[11] D Ringold, *Roma and the Transition in Central and Eastern Europe: Trends and Challenges* (Washington DC, The World Bank, 2000). Available at: http://siteresources.worldbank.org/EXTROMA/Resources/transition.pdf.

[12] ibid, 10.

Hungary. For example, a comparative sociological study conducted by researchers from Yale University in 2000 (the Yale dataset) found that Hungarian Roma were 13 times more likely than a non-Romani Hungarian to live below the absolute poverty line of $2.15 a day, and 40.3 per cent of Hungarian Roma lived at the relative poverty line of $4.30 a day, compared to only 6.9 per cent of the non-Romani population.[13]

The Yale dataset also detailed significantly inferior living conditions for Romani populations. Romani dwellings were significantly smaller in size than the national average and a lack of access to utilities, such as water, gas, electricity and of access to public services, such as waste collection was a significant issue in many Roma neighbourhoods across the region. Access to running water was a problem for 3.2 per cent of the majority population in Bulgaria but 32.4 per cent of Bulgarian Roma lacked access. The disparity was even greater in relation to connection to sewage (90.3% compared to 52.3%), access to a telephone (80.6% to 12.1%) or to an indoor toilet (65.2% to 15%). A 1999 Council of Europe report thus concluded that '[t]here is evidence … that confirms that the housing of the poor Roma is worse than the most destitute among the dominant society'.[14] Further, Roma frequently lived in settlements or dwellings that were geographically or spatially isolated from their non-Romani neighbours, compounding difficulties in access to services such as health care and education as well as entrenching social isolation.

With regard to educational attainment, Roma were also at a significant disadvantage – they were far less likely to have completed secondary education than the majority population. While over 40 per cent of the Bulgarian majority had completed secondary education in 1997, less than 6 per cent of Romani adults had done so, although this represented a substantial improvement over figures from the beginning of the 1990s.[15] The Yale figures confirmed the achievement gap between Roma and non-Roma and highlighted that the majority of Romani children not only did not complete secondary education but also did not complete primary education. Low educational attainment was also strongly visible in 2000 in western European Romani populations.[16]

[13] D Ringold, MA Orenstein and E Wilkens, *Roma in an Expanding Europe. Breaking the Poverty Cycle* (Washington DC, The World Bank, 2005), 29–30. The Yale dataset is analysed in greater detail in an earlier report: A Revenga, D Ringold and W Tracy, *Poverty and Ethnicity: A Cross-Country Study of Roma Poverty in Central Europe* (Washington DC, The World Bank, 2002).

[14] V Macura, *Housing, Urban Planning and Poverty: Problems Faced by Roma/Gypsy Communities with Particular Reference to Central and Eastern Europe*, Council of Europe Doc. MG-S-ROM (99) 1, Strasbourg, 22 February 1999, 16.

[15] Ringold, Orenstein and Wilkens (n 13) 17–18.

[16] Data from Spain, for example from 1999, suggested adult literacy rates of around 70 per cent for Spanish Roma. Moreover, a 2002 study found that between 1994 and 2001, a majority of Romani children (54%) did not attend school regularly and school dropout rates during secondary school were very high for Romani children: 60 per cent for boys and 80 per cent for girls; Ringold (n 11) 169. The OSCE Report confirmed the general thrust of a disparity between educational attainment for Romani and non-Romani populations across the OSCE area; Organization for Security and Co-operation in Europe, Report on the Situation of Roma and Sinti in the OSCE Area (The Hague, 2000) 65. Available at: www.osce.org/hcnm/42063?download=true.

However, it is in employment that the starkest differences between the Romani and majority populations were to be seen in 2000. In the Czech Republic, for example, whereas 70 per cent of the Romani adult population were unemployed, the figure was only 10 per cent for the population as a whole.[17] Although such figures do not take account of work in the informal sector and thus far more Roma will have been earning income than such figures suggest, the lack of access to formal employment undoubtedly contributed to higher poverty levels. Informal work is less secure, does not provide additional benefits, such as training, and is not protected by health and safety regimes; this entails that informal work is much more likely to be dangerous or cause damage to health than work in the formal sector. Even within the formal sector, Roma were disproportionately to be found in low-skilled jobs, which are likely to be the most hazardous in terms of contamination or accidents.[18]

Data on Romani health in 2000 was scarce and fragmented; however, information from the 1990s suggested a reduced life expectancy of between 10 and 15 years for Roma in relation to the majority population. Estimates for infant mortality showed a similar gap, being almost double that of the non-Romani population.[19] Roma were also more at risk from communicable diseases, as a result of poor nutrition, poor living conditions and overcrowding and a lack of access to health care services. The reality that Roma were more likely to be sick than the majority population not only led to higher mortality rates but also had an impact on the ability to work and to attend school, further aggravating already dire poverty levels.

Based on the evidence above of interrelated and mutually aggravating elements, World Bank researchers drew the conclusion that at the turn of the century, Romani poverty was pervasive, inter-generational and multi-faceted.[20] Given this, it is not surprising that the UNDP concluded in 2003 of Roma living in Bulgaria, the Czech Republic, Hungary, Romania and Slovakia that 'by such measures as literacy, infant mortality and basic nutrition, most of these countries' four to five million Roma endure conditions closer to sub-Saharan Africa than Europe'.[21] However, while Romani communities in CEE were trapped in a poverty cycle in 2000, the basis of their marginalisation was not solely due to the multi-faceted nature of poverty itself.[22] Rather, it is a complex inter-play of poverty and discrimination. In an OSCE report published in 2000, the High Commissioner for

[17] OSCE Report (n 16) 28.

[18] Ringold (n 11), 52.

[19] ibid, 48. Figures are similar for the one western European country studied – Spain. The report notes that Romani life expectancy is on average 13 years lower than that of the majority Spanish population; 165.

[20] ibid, xix.

[21] United Nations Development Programme, *Avoiding the Dependency Trap. The Roma Human Development Report 2003* (UNDP, 2002). Available at: http://hdr.undp.org/en/content/avoiding-dependency-trap.

[22] On unravelling the plural nature of disadvantage, see the excellent work of J Wolff and A de-Shalit, *Disadvantage* (Oxford, Oxford University Press, 2007).

Minorities, Max van der Stoel, stated boldly: 'Discrimination is a defining feature of the Romani experience.'[23] He went on to note that '[a]nti-Romani bias has a profound impact on access to employment opportunities, education, housing and health care'.[24] This anti-Romani bias was both individual and structural (eg in the case of Roma facing structural racial segregation in access to education via placement in 'special' schools or 'special' classes).[25] Moreover, beyond discrimination in all areas of life, anti-Romani bias manifested itself in the years around 2000 in widespread negative stereotyping and in racially motivated violence, both at the hands of state institutions, notably the police and military and from the civilian population, most visible – although certainly not limited to – as attacks by skinhead gangs or individuals.[26]

If we are to sum up the state of Romani marginalisation at the beginning of the twenty-first century, we need to note not only the drastically unequal life chances of Romani individuals when compared to their non-Romani neighbours and compatriots, but also to highlight the widespread nature of violence and public expressions of anti-Romani hostility prevalent in many European countries, not only those of CEE. Moreover, and perhaps more damning even than that conclusion, is that these actions took place within a broad culture of impunity.[27]

If this was the state of Romani life around 2000, what picture emerges in 2015? Again, the data in reports published in or around 2015 are often based on data collected several years previously. In a 2014 report from the UNDP, based on data collected in 2011, the percentage of Roma living in poverty (less than $4.30 a day) declined in the period 2004 to 2011 across all the countries studied.[28] Despite this, the relative poverty rate for Roma remained three to four times higher than the national average, and – perhaps more importantly – twice as high as their non-Romani neighbours (i.e. those living in close proximity who would be expected to share the same low level socio-economic conditions).[29] Roma remain 'educationally poor' compared to their non-Romani neighbours, and overwhelmingly

[23] OSCE Report (n 16) 23.

[24] ibid.

[25] Special education is a euphemism for remedial education and is where a large percentage of Romani children ended up. This education was often of a drastically lower standard than the regular system. For details of Roma and special education, see ERRC, *A Special Remedy: Roma and Schools for the Mentally Handicapped in the Czech Republic* (Budapest, European Roma Rights Centre, 1999). Available at: www.errc.org/article/a-special-remedy-roma-and-schools-for-the-mentally-handicapped-in-the-czech-republic/3680.

[26] Reports of violence against Roma have been well documented by the European Roma Rights Centre across their many types of publications, which can be found on their website by year or by country. Available at: http://errc.org. A good summary of the situation in 2000, largely based on ERRC reporting, is available in the OSCE 2000 Report (n 16) 36–47.

[27] OSCE Report (n 16).

[28] A Ivanov and J Kagin, *Roma Poverty from a Human Development Perspective* (Istanbul, United Nations Development Programme, 2014). The countries studied for the report are Albania, Bosnia and Herzegovina, Bulgaria, Hungary, Croatia, Czech Republic, Moldova, Montenegro, Macedonia and Romania.

[29] ibid, 26.

more likely to be affected by placement in special schools or classes. Many Roma in 2011 were still not completing secondary education; in Slovakia and Hungary, the rates of Roma failing to complete secondary education were 20 and 13 per cent respectively, where the national average is 1 per cent or less.[30] That said, the period did mark an improvement in the number of Romani children completing primary education,[31] as well as in the percentage of children who said that they were able to read and write.

Unemployment rates remain significantly higher for Roma than non-Roma across the region, although the differences appear to be less pronounced than at the start of the period. This has, however, been attributed to the increase in unemployment in general, rather than an increase in Roma joining the labour market.[32] Although there are no cross-country studies on employment discrimination, on the basis of the collected 2011 data, Higgins has concluded that 'differences in educational level – and other individual characteristics – are not on the whole sufficient to explain the gap in employment opportunities and wages between Roma and non-Roma.'[33] The gap, then, is to be explained by discrimination. Roma remain far more likely to be employed in the informal sector than their non-Romani peers, with all the attendant risks which that entails, as noted above. For example, in Bulgaria in 2011, some 46 per cent of Romani men and 32 per cent of Romani women worked in the informal sector as opposed to 10 per cent of men and 5 per cent of women in non-Romani communities. In Hungary, the numbers are triple and in Slovakia, they are double.

The UNDP 2011 survey data notes significant disparities in health between Roma and non-Roma and suggests that the leading cause of Romani health vulnerabilities is the lack of formal employment and attendant access to medical insurance programmes.[34] The UNDP reports that, as of 2011, the gap between the ability of Roma and non-Roma to access medicines was more than 20 percentage points in all countries except Montenegro. Moreover, in Bulgaria, the Czech Republic and Romania, the gap in the ability to afford medicines had increased over the period, suggesting that Roma are falling ever-further behind in their ability to access health care.[35]

In relation to housing and living standards, the 2011 survey found that a third of Romani households across the region lack access to clean water within their dwelling – a figure similar to that in 2000.[36] A large improvement has been realised

[30] ibid, 36–37.

[31] This was the case for all countries except Serbia and the Former Yugoslav Republic of Macedonia; Friedman, *Decade of Roma Inclusion Progress Report* (n 8) 18–19.

[32] ibid, 22.

[33] N O'Higgins, *Roma and Non-Roma in the Labour Market in Central and South Eastern Europe* (Bratislava, United Nations Development Programme, 2012) 45; cited in Friedman (n 8) 22.

[34] Ivanov and Kagin (n 28) 47.

[35] Friedman (n 8) 26–27.

[36] Ivanov and Kagin (n 28) 49.

across the period in the Czech Republic, however, where the share of Roma living without access to water is now on parity with their non-Romani neighbours. Such improvement is not noted in relation to the access to sanitation facilities; Roma continue to lack access compared to their non-Romani neighbours living in close proximity. Sixty-two per cent of Bulgarian Roma lack access to sanitation compared to 18 per cent of similarly situated non-Roma. Roma are less likely to have access to electricity and heating and more Romani households communicate that they are unable to keep their houses warm than their non-Romani neighbours. Likewise, Roma are much more likely to live in substandard accommodation, to have no access to public waste collection and to lack security of tenure than their non-Romani counterparts.

In sum, while improvements in living conditions and access to public services were registered across a 10–15-year period in most countries, they are frequently explained by either rising standards overall – so that the gap between Roma and non-Roma barely changes – or, where the gap closes, it is often a result of falling living standards or lower participation in the labour market by non-Roma rather than an improvement in the Romani position. Moreover, the biggest improvements in Romani socio-economic conditions are registered in non-EU countries, such as Albania,[37] suggesting that EU law and policy are not necessarily the cause of any positive change. The 2011 and 2013 data suggests that most Roma in CEE – despite the improvements that the reports detail – continue to live in 'severe material deprivation' in contrast to the majority average, who are either mainly 'non-materially deprived' (as in the Czech Republic or Hungary) or who are either 'non-materially deprived' or 'materially deprived but not severely', as in Bulgaria or Slovakia.[38] Or, in the opening words of the Fundamental Rights Agency 2011 report on the situation of Roma in 11 EU countries:

> Roma – Europe's largest minority of 10–12 million people – are victims of racism, discrimination and social exclusion. Of those surveyed in this report, one in three is unemployed, 20% are not covered by health insurance, and 90% are living below the poverty. Many face prejudice, intolerance, discrimination and social exclusion in their daily lives. They are marginalised and mostly live in extremely poor socio-economic conditions.[39]

These words were jointly written by the EU Commissioner for Justice, Fundamental Rights and Citizenship, Viviane Redding; the Commissioner for Regional Policy, Johannes Hahn; and the Commissioner for Employment, Social Affairs and Inclusion, László Andor – and they were written 13 years after the enactment of the Race Equality Directive.

[37] ibid, 48.
[38] ibid, 53.
[39] European Union Agency for Fundamental Rights (FRA), *The Situation of Roma in 11 EU Countries – Survey Information at a Glance* (Luxembourg, Publications Office of the European Union, 2012).

III. So What has the Directive Achieved?

It could be argued that I am judging the RED on the basis of unfair criteria: it was never intended to have a direct impact on the improvement of Romani socio-economic conditions. A better judge of the Directive would then be whether or not it is being used by individuals or institutions to tackle instances of discrimination and gain redress for victims. If this is the criteria by which it should be judged, perhaps it is not doing too badly. While the RED may not have inspired substantial improvements to the material conditions in which the majority of Europe's Romani population live, it is being used to tackle anti-Romani discrimination. This alone suggests an impact of sorts. As the Commission reported in 2014, it has led directly to a number of court cases, primarily before national courts, relying upon the transposed Directive.[40] These cases concerned the areas of education, employment and access to services, in Member States from Hungary to Sweden.[41]

Moreover, the Commission's assessment that 'Roma-specific problems often derive from how the legislation is applied at regional or local level'[42] has led to the launch of infringement proceedings against two Member States. In September 2014, the Commission launched proceedings against the Czech Republic in relation to the continuing segregation of Romani children in education; and in 2015, proceedings were launched against Slovakia on similar grounds. The Commission, according to its own report, is also considering proceedings in relation to structural discrimination against Roma in the areas of housing and education in several Member States. There seems little doubt that the Directive is being taken seriously by the Juncker Commission and it seems likely that further examples of enforcement procedures can be expected in the coming period. This, of course, contrasts with the relative inaction of the Commission in relation to the deliberate targeting of Romani EU migrants for expulsion by French authorities in the summer of 2010.[43]

[40] Most Member States do not collect or publish data on the number of court cases on racial or ethnic discrimination, although where data is available (e.g. in the UK) it suggests that the number is very low for most Member States. See FRA, *The Racial Equality Directive: Applications and Challenges* (Luxembourg, Publications Office of the European Union, 2012) 12.

[41] Note, however, that the FRA saw one of the key challenges for the Directive, its lack of use, being due to a low level of awareness in certain Member States (of 550 complaints in relation to housing across the EU between 2000 and 2009, 376 came from only two Member States: Ireland and Finland); FRA, *The Racial Equality Directive* (n 40) 19–20.

[42] European Commission Report (n 6) 9–10.

[43] For more on this, see M Dawson and E Muir, 'Individual, Institutional and Collective Vigilance in Protecting Fundamental Rights in the EU: Lessons from the Roma' (2011) 48 *Common Market Law Review* 751. Also, A McGarry and H Drake, 'The Politicization of Roma as an Ethnic Other: Security Discourse in France and the Politics of Belonging' in U Korkut, G Bucken-Knapp, A McGarry, J Hinnfors and H Drake (eds), *The Politics and Discourses of Migration in Europe* (New York, Palgrave Macmillan, 2013).

Moreover, while the Directive has made little impact on European-level jurisprudence,[44] when presented with a second opportunity to examine it, the Court of Justice of the European Union (CJEU) delivered a ruling that both cemented and extended its protection.[45] This is doubly significant for our consideration here because the case – *CHEZ v Nikolova* (2015)[46] – concerned the allegation of discrimination again Roma, albeit that the applicant was non-Romani. The CJEU confirmed that one does not need to be a member of the targeted group to be adversely affected by discrimination on ethnic or racial grounds and thus to benefit from the Directive's protections.[47] More significantly, the Court took a flexible line on the use of comparators when adducing unequal treatment, finding that the comparator was not districts that were plagued (allegedly, as no evidence of a problem was put forward by the electricity company) by similar problems of interference with electricity meters but all 'consumers of electricity who are supplied by the same distributor within an urban area'.[48] This finding is likely to expand the scope of application of the Directive to new situations. Further, and very much to be welcomed, the Court found that the disadvantage suffered concerned not only the practical difficulty as a consumer of being able to monitor one's own electricity consumption, but also the 'offensive and stigmatizing nature of the practice'.[49] This last finding of the destructive psychological impact of racial discrimination may not seem particularly significant; it is arguably important, however, in a context in which the European Court of Human Rights has failed to emphasise the psychological damage done by the racial segregation of Romani children into inferior education alongside the damage to their education.[50] It is also perhaps worth noting that this case concerned the Bulgarian National Anti-Discrimination Commission as the respondent party – a body that itself is a product of the RED and one, on the evidence of this case, that seems to be working rather well.[51]

[44] In the opinion of the Commission, there have been very few cases before the CJEU under the preliminary reference procedure; Annexes to the Joint Report on the application of Council Directive 2000/43/EC of 29 June 2000 implementing the principle of equal treatment between persons irrespective of racial or ethnic origin ('Racial Equality Directive') and of Council Directive 2000/78/EC of 27 November 2000 establishing a general framework for equal treatment in employment and occupation ('Employment Equality Directive'), COM(2014) 2 final, 19.

[45] The CJEU refused jurisdiction to hear an earlier case on the same topic, also from Bulgaria, but in which the applicant was Romani, because it ruled – against the advice of AG Kokott – that the Commission for Protection against Discrimination ('the KZD') did not have standing to make a preliminary ruling request because it did not accept the capacity of the referring authority as a court or tribunal within the meaning of Article 267 TEU – Case C-394/11 *Valeri Hariev Belov v CHEZ Elektro Balgaria AD* EU:C:2012:585.

[46] Case C-83/14 *CHEZ Razpredelenie Bulgaria AD v Komisia za zashtita ot diskriminatsia* EU:C:2015:480 (*CHEZ*). For more on this case, see the chapter by M Möschel in this volume.

[47] On the allocation of the burden of proof in this case, see the chapter by K Henrard in the present volume.

[48] Case C-83/14 *CHEZ* (n 46) para 90.

[49] ibid, paras 87, 108.

[50] M Goodwin, 'Taking on Racial Segregation: the European Court of Human Rights at a Brown v Board of Education moment?' (2009) 170 *Rechtsgeleerd Magazijn Themis* 93.

[51] Article 13 of Directive 2000/43/EC requires Member States to establish a national body for the promotion of equal treatment without regard to racial or ethnic difference.

Putting aside, then, the fact of the sheer paucity of cases at the European level involving the RED, when it gets a case, the CJEU is willing to enforce it.[52]

In addition, one can make an argument for the indirect impact of the RED on the campaign for Roma rights. It is perhaps not unreasonable to suggest that the (eventual) victory in *DH and Others v Czech Republic* (2007) before the European Court of Human Rights was inspired to some extent by the Directive and by the Strasbourg Court's desire not to see the EU steal its leadership position on fundamental rights issues. The Court's decision to reverse its position and accept the shift in the burden of proof once a *prima facie* case has been established – central to the applicant's case in *DH* – was likely made easier by the Directive's clear stance on burden of proof shifting.[53]

Clearly, then, the RED has raised the standard of legal protection against racial discrimination in Europe, in the national courts, at the EU level and within the Council of Europe system and these protections have been of some significance to Romani applicants. Yet, another standard by which we might judge the success of the Directive is the extent to which it has affected or inspired changes in approach or attitude towards Roma. In other words, has the Directive helped to create the tolerant Europe that it identifies in its preamble? Unfortunately not. The Commission has acknowledged in a recent report that what it calls 'anti-Gypsyism', as well as hate speech and hate crime towards Roma, has been on the rise in the last few years.[54] A 2014 Pew Research Centre study found that the populations of nearly all Member States hold deeply unfavourable views of the Roma, reaching majorities in several Member States of Western Europe (Italy: 85%; France: 66%; Greece: 53%; UK: 50%).[55] More worryingly, the report also notes that politicians and public authorities frequently fail to condemn such activities. While the Commission report appears to suggest that this rise in anti-Romani sentiment is due to the economic crisis, this explanation is too simplistic. The 2016 study by the same organisation found similar levels of anti-Romani sentiment in comparison to 2014 levels, despite the improving economic climate in most of the countries surveyed. Another reason for distrusting the Commission's causal explanation is that Roma remain the most negatively viewed group in Europe in the 2016 survey, despite the refugee crisis and the attendant challenges to European self-identity.[56]

[52] On this point, see also the chapter by K Henrard in this volume.

[53] Goodwin, 'Taking on Racial Segregation' (n 50). See also the chapter by K Henrard in the present volume.

[54] European Commission Report (n 6) 9. See also U Belavusau, 'Anti-Roma Hate Speech in the Czech Republic, Hungary, and Poland' in M Goodwin and P De Hert (eds), *European Roma Integration Efforts – A Snapshot* (Brussels, Brussels University Press, 2013) 141.

[55] Pew Research Center, *A Fragile Rebound for EU Image on Eve of European Parliament Elections* (2014), 30–33. Available at: www.pewglobal.org/2014/05/12/chapter-4-views-of-roma-muslims-jews/; cited in European Commission Report (n 6) 9.

[56] R Wike, B Stokes and K Simmons, *Europeans Fear Wave of Refugees Will Mean More Terrorism, Fewer Jobs* (Pew Research Center, 2016). Available at: www.pewglobal.org/2016/07/11/europeans-fear-wave-of-refugees-will-mean-more-terrorism-fewer-jobs/lede-chart-2/.

Dislike and distrust of Romani neighbours remains stronger than dislike of immigrants, even following incidents such as those in Cologne at the 2015 New Year celebrations. Even more noteworthy are the study's findings that although anti-Muslim sentiment has unsurprisingly risen since the Daesh-inspired attacks in France, Belgium and elsewhere in the last two years, anti-Romani sentiment is still higher than dislike of Muslims.[57]

Moreover, more detailed consideration of the figures suggests a broadly negative view of Roma across the political spectrum: while voters on the right dislike Roma in significantly higher numbers, left-leaning voters still record high levels of anti-Romani views. The 2014 figures suggest, for example, that at least 30 per cent in Germany and 54 per cent in France of those who placed themselves on the ideological left had strongly negative attitudes towards Roma.[58]

All of this suggests that anti-Romani sentiments remain a strong undercurrent of mainstream European society, as well as European identity.[59] Further, while the figures have improved over the longer term since 1991, the RED appears to have had no noticeable effect on the degree or depth of hostility towards Roma; gradual declines in anti-Romani sentiments, if any, appear to be part of a longer-term trend and there is no significant departure from that trend in the years following the Directive.[60] Unscrupulous politicians continue to – successfully – use Roma as a scapegoat for circumstances or policies that the majority do not like, whether in Hungary or France; correctly understanding that targeting Roma with their prejudiced rhetoric will often refocus discontent.[61]

In addition to widespread anti-Romani sentiment, actual discrimination against Roma – in education, housing, the workplace, and access to services – remains an equal constant. In the countries of Central and Eastern Europe, between a quarter and nearly two-thirds of Romani children attend segregated schools or classes; the problem of Romani children being placed in special schools for children with mental disabilities is still present, with an average of 20 per cent of all Romani children being so placed in the Czech and Slovak Republics.[62] Moreover, discrimination continues into adulthood, with the majority of Roma surveyed across the Member States reporting discrimination in their search for employment.

[57] For more on the depth and breadth of anti-Romani feeling across Europe as a whole, see McGarry, *Romophobia* (n 4).

[58] Pew Research Center, *A Fragile Rebound for EU Image* (n 55).

[59] On the importance of anti-Romani sentiment in relation to migration for the formation of European identity, see McGarry (n 4) 211–245.

[60] Pew Research Center report (n 55) suggests that since 1991 anti-Romani sentiment has been declining: in 1991, levels of anti-Romani sentiment were significantly higher (e.g. in Germany there was a drop from 60 per cent to 42 per cent between 1991 and 2014).

[61] See, e.g. B Rorke, '10 Things They Said about Roma in Hungary' (*European Roma Rights Centre blog*, 27 October 2015) Available at: www.errc.org/blog/10-things-they-said-about-roma-in-hungary/83. The 'they' of the title are senior Hungarian politicians.

[62] FRA, *Roma Survey – Data in Focus. Education: the Situation of Roma in 11 Member States* (Luxembourg, Publications Office of the European Union, 2014).

All in all, the Fundamental Rights Agency has concluded that discrimination against Roma in the areas of education, housing and employment continues to constitute a structural barrier preventing their full participation in society.[63] Moreover, while the most recent Commission report on Romani integration takes stock of measures introduced within the Member States to address discrimination – such as promoting inter-cultural dialogue, introducing segments on Romani culture and history into school curricula or providing inter-cultural training for civil servants and frontline public service providers – it concludes, in its own words, that 'no real improvements can be seen on the ground'.[64] In other words, discrimination and anti-Romani feeling are as ripe as ever.

At the same time, therefore, that the Directive is actively being used, albeit in a limited way, it appears to be needed more than ever. In the 15 years since the Directive's launch, the dire socio-economic conditions of Romani communities have barely improved; discrimination against Roma across all areas of life continues to constitute a barrier to their participation in European societies; and anti-Romani sentiment is, by the Commission's own reckoning, not only not declining but is actually on the rise. It seems fair to conclude that the Directive has had little impact in reducing racial discrimination against members of Romani communities, in improving their material lives or in changing attitudes towards Romani neighbours. That said, the Directive has arguably been fairly successful in providing a legal remedy to Romani victims and in creating a standard to which Member States can be held accountable. This is not nothing. If the prime purpose of the Directive is to provide a legal frame for tackling racial discrimination, it goes some way to achieving this. And yet, another of its stated purposes is to give effect to the principle of equal treatment. If this is the standard to which we hold the Directive, it has indisputably failed in relation to the most vulnerable of Europe's peoples.[65]

IV. Respecting 'Relevant' Difference?

Notwithstanding the above, taking the RED to task for failing to tackle racial discrimination against Roma would arguably be unreasonable. It is well known that law alone is unlikely to bring about social change: the European institutions are clearly aware of this. The RED is only part of the picture of Romani integration efforts. Indeed, as the Commission itself states: 'The Commission recognises that legislation alone is not enough to resolve the deep-rooted social exclusion

[63] ibid. This data is also drawn from Western European states.

[64] European Commission, Assessing the implementation of the EU Framework for National Roma Integration Strategies and the Council Recommendation on Effective Roma integration measures in the Member States 2016, COM(2016) 424, 8.

[65] The Directive's title states that it is to implement the principle of equal treatment. See also FRA, *The Racial Equality Directive* (n 40) 9.

of the Roma and the prejudice they still face.'[66] Integration is instead to be achieved by combining the RED with policy, funding and national legislation in the context of the Framework for National Roma Integration Strategies, adopted in 2011.[67]

I have taken issue with the neo-liberal approach that the Framework takes to European citizenship elsewhere.[68] Here, I wish to focus on anti-discrimination law to make a similar point. My deeper disagreement with the RED concerns the reasons that it has failed to tackle the mistreatment and abuse of Romani individuals and communities over the last 15 years. Moreover, I am not interested in the external factors that have contributed to that failure, such as the economic crisis, the refugee crisis or the depth of historical hostility, but on why the Directive fails on its own terms – and this concerns its relationship to difference. What I wish to suggest is that the Directive is not interested in difference but only in 'surface' or 'skin' difference. The RED focuses on the difference that is *visual* and not *substantive*. This point is not new and the Directive has long been subject to criticism by those who contest its focus on formal rather than substantive equality.[69] This discussion concerns the focus of most anti-discrimination standards – the RED is not unique here – on equality of opportunities rather than equality of results; that is, they focus on smaller, individual wrongs in the present rather than on the position of discriminated groups as a result of historical wrongs.[70] As a consequence, the position of a group within society or systemic discrimination, as opposed to individual acts of discrimination, go unaddressed. It is for this reason, of course, that the Directive includes a provision on positive action. Article 5 exempts positive or remedying action from the prohibition on equal treatment but it does not require Member States to take such action. EU gender equality rules – an older, more developed, part of the body of EU equal treatment rules – suggest that any scope for action under this provision will be strictly reviewed and thus limited.[71] The Directive thus only pays lip service to the problem. This focus on individual equality rather than the position of groups within society entails that it is of little use in tackling the socio-economic deprivation that is so entangled with anti-Romani discrimination in together creating

[66] European Commission, Joint Report on the application of Council Directive 2000/43/EC and of Council Directive 2000/78/EC, COM(2014) 2 final, 13.

[67] European Commission, An EU Framework for National Roma Integration Strategies up to 2020, COM(2011) 173 final.

[68] M Goodwin and R Buijs, 'Making Good Citizens of the Roma: A Closer Look at the EU Framework for National Roma Integration Strategies' (2013) 14 *German Law Journal* 2041.

[69] See, e.g. E Howard, 'The EU Race Directive: Time for Change?' (2007) 8 *International Journal of Discrimination and the Law* 237, 241–243.

[70] See, e.g. M Bell, *Anti-Discrimination Law and the European Union* (Oxford, Oxford University Press, 2002); S Fredman, *Discrimination Law* (Oxford, Oxford University Press, 2002); B Hepple, *Equality. The New Legal Framework* (Oxford, Hart Publishing, 2011).

[71] See M Poiares Maduro, 'The European Court of Justice and Anti-Discrimination Law' (2005) 2 *European Anti-Discrimination Law Review* 21.

Romani marginalisation.[72] Moreover, the focus on an individual *instance* of discrimination also prevents the Directive from addressing the complexity of discrimination across inter-locking areas, such as housing, health, education and so on.[73] What is so pernicious about the intersection of poverty and discrimination that constitutes group-based social marginalisation is the way in which disadvantage spreads from one area of life to another. As we know from the excellent work of Jonathan Wolff and Avner de-Shalit, marginalisation (or disadvantage, which is the term that they use) is plural.[74] This is an important reason why the Directive is not a particularly helpful tool in addressing Romani social exclusion or marginalisation.

I want to go a step further, however, and suggest that the Directive's main failure in tackling Romani marginalisation comes not because it does not recognise or convincingly attempt to rectify historical inequalities, nor because it sees racial discrimination as a deviation from a norm and thus as a series of isolated incidents instead of acknowledging it as an institutionalised practice;[75] but because it fails at a conceptual level to recognise deeper difference. We view discrimination against a base norm that assumes a shared understanding of what social inclusion is or looks like. This is true for all non-discrimination instruments, whether they are tackling discrimination on gender grounds, sexuality, religion, disability or any other protected ground. Why this matters for racial or ethnic equality is that this ground is far more likely to involve cultural difference from the majority. Marginalisation or social exclusion is most often an interaction between discrimination and poor socio-economic conditions, in which group-based discrimination feeds off poverty which, in turn, ensures that this poverty becomes a trap.[76] This is certainly the case for Roma.

[72] The RED does, of course, include a provision on indirect discrimination, which speaks to the notion of broader systemic discrimination, but it nonetheless addresses only individual acts of discrimination. For more on the need for a focus on the position of Roma within European societies as a group, see McGarry (n 4). For a broader critique that the EU focuses too much on justice as individual rights at the expense of redistributive justice, see A Somek, 'The Preoccupation with Rights and the Embrace of Inclusion: A Critique' in D Kochenov, G de Búrca and A Williams (eds), *Europe's Justice Deficit* (Oxford, Hart Publishing, 2015).

[73] For more on the inter-locking nature of discrimination against Roma, see M Goodwin, 'Multidimensional Exclusion: Viewing Romani Poverty through the Nexus of Race and Poverty' in D Schiek (ed), *European Union Discrimination Law: Comparative Perspectives on Multidimensional Equality Law* (Abingdon, Routledge, 2008). On the inter-locking and plural nature of social exclusion more generally, Wolff and de-Shalit, *Disadvantage* (n 22). This point has been made more recently by the FRA; see FRA, *The Racial Equality Directive* (n 40) 23.

[74] For more on disadvantage spreading, see Wolff & de-Shalit (n 22). See also M Goodwin, 'Understanding Social Exclusion in Under 7 Minutes'. Available at: https://videocollege.uvt.nl/Mediasite/Play/b6caaf31c57f4513bfec355b1f5c5ce21d.

[75] On this last point see Z Jovanovic, 'Why Europe's "Roma Decade" Didn't Lead to Inclusion' (*Open Society Foundations*, 21 September 2015). Available at: www.opensocietyfoundations.org/voices/why-europe-s-roma-decade-didn-t-lead-inclusion.

[76] For a quick guide to the interplay between poverty and prejudice, see Goodwin, 'Multidimensional Exclusion' (n 73).

However, in addition to knowing that this type of marginalisation is structured and sustained by a web of institutionalised practices and relations, we also know that the experience of marginalisation is specific to each community and group. While it is possible to deduce the existence of marginalisation from the outside by measuring living standards and levels of discrimination and abuse, this at best projects our understanding of what it is to be marginalised onto the targeted. It does not tell us how marginalisation is experienced or felt: whether it is experienced as marginalisation and, if so, in what way. Nor does it not tell us the necessary details for understanding what the enabling factors or, conversely, the corrosive factors are – keys, as it were, to unlocking the inter-connectedness across the plural areas of disadvantage.[77] Should one focus, for example, on education or on health or housing, as the place to begin in breaking open the inter-locking nature of disadvantages? While exclusion is plural and inter-locking, it is not possible to target everything all at once: so where is action prioritised, and who decides? More importantly, an external perspective cannot tell us what changes those affected would be willing to make to see their living standards increase or the exclusion decline. If change always includes losses as well as gains, if it involves destruction as well as new opportunities, what can be sacrificed and, again, who decides? Acknowledging the depth of cultural diversity across Europe means accepting that there are some practices that groups may not be willing to give up in order to overcome their marginalisation – whether because the practice has become too central to their identity or because they do not experience marginalisation in the way that we assume they must.[78]

An external perspective on marginalisation, moreover, assumes an end-goal that may not be shared by the community affected. To be viewed as marginalised solely from an external perspective is purely to be understood as marginalised *from* something; this something is the norm or baseline for a society. Social inclusion for EU policies and instruments – as reflected, *inter alia*, in the Commission's 2020 Strategy – is integration into the life that the majority live.[79] This much seems obvious, albeit worth stating. Yet that way of life can be defined in any number of ways. Within the European Union, however, the majority way of life is defined primarily in economic terms, despite the professed commitments to the social ones.[80] This primarily economic understanding of what the EU is about also conditions the conceptual underpinning of the RED, where the underlying

[77] Wolff and de-Shalit (n 22) 133–154.

[78] It is important to note here that not only is Romani identity non-homogenous across Europe's Romani communities (i.e. there are a wide variety of cultural practices and identification with these practices) but that it is obviously subject to change via both internal and external interaction.

[79] European Commission, *Europe 2020: A Strategy for Smart, Sustainable and Inclusive Growth* (3 March 2010). Available at: http://ec.europa.eu/europe2020/index_en.htm.

[80] From a wealth of literature on this subject, see C Joerges, 'Will the Welfare State Survive European Integration?' (2011) 1 *European Journal of Social Law* 4; E Christodoulidis 'The European Court of Justice and "Total Market" Thinking' (2013) 14 *German Law Journal* 2005. See also this discussion in reference to EU Romani policy, Goodwin and Buijs (n 68).

base norm is participation in a market economy. Put more bluntly, the Directive is concerned only with that difference that is irrelevant to integration into the European economy.[81]

That the market is central to the aims of the Directive can be seen in the text itself. Paragraph 8 of the preamble highlights the 2000 Employment Guidelines agreed at the 1999 Helsinki summit and stresses the need 'to foster conditions for a socially inclusive labour market by formulating a coherent set of policies aimed at combating discrimination against groups such as ethnic minorities'. Paragraph 9 mentions the importance of tackling racial and ethnic discrimination for 'the attainment of a high level of employment and of social protection, the raising of the standard of living and quality of life, economic and social cohesion and solidarity'. The importance of avoiding distortions to the labour market is thus front and centre and provides the frame in which social goals, such as social protection and social cohesion are to be understood. This interpretation is given weight by an FRA report, which highlights that the Directive was drafted at a time when economic growth was producing labour market shortages.[82] These shortages were to be filled by foreign workers and the Directive was needed to ensure the cohesion of a mixed workforce.[83] In addition, the report notes as part of its background to the creation of the Directive that it was deemed important for the continued well-being of the European economy and to 'maximise performance', to be able to attract workers with the best skills and qualifications without regard to race or ethnicity. Moreover, that a diverse workforce was more attractive to an increasingly diverse consumer base was also highlighted. Seen in this light, the Directive is not a manifestation of the EU's commitment to cultural diversity. It is not a cherishing of difference. Instead it aims to remove irrelevant differences between workers who create instability in the workforce and threaten economic growth, at the same time as being a statement of European values as given in Article 6 TEU.[84] It is, of course, a central part of market liberalism that our values are those that support the functioning of the market.[85]

The Race Equality Directive therefore forms part of a broader shift within the European Union in the approach to Roma from minority rights to social inclusion;[86] from a focus on difference to one that stresses integration into the

[81] McGarry makes a similar point when he characterises EU policy towards Roma as being focused on redistribution at the expense of recognition. As McGarry puts it, EU policy focuses on job creation and market participation and neglects anti-Romani sentiment, as well as the need for a positive recognition of the contribution of Roma and Romani culture to European society. See A McGarry, 'The Dilemma of the European Union's Roma Policy' (2011) 32 *Critical Social Policy* 126, 131.

[82] FRA, *The Racial Equality Directive* (n 40) 10.

[83] ibid. These views are not the FRA's own but the result of conversations about the Directive with unidentified social partners.

[84] Treaty on European Union [2016] OJ C202/1 (TEU).

[85] See, *inter alia*, the contributions by S Roy, 'Justice as Europe's Signifier' and D Augenstein 'We the People: EU Justice as Politics' in Kochenov, de Búrca and Williams (eds), *Europe's Justice Deficit* (n 72).

[86] This has been well argued in the context of the EU's approach to Roma in E Sobotka and P Vermeersch, 'Governing Human Rights and Roma Inclusion: Can the EU be a Catalyst for Local Change?' (2012) 34 *Human Rights Quarterly* 800, 802–809.

majority way of life. This integration, provided for in the Framework for National Roma Integration Strategies, is centred on formal participation in the labour market, whereby economic integration is a pre-condition for social integration. Integration, therefore, at least as it is envisaged for EU citizens of Romani origin, must be preceded by participation in the formal wage economy.[87]

This matters because equal treatment that has a pre-determined end goal of integration into the formal economy is not equal treatment. It is coercive, even if we cannot imagine that anyone would want any other way of life than the one that we enjoy. Moreover, it fails to accept the marginalised group as equal participants in society but sees them instead as grateful recipients of inclusion. While ostensibly concerned about equal treatment, the end-goal of integration fails to acknowledge the equality of those who are marginalised. To treat Roma as equals means to allow Romani individuals and communities to give concrete form to their own marginalisation, based on what matters to them, and to allow that to form the basis of an open dialogue about changing institutionalised practices of discrimination and exclusion. Inclusion and integration must have a mutually defined outcome; it cannot be a march towards a pre-determined end goal. To be clear, I am not suggesting that Romani communities enjoy their marginalisation and prefer it to participation in the wage economy; nor am I suggesting that any cultural difference is a cause or justification for discriminatory practices or dire living conditions. I am arguing instead for a recognition that integration into the formal economy comes at a price and to note that we cannot assume that we know what culturally different communities actually want (ie whether communities are willing to make the trade-off of a higher standard of living for a more conformist lifestyle). Maybe it is a price that Romani individuals and communities wish to pay, but maybe it is not. The only way that we will know the answer to what marginalisation means to Romani communities is to ask in a manner in which the answer we receive is not already pre-conditioned by the construction of the question.[88]

V. Concluding Reflections

There is nothing new in highlighting that the history of European integration has been dominated by economic priorities from the start; more recent criticisms, particularly in relation to the European response to the 2008 economic meltdown, have noted the dominance of neo-liberal thinking within the European institutions.[89] Yet the impact of this has not yet been explored in any detail in

[87] Goodwin and Buijs (n 68) 2052–2054.

[88] On the use of public reflexive equilibrium as a methodology for asking open questions, see Wolff and de-Shalit (n 22) 119–128.

[89] See, e.g. Christodoulidis (n 80).

relation to the EU's strategies on inclusive growth and integration or to its anti-discrimination framework in particular. This chapter has barely scratched the surface of the work that needs to be done here.

Returning to the question of whether or not the creation of the RED should still be celebrated today, the FRA report notes that the 'social actors' with whom it spoke to gauge opinions on its success report that the importance of the Directive lies in its symbolic role – that it sent, and continues to send, an unambiguous message that discrimination on the basis of racial or ethnic origin was (and is) unacceptable. This is undoubtedly true and the Directive is an important part of a European legal framework for those who face discrimination purely on the basis of the colour of their skin or ethnic origin. However, group-based social exclusion is vastly more complex and requires instruments that are able to see, accept and promote difference. The Directive, then, is also a symbol of another Europe: one that sees formal economic participation as central to what it is to be European; a Europe that, despite its commitment to respect cultural diversity, is only interested in diversity that is skin deep. I am still glad that the Race Equality Directive exists but, seen from the perspective of Romani marginalisation, I am no longer sure that it is worth celebrating.

The title of this volume asks contributors to reflect on the achievements, pitfalls and prospects of EU anti-discrimination law and I have been asked to suggest reforms to the RED that would ensure better ('proper') protection for Roma in Europe. The easiest response to this is that the law is not able to bring about the celebration of Romani difference and European diversity that is needed to begin the process of addressing anti-Romani sentiment and discrimination.[90] The battle for hearts and minds cannot be won by legal claims about individual instances of discrimination. If it was needed, this chapter has provided evidence of this. Yet it is possible to imagine legal reforms that could make a difference – in conjunction with the celebration of difference – but it requires a sea-change in thinking about discrimination within the EU. It would require a shift away from individual actions to compulsory (as opposed to voluntary) group-based positive measures to rectify historical wrongs and provide genuine equal opportunities. More importantly, it would require an open conversation at all levels, but above all at the local level, about Romani experiences of marginalisation, and about hopes and fears for integration. Positive measures will need to be tailored to each context and be the product of co-creation between Romani and non-Romani communities, and between these communities and the state that must pay for and enforce positive measures. If EU anti-discrimination policy can provide a frame in which such processes can begin, I will happily join in the celebrations 15 years from now.

[90] For a good example of such celebration, see the launch in June 2017 of the European Roma Institute for Arts and Culture in Berlin; K Connolly, '"A place to call our own": Europe's first Roma cultural centre opens in Berlin' (*The Guardian*, 8 June 2017). Available at: www.theguardian.com/world/2017/jun/08/roma-artists-launch-art-cultural-centre-institute-berlin.

PART III

Religion

8

Religious Discrimination in the Workplace

Achbita and *Bougnaoui*

EUGENIA RELAÑO PASTOR

> When the employer concludes a contract of employment with an employee, he does not buy that person's soul.
>
> Advocate General Sharpston in *Bougnaoui*[1]

I. Introduction

In the first cases to reach the Court of Justice of the European Union (CJEU) concerning discrimination on the grounds of religion under the Framework Equality Directive (FED),[2] national courts in Belgium and France asked whether the dismissal of two Muslim women by a private employer because they wore a religious headscarf at work were direct discrimination or whether exceptions to FED allow for such dismissals. The questions asked by the referring national courts were different. In *Achbita* (2017),[3] the Belgian court asked whether the employer's neutrality rule amounts to direct discrimination, while in *Bougnaoui* (2017),[4] the French court asked whether the neutrality requirement can amount to an *occupational requirement* (Article 4(1) FED),[5] if based on a client's demand.

[1] Case C-188/15 *Asma Bougnaoui and Association de défense des droits de l'homme (ADDH) v Micropole SA* EU:C:2016:553, Opinion of AG Sharpston, para 73.

[2] Council Directive 2000/78/EC establishing a general framework for equal treatment in employment and occupation [2000] OJ L303/16 (Framework Equality Directive).

[3] Case C-157/15 *Samira Achbita, Centrum voor gelijkheid van kansen en voor racismebestrijding v G4S Secure Solutions NV* EU:C:2017:203.

[4] Case C-188/15 *Asma Bougnaoui and Association de défense des droits de l'homme (ADDH) v Micropole SA* EU:C:2017:204.

[5] Art 4 FED describes occupational requirements as follows: 'Notwithstanding Article 2(1) and (2), Member States may provide that a difference of treatment which is based on a characteristic related to

In the *Achbita* case, a claim was brought by an employee in Belgium working as a receptionist for G4S, a global security company. No uniform was provided for Ms Achbita, but when she began wearing the Muslim headscarf, the company claimed to have a written policy of 'neutrality' in the workplace, meaning a bar on clothing expressing a religious, philosophical or political belief. G4S dismissed Ms Achbita and the next day, a written policy came into force. Advocate General Kokott suggested in her opinion that G4S's policy constituted only indirect discrimination that could be justified.[6] In the *Bougnaoui* case, an employee was ordered by her French employer not to wear her headscarf following an objection from a customer. When Ms Bougnaoui refused to remove her headscarf, she was dismissed. In her opinion, Advocate General Sharpston concluded that Ms Bougnaoui had been subject to direct discrimination.

On 14 March 2017, the Grand Chamber of the CJEU issued its judgments in these cases. In both cases, the CJEU interpreted the FED to imply that limitations on employees wearing religious headscarves can be acceptable if they are based on an internal policy of political, philosophical or religious neutrality set by the employer. Still, the Court in its judgments arguably veers towards direct discrimination in *Bougnaoui* and towards indirect discrimination in *Achbita*.

These two cases raise fundamental questions about the right to manifest one's religion and belief in the workplace, particularly in light of the divergent views of the Advocates General, as to the type of discrimination that occurred. This contribution will start with an analysis of the Advocates General's opinions, as the very divergent approaches taken in the two opinions deserve to be highlighted. Since *Achbita* and *Bougnaoui* are the first cases raising grounds of religious discrimination in the form of a lack of reasonable accommodation under the FED, the assessment by the European Union (EU) judiciary of these cases will have an impact on thousands of women across the EU who wear headscarves as a matter of religious conviction.[7] Furthermore, the more extensive reasoning in the opinions, as compared to the judgments, serve as means to highlight several problematic aspects of the underlying assumptions and conceptual choices. Subsequently, the most relevant holdings by the CJEU are considered, with particular attention being paid to the Court's lack of engagement with the concept of duties of reasonable accommodation. By way of conclusion, some recommendations are formulated on how EU anti-discrimination law can be improved. The following chapter in

any of the grounds referred to in Article 1 shall not constitute discrimination where, by reason of the nature of the particular occupational activities concerned or of the context in which they are carried out, such a characteristic constitutes a genuine and determining occupational requirement, provided that the objective is legitimate and the requirement is proportionate.'

[6] Case C-157/15 *Samira Achbita, Centrum voor gelijkheid van kansen en voor racismebestrijding v G4S Secure Solutions NV* EU:C:2016:382, Opinion of AG Kokott.

[7] European Union Agency for Fundamental Rights, *Second European Union Minorities and Discrimination Survey. Muslims – selected findings* (Luxembourg, Publications Office of the European Union, 2017).

this volume will then zoom in on the reasoning developed by the Court in these two cases.[8]

II. Complex Questions Raised by the AG Opinions in *Achbita* and *Bougnaoui*: Religion, Personal Identity, Neutrality and Causality

One of the most problematic and forgotten kinds of discrimination is that based on religious manifestation.[9] Before the EU Equality Directives were adopted in 2000, the CJEU had only once before ruled on a claim of discrimination on grounds of religion – in 1976, almost a quarter of a century earlier. In *Prais* (1976),[10] the plaintiff complained about the scheduling of a written recruitment test on a Jewish holiday on which, according to her religion, she was not permitted to travel or write. The Court carried out a balancing exercise, weighing the interest of the candidate's religious practices against the principle of equality, according to which all written tests should be administered under the same conditions and on the same dates for all candidates. The Court admitted that 'if a candidate informs the appointing authority that religious reasons make certain dates impossible for him, the appointing authority should take this into account in fixing the date for written tests, and endeavour to avoid such dates'.[11] Arguably, a reasonable accommodation, albeit in its embryonic stage, was visible in the legal reasoning of *Prais*.[12]

A decade after *Prais*, the Luxembourg Court in *Steymann* (1988) ruled on another religious issue relating to economic activities carried out by members of a religious or spiritual community.[13] The Court accepted that remuneration can be fulfilled in other forms than money (e.g. services provided by the employer to

[8] As will be argued more fully in Section III of this chapter and in Chapter 9, the judgments are rather disappointing as they do not provide enough guidance to national courts on the criteria to be taken into consideration when assessing alleged religious discrimination. In the process, the CJEU has lost a golden opportunity to better position itself as regards reasonable accommodation for religion and belief in the workplace. For a wider overview of the concept of reasonable accommodation, albeit in the context of disability, see the chapter by L Lourenço and P Pohjankoski in the present volume.

[9] In some countries, such as Austria, Denmark or Sweden, courts have found that a prohibition on wearing a headscarf during work could only be deemed indirect discrimination. See, e.g. E Relaño Pastor, 'Towards Substantive Equality for Religious Believers in the Workplace? Two Supranational European Courts, Two Different Approaches' (2016) *Oxford Journal of Law and Religion* 19. For some authors, like Katayoun Alidadi, if discrimination based on religious manifestations can only constitute indirect discrimination, there is 'a "cloak of legitimacy" attached to wide-ranging corporate "neutrality policies"' – in K Alidadi, *Religion, Equality and Employment in Europe. The Case of Reasonable Accommodation* (Oxford, Hart, 2017) 92.

[10] Case 130/75 *Vivien Prais v Council* EU:C:1976:142.

[11] ibid para 16.

[12] See the chapter by Lourenço and Pohjankoski in the present volume.

[13] Case C-196/87 *Udo Steymann v Staatssecretaris van Justitie* EU:C:1988:475.

the employee).[14] The next case which addressed the accommodation of religious practices of minorities was *UK v Council* (1996) regarding the annulment of Council Directive 93/104/EC of 23 November 1993 concerning certain aspects of the organization of working time.[15] In its judgment, the Court showed a degree of sensibility towards religious and cultural diversity. It upheld that although the question whether to include Sunday in the weekly rest period is ultimately left to the assessment of Member States, diversity of cultural, ethnic and religious factors in those States should be taken into account.[16]

Turning to the two 'religious' cases that have arisen under the FED until now, the Advocate General in the *Achbita* case began her opinion with asking a fundamental question of 'how much difference and diversity must an open and pluralistic European society tolerate within its borders and, conversely, how much assimilation is it permitted to require from certain minorities?'[17] The wording used by the Advocate General clearly implies a particular starting position, namely that Europe seeks to assimilate its minorities, while merely tolerating diversity and only to the extent that it must. That starting position and the related mindset also explain some of the Advocate General's later statements, such as 'While an employee cannot "leave" his sex, skin colour, ethnicity, sexual orientation, age or disability "at the door" upon entering his employer's premises, he may be expected to moderate the exercise of his religion … in relation to his clothing'.[18] It would appear that sex or skin colour is part of a person's identity in a way that religion is not. It is submitted that there are conceptual flaws in the reasoning of the Advocate General, specifically regarding her understanding of terms such as 'religion', 'personal identity' and 'neutrality'. In addition, her vague and feeble argumentation of what constitutes 'direct discrimination' must also be criticised.

A. Religion and Belief

The Advocate General in *Achbita* started by accepting that 'religion' must be interpreted broadly to include not only the beliefs of an individual, but also their religious practice (*forum internum* and *forum externum*).[19] Therefore, any policy which bars religious practices, especially one which bars them because of the religious nature of such practices, will inevitably mean that the affected persons are

[14] In this case, activities were performed by members of a religious community as part of commercial activities of that community. Those activities constitute economic activities within the meaning of EU law insofar as the services may be considered as indirect compensation for genuine and effective work.

[15] Case C-84/94 *United Kingdom of Great Britain and Northern Ireland v Council of the European Union* EU:C:1996:431.

[16] ibid para 37.

[17] Case C-157/15 *Achbita* (AG Opinion) (n 6) para 3.

[18] ibid para 116.

[19] ibid para 35.

treated less favourably than others 'on grounds of religion'. Thus, the Advocate General views the difference in treatment as 'between employees who wish to give active expression to a particular belief – be it religious, political or philosophical – and their colleagues who do not feel the same compulsion. However, this does not constitute "less favourable treatment" that is directly and specifically linked to religion'.[20] Consequently, she implies that those individuals who express their religion by wearing particular clothing should not be protected from the prohibition of discrimination on the grounds of religion.

It seems that the manifestation of one's protected religion deserves less protection than other grounds such as race, ethnicity or sex. This could be the expected result if one considers religion as a sort of 'external layer' added to the individual, something mutable that one could change. In the view of Advocate General Kokott, religion is different from other characteristics because 'the practice of religion is not so much an unalterable fact as an aspect of an individual's private life'.[21] Consequently, according to the Advocate General's reasoning, since one can choose a religion, it is fair to restrict protection on the basis that one's religion is not immutable. As Vickers points out, this argument can be challenged.[22] Even when religion is chosen, the cost to the individual of renouncing a key aspect of their identity is high. Other characteristics can involve an element of choice, such as pregnancy, and yet the choice argument is not accepted as a reason to deny protection, since the decision could be fundamentally related to the person's identity. On this basis, the choice to manifest religion through clothing should be protected.

Holding the opposite position from AG Kokott, Advocate General Sharpston stated in *Bougnaoui* that 'it would be entirely wrong to suppose that, whereas one's sex and skin colour accompany one everywhere, somehow one's religion does not'.[23] European Union law should protect the manifestations of core beliefs not because they are immutable but because of their central and nuclear role in the dignity of the individual. One should not forget that the EU is founded, among other principles, on the value of respect for human dignity and freedom (Article 2 TEU).[24] The fact that the intensity of religious observance may fluctuate over a person's lifetime does not mean that the faith or beliefs should not merit protection. In a previous case, *Y and Z* (2012),[25] the CJEU highlighted that the right to act upon religious or moral beliefs clearly includes manifestations of beliefs which can take many different forms. In the opinion in this case, Advocate General Bot

[20] ibid para 53.
[21] ibid para 116.
[22] L Vickers, 'ECJ Headscarf Series 2: The Role of Choice; and the Margin of Appreciation' (*Strasbourg Observers*, 8 September 2016). Available at: https://strasbourgobservers.com/2016/09/08/blog-series-the-role-of-choice-and-the-margin-of-appreciation.
[23] Case C-188/15 *Bougnaoui* (AG Opinion) (n 1) para 118.
[24] Treaty on European Union [2016] OJ C202/1 (TEU).
[25] Joined Cases C-71/11 and C-99/11 *Y and Z* EU:C:2012:518.

provided an insight into the understanding of Article 9 ECHR[26] by addressing the scope of protection for freedom of thought, conscience and religion under EU law.[27] He also reiterated the idea that freedom of religion is an essential aspect of a believer's identity and philosophy.[28] Likewise, in the final judgment of *Y and Z*, the CJEU highlighted that the right to act upon one's religious or moral beliefs clearly includes manifestations of those beliefs, which can take many different forms. The critical aspect is to protect the choices of an individual and to guarantee the right to act upon sincerely held religious or moral beliefs. More precisely, regarding religion as a matter of choice, the European Court of Human Rights (ECtHR) noted in *SAS v France* (2014) 'that personal choices as to an individual's appearance … relate to the expression of her personality and thus fall within the notion of private life'.[29] Consequently, it is irrelevant whether the applicant wears a religious garment both in public and private or does so at will, rather than constantly.

Therefore, EU law should protect manifestations of core beliefs because of their central and nuclear role in the dignity of the individual, irrespective of whether they are immutable or result from individual choice. There are no 'degrees' of one's religion, as Advocate General Kokott seems to imply in her reasoning when suggesting that 'moderate' religion should be more appropriate at workplace. By doing so, AG Kokott is patronising about what 'religion' means to a particular person.

B. Personal Identity

Precisely because there exists a link between human dignity, personal identity and the actions pursued on the basis of one's identity, EU law protects personal autonomy as being essential for one's ability to fulfil one's potential. In *Coleman* (2008), Advocate General Poiares Maduro associates equality with human dignity and personal autonomy in the employment sector. He bases the protection of equality on grounds of religion and belief on the autonomy and self-fulfilment of the person.[30] In *SAS v France*, the Strasbourg Court noted that the full-face veil could be perceived as strange in public spaces, but that 'it is the expression of a cultural identity which contributes to the pluralism that is inherent in democracy'.[31] However, the manifestation of personal identity could be subject

[26] Convention for the Protection of Human Rights and Fundamental Freedoms (European Convention on Human Rights, as Amended) (ECHR).

[27] Joined Cases C-71/11 and C-99/11 *Y and Z* EU:C:2012:224, Opinion of AG Bot, paras 33–35.

[28] ibid para 33.

[29] *SAS v France* App no 43835/11 (ECtHR, 1 July 2014) para 107.

[30] Case C-303/06 *S Coleman v Attridge Law and Steve Law* EU:C:2008:61, Opinion of AG Poiares Maduro, para 11.

[31] *SAS v France* (n 29) para 120.

to some restrictions when there are conflicting interests, such as a neutral image of a company.

According to Advocate General Kokott, national authorities are in a better position to take into consideration the circumstances of each case, particularly regarding the size and conspicuousness of the religious symbol, the nature of the activity, and the context in which the employer must perform her activity, as well as the national identity of the country.[32] Therefore, the Advocate General recommended the Court to grant national authorities guidance for a proportionality assessment in each particular case. In this way, the Advocate General seems to imply that national identity could be a factor which potentially limits the manifestation of personal identity and it is a factor that plays a role in the proportionality test. However, if national identity (in this case, Belgian) is apparently built upon a dominant, neutral and 'autochthonous' population who live in a 'neutral' setting where visible religious signs are not included, how could the manifestation of religious diversity in national 'neutral' contexts be protected?

Furthermore, Advocate General Kokott's position on giving a 'measure of discretion' to national authorities, in particular to national courts in applying the proportionality test, could lead to any EU country with symbolic or historic religious references in their constitutions to use these in a discretionary way to undermine diversity within their borders. Many European constitutions, such as the Constitution of the Republic of Poland (1997), the Constitution of Ireland (1937) and the Constitution of Greece (1975), to name but a few, contain explicit Christian references as part of their constitutional traditions.[33] Should religious references as part of national identity be allowed to justify discrimination on the grounds of religion?[34] Vickers notes that the CJEU case law on equality sets the standards to eradicate inequality rather than to reflect different national traditions,

[32] Case C-157/15 *Achbita* (AG Opinion) (n 6) para 141.

[33] The Constitution of the Republic of Poland (1997): 'We, the Polish Nation – all citizens of the Republic, both those who believe in God as the source of truth, (…) for our culture rooted in the Christian heritage of the Nation and in universal human values, (…) recognizing our responsibility before God or our own consciences, hereby establish this Constitution of the Republic of Poland.' The Constitution of Ireland (1937): 'In the Name of the Most Holy Trinity, from Whom is all authority and to Whom, as our final end, all actions both of men and States must be referred." The Constitution of Greece (1975): 'In the name of the Holy and Consubstantial and Indivisible Trinity.'

[34] Article 4(2) TEU provides that '[t]he Union shall respect the equality of Member States before the Treaties as well as their national identities, inherent in their fundamental structure, political and constitutional, inclusive of regional and local self-government. It shall respect their essential State functions, including ensuring the territorial integrity of the State, maintaining law and order and safeguarding national security. In particular, national security remains the sole responsibility of each Member State'. Article 4(2) TEU and the concept of national identity have the potential to protect aspects fundamental to the Member States on the basis of EU law. As the concept of national identity is neither specific nor objectively clear, the difficult question is to determine whether a specific religious identity or secularism, as part of a particular national identity, could work as a limitation to the manifestation of religion. For an analysis of Article 4(2) TEU and the respect the national identities of Member States, M Dobbs, 'Sovereignty, Article 4(2) TEU and the Respect of National Identities: Swinging the Balance of Power in Favour of the Member States?' (2014) 33 *Yearbook of European Law* 298–334.

stating: 'Given that it would seem inconceivable that a court would allow a state to argue that national traditions should be allowed to justify sex or race discrimination in employment, it is questionable whether such reasoning should be accepted in the different context of religion'.[35]

C. Neutrality

Certain kinds of labour can require a worker to possess certain characteristics. Article 4(1) FED permits Member States to provide an exemption from the prohibition on direct discrimination where this characteristic is a genuine and determining occupational requirement, provided that the objective is legitimate and the requirement is proportionate. While AG Kokott concluded that the discrimination in *Achbita* was not direct, she did turn to the latter exemption in the analysis of the justification of indirect discrimination since 'legitimate aims within the meaning of Article 2(2)(b)(i) of Directive 2000/78 include without any doubt the aims expressly recognised by the EU legislature itself, that is to say, … compliance with special occupational requirements (Article 4(1) of the Directive)'.[36]

Applying Article 4(1) FED to *Achbita*, the Advocate General concludes that the 'occupational requirement' at issue is willingness not to wear clothing which would amount to a visible sign of one's religion. The objective of such a company policy is to uphold the image of G4S as a 'neutral' employer where no staff member wears a sign of religion.[37] Accordingly, this neutrality policy was deemed to be within the margin of discretion granted to a business.[38] The Advocate General stated that:

> a policy of neutrality is absolutely crucial, not only because of the variety of customers served by G4S, but also because of the special nature of the work which G4S employees do in providing those services, which is characterized by constant face-to-face contact with external individuals and has a defining impact not only on the image of G4S itself but also and primarily on the public image of its customers.[39]

Surprisingly, there was no reference to any evidence that the policy of neutrality was necessary to preserve the image of G4S. The Advocate General argued that 'the desire to display, in relations with both public and private sector customers, a policy of political, philosophical or religious neutrality must be considered legitimate' because it relates to the freedom to conduct a business as guaranteed by Article 16 of the Charter of Fundamental Rights (CFR, Charter),[40] notably where only those workers who are in contact with the employer's

[35] Vickers (n 22).
[36] Case C-157/15 *Achbita* (AG Opinion) (n 6) para 60.
[37] ibid paras 73–76.
[38] ibid para 93.
[39] ibid para 94.
[40] Charter of Fundamental Rights of the European Union [2016] OJ C202/2 (CFR).

customers are covered.[41] The wish to project an image of neutrality relates to the freedom to conduct a business recognised in Article 16 CFR and is, in principle, legitimate.

This line of reasoning could prove problematic for members of religious minorities whose practices could be subject to the right to conduct business as protected by the Charter.[42] Consequently, one would need convincing and cogent reasons for how a policy of neutrality can be a legitimate aim according to Article 2(2)(b) of the Framework Equality Directive.

However, such convincing reasoning is missing, while at least three counterarguments can be made. First of all, many employers permit staff to wear clothing which represents a visible sign of their religion, ethnic origin or culture.[43] Interestingly, G4S itself 'incorporated the headscarf into the uniform worn by their security guards at the London Olympics', six years after having dismissed Ms. Achbita for wearing it.[44] Second, it is not clear how the 'neutrality' argument could play the same role as the principle of secularism when applied to the public sector as a basis for restrictions on religious freedom. Wearing a headscarf is neutral as to the character of the employer and it has not been proven to impair the ability to perform work duties, in the case of Achbita, as a receptionist. Brems has stated that extending neutrality to the private sector is 'a big leap' and that 'neutrality can be an easy cover-up for prejudice'.[45] Third, and as nicely put forward by Advocate General Sharpston when balancing religious and business interests in *Bougnaoui*:

> I draw attention to the "insidiousness" of the argument, "but we need to do X because otherwise our customers won't like it". Where the customer's attitude may itself be indicative of prejudice based on one of the "prohibited factors", such as religion, it seems to me particularly dangerous to excuse the employer from compliance with an equal treatment requirement in order to pander to that prejudice.[46]

D. Causality: Direct v Indirect Discrimination

The Framework Equality Directive prohibits direct and indirect discrimination, harassment, and instructions to discriminate, along with victimisation on grounds

[41] Case C-157/15 *Achbita* (n 3) paras 37–38.

[42] E Spaventa, 'What is the Point of Minimum Harmonization of Fundamental Rights? Some Further Reflections on the Achbita Case' (*EU Law Analysis*, 21 March 2017). Available at: http://eulawanalysis.blogspot.co.uk/2017/03/what-is-point-of-minimum-harmonization.html.

[43] See, e.g. 'Scotland Police Adds Hijab to Uniform' (*About Islam*, 8 June 2016). Available at: http://aboutislam.net/muslimissues/europe/scotland-police-adds-hijab-uniform.

[44] M Privot, 'Ban on headscarves and religious clothing is discrimination' (*EURACTIV*, 15 July 2016). Available at: www.euractiv.com/section/social-europe-jobs/opinion/ban-on-headscarves-and-religious-clothing-is-discrimination/.

[45] E Brems, 'Analysis: European Court of Justice Allows Bans on Religious Dress in the Workplace' (*Blog of the IACL, AIDC*, 25 March 2017). Available at: https://iacl-aidc-blog.org/2017/03/25/analysis-european-court-of-justice-allows-bans-on-religious-dress-in-the-workplace/.

[46] Case C-188/15 *Bougnaoui* (AG Opinion) (n 1) para 133.

of religion or belief. Direct discrimination occurs where a person is treated less favourably on grounds of religion or belief, in particular when employers refuse to employ religious or non-religious staff altogether or to employ those of one religion on more favourable terms than those of a different religion. It also covers treatment based on the discriminator's assumption about a person's religion, even though this may be mistaken, as well as discrimination based on a person's association with people of a particular religion.[47]

One of the challenges of EU equality law is the dichotomy of direct–indirect discrimination and how to deal with rooted forms of discrimination, disadvantage, stereotyping and situations that do not fit easily in the EU anti-discrimination law framework. In the *Achbita* case, the first question to tackle is whether there is an instance of direct or indirect discrimination. It is critical to choose one departure point or the other because of the notable differences in possible justifications. The Advocate General's opinion concluded that there is no direct discrimination on grounds of religion when an Muslim employee is banned from wearing an Islamic headscarf in the workplace, provided that the ban is founded on a general company rule prohibiting visible political, philosophical and religious symbols in the workplace and not on stereotypes or prejudices against one or more particular religions or against religious beliefs in general.[48] Such a ban does not imply less favourable treatment based on religion, but may constitute indirect discrimination based on religion. However, such indirect discrimination may be justified as proportionate for enforcing a legitimate policy of religious and ideological neutrality pursued by the employer in the company concerned. The question here is how a general rule at work has the effect of treating some people differently from others in a comparable situation on grounds of religion or belief. G4S argued that the rule is 'neutral' because it barred all visible signs of every political, philosophical or religious belief. The Advocate General agreed and highlighted that this company rule applies without distinction, and is neutral from the standpoint of religion and ideology. She also pointed out that:

> the position would certainly be different … if a ban such as that at issue here proved to be based on stereotypes or prejudice in relation to one or more specific religions – or even simply in relation to religious beliefs generally. In that event, it would without any doubt be appropriate to assume the presence of direct discrimination based on religion. According to the information available, however, there is nothing to indicate that that is the case.[49]

[47] See, e.g. L Vickers, *Religion and Belief Discrimination in Employment – the EU Law* (Brussels, Publications Office of the European Union, 2007) 12; Case C-303/06 *Coleman* (n 30) para 38.

[48] Case C-157/15 *Achbita* (n 3) paras 30–32; Case C-157/15 *Achbita* (AG Opinion) (n 6) paras 55–57.

[49] Case C-157/15 *Achbita* (AG Opinion) (n 6) para 55.

I respectfully disagree with Advocate General Kokott's conclusion, for several reasons:

(1) In its previous case law concerning various EU law prohibitions on discrimination, the Court has generally adopted *a broad understanding* of *the concept of direct discrimination* and has always assumed such discrimination to be present where a measure was inseparably linked to the relevant reason for the difference of treatment.[50] As the CJEU recently noted, the key element for differentiating between direct and indirect discrimination is that 'if it is apparent that a measure which gives rise to a difference in treatment has been introduced for reasons relating to [the protected characteristic], that measure must be classified as "direct discrimination" within the meaning of [EU law]'.[51] Ms. Achbita was dismissed on 12 June 2006 and the written rule came into force on 13 June 2006. This suggests that there might be a causal link between the employer's decision to ban the wearing of visible religious symbols and Achbita's dismissal. There is enough evidence to suggest that this prohibition was introduced because of the religious conflict that arose between Achbita and the company, so her dismissal could arguably amount to direct discrimination. Ms Achbita genuinely considered a headscarf as part of her Muslim identity, and her employment could be at risk if she refused to remove it. She was placed in a position of choosing between preserving her identity or her job. When the employer addressed Achbita's situation, he adopted a rule specifically to avoid any other conflicts in the company. Therefore, G4S adopted a general ban, taking into consideration Achbita's dismissal.

(2) Direct discrimination could also be detected by comparing the treatment of those whose world views, beliefs or religions require certain 'behaviour' practices (e.g. wearing particular clothing and those whose worldviews, beliefs or religions do not). Unfortunately, Advocate General Kokott compared Ms Achbita with people who wanted to manifest their religion or belief through the wearing of religious symbols at work, concluding that all such people were also banned from doing so. Consequently, there was no less favourable treatment. However, such reasoning starts from an incorrect comparison. It compares the different manifestations of political, philosophical or religious

[50] See Case C-177/88 *Dekker* EU:C:1990:383, paras 12 and 17; Case C-179/88 *Handels-og Kontorfunktionærernes Forbund* EU:C:1990:38, para 13; Case C-320/01 *Busch* EU:C:2003:114, para 39; Case C-116/06 *Kiiski* EU:C:2007:536, para 55; Case C-356/09 *Kleist* EU:C:2010:703, para 31; Case C-499/08 *Ingeniørforeningen i Danmark* EU:C:2010:600, paras 23–24; Case C-267/06 *Maruko* EU:C:2008:179, para 72; Case C-147/08 *Römer* EU:C:2011:286, para 52; Case C-267/12 *Hay* EU:C:2013:823, paras 41 and 44. To that effect, see also Case C-83/14 *CHEZ Razpredelenie Bulgaria* EU:C:2015:480, paras 76, 91 and 95.

[51] C-83/14 *CHEZ Razpredelenie Bulgaria* (n 50) para 95.

beliefs targeted by a neutral policy with each other, while the true comparator should be the 'other' employee who does not manifest any belief.[52] Any company policy forbidding employees to wear visible signs of their political, philosophical or religious belief treats those employees who believe in wearing external signs of their beliefs less favourably on grounds of religion. As Brems writes, 'it is astonishing that … direct discrimination on grounds of religion or belief exists only when a measure targets a single religion or a selection of religions, but not when a measure targets all religions and beliefs. Generalized hostility toward religions is apparently a manifestation of neutrality'.[53]

(3) The legal reasoning of the Advocate General in *Achbita* arguably implies that any blanket ban on 'active expression' of any characteristic protected by EU law would not be direct discrimination. As Vickers points out, 'the allegations of direct discrimination were, unsurprisingly, rejected. Discrimination based on a generally applicable dress code is not direct discrimination'.[54] It follows then that a bar on 'active expression' of ethnicity, sex or sexual orientation would not be direct discrimination. Under such an interpretation, an employer could require all employees to wear 'sex-neutral' clothing. Thereupon, Advocate General Kokott may conclude that disadvantaged persons would only be those who wish to give active expression to a 'particular' ethnicity, sex or sexual orientation, while the neutrality of the general policy would justify this restriction. Clearly, such a restriction contradicts the founding values of the European Union, such as pluralism, non-discrimination, justice and solidarity (Article 2 TFEU).[55]

(4) As the Open Society remarked in reference to both cases: 'Paradoxically, wrongly characterizing religion-based bans as "neutral" would lead to the very result the French Government fears. Employers who do not ban religious clothing would be reasonably perceived or portrayed as "taking sides" in favour of religious expression and of the religion of their employees. This would promote intolerance of people with religious beliefs'.[56] As a matter of fact, there is an ongoing pattern of hostility towards headscarf wearers

[52] S Ouald Chaib and V David, 'European Court of Justice Keeps the Door to Religious Discrimination in the Private Workplace Opened. The European Court of Human Rights Could Close it' (*Strasbourg Observers*, 27 March 2017). Available at: https://strasbourgobservers.com/2017/03/27/european-court-of-justice-keeps-the-door-to-religious-discrimination-in-the-private-workplace-opened-the-european-court-of-human-rights-could-close-it/.

[53] Brems (n 45).

[54] L Vickers, 'Direct Discrimination and Indirect Discrimination: Headscarves and the CJEU' (*Oxford Human Rights Hub*, 15 March 2017). Available at: http://ohrh.law.ox.ac.uk/direct-discrimination-and-indirect-discrimination-headscarves-and-the-cjeu/.

[55] Treaty on the Functioning of the European Union [2016] OJ C202/1 (TFEU).

[56] Open Society Justice Initiative, *Employer's Bar on Religious Clothing and European Union Discrimination Law*, Briefing Paper (2016) 6. Available at: www.opensocietyfoundations.org/briefing-papers/employers-bar-religious-clothing-and-european-union-discrimination-law.

> in Belgian society.[57] The majority of cases of discrimination reported at the Inter-federal Centre for Equal Opportunities are claims of discrimination on the basis of wearing religious attire.[58]

Moreover the Charter of Fundamental Rights is now part of primary EU law and thus needs to influence reasoning both by the Court and its Advocates General. Furthermore, Article 10 of the Charter should be interpreted according to the ECHR and the case law of the ECtHR, as prescribed by Article 52(3) of the Charter. Indeed, in *Achbita* both the Court and the Advocate General referred to ECHR and specifically to *Eweida and Others v the UK* (2013).[59] As the Advocate General highlights at the beginning of her opinion:

> Ms Achbita, like many other Muslim women, wears her headscarf for religious reasons, and there is no reason to doubt the sincerity of her religious motivation. Following the approach taken by the European Court of Human Rights in relation to Article 9, and the practice of many national courts and institutions, the Court of Justice should regard the foregoing as a factor linking this case to religion to an extent sufficient to bring it within the substantive scope of European Union law prohibition on religious discrimination.[60]

Taking into consideration the importance of being able to manifest a religion through wearing a headscarf, the question is raised why AG Kokott in *Achbita* did not conduct a strict review, when balancing the interests of the employer in having a neutral company image with the importance for an employee of manifesting their religion at work, as the ECtHR did in the previously mentioned case of *Eweida*.

In this vain, Advocate General Sharpston stated in *Bougnaoui* that, in the context of examining whether a proper balance had been struck, the starting point 'must be that an employee has, in principle, the right to wear religious apparel or a religious sign but that the employer also has, or may have, the right to impose restrictions'.[61] The Advocate General suggested that 'the employer and employee will need to explore the options together to arrive at a solution that accommodates both the employee's right to manifest his religious belief and the employer's right to conduct his business'.[62]

[57] See D Seta, *Forgotten Women: The Impact of Islamophobia on Muslim Women* (Brussels, European Network Against Racism, 2016). Available at: www.enar-eu.org/Forgotten-Women-the-impact-of-Islamophobia-on-Muslim-women.

[58] Centre for equal Opportunities and Fight against Racism, *Jaarverslag Discriminatie/Diversiteit 2013*. Available at: http://unia.be/files/Z_ARCHIEF/cgkr_00668_01_jvs_discdiv_nl.pdf. In 2014, 90 per cent of the complaints submitted at the Interfederal Centre for Equal Opportunities concerned Muslims. 268 of the 297 claims and 50 of the dossiers concerned prohibitions on the wearing of religious attire by Muslim women.

[59] *Eweida and others v UK* Apps nos 48420/10, 59842/10, 36516/10 (ECtHR, 15 January 2013).

[60] Case C-157/15 *Achbita* (AG Opinion) (n 6) para 38.

[61] Case C-188/15 *Bougnaoui* (AG Opinion) (n 1) para 122.

[62] ibid para 128.

These two cases exemplify the increasing controversy over balancing 'competing' rights at work, when the rights that need to be protected are: (1) the right to hold and manifest one's religion and (2) the freedom to carry on a business. An accommodation should be found so that the two rights can be safeguarded in a harmonious and balanced way. Therefore, the starting point for any analysis should be that, in principle, an employee has the right to wear religious signs but the employer also has the right to impose some restrictions. Consequently, an equitable balancing exercise is called for that gives proper weight to the importance of the manifestation of belief by the applicants.[63]

III. The CJEU Judgments in *Achbita* and *Bouganoui*, Religious Equality and Duties of Reasonable Accommodation

The values of equality and pluralism, as well as the commitment to combat discrimination and social exclusion, are deeply embedded in the documents of the EU.[64] European Union anti-discrimination law relies on the provisions of the treaties and it has been extended through the interplay of jurisprudence on the general principles of EU law and the Equality Directives.[65] The recitals to the directives make clear that EU action to counter discrimination is no longer driven by market integration alone, but also by the goal of attaining economic and social cohesion, solidarity, and the development of the EU as an area of freedom, security and justice. In order to achieve social cohesion, one factor to take into consideration is the protection of vulnerable groups. Any action that could undermine the effective integration of specific groups, such as Muslim women, into the labour market should be carefully scrutinised.[66] Additionally, the European Social

[63] E Howard, 'Islamic Headscarves and the CJEU: *Achbita and Bougnaoui*' (2017) 24 *Maastricht Journal of European and Comparative Law* 348.

[64] Art 2 TEU: 'The Union is founded on the values of respect for human dignity, freedom, democracy, equality, the rule of law and respect for human rights, including the rights of persons belonging to minorities. These values are common to the Member States in a society in which pluralism, non-discrimination, tolerance, justice, solidarity and equality between women and men prevail.' Art 3(3) TEU: 'The Union shall establish an internal market (…) It shall combat social exclusion and discrimination, and shall promote social justice and protection, equality between women and men, solidarity between generations and protection of the rights of the child.'

[65] Race Equality Directive, Framework Equality Directive, Equal Treatment Directive, Council Directive 2004/113/EC implementing the principle of equal treatment between men and women in the access to and supply of goods and services [2004] OJ L373/37.

[66] See European Union Agency for Fundamental Rights, *Second European Union Minorities and Discrimination Survey: Muslims – Selected findings* (Luxembourg, Publications Office of the European Union, 2017). This report examines how Muslims living in the EU face discrimination in a broad range of settings – and particularly when looking for work, on the job, and when trying to access public or private services.

Charter (ESC)[67] – a Council of Europe treaty that guarantees social and economic human rights which was adopted in 1961 and revised in 1996 – and the jurisprudence of the European Committee on Social Rights (ECSR) are also recognised as general principles of EU law. The ECSR encourages States Parties to conduct an active labour policy, seeking to promote the integration of minorities, emphasising how one pillar of the European Employment Strategy concerns the integration of disadvantaged groups into the employment market.

When the CJEU obtained its first opportunity to rule on religious discrimination at work, the legal reasoning should have been in line with EU law as a whole, including the ECSR. The Court should have supported the integration of individuals belonging to groups facing social exclusion. A message of inclusion would have been particularly appropriate in light of the widespread existence of negative stereotypes about Muslim women in Europe,[68] particularly at work. Unfortunately, the pronounced judgments provide too many opportunities for private companies to introduce general restrictions on religious and cultural symbols, in particular for employees with contact jobs. In practice, these kinds of general restrictions specifically affect Muslim women like the applicants in the cases considered here.[69]

In *Achbita*, the CJEU was asked for guidance on whether the adoption by an employer of a rule which requires all workers to dress neutrally – an unwritten rule at the time Achbita was dismissed – amounts to direct or indirect discrimination. The CJEU followed the opinion of the Advocate General in *Achbita* that since the rule was not based on stereotypes or prejudice against religious beliefs in general or against particular religions, the fact that someone is prohibited from wearing an Islamic headscarf at work does not constitute direct discrimination.

The Court continued its reasoning by highlighting that such an internal rule of a private undertaking may constitute indirect discrimination within the meaning of Article 2(2)(b) FED if it is established that the apparently neutral obligation it imposes results, in fact, in persons adhering to a particular religion or belief being put at a particular disadvantage, unless it is objectively justified by a legitimate aim, such as the pursuit by the employer, in its relations with its customers, of a policy of political, philosophical and religious neutrality, and the means of achieving that aim are appropriate and necessary, which it is for the referring Court to ascertain.[70] Put differently, the Court accepts that the neutrality policy of an employer constitutes a legitimate aim for a measure that disproportionately

[67] Art 1(2) of the European Social Charter, in combination with the Preamble of the Charter, as prohibiting all forms of discrimination in employment.

[68] E Brems (ed), *The Experiences of Veil Wearers in Europe and the Law* (Cambridge, Cambridge University Press, 2014).

[69] Seta (n 57) 21; Amnesty International, *Wearing the Headscarf in the Workplace. Observations on Discrimination Based on Religion in the Achbita and Bougnaoui Cases* (28 October 2016). Available at: www.amnesty.org/en/documents/eur01/5077/2016/en/.

[70] Case C-157/15 *Achbita* (n 3) para 45.

disadvantages women wearing a headscarf for religious reasons. As Howard points out, 'the CJEU appears to have opted for [a lenient justification test] and has been criticized for doing so'.[71] It is hard to understand why the CJEU in *Achbita* did not explain in detail how a policy of neutrality for a private company can be a legitimate aim for restricting Ms Achbita's freedom in manifesting her religion at work. Furthermore, while in the context of race and gender discrimination, the standard of review has been very strict, but it is yet unclear whether the same strict standard of proportionality will apply to religion or belief cases.[72] Hence, in *Achbita*, the CJEU seems to virtually give private employers *carte blanche* to introduce general restrictions on religious dress that could *potentially* affect believers who want to manifest their religion through clothing.

In *Bougnaoui*, the CJEU clarified that if, on referral, the national Court establishes that Ms Bougnaoui had been dismissed for wearing a headscarf not based on an internal rule but in order to satisfy the customers' wishes, this would amount to direct discrimination on grounds of religion. Although direct discrimination cannot be justified, there are some exceptions to this position where a religion or belief constitutes an occupational requirement for the job in question because of the nature of the occupation, or the context in which the work is carried out (e.g. requiring that a priest be Catholic, or that a teacher of Islam be Muslim). In such a case, discrimination will be lawful if it is proportional.[73] In *Bougnaoui*, the CJEU pointed out that 'in accordance with Recital 23 of FED, it is only in very limited circumstances that a characteristic related, in particular, to religion may constitute a genuine and determining occupational requirement'.[74] The Court then elaborated that this concept in Article 4(1) FED

> refers to a requirement that is objectively dictated by the nature of the occupational activities concerned, or of the context in which they are carried out. It cannot, however, cover subjective considerations, such as the willingness of the employer to take account of the particular wishes of the customer.[75]

Therefore, the CJEU concluded in line with the opinion of AG Sharpston that a particular characteristic was not a genuine and determining occupational requirement.

In both *Achbita* and *Bougnaoui*, the CJEU highlighted that it was up to the referring court to ascertain whether there was direct or indirect discrimination. Strikingly, it missed the opportunity to develop the factors that could play a role in the proportionality test in religion or belief cases.[76]

[71] Howard (n 63) 10.
[72] Vickers, 'ECJ Headscarf Series 2' (n 22).
[73] Art 4(1) FED.
[74] Case C-188/15 *Bougnaoui* (n 4) para 38.
[75] ibid para 40.
[76] P Edge and L Vickers, 'Review of Equality and Human Rights Law Relating to Religion of Belief', Equality and Human Rights Commission, Research Report 97 (2015) 27.

Surprisingly, the CJEU also missed the opportunity to bring the concept of 'reasonable accommodation' into the framework of indirect discrimination.[77] One aspect of indirect discrimination is the question of whether the employer has a duty to accommodate religious beliefs. Article 5 of the FED envisages a duty of reasonable accommodation only with regard to disability.[78] The question is whether that duty should be extended to grounds of religion. This matter has generated ample debate and controversy among scholars.[79] In a few European countries, reasonable accommodation has been applied to other grounds apart from disability.[80] The failure to accommodate a request for different treatment by religious employees may amount to indirect discrimination, unless the refusal can be justified.[81] This leads to the conclusion that the duty to accommodate could be intrinsically linked to indirect discrimination.

One of the main arguments for differentiating the duty of *reasonable accommodation* from *indirect discrimination* is that EU law requires a group disadvantage as established by a comparison exercise.[82] It is hard to prove a group disadvantage with a statistical approach in some reasonable accommodation claims.[83] However, it may also be sufficient, as *prima facie* evidence of indirect discrimination, to show that a practice prohibiting a specific expression of religion is intrinsically liable to put a group of workers who are sincere believers at a

[77] See the chapter by A Śledzińska-Simon in the present volume.

[78] EU law also foresees a duty to accommodate working conditions for women who are pregnant or are breastfeeding, if the normal working conditions would entail any risk for their health and safety – see Directive 92/85/EEC Art 5(1). See also L Waddington, 'Reasonable Accommodation. Time to Extend the Duty to Accommodate Beyond Disability?' (2011) 36 *NTM/NJCM-Bulletin* 186; see the chapter by Lourenço and Pohjankoski in the present volume.

[79] K Alidadi, *Religion, Equality and Employment in Europe: The Case for Reasonable Accommodation* (Oxford, Hart, 2017); K Alidadi, 'Reasonable Accommodations for Religion and Belief: Adding Value to Article 9 ECHR and the European Union's Anti-Discrimination Approach to Employment?' (2012) 37 *European Law Review* 693.

[80] Reasonable accommodation has extended to religious grounds in Bulgaria (Protection against Discrimination Act, Art 13); Croatia (Act on Holidays, Remembrance Days and Non-working Days of 30 April 1996, Art 3); Former Yugoslav Republic of Macedonia (The Law on Holidays of the Republic of Macedonia, Arts 1 and 2); and partially extended in Germany and France. In France, accommodations result from judicial decisions relating to the application of freedom of religion (see the jurisprudence of the Administrative Supreme Court regarding reasonable accommodation on religious grounds of the pupil's duty to attend school and Ministerial Instruction of the Ministry of Public Service No 2106 of 14 November 2005 regarding authorisations of absence on religious grounds). In Germany, it depends on judicial interpretation of Article 4 of the Basic Law (Constitution). See, e.g. European Commission, *Developing an Anti-discrimination Law in Europe* (Luxembourg: Publications Office of the European Union, 2015) 29–30.

[81] See, e.g. Vickers, *Religion and Belief Discrimination in Employment* (n 47) 12.

[82] S Havekort-Speekenbrink, *European Non-Discrimination Law. A Comparison of EU Law and the ECHR in the Field of Field of Non-Discrimination and the Freedom of Religion in Public Employment with an Emphasis on the Islamic Headscarf Issue* (Cambridge, Intersentia, 2012).

[83] Indirect discrimination requires that the applicant demonstrates that a specific measure would put Muslim women – as the cases discussed here – at a particular disadvantage compared to other persons. This is referred as a disparate impact test and this kind of test could be an obstacle for the applicant for many reason – see Haverkort-Speekenbrink (n 82) 96.

disadvantage compared to other workers.[84] If the CJEU had considered the impact of the ban on wearing religious signs in the workplace by correctly balancing all interests and rights involved, indirect discrimination on grounds of religion and belief could have been extended, thereby reinforcing the concept of substantive equality.[85] Although the term 'reasonable accommodation' appears only in the context of disability, the CJEU could have used it, particularly in *Achbita*, as a principle embedded in the logic of the Framework Employment Directive as a whole in order to combat all kinds of discrimination at the workplace. As Tourkochoriti states referring to *Achbita*, 'the principle of reasonable accommodation, just like the principle of practical harmonization, are principles embedded within the European legal culture which help courts find a solution to similar cases of rights in conflict'.[86]

IV. An Opportunity to Improve EU Anti-discrimination Law

The preceding analyses allows us to conclude that the Luxembourg Court has missed a golden opportunity to increase, strengthen and provide better coherence as to the application of EU anti-discrimination law. Following Article 52(3) CFR, EU law can provide more extensive protection than the ECHR. In interpreting the ECHR, the Strasbourg Court considered the national Court of appeal in *Eweida* not to have correctly balanced the interest of the employer and employee's freedom of religion. In *Eweida*, the ECtHR concluded that manifesting one's religious belief is a fundamental right since 'a healthy democratic society needs to tolerate and sustain pluralism and diversity' and also due to 'the value to an individual who has made religion a central tenet of his or her life is to be able to communicate that belief to others'.[87] This demonstrates that reasonable requests from employees cannot be refused without due consideration. Taking that into account, the CJEU should have conducted a stronger proportionality assessment in the *Achbita* judgment. Unfortunately, the Court did not show any evidence by way of explaining the weight attributed to one side of the balance (ie the employer), while ignoring the value of religious manifestation to the applicant.

[84] See F Ast, 'Reflection on the Recognition of a Right to Reasonable Accommodation in EU Law' in MC Foblets, K Alidadi, JS Nielsen and Z Yanasmayan (eds), *Belief, Law and Politics: What Future for a Secular Europe* (Farnham, Ashgate Publishing Limited, 2014).

[85] See A Stein, 'Reasonable Accommodation for Religion and Belief: Can it Be Accommodated in EU Law without an Express Duty?' in Foblets et al (n 84).

[86] I Tourkochoriti, 'Protection with Hesitation: On the recent CJEU Decisions on Religious Headscarves at Work' (*Vervassungsblog*, 21 March 2017). Available at: http://verfassungsblog.de/protection-with-hesitation-on-the-recent-cjeu-decisions-on-religious-headscarves-at-work/.

[87] *Eweida* (n 59) para 94.

One should keep in mind that religion – as much as race, ethnicity, sex or language – is part of a person's 'inherent identity', therefore, 'all [such] discrimination grounds should be afforded the same level of protection', irrespective of whether the protected grounds are 'biologically determined, socially established or personally chosen'.[88] Although different levels of protection are afforded to different discrimination grounds in the EU approach to equal treatment, there also exists a common goal to achieve substantive equality. As Advocate General Sharpston suggested in *Bougnaoui*, different standards of protection should not be applied to different equality grounds.

Thus, if national identity would not be allowed to justify gender discrimination, by implication, it should not justify religious discrimination. The CJEU implicitly relied on a substantive approach to equality to deliver landmark decisions such as *Coleman*. In that case, the Court linked substantive equality to the notion of dignity: all human beings deserve equal respect and treatment, regardless of their personal characteristics. Several Advocates General have also referred to dignity as an underlying value of equality.[89] Closely linked to non-discrimination and equality is the protection of cultural, religious and linguistic diversity.[90] As a matter of fact, Article 22 of the Charter regarding diversity immediately follows the general principle of equality as laid down in Article 21.

The role of the CJEU is to give guidance in applying EU law in a way that strengthens the harmonious interaction of persons and groups with varied identities in every area of life, including education, housing and the workplace. Without due respect for diversity, it is not possible to achieve social cohesion. *Achbita* and *Bougnaoui* are both cases that touch the very heart of EU law – the working sector. Any ban on wearing religious garments at work would result in blocking many believers, mostly Muslim women, from the entire field of private employment or, at least, in making access to private employment more difficult.[91] Any kind of discrimination that may have the effect of restricting, if not precluding, access to professions for certain groups would have structural repercussions on the labour market and on social cohesion. Erasing religious or cultural expression from visible places at work is not a neutral project, as Amnesty International

[88] S Benedi Lahuerta, 'Taking EU Equality Law to the Next Level: In Search of Coherence' (2016) 7 *European Labour Law Journal* 348, 353–54.

[89] Case C-303/06 *Coleman* (AG Opinion) (n 30) para 8; Case C-447/09 *Reinhard Prigge and Others v Deutsche Lufthansa AG* EU:C:2011:573, Opinion of AG Cruz Villalon, para 31. See K Alidadi, 'Cultural Diversity in the Workplace: Personal Autonomy as a Pillar for the Accommodation of Employees Religious Practices?' in MC Foblets, M Graziadei and A Dundes Renteln (eds), *Personal Autonomy in Plural Societies: A Principle and its Paradoxes (Law and Anthropology)* (Abingdon, Routledge, 2017).

[90] See, further, eg D Kochenov and T Agarin, 'Expecting too Much: European Union's Minority Protection Hide-and Seek' (2017) 1 *Anti-Discrimination Law Review* 7; B De Witte and S Mancini, 'Language Rights as Cultural Rights – a European Perspective' in F Francioni and M Scheinin (eds), *Cultural Human Rights* (Martinus Nijhoff, 2008); K Henrard (ed), *The Interrelation between the Right to Identity of Minorities and their Socio-economic Participation* (Martinus Nijhoff, 2013).

[91] See Seta (n 57).

points out.[92] The alternative suggested by the CJEU – that employees such as Ms Achbita could be moved to back-office positions where there would not be face-to-face contact with customers is not a human rights solution. Any restriction, such as a 'back-room' non-client facing role, undermines the values on which EU law is founded – pluralism, non-discrimination, tolerance, justice, solidarity and equality. If the Luxembourg Court confirms the legal reasoning taken in *Achbita* in the next religious discrimination case to reach the CJEU, the EU's commitment to the principle of non-discrimination will be compromised.

[92] Amnesty International, *Wearing the Headscarf in the Workplace. Observations on Discrimination Based on Religion in the Achbita and Bougnaoui cases* (28 October 2016). Available at: www.amnesty.org/en/documents/eur01/5077/2016/en/.

9

Unveiling the Culture of Justification in the European Union

Religious Clothing and the Proportionality Review

ANNA ŚLEDZIŃSKA-SIMON

I. Introduction

Today, the vision of an 'ever closer Union' is fading away because populist leaders, parties, and governments openly contest European Union (EU) policies and fail to respect the rule of law and fundamental values upon which the Union was based.[1] As a consequence of increasing immigration and refugee flows, national and ethnic diversity and terrorist threats, the common European identity and values raise more questions than economic integration. One of the key questions in several European states is how to respond to individual claims for recognition of the right to practice a religion and manifest a religious identity in public.[2]

EU law not only guarantees freedom of religion, but also prohibits discrimination on the grounds of religion.[3] Religion is among several characteristics protected by EU equality law, but it is a deeply troubled category because it is often a target of secular laws or business policies endorsing the principle of neutrality. Moreover, there are deep differences among religions and individuals practising

[1] See, e.g. L Pech, KL Scheppele, 'Illiberalism Within: Rule of Law Backsliding in the EU' (2017) 19 *Cambridge Yearbook of European Legal Studies* 3; W Sadurski, 'How Democracy Dies (in Poland): A Case Study of Anti-Constitutional Populist Backsliding' (2018) *Sydney Law School Research Paper* No 18/01.

[2] See, A Triandafyllidou, 'The Role of Religion and Secularism in Defining European Identity and Culture: Challenges, Scenarios and Ways Forward of the Document' (2016) Vision Document (cultural inclusion axis). Available at: www.culturalbase.eu.

[3] See Charter of Fundamental Rights of the European Union [2016] OJ L202/2 (CFR), Art 22 (prohibition of discrimination) and Art 23 (respect for cultural, religious and linguistic diversity).

religion.[4] On the one hand, some religions prescribe strict rules concerning religious clothing or dietary laws. On the other hand, some individuals freely choose to manifest their religious beliefs by wearing religious symbols or practising certain religious traditions in public.[5]

While neither protection of freedom of religion, nor protection against religious discrimination is absolute, the question of how to reconcile two conflicting claims of neutrality and religious freedom requires a fair balance to be struck.[6] Therefore, courts carry a heavy burden of responsibility when they rule on the place of religion in a secular state. In particular, when courts solve conflicts between freedom of religion and other fundamental rights and freedoms or decide whether differentiation on grounds of religion amounts to discrimination, they shape the common understanding of what is acceptable in a democratic society. What the general public may learn from such decisions is how to justify a rule that gives preference to either religion or neutrality. It would be thus a worrying sign if banning a religion from a public place or sight can be justified by any reason or if reasons for such bans are inherently discriminatory.

In essence, what is at stake in cases concerning religious freedoms (and clothing in particular) is the 'equal' protection against discrimination. Since belonging to a certain religious, and usually also a national, ethnic or immigrant community is often a factor determining one's social and economic status, the transformative potential of the EU equality legislation may be thwarted if religious claims are not given adequate attention. Evidently, weak protection against discrimination on the grounds of religion may augment the segregation, isolation or ghettoisation of religious groups and, in effect, lead to a status-based society with unequal classes of people such as those that existed in Feudalism.[7]

European Union law endorses not only formal, but also substantive equality which takes difference into account.[8] Yet, it does not provide an answer for

[4] J Weiler, 'Je suis Achbita' (2017) 28 *European Journal of International Law* 989 (arguing that there is a difference between the obligatory and voluntary wearing of religious symbols as 'practice' and 'manifestation' of a religion).

[5] Religious clothing is often considered together with other religious symbols, which include skull caps, headscarves, face covering veils, burqas, burkinis, crosses or crucifixes, turbans, Kara bangles and dreadlocks. As explained by E Howard, religious symbols are worn or displayed not only because they are seen as an obligation of religious faith or belief, but linked to, or inspired by religion or belief, even if there is no obligation. E Howard, 'Religious symbols' in A Wiesand, K Chainoglou and A Śledzińska-Simon (eds), *Culture and Human Rights: Wroclaw Commentaries* (Berlin, De Gruyter, 2016). See also M Evans, *Manual on the Wearing of Religious Symbols in Public Areas* (Strasbourg, Council of Europe Publishing, 2009).

[6] See *Eweida and Others v the United Kingdom*, Apps nos 48420/10, 59842/10, 51671/10 and 36516/10 (ECtHR, 15 January 2013).

[7] M Rosenfeld, 'Equality and the Dialectic between Identity and Difference' (2005) Cardozo Legal Studies Research Paper No 133.

[8] S Fredman, *Discrimination Law* (Oxford, Oxford University Press, 2002) 1–26. See also S Fredman, 'Emerging from the Shadows: Substantive Equality and Article 14 of the European Convention of Human Rights' (2016) 16 *Human Rights Law Review* 273.

how to accommodate religion or to recognise cultural differences in public or private settings.[9] This question is even more pressing nowadays because cultural pluralism – or multiculturalism specifically[10] – has increasingly been seen as a fiasco.[11] Thus, a real challenge for the future of the EU as an area of justice, freedom, and security is to address pluralist claims in the face of growing nationalism and scepticism towards the politics of identity.[12] What is also needed is a method of distinguishing benign religious identity claims from claims which should be discarded as contrary to the values of an open, democratic society.

The aim of this chapter is to examine how European courts assess laws, policies or practices that either directly target religious groups or have deleterious effects on their members. On this ground, it is argued that the judicial approach to such limitations reveals a culture of justification which may either strengthen or diminish the legal protection of fundamental rights.[13] The chapter explores veil ban decisions rendered by the Court of Justice of the European Union (CJEU) and the European Court of Human Rights (ECtHR), as well as constitutional courts and highest domestic courts in European states. Assuming that the judicial review in cases concerning fundamental rights is based on the proportionality test, the chapter aims to analyse how courts carry out this test with regard to laws, policies or practices that infringe upon religious freedoms or the right not to be discriminated on the grounds of religion. The chapter intends to contribute to a wider debate on religious accommodation,[14] and re-appraise the impact of EU equality law on the protection of religiously motivated identity claims.[15]

[9] The EU equality law does not contain an explicit obligation to accommodate religion. Therefore, this concept needs to be established by the judicial branch as a derivative from the principle of equality in its substantive reading.

[10] See, e.g. W Kymlicka (ed), *The Rights of Minority Cultures* (Oxford, Oxford University Press, 1995); I Shapiro and W Kymlicka (eds), *Ethnicity and Group Rights* (New York, New York University Press, 1997; Jeremy Waldron, 'One Law for All? The Logic of Cultural Accommodation' (2002) 59 *Wash and Lee Law Review* 3.

[11] See, Merkel erklärt Multikulti für gescheitert (*Spiegel online*, 16 October 2010). Available at: www.spiegel.de/politik/deutschland/integration-merkel-erklaert-multikulti-fuer-gescheitert-a-723532.html.

[12] See, e.g. A Gutman, *Identity in Democracy* (Princeton, Princeton University Press, 2003).

[13] M Cohen-Eliya and I Porrat, *Proportionality and Constitutional Culture* (Cambridge, Cambridge University Press, 2012) 7 (explaining that proportionality epitomises a legal culture, which requires substantive justification for all government actions in terms of rationality and reasonableness, and the necessary tradeoffs they entail).

[14] On the concept of reasonable accommodation, see the chapter by L Lourenço and P Pohjankoski in the present volume.

[15] See, e.g. E Brems (ed), *The Experiences of Veil Wearers in Europe and in Law (Cambridge Studies in Law and Society)* (Cambridge, Cambridge University Press 2014); M-C Foblets and K Alidadi (eds), *A Test of Faith? Religious Diversity and Accommodation in the European Workplace* (Abingdon, Routledge, 2012); E Howard, *Law and the Wearing of Religious Symbols. European Bans on the Wearing of Religious Symbols in Education* (Abingdon, Routledge, 2011).

II. Limits to the Protection against Religious Discrimination in EU Law

There are a number of limitations to the effective protection against religious discrimination in EU law. First, EU law has a limited scope of application. Second, it is deeply fragmented with regard to its normative foundations and the implementation, leading to *de iure* and *de facto* hierarchies of the protected grounds.[16] Third, the EU is bound to respect the national identity of Member States, which implies the need to create exceptions to the uniform application of EU law with regard to the church – state relationship and the status of religion in the public space.[17]

The limited scope of application of EU law is the result of a division of competences between the Union and its Member States. Although equality has been recognised as a general principle of EU law,[18] a value common to the Member States[19] and the objectives of the EU,[20] combating discrimination in the EU is constrained by the objectives and powers conferred upon the Union by the treaties.[21] While the primary function of the prohibition of discrimination (initially on the grounds of nationality and sex) was to enable European integration through the realisation of the internal market and, subsequently, with the addition of other grounds, to facilitate the EU citizenship and fundamental rights protection project, by virtue of the Treaty of the European Union,[22] these goals are limited to areas of EU competence. As a result, the scope of EU law does not cover several subject matters pertinent to fighting discrimination against minority groups, such as relations between church and state, laws regulating public service, education systems or the content of school curricula. Moreover, the equality guarantees contained in the Charter of Fundamental Rights of the European Union (CFR) are binding only within the limits of EU law.[23]

Moreover, the principle of equality and non-discrimination was given expression predominantly in EU directives related to the areas essential for the internal market and labour law. Although the Race Equality Directive[24] and the Gender

[16] R Xenidis, 'Shaking the Normative Foundations of EU Equality Law: Evolution and Hierarchies between Market Integration and Human Rights Rationales' (2017) EUI Working Paper No 2017/04; S Prechal, 'Discrimination Does Not Fall Down from Heaven': The Context and Evolution of Nondiscrimination in EU law (2009) Eric Stein Working Paper No. 4.

[17] Declaration No 11 to the Final Act of the Treaty of Amsterdam. See also Recital 24 of the Directive 2000/78/EC.

[18] See, e.g. Cases C-117/76 and C-16/77 *Ruckdeschel* ECLI:EU:C:1977:160 and in particular Case C-144/04 *Mangold* ECLI:EU:C:2005:709.

[19] Art 2 TEU.

[20] Art 3(3) TEU.

[21] Art 10 TFEU.

[22] Treaty on European Union [2016] OJ C202/1 (TEU).

[23] Art 51(1) CFR.

[24] Directive 2000/43/EC implementing the principle of equal treatment between persons irrespective of racial or ethnic origin [2000] OJ L180/22 (Race Equality Directive).

Equality (Recast) Directive[25] also apply this prohibition to other areas such as social protection, the transformative potential of EU equality law[26] is certainly driven by an economic rationale.[27] As a result, the principle of equality and non-discrimination still continues to denote merely a market value rather than a true human right with a universal scope of application.[28]

Currently, EU equality law remains deeply fragmented into sub-regimes related to the selected protected grounds which differ with regard to the material scope and the institutional framework. As a result, under EU law, one cannot complain about all instances of discrimination, but only raise complaints that fall within the material scope of a relevant directive. In fact, only political reasons explain why the EU legislator set out the broadest scope of protection against discrimination with regard to racial and ethnic origin, while the Framework Equality Directive (FED) covering religion, age, disability and sexual orientation is limited to the sphere of employment.[29] Moreover, the absence of a directive implementing the principle of equality with regard to religion, age, disability and sexual orientation beyond employment[30] lends support to the claim of an internal hierarchy of protected categories in EU law.[31]

In consequence, in the current state of EU legislation, even certain areas that form part of Union competence are not covered by EU equality law. For example, under EU law, it would be 'lawful' to deny services to a Jew wearing a yalmulke, as there are no rules that proscribe discrimination on the grounds of religion as regards access to goods and services available to the public. However, if this case is presented as discrimination with regard to racial or ethnic origin, it would be prohibited by the Race Equality Directive (RED). Likewise, a rule prohibiting women from wearing headgear could be effectively challenged as gender discrimination in employment and social services,[32] as well as in access to goods and services,[33] but not in education which falls outside the scope of the EU gender

[25] Directive 2006/54/EC of the European Parliament and of the Council on the implementation of the principle of equal opportunities and equal treatment of men and women in matters of employment and occupation (recast) [2006] OJ L204/23 (Gender Equality (Recast) Directive).

[26] E Muir, 'The Transformative Function of EU Equality Law' (2013) 5 *European Review of Private Law* 1231.

[27] See also the introductory chapter to this volume by U Belavusau and K Henrard.

[28] See, e.g. Case C-167-12 *X*. ECLI:EU:C:2014:169 and Case C-363/12 *Z* ECLI:EU:C:2014:159 (rejecting a gender discrimination claim raised by 'IVF mothers' who sought the right to adoption and maternity leave in absence of 'surrogacy leave').

[29] Council Directive 2000/78/EC establishing a general framework for equal treatment in employment and occupation [2000] OJ L303/16 (Framework Equality Directive).

[30] Proposal for a Council Directive on implementing the principle of equal treatment between persons irrespective of religion or belief, disability, age or sexual orientation, COM (2008) 426.

[31] H Meenan, 'Conclusions' in H Meenan (ed), *Equality Law in an Enlarged Union. Understanding the Article 13 Directives* (Cambridge, Cambridge University Press, 2009) 342.

[32] Directive 2006/54/EC of the European Parliament and of the Council on the implementation of the principle of equal opportunities and equal treatment of men and women in matters of employment and occupation (recast) [2006] OJ L204/23.

[33] Directive 2004/113/EC implementing the principle of equal treatment between men and women in the access to and supply of goods and services [2004] OJ L 373/37.

equality directives. Still, it is possible to remedy the existing gaps in the equality protection at the national level. Specifically, Member States may adopt or maintain provisions which offer more protection to the persons concerned than those laid down in EU law.[34]

Although the limited scope of EU equality protection may also, in some cases, be compensated by the European Convention of Human Rights (ECHR), the Convention system is focused on the protection of personal and political rights and freedoms in addition to the rights to property, education and participation in elections (provided in additional protocols). Furthermore, the prohibition of discrimination stipulated in Article 14 ECHR does not enshrine an autonomous subjective right to non-discrimination. Rather, discrimination can be alleged only in relation to breaches of other Convention rights and freedoms.[35] In consequence, potential victims of discrimination may claim discrimination without the need to invoke another Convention right or freedom only against a State Party to Protocol 12. Still, the current number of such states is only ten.[36] In addition, in some cases, the Strasbourg Court persistently decides on the merits of a case solely in relation to provisions other than Article 14 ECHR.[37] As a result, all veil ban cases before the ECtHR appear solely as concerning solely freedom of religion (Article 9 ECHR) because the Court declined to decide whether the impugned law or practice amounted to discrimination on the grounds of religion.

Finally, the application of EU equality law is also constrained by the constitutional traditions of Member States. On the one hand, constitutional principles and norms regarding relations between church and state undermine the uniform application of EU equality law, particularly in Member States who favour a strict separation between church and state (*laïcité*) (such as Belgium or France). In this context, one could note that there are multiple interpretations of the concept of state neutrality, and there is no agreement on whether secularism could be regarded as a common European constitutional tradition.[38] Since there are no common

[34] See Art 6(1) and recital 25 in the preamble to the RED.

[35] In comparison in *Belov*, AG Kokott explained that conditions for the existence of discrimination are not conditioned on the invocation or infringement of other rights or interests defined in law. Case C-394/11 *Belov* EU:C:2012:585, Opinion of AG Kokott, paras 7–72. Also, the CJEU in *Nikolova* held that Art 2(1), (2)(a) and (b) of Directive 2000/46 must be interpreted as precluding a national provision which makes the existence of direct discrimination or indirect discrimination conditional on a prejudice to rights or legitimate interests – Case C-83/14 *CHEZ Razpredelenie Bulgaria AD (Anelia Nikolova)* EU:C:2015:480.

[36] Protocol No. 12 to the Convention for the Protection of Human Rights and Fundamental Freedoms, ETS No 177.

[37] There is a line of cases in which the ECtHR held that a State Party to the Convention failed to comply with its positive obligations regarding a group of particularly vulnerable persons to enable them to effectively enjoy Convention rights or freedoms. Yet the Court found that it was 'not necessary to separately determine whether the facts of the case also gave rise to a breach of Article 14 of the Convention'. See, e.g. *VC v Slovakia*, App no 18968/07 (ECtHR, 8 November 2011); *Winterstein and Others v France*, App no 20713/07 (ECtHR, 17 October 2013).

[38] Weiler (n 4) at 1003. Also J Kis, '*The Principle of State Neutrality*' in M Rosenfeld and A Sajó (eds) *The Oxford Handbook of Comparative Constitutional Law* (Oxford, Oxford University Press, 2012) 328.

European standards on the place of religion and religious symbols in public sphere,[39] national authorities have a wide margin of appreciation with respect to the principles governing public service,[40] school systems and curricula,[41] and even rules of peaceful social co-existence.[42] Moreover, public administration traditions and the notion of public service, which determines the public-private divide, vary between Member States.[43]

Last but not least, the principle of equality may come into conflict with the obligation of the EU to respect the national identity of Member States with distinctive constitutional traditions.[44] Relying on Article 4(2) of the Treaty on the Functioning of the European Union,[45] Member States may claim derogations from the uniform application of the principle of equality with regard to public service.[46] Arguably, if accepted, the national identity exception applied in the context of EU equality law would have much wider implications than derogations from freedom of movement established in other cases.[47] In Belgium or France, it may actually apply to the entire public sector and seriously undermine chances for the

[39] For an overview of law and practice in the Member States of the Council of Europe with regard to the presence of religious symbols in state schools, *see Lautsi v Italy*, App no 30814/06 (ECtHR, 18 March 2011) paras 26–28. In *Sahin v Turkey*, the Grand Chamber emphasised that '[i]t is not possible to discern throughout Europe a uniform conception of the significance of religion in society (…), and the meaning or impact of the public expression of a religious belief will differ according to time and context (…). Rules in this sphere will consequently vary from one country to another according to national traditions and the requirements imposed by the need to protect the rights and freedoms of others and to maintain public order (…). Accordingly, the choice of the extent and form such regulations should take must inevitably be left up to a point to the State concerned, as it will depend on the specific domestic context (…)' – *Sahin v Turkey*, App no 44774/98 (ECtHR, 10 November 2005) para 109.

[40] *Dahlab v Switzerland*, App no 42393/98 (ECtHR, 15 February 2001); *Kurtulmus v Turkey*, App no 65500/01 (ECtHR, 24 January 2006); *Ebrahimian v France*, App no 64846/11 (ECtHR, 26 November 2015).

[41] *Aktas and Others v France*, App no 43563/08 (ECtHR, 30 June 2009); *Dogru v France*, App no 27058/05 (ECtHR, 4 December 2008); *Sahin v Turkey*, App no 13279/05 (ECtHR, 20 October 2011).

[42] *SAS v France*, App no 43835/11 (ECtHR, 26 June 2014); *Belkacemi and Oussar v Belgium*, App no 37798/13 (ECtHR, 11 July 2017). Compare *Ahmed Arslan and Others v Turkey*, App no 41135/98 (ECtHR, 23 February 2010) holding that wearing a religious garment in public does not pose a threat to public order, in particular if there is no evidence of engaging in proselytism.

[43] See S Ferrari and S Pastorelli, *Religion in Public Spaces: a European Perspective* (Abingdon, Routledge, 2016).

[44] See, e.g. LFM Besselink, 'National and Constitutional Identity Before and After Lisbon' (2010) 6 *Utrecht Law Review* 36.

[45] Treaty on the Functioning of the European Union [2016] OJ C202/1 (TFEU).

[46] Case C-157/15 *Samira Achbita* EU:C:2016:382, Opinion of AG Kokott, para 32: 'National identity does not therefore limit the scope of the Directive as such, but must be duly taken into account in the interpretation of the principle of equal treatment which it contains and of the grounds of justification for any differences of treatment.'

[47] See, e.g. Case C-36/02 *Omega Spielhallen* ECLI:EU:C:2004:614; Case C-208/09 *Sayn-Wittgenstein* ECLI:EU:C:2010:806; Case C-391/09 *Malgožata Runevič-Vardyn and Łukasz Paweł Wardyn* ECLI:EU:C:2011:291.

economic and social integration of certain minority groups.[48] Nevertheless, the last word in such cases belongs to the CJEU which has the sole authority to decide whether a derogation goes beyond what is necessary to protect national identity.[49]

III. The Prohibition of Discrimination and its Limits

The standard understanding of EU equality law is that the prohibition of discrimination is not absolute. In other words, not all differentiations even with regard to the protected categories amount to discrimination which is prohibited. The limitation test which serves to assess whether a law, policy or practice is acceptable is commonly known as the proportionality test.

The proportionality test is a part of the standard judicial analysis of limitations imposed on individual rights or freedoms.[50] In a standard case, the judicial inquiry into the limitations of rights comprises two sets of questions. First, a court examines the scope of protection. In essence, this stage concerns the question whether there has been an interference with a right or freedom. Once a limitation falls in the ambit of legal protection, the Court can move to assess any justification for the interference. The justification analysis can be broken down into three stages. First, it must be established whether the interference is provided for by law. Second, it is examined whether the interference pursues any legitimate aim. Third, the interference needs to pass the proportionality *sensu stricto* test.

The proportionality analysis typically includes the following questions:

(a) whether there was a rational connection between the aim and the means (suitability);

(b) whether the impairment of the right was minimal, and there are no alternative, less impairing means that would serve the aim equally well (necessity); and

(c) whether a fair balance has been struck between the benefit of achieving the aim and the harm resulting from the infringement of the right.[51]

[48] See, e.g. *Ebrahimian v France* (n 40). See further E Brems, 'Ebrahimian v. France: Headscarf ban upheld for the entire public sector' (Strasbourg Observers Blog, 27 November 2015). Available at: https://strasbourgobservers.com/2015/11/27/ebrahimian-v-france-headscarf-ban-upheld-for-entire-public-sector/.

[49] LFM Besselink, 'Case C-208/09 *Ilonka Sayn-Wittgenstein v Landershauptmann von Wien*, Judgment (Second Chamber) of 22 December 2010' (2012) 49 *Common Market Law Review* 671.

[50] See, e.g. A Barak, *Proportionality: Constitutional Rights and their Limitations* (Cambridge, Cambridge University Press, 2012); E Ellis (ed), *The Principle of Proportionality in the Laws of Europe* (Oxford, Hart Publishing, 1999).

[51] A Stone Sweet and J Mathews, 'Proportionality, Balancing and Global Constitutionalism' (2008) 19 *Columbia Journal of Transnational Law* 72; M Kumm, 'Institutionalising Socratic Contestation: The Rationalist Human Rights Paradigm, Legitimate Authority and the Point of Judicial Review' (2007) 1 *European Journal of Legal Studies* 17; M Kumm, 'The Idea of Socratic Contestation and the Right to Justification: The Point of Rights-based Proportionality Review' (2010) 4 *Law and Ethics of Human Rights* 142.

The same standard of limitation analysis is enshrined in Article 52(1) of the Charter of Fundamental Rights which reads as follows:

> Any limitation on the exercise of the rights and freedoms recognised by this Charter must be provided for by law and respect the essence of those rights and freedoms. Subject to the principle of proportionality, limitations may be made only if they are necessary and genuinely meet objectives of general interest recognised by the Union or the need to protect the rights and freedoms of others.

In consequence, any limitation imposed on the rights and freedoms provided in the Charter needs to pass three stages: 'provided by law', 'legitimate aim' and 'proportionality test'.

In this context, it is characteristic that the prohibition of discrimination entailed in Article 21 of the Charter does not use the term 'right'. Yet, it is recognised that this provision guarantees individuals protection against discrimination which may be invoked independently of whether there is a breach of other Charter rights or freedoms. Hence, one could speak of a subjective *right* not to be discriminated against with regard to a specific protected ground.[52]

In practice, the prohibition of discrimination may be invoked in case a measure (e.g. national law implementing EU law) treats two categories of similarly situated subjects unequally. In such instances, it could thus be assumed that there is an 'interference' with the right not to be discriminated against and the measure needs to further pass the legitimate aim and the proportionality *sensu stricto* tests. In the words of the Court of Justice, the proportionality test implies that the measure does not 'exceed the limits of what is appropriate and necessary in order to attain the relevant legitimate objectives' and 'when there is a choice between several appropriate measures, recourse must be had to the least onerous among them, and the disadvantages caused must not be disproportionate to the aims pursued'.[53]

The proportionality test also plays a role in the context of EU equality law. First, it applies to derogations from the prohibition of direct discrimination, where the concept of 'legitimate aims' is very specific. Second, it is also used to assess whether indirect discrimination has sufficient justification.[54]

[52] As a matter of fact, neither EU law nor the CJEU use the term 'right' in relation to equality. Hence, in the EU vocabulary, there is no subjective right to equal treatment and non-discrimination. Instead, the CJEU speaks of the principle of non-discrimination in relation to a specific protected ground (ie gender, age, sexual orientation, etc.) enshrined in Art 21 CFR and given specific expression by the EU Equality Directives.

[53] Case C-528/13 *Léger* EU:C:2015:288. For an overview of proportionality in this case, see U Belavusau, 'Towards EU Sexual Risk Regulation: Restrictions on Blood Donation as Infringement of Active Citizenship' (2016) 7 *European Journal of Risk Regulation* 801.

[54] See also *Eweida* (n 6) para 104: 'The Court considers that the relevant comparator in this case is a registrar with no religious objection to same-sex unions. It agrees with the applicant's contention that the local authority's requirement that all registrars of births, marriages and deaths be designated also as civil partnership registrars had a particularly detrimental impact on her because of her religious beliefs. In order to determine whether the local authority's decision not to make an exception for the applicant and others in her situation amounted to indirect discrimination in breach of Article 14, the Court must consider whether the policy pursued a legitimate aim and was proportionate.'

In the light of the FED, direct discrimination on the grounds of religion occurs where one person is treated less favourably than another is, has been or would be treated in a comparable situation.[55] It means that less favourable treatment on the grounds of religion is prohibited unless (1) it is not less favourable, or (2) it falls in the scope of a derogation. The Directive provides three types of derogations regarding religion which include (1) genuine and determining occupational requirements,[56] (2) religious institutions,[57] and (3) positive actions.[58] Consequently, courts need to use the proportionality analysis to review the relationship between the legitimate objectives for which a derogation was established and the means employed to achieve these objectives.

By contrast, indirect discrimination occurs when an apparently neutral provision, criterion or practice has a discriminatory effect on a protected category compared with other persons, unless it can be objectively justified.[59] An objective justification requires showing that unequal treatment serves a legitimate interest and is appropriate and necessary. The conditions of appropriateness and necessity follow the standard proportionality test, which implies that a measure is appropriate and necessary when there are no other appropriate and less restrictive measures to achieve the aim, and the disadvantages caused are not disproportionate to the objectives thereby pursued.[60]

IV. Proportionality Test

The proportionality test is not only used by the European Court of Human Rights and domestic (constitutional) courts to review limitations of human rights, but also by the Court of Justice in cases concerning discrimination.[61] While there is a difference in the scope of inquiry carried out by international Courts in human rights cases, in particular between the ECtHR, which uses the notion of margin of

[55] Directive 2000/78/EC, Art 2(1)(a).

[56] ibid Art 4(1).

[57] ibid Art 4(2) and (3).

[58] ibid Art 7.

[59] Art 2(1)(b) Directives 2000/78/EC, 2000/43/EC, 2004/13/EC, 2006/54/EC.

[60] In *CHEZ*, the CJEU set the proportionality test in the following way:

> 'a measure would be capable of being objectively justified:
>
> (1) by the intention to ensure the [*legitimate* aim]
>
> only if that measure did not go beyond what is:
>
> (2) appropriate and
> (3) necessary to achieve those legitimate aims and
> (4) the disadvantages caused were not disproportionate to the objectives thereby pursued'. – Case C-83/14 *CHEZ* (n 35) para 129.

[61] The proportionality test is also central in cases in which the CJEU assesses legality of national measures affecting the functioning of the Single Market. See, e.g. N Emiliou, *The Principle of Proportionality in European Law: A Comparative Study* (London, Kluwer Law International, 1995).

appreciation to defer to national authorities in their means-ends assessment and the CJEU, which usually leaves the actual balancing to the national courts, the proportionality test appears to be a harmonising element in the fragmented body of human rights law.

One of the major reasons for the almost universal recognition of the proportionality analysis stems from the open-ended character of its questions and its focus on balancing competing values rather than predetermined constitutional commitments.[62] Unlike the model of judicial review based on the priority of rights, the proportionality test does not measure their abstract weight, but the relative importance of competing values. The test thus entails the possibility of adapting the 'balancing scale' to local conditions. More importantly, its structure acknowledges that disagreement about the relative weight of fundamental rights is inherent in a democratic society.[63]

The proportionality test is only a tool to assess limitations of rights rather than to establish their abstract priority. Therefore, in judicial review based on the concept of rights as principles,[64] particular attention needs to be given to justifications. Otherwise, the virtue of having rights becomes particularly weak.[65] It is even argued that a meaningful analysis of rights limitations needs to involve both the evaluation of the 'process of reasoned justification' and the 'justifiability of the actual decision'.[66] The emphasis on the procedural aspect takes into account the quality of the decision-making process, while the focus on the merits refers to the acceptability of the outcome of this process in the form of a law or policy. Therefore, it is recommended that courts integrate these two approaches and scrutinize both the process and the substance of a law or policy.

In the process-orientated analysis, courts may actually inquire whether rights have been duly considered by decision makers, and more specifically, whether the fact of adopting a law or policy was known to all those concerned, and whether the policy was consistently applied. The process-orientated review also addresses the question whether those concerned were heard, or ultimately, whether their point of view was taken into account. In contrast, the substance-orientated analysis focuses on the practical outcome of the process. It verifies whether the aims are legitimate and whether the relationship between means and ends is proportional.

[62] LB Tremblay, 'An Egalitarian Defense of Proportionality-based Balancing' (2014) 12 *International Journal of Constitutional Law* 864.

[63] J Waldron, *Law and Disagreement* (Oxford, Oxford University Press, 1999); G Webber, *Negotiable Constitution: On Limitation of Rights* (Cambridge, Cambridge University Press, 2009).

[64] R Alexy, *Theory of Constitutional Rights* (Oxford, Oxford University Press, 2010).

[65] M Kumm, 'What Do You Have in Virtue of Having a Constitutional Right? On the Place and Limits of the Proportionality Requirement' (2006) New York University Public Law and Legal Theory Working Paper No 46.

[66] D Dyzenhaus, 'Proportionality and Deference in a Culture of Justification' in G Huscroft, BW Miller, and G Webber (eds), *Proportionality and the Rule of Law* (Cambridge, Cambridge University Press, 2014) 234–258.

This integrated approach to the proportionality review requires that courts apply the necessity test rigorously. In case of regulations concerning religious clothing, the process-orientated analysis of the necessity requirement would mean that main stakeholders are invited to participate in determining the scope of a law or policy and are able to suggest modifications to or exceptions from the general rule. In turn, the substance-orientated analysis of the necessity test permits a substantive assessment of the reasons for rejecting less restrictive solutions. As specifically regards Islamic veils, it thus implies that employers consider introducing a customized company headgear (cap) in a company dress code.

V. Proportionality of a Veil Ban

A. Interference with the Scope of Rights

The following analysis aims to reconstruct arguments examined by courts in veil ban cases, where the first question is whether there had been an interference with freedom of religion. Notably, such an interference is usually easily acknowledged as Courts prefer to deal with the question of whether an interference is justified. Even less contestable is whether wearing religious clothing or symbols constitutes a practice of a religion or its mere manifestation.

There are a variety of Islamic dresses and headgears and many ways to wear them.[67] In the second headscarf case before the German Federal Constitutional Court (FCC), the applicant, a teacher in a public school, was forced to abandon the Islamic veil, but insisted on covering her head with a cap (*Mütze*) that was available in shops.[68] In *SAS v France* [2014], the applicant claimed to be 'a devout Muslim' but she wore *burca* and *nijab* not systematically, but according to her liking.[69] In *Achbita* [2017], the applicant was a Muslim woman who decided to wear the Islamic headscarf at work three years after the commencement of her employment. Also in the British case decided by the House of Lords, *Begrum* [2006] the applicant originally accepted her school uniform as the modest dress without complaint, but after two years refused to attend the school without a headscarf and a long coat-like garment prohibited by the school.[70]

[67] The term 'veil' refers to different types of Islamic headgear ('hijab', 'al-amira', 'sharia', 'khimar', 'chador', 'niqab' and 'burca'). Yet, their shape and size may, in fact, make a difference in the policy context.

[68] Judgment of the German Federal Constitutional Court of 27 January 2015, 1 BvR 471/101.

[69] *SAS* (n 42) paras 11–12: 'The applicant added that she wore the niqab in public and in private, but not systematically: she might not wear it, for example, when she visited the doctor, when meeting friends in a public place, or when she wanted to socialise in public. She was thus content not to wear the niqab in public places at all times but wished to be able to wear it when she chose to do so, depending in particular on her spiritual feelings. There were certain times (for example, during religious events such as Ramadan) when she believed that she ought to wear it in public in order to express her religious, personal and cultural faith. Her aim was not to annoy others but to feel at inner peace with herself.'

[70] *R (Begum) v Governors of Denbigh High School* [2006] UKHL 15.

Imputing that a veil ban infringes upon freedom of religion can be subjected to a number of objections. First, it could be argued that an Islamic veil is not a religious symbol; second, its mandatory character could be contested even by religious leaders; and third, the motivation to wear a veil does not need to be strictly religious. It could also be argued that 'unlike the Christian cross (…), the headscarf is not in itself a religious symbol. Only in connection with the person who wears it and with the conduct of that person in other respects can it have such an effect'.[71] In contrast, some commentators view an Islamic veil simply as a piece of cloth which should be regarded as such, while a suspicious reaction to veils is an example of 'cultural chauvinism'.[72]

Nevertheless, it appears that courts commonly accept that an Islamic veil is a symbol of religious identity and affiliation with a religious community.[73] Consequently, a veil ban is seen as a limitation of freedom of religion. It is clear that courts avoid examination of whether a person wearing a veil was actually fulfilling a religious duty.[74] Evidently, judges understand that it is not their task either to examine the genuineness of religious convictions or to provide an interpretation of a holy script. Any such attempt may be contested by religious authorities and undermines the position of a judge as a neutral arbiter. They also seem to assume that wearing a headscarf is an act of free will[75] rather than gender oppression,[76] provided that no circumstances of the case prove the contrary.[77]

However, there is an additional difficulty regarding the interference analysis in public service employment cases. In the past, some courts accepted that rules affecting public servants do not infringe upon individual rights but specify the official duties. Hence, the prohibition to manifest religious views in public service

[71] Judgment of the German Federal Constitutional Court of 24 September 2003, 2 BvR 1436/02 (further referred to as *Ludin*), para 50.

[72] W Brown, *Regulating Aversion: Tolerance in the Age of Identity and Empire* (Princeton, Princeton University Press, 2006).

[73] A Vakulenko, 'Islamic Dress in Human Rights Jurisprudence: A Critique of Current Trends' (2007) 4 *Human Rights Law* 717 (noting that 'the very construction of hijab issues as those of "religious identity", sustained by the use of Article 9 of the ECHR as the primary legal basis for their resolution, has shaped a number of counterproductive trends. These are: avoiding difficult questions through a judicial technique of deference to local knowledge; using a language of choice to produce an obscure and unsatisfactory account of Muslim women's agency; false dichotomising of culture and gender; and producing an ever more docile and exposed subject through the subtle mechanisms of public scrutiny and moralising.').

[74] *Sahin* (n 41) para 71.

[75] Sahin (n 41) Dissenting opinion of Judge Tulkens, para 12: 'It is not the Court's role to (…) determine in a general and abstract way the signification of wearing the headscarf or to impose its viewpoint on the applicant. The applicant, a young adult university student, said – and there is nothing to suggest that she was not telling the truth – that she wore the headscarf of her own free will. In this connection, I fail to see how the principle of sexual equality can justify prohibiting a woman from following a practice which, in the absence of proof to the contrary, she must be taken to have freely adopted.'

[76] In contrast, a veil may be construed as a symbol of Islamic feminism.

[77] See *Aishah Azmi*, Employment Appeal Tribunal decision of March 2007, Appeal no UKEAT/0009/07/MAA; *SAS* (n 42) para 11: 'The applicant emphasised that neither her husband nor any other member of her family put pressure on her to dress in this manner.'

was considered as an internal part of public service employment rather than a limitation of human rights of public servants. This position follows the *quid pro quo* logic which implies that public employment is conditional upon giving up some individual rights and freedoms.[78] This approach was also adopted by the ECtHR in a case concerning higher education, where it was found that a veil ban does not constitute an interference with freedom of religion.[79] The Court stated that 'by choosing to pursue her higher education in a secular university a student submits to those university rules, which may make the freedom of students to manifest their religion subject to restrictions as to place and manner intended to ensure harmonious coexistence between students of different beliefs'.[80]

Today, the ECtHR has departed from this position and regards all national laws concerning religious symbols or clothing as an interference in the scope of protection enshrined in Article 9 ECHR.[81] Even more progressive was the FCC which recognised not only that public school teachers have the right to enjoy freedom of religion in their workplace,[82] but also that an Islamic veil worn by a teacher should not be attributed to the state.[83] In this regard, the FCC differentiated between religious symbols carried by individual persons and exhibited by the school administration.[84]

B. Prescribed by Law

The question whether the measure was provided for by law was not decisive in most of the analysed veil ban cases. One could even note that rules regarding dress code are not necessarily a matter of statutory law. In *Begrum*, for example, the powers to establish such rules were expressly delegated to the local school authority. Still, it is important that there is a clear statutory authorisation to adopt rules restricting manifestations of religious faith.

Most recently, the Hungarian Constitutional Court invalidated a local decree banning Islamic veils, as well as other religious activities as the law lacked a

[78] See, e.g. GS Morris, 'Fundamental Rights: Exclusion by Agreement?' (2001) 30 *Industrial Law Review* 49; F Wind, R Schimana, M Wichmann, *Öffentliches Dienstrecht. Das Beamten- und Arbeitsrecht für den öffentlichen Dienst* (Kohlhammer 1999) 18.

[79] *Karaduman v Turkey*, App no 8810/03 (ECtHR, 17 June 2008).

[80] ibid para 109.

[81] Compare with *Dahlab v Switzerland* (ECtHR, 15 February 2001); *Kurtulmus v Turkey* (ECtHR, 24 January 2006); *Köse and 93 others v Turkey* (ECtHR, 24 January 2006); *Aktas v France* (ECtHR, 30 June 2009).

[82] BVerfGE 39, 334 (366–67); BVerfGE 108, 282, para 34: 'Even for those with the status of civil servants, the fundamental rights apply, although the civil servant's sphere of responsibilities under Article 33 (5) of the Basic Law restricts the civil servant's exercise of fundamental rights in office; these limits follow from general standards imposed on the civil service of from particular requirements of the public office in question.'

[83] 1 BvR 471/10.

[84] ibid para 104.

statutory basis.[85] As this decision was exclusively based on this formal grounds, three concurring judges noted 'with a view to the problems stemming from the obvious threats caused by the Islamisation of Europe' that it should not preclude the adoption of a similar ban by the Parliament.

Also in *Ludin* [2003], the first judgment of the German FCC on the Islamic veil in public service, the ban was held to be unconstitutional as it did not have a sufficiently clear statutory basis. In this case, the FCC found that the prohibition to wear a veil imposed on public school teachers could be introduced only by the democratically legitimised state legislator. It also emphasised that it is the duty of state legislatures to define teachers' obligation under civil-service law and to determine the limits of the conflicting rights.[86] On this basis, the Court also emphasised that legislation introducing limitations on public servants' rights must 'seek a compromise that is reasonably acceptable to everyone'.[87]

C. Legitimate Aim

The legitimate aim stage is used to establish whether the law infringing upon rights and freedom pursued a legitimate legislative goal or, conversely, whether it was motivated by illegitimate reasons.[88] While courts seem to be generally inclined not to question the legislative motives in the legitimate aim stage, a rigorous approach to the proportionality test could, in some cases, help to 'smoke out' any discriminatory intentions.[89] Still, some of the aims invoked in the veils decisions were not accepted exactly because they were based on prejudice.

The standard defence of a veil ban (i.e. neutrality) is usually approved. For example, the German FCC agreed that the legislation adopted by North Rhine Westphalia intended 'to safeguard the educational mandate of the state, to protect conflicting fundamental rights of pupils and parents and thereby to prevent conflicts from the outset'.[90] It thus acknowledged that the law was legitimate as it aimed to ensure state neutrality and religious peace in schools.

[85] Judgment of the Hungarian Constitutional Court of 11 April 2017, no II/2034/2016.

[86] *Ludin* (n 71) para 67.

[87] ibid.

[88] For example, the Hungarian local ban on Islamic headscarves, Mosque buildings and other Islamic activities was justified by the aim to defend local community and traditions and presented as necessary in the view of the EU refugee redistribution plans.

[89] W Sadurski, 'Standards of Constitutional Scrutiny and Motive-based Theory of Discrimination' in M Zubik (ed), *Human Rights in Contemporary World. Essays in Honour of Professor Lech Garlicki* (Warszaw, Wydawnictwo Sejmowe, 2017) 253–262, 255 ('A heightened scrutiny of laws may be seen as vigorous enquiry into the reasons behind the law, stemming from an uncertainty, skepticism or suspicion as to the nature of the reasons behind the law – or at least frustration that no such reasons have been provided by the legislator').

[90] 1 BvR 471/10, para 99. In this decision, the FCC took into account that different states adopt different rules because the compromise may require taking into account school traditions or religious convictions of the population living in a given state.

In other cases before national courts, veil bans were justified by the protection of public order and the rights of others. For example, the French Constitutional Council accepted that a full-face veil could be dangerous in terms of public safety and also that it fails to comply with the minimum requirements of a common life. It agreed with the position that women who conceal their face experience exclusion and inferiority. In effect, it found that it is not the ban, but the full-face cover that is 'patently incompatible with the constitutional principles of liberty and equality'.[91]

In contrast, the Spanish Supreme Court disagreed with the Catalonian High Court of Justice which held that a full-face veil ban serves the protection of public tranquillity, public safety or public order in the absence of evidence that wearing the veil was detrimental to those interests.[92] It also observed that the ban could not be justified by the protection of women who wear it under duress. On the contrary, it found that the ban could result in the isolation of and discrimination against immigrant women and was incompatible with the objective of ensuring their social integration.

In *SAS v France* (2014), the ECtHR Grand Chamber accepted that the law prohibiting full-face veils serves the 'protection of the rights and freedoms of others' and regarded it as a barrier to 'living together in diversity'.[93] Still, it rejected the government's position invoking the protection of gender equality and the dignity of others. It first noted that the government may not rely on gender equality to ban a practice that is defended by women. It would mean that states could use such justification to 'protect individuals from the exercise of their own fundamental rights and freedoms'.[94] The ECtHR also observed that wearing a veil is not aimed at insulting anyone, in absence of evidence to the contrary.[95] Similarly, the Court did not accept that the law prohibiting the concealment of the face in the public could be justified by the interest of 'public safety'. In this context, it pointed out that the government did not provide evidence that wearing a veil poses a threat to public safety.

Nevertheless, in *SAS*, the ECtHR noted that the national legislator adopting the ban could be motivated by a discriminatory intent. It emphasised that 'a State which enters into a legislative process of this kind takes the risk of contributing to the consolidation of the stereotypes which affect certain categories of the population and of encouraging the expression of intolerance, when it has a duty, on the contrary, to promote tolerance'.[96] This observation did not lead the

[91] Decision of the French Constitutional Council of 7 October 2010, no 2010-613 DC.

[92] Judgment of the Spanish Supreme Court of 6 February 2013, Case No 693/2013, Appeal no 4118/2011.

[93] *SAS* (n 42) para 121.

[94] ibid para 119.

[95] ibid: '[a State Party] does not have any evidence capable of leading it to consider that women who wear the full-face veil seek to express a form of contempt against those they encounter or otherwise to offend against the dignity of others.'

[96] ibid para 149.

Court to disqualifying the legislative motives altogether since it accepted that the impugned law did not aim to ban a religious practice, but the concealment of the face.[97]

D. Necessary in a Democratic Society

For the purpose of a judicial review of a limitation imposed on a right or freedom, the necessary in a democratic society clause implies that the proportionality test applies. Although the first stage concerning suitability of a measure could actually pose a substantive hurdle to a veil ban, this question was usually not addressed *in extensu* or was even entirely skipped in the analysed veil cases. In turn, the necessity test entails the least restrictive means test. Thus, the necessity test is meaningless if courts do not truly engage with the examination of alternative solutions to the adopted ones or ponder upon their comparative effectiveness.

It is particularly puzzling if courts defer to the legislative choice in the necessity stage in cases concerning bans subject to criminal or disciplinary sanctions. It could be expected that in such cases, courts seek to establish whether there are less-restrictive solutions that could serve the aims of the law equally well. For example, in their decisions, courts could explain why the prohibition of an Islamic dress is to be considered the least restrictive way to protect women from 'external pressures', or conversely, why the pressure to wear a particular type of Islamic clothing is worse than the pressure to remove it.[98]

In general, it could be observed that domestic courts upholding the full-face veil bans were be persuaded by a limited scope of the considered adopted measure. Also in cases where the law provided some exceptions from the general rule, a veil ban could be found to be not overly restrictive. Characteristically, the full-face veil bans in both France and Belgium were upheld because there were more restrictive solutions than those actually chosen by the legislator. Thus, a yardstick in the test was not less restrictive, but the most restrictive means. In this comparison, the impugned laws easily passed the necessity stage.

In France, the law applied only to full-face veils worn in public places, but not to places of worship open to the public. Thus, religious women could wear a *burca* or *nijab* in private and in places of worship. In comparison, the Belgian Constitutional Court found a similar prohibition proportionate for the reason that 'the legislature opted for the most lenient criminal sanction'.[99] Taking into account the mechanism of individualisation of criminal sanctions, the Court held that the 'recourse to a criminal sanction to guarantee compliance with the prohibition imposed by the Law has no disproportionate effects in relation to the

[97] ibid para 151.
[98] *Vakulenko* (n 73) 724.
[99] Belgian Constitutional Court, judgment of 6 December 2012, B.29.1.

aims pursued'.[100] It also observed that the law does not apply to persons acting upon duress and in places of worship.

Similarly, in the *SAS* case, the Strasbourg Court attenuated the importance of criminal sanctions by emphasising that they were 'the lightest that could be envisaged' and thus proportionate. As a result, instead of giving weight to individual freedom, the Court gave special weight to the 'role of the domestic policy-maker'.[101] Regrettably, as noted in a dissenting opinion:

> [t]he Government have not explained why it would have been impossible to apply less restrictive measures, instead of criminalising the concealment of the face in all public places. No account has been given as to whether or to what extent any efforts have been made to discourage the relatively recent phenomenon of the use of full-face veils, by means, for example, of awareness-raising and education.[102]

Exactly because less intrusive measures were discussed in the legislative process, but nevertheless rejected, did the Court not feel competent to intervene with the legislative choice, lacking more specific information about why the 'soft' measures were not adopted.

Even more striking in the veil cases is the weak role of evidence demonstrating the necessity of a legislative intervention. In fact, only the FCC found that prohibiting public school teachers to wear a veil in school was unacceptable as it was based on an erroneous assumption that the mere presence of a veil causes a risk of disturbance. In the majority opinion, the Court conceded that the realisation of the duty of the state to observe religious neutrality does not preclude teachers from wearing a veil as a passive symbol. However, in the opinion of the FCC, the law could prohibit an external religious conduct which results in a sufficiently concrete danger for the school peace or state neutrality.[103]

In the end, it is worth noting that there is not a single decision of the European Court of Human Rights finding a breach of freedom of religion in veil cases. It seems that in case of Islamic clothing, the Court is more willing to accept that the national authorities struck a fair balance between individual freedoms and the protection of public interests than in case of Christian symbols. In particular, if a veil ban is introduced in the context of public education or employment, the Court was eager to emphasise that national authorities have a wide margin of appreciation to regulate questions concerning the relationship between state and religion.[104]

Although, in some cases, courts took into account the decision-making process leading to the adoption of a veil ban, this aspect was never used to discredit the content of the law. In *Sahin*, the Court noted that students are free to manifest their

[100] ibid B.24.
[101] ibid para 154.
[102] *SAS* (n 42) Joint partly dissenting opinion by Judges Nussberger and Jäderblom, para 24.
[103] 1 BvR 471/10, para 108.
[104] *Sahin* (n 41) para 110.

beliefs 'within the limits imposed by the constraints of educational organisation',[105] and stressed that the impugned legislation was based on a dialogue between the university and the students.

Also in the *Begrum* case, the UK House of Lords, acting in its judicial capacity, was satisfied with the school's process for devising its uniform policy, which included consultations with local Muslim authorities.[106] The Lords emphasised that they lacked 'local knowledge' (i.e. 'the experience, background and detailed knowledge of the head teacher, staff and governors').[107] In effect, they held that 'the justification must be sought at the local level and it is there that an area of judgment, comparable to the margin of appreciation, must be allowed to the school'.[108]

VI. Justification Analysis in the Veil Ban Cases before the CJEU

The two veil ban decisions rendered by the CJEU are the first to provide an interpretation of the EU Equality Directives with regard to religion.[109] In essence, the CJEU had to determine whether a ban on religious symbols in the workplace may be justified by the economic interests of private employers.[110] The French and Belgian courts asked in their preliminary references whether the promotion of the company's image and catering to customer preference warrants a derogation from the prohibition of discrimination with regard to religion. In a broader sense, answering this question, the CJEU was expected to suggest how to reconcile the principle of non-discrimination with the protection of economic freedoms guaranteed in EU law.

The preliminary question in *Bougnaqoui* [2017] was whether a requirement not to wear the religious clothing is capable of constituting an occupational requirement in the meaning of Article 4(1) of the FED.[111] In *Achbita* [2017], the problem

[105] ibid para 118.

[106] The House of Lords noticed that the policy-making process regarding the school uniform was participatory and inclusive as the school consulted its policy with parents, students, staff and the Imams of the three local mosques and received no objection to the chosen dress (*shalwar kameeze*) that was worn by Muslim, Hindu and Sikh girls. Specifically, the Islamic authorities advised that the school uniform did not offend the Islamic dress code. Yet, the school authorities did not consider other options than shalwar kameeze for religious students.

[107] *Begum* (n 70) para 34.

[108] ibid.

[109] Cases C-157/15 *Achbita* EU:C:2017:203 and C-188/15 *Bougnaqoui and ADDH* EU:C:2017:204. See further A. Śledzińska-Simon, 'Is there a place for the Islamic veil in the workplace? Managerial prerogatives and the duty of reasonable accommodation in the EU anti-discrimination governance' (2016) 17 *ERA Forum* 203.

[110] See also the chapter written by E Pastor in the present volume.

[111] Recital 23 of the Preamble and Art 4(1) FED ('Member States may provide that a difference of treatment which is based on a characteristic related to any of the [prohibited] grounds (…) shall

was qualified by the CJEU as indirect discrimination,[112] even though Belgian courts approached it as a case of direct discrimination.[113] Ultimately, in both cases the decision had to be based on the proportionality analysis – in *Bougnaoui* the CJEU dealt with the proportionality of a derogation from the prohibition of direct discrimination, while in *Achbita* it reviewed allegedly neutral provisions having a deleterious impact on Muslim women.

In both instances, the employers had to demonstrate that their policies serve a legitimate interest, and are necessary and proportionate. Nevertheless, the scope of permissible justification in case of occupational qualifications is much narrower than in case of indirect discrimination as it presupposes a very precise legitimate aim. In the words of Article 4(1) FED, the genuine and determining occupational requirement should be closely related to the nature of the particular occupational activities or the context in which they are carried out.

In *Bougnaqoui*, the employer required that a person who takes the position of a design engineer should not visibly affiliate with any religion, in particular through religious conduct when in contact with customers. Hence, the CJEU had to determine whether religion (defined in a negative way by reference to religious conduct) can constitute an occupational requirement which is 'genuine and determining'. The Court had previously ruled in *Feryn* [2008] that a company owner who publicly declared he would not recruit Moroccans could not claim that ethnic origin – or precisely, the fact of not belonging to a particular ethnic group – is a genuine and determining occupational qualification.[114] Moreover, the CJEU explained that 'it is not the ground on which the difference of treatment is based but a characteristic related to that ground which must constitute a genuine and determining occupational requirement'.[115] It also emphasised that it is only in very limited circumstances that a characteristic related, in

not constitute discrimination where, by reason of the nature of the particular occupational activities concerned or of the context in which they are carried out, such a characteristic constitutes a genuine and determining occupational requirement, provided that the objective is legitimate and the requirement is proportionate.').

[112] The CJEU could reach this conclusion since the employer did not prohibit wearing the Islamic veil but all religious symbols at work. See also Weiler (n 4) 'In our case the purpose is to ensure "neutrality" for the presumed purpose of offering a more "professional" contact between company employees or some such objective, but the metrics used are precisely the protected classes – religion; "convictions." If you use as your metric the protected class itself, this seems to me to take it squarely out of "indirect" discrimination and into direct discrimination.'

[113] In Case C-157/15 *Achbita* (n 109), the Belgian Court asked the CJEU whether Article 2(2)(a) FED should be interpreted as meaning that the prohibition to Muslims to wear the headscarf at work does not imply any direct discrimination when the rule forbids all the workers to wear any visible symbol expressing their political, philosophical or religious belief.

[114] Case C-54/07 *Feryn* EU:C:2008:397, para 25: 'The fact that an employer declares publicly that it will not recruit employees of a certain ethnic or racial origin, something which is clearly likely to strongly dissuade certain candidates from submitting their candidature and, accordingly, to hinder their access to the labour market, constitutes direct discrimination in respect of recruitment within the meaning of Directive 2000/43.' Hence, the only permissible defence was to prove that the undertaking's actual recruitment practice did not correspond to the discriminatory statements.

[115] Case C-229/08 *Wolf* EU:C:2010:3.

particular, to religion may constitute a genuine and determining occupational requirement.[116]

Having regard to the facts of the case at hand, the CJEU underlined that the genuine and determining occupational requirement refers to objective characteristics 'dictated by the nature of the occupational activities concerned or of the context in which they are carried out' rather than to 'subjective considerations, such as the willingness of the employer to take account of the particular wishes of the customer'.[117] However, here, the CJEU could have followed the process-orientated path of the proportionality analysis and centred on the communication process between the employer and current or potential employees. This argument was raised by Advocate General Sharpston who noted that the employer and employee need to 'explore the options together to arrive at a solution that accommodates both the employee's right to manifest his religious belief and the employer's right to conduct his business'.[118] Ultimately, the CJEU could have established that an employer bears a duty not only to justify its internal policies, but also to specify why it was not possible to reasonably accommodate the religious identity claims of particular employees.

In contrast, *Achbita* was decided on formal grounds. The Court first accepted that 'the desire to display, in relations with both public and private sector customers, a policy of political, philosophical or religious neutrality must be considered legitimate'.[119] Yet, in the end, it focused on the question of whether the policy was 'prescribed by law'. It specifically required that a private company introduces an official policy banning all manifestations of political, philosophical or religious beliefs in the workplace and ensures that it is consistently applied. It also emphasised that such policy needs to be 'genuinely pursued in a consistent and systematic manner'.[120]

Although the CJEU made a general suggestion regarding the narrowly tailored means in relation to the company rules applying only to employees who are required to come into direct contact with customers, it did not pursue the least restrictive means test or balancing between the principle of non-discrimination and the right to economic freedom enshrined in Article 16 of the Charter. Instead, the CJUE required that to be considered strictly necessary, the prohibition on the visible wearing of any sign or clothing capable of being associated with a religious faith or a political or philosophical belief needs to cover only employees who interact with customers.[121] In effect, it suggested that such a narrowly-tailored measure could be considered appropriate and necessary. Clearly, the Court failed to engage in a meaningful proportionality analysis that should be at the heart of a fundamental rights case such as that at hand.

[116] Case C-157/15 *Achbita* (n 109) para 34.
[117] ibid para 40.
[118] Case C-157/15 *Achbita* EU:C:2017:203, Opinion of AG Sharpston, para 128.
[119] Case C-157/15 *Achbita* (n 109) para 37.
[120] ibid para 40.
[121] ibid para 42.

VII. Conclusions

The veil ban decisions rendered by the CJEU seem to follow the reasoning of most other courts in these veil controversy cases, which similarly deferred to the relevant decision-making authority. The ECtHR accepted that since there is no consensus about the relationship between church and state in Europe, national authorities have a broad margin of appreciation in this area. Consequently, it held that banning the Islamic veil in public education, public service and in public does not violate freedom of religion. In comparison, its approach to religious symbols still related to Christianity in the context of private employment was much less deferential.[122] One could thus get the impression that the Strasbourg Court treats these two religions unequally.

Among national courts, only the German FCC and the Spanish Constitutional Court disagreed with the legislative choice to ban the veil, basing this on a lack of clear evidence that the mere presence of a veil can disturb social peace and public order. Remarkably, the Spanish decision concerning the full-face veil needs to be contrasted with the position of the French and Belgian constitutional adjudicators in favour of banning the *burca* and *nijab*.

It could thus be argued that the current protection of freedom of religion and the protection against religious discrimination in Europe is based on a multilevel normative framework, which leaves a significant margin of discretion to 'local' decision-makers. The political and social sensitivity of the subject matter seems to prevent courts from applying a more demanding scrutiny in the context of the proportionality analysis that could help to identify and address the existing patterns of religious discrimination.

In the context of the veil case judgments, it is striking that courts tend to apply the proportionality test loosely. They either inadequately address the least restrictive means test or refuse to actually balance between the competing values. Moreover, they seem not to look behind the officially stated purposes of the law or policy in suspicion of discriminatory motives. They also do not actually weight the wider social consequences of such laws or policies. This tendency is even more saddening where followed by the CJEU which has clearly avoided the proportionality test in the relevant cases. The Luxembourg Court was driven by the aim of 'projecting an image of neutrality', but actually subsumed the means-aims analysis into the legitimate aim test. Not only did it fail to involve this test in the actual stages of the justification analysis, but also to determine the parameters of such analysis for the referring court.[123]

Regrettably, the CJEU lacked the courage to strengthen the requirements concerning the justification of discriminatory rules in cases regarding religion and to instruct domestic courts on how to examine such cases both normatively

[122] See, in particular, *Eweida v UK* (n 6).
[123] Weiler (n 4) 890.

and empirically. The CJEU should clearly explain that achieving neutrality in business operations could not be done by accommodating any discriminatory views of clients. In addition, the Court did not suggest that private companies bear the duty to engage in a meaningful dialogue with their employees in order to consider alternative solutions to a veil ban and, ultimately, to justify a denial of reasonable accommodation of religious identity claims. Instead, the CJEU simply moved Muslim women from the front desk to the back office. It thus acknowledged that, *in principle*, a private company may prohibit employees in direct contact with customers from manifesting their religious beliefs. In this way, it missed the chance to enhance the effective legal protection of freedom of religion and freedom from discrimination in private employment and beyond.

In the light of these developments, the future of EU anti-discrimination law seems to depend on the judicial response to the problem of structural discrimination and the endorsement of diversity as a legal value. In this context, the shift from norm compliance to management needs to be seen as a consequence of the normative deficiency of the EU anti-discrimination law. Evidently, the uniform interpretation and application of the EU Equality Directives is challenged by national identities, private–public divide and the customer orientation of private business. There is also a risk that these shortcomings of EUn law will result in a re-nationalisation of equality protection and a reinforcement of the existing hierarchies of the protected categories, leading to an even greater divide between secular Europe and its religious communities.

PART IV

Sexual Orientation

10

The Impact of the Framework Equality Directive on the Protection of LGB Persons and Same-Sex Couples from Discrimination under EU Law

ALINA TRYFONIDOU*

I. Introduction

This chapter aims to assess the impact of the Framework Equality Directive 2000 (Directive 2000/78)[1] on the protection of lesbian, gay and bisexual (LGB) individuals and same-sex couples from discrimination under European Union (EU) law.[2] The analysis will begin by explaining that until the adoption of the Framework Equality Directive (FED) 2000, the only steps that the EU took for the protection of the rights of LGB persons and same-sex couples consisted of soft law measures which, as such, lacked teeth. In addition, unlike discrimination on the grounds of gender reassignment, discrimination on the grounds of sexual orientation was held by the Court of Justice of the EU (CJEU) not to be included in the prohibition of discrimination on the grounds of sex and, hence, the various EU law provisions prohibiting the latter could not be applied to assist LGB individuals. The chapter will then analyse the Framework Equality Directive 2000, demonstrating how it has improved the position of LGB persons and same-sex couples under EU law but also highlighting its shortcomings. Moreover, it will be considered whether the gaps in protection left by the Directive are satisfactorily filled by other instruments, in particular by the EU Charter of Fundamental Rights (CFR)[3] which,

* I would like to thank the editors of this book and Phillip M Ayoub for their very helpful comments on previous drafts of this chapter. Needless to say, all errors remain mine.

[1] Council Directive 2000/78/EC establishing a general framework for equal treatment in employment and occupation [2000] OJ L303/16 (Framework Equality Directive, FED).

[2] It should be noted that for ease of reference the umbrella terms 'EU' and 'EU law' will be used throughout this chapter, even when referring to periods preceding the establishment of the EU when the matters of equality were addressed as pertaining to the competence of the E(C)C.

[3] Charter of Fundamental Rights of the European Union [2016] OJ C202/393.

in Article 21, prohibits discrimination on, *inter alia*, the grounds of sexual orientation. Finally, it will be examined whether other legal instruments potentially coming into force in the future will be able to cover these gaps. Specifically, the proposed Equality Directive,[4] which is currently in a state of legal limbo, will be considered. Apart from a detailed analysis of the FED and other relevant legislation, the chapter will also critically assess the judgments by the CJEU that offer an interpretation of the above instruments.

II. LGB Rights under EU Law before the Introduction of the Framework Equality Directive

The recognition of gay and lesbian rights only began in the 1970s, following the awareness raised by the Stonewall riots in New York in June 1969 and the vocalisation of the concerns of the gay and lesbian community through the activities of early gay rights organisations.[5] Nonetheless, gay and lesbian rights as a new 'genre' of human rights found their place in human rights protection much later and usually as a result of purposive judicial interpretation rather than the amendment of human rights instruments to make explicit reference to them.

Thus, the Council of Europe's European Convention on Human Rights (ECHR) did not – and still does not – include any reference to gay and lesbian rights. Similarly, the prohibition of discrimination in Article 14 does not make explicit reference to sexual orientation as a protected ground. Nevertheless, the Strasbourg Court has held that sexual orientation is covered by the open 'or other ground' clause in this provision.[6] Moreover, the Court's jurisprudence has revealed that a number of other ECHR provisions can be employed either alone or in combination with Article 14 ECHR to vindicate the human rights of LGB persons.[7]

Similarly, the founding Treaties of what later became the EU (ie the three Community Treaties)[8] made no reference to fundamental human rights, let alone to LGB rights. This does not appear surprising, given that some of the founding states of the EU and the Council of Europe maintained a criminal

[4] Proposal for a Council Directive implementing the principle of equal treatment between persons irrespective of religion or belief, disability, age or sexual orientation COM (2008) 426 (Proposal for Equality Directive). This was accompanied by a Communication from the Commission to the European Parliament, the Council, the European Economic and Social Committee and the Committee of the Regions. Non-Discrimination and Equal Opportunities: A renewed commitment, COM (2008) 420.

[5] For an excellent account of the history of the gay rights movement in the US, see L Faderman, *The Gay Revolution: The Story of the Struggle* (New York, Simon & Schuster, 2015).

[6] *Salgueiro da Silva Mouta v Portugal*, App no 33290/96 (ECtHR, 21 December 1999), para 28 (sexual orientation).

[7] Eg Arts 3 (freedom from torture and inhuman or degrading treatment), 8 (right to private and family life), and 12 (right to marry) ECHR.

[8] The European Coal and Steel Community (ECSC) Treaty, the European Economic Community (EEC) Treaty, and the European Atomic Energy (Euratom) Community Treaty.

provision prohibiting sodomy (ie male-to-male consensual sex) at the time that both of these organisations were conceived.[9] Nevertheless, tentative steps towards protecting the rights of this segment of the population had already been taken by the EU in the 1980s. Admittedly, until 1999, all such initiatives were confined to soft law measures.[10]

The very first of these soft law measures was taken in 1984, when the European Parliament adopted a resolution on sexual discrimination, inviting the Commission to propose legislation on combating discrimination of homosexual persons in access to employment.[11] Two further resolutions were adopted in 1986 – one on fascism and racism in Europe and one on violence against women – both mentioning sexual orientation as relevant to acts of intolerance.[12]

The following decade saw the adoption of a European Parliament resolution on a plan of action in the context of the 1991–1992 'Europe against AIDS' programme, which stressed the need to include gay men in preventive measures against AIDS.[13] There were, also, actions which sought to raise awareness of the issues affecting the gay and lesbian community, the best example being an EU-funded project which considered the impact on lesbians and gays of the completion of the European internal market.[14] In 1994, the European Parliament Committee on Civil Liberties and Internal Affairs decided to draw up a report – the so-called 'Roth Report'[15] – which identified the various problems faced by 'homosexuals' at the time and called on the Member States as well as the EU institutions to take action to remedy them. Among other things, the report asked the Commission to present a draft Council Directive on combating discrimination on the basis of sexual orientation in a wide range of areas of human life. The report also 'affirmed' the European Parliament's 'conviction that all citizens must be treated equally, irrespective of their sexual orientation'[16] and noted that it '[c]onsiders that the European Community is under the obligation to apply the fundamental principle of equal treatment, irrespective of each individual's sexual orientation, in all legal provisions already adopted or which may be adopted in future'.[17] The European Parliament subsequently issued a 'Resolution on equal rights for homosexuals and lesbians in the EC', which was

[9] This was the case in Germany, Ireland, the United Kingdom and Norway.

[10] See, eg PM Ayoub and D Paternotte, *LGBT Activism and the Making of Europe* (Hampshire, Palgrave Macmillan, 2014).

[11] European Parliament Resolution on sexual discrimination at the workplace [1984] OJ C104/46.

[12] European Parliament Resolution on the rise of fascism and racism in Europe [1986] OJ C141/461; European Parliament Resolution on violence against women [1986] OJ C176/73.

[13] European Parliament Resolution on a plan of action in the context of the 1991–1992 'Europe against AIDS' programme [1991] OJ C158/54.

[14] K Waaldijk and A Clapham (eds), *Homosexuality: A European Community Issue – Essays on Lesbian and Gay Rights in European Law and Policy* (Dordrecht, Martinus Nijhoff, 1993).

[15] European Parliament, Report of the Committee of Civil Liberties and Internal Affairs on equal rights for homosexuals and lesbians in the EC (26 January 1994) A3-0028/94.

[16] Roth Report (n 15).

[17] ibid para 2.

a (much) watered-down version of the Roth Report.[18] This resolution, instead of calling on the Commission to present a draft Directive prohibiting discrimination on the grounds of sexual orientation, merely requested it 'to present a draft Recommendation on equal rights for lesbians and homosexuals'.[19]

In response to these initiatives, the Commission took a number of similarly modest steps. For instance, it included sexual harassment on the grounds of sexual orientation in its code of practice on measures to combat sexual harassment.[20] Similarly, in 1998, the staff regulations for officials of the European Communities were amended to include a clause prohibiting discrimination on grounds of sexual orientation.[21]

During this period, the CJEU, was likewise for the first time confronted with cases involving LGBT persons. Strikingly, the Court showed itself to be rather reticent in relation to the protection of LGB rights, in contrast to its willingness to protect the rights of trans persons.

The first case that reached the CJEU – *P v S and Cornwall* [1996][22] – involved a male-to-female trans person who sought to rely on EU law to challenge the decision of her employer to dismiss her as a result of her decision to undergo gender reassignment surgery. Given that, in the mid-1990s, only discrimination on the grounds of sex and nationality was prohibited by EU law, the claimant argued that the contested dismissal amounted to discrimination based on sex. Since dismissal falls within the scope of 'working conditions', it was argued that the discrimination complained of amounted to a breach of the Equal Treatment Directive 1976 (Directive 76/207).[23] The Court was receptive to these arguments, holding that discrimination on the grounds of gender reassignment amounts to discrimination on the grounds of sex and is thus contrary to EU law.

Shortly after this ruling, in *Grant* [1998][24] the Court was called on to decide whether the prohibition of discrimination on the grounds of sex also included

[18] European Parliament Resolution on equal rights for homosexuals and lesbians in the EC [1994] OJ C61/40.

[19] ibid.

[20] European Commission, A code of practice on measures to combat sexual harassment, Annex to the Commission Recommendation on the dignity of women and men at work [1992] OJ L49/1.

[21] Regulation 781/98 amending the Staff Regulations of Officials and Conditions of Employment of Other Servants of the European Communities in respect of equal treatment [1998] OJ L113/4.

[22] Case C-13/94 *P v S and Cornwall City Council* EU:C:1996:170. For comments, see L Flynn, 'Annotation of Case C-13/94, *P v S and Cornwall County Council*, Judgment of the Full Court of 30 April 1996, [1996] ECR I-2143' (1997) 34 *Common Market Law Review* 367; R Wintemute, 'Recognising New Kinds of Direct Sex Discrimination: Transsexualism, Sexual Orientation and Dress Codes' (1997) 50 *Modern Law Review* 334, 339–344.

[23] Council Directive 76/207/EEC on the implementation of the principle of equal treatment for men and women as regards access to employment, vocational training and promotion, and working conditions [1976] OJ L39/40.

[24] Case C-249/96 *Grant v South-West Trains* EU:C:1998:63. For comments, see KA Armstrong, 'Tales of the Community: Sexual Orientation Discrimination and EC Law' (1998) 20 *Journal of Social Welfare and Family Law* 455; J McInnes, 'Annotation of Case C-249/96, *Lisa Jacqueline Grant v South West Trains Ltd*, Judgment of the Full Court of 17 February 1998, [1998] ECR I-636' (1999) 36 *Common*

discrimination on the grounds of sexual orientation or, if not, whether the latter form of discrimination was prohibited by EU law at the time. This case involved a lesbian employee of South-West Trains (in the UK) who was refused travel concessions for her (long-term) female partner, although her (male) predecessor in the post did receive these concessions for his (long-term) female partner. Ms Grant claimed that this amounted to (direct) discrimination on the grounds of sex prohibited by EU law relying on the requirement of equal pay for equal work in Article 119 EC (now Article 157 TFEU) and the directives on equal treatment of men and women.[25]

However, Grant's argument was not accepted by the Court. In relation to the claim that the contested refusal amounted to discrimination on the grounds of sex, the Court employed the 'equal misery' argument, comparing Ms Grant with a (hypothetical) *male* employee claiming the same concessions for his (*male*) partner.[26] This methodology has been widely criticised in the literature for using the wrong comparator. The correct comparator would have been a male colleague with a *female* partner, since, in this way, the *only* characteristic changed in the comparison is the sex of the claimant, whereas under the comparison drawn by the Court, both the sex of the claimant *and* the sex of the partner were changed.[27] The Court then pointed out that:

> in the present state of the law within the Community, stable relationships between two persons of the same sex are not regarded as equivalent to marriages or stable relationships outside marriage between persons of opposite sex. Consequently, an employer is not required by Community law to treat the situation of a person who has a stable relationship with a partner of the same sex as equivalent to that of a person who is married to or has a stable relationship outside marriage with a partner of the opposite sex.[28]

Finally, the Court noted that discrimination on the grounds of sexual orientation is not covered by the prohibition of discrimination on the grounds of sex.[29]

III. Directive 2000/78

As seen in the previous section, until the promulgation of Directive 2000/78, EU law did not grant any protection from discrimination based on sexual

Market Law Review 1043; M Bell, 'Shifting Conceptions of Sexual Discrimination at the Court of Justice: from *P v S* to *Grant v SWT*' (1999) 5 *European Law Journal* 63.

[25] Namely, Council Directive 75/117/EEC on the approximation of the laws of the Member States relating to the application of the principle of equal pay for men and women [1975] OJ L45/19 and Council Directive 76/207/EEC on the implementation of the principle of equal treatment for men and women as regards access to employment, vocational training and promotion, and working conditions [1976] OJ L39/40.

[26] Case C-249/96 *Grant* (n 24) para 27.

[27] Flynn (n 22) 382; Wintemute (n 22) 347–348; McInnes (n 24) 1049–1050.

[28] Case C-249/96 *Grant* (n 22) para 35.

[29] The CJEU followed the same approach in Joined Cases C-122 and 125/99 *P D and Sweden v Council* EU:C:2001:304.

orientation to LGB individuals. Moreover, unlike discrimination on the grounds of gender reassignment, discrimination on the grounds of sexual orientation was held not to amount to discrimination on the grounds of sex. Thus, there was a lacuna in the protection of this segment of the EU population. However, this gap was filled by the Treaty of Amsterdam, which introduced Article 13 EC[30] (now Article 19 TFEU), stipulating:

> Without prejudice to the other provisions of the Treaties and within the limits of the powers conferred by them upon the Union, the Council, acting unanimously in accordance with a special legislative procedure and after obtaining the consent of the European Parliament, may take appropriate action to combat discrimination based on sex, racial or ethnic origin, religion or belief, disability, age or sexual orientation.

This provision does not prohibit discrimination on, *inter alia*, the grounds of sexual orientation but is merely a competence-giving provision which, as such, lacks direct effect. Accordingly, the prohibition of discrimination on the grounds of sexual orientation did not automatically emerge from the insertion of Article 13 into the EC Treaty, but was only introduced when the EU legislature promulgated Directive 2000/78.

The latter instrument prohibits (direct and indirect) discrimination on the grounds of religion or belief, disability, age or sexual orientation, in the areas of employment, vocational training, and membership of a professional organization. It makes clear that harassment based on any of these grounds is a prohibited form of discrimination.[31] Similarly, an instruction to discriminate on these grounds is unlawful.[32] Furthermore, the Directive makes provision for a general occupational requirements exception applicable to all grounds.[33] More specific exceptions only apply to discrimination on the grounds of disability and age.[34] Indirect discrimination on any of the grounds laid down in the Directive can be objectively justified.[35] The Directive is also 'without prejudice to measures laid down by national law which, in a democratic society, are necessary for public security, for the maintenance of public order and the prevention of criminal offences, for the protection of health and for the protection of the rights and freedoms of others'.[36] Taking a substantive equality approach, the Directive facilitates positive action, noting that 'the principle of equal treatment shall not prevent any Member State from maintaining or adopting specific measures to prevent or compensate for disadvantages

[30] For commentary on the steps that led to the introduction of this provision by the Treaty of Amsterdam, see M Bell and L Waddington, 'The 1996 Intergovernmental Conference and the Prospects of a Non-Discrimination Treaty Article' (1996) 25 *Industrial Law Journal* 320. For comments on Article 13 EC generally, see L Flynn, 'The Implications of Article 13 EC – After Amsterdam, Will Some Forms of Discrimination be More Equal than Others?' (1999) 36 *Common Market Law Review* 1127.

[31] FED Arts 2 (prohibition) and 3 (scope).

[32] ibid Art 2(4).

[33] ibid Art 4.

[34] ibid Arts 5 and 6 respectively.

[35] ibid Art 2(2)(b)(i).

[36] ibid Art 2(5).

linked to any of the grounds referred to in Article 1'.[37] The legislation is a minimum harmonisation measure, enabling Member States to introduce or maintain provisions which are more favourable than those laid down in it.[38] In addition, provision is made for remedies and enforcement, with particular attention on the promotion of dialogue between social partners, the encouragement of dialogue with appropriate NGOs that have a legitimate interest in contributing to the fight against discrimination, and the promotion of the principle of equality.[39]

The Framework Equality Directive (FED) is important in that it is the first instrument in EU law to establish a binding prohibition of discrimination on the grounds of sexual orientation. Yet it has been criticised for not going far enough, especially when compared to the instruments prohibiting discrimination on the grounds of sex, and racial or ethnic origin. In particular, the protection afforded by the Directive appears to be inferior to that provided by (its sister) Race Equality Directive 2000 (Directive 2000/43),[40] which was also adopted on the basis of Article 13 EC and promulgated just months before. Admittedly, the material scope of application is much more limited for Directive 2000/78 – it only applies to employment, vocational training and membership of a professional organisation, whereas Directive 2000/43 also encompasses social protection (including social security and healthcare), social advantages, education, and access to and supply of goods and services which are available to the public, including housing.[41] Moreover, the relatively large amount of exceptions from discrimination in Directive 2000/78 means the categories of persons that fall within its scope are less protected than those under Directive 2000/43, which has a more limited scope for exceptions. Moreover, the Race Equality Directive 2000 obliges Member States to designate a body for the promotion of equal treatment of all persons without discrimination on the grounds of racial or ethnic origin,[42] whereas no such duty is imposed by Directive 2000/78. Hence, a number of commentators have criticised the current anti-discrimination policy of the EU for creating a hierarchy among the various grounds on which discrimination is prohibited, with discrimination on the grounds of racial or ethnic origin at the top, and discrimination on the grounds of age at the bottom of the hierarchy.[43]

[37] ibid Art 7.

[38] ibid Art 8.

[39] ibid Arts 13 and 14 respectively. For a discussion of the role that transnationally connected LGBT NGOs play as catalysts in the adoption of legislation protecting LGBT rights, especially in more recent EU Member States, see the chapter by Phillip M Ayoub in the present volume.

[40] Council Directive 2000/43/EC implementing the principle of equal treatment between persons irrespective of racial or ethnic origin [2000] OJ L180/22 (Race Equality Directive).

[41] For their material scope, see Art 3 of each Directive.

[42] Directive 2000/43 (n 40) Article 13.

[43] D Schiek, 'A New Framework on Equal Treatment of Persons in EC Law? Directives 2000/43/EC, 2000/78/EC and 2002/73/EC Changing Directive 76/207/EEC in context' (2002) 8 *European Law Journal* 290; M Bell and L Waddington, 'Reflecting on Inequalities in European Equality Law' (2003) 28 *European Law Review* 349; E Howard, 'The Case for a Considered Hierarchy of Discrimination Grounds in EU Law' (2007) 13 *Maastricht Journal of European and Comparative Law* 445.

Unfortunately, such a hierarchical relationship among the various grounds makes the law in this area ill-suited for dealing with multiple discrimination, since in certain areas (e.g. housing) discrimination on the grounds of racial origin is prohibited whilst discrimination on the grounds of sexual orientation is not. For example, if a gay Asian man is discriminated against on grounds of ethnic origin *and* sexual orientation, he can rely on Directive 2000/43 to challenge the former but he cannot rely on Directive 2000/78 to challenge the latter.[44] Finally, neither of the 2000 Directives makes it clear that discrimination by assumption and discrimination by association are also prohibited. Nevertheless, this has been established by the Court of Justice in its jurisprudence interpreting the directives.[45]

The prohibition of discrimination on the grounds of sexual orientation, as laid down in the FED, was interpreted by the CJEU through a number of preliminary rulings. The first such ruling was delivered eight years after the promulgation of the Directive. *Maruko* [2008][46] concerned a reference from proceedings between Mr Maruko and the German Theatre Pension Institution ('VddB') relating to the refusal by VddB to recognise Mr Maruko's entitlement to a widower's pension as part of the survivor's benefits provided for under the compulsory occupational pension scheme, of which his deceased registered life partner had been a member. The refusal by VddB was based on the fact that its regulations only provided for such an entitlement for spouses, excluding surviving registered life partners.

When considering whether the contested refusal amounted to discrimination on the grounds of sexual orientation contrary to Directive 2000/78, the Court pointed out that:

> from 2001 [...] the Federal Republic of Germany altered its legal system to allow persons of the same sex to live in a union of mutual support and assistance which is formally constituted for life. Having chosen not to permit those persons to enter into marriage, which remains reserved solely to persons of different sex, that Member State created for persons of the same sex a separate regime, the life partnership, the conditions of which have been gradually made equivalent to those applicable to marriage.[47]

The Court then summarised the views of the referring court and, without providing its own conclusion as to whether registered partnerships are treated as equivalent to marriage under German law, stated:

> If the referring Court decides that surviving spouses and surviving life partners are in a comparable situation so far as concerns that survivor's benefit, legislation such as that at

[44] M Bell, 'Advancing EU Anti-Discrimination Law: the European Commission's 2008 Proposal for a New Directive' (2009) 3 *The Equal Rights Review* 7, 9.

[45] Case C-81/12 *Asociația Accept v Consiliul Național pentru Combaterea Discriminării* EU:C:2013:275 (discrimination by assumption); Case C-303/06 *Coleman v Attridge Law and Steve Law* EU:C:2008:415 (discrimination by association).

[46] Case C-267/06 *Maruko v Versorgungsanstalt der deutschen Bühnen* EU:C:2008:179. For a comment, see C Tobler and K Waaldijk, 'Annotation of Case C-267/06, *Tadao Maruko v Versorgungsandstalt der deutschen Bühnen*, Judgment of the Grand Chamber of the Court of Justice of 1 April 2008, not yet reported' (2009) 46 *Common Market Law Review* 723.

[47] Case C-267/06 *Maruko* (n 46) para 67.

> issue in the main proceedings must, as a consequence, be considered to constitute direct discrimination on grounds of sexual orientation, within the meaning of Articles 1 and 2(2)(a) of Directive 2000/78.[48]

To put it differently, if for a certain purpose (e.g. grant of a survivor's pension) *a Member State considers* same-sex registered partnerships as equivalent to marriage, it must treat them in the same way. If it treats the two types of relationships differently, *despite the fact that it considers them equivalent*, this amounts to direct discrimination on the grounds of sexual orientation which is contrary to the Directive. The *Maruko* judgment gave cause for both praise and criticism.

Starting with the former, the Court should be commended for taking a pragmatic approach when determining what type of discrimination is at issue in such a case. As noted above, it ruled that on the facts of the case, there was direct discrimination on the grounds of sexual orientation. Since marriage was not available to same-sex couples, legislation which limits the availability of a certain entitlement to married couples amounts to (direct) discrimination on the grounds of sexual orientation, if said entitlement is refused to a couple who is not married (because marriage is not open to it) but has entered into a registered partnership.[49] This finding 'renders Maruko remarkable'.[50]

On the other hand, the view in Maruko that equality of treatment between same-sex registered partners and opposite-sex married persons is only required if a Member State considers the two as being in a comparable situation for a specific purpose has been criticised: by deferring this matter to the Member States, the Court was in effect leaving same-sex couples to the mercy of the latter.

The Court followed exactly the same approach in the subsequent case of *Römer* [2011].[51] At issue in that case was the refusal of the German authorities to adopt for former employees, who had entered into a life partnership in Germany with their same-sex partners, the same method of calculating the supplementary pension to which they were entitled as that which was used for former employees who were married to their (opposite-sex) partner. The Court held that the Directive precludes the use of such a different method of calculating the supplementary pension if 'in the Member State concerned, marriage is reserved to persons of different gender and exists alongside a registered life partnership' which is reserved to persons of the same gender; moreover, it found that there is direct discrimination on the grounds of sexual orientation because, under national law 'that life partner is in a legal and factual situation comparable to that of a married person as regards that pension. It is for the referring court to assess the comparability, focusing on

[48] ibid para 72.

[49] According to Tobler and Waaldijk, *Maruko* can be viewed as a 'move away from an approach under which only measures that are explicitly based on the prohibited criterion or on a criterion that is by nature indissociably linked to it (such as pregnancy in the case of sex) amount to direct discrimination.' – see Tobler and Waaldijk (n 46) 739–740.

[50] A Eriksson, 'European Court of Justice: Broadening the scope of European nondiscrimination law' (2009) 7 *International Journal of Constitutional Law* 731, 742.

[51] Case C-147/08 *Römer v Freie und Hansestadt Hamburg* EU:C:2011:286.

the respective rights and obligations of spouses and persons in a registered life partnership, as they are governed within the corresponding institutions, which are relevant taking account of the purpose of and the conditions for the grant of the benefit in question'.[52]

The next case on the prohibition of discrimination based on sexual orientation under Directive 2000/78 was *Asociaţia Accept* [2015],[53] which emerged from proceedings between Accept, a Romanian NGO which defends and promotes the rights of LGBT persons, and the Romanian Council for Combatting Discrimination. The latter had partially dismissed a complaint lodged following public statements made by a person (Mr Becali) who presented himself as having – and was considered by public opinion to play – a leading role in a Romanian professional football club (FC Steaua). Mr Becali had ruled out the recruitment by FC Steaua of a footballer alleged as being gay. Consequently, Accept claimed that the principle of equal treatment had been breached in regard to recruitment.

In its judgment, the Court first pointed out that to establish direct discrimination on the grounds of sexual orientation, an identifiable complainant who claims to have been the victim of such discrimination is not required.[54] Instead, it suffices if the claim is brought by an NGO without identifying the person that has been harmed by the action forming the basis of the complaint. The Court then explained that it is not relevant if the statements which amount to discrimination come from a person who does not have legal capacity to bind or represent the club in recruitment matters, when this person is considered by public opinion to have such capacity. The fact that the club has not distanced itself from the statements concerned is a factor which the referring court may take into account when making its judgment.[55] The Court also made it clear that discrimination *by assumption* is prohibited by the Framework Equality Directive 2000. In other words, for discrimination on the grounds of sexual orientation to be proved, it suffices if someone discriminates against a person because *they think* that he or she is gay, irrespective of the actual sexual orientation of the latter.

This judgment must clearly be applauded, as the Court demonstrated its willingness to adopt a broad pragmatic approach when interpreting the prohibition of discrimination on the grounds of sexual orientation. It seems to have achieved substantive rather than merely formal equality, by seeking to ensure that even potential obstacles to access to the employment market which are liable to occur as a result of the existence of discriminatory measures or practices are prohibited.

[52] ibid, para 52.

[53] Case C-81/12 *Asociaţia Accept* (n 45). For excellent commentary on the case, see U Belavusau 'A Penalty Card for Homophobia from EU Non-Discrimination Law: Comment on *Asociaţia Accept* (C-81/12)' (2015) 21 *Columbia Journal of European Law* 329 and the chapter by Kristin Henrard in this volume.

[54] Case C-81/12 *Asociaţia Accept* (n 45) para 36. The Court had already held this in relation to the prohibition of discrimination on the grounds of race in Case C-54/07 *Centrum voor gelijkheid van kansen en voor racismebestrijding v Firma Feryn* EU:C:2008/397.

[55] Case C-81/12 *Asociaţia Accept* (n 45) paras 46–53.

Thus, the Court's analysis is no longer confined to a consideration of whether a specific person has been discriminated against in comparison to another person in similar circumstances at a particular instance. Instead, it more broadly considers whether a certain practice or action of a person or body is such as to create a discriminatory climate against a segment of the population which shares a characteristic which is a prohibited ground of discrimination under the Directive. Moreover, the Court's approach in *Asociaţia Accept* demonstrates its desire to be sensitive to the specific considerations that pertain to minorities in general,[56] and LGB individuals in particular (namely, that they may not wish to 'come out' by bringing an action claiming that they have been the victims of sexual orientation discrimination), especially in Member States where homophobia is still (highly) prevalent. Allowing actions to be brought by NGOs in situations without an identifiable victim is especially important. It ensures that LGB individuals who are not 'outed' are not faced with the difficult dilemma of either refraining from bringing an action to continue hiding their sexuality or to bring an action and thus 'come out' at a time when they may not be ready or in circumstances that will make them suffer negative consequences.

The same positive approach towards the protection of LGB persons from discrimination is evident in the subsequent case of *Hay* [2013],[57] with facts quite similar to those in *Maruko* and *Römer*. Here, the Court took the opportunity to react to the criticisms levelled against its approach in the previous cases by conducting the comparability assessment (between same-sex and opposite-sex couples) itself, instead of leaving it to the Member States.

The case involved the refusal by a French bank to award one of its employees, Mr Hay who concluded a civil solidarity pact with his male partner, special leave and a bonus granted to staff who marry. After finding that the issue related to Mr Hay's 'pay', the Court decided that Directive 2000/78 was applicable. It then proceeded to consider whether same-sex couples who entered into a Pacte Civil de Solidarité (PACS) were in a position comparable to opposite-sex married couples as regards the special leave and the bonus, concluding that they are.[58] In contrast, in the *Maruko* and *Römer* judgments, the Court merely provided guidelines as to how the comparability assessment should be conducted without making the assessment itself.

In line with *Maruko* and *Römer*, the Court upheld that discrimination against same-sex couples who have entered into a form of registered partnership because marriage is not available to them amounts to *direct* discrimination on the grounds of sexual orientation.[59] It noted:

> The fact that the PACS, unlike the registered life partnership at issue in the cases which gave rise to the judgments in *Maruko* and *Römer*, is not restricted only to homosexual

[56] As first demonstrated in Case C-54/07 *Feryn* (n 54).

[57] Case C-267/12 *Hay v Crédit agricole mutuel de Charente-Maritime et des Deux-Sèvres* EU:C:2013:823.

[58] ibid para 36.

[59] ibid para 41.

couples is irrelevant and, in particular, does not change the nature of the discrimination against homosexual couples who, unlike heterosexual couples, could not, on the date of the facts in the main proceedings, legally enter into marriage'.[60]

Accordingly, for a finding of direct discrimination it is not necessary that the status which is treated worse (here, the PACS) is only open to same-sex couples. Rather, what is required is simply that the status through which additional rights or benefits are granted (in this case, marriage) is not open to same-sex couples.

Overall, *Hay* – in line with *Asociația Accept* – can be considered an example of a case which has improved the position of LGB persons and same-sex couples under EU law, by interpreting the prohibition of discrimination on the grounds of sexual orientation broadly, and appearing less hesitant to sanction clearly discriminatory actions. The Court now seems willing to conduct the comparability assessment itself and to determine whether under national law, same-sex registered partners are similarly situated with opposite-sex married couples for a particular purpose. In case of a positive determination, Member States would be required to extend entitlements which they might have preferred to bestow only on married couples also to same-sex couples who have formalised their relationships.

The most recent case concerning the prohibition of discrimination on the grounds of sexual orientation under Directive 2000/78 is *Parris* [2016].[61] Dr Parris, a retired academic, brought an action against Trinity College Dublin (his former employer) and a number of Irish government departments, arguing that he had been discriminated against by the defendants by reason of his age and sexual orientation. Trinity College Dublin had refused to accept Dr Parris's request that on his death, the survivor's pension provided for by the occupational benefit scheme, of which he was a member, should be granted to his civil partner. The refusal was based on the fact that Dr Parris entered into a civil partnership with his male partner only after he had turned 60 and the occupational scheme provided that the survivor's pension was payable only if the claiming member had married or entered into a civil partnership before reaching the age of 60. However, in Ireland, civil partnerships could only be entered into since January 2011, and civil partnerships entered into abroad could be recognised only prospectively from January 2011. Thus, LGB persons born before 1 January 1951 (ie LGB persons who turned 60 before they could enter into a same-sex civil partnership in Ireland) were, in effect, excluded in all instances from claiming a survivor's benefit for their same-sex civil partner. The main question of the referring court was whether the contested rule of the occupational scheme amounted to discrimination on the grounds of age and/or sexual orientation, contrary to Directive 2000/78.

The Court held that the contested rule did not give rise to direct discrimination on the grounds of sexual orientation because it did not refer directly to the worker's sexual orientation. The Court also found that the contested rule did not give rise to indirect discrimination on these grounds either, as 'the fact that

[60] ibid para 43.
[61] Case C-443/15 *Parris v Trinity College Dublin and Others* EU:C:2016:897.

Mr Parris is unable to satisfy that condition is a consequence, first, of the state of the law existing in Ireland at the time of his 60th birthday, in particular the absence at that time of a law recognising any form of civil partnership of a same-sex couple, and, secondly, of the absence, in the rules governing the survivor's benefit at issue in the main proceedings, of transitional provisions for homosexual members born before 1951'.[62]

Referring to Recital 22 of Directive 2000/78, the Court proceeded to highlight the deference it shows towards Member State laws regarding the regulation of marital status in their territory and, in particular, the legal recognition of same-sex relationships: these are matters with respect to which Member States have maintained their full competence, and thus have regulatory freedom over, provided that obligations under EU law are complied with.[63] The Court then explained that the 'Member States are thus free to provide or not provide for marriage for persons of the same sex, or an alternative form of legal recognition of their relationship, and, if they do so provide, to lay down the date from which such a marriage or alternative form is to have effect'.[64] From this, the Court concluded that:

> EU law, in particular Directive 2000/78, did not require Ireland to provide before 1 January 2011 for marriage or a form of civil partnership for same-sex couples, nor to give retrospective effect to the Civil Partnership Act and the provisions adopted pursuant to that act, nor, as regards the survivor's benefit at issue in the main proceedings, to lay down transitional measures for same-sex couples in which the member of the scheme had already reached the age of 60 on the date of entry into force of the act.[65]

Accordingly, the CJEU deemed the contested rule not to violate the prohibition of discrimination on the grounds of sexual orientation, laid down in the FED. Nevertheless, the contested measure was held to establish a difference in treatment directly based on the criterion of age, which however fell within one of the exceptions provided by the Directive and was thus not prohibited.

Finally, the question was raised whether the contested rule gave rise to (multiple) discrimination on the combined grounds of age and sexual orientation. The Court did not examine this in substance, merely indicating that multiple discrimination is not prohibited by the FED.[66]

As argued elsewhere,[67] the judgment can be characterised as a failed opportunity for the CJEU to offer effective protection to LGB persons and same-sex couples under EU law. In particular, the *Parris* case seems to be treading cautiously around matters that are delicate from the standpoint of the Member States. The Court appears wary of being accused of imposing its own views with regard to

[62] ibid para 56.
[63] ibid paras 57–58.
[64] ibid para 59.
[65] ibid para 60.
[66] ibid para 80.
[67] A Tryfonidou, 'Another Failed Opportunity for the Effective Protection of the Rights of Same-Sex Couples under EU law: *Parris v. Trinity College Dublin and Others*' (2017) 2(2) *Anti-Discrimination Law Review* 83–95.

a matter (namely, the legal recognition of same-sex relationships) for which there is still great diversity of opinion among the Member States.[68] By hiding behind Recital 22, the Court avoided intervening in this case. The legal recognition of same-sex relationships and the derived rights is indeed a matter wholly to be regulated at Member State level. However, the *Parris* judgment allows Member States to discriminate against LGB persons who are unable to enter into a marriage or registered partnership in a certain Member State until a certain date. These persons are differently situated from heterosexual persons who had the (legal) option of entering into a marriage or registered partnership by the required age, but chose not to do so and, thus, should be treated differently.

As in other areas where the Member States have maintained their full legislative competence, they must comply with their obligations under EU law when making legislation regulating the legal recognition of family relationships (including same-sex relationships) and the economic consequences that ensue from entering into such relationships. Accordingly, it is not correct for the CJEU in this case to simply state that the legal recognition of same-sex relationships is a matter that falls to be regulated exclusively by the Member States. Rather, it must ensure that Member State rules governing occupational pensions in situations involving same-sex couples comply with Directive 2000/78. Such compliance would require the removal of discrimination on the (combined) grounds of sexual orientation and age, without however requiring Ireland to recognise such relationships retrospectively – indeed a matter that falls to be regulated exclusively by Ireland. Compliance could be achieved by amending the rule and permitting LGB persons born before 1951 to claim the survivor's benefit for their same-sex partner even if they entered into a civil partnership or marriage after turning 60.

Notwithstanding its rather disappointing approach in *Parris*, the Court's interpretation of the Directive in other recent cases has in several respects played an important role in improving the position of LGB persons and same-sex couples under EU law.

IV. Other (Actual or Potential) Sources of Legal Protection of LGB Persons and Same-Sex Couples from Discrimination under EU Law

The aim of this section is to consider whether the other (actual or potential) main sources of protection of LGB persons and same-sex couples under EU law can fill the gaps left by Directive 2000/78.

[68] For a discussion of the different approaches to the legal recognition of same-sex relationships and the protection of LGBT rights among EU Member States, as well as the factors that influence the diffusion of new norms and laws in different groups of Member States, see the chapter by Phillip M Ayoub in the present volume.

A. The EU Charter of Fundamental Rights

The Treaty of Lisbon came into force in December 2009. It amended the EU and EC Treaties, and changed the name of the latter to 'TFEU'. In addition, it made the EUCFR binding, by providing in Article 6(1) TEU (as amended) that this document now has the same legal value as the treaties. The coming into force of the Treaty of Lisbon has been immensely important for the protection of LGB rights for a number of reasons.

Firstly, the treaty added a new mainstreaming provision – Article 10 TFEU – which provides that '[i]n defining and implementing its policies and activities, the Union shall aim to combat discrimination based on sex, racial or ethnic origin, religion or belief, disability, age or sexual orientation'. This provision proactively ensures that all EU policies should now be free from discrimination on, *inter alia*, the grounds of sexual orientation. Thus, it suitably complements the reactive protection from this sort of discrimination offered by secondary legislation (Directive 2000/78) and by the EUCFR (as will be seen below).

Secondly, as noted above, the Treaty of Lisbon made the EUCFR binding. This means that its provisions *bind* the EU institutions, and individuals can bring actions against Member States for breaching their rights under the Charter in situations that fall within the scope of EU law. As regards LGB individuals, this is significant because Article 20 of the Charter states that 'Everyone is equal before the law'. More significantly, Article 21 provides that 'Any discrimination based on any ground such as sex, race, colour, ethnic or social origin, genetic features, language, religion or belief, political or any other opinion, membership of a national minority, property, birth, disability, age or *sexual orientation* shall be prohibited' (emphasis added). Therefore, LGB individuals can rely on this provision to challenge instances of discrimination based on their sexual orientation even in situations which are not related to employment, vocational training, and membership of professional organisations. Put differently, the Charter has expanded the material scope of the prohibition of discrimination on the grounds of sexual orientation.

Yet, one should not overestimate the ability of the Charter to protect the rights of LGB individuals. Indeed, the Member States are only bound when they are 'implementing EU law'.[69] Since it is still not entirely clear when this requirement is satisfied,[70] the extent to which this provision can be relied on against Member States will be dependent on the Court's willingness to interpret it broadly.

[69] Art 51 CFR.

[70] The Explanations Relating to the Charter of Fundamental Rights ([2007] OJ C303/17) state that the Charter is binding on the Member States 'when they act in the scope of Union law'. The most recent case-law interpreting Article 51 also adopts a broad reading of this provision: 'The applicability of European Union law entails applicability of the fundamental rights guaranteed by the Charter' (Case C-617/10 *Fransson* EU:C:2013:105 para 21). However, it is yet to be clarified *when* a situation falls within the scope of EU law for this purpose. In some of its latest case-law, the Court appears

Thirdly, apart from Article 21 TFEU, the Charter also includes a number of other rights that can be of help to LGB persons, most significantly the right to human dignity and the right to private and family life. However, this is not really an innovation, since even before the coming into force of the Charter, these rights were already protected as general principles of EU law and, could therefore be relied on by LGB persons.

To date, the Court has only had the chance to apply the Charter in a single case involving LGB individuals – *Léger*[71] – concerning alleged discrimination on the grounds of sexual orientation outside the field of employment. The case considered the compatibility with EU law of the blanket ban in France on blood donation by men who have had sex with other men (MSM). It was argued that this amounted to discrimination on the grounds of sexual orientation since this category of persons essentially comprised of gay and bisexual men. The Charter was deemed applicable because the contested French legislation was implementing relevant EU secondary legislation.[72] Thus, it was necessary to consider whether a permanent ban on blood donation by the MSM population is compatible with the fundamental rights recognised by the EU legal order.[73] The Court noted, in particular, that the French legislation 'must respect inter alia Article 21(1) [of the Charter] … according to which any discrimination based on sexual orientation must be prohibited. Article 21(1) is a particular expression of the principle of equal treatment, which is a general principle of EU law enshrined in Article 20 of the Charter'.[74] The Court found that the contested ban 'may discriminate against homosexuals on grounds of sexual orientation',[75] since the challenged legislation 'determines the deferral from blood donation on the basis to the homosexuality of the male donors who, on account of the fact that they have had homosexual sexual relations, are treated less favourably than male

to have adopted a rather restrictive approach to this question (see, eg Case C-45/12 *Hadj Ahmed* EU:C:2013:390; Case C-198/13 *Hernández* EU:C:2014:2055).

[71] Case C-528/13 *Léger v Ministre des Affaires sociales, de la Santé et des Droits des femmes and Etablissement français du sang* EU:C:2015:288. For comments, see P Dunne, 'A Right to Donate Blood? Permanent Deferrals for "Men Who Have Sex with Men" (MSM): *Léger*' (2015) 52 *Common Market Law Review* 1661; A Tryfonidou, 'The *Léger* Ruling as Another Example of the ECJ's (Disappointingly) Reticent Approach to the Protection of the Rights of LGB Persons under EU Law' (2016) 41 *European Law Review* 91; U Belavusau, Towards EU Sexual Risk Regulation: Restrictions on Blood Donation as Infringement of Active Citizenship' (2016) 7 *European Journal of Risk Regulation* 801.

[72] Directive 2002/98/EC of the European Parliament and of the Council setting standards of quality and safety for the collection, testing, processing, storage and distribution of human blood and blood components and amending Directive 2001/83 [2003] OJ L33/30; Commission Directive 2004/33/EC implementing Directive 2002/98/EC of the European Parliament and of the Council as regards certain technical requirements for blood and blood components [2004] OJ L91/25.

[73] Case C-528/13 *Léger* (n 71) paras 45–47.

[74] ibid para 48. However, as explained by Belavusau, the CJEU in its judgment in this case demonstrates a 'narrow understanding of the EU discrimination regime' which 'suggests that the Court is unwilling to stretch the material scope of the Equality Directive beyond the employment market and labour relations […] by calling 'into question the very existence of a general principle of non-discrimination on the grounds of sexual orientation' – see Belavusau (n 71) 808.

[75] Case C-528/13 *Léger* (n 71) para 50.

heterosexual persons'.[76] Nevertheless, the measure may be justified if it satisfies the conditions laid down by Article 52 of the Charter. While the CJEU left it to the national Court to make the final decision, it provided detailed guidelines, specifically pointing out that the national Court must examine whether there are measures which can achieve the same aim (a high level of human health protection) without requiring the imposition of a complete lifetime ban on blood donation by the MSM population.[77]

As explained elsewhere, the Court's judgment is disappointing.[78] Although it found that the measure 'may' amount to discrimination on the grounds of sexual orientation contrary to Article 21 of the Charter, it proceeded to consider whether it is justified under Article 52. Instead, it should have ruled that the measure could under no circumstances be justified. There may indeed be some gay and bisexual men who engage in risky sexual behaviour through unprotected sex with multiple partners. Yet, this is also the case for some heterosexual men and for some heterosexual, bisexual or lesbian women. Accordingly, imposing a blanket ban only on gay and bisexual men appears to be unjustifiable. Moreover, the exclusion from blood donation applies to *all* men who have had sex with other men, even if only once in their life. Such a wide extent and duration cannot be justified on medical grounds. Indeed, medical advances have made it possible to easily detect a virus such as HIV after a certain period of time has passed since it has been contracted. Therefore, the contested *blanket* ban is unnecessary for ensuring the protection of public health. Moreover, the hands-off approach of the Court leaving it to the national Courts to decide on the justifiability of the measure in effect condones a national measure based on deep-seated homophobia and on stereotypical misconceptions about the sexual behaviour of gay and bisexual men.

Admittedly, the main reason behind the Court's reticent approach in the judgment is likely to stem from its wish not to be seen as interfering in a matter which is sensitive from the point of view of the Member States. The contested measure touches on matters of public health and sexuality, in relation to which a wide margin of appreciation is often left to the Member States. Yet, in situations where there is a clear breach of the fundamental rights of a segment of the EU population – as was the case in *Léger* – wishing to keep the Member States happy by not interfering with their freedom to regulate sensitive matters is not acceptable.

Although the Charter does have the potential to complement Directive 2000/78 by protecting LGB individuals from discrimination outside employment, provided that the situation falls within the scope of application of the Charter, the signs so far are not very encouraging. The Court's political and social considerations appear to form an obstacle to protecting the rights of LGB persons.

[76] ibid para 49.

[77] ibid paras 51–69.

[78] Tryfonidou, 'The *Léger* Ruling' (n 71). In contrast, Dunne noted that the judgment 'appears to create a practical EU blueprint both for protecting the integrity of Member State blood supplies and guaranteeing the equal treatment of MSM donors' – see Dunne (n 71) 1662.

B. The (Proposed) Equality Directive

As noted earlier, one of the main weaknesses of Directive 2000/78 is its limited material scope, which only covers the areas of employment and vocational training. This gap in protection will be filled if the proposed Equality Directive becomes law.[79] However, notwithstanding extensive discussion since 2008 regarding the substance of the proposed Directive and the amendments to the original proposal, there are no signs that unanimity in Council will be achieved any time soon (if at all).

The proposed directive would complement the existing FED by extending the prohibition of discrimination therein beyond the employment field to all areas covered by the RED. Moreover, the Equality Directive provides for a duty to be imposed on Member States to designate a body for the promotion of equal treatment irrespective of religion or belief, disability, age or sexual orientation, which is currently missing from Directive 2000/78.

Nonetheless, the proposed directive does not fill other gaps in protection left by Directive 2000/78. Like the latter instrument, the Equality Directive contains a wider range of exceptions from the prohibition of discrimination on the grounds of religion, disability, age or sexual orientation than the other instruments regarding the prohibition of discrimination on the grounds of gender, nationality and race.[80] Moreover, the proposal misses the opportunity to not only cater for multiple discrimination but also to enshrine the CJEU's case law on discrimination based on assumption and discrimination based on association as falling under the prohibition of discrimination.

One may ask why adopting the proposed directive would be important from a practical point of view. After all, discrimination on the grounds of sexual orientation is already prohibited in areas outside employment and vocational training by Article 21 EUCFR. Indeed, the Charter can help LGB persons who are discriminated against either by the EU institutions or by the Member States when the latter implement EU law. However, the lack of clarity about interpreting the latter requirement should not be forgotten. A restrictive interpretation is possible which considers the prohibition of discrimination on the grounds of sexual orientation outside employment and vocational training as applicable only in situations where a Member State is implementing EU law. However, by adopting the proposed directive, the EU will impose an obligation on *all* Member States to prohibit discrimination on the grounds of, *inter alia*, sexual orientation outside employment and vocational training. Hence, the uniform protection of LGB

[79] Proposal for Equality Directive (n 4).

[80] For an analysis of the proposal and/or the suggestions made by other institutions (in particular, the European Parliament) in relation to it, see Bell, 'Advancing EU Anti-Discrimination Law' (n 44); E Howard, 'EU Equality Law: Three Recent Developments' (2011) 17 *European Law Journal* 785, 788–92.

persons from discrimination *in all Member States* would be ensured.[81] Moreover, requiring the promulgation of *national law* which will prohibit discrimination on the grounds of sexual orientation in a wide range of areas will protect LGB individuals from discrimination in these areas *even in situations that are entirely unrelated to, and thus fall outside the scope of, EU law*. Finally, since the proposed Equality Directive – like Directive 2000/78 – provides that the prohibition of discrimination will have to apply *both* in the public and the private sectors, LGB individuals will be able to rely on the implementing national legislation even against private individuals. For instance, if a same-sex couple is refused a hotel room, this will be prohibited by national law implementing the proposed directive, allowing for an action to be brought against the hotel owners.

Thus, and for the reasons summarised above, it is important to ensure that the proposed Equality Directive is promulgated soon because it will significantly improve the position of LGB persons under EU law and their protection from discrimination. Given that Commissioner Frans Timmermans, whose portfolio includes the protection of fundamental rights, has made the passing of the proposed Equality Directive one of his priorities, there is reason to feel optimistic about the possibility of this instrument becoming law in the next few years.

V. Conclusion

Overall, the FED, as interpreted and applied by the CJEU, can be deemed a success story. As O'Cinneide has noted, 'the equality directives have come to exert a significant "destabilizing" effect on structural forms of inequality hitherto accepted as "normal" at national level, by opening up new legal avenues for individuals, NGOs, trade unions and other organizations to challenge discriminatory practices'.[82] Yet, this does not mean that LGB individuals in the EU now enjoy complete equality with heterosexual individuals, and that they are free from discrimination in all areas of human life. As we have seen, the material scope of the FED is still confined to employment and vocational training. Consequently, Member States are only obliged to have provisions in their legislation which prohibit discrimination on the grounds of sexual orientation in this context. While in cases which fall outside the scope of the Directive, Article 21 EUCFR can come to the rescue, this is not a panacea. Unlike the FED, which requires Member States to prohibit discrimination on the grounds of, *inter alia*, sexual orientation even in situations

[81] As Bell has noted, 'A mapping study for the Commission published in 2006 found that although there was a wide range of legislation in the Member States on discrimination outside employment, this was often variable in its material scope and it was not always consistent in the range of discrimination grounds covered' – see Bell (n 44) 16.

[82] C O'Cinneide, 'The Constitutionalization of Equality within the EU Legal Order: Sexual Orientation as a Testing Ground' (2015) 22 *Maastricht Journal of European and Comparative Law* 370 at 373.

involving private bodies and parties, Article 21 of the Charter can only be relied on against the EU and against the Member States when implementing EU law. Furthermore, the Charter requires the existence of a link with EU law, such as Member State discrimination against LGB individuals when implementing EU legislation or discrimination on the grounds of sexual orientation against persons who have exercised their free movement rights. Conversely, the proposed Equality Directive requires the Member States to adopt legislation to implement it, which would then apply as part of the national legal system in *all* situations, irrespective of the existence of a link with EU law. Accordingly, the EU legal framework which seeks to protect LGB individuals and same-sex couples from discrimination will only be complete once the proposed Equality Directive becomes law.

11

EU Law as an (In)Direct Source of LGB Rights across Europe[1]

PHILLIP M AYOUB

I. Introduction

For affluent democracies, the birth of the gay liberation movement and the dawn of the 1970s heralded a marked, albeit gradual, expansion in the forms of legal protections that states provided to gay and lesbian minorities. By 1 October 1989, the first same-sex couples had entered into registered partnerships in Denmark. Although progress has been slow and has provoked counter-movements intended to block progressive legislation, the proliferation of pro-LGB[2] legislation has amplified the voice of a once politically invisible group and has become a recurrent theme in modern European politics. More recently, advances at the regional level have fuelled LGB rights in Europe. Notably, the European Union's (EU) Framework Equality Directive (2000/78/EC), a ground-breaking Directive that enshrined sexual orientation in international law, has contributed to the spread of LGB rights, both directly and indirectly.[3] Beyond the Framework Equality Directive (FED), the chapter also looks at broader transformations institutionally at the supranational level that contribute to the profound developments in the realm of LGB rights.

[1] This chapter is a reprint adapted from the original: P Ayoub, 'Contested Norms in New-Adopter States: International Determinants of LGBT Rights Legislation' (2015) 21 *European Journal of International Relations* 293. Copyright © 2015 by the Author. Reprinted by (paid) permission of SAGE Publications, Ltd.

[2] It should be noted that 'LGB' (lesbian, gay, and bisexual) and 'sexual minorities' are used broadly, as umbrella terms in this chapter, to describe people who do not fit heteronormative categories. While trans people are affected by several of the pieces of legislation mentioned below, the coding here regrettably does not account for legislation pertaining specifically to trans people.

[3] Council Directive 2000/78/EC establishes a general framework for equal treatment in employment and occupation [2000] OJ L303/16 (Framework Equality Directive (FED)). Throughout this chapter, any references to the Framework Equality Directive exclusively consider how it relates to LGB people. Please note also, for example, that there exists a parallel and more expansive 'Race Equality' Directive 2000/43/EC. Furthermore, the FED also covers the grounds of sexual orientation, age, disability, and religion. For a detailed history, see the chapter by A Tryfonidou in the present volume.

For example, Article 21 Charter of Fundamental Rights[4] and Article 10 TFEU (the mainstreaming provision)[5] have surely contributed, directly *and* indirectly, to the further protection of LGB rights in EU Member States.

The achievement of the legal recognition of LGB minorities, however, varies greatly across European states. Europe is distinctive in that it houses states at both ends of the spectrum of global LGB egalitarianism. While some European states (e.g. Denmark) became the world's leading advocates for LGB rights, providing the most extensive legal protections to their citizenry, others have only relatively recently decriminalised same-sex relations (e.g. Romania in 1996). Figures 11.1 and 11.2 show the varied adoption of LGB legislation over three decades in old and new Member States respectively – the countries are listed in the order of their standing in 2010. The chapter examines this variation, exploring why LGB rights legislation is passed at higher levels in some cases and less so in others.

The observed variation raises important questions for scholars of European law, international relations, and social movements: What accounts for such different levels of legal recognition of sexual minorities across European states? Is change a result of heightened transnational cooperation with groups in states that have previously adopted the legislation? Or is it a result of the domestic preconditions of the state that allow international norms (which are furthered by institutional rules, as in this case of the EU Framework Equality Directive) regarding the legal rights for sexual minorities to proliferate? The answers to these questions

Figure 11.1

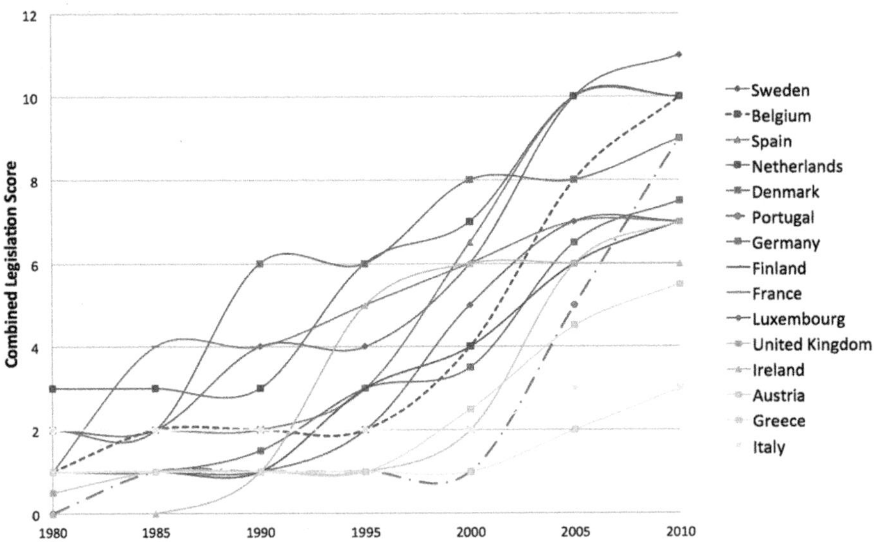

[4] Charter of Fundamental Rights of the European Union [2016] OJ C202/2 (consolidated version).
[5] Treaty on the Functioning of the European Union [2016] OJ C202/1 (consolidated version).

Figure 11.2

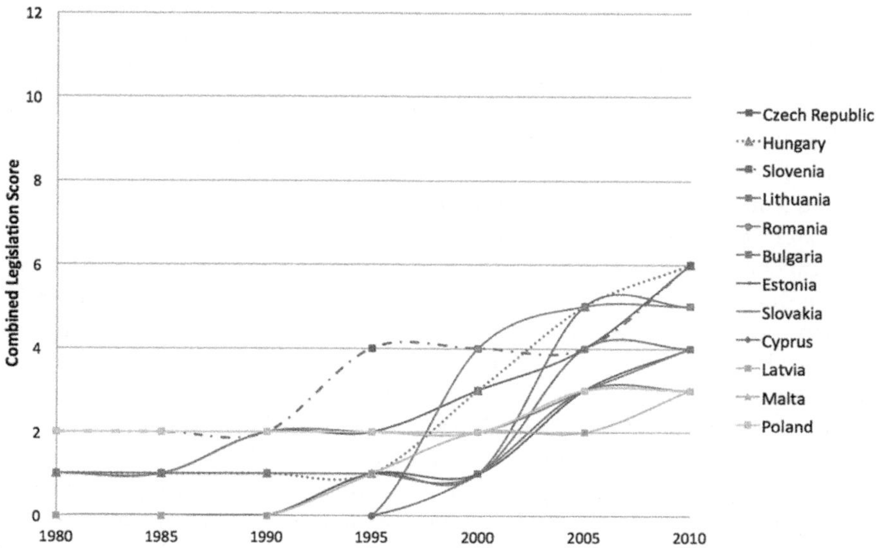

are theoretically and practically important for the study of politics. There are few social issues that incite as much controversy in contemporary world politics as LGB rights, yet, despite their contested nature, a growing number of states have adopted these norms into their legal frameworks.[6] Understanding the differential levels of adoption brings to light the international channels and domestic conditions of diffusion.

To explain this variation, it is argued that transnational and domestic explanations depend on the political identities of the groupings that states find themselves in within the international system. These state groupings are thought of in terms of new-adopter and first-mover status, which have different political identities in relation to the international society of states, and subsequently also different political imperatives to adopt pieces of legislation that have become symbolic of political modernity. Thus, looking at the EU, the adoption patterns are expected to differ according to newly admitted EU Member States (EU-12) and long-standing EU Member States (EU-15).[7]

[6] S Barclay, M Bernstein, and A-M Marshall (eds), *Queer Mobilizations: LGBT Activists Confront the Law* (New York, New York University Press, 2009); JJ Fernández and M Lutter, 'Supranational Cultural Norms, Domestic Value Orientations and the Diffusion of Same-sex Union Rights in Europe, 1988–2009' (2013) 28 *International Sociology* 102; L Helfer and E Voeten, 'International Courts as Agents of Legal Change: Evidence from LGBT Rights in Europe' (2014) 68 *International Organization* 77; K Waaldijk and M Bonini-Baraldi, *Sexual Orientation Discrimination in the European Union: National Laws and the Employment Equality Directive* (The Hague, TMC Asser Press, 2006).

[7] EU-15 states include those states admitted in the first five waves of accession: (1952) Belgium, France, Germany, Italy, Luxembourg, and the Netherlands; (1973) Denmark, Ireland, and the United Kingdom; (1981) Greece; (1986) Portugal and Spain; and (1995) Austria, Finland and Sweden. EU-12

The EU Equality Directives[8] were adopted slightly preceding the 2004 eastward enlargement, and the newly accepted Member States were compelled to adapt their non-discrimination frameworks in accordance with the newly adopted EU secondary law. While levels of adoption also vary within both groupings, different factors can explain this. In EU-15 states, where the norm was politicised earlier (through the gay liberation movement of the 1970s and the HIV-AIDS Crisis of the 1980s), domestic factors such as the commonly theorised level of modernity are expected to play a greater role in increasing the likelihood and extent of diffusion. By contrast, transnational interactions via social and political channels that tie states to the international community should accelerate the diffusion of LGB norms in contexts where the issue has only recently become politicised (the EU-12 states). In new-adopter states, transnational channels have the capacity to enhance the salience of international norms and laws, and transnationally-connected LGB organisations can act as catalysts in the adoption of legislation by signalling to decision makers that LGB rights are connected to the state's reputation within the international community. Not only do LGB organisations help states and the wider society to interpret external information, they also help to frame that information in ways that resonate in local contexts. Thus, a distinction is made between domestic and transnational factors, suggesting that their influence should vary across groupings of first-mover and new-adopter states.

The analysis looks at the adoption of LGB legislation between 1970 and 2009. The focus is on pieces of LGB legislation, and also in particular the FED adopted within this period, because these constitute an observable consequence of norm diffusion. The latter concept refers to the spread of new standards of acceptable behaviour across borders. Following the efforts of international relations, social movements, and Europeanisation scholars, the chapter seeks to explain the diffusion of LGB rights policies by using their carefully conceptualised theories of cognitive change among social actors and relational channels between states. Calls for further research are addressed by systematically exploring the (non-)diffusion of five categories (anti-discrimination, criminal law, partnership, parenting rights, and equal sexual offenses provisions) of LGB legislation, as well as anti-discrimination legislation specifically, in multiple domestic contexts and by specifying the international channels, domestic actors, and conditions responsible for change. The analysis uses a large-*n* cross-national dataset of changed LGB rights legislation in Europe.

The findings suggest that the transnational embeddedness of a state's LGB advocacy organisations – a brokered transnational channel – is a powerful

states include those admitted in the 2004 and 2007 waves: (2004) Czech Republic, Cyprus, Estonia, Hungary, Latvia, Lithuania, Malta, Poland, Slovakia, and Slovenia; and (2007) Bulgaria and Romania. This imperfect distinction is used for analytical purposes. It is not meant to conceal the intolerance and injustice that LGB people still experience in EU-15 states, nor is it intended to 'other' EU-12 states as an abnormality to 'Western' scripts. In this respect, see CF Stychin, *A Nation By Rights: National Cultures, Sexual Identity Politics, and the Discourse of Rights* (Philadelphia, Temple University Press Office, 1998).

[8] Framework Equality Directive and Race Equality Directive.

explanation for successful policy diffusion to new EU-12 Member States, alongside other transnational channels that lead to LGB visibility in society and in the minds of state authorities. In this sense, the external mechanism introduced by the EU Framework Equality Directive was important for the diffusion of rights, not only by directly influencing anti-discrimination in employment, but also through the spill-over effect of cementing LGB rights beyond employment matters as a part of European values. While the results lend cross-national, empirical reinforcement to some of the theoretical expectations regarding the transnational sources of diffusion, they show substantial variability in the determinants of LGB policy adoption between first-mover EU-15 and new-adopter EU-12 state groupings. Domestic factors, especially economic modernisation, are more relevant for policy adoption in EU-15 states, whereas new EU-12 states display greater dependence on transnational actors and are more influenced by international social and political channels. In sum, first-mover or new-adopter status matters for how international and domestic factors influence the diffusion of new norms and laws, such as the EU Equality Directives.

The chapter proceeds in three parts. First, a set of hypotheses is drawn from previous literature. Second, an elaboration on the main argument will show how the expectations of scholars regarding the diffusion of law might vary across first-mover EU-15 Member States and new-adopter EU-12 Member States. This entails a consideration of legislation on anti-discrimination in EU-12 Member States, which were influenced greatly by the FED which established a general framework for equal treatment in employment and occupation. The third section discusses the results of the quantitative analysis. By way of conclusion, the significance of the findings for the study of norm diffusion and global trends in policy adoption is discussed.

II. Explaining the Diffusion of Rights Legislation

Previous scholarship explaining the international diffusion of social policies has generally fallen into one – or a combination – of three camps, wherein successful diffusion is linked to the presence of: (1) advocacy networks connecting international and domestic politics, (2) international channels of socialisation and/or sanctioning pressure, and (3) bottom-up domestic resonance. These frameworks inform the core hypotheses tested in this analysis.

A. Transnational Advocacy Networks

International relations and social movement scholars have noted the importance of advocacy groups in influencing the international diffusion of rights legislation.[9]

[9] ME Keck and K Sikkink, *Activists Beyond Borders: Advocacy Networks in International Politics* (Ithaca, NY Cornell University Press, 1998); C Roggeband, 'Transnational Networks and Institutions'

Social movement organisations are commonly theorised as the most experienced type of organisation in channelling a social group's grievances to the relevant authorities.[10] In particular, Soule and King's work on minority rights legislation offers substantial evidence that social movement activity affects the introduction and diffusion of rights and anti-discrimination legislation for various minorities in the United States.[11] Focusing particularly on LGB rights, the works of Kollman,[12] Holzhacker,[13] and Paternotte[14] have emphasised the centrality of advocacy networks fostered by organisations such as the International Lesbian, Gay, Bisexual, Trans, and Intersex Association (ILGA) in addition to a series of domestic factors.

Hypothesis 1: *The likelihood of passing higher levels of LGB legislation increases when domestic LGB organisations become embedded in the transnational activist networks Europe provides.*

B. International Pressure and Socialisation

For many international relations scholars, rights legislation diffuses to states when those states are convinced of the social appropriateness of the norm or when they fear the costs of international pressures. These theories – the first linked to mechanisms of socialisation and the second to political conditionality and material incentives – posit logics of appropriateness and consequences, respectively. World polity and constructivist scholars focus on the first set of informal processes of influence, arguing that international norms exert an influence on states by defining the contours of appropriate behaviour.[15] Interactions between states in an international community lead to different cognitive understandings of what is acceptable. These indirect channels can engender change via socialisation through mechanisms of learning and deliberation.[16]

in R Givan, K Roberts, and SA Soule (eds), *The Diffusion of Social Movements* (Cambridge, Cambridge University Press, 2010); C Montoya, *From Global to Grassroots: The European Union, Transnational Advocacy, and Combating Violence against Women* (Oxford, Oxford University Press, 2013).

[10] PM Ayoub, 'Repressing Protest: Threat and Weakness in the European Context, 1975–1989' (2010) 15 *Mobilization* 465, 473.

[11] SA Soule and BG King, 'The Stages of the Policy Process and the Equal Rights Amendment, 1972–1982' (2006) 11 *American Journal of Sociology* 1871; SA Soule, 'Going to the Chapel? Same-Sex Marriage Bans in the United States, 1973–2000' (2004) 51 *Social Problems* 453.

[12] K Kollman, *The Same-Sex Unions Revolution in Western Democracies: International Norms and Domestic Policy Change* (Manchester, Manchester University Press, 2013).

[13] R Holzhacker, 'National and Transnational Strategies of LGBT Civil Society Organizations in Different Political Environments' (2012) 10 *Comparative European Politics* 23.

[14] D Paternotte and D Kollman, 'Regulating Intimate Relationships in the European Polity: Same-Sex Unions and Policy Convergence' (2013) 20 *Social Politics* 510.

[15] M Finnemore and K Sikkink, 'International Norm Dynamics and Political Change' (1998) 52 *International Organization* 887; A Klotz, *Norms in International Relations: The Struggle Against Apartheid* (Ithaca, Cornell University Press, 1995); JW Meyer et al, 'World Society and the Nation-State' (1997) 103 *American Journal of Sociology* 144.

[16] T Risse, '"Let's Argue!": Communicative Action in World Politics' (2000) 54 *International Organization* 1.

When states are members of international organisations, their representatives are often required to confront the LGB issue and take a stand. The FED is a case in point, in that more porous states – in terms of political and social connectedness to other states – are more susceptible to outside legal pressures.[17] For many, adopting the Directive into national law was the first step in providing protective measures for their LGB citizens. Other indirect channels of diffusion are social, such as importing television shows featuring gay characters from cultural powers like the United States, which has increased rapidly since the 1990s. Studies show that exposure to media with gay themes positively influences social attitudes as well as the actions of policymakers regarding LGB issues.[18] Social channels reconfigure the threat associated with minorities by making them familiar. These channels of interaction lead to social learning, providing images and understandings of what it means to be a member of an international political and social community.

Hypothesis 2a: *The likelihood of passing higher levels of LGB legislation increases when the state's level of political porosity is higher.*

Hypothesis 2b: *The likelihood of passing higher levels of LGB legislation increases when the state's level of social porosity is higher.*

Rational institutionalists attribute domestic change to the incentives provided by international organisations and focus on the costs associated with norm adoption.[19] According to this perspective, political leaders weigh the costs and benefits of adopting a norm. In the EU, non-adoption of the LGB norm can mean lost material benefits linked to economic and security cooperation at the European level. Scholars have emphasised the unique and direct role of EU conditionality in the adoption of new laws in the EU Member States, with sanctions and competition representing the central mechanisms by which this type of process occurs.[20] There are reasons to expect that states will adopt LGB rights legislation through these mechanisms, especially since the EU required applicant states to decriminalise homosexuality and to adopt the employment anti-discrimination measures in their legal frameworks in the 1990s and early 2000s.[21] Since EU conditionality

[17] An example of political porosity is the degree to which states enter international organisations, while the circulation of media across borders is an example of social porosity.

[18] J Cooley and G Burkholder, 'Using Video and Contact to Change Attitudes Toward Gay Men and Lesbians' (2011) 5 *Journal of Social, Behavioral, and Health Sciences* 83; PM Ayoub and J Garretson, 'Getting the Message Out: Media Context and Global Changes in Attitudes Toward Homosexuality' (2017) 50 *Comparative Political Studies* 1055.

[19] LL Martin and B Simmons, 'Theories and Empirical Studies of International Institutions' (1998) 52 *International Organization* 729.

[20] F Schimmelfennig and U Sedelmeier (eds), *The Europeanization of Central and Eastern Europe* (Ithaca, Cornell University Press, 2005); D Toshkov, 'Embracing European Law: Compliance with EU Directives in Central and Eastern Europe' (2008) 9 *European Union Politics* 379; MA Vachudova, *Europe Undivided: Democracy, Leverage, and Integration After Communism* (Oxford, Oxford University Press, 2005).

[21] PM Ayoub and D Paternotte (eds), *LGBT Activism and the Making of Europe – A Rainbow Europe?* (Basingstoke, Palgrave Macmillan, 2014); M Mos, 'Of Gay Rights and Christmas Ornaments: The Political History of Sexual Orientation Non-Discrimination in the Treaty of Amsterdam' (2014) 52 *Journal of Common Market Studies* 632.

should have a greater effect in the years leading up to accession, especially when concerning the FED, an indicator of a state's application to join the EU is also included.[22]

Hypothesis 2c: *The likelihood of passing higher levels of LGB legislation increases when a state accedes to join the EU.*

Hypothesis 2d: *The likelihood of passing higher levels of LGB legislation increases when a state applies to join the EU.*

C. Domestic Resonance

Other scholars have taken a 'bottom-up' approach, emphasising the domestic political and cultural variables that condition the reception of contentious international ideas.[23] This literature focuses on the congruence between international norms and elements of the domestic context, outlining several domestic factors that influence the receptivity of norms concerning social minorities. Post-materialists expect higher levels of democracy and affluence to correspond with a state's readiness to legislate minority rights issues.[24] Social movement scholars have focused on domestic spaces for LGB identities and culture, which may influence the reception of legal norms by making the context more susceptible. Various minority movements rely on 'free' or 'safe' spaces to form associational ties and to mobilise counter-hegemonic identities.[25] Finally, the dominant religious institution and orientation of the state may influence its receptivity to LGB rights norms.

[22] C O'Dwyer, 'From Conditionality to Persuasion? Europeanization and the Rights of Sexual Minorities in Post-Accession Poland' (2010) 32 *Journal of European Integration* 229; F Schimmelfennig, 'European Regional Organizations, Political Conditionality, and Democratic Transformation in Eastern Europe' (2007) 21 *East European Politics and Societies* 126; D Kochenov, *EU Enlargement and the Failure of Conditionality: Pre-Accession Conditionality in the Fields of Democracy and the Rule of Law* (Alphen aan den Rijn, Kluwer Law International, 2008); D Toshkov, 'Embracing European Law' (2008) 9 *European Union Politics* 379; K Slootmaeckers, H Touquet, and P Vermeersch (eds), *The EU Enlargement and Gay Politics: The Impact of Eastern Enlargement on Rights, Activism and Prejudice* (Basingstoke, Palgrave Macmillan, 2016).

[23] AP Cortell and JW Davis, 'How Do International Institutions Matter? The Domestic Impact of International Rules and Norms' (1996) 40 *International Studies Quarterly* 451; L Seybert, 'The Trouble with "Returning to Europe": New European Union Members' Reluctant Embrace of Nuclear Safety and Minority Rights' (unpublished PhD Dissertation – on file with author, Cornell University, 2012); M Zürn and JT Checkel, 'Getting Socialized to Build Bridges: Constructivism and Rationalism, Europe and the Nation-State' (2005) 59 *International Organization* 1045.

[24] R Inglehart and P Norris, *Rising Tide: Gender Equality and Cultural Change around the World* (Cambridge, Cambridge University Press, 2003).

[25] F Polletta, '"Free Spaces" in Collective Action' (1999) 28 *Theory and Society* 1; C Zepeda-Millán, 'Weapons of the (Not So) Weak: Immigrant Mass Mobilization in the US South' (2014) 40 *Critical Sociology* 1; C Zepeda-Millán, 'Perceptions of Threat, Demographic Diversity, and the Framing of Illegality: Explaining (Non)Participation in New York's 2006 Immigrant Protests' (2014) 67 *Political Research Quarterly* 880.

Byrnes and Katzenstein[26] find the variation in the type of religion across Europe to be an obstacle to EU integration. In post-socialist societies, the Catholic and Orthodox churches have both been opposed to the import of EU standards on sexuality.[27] A series of domestic variables are included in the models in order to tap into these concepts.

Hypothesis 3a: *The likelihood of passing higher levels of LGB legislation increases when more domestic social spaces for LGB people exist.*

Hypothesis 3b: *The likelihood of passing higher levels of LGB legislation increases when a state's level of democracy is higher.*

Hypothesis 3c: *The likelihood of passing higher levels of LGB legislation increases when a state is wealthier.*

Hypothesis 3d: *The likelihood of passing higher levels of LGB legislation depends on a state's dominant religious institution.*

D. Theory

Taken individually, existing explanations are simplistic because they ignore the multiple dimensions of diffusion in a complex, multi-level interactive environment.[28] Following the call from Sil and Katzenstein to move beyond grand narratives,[29] several of the above mechanisms are combined here with added insights from the contentious politics literature to argue that international explanations should be more compelling in new-adopter states where issues have been more recently politicised (Hypotheses 1 and 2), while domestic explanations should be more powerful in first-mover states (Hypothesis 3).

This expectation rests on the idea that actors in new-adopter states are more dependent on international resources for making new issues visible and are more inclined to see adoption as a means to gain external legitimacy and improve reputation. When states become more transnationally connected in the international system, this process can occur even before domestic audiences are prepared to embrace the issue. For first-mover states, domestic factors should be more likely to explain the expansion of LGB rights. Their membership in a club that began to address the issue earlier paradoxically relieves the need to respond to international

[26] TA Byrnes and PJ Katzenstein (eds), *Religion in an Expanding Europe* (Cambridge, Cambridge University Press, 2006).

[27] S Ramet, 'Thy Will Be Done: The Catholic Church and Politics in Poland since 1989' in Byrnes and Katzenstein (n 26); S Ramet, 'The Way We Were – and Should Be Again? European Orthodox Churches and the "Idyllic Past"' in Byrnes and Katzenstein (n 26).

[28] ER Graham, CR Shipan, and C Volden, 'The Diffusion of Policy Diffusion Research in Political Science' (2013) 43 *British Journal of Political Science* 673.

[29] R Sil and PJ Katzenstein, *Beyond Paradigms: Analytic Eclecticism in the Study of World Politics* (Basingstoke, Palgrave Macmillan, 2010).

political pressures to expand on basic LGB rights. However, such a distinction between first-movers and new-adopters is often overlooked. Many studies find that a mix of international and domestic theoretical factors matters, but they do not take into account the sub-regional and state identities that others have found to privilege some diffusion factors over others.[30] According to Towns, states that have historically failed to gain international recognition are often the first to reach higher levels of norms to improve their reputation in international hierarchies.[31] In this sense, reputation serves 'as an umbrella term for the subjective image of a state that is held by other actors, both on its own and in relation to others'.[32] Since states occupy different positions within the international system, and have distinctive histories related to LGB rights at the international level, state authorities are presumed to be motivated to adopt pro-LGB legislation by different factors in two subsets of states: the EU-15 and the EU-12.

Thus, systematic differences between contexts in which the LGB issue was politicised during the early phases of LGB norm development in the 1970s (i.e. EU-15 states), and contexts in which the issue only recently gained widespread public visibility (i.e. the EU-12 states), should be hypothesised. Drawing on the work of sociologists like Tolbert and Zucker,[33] Strang,[34] and Soule,[35] the diffusion and institutionalisation of norms is then a two-stage process. The process may thus be more 'internal' in a set of states that identify with a first-mover grouping, where local communities responded to domestic political problems and then crystalised a norm, which new EU states adopt later as they seek external legitimacy. In her study of policies on same-sex unions, Kollman makes a similar point, arguing that domestic facilitating factors were less imperative for 'second wave' countries, which followed the example of European norm pioneers.[36] This is reminiscent of the distinction between early and late industrialisers in international political economy: whereas early industrialisers had to come up with technological and social innovations through trial and error, late adopters were able to adapt and replicate templates that were demonstrated to work.[37] Norm evolution

[30] A Gurowitz, 'The Diffusion of International Norms: Why Identity Matters' (2006) 43 *International Politics* 305; AE Towns, 'Norms and Social Hierarchies: Understanding International Policy Diffusion "From Below"' (2012) 66 *International Organization* 179.

[31] Towns (n 30).

[32] J Erickson, 'Saving Face, Looking Good, and Building International Reputation in East and West' in LW Pauly and BW Jentleson (eds), *Power in a Complex Global System* (London, Routledge, 2014) 181.

[33] PS Tolbert and LG Zucker, 'Institutional Sources of Change in the Formal Structure of Organizations: The Diffusion of Civil Service Reform, 1880–1935' (1983) 28 *Administrative Science Quarterly* 22.

[34] D Strang, 'From Dependency to Sovereignty: An Event History Analysis of Decolonization 1870–1987' (1990) 55 *American Sociological Review* 846.

[35] SA Soule, 'The Student Divestment Movement in the United States and Tactical Diffusion: The Shantytown Protest' (1997) 75 *Social Forces* 855.

[36] Kollman, *The Same-Sex Unions Revolution in Western Democracies* (n 12) 185.

[37] A Gerschenkron, *Economic Backwardness in Historical Perspective: A Book of Essays* (Cambridge, Cambridge University Press, 1962). Pablo Yanguas is thanked for suggesting this theoretical link.

in first-mover states was incremental and driven by domestic groups, which had to work within the constraints of the local institutional and normative context. By the time new-adopter EU-12 states became EU members, they were obliged to confront an established and institutionalised European norm – in large part through the FED – leaving less room for incremental adaptation.

In new-adopter EU-12 states, a greater norm diffusion was expected as (1) domestic LGB organisations become embedded in transnational advocacy networks and (2) states become more permeable to international influences. Thus, a greater role is envisaged for international sources of change in these states, in which LGB people are more likely to depend on external resources and frames to make the issue resonant and legitimate in the domestic sphere. Within this group, the states most likely to adopt LGB legislation are then those that are the most porous.[38] Political and social porosity primes these contexts by allowing transnational actors to send a clear and legitimate signal to both society and the state that adopting the norm is part of what it means to belong to modern Europe. Such actors – usually transnationally embedded domestic LGB organisations – can harness the ideas behind new norms and adapt them, manufacturing a narrative of resonance in their domestic contexts, even when LGB people were previously invisible locally.[39] Thus, it must be noted that in the case of LGB rights, states do not passively emulate international examples. The norms governing LGB rights remain contested, even when enshrined in EU law.[40] Therefore, careful interpretation is required by domestic LGB groups who can channel international examples to legitimise them locally. These actors help to interpret the norm, and send a clear signal to the state that norm compliance is necessary for fulfilling its role in international society. When such actors are absent, international norms risk being painted as external imposition, precisely because the opposition can more easily frame LGB rights as 'external' within states that have only recently deliberated the issue. The more internationalised the context, the easier it is for actors to frame the norm as legitimate to policymakers, a process that is particularly important within new-adopter contexts. This also explains why much of the effect of the Framework Equality Directive on states is indirect (i.e. giving legitimacy to such actors).

In regard to EU-15 states, policymakers should be less likely to feel the pressure to conform to international standards. Their international reputations do not suffer if they do not achieve the highest benchmarks of LGB recognition. For example, the German Government, led by Angela Merkel, balked at international

[38] As Katzenstein has argued, the interaction of globalisation and internationalisation ('territorially based exchanges across borders') enhances the 'porousness' of states. PJ Katzenstein, *A World of Regions: Asia and Europe in the American Imperium* (Ithaca, NY: Cornell University Press, 2005).

[39] As elsewhere, many new EU Member States have long and rich histories of LGB life, but this identity was expressed less openly in public, compared to many EU-15 states. See A Chetaille, 'Poland: Sovereignty and Sexuality in Post-socialist Times' in M Tremblay, D Paternotte and C Johnson (eds), *The Lesbian and Gay Movement and the State* (Abingdon, Routledge, 2011).

[40] ZI Búzás, 'Evading International Law: How Agents Comply with the Letter of the Law but Violate Its Purpose' (2017) 23(4) *European Journal of International Relations* 857–883.

activist demands to implement same-sex marriage after the American movement successfully won rhetorical support from President Barack Obama in 2012.[41] German authorities could reference their leading status on other types of LGB legislation. By contrast, Prime Minister Sali Berisha of Albania expressed his support for same-sex marriage years earlier, in 2009. He quite clearly geared his rhetoric on same-sex marriage to the international community and used European standards to justify the position to his domestic audience.[42] The following analysis tests the three hypotheses within each subset of states (new-adopters and first-movers) to explore the statistical explanations for why the LGB norm spreads more rapidly and abundantly to some states rather than others.

E. Data and Methods

This chapter utilises panel data to explore changes in the extent of the adoption of LGB legislation across states over 40 years. The complete dataset includes data on the passage of LGB legislation in EU Member States between 1970 and 2009. It goes without saying that the period from 2009 until today has seen many further advances in the protection of LGB (and trans) rights in EU Member States, advances that continue the trend seen in the 40 years analysed here.[43] The 1970–2009 timeframe is due to data constraints stemming from the fact that this chapter is a reprint of an earlier data collection and study. The dataset combines data collected on LGB legislation (the dependent variable, DV) with other country contextual data by year (the independent variables, IVs). The data used for the independent variables were collected from organisational membership lists and five existing cross-national datasets containing information on levels of globalisation (KOF Index of Globalization),[44] democracy (Polity IV),[45] GDP measures (Penn World Table),[46] and LGB social spaces.[47]

[41] In Germany marriage had not traditionally been at the centre of the movement's agenda, but within days of President Obama's announcement, transnational organisations like AllOut! staged protests in Berlin, painting Germany – which has a better record than the United States – as a laggard on LGB rights.

[42] See M Michels, 'Albania: The Gay Movement You Never Imagined' (*The Huffington Post*, 11 May 2012). Available at: www.huffingtonpost.com/american-anthropological-association/albania-gay-rights_b_1497865.html and S Barris, 'Albania Protects LGBT People from Discrimination' (*ILGA Europe*, 23 February 2010). Available at: http://ilga.org/albania-protects-lgbt-people-from-discrimination/.

[43] PM Ayoub, *When States Come Out: Europe's Sexual Minorities and the Politics of Visibility* (New York, Cambridge University Press, 2016).

[44] A Dreher, N Gaston and W Martens, *Measuring Globalisation: Gauging Its Consequences* (New York, Springer, 2008).

[45] M Marshall, K Jaggers, and TR Gurr, 'POLITY IV PROJECT Dataset Users' Manual: Political Regime Characteristics and Transitions, 1800–2010' (2016). Available at: www.systemicpeace.org/inscr/p4manualv2015.pdf>.

[46] A Heston, R Summers, and B Aten, 'Penn World Table Version 7.0, Center for International Comparisons of Production, Income and Prices at the University of Pennsylvania' (2011). Available at: https://knoema.com/PWT2011Jun/penn-world-table-7-0.

[47] DJ Frank, BJ Camp, and SA Boutcher, 'Worldwide Trends in the Criminal Regulation of Sex, 1945 to 2005' (2010) 75 *American Sociological Review* 867.

In line with the propositions of this research, the analysis is limited to: (1) the 27 states that had joined the EU by 2009, since all states are embedded in the EU's institutional structures, and (2) the years 1970–2009. The analysis begins in 1970 because it roughly coincides with the time of the 1969 Stonewall Rebellion – the first broadly publicised instance of LGB resistance – and the birth of the gay liberation movement, which began in the United States in 1965 and found its way to Europe by 1971.[48] As was described above, new and old EU Member States are analysed separately due to their differing political histories. As such, different conditions are expected to hold for these distinct subsets of states.

Governments select from a set of legislative measures that grant LGB people state-sanctioned recognition in their respective states. The outcome of interest in this study focuses on 12 pieces of pro-LGB legislation that fall under the following five categories: anti-discrimination (employment, goods and services, constitution), criminal law (prohibition of incitement to hatred), partnership (cohabitation, registered partnership, and marriage equality), parenting rights (joint and second parent adoption, fertility treatment), and equal sexual offence provisions (age of consent and legality of sex-same relations). The analysis uses both a five-point categorical LGB legislation DV based on the five categories and a 12-point legislation DV based on the key legislation components.[49] Table 11.2 also employs a measure that looks specifically at anti-discrimination, which is most directly relevant to the FED.

The hypotheses are tested using ordered logit regression and Poisson regression (depending on the DV used) to explore the determinants of the successful passage of legislation. The ordered logit analysis assigns an ordered value according to the extent to which a state passes categories of LGB legislation (5-point DV), taking into account that some states go much farther (e.g. legalizing LGB partnerships) than others (e.g. decriminalising same-sex sexual relations). The Poisson analysis uses a count of all pro-LGB legislation passed (12-point DV). The original study on which this analysis is based provides more detailed information on the methods of analysis, including conceptualisation and coding of dependent and independent variables, as well as the descriptive statistics for the variables used in this study.[50]

F. Results

Table 11.1 presents the results for the ordered logit and Poisson models, reflecting the extent to which states adopt LGB legislation. It divides results into two groups,

[48] B Adam, J Willem Duyvendak, and A Krouwel (eds), *Global Emergence of Gay & Lesbian Politics* (Philadelphia, Temple University Press, 1998).

[49] PM Ayoub, 'Contested Norms in New-Adopter States: International Determinants of LGBT Rights Legislation' (2015) 21 *European Journal of International Relations* 293.

[50] ibid. This is an important point to keep in mind, also in relation to the soft law measures discussed at the outset of the chapter by Tryfonidou in this volume. Soft law processes, even if without 'teeth', are part and parcel of transformative change for LGB people.

Table 11.1 Ordered Logit and Poisson regression models predicting the passage of pro-LGBT legislation†, 1970–2009

	EU-12				EU-15			
	Ordered Logit Regression, 5-point DV		**Poisson Regression, 12-point DV**		**Ordered Logit Regression, 5-point DV**		**Poisson Regression, 12-point DV**	
	1	2	3	4	5	6	7	8
Transnationally-linked LGBT organisations	1.070*	1.222*	0.156*	0.179*	−0.182	−0.229	−0.030	−0.040
	(0.368)	(0.384)	(0.068)	(0.070)	(0.615)	(0.442)	(0.090)	(0.083)
International channels								
Social channels	0.147*		0.041*		−0.058		−0.012	
	(0.072)		(0.015)		(0.073)		(0.011)	
Political channels	0.067+		0.011*		0.042		0.015*	
	(0.038)		(0.005)		(0.039)		(0.007)	
Overall porousness		0.126*		0.013+		0.013		0.014+
		(0.066)		(0.007)		(0.057)		(0.008)
EU accession	0.780	1.287	−0.015	0.135	0.793	0.879	0.235	0.241
	(1.050)	(1.037)	(0.148)	(0.140)	(1.010)	(0.984)	(0.179)	(0.194)
EU application issued	−0.319	0.411	−0.296	−0.013	−1.149	−1.210	0.026	0.009
	(0.750)	(0.394)	(0.176)	(0.074)	(1.730)	(1.597)	(0.258)	(0.236)
Domestic conditions								
LGBT social spaces	1.581+	1.424	0.146	0.138	0.052	0.111	−0.109	−0.089
	(0.857)	(0.928)	(0.124)	(0.135)	(0.817)	(0.929)	(0.118)	(0.149)
Democracy level	−0.038	−0.10+	−0.037*	−0.043*	0.018	0.065	−0.041	−0.024
	(0.064)	(0.054)	(0.011)	(0.015)	(0.134)	(0.125)	(0.026)	(0.025)
GDP	−0.000	−0.000	−0.000	−0.000	0.0004*	0.0004*	0.000*	0.0001*
	(0.000)	(0.000)	(0.000)	(0.000)	(0.000)	(0.000)	(0.000)	(0.000)
Protestant	–	–	–	–	0.299	0.919	0.290	0.279
					(1.216)	(2.067)	(0.210)	(0.259)
Catholic	0.535	−0.774	−0.159	−0.439*	−1.892+	−1.128	−0.214	−0.022
	(2.586)	(2.031)	(0.209)	(0.176)	(0.981)	(1.056)	(0.132)	(0.165)

(continued)

Table 11.1 ***(Continued)***

	EU-12				EU-15			
	Ordered Logit Regression, 5-point DV		Poisson Regression, 12-point DV		Ordered Logit Regression, 5-point DV		Poisson Regression, 12-point DV	
Other	-1.566	-3.347*	-0.605*	-0.868*	-4.506*	-3.252	-1.331*	-0.964*
	(1.429)	(1.243)	(0.151)	(0.196)	(1.883)	(2.061)	(0.302)	(0.378)
Observations	266	266	266	266	560	560	560	560
Clustered by nation	10	10	10	10	14	14	14	14

Notes: Luxembourg, Cyprus, and Malta not included (data limitations), robust standard errors in parentheses, *p<0.05, +p<0.1.

according to the subset of states: the new EU Member States (Models 1–4) and the old EU Member States (Models 5–8). All models reported are run with either the *social* and *political channels* variables (Models 1, 3, 5 and 7) or the *combined channels* variables (Models 2, 4, 6 and 8).

In analysing the adoption of LGB legislation in Europe, the results are complex, supporting different theoretical approaches according to the subset of states analysed. The results surrounding the EU-12 models (Models 1–4) provide a measure of support for the hypothesis that transnational and international channels influence the extent to which LGB-friendly policies diffuse. The variables *transnationally-embedded LGB organisations, social channels,* and *political channels* are all significant at the customary level ($p \leq .05$), controlling for all other variables in the models. The *combined channels* variables are also significant at the .05 (Model 2) or .1 (Model 4) levels. An examination of Models 1–4 in Table 1 indicates that, on average, as states have more transnationally-embedded LGB organisations, they are more likely to adopt more LGB-friendly policies. The findings related to international channels are also in line with the hypothesis that diffusion depends on the international porosity of states.

The *EU accession* and *EU application* variables fail to reach significance across models, which privilege policy adoption via mechanisms of transnational socialisation over hard law and EU conditionality.[51] This is likely also to be related to the fact that the EU's direct pressure mechanism only encourages states to pass anti-discrimination legislation (explained below). What is striking are the inconclusive findings for the role that domestic variables play in any new EU-12 states. The results suggest that *GDP wealth* is not significantly correlated with higher levels of policy adoption in any of the models concerning new EU Member States. Furthermore, the positive effect of *LGB social spaces* on the diffusion of legislation only reaches significance at the .1 level, and only in Model 1. States in which

[51] Kollman, *The Same-sex Unions Revolution in Western Democracies* (n 12).

the dominant religion is *Catholic* or *other* (generally Orthodox in this analysis) are less likely than *mixed Christian* states to pass LGB legislation, but the significance levels of the results remain mixed across models. The *other* religion variable performs the best, reaching significance in Models 2–4, which supports research on the particularly strong opposition by the Orthodox Church to LGB rights.[52]

Surprisingly, *democracy level* is not positively correlated with greater levels of LGB policy adoption. Instead, it challenges the expectations of the domestic resonance camp by being negatively correlated with passing higher levels of LGB legislation in new EU Member States. While it should be noted that this finding applies to one of the most democratic regions in the world – and may be reversed if the analysis went beyond the regional scope of this study – it is interesting to find that among new EU Member States, the strongest democracies are not the most successful LGB rights adopters. This might be related to a similar international society rationale involving state reputation, in that states with strong democratic reputations need not worry about their international image to the extent that weaker democracies do.[53] For example, while the Danes were the first movers on registered partnership, they waited until 2012 to approve same-sex marriage, without international criticism. Newer democracies have incentives to make credible human rights commitments for foreign audiences.[54] In many parts of the world (including some states in Latin America, and Spain and Portugal in the EU-15 states), such states went farther when it came to adopting various pieces of LGB legislation despite being followers on LGB rights in earlier years.

The image is somewhat reversed for the EU-15 states (Models 5–8), many of which were early movers in the global expansion of LGB rights. For this subset of states, a key measure of domestic conditions is significant ($p \leq .05$) across models. The results indicate that *economic wealth* is positively correlated with high levels of LGB-friendly policies, suggesting that more affluent EU-15 states were particularly likely to adopt extensive LGB legislation. In line with the modernisation theory, domestic affluence is a significant predictor of the extent of policy diffusion, but only in the leading EU-15 states. It matters less for EU-12 adopters, where the diffusion of LGB legislation is influenced by a host of other transnational and international variables. Of the transnational and international channels, only *political* and *combined channels* are significant, at the .05 and .1 level respectively and positively correlated with LGB policy adoption, but only in Models 7 and 8. The later timing of LGB visibility may also explain why EU-12 states are more susceptible to international channels.[55] EU-15 states began responding to the issue in a less connected world, with fewer outside pressures, but the game

[52] Ramet, 'The Way We Were – and Should Be Again?' in Byrnes and Katzenstein (n 26).

[53] Towns (n 30).

[54] A Moravcsik, 'The Origins of Human Rights Regimes: Democratic Delegation in Postwar Europe' (2013) 54 *International Organization* 217.

[55] MD Kane, 'Timing Matters: Shifts in the Causal Determinants of Sodomy Law Decriminalization, 1961–1998' (2007) 54 *Social Problems* 211.

changed as such pressures intensified and such state decisions could no longer be made in a vacuum.[56]

Religion also plays a role in some EU-15 models, suggesting that states falling under the *other* religion category (in this case, Orthodox Greece) are significantly less likely than mixed religious states to pass higher levels of LGB legislation (Models 5, 7, and 8). The results of Model 5 also suggest that *Catholic* states are less likely than mixed religious states to pass higher levels of pro-LGB legislation at the .1 level of significance. Finally, the null effect for domestic LGB social spaces does not necessarily diminish the historical importance of these spaces in the development of the LGB movement. Social spaces brought together an invisible group of people and helped to ferment a movement in first-mover countries. However, for several reasons, these spaces matter less for the passage of higher levels of LGB legislation, which generally occurs later. The finding may also reflect the fact that Europeanisation has given some actors, especially rooted cosmopolitans, greater access to established spaces in external contexts.[57] The notable differences between the EU-12 and EU-15 states in the extent to which LGB friendly policies diffuse supports the theoretical expectations outlined in this chapter.

Table 11.2 EU-12 Determinants of year passing anti-discrimination, 1970–2010

	Anti-Discrimination
Transnational LGBT organisations	9.09*
	(2.19)
Combined channels	.99*
	(.36)
EU accession	27.49*
	(7.58)
Democracy level	10.62*
	(4.12)
GDP (log)	11.43
	(9.22)
Diffusion of anti-discrimination	2.82*
	(.435)

(continued)

[56] This point does not suggest that international pressures were absent in earlier times. Even before ILGA's founding in 1978, there was a long history of transnational activism in Europe, dating back to Magnus Hirschfeld's Scientific Committee in 1928, followed by transnational organising during the time of the homophile movement. Various European Parliament resolutions and supranational Court rulings also constituted international pressures for EU-15 states.

[57] PM Ayoub, 'Cooperative Transnationalism in Contemporary Europe: Europeanization and Political Opportunities for LGBT Mobilization in the European Union' (2013) 5 *European Political Science Review* 279.

Table 11.2 ***(Continued)***

	Anti-Discrimination
Constant	–359.49*
	(77.39)
Observations	306
Clustered by nation	11

Notes: Malta not included due to data limitations in Polity IV Dataset, discrete time logit models, robust *z*-statistics in parentheses, * significant at <5% level.

Source: Ayoub, *When States Come Out* (n 40), 114.

Turning to Table 11.2, the focus now specifically shifts to the outcome of anti-discrimination legislation in new-adopter states. Unsurprisingly, *EU accession*, alongside other international channels, has a pronounced and significant effect on the likelihood of adopting anti-discrimination measures for LGB people. Since the FED applied to all the applicant states in this sample, joining the EU in the 2004 and 2007 waves of accession, it is reflected centrally in these findings and supports the direct effect of conditionality in this area. That said, when looking at LGB rights more holistically, one should remain conscious of the fact that many other laws diffuse indirectly, via soft mechanisms of diffusion. Indeed, the direct effect of EU conditionality is particularly pronounced in the area of LGB rights law shaped by the FED.[58] Indirect transnational sources of change, such as mimicking laws adopted by other EU states, matters a great deal for many rights issues, including anti-discrimination. In Table 11.2, this is captured by the *Diffusion* variable, which measures the amount of other EU states that have such laws in place. The presence of *transnational LGB organisations* and *combined channels* also helps pressure states to adopt such policies. In sum, the FED has both a direct and indirect role in shaping the spread of laws around sexual orientation in the EU space.

III. Conclusions

This analysis has sought to contribute to, as well as test, four theoretical explanations for the diffusion of contentious pieces of legislation: rights legislation diffuses to states (1) when those states fear the costs of international pressure, (2) when they become convinced of the appropriateness of the international norm, (3) when their advocacy organisations are embedded in transnational networks, and (4) when their pre-existing domestic norms resonate with the international norms. Differences among new-adopter and first-mover states were hypothesised, with the expectation that the presence of transnationally-embedded LGB organisations and channels of internationalisation would matter more for diffusion in

[58] Ayoub, *When States Come Out* (n 40).

new-adopter states because they make the issue initially salient in the domestic realm. These organisations and channels of influence depend heavily on EU law, such as the Framework Equality Directive, to send signals to state decision makers that the issue is a standard in their international community.

A comparison between the EU-12 and EU-15 revealed variation in the extent to which a state passes higher levels of LGB legislation, according to the state-grouping's position in the international system. All international channels and the presence of transnationally embedded LGB organisations proved significant for diffusion in the new-adopter states. In EU-15 states, the results related to these variables were less consistent, with only the combined and political channels appearing as significant predictors of diffusion in some models. Where domestic predictors were not significantly and consistently correlated with adoption in EU-12 states, economic wealth had explanatory power in all models across EU-15 states. International and transnational sources provide the resources to make the issue visible, as well as the legitimising frames to associate the issue with modernity in the contemporary international society that EU states find themselves in.

Future research would benefit from more carefully exploring the relationship between international norms and the domestic resistances that moderate their reception,[59] as well as global processes of norm polarisation.[60] Such work can offer important insights into studies on LGB rights, since these rights remain hotly contested in multiple contexts. In a context like Europe, riddled with Brexit and populist movements, one must proceed with caution when theorising conditionality without also exploring the repercussions it can provoke if LGB rights are experienced as externally imposed. As demonstrated here, the legacy of the Framework Equality Directive also concerns its more subtle and indirect effect on the broader diffusion of various types of LGB rights. Supporting LGB rights in EU law has led to protections for sexual minorities, both through direct and indirect mechanisms. That said, the presence of local movement actors to help channel and interpret laws for domestic processes plays a central role. Furthermore, an area that calls for much of our attention is the intersectional connection of this posturing by Europe to other groups that remain equally marginalised in the European public sphere. For example, in some contexts, LGB rights – as a European value – have been used instrumentally to discriminate against other marginalised groups in the EU, such as refugees and migrants.[61] Indeed, improving equality in Europe is always best served in a process that views the struggles of various groups as intersectionally linked across race, class, gender, and ability.[62]

[59] PM Ayoub, 'With Arms Wide Shut: Threat Perception, Norm Reception, and Mobilized Resistance to LGBT Rights' (2014) 13 *Journal of Human Rights* 337.

[60] J Symons and D Altman, 'International Norm Polarization: Sexuality as a Subject of Human Rights Protection' (2015) 7 *International Theory* 61.

[61] P Mepschen, JW Duyvendak, and EH Tonkens, 'Sexual Politics, Orientalism and Multicultural Citizenship in the Netherlands' (2010) 44 *Sociology* 962.

[62] J Kantola and K Nousiainen, 'Institutionalizing Intersectionality in Europe' (2009) 11 *International Feminist Journal of Politics* 459; A Krizsan, H Skjeie and J Squires (eds), *Institutionalizing*

While the analysis focused exclusively on the rights of sexual minorities, there is reason to believe that the results may play out similarly for several other issues concerning marginalised groups in international politics. In particular, the findings hold broad implications for research on the spread of policies against domestic violence,[63] sexual harassment in the workplace,[64] and the introduction of gender quotas,[65] where scholars have shown that state behaviours towards women are linked to both domestic *and* international politics, such as transnational networks and hierarchies in international society. Given the politically salient and contentious nature of LGB rights policies, the findings also have important theoretical and practical implications, supporting the notion that state decision makers in new-adopter states are drawn to internationally visible issues, even if the national debate concerning these issues is not resolved.[66] Most generally, the evidence concerning the role of state groupings and hierarchies contributes to the knowledge about processes of state socialisation and norm transfer in international politics,[67] as well as suggests pathways for explaining the effectiveness of transnational activism in cross-national comparison.[68]

In conclusion, states care about their image and reputation on the world stage and new-adopters are willing to take risky policy decisions when they receive strong signals that the international community expects it of them. In the year after President Obama first expressed his support for same-sex marriage in May 2012, four countries in three world regions passed such legislation, and several others had it tabled. In 2014, lawmakers in Catholic Malta voted 37–0 (with some abstentions) to legalise both same-sex unions and joint adoption by same-sex couples, and Estonia has placed a gender-neutral cohabitation bill on parliament's agenda. After Malta's votes, Prime Minister Joseph Muscat said, 'Malta is now more liberal and *more European*,' before adding that the legislation also gives 'equality to all its people'.[69] Indeed, Malta, an EU-12 state, has also made gains in many other areas, including gender recognition (2015) and full marriage rights (2017), to top ILGA Europe's Rainbow map in recent years. It is a case that thus supports the conclusions of this chapter: a strong and internationally connected

Intersectionality: The Changing Nature of European Equality Regimes (Basingstoke, Palgrave Macmillan, 2012).

[63] Montoya (n 9).

[64] Roggeband in Givan, Roberts and Soule (n 9).

[65] Towns (n 30).

[66] A Karch, 'Vertical Diffusion and the Policy-making Process: The Politics of Embryonic Stem Cell Research' (2012) 65 *Political Research Quarterly* 48.

[67] B Greenhill, 'Recognition and Collective Identity Formation in International Politics' (2008) 14 *European Journal of International Relations* 343; T Flockhart, '"Complex Socialization": A Framework for the Study of State Socialization' (2006) 12 *European Journal of International Relations* 89; AE Towns, 'The Status of Women as a Standard of "Civilization"' (2009) 15 *European Journal of International Relations* 681.

[68] Keck and Sikkink (n 9); S Tarrow, *The New Transnational Activism* (Cambridge, Cambridge University Press, 2005).

[69] N Nielsen, 'Malta Legalises Same-Sex Unions and Adoption' (*EUobserver.Com*, 15 April 2014). Available at: http://euobserver.com/social/123858.

local movement, combined with social and political international pressures can lead to transformative change.

In these historically unprecedented times of LGB visibility, international sources of change should have currency in explaining the proliferation of sexual minority rights, especially among new-adopter states. As also argued by Tryfonidou in this volume, the FED surely has contributed to those international sources. This chapter has shown that it does so both directly and indirectly, by championing a norm and giving it teeth to effect change across the European polity. Indeed, it has also played a role globally by further establishing international norms that recognise LGB people as part of the social fabric of many societies, and as having a due claim to rights protections. There is a long way to go for LGB (and even more so for trans and intersex) people, but the path-breaking role of the FED in pushing Member States towards LGB rights and empowerment is paramount, despite the pitfalls encountered on that way.[70]

[70] PM Ayoub, 'Protean Power in Movement: Navigating Uncertainty in the LGBT Rights Revolution' in PJ Katzenstein and L Seybert (eds), *Power in Uncertainty: Exploring the Unexpected in World Politics* (Cambridge, Cambridge University Press, 2018).

PART V

Age

12

Justifying Age Discrimination in the EU

RACHEL HORTON

I. Introduction

The EU is 'turning increasingly grey',[1] with the population share of those over the age of 65 projected to rise to 28 per cent by 2050 from 19 per cent in 2015.[2] Demographic ageing poses a range of complex policy challenges, including for the labour market. The European Social Partners in their 2015–2017 Work Programme have identified the need to increase the active workforce, young and old, as one of the most important of such challenges.[3] Legal protection from age discrimination is a fundamental tool in meeting the needs and protecting the rights of this changing workforce.

However, the legal framework for protection from age discrimination is a 'weaker template' than that governing other protected grounds.[4] Distinct from such other grounds protected by EU anti-discrimination law, the Framework Equality Directive (FED) provides that differences in treatment on grounds of age, which would amount to direct discrimination on other grounds, may be permitted where it can be objectively justified.[5] In the absence of clear political or social consensus on the nature of age discrimination and with only limited guidance in the legislation itself, the Court of Justice of the European Union (CJEU) has been

[1] European Commission, *The 2015 Ageing Report: Economic and budgetary projections for the 28 EU Member States (2013–2060)*, European Economy 3/2015 (Luxembourg, Publications Office of the European Union, 2015).

[2] For a useful analysis of demographic changes, see K Scott 'Demographic Developments and Economic Challenges in an Ageing Europe' in A Numhauser-Henning (ed), *Elder Law: Evolving European Perspectives* (Cheltenham, Edward Elgar, 2017).

[3] ETUC et al, *The 2015–2017 Work Programme of the European Social Partners. Partnership for Inclusive Growth and Employment* (2015). Available at: www.etuc.org/publications.

[4] A Numhauser-Henning, JJ Votinius and A Zbyszeweska, 'Equal Treatment and Age Discrimination – Inside and Outside Working Life' in Numhauser-Henning (n 2).

[5] Council Directive 2000/78/EC establishing a general framework for equal treatment in employment and occupation [2000] OJ L303/16 (Framework Equality Directive), Art 6.

tasked with navigating a difficult course in establishing the boundaries of permissible justification. In the significant body of case law that has emerged since the adoption of the FED, the Court has produced some clear guidance for Member States and national Courts and, as will be seen, has taken a more robust approach to the justification test in some respects than had perhaps been anticipated.[6]

Nonetheless, in one respect at least, the case law is frustrating. The differences between the approach the Court has taken to age discrimination and its approach to discrimination on other grounds are often striking. Such divergence, it will be argued, is not simply an inevitable consequence of the admittedly significant differences in the legislative provisions themselves. It is also a result of the choices that the Court has made in applying the test for justification. The case law is missing an account of *whether* and, if so, *when* and *why* age discrimination is different in nature from discrimination on grounds of, for example, sex and race. Without such an account, the case law on age is difficult to reconcile with the case law on other protected grounds, and in particular, with the Court's identification of the prohibition from discrimination as a fundamental right which protects human dignity and autonomy.[7]

First outlining the background to the legislation, and considering the arguments on the fundamental differences between age and other protected grounds of discrimination, this chapter will then focus on the Court's approach to two issues – stereotyping and positive action. These were chosen as illustrating the most striking contrast between permissible treatment in relation to age as compared to other grounds. It will be argued that while some differences in the Court's approach between grounds may be well-founded conceptually, it has failed to consistently articulate what age discrimination has in common with discrimination on other grounds. In particular, the full range of harms to which age discrimination may give rise have not been identified; an approach which risks diluting the strength of the legal protection available. Moving forward, it will be suggested that a more transparent and principled account of the similarities and differences between age and other grounds is needed.

II. Age as a Protected Ground

A. Background and Legislative Framework

The inclusion of age within the EU legislative framework prohibiting discrimination and promoting equality resulted from a number of competing perspectives

[6] C O'Cinneide, 'Age Discrimination and the European Court of Justice: EU Equality Law Comes of Age' (2009–2010) 2 *Revue des Affaires Européennes* 253.

[7] See, e.g. Case C-13/94 *P v S and Cornwall County Council* EU:C:1996:170 para 22, where the Court made clear that to tolerate discrimination against an individual (in that case against transsexuals) would be tantamount to 'a failure to respect the dignity and freedom to which her or she is entitled, and which the Court has a duty to safeguard'.

and priorities.[8] The legislation was drafted in the context of anxiety about the challenge to the labour market of an ageing population.[9] Action was needed to increase participation in the labour market of older workers, and age discrimination – or at least the use of age to control the conditions of exit and entry into the labour market – was seen as a barrier to achieving this. Thus, the original Commission proposal noted that while 'demographic trends make it essential to ensure that as high a percentage as possible of people of working age are in jobs', a number of discriminatory practices were undermining this goal, particularly in relation to older workers.[10] Recital 11 of the FED provides that age discrimination (in common with discrimination on other grounds):

> may undermine the achievement of the objectives of the EC treaty, in particular the attainment of a high level of employment and social protection, raising the standard of living and the quality of life, economic and social cohesion and solidarity, and the free movement of persons.

However, and as will be evident from the discussion on the CJEU case law below, age discrimination is also often seen as a potential solution to improve labour market access for disadvantaged age groups. Employers may be incentivised to employ the young or the old when permitted to use less generous or secure terms and conditions of employment for these age groups; and mandatory retirement may be used to ensure new openings are available for younger workers.[11] In addition, as Freedland and Vickers have argued, the use of age is deeply entrenched in structures of the labour market (particularly in relation to retirement) and there has been reluctance, both on the part of EU institutions and the Member States, to engage in the extensive and undoubtedly expensive and disruptive structural reform a full-scale prohibition of age discrimination would require.[12] As Recital 25 FED explains:

> The prohibition of age discrimination is an essential part of meeting the aims set out in the Employment Guidelines and encouraging diversity in the workforce. However, differences in treatment in connection with age may be justified under certain circumstances and therefore require specific provisions which may vary in accordance with the situation in Member States.

In common with the other protected grounds, there is also evidence that age equality, and the right not to be discriminated against because of age, are deserving

[8] See, e.g. D Schiek, 'Age Discrimination before the ECJ – Conceptual and Theoretical Issues' (2011) 48 *Common Market Law Rev* 777; M Sargeant, 'The European Court of Justice and Age Discrimination' (2011) 2 *Journal of Business Law* 144.

[9] European Commission, 'Proposal for a Council Directive Establishing a General Framework for Equal Treatment in Employment and Occupation – Explanatory Memorandum' COM(1999) 565 final.

[10] ibid.

[11] For detailed discussion on the position of young people in the labour market, see chapter by B ter Haar in the present volume.

[12] M Freedland and L Vickers, 'Age Discrimination and EU Labour Rights Law' in A Bogg, C Costello and A Davies (eds), *A Research Handbook on EU Labour* Law (Cheltenham, Edward Elgar, 2016). The authors note that age is not alone in this respect – implementing gender discrimination law also involves deep structural changes (528).

of protection as fundamental rights. Thus, the preamble to the FED notes that 'the right of all persons to equality before the law and protection against discrimination constitutes a universal right' recognised in a number of international human rights instruments.[13] Further, the European Charter of Fundamental Rights (CFR), proclaimed in the same year as the FED, lists age among the protected grounds of discrimination and proclaims the right of the elderly to a life of dignity and independence and to social inclusion.[14]

Lack of social and political consensus on the status of age discrimination was evident in the drafting phase of the Directive.[15] In particular, there was debate as to the possibility, or desirability, of identifying at the outset the situations in which direct age discrimination could be justified. Consideration was given as to whether or not the Directive should contain a list of specific exceptions to the principle of non-discrimination on grounds of age rather than a general justification provision.[16] There was concern that a specific exceptions approach gave the impression that particular categories of discrimination were automatically justified without the need for objective justification. There was also concern that the absence of agreement on the status of age – the social importance of which was undergoing rapid change – would make such an approach unrealistic.[17] The compromise was a piece of legislation which prohibits age discrimination but provides that, unlike for the other grounds, the prohibition of direct as well as indirect age discrimination is subject to an open-ended justification test. Article 6 FED sets out the test for justification together with non-exhaustive examples of the categories of aims which may be legitimate:

> Member States may provide that differences of treatment on grounds of age shall not constitute discrimination, if, within the context of national law, they are objectively and reasonably justified by a legitimate aim, including legitimate employment policy, labour market and vocational training objectives, and if the means of achieving that aim are appropriate and necessary.

This is followed by a non-exhaustive list of the types of differences in treatment which may be justifiable, subject to the requirement of proportionality. In addition to Article 6 FED, and in common with the other protected grounds, exceptions to the prohibition against direct discrimination are also made where the uses of age amount to positive action (Article 7 FED) or where a characteristic related to age amounts to a genuine and determining occupational requirement (Article 4 FED).

[13] Framework Equality Directive, Recital 4.

[14] Charter of Fundamental Rights of the European Union [2016] OJ C202/393, Arts 21 and 25; See also Art 24 which protects the rights of the child to have their views taken into account according to their age and maturity.

[15] European Parliament, 'Report on the proposal for a Council directive establishing a general framework for equal treatment in employment and occupation' A5-0264/2000 final.

[16] ibid.

[17] Prior to FED, very few Member States had legislation prohibiting age discrimination – see C O'Cinneide, 'Comparative European Perspectives on Age Discrimination' in S Fredman and S Spencer, *Age as an Equality Issue: Legal and Policy Perspectives* (Oxford, Hart, 2003).

B. Conceptual Issues

There are a number of arguments as to why age equality and age discrimination are fundamentally different in nature from equality and discrimination on grounds of, say, race or sex. These arguments suggest that at least some forms of age discrimination are less harmful than discrimination on other grounds.

The first two – related – arguments concern the temporal dimension to equality, often referred to as the 'complete life view' and 'fair innings arguments'. Both appeal to the idea that (some forms of) equality between individuals should be assessed not at a particular moment in time but across the whole life course. McKerlie defines the complete life view as the normative principle 'that different people's share of resources, or welfare, should be equal when we consider the amounts of those things that they receive over the complete course of their lives'.[18] From this perspective, using age as a criterion for determining access to various goods, provided this is done consistently over time, appears not to create inequality because, over the course of a lifetime, everyone will be eligible for the same benefits and subject to the same burdens. Less favourable treatment because of age today is only a part of the story since it is compensated for by the more favourable treatment received in the past or to be received in the future. Thus, across the entire course of our lives, we will not have been treated unequally with others. On this view, as Cupit notes, age discrimination appears to be simply a matter of taking turns.[19]

The complete life view of equality suggests that we *may* discriminate on grounds of age (i.e. use chronological age to organise and ration access to various goods or benefits such as jobs) because no inequality is thereby created. The fair innings argument says we *should*, sometimes, discriminate on grounds of age to avoid inequality or to achieve substantive equality between generations. Since older generations have lived or worked longer, they have acquired advantages (e.g. a long career, adequate pension savings) over the young. Treating both groups equally today may preserve this advantage for the older generation at the expense of the younger, and may further serve to permanently exclude younger generations from the opportunities enjoyed by those who have gone before them. There are several versions of the fair innings argument but, typically, its advocates argue that where resources such as jobs are scarce, priority in their distribution should be given to the younger generations without a long career and the opportunity to save resources for retirement. In essence, this is an argument for a form of positive discrimination. Unlike sex or race discrimination, the substantive inequality the fair innings approach aims to correct is not rooted in historical discrimination against a particular group, but inevitably generated by the passage of time.[20]

[18] D McKerlie, 'Equality and Time' (1989) 99 *Ethics* 475.

[19] G Cupit, 'Justice, Age, and Veneration' (1998) 108 *Ethics* 702.

[20] In some cases, the inequality is caused by changing circumstances which preclude the younger generation from accessing the same opportunities as the older generation once enjoyed.

The complete life view of equality has been endorsed by a number of influential egalitarian thinkers. Both Dworkin and Daniels, for example, advance (different) conceptions of equality which accept that a fair distribution of resources may include an uneven distribution over the life course for each individual.[21] For similar reasons, some economists justify mandatory retirement as a necessary consequence of the maximally efficient distribution of wages across a lifetime.[22] This distribution is uneven across different stages of working life – lower wages on first entry into the workforce which then increase until retirement – but serves to maximise wealth for workers across their whole lives. It is argued that mandatory retirement is necessary for this scheme to be sustainable. Thus, even though one may be unhappy about mandatory retirement when the time comes, it is a necessary part of an implicit bargain – if not one made explicitly through contract or collective agreement – which rational workers would choose as a means of maximising wealth.

Although intuitively appealing, at least three empirical and conceptual difficulties with the complete life and fair innings accounts of equality should be noted. First, the fair innings argument has been criticised as relying on flawed assumptions in its application to the labour market. In particular, the premise that there is a fixed number of jobs, a 'lump of labour' to be shared among the generations has been disputed.[23] In many policy documents issued prior to the introduction of age-discrimination legislation, the UK Government dismissed this contention as fallacious, arguing that, on the contrary, the retention of older workers is capable of generating growth and hence more jobs.[24] In addition, the argument that mandatory retirement is an effective way of improving youth unemployment is challenged as failing to recognise that in many cases the exit of an older worker does not necessarily create a vacancy for a younger worker.[25]

Second, the notion of complete life equality relies on the idea that everyone will enjoy the same provision (or denial) of benefits, opportunities and services over a lifetime. However, differing circumstances or other barriers clearly mean that not everyone is able to take advantage of the benefits theoretically on offer at one stage of life to compensate for the lack of benefits available at other times. As Fudge notes, many groups simply do not fit the 'normative model' of intergenerational solidarity on which many policies permitting direct age

[21] N Daniels, 'Am I My Parents' Keeper?' in N Daniels, *Just Health Care* (Cambridge, Cambridge University Press, 1985); R Dworkin, *Sovereign Virtue: The Theory and Practice of Equality* (Cambridge MA, Harvard University Press, 2000).

[22] See, e.g. E Lazear, 'Why is There Mandatory Retirement' (1979) 87 *Journal of Political Economy* 1261; see also discussion in S Issacharoff and E Worth Harris, 'Is Age Discrimination Really Age Discrimination? The ADEA's Unnatural Solution.' (1997) 72 *New York University Law Review* 780.

[23] See, e.g. discussion in S Fredman 'The Age of Equality' in Fredman and Spencer (n 17).

[24] Cabinet Office: Performance and Innovation Unit, *Winning the Generation Game* (London, Her Majesty's Stationery Office, 2000).

[25] ibid.

discrimination are based.[26] For those who have had unequal opportunities in the labour market, differential treatment of one age group may serve to entrench existing disadvantage.

A third objection is the argument that the harm of discrimination does not reside – at least solely – in the distributive inequality which it may create. Excluding members of a particular age group from valuable benefits today may be harmful even if no lifetime inequality results, because it harms other important interests such as dignity, autonomy or social inclusion, the protection of which is usually regarded as a fundamental aim of anti-discrimination law.[27] While the complete life view may address worries about *comparative* injustice, it does nothing to allay concerns about other harms which it may create. In this respect, the complete life view is susceptible to the same problems as other conceptions of formal equality. It has long been recognised that adherence to formal equality, or consistency of treatment, while crucially important in some contexts, is insufficient to meet the broader aims of anti-discrimination law.[28]

A further argument often made in relation to age, though one less examined in the theoretical literature, is that basing decisions on age is less demeaning to the individual who is denied some benefit as a result. This is because age, unlike other protected characteristics, does not have the same long history of oppression as a group.[29] Even accepting this, the argument is again susceptible to the objection that while some uses of age are *less* harmful than comparable uses of sex or race to determine access to the labour market, it does not mean that there is no harm caused. While historical discrimination and group disadvantage may be important or indeed sufficient conditions to conclude that the use of particular personal characteristics is demeaning or undermines dignity or autonomy, they are not *necessary* conditions. This is certainly reflected in the protection afforded by the EU anti-discrimination framework which is, at least in relation to direct discrimination, largely symmetrical, with members of the majority or advantaged groups receiving equal protection alongside the minority.

Therefore, there are reasons to be cautious in deploying arguments that age is different in justifying age discrimination. The claims considered above tend to concentrate on only one aspect of the potential harm caused by discrimination. However, literature has explored the harm caused by discrimination from more

[26] J Fudge, 'Dignity, Disadvantage and Age: Putting Constitutional and Fundamental Rights to Work for Older Workers' in Numhauser-Henning (n 2).

[27] S Fredman, *Discrimination Law* 2nd edn (Oxford, Oxford University Press, 2011). In relation to age, see also B Hepple, 'Age Discrimination in Employment: Implementing the Framework Directive 2000/78/EC' in Fredman and Spencer (n 17).

[28] Fredman, *Discrimination Law* (n 27).

[29] See G Rutherglen, 'From Race to Age: The Expanding Scope of Employment Discrimination Law' (1995) 24 *Journal of Legal Studies* 491; C Cinneide, 'Constitutional and Fundamental Rights Aspects of Age Discrimination' in A Numhauser-Henning and M Ronnmar (eds), *Age Discrimination and Labour Law: Comparative and Conceptual Perspectives in the EU and Beyond* (Alphen aan den Rijn, Kluwer Law International, 2015).

than one perspective. Fredman, among others, has proposed a multi-dimensional approach to understanding the values which underpin substantive equality.[30] This implies a recognition of the range of wrongs associated with discrimination and inequality and of the range of harms discriminatory treatment can cause. Any attempt to justify age discrimination, and certainly one which relies on the differences between age and other characteristics, must also account for the full range of wrongs and harms potentially caused by differences in treatment because of age.

III. The Case Law of the CJEU

A. Introduction

From the outset, the CJEU signalled it would take a robust approach to the adjudication of age discrimination claims. Indeed in *Mangold v Helm* (2005), the first case on the scope of the age discrimination provisions in the FED, the Court controversially suggested that non-discrimination on grounds of age was a fundamental principle of EU law, aligning it with non-discrimination on other grounds.[31] The Court has since made clear that Article 6 FED is a very specific derogation from the principle of equal treatment and that a high standard of proof is required in establishing the legitimacy of aims for the purposes of the justification test.[32] The Court noted in *Age Concern* (2009) that:

> mere generalisations concerning the capacity of a specific measure to contribute to employment policy, labour market or vocational training objectives are not enough to show that the aim of the measure is capable of justifying derogation from that principle and do not constitute evidence on the basis of which it could reasonably be considered that the means chosen are suitable for achieving that aim.[33]

Generally, the Court has had little difficulty in accepting a wide range of aims as legitimate and therefore, in principle, capable of justifying discriminatory measures.[34] Such aims have included promoting employment for younger and

[30] Fredman (n 27); see also S Moreau, 'The Wrongs of Unequal Treatment' (2004) 57 *University of Toronto Law Journal* 291.

[31] Case C-144/04 *Werner Mangold v Rüdiger Helm* EU:C:2005:709. See also Case C-555/07 *Kücükdeveci v Swedex GmbH & Co KG* EU:C:2010:21.

[32] Case C-388/07 *The Queen, on the Application of the Incorporated Trustees of the National Council for Ageing (Age Concern England) v Secretary of State for Business, Enterprise and Regulatory Reform* EU:C:2009:128; Joined Cases C-159/10 and C-160/10 *Fuchs and another v Land Hessen* EU:C:2011:508.

[33] Case C-388/07 *Age Concern* (n 32) para 51.

[34] See, further M Sargeant, 'The Default Retirement Age: Legitimate Aims and Disproportionate Means' (2010) 39 *Industrial Law Journal* 244.

older workers,[35] sharing employment opportunities between generations,[36] ensuring a mix of generations in the workplace,[37] and avoiding the need to dismiss employees for reasons of incapacity.[38] In this respect, perhaps the Court has to an extent gone beyond the view expressed in the original Commission proposal that 'only in very exceptional circumstances' could a difference in treatment on grounds of age be justified.[39] However, it has tended to be more rigorous in its examination of the necessity or appropriateness of proposed measures in achieving the invoked aims, thus ultimately providing meaningful protection against age discrimination. The Court has shown willingness to reject measures based on poorly evidenced or inconsistent claims. For example, a maximum age for practising dentists in Germany was not proportionate to the legitimate aim of protecting the health of patients because it did not equally apply to the private sector.[40] Similarly, a provision which excluded service before the age of 25 from the calculation of minimum notice periods was not appropriate for achieving the legitimate aim of affording employers greater flexibility in personnel management, because it affected all those who had begun employment before the age of 25 regardless of their age at dismissal.[41]

As O'Cinneide explains, age has therefore been treated 'as both similar and different to the other discrimination grounds: it is treated as a "suspect" category which warrants the rigorous application of the objective justification test, but nevertheless the special nature of age and the potential for age-based distinctions to serve rational ends is also factored into the application of this test'.[42] It should also be noted that the Court has not taken a uniform approach to its scrutiny of potentially discriminatory measures on grounds of age. As has been well documented elsewhere, it has tended to adopt a light touch 'rationality' approach in respect of mandatory retirement policies, but has imposed a stricter standard where measures have involved, for example, the denial of social benefits.[43]

Nonetheless, the Court itself has thus far remained silent on the issue of whether and why age is 'different' from other grounds protected by the legislation; and on the implications of this question for establishing its approach to justification.

[35] Case C-411/05 *Felix Palacios de la Villa v Cortefiel Services SA* EU:C:2007:604; Case C-88/08 *David Hütter v Technische Universität Graz* EU:C:2009:381; Joined Cases C-159/10 and C-160/10 *Fuchs* (n 32); Case C-144/04 *Mangold* (n 31); Case C-555/07 *Kücükdeveci* (n 31).

[36] Case C-341/08 *Domnica Petersen v Berufungsausschuss für Zahnärzte für den Bezirk Westfalen-Lippe* EU:C:2010:4; Case C-45/09 *Gisela Rosenbladt v Oellerking Gebäudereinigungsges. mbH.* EU:C:2010:601; Joined Cases C-159/10 and C-160/10 *Fuchs* (n 32).

[37] Joined Cases C-250/09 and C-268/09 *Vasil Ivanov Georgiev v Tehnicheski universitet – Sofia, filial Plovdiv* EU:C:2010:699; Joined Cases C-159/10 and C-160/10 *Fuchs* (n 32).

[38] Joined Cases C-159/10 and C-160/10 *Fuchs* (n 32); Case C-45/09 *Rosenbladt* (n 36).

[39] European Commission, 'Proposal for a Council' (n 9) Art 5.

[40] Case C-341/08 *Petersen* (n 36).

[41] Case C-555/07 *Kücükdeveci* (n 31).

[42] C O'Cinneide, 'Age Discrimination and the European Court of Justice' (n 6) 265.

[43] See discussion in Fudge (n 26), Freedland and Vickers (n 12).

In contrast, several of the Advocates General have proved more willing to engage with this question and have offered a number of reasons for treating age differently from other grounds. Some explanations simply relate to the fact that age is both a 'new' ground in the legal framework and one the use of which is still widespread in structuring the labour market. Thus, Advocate General Cruz Villalón noted in *Prigge* (2011):

> The position of age in the list set out in Article 21 [of the CFR] is itself an indication that this is not exactly the oldest or most "classical" of the prohibitions of discrimination. This does not, of course, imply that it ranks below the others. But it does give grounds for arguing that its undisputed modernity makes it a type of non-discrimination the principles of which remain to be fully consolidated, and which, in some respects at least, continues to evolve through the construction of a political and social consensus.[44]

Moreover, Advocate General Jacobs argued in *Lindorfer* (2005) that 'the idea of equal treatment irrespective of age is subject to very numerous qualifications and exceptions, such as agelimits of various kinds, often with binding legal force, which are regarded as not merely acceptable but positively beneficial and sometimes essential'.[45] On this view, the differences between age and other characteristics are rooted largely in the evolving perceptions and structures of society.

Other Advocates General have suggested that the differences are rather more fundamental. In *Test Achats* (2011), Advocate General Kokott, having argued that it was impermissible to use sex as a proxy for motor insurance risk, went on to differentiate sex from age by reference to the complete life view of equality:

> It is true that age is a characteristic which is also inseparably linked to an individual but every human being passes through different categories of age in his life. If insurance premiums and benefits are therefore calculated differently according to age, that does not yet as such give rise to any fear that the insured person will be disadvantaged as an individual. Everyone may, on the basis of age, in the course of his life be in receipt of insurance products which are more or less favourable to him.[46]

In *Vital Pérez* (2014), Advocate General Mengozzi argued that age was fundamentally different for another reason: 'age is not, as a rule, considered to be a "suspect" ground on a par with race or gender, not sharing their long history of discrimination'.[47]

[44] Case C-447/09 *Reinhard Prigge and Others v Deutsche Lufthansa AG* EU:C:2011:321, Opinion of AG Cruz Villalón, para 32.

[45] Case C-227/04 *Maria-Luise Lindorfer v Council of the European Union* EU:C:2005:656, Opinion of AG Jacobs, para 85.

[46] Case C-236/09 *Association Belge des Consommateurs Test-Achats ASBL and Others v Conseil des ministers* EU:C:2010:564, Opinion of AG Kokott, para 50. For a similar argument, see also judgment of Lady Hale in the UK case of *Seldon v Clarkson, Wright and Jakes (A Partnership)* [2012] UKSC 16 at 4.

[47] Case C-416/13 *Mario Vital Pérez v Ayuntamiento de Oviedo* EU:C:2014:2109, Opinion of AG Mengozzi, para 4 citing the US Supreme Court decision in *Massachusetts Board of Retirement v Murgia* [1996] (427 US 307).

The extent to which the Court has adopted these perspectives is unclear. However, there are two issues on which differences in its approach to age as compared to other grounds have been particularly striking. These are firstly, its consideration of the use of age as a proxy or stereotype; and secondly, its approach to the scope of 'positive action' – here broadly defined as measures taken with the aim of remedying disadvantage suffered by a protected group. The next two sections will assess the view of the Court in relation to these two issues and will suggest that a more transparent approach to its assessment of the status of age is needed.

B. Using Age as a Proxy or Stereotype

The CJEU has been asked to consider a number of situations in which age has been used as a proxy or substitute for some other characteristic.[48] These characteristics include physical capacity,[49] general capacity for work,[50] ability to keep up-to-date with recent developments,[51] ability to integrate into a new society,[52] experience,[53] financial needs,[54] ability to find work[55] and future employment plans.[56] Ordinarily, the use of age as a proxy has been assessed with reference to the general justification test in Article 6 FED. On a few occasions, however, it has been assessed under Article 4 FED as an occupational requirement. In general, the CJEU has been receptive to the idea that chronological age is a good proxy for a number of biological or social and economic facts although it has been willing to challenge specific examples of this approach where evidence is insufficient or otherwise lacking. Nonetheless, the Court's willingness to use age *in principle* as a proxy is striking. This contrasts with the approach taken by the CJEU as well as other courts in respect of sex or race, where even the use of statistically sound and well-evidenced proxies have largely been deemed unjustifiable.[57]

[48] Here, 'proxy' means the use of one (normally easy to identify) characteristic as a substitute for another (normally harder, more expensive, or impossible to test for). The use of proxies is closely related to the idea of stereotyping – understood as the assumption that an individual holds the characteristics of a group to which they belong.

[49] Case C-229/08 *Colin Wolf v Stadt Frankfurt am Main* EU:C:2010:3; C-447/09 *Prigge* EU:C:2011:573; Case C-416/13 *Vital Pérez* EU:C:2014:2371.

[50] Case C-45/09 *Rosenbladt* (n 36); Joined Cases C-159/10 and C-160/10 *Fuchs* (n 32); Case C-141/11 *Torsten Hörnfeldt v Posten Meddelande AB* EU:C:2012:421.

[51] Case C-286/12 *European Commission v Hungary* EU:C:2012:687. See also U Belavusau, 'On Age Discrimination and Beating Dead Dogs: Commission v Hungary' (2013) 50 *Common Market Law Review* 1145.

[52] Case C-540/03 *European Parliament v Council of the European Union* EU:C:2006:429.

[53] Case C-88/08 *Hütter* (n 35); Joined Cases C-297/10 and C-298/10 *Sabine Hennigs v Eisenbahn-Bundesamt and Land Berlin v Alexander Mai* EU:C:2011:560.

[54] Joined Cases C-297/10 and C-298/10 *Hennigs* (n 53).

[55] Case C-555/07 *Kücükdeveci* (n 31).

[56] Case C-515/13 *Ingeniorforeningen i Danmark v Tekniq* EU:C:2015:115.

[57] See, eg *R (European Roma Rights Centre and Others) v Immigration Officer at Prague Airport and Another* [2004] UKHL 55; *Timishev v Russia* [2007] 44 EHRR 37; Case C-236/09 *Association Belge*

It would be wrong to suggest that the CJEU has always taken a strict or consistent view as regards stereotyping on other grounds.[58] Particularly in its early jurisprudence on pregnancy and maternity rights, it was criticised for perpetuating and reinforcing gender stereotypes relating to the roles of mother and father in childcare.[59] More recently, however, the CJEU has been willing to challenge these stereotypes, albeit not consistently. In 2010, the Court had the rare opportunity to directly address the question of if, and when, it may be permissible to use sex as a proxy. In *Test-Achats* (2011), the Court was asked to review the compatibility of Directive 2004/113 EC (regulating sex discrimination in the provision of goods and services) with one of the fundamental rights of EU law – the prohibition on sex discrimination.[60] Specifically, the challenge concerned Article 5(2) of that Directive which provided that Member States may (temporarily) continue to permit differences related to sex in respect of insurance premiums and benefits where sex was a determining risk factor which could be substantiated by relevant and accurate actuarial data. The defendant company argued that their purpose in using statistical data based on sex to calculate premiums was to avoid increasing premiums for all. Advocate General Kokott – whom the Court followed – argued that although using proxies in the calculation of risk is not wrong in principle, using *sex* as a substitute criterion in this way was incompatible with the principle of equal treatment and inappropriate in a Union which had declared respect for dignity, equality and non-discrimination.[61] Aside from situations where the relevant differences between men and women could be established 'with certainty', positive action was the only reason to justify differentiations on grounds of sex.[62] Thus, it was the very *idea* of using sex as a proxy that troubled the Court rather than simply the quality of evidence used to support it.

This strict approach to the use of sex contrasts with that taken in relation to age. In many cases, the Court has left the use of age-based stereotypes unchallenged. In *Wolf* (2010), the requirement in question was the maximum recruitment age for fire fighters.[63] The employer wanted new recruits to be able to maintain the required level of fitness for working as an operational firefighter for a minimum of 15 years. On the basis of evidence produced by the German Government that physical fitness declines with age, the Court agreed that it was

des Consommateurs Test-Achats ASBL and Others v Conseil des ministres EU:C:2011:100. For a helpful account of the legal framework relating to ethnic profiling see O De Schutter and J Ringelheim 'Ethnic Profiling: A Rising Challenge for European Human Rights Law' (2008) 71(3) *Modern Law Review* 358–384.

[58] See A Timmer, 'Gender Stereotyping in the Case Law of the EU Court of Justice' (2016) 1 *European Equality Law Review* 37.

[59] C McGlynn, 'Ideologies of Motherhood in European Community Sex Equality Law' (2000) 6 *European Law Journal* 29.

[60] Case C-236/09 *Test-Achats* (n 57).

[61] Case C-236/09 *Test-Achats* (Opinion of AG Kokott) (n 46) para 67.

[62] ibid para 60.

[63] Case C-229/08 *Wolf* (n 49).

unlikely for most individuals to have the required level of fitness beyond the age of 45–50. Therefore, the use of a minimum age requirement of 30 for recruitment was proportionate. Put differently, according to the Court, age could be used as a proxy for physical fitness. The possibility of an alternative method of testing for physical fitness was not considered. It is true that here the employer required a certain level of physical fitness from the recruits 15 years in the future, for which it may be very difficult to test at the time of application. However, the availability or otherwise of an appropriate alternative test does not appear to have been a relevant consideration at all.

Rosenbladt (2010), *Fuchs* (2011), and *Hörnfeldt* (2012)[64] all concerned the use of mandatory retirement ages and the (potentially) legitimate aims at issue included the avoidance of humiliating capability proceedings which, it was assumed, would eventually be required if workers were not compulsorily retired. Such an aim assumes first, that the relevant retirement age is a sensible proxy for the point at which an employee's capabilities would start to decline and second, that older workers find capability proceedings more humiliating than they do mandatory retirement. The Court accepted the aim as legitimate and made no comment about the assumptions on which its decision is based. There was no reference to the capabilities needed for the jobs or sector in question nor discussion of any evidence that the ages chosen were a reliable proxy. It is possible that the lack of close scrutiny here was related to what other commentators have identified as a reluctance to unduly interfere with Members States' margin of discretion in relation to retirement in particular.[65] Yet, the acceptance of age stereotypes was not needed to achieve this objective. In each of the cases above, there were other legitimate aims upon which the Court could have relied to sanction the measure in question.

Where the CJEU has challenged the use of age as a proxy, this has primarily been based on the inadequacy of evidence presented to support the use of (a particular) age in this way. In *Hennigs* (2011), for example, in deciding whether an age-gradated basic pay scheme could be justified under Article 6 FED, the Court challenged the argument that older workers have greater financial needs than younger workers, noting that 'it has not been shown that there is a direct correlation between the age of employees and their financial needs. Thus, a young employee may have substantial family burdens to bear while an older employee may be unmarried without children'.[66] Here, the Court also pointed out that it is a mistake to assume that length of service – and therefore age – is a good proxy for the amount of professional experience a worker possesses because 'professional experience does not always increase with length of service. Sometimes it even

[64] Case C-45/09 *Rosenbladt* (n 36); Joined Cases C-159/10 and C-160/10 *Fuchs* (n 32); Case C-141/11 *Hörnfeldt* (n 50).

[65] Freedland and Vickers (n 12).

[66] Joined Cases C-297/10 and C-298/10 *Hennigs* (n 53) para 70.

diminishes'.[67] Likewise in *Prigge* (2011), a case concerning a provision in a collective agreement requiring compulsory retirement of commercial airline pilots at the age of 60, the Court determined that certain physical capacities were indeed essential for the safe performance of the duties of an airline pilot.[68] As it 'is undeniable that those capabilities diminish with age',[69] in this context age was capable, in principle, of being a genuine and determining occupational requirement. Nevertheless, the use of age was not proportionate on the facts because international rules set the relevant limit at 65 rather than 60. The problem was the lack of evidence to support the choice of the particular age, not the fact that age was used as a proxy in the first place.

In *Vital Pérez* (2014), the Court had to assess a measure which set a maximum recruitment age of 30 for the local Spanish police force. It had been argued by the defendant local authority in Spain that age was a good proxy for physical capacity. Holding that the measure was disproportionate under both Article 4(1) and Article 6(1) FED, the Court noted that entry to the force also depended on 'stringent, eliminatory physical tests which … would make it possible to attain the objective of ensuring that local police officers possess the particular level of physical fitness required for the performance of their professional duties in a less binding manner than the fixing of a maximum age limit'.[70] The age limit was therefore unnecessary. This approach arguably brings the treatment of age proxies more in line with the use of proxies on other grounds.[71] While individual assessment may not always be possible or appropriate, it is difficult to understand why it should be permissible to use age as a substitute for individual assessment when the latter is feasible.[72] Nonetheless, this remains the only case where attention has been paid to the availability of a less discriminatory alternative than using age as a proxy for capacity. Yet, even here the Court did not suggest, as it did with sex in *Test-Achats*, that using a protected characteristic in this way was entirely unacceptable.[73]

Thus, while the Court has, albeit not consistently, shown concern about age being a good statistical predictor of something else and has demanded current evidence of this in a number of cases, it has generally accepted the use of age as a proxy in circumstances where it is difficult to imagine it doing so for other grounds. This difference in approach could theoretically be justified on a number of grounds. On the complete life view, where age is used as a gateway to inclusion in the labour

[67] ibid para 30.

[68] C-447/09 *Prigge* (n 49).

[69] ibid para 67.

[70] Case C-416/13 *Vital Pérez* (n 49) para 24.

[71] See assessment by Lady Hale on the impermissibility of using sex as a proxy for physical strength in *Seldon* (n 46) at 58.

[72] See also Fudge (n 26) who contrasts the approach of the CJEU with that of the Supreme Court of Canada which has imposed a requirement to demonstrate that individual assessment is not feasible to establish that using age as a proxy is necessary.

[73] Case C-236/09 *Test-Achats* (n 57).

market or to certain benefits within it, the impact on those disadvantaged or excluded may not result in inequality over a lifetime. This was precisely the type of reasoning used by Advocate General Kokott in *Test-Achats* to justify the view that the use of age as a proxy in calculating insurance risk would be acceptable whereas the use of sex as a proxy was not.[74] Age stereotypes may also be seen as less harmful because of the lack of association between age and historical inequality and discrimination.[75] However, as noted above, (even accurate) stereotypes are argued to often be harmful simply because they fail to respect individuality. Eidleson, for example, claims that the wrong of basing decisions on statistical generalisations without regard for individual characteristics is a result of failing to pay attention to the unique character traits individuals have developed through their own autonomous choices.[76] If one accepts this view, well-founded age stereotypes may cause less harm than sex or race stereotypes, but may be harmful nonetheless. These disadvantages should be properly addressed by anti-discrimination law. There is scope for the Court to take account of such harm within the proportionality test, weighing it against other needs and interests if necessary. It should do so explicitly to provide reassurance that, even where such harms are outweighed by other important interests, they are not discounted or ignored.

C. Positive Action

Under Article 3 of the Recast Equal Treatment Directive[77] and equivalent provisions of the Race Equality Directive (Article 5) and Framework Equality Directive (Article 7), Member States are permitted to adopt specific measures to prevent or compensate for disadvantages linked to protected grounds 'with a view to ensuring full equality in practice'. These provisions recognise that a requirement to treat individuals equally is unlikely to result in equality in practice because, by reason of stereotypes and prejudice in particular, two equally qualified individuals may not have had the same opportunities.[78]

Despite this 'legislative' recognition, the CJEU has set restrictive limits to what is permissible in the name of positive action on gender and has characterised the positive action provision as a narrow derogation from the non-discrimination principle rather than a crucial part of achieving substantive equality. In *Kalanke* (1995), it was held that the positive action provisions of the Equal Treatment

[74] Case C-236/09 *Test-Achats* (Opinion of AG Kokott) (n 46) para 50.

[75] F Schauer, *Profiles, Probabilites and Stereotypes* (Cambridge MA, Harvard University Press, 2003).

[76] B Eidelson, *Discrimination and Disrepsect* (Oxford, Oxford University Press, 2016).

[77] Directive 2006/54/EC of the European Parliament and of the Council on the implementation of the principle of equal opportunities and equal treatment of men and women in matters of employment and occupation (recast) [2006] OJ L204/23 (Equal Treatment Directive).

[78] Case C-409/95 *Hellmut Marschall v Land Nordrhein-Westfalen* EU:C:1997:533 paras 29–30.

Directive[79] should be interpreted strictly and that national rules which guarantee women absolute and unconditional priority for appointment or promotion overstepped the limits of these provisions.[80] This was because the national rules went beyond promoting equal opportunities in attempting to arrive at equal results. The judgment made clear that equal results could only be permitted to arise as a natural result of equal opportunities.[81] In *Marschall* (1997)[82] and in *Badeck* (2000),[83] the Court gave a closed list of circumstances in which a measure aiming to prioritise the promotion of women in an industry where they were underrepresented would be permitted. These were: first, if the male and female applicants were equally well qualified; second, if the measure did not give automatic unconditional priority to women; and third, if each candidate was subject to objective assessment which took into account their specific personal situation.

Reticence to expand the scope of positive action further is, of course, tied to the difficulties in reconciling a perceived tension between the twin goals of promoting equality and prohibiting discrimination. As Advocate General Tesauro explained in *Kalanke*:

> What is under discussion above all is the significance of the principle of equal treatment, the contrast between formal equality, in the sense of equal treatment as between individuals belonging to different groups, and substantive equality, in the sense of equal treatment as between groups. In the final analysis, must each individual's right not to be discriminated against on grounds of sex – which the Court itself has held is a fundamental right the observance of which it ensures – yield to the rights of the disadvantaged group?[84]

The limits the Court has chosen to set to reconcile this tension demonstrates a strong adherence to the primacy of merit and individualism.[85] In the view of the Court, it seems, inequality between groups should not be solved by an employer's policy measures which pay no or insufficient regard to the merit and individual circumstances of those affected because this would undermine the objectives of the equality law framework.

This reticence contrasts strongly with the approach the Court has taken to what can (broadly) be characterised as positive action measures in relation to age.[86]

[79] Council Directive 76/207/EEC on the implementation of the principle of equal treatment for men and women as regards access to employment, vocational training and promotion, and working conditions [1976] OJ L39/40 (Equal Treatment Directive), Art 2(4).

[80] Case C-450/93 *Eckhard Kalanke v Freie Hansestadt Bremen* EU:C:1995:322.

[81] ibid paras 22–23.

[82] Case C-409/95 *Marschall* (n 78) para 35.

[83] Case C-158/97 *Georg Badeck and Others* EU:C:2000:163 para 38.

[84] Case C-450/93 *Eckhard Kalanke v Freie Hansestadt Bremen* EU:C:1995:105, Opinion of AG Tesauro, para 7.

[85] See, e.g. S Fredman, 'Affirmative action and the European Court of Justice: A Critical Analysis' in J Shaw (ed), *Social Law and Policy in and Evolving European Union* (New York, Hart, 2000).

[86] For a useful account of the key features of affirmative or positive action, see T Khaitan, *A Theory of Discrimination Law* (Oxford, Oxford University Press, 2015).

These have the stated or implied aim of redressing disadvantages faced by a particular age group in the labour market and/or promoting intergenerational equality. So far, such measures have not been analysed by the Court under the positive action provisions of Article 7 FED,[87] but have instead been treated as instances of direct discrimination which may be justified under Article 6 FED. However, these types of measures share similar aims with those normally assessed as positive action measures on gender equality where the goal is typically to reduce the disadvantage faced by a particular gender or to advance gender equality. It is therefore instructive to compare the Court's approach to age and gender in this respect.

There are two broad categories of age-based measures worth considering here – the use of contractual terms and conditions to make certain age groups more attractive to employers and the exclusion of certain age groups from the workplace to free up opportunities for others. *Mangold* is a prime example of the first category, as it involved a national measure permitting employers to use fixed-term contracts for employees who had reached the age of 52 without having to justify this use by reference to other reasons. The Court found that 'the legitimacy of such a public interest aim – to promote the vocational integration of older workers – cannot reasonably be thrown into doubt'.[88] Nevertheless, the measure was deemed disproportionate because it enabled employers to switch their existing older workforce from open-ended onto fixed-term contracts as well as to use fixed-term contracts when recruiting new older workers, thus going beyond what was necessary.[89] In *Hütter* (2009),[90] the Court had to consider a law that permitted experience acquired before the age of 18 not to be counted when calculating entitlements based on length of service. Among others, the aim of promoting the integration of younger workers into the labour market was found to be legitimate. However, the measure was not proportionate because it applied irrespective of the actual age of the employee and was therefore deemed inappropriate for promoting the entry of young workers into the labour market.[91] In this respect, the Court distinguished the policy from minimum wage policies which provide lower minimum pay for younger than for older workers (and which, presumably, would be capable of being both appropriate and necessary).[92] Thus, while the Court found the relevant provisions to be flawed, there was no indication

[87] In Case C-143/16 *Abercrombie & Fitch Italia Srl v Antonino Bordonaro* EU:C:2017:235, AG Bobek considered the legality of a measure which provided that 'on call' contracts could be used without restriction for workers in certain age groups in order to improve their access to the labour market. He argued that measure did not fall within the category of positive action under Article 7 because '[f]rom a certain vantage point, it could be seen as perpetuating the more precarious position of the younger part of the population in the labour market' (para 58).

[88] Case C-144/04 *Mangold* (n 31) para 60.

[89] ibid para 64.

[90] Case C-88/08 *Hütter* (n 35).

[91] ibid para 49.

[92] See also Case C-555/07 *Kücükdeveci* (n 31).

that measures in this category were not justifiable in principle. By contrast, it is unthinkable that such an approach would be condoned by the CJEU in relation to comparable measures to improve labour market participation for women or underrepresented ethnic minorities (even without the obvious constraints of equal pay regulation).

Secondly, mandatory retirement measures can be justified by reference to the aims of improving intergenerational equality or redressing the disadvantage affecting a particular group. In a number of cases, the CJEU has accepted that the aim of ensuring the availability of jobs for younger workers is in principle capable of justifying mandatory retirement. Nonetheless, the need for such measures in particular industries and sectors has been questioned. The Court has been alert to the potential impact of compulsory retirement on those affected, sometimes utilising a proportionality assessment. In *Palacios* (2007) for example, a compulsory retirement clause contained in a collective agreement was justified as a means to improve intergenerational equality in the labour market against a backdrop of high youth unemployment.[93] Important to this finding was the fact that in the view of the Court, the relevant legislation was not based solely on age but also on access to an adequate pension.[94] In *Petersen* (2010), the promotion of access of young people to the dental profession was in principle a legitimate aim but the national Court was asked to satisfy whether a shortage of jobs was indeed putting new entrants to the profession at a disadvantage.[95]

In *Rosenbladt,* the claimant, a part-time cleaner, challenged a mandatory retirement provision in a collective agreement. The Court recognised that mandatory retirement may cause particular financial hardship for Ms Rosenbladt and others in the same sector due to the inadequacy of the state pension. However, this did not prevent the mandatory retirement provision from being justified by the aim of (among others) sharing jobs more equally among the generations and facilitating access to the labour market by young workers at a time of chronic unemployment.[96] In relation to determining the proportionality of the measure, the Court noted the importance of national law permitting Ms Rosenbladt to seek fresh employment elsewhere after retirement, free from age discrimination.[97] Interestingly, Advocate General Trstenjak argued that the problem of inadequate pension savings faced by Ms Rosenbladt (and others like her) as a part-time worker in the cleaning sector could not be solved by using the prohibition on age discrimination to preclude mandatory retirement.[98] In *Fuchs*, the Court held that the prohibition on age discrimination, again in relation to mandatory retirement,

[93] Case C-411/05 *Palacios* (n 35).

[94] ibid para 73.

[95] Case C-341/08 *Petersen* (n 36). See also Joined Cases C-250/09 and C-268/09 *Georgiev* (n 37) where the Court raised similar concerns in the context of the university sector.

[96] Case C-45/09 *Rosenbladt* (n 36) paras 70–77.

[97] ibid.

[98] ibid para 165.

must be read in the light of the right to work in the CFR.[99] It argued that particular attention should be paid to the 'participation of older workers in employment and thus in economic, social and cultural life'.[100] This acknowledges the close relationship between employment and access to other forms of social inclusion. However, the rights of older workers in this respect were to be balanced against the needs of younger workers.

Therefore, as with stereotyping, the Court has been willing to question the accuracy of claims about the existence of disadvantage attaching to a particular age group in the labour market and claims about the ability of the proposed measure to improve the situation. In this respect, the CJEU has shown its receptiveness to the concerns expressed by those who question the empirical assumptions on which fair innings arguments are based. In addition, and unlike with stereotyping, the Court has also made clear references to (some of) the harmful impacts of the measure under consideration. Furthermore, it has sometimes been willing to balance these harms against the rights and interests of those whom the disputed measure is intended to benefit. Nonetheless, the contrast with the approach to positive action measures on other grounds is significant. In particular, a far broader range of measures appear to be in principle permissible than is the case for discrimination on grounds of sex.

The reason that the CJEU and courts more generally have appeared less anxious about the appropriate boundaries of positive discrimination in relation to age as compared to other grounds may be linked to the complete life view of equality. The UK Supreme Court certainly appeared to take this approach in *Seldon* (2012) where, in justifying a mandatory retirement measure, it was noted that '[i]n the particular context of inter-generational fairness, it must be relevant that at an earlier stage in his life, a partner or employee may well have benefited from a rule which obliged his seniors to retire at a particular age'.[101] Among the concerns often raised about positive action is the unfairness of placing the burden to redress group disadvantage on individuals who may have had no part in creating or benefitting from the disadvantage in the first place.[102] An individual who loses out on a particular job because it has been given to a member of a disadvantaged group may not have been a perpetrator or even a beneficiary of past discrimination. A complete life approach to equality appears to (at least partially) solve this problem in relation to age because it assumes that a burden suffered by an individual in furtherance of intergenerational equality has been or will be compensated by a corresponding benefit at a different time.

However, as noted above, this compensation model does not always work in practice. In relation to retirement, there is very good reason to think that the

[99] Art 15(1) CFR.
[100] Joined Cases C-159/10 and C-160/10 *Fuchs* (n 32) para 64.
[101] *Seldon* (n 46) at 65.
[102] For a helpful account of the arguments see Fredman, *Discrimination Law* (n 27) chapter 5.

access of individuals to labour market opportunities at an earlier stage in their careers is profoundly unequal. Even without this obvious problem, the deprivation of a benefit which may have been available at an earlier stage in life (or which may become available later on) may not be the only harm or wrong caused by using age to ration access to the labour market or other goods. Other consequences may include the harm associated simply with a failure to base important decisions about people on their individual needs and merits, or social exclusion which may result from the inability to access a particular benefit or institution. These may not be meaningfully compensated for or eliminated by other experiences at different stages of life. Of course, the view may be taken that (some of) these other harms are outweighed by the need to remedy the disadvantage to different age groups. However, as with the use of age as a proxy, this balancing must be done transparently, taking full account of all of the harms less favourable treatment may cause. This is not to suggest an unduly restrictive approach to permitting action to remedy disadvantage to particular generations, where evidence supports taking such steps. Indeed, the current limits on positive discrimination, and the aims of anti-discrimination law, have been criticised as unduly restrictive and therefore unlikely to facilitate progress towards greater equality in practice.[103] The possibility of doing more in the name of substantive age equality than is permitted in respect of other grounds should perhaps be welcomed.

IV. Conclusion

This chapter has argued that, within the relatively broad discretion afforded to it by the legislative framework, the approach chosen by the CJEU to justifying age discrimination is difficult to reconcile with its view of discrimination on other grounds. Furthermore, the CJEU has not articulated its reasons for this approach. Of course, it would be naive to ignore the considerable political and economic challenges created by the introduction of the prohibition on age discrimination. It is against this background that the Court has been required to develop its guidance. As Freedland and Vickers note, it is then perhaps unsurprising that the Court has left more discretion to Member States, at least in some respects, than a deep and comprehensive approach to age equality may require.[104]

Nevertheless, the nature of age discrimination remains contested. This chapter has sought to suggest that while there are reasons for accepting the argument that age as a grounds is different from other characteristics, this must be done with careful attention to the full range of harms recognised in the Court's

[103] S Fredman, 'After Kalanke and Marschall: Affirming Affirmative Action' (1998) 1 *Cambridge Yearbook of European Legal Studies* 199.

[104] Freedland and Vickers (n 12).

jurisprudence on other grounds to which age discrimination may give rise. A principled approach to justifying age discrimination requires a clear account of *all* such harms, and the respects in which they differ (if at all) from those caused by discrimination on other grounds. This enables a proper balancing in an assessment of proportionality.

It is likely that the case law on age discrimination will continue to evolve alongside society's understanding of it. As Advocate General Sharpston noted in *Bartsch* (2008), '[w]hat has happened over the intervening years is that society's perception of more subtle forms of differential treatment on grounds of age has changed from unthinking acceptance to focused examination'.[105] As with gender, therefore, it may be possible to see age being at an early stage of a journey towards a more robust rejection by society of many of the forms of age discrimination which at the moment remain widely accepted. In order to play its part in such an evolution, however, it is hoped that the CJEU, whose importance in transforming perceptions of gender equality and discrimination can hardly be overstated, will develop a more transparent and coherent account of age equality.

[105] Case C-427/06 *Birgit Bartsch v Bosch und Siemens Hausgerate (BSH) Altersfursorge GmbH* EU:C:2008:297, Opinion of AG Sharpston, para 58.

13

EU Age Discrimination Law

A Curse or a Blessing for EU Youth Policy?

BERYL P TER HAAR

I. Introduction

There are many occasions when society differentiates on the basis of age – for example setting a minimum age to drive a car,[1] to buy and drink alcohol,[2] to vote, or to become a constitutional judge.[3] Many such distinctions are generally accepted as common sense.[4] Differentiation based on age is also made in employment and occupation, including, for example, working time as well as health and safety measures at the workplace. The fact that these issues have been regulated by a specific EU Directive[5] confirms the common acceptance of such differential treatment of young people in the EU. It is similarly accepted that specific policy efforts are needed to support young people in finding their place in society and on the labour market.

At the same time, it is widely acknowledged that not all distinctions based on age are acceptable, particularly when the difference in treatment is based on stereotypes that affect human dignity[6] (e.g. presuming that young people are inexperienced, less reliable or loyal than older workers).[7] Additionally, measures

[1] For instance, in the Netherlands the age for driving a car is set at 18.

[2] In Europe, the legal age to drink alcohol is widely accepted as 18; *cf* Dutch Institute for Alcohol Policy (STAP), 'New European overview shows that alcohol age limit of 18 is widely accepted, but lacks compliance in many countries' (October 2013).

[3] U Belavusau, 'On Age Discrimination and Beating Dead Dog: *Commission v. Hungary*' (2013) 50 *Common Market Law Review* 1145.

[4] M Sargeant, 'Young People and Age Discrimination' (2013) 2 *E-Journal of International and Comparative Labour Studies* 1–16.

[5] Council Directive 94/33/EC on the Protection of Young People at Work [1994] OJ L216/12.

[6] For an elaboration on this point in relation to age discrimination, see the chapter by R Horton in this volume.

[7] See Sargeant (n 4).

targeting one age group such as young workers may negatively affect another age group. Furthermore, some means for protecting or improving the opportunities of a particular age group may not turn out to as effective as expected. In these situations, it is good, or even necessary, to be able to challenge the legality of such a measure.[8]

The EU Framework Directive on Equal Treatment in Employment and Occupation (Framework Equality Directive (FED))[9] offers a legal basis to challenge such measures. Article 1 FED enlists age as one of the discrimination grounds and Article 2 prohibits direct and indirect discrimination on the grounds defined in Article 1. However, Article 6 FED allows for explicit justification of indirect as well as direct discriminatory measures on the grounds of age when the measure serves a legitimate aim and is necessary as well as proportionate to achieve that aim. Legitimate aims are rather open and include employment policy as well as labour market and vocational training objectives.

Over the course of 15 years, the Court of Justice of the European Union (CJEU) has developed a considerable body of jurisprudence on age discrimination. Approximately 30 cases is indeed a notable figure, especially when compared with other discrimination grounds enlisted in Article 1 FED.[10] The vast majority of these cases deal with measures affecting older workers, particularly regarding retirement age or pension schemes.[11] A significantly smaller number of cases – only five – concern measures affecting younger workers.[12] Research analysing these cases indicates that the CJEU has been rather lenient in accepting measures regarding older workers and more strict in accepting measures targeting younger workers.[13] However, this approach potentially puts EU Youth Policy under pressure. Moreover, it raises the question of whether the FED is, in fact, hampering measures to improve the situation of young people. In other words, it should be determined whether the FED is a curse or a blessing for EU Youth Policy.

The aim of this chapter is to analyse the effect of the FED, in particular Article 6, on EU Youth Policy. To that end, the chapter is structured as follows. In section II, EU Youth Policy is described, with a focus on youth employment policy. Section III will briefly discuss age as discrimination grounds and elaborate

[8] Case C-88/08 *David Hütter v Technische Universität Graz* EU:C:2009:381 discussed in section IV is a good example.

[9] Council Directive 2000/78/EC establishing a general framework for equal treatment in employment and occupation [2000] OJ L303/16 (Framework Equality Directive).

[10] For an overview of cases until 2014 see BP ter Haar and M Rönnmar, 'Intergenerational Bargaining, EU Age Discrimination Law and EU Policies – An Integrated Analysis' Report for the project 'Intergenerational Bargaining: Towards Integrated Bargaining for Younger and Older Workers in EU Countries' (2014) 18; D Schiek, 'Age Discrimination before the CJEU – Conceptual and Theoretical Issues (2011) 48 *Common Market Law Review* 777.

[11] See, eg Joined Cases C-159/10 and C-160/10 *Fuchs and Köhler v Land Hessen* EU:C:2011:508; Case C-190/16 *Werner Fries v Lufthansa CityLine GmbH* EU:C:2017:513; Case C-447/09 *Prigge & Others* EU:C:2011:573.

[12] See, nn 14–18.

[13] See, eg ter Haar and Rönnmar (n 10).

on Article 6 FED. Section IV analyses the CJEU's case law dealing with measures targeting or affecting young people. More specifically, it will critically discuss the following cases: *Hütter* (2009),[14] *Kücükdeveci* (2010),[15] *O* (2015),[16] *De Lange* (2016),[17] and *Abercrombie & Fitch* (2017)[18]. In section V, the chapter concludes with an analysis of the findings in the three parts in light of the central question of whether EU age-discrimination law is a curse or a blessing for EU Youth Policy.

II. EU Youth Policy

This section explores three relevant aspects of EU Youth Policy. First, it looks into the legal basis for the EU to adopt measures in the field of youth policy, defining the competence of the EU to deal with youth matters. Second, it explores why youth has become such a prominent target group for EU policies. Third, it delves into the governance regime and the changing approach of EU youth policies over the course of time, unfolding some examples of national measures for young people.

A. Legal basis for EU Youth Policy

In the EU's legal doctrine, the field of youth policy is relatively under explored. That in itself is not surprising, since the EU treaties do not include youth policy as an independent policy field (eg unlike employment (Title IX TFEU) or social policy (Title X TFEU)). Indeed, only two provisions mention youth as specific target group. The first is Article 47 TFEU, which states that 'Member States shall, within the framework of a joint programme, encourage the exchange of young workers'. This provision was already part of the chapter on the free movement of workers in the Treaty Establishing the European Economic Community (EEC) adopted in 1957.[19] The second provision, now Article 165 TFEU, was introduced in 1992 in the Treaty of Maastricht,[20] and provides the EU with the competence to adopt supportive measures to encourage 'the development of youth exchanges and of exchanges of socio-educational instructions, and encouraging the participation of young people in democratic life in Europe'.[21]

The legal basis for fostering a specific EU youth policy is, thus, limited. Firstly, the material scope is restricted to the context of the free movement of workers,

[14] Case C-88/08 *Hütter* (n 8).

[15] Case C-555/07 *Seda Kücükdeveci v Swedex GmBH& Co* EU:C:2010:21.

[16] Case C-432/14 *O v Bio Philippe Auguste SARL* EU:C:2015:643.

[17] Case C-548/15 *JJ de Lange v Staatssecretaris van Financiën* EU:C:2016:850.

[18] Case C-143/16 *Abercrombie & Fitch Italia Srl v Antonino Bordonaro* EU:C:2017:566.

[19] Art 50 Treaty Establishing the European Economic and Steel Community (EEC Treaty).

[20] Art 126 Consolidated Version of the Treaty on European Union, Treaty of Maastricht [1992] OJ C 325/5.

[21] TFEU Art 165(2).

education and participation in democratic life in Europe. Secondly, the EU's competence is narrowed down to coordination and support.[22] Moreover, paragraph 4 of Article 165 TFEU explicitly excludes any harmonising effect of measures adopted on the legal basis of this provision.[23] This implies that measures cannot be adopted by instruments such as directives and regulations, since by definition their purpose is to harmonise laws and policies of the Member States.[24]

Despite these limitations, the EU has developed a comprehensive youth policy, also addressed as EU Youth Strategy,[25] which comprises the following eight actions fields: (1) education and training; (2) employment and entrepreneurship; (3) health and wellbeing; (4) participation; (5) voluntary activities; (6) social inclusion; (7) youth and the world; and (8) creativity and culture.[26] These action fields aim to achieve two objectives: (a) more and equal opportunities for young people in education and in the labour market; and (b) active citizenship, social inclusion and solidarity of young people.[27] These objectives target an overarching goal, namely 'to enable all young women and men to make the best of their potential'.[28] The regulatory mechanism of the Youth Strategy is that of the Open Method of Coordination (OMC).[29]

B. Why Youth as a Target Group for EU Policy?

Why is the EU so concerned with youth as a specific target group for policy? What differentiates the position of young people from that of others? It is not merely because they are of a certain age – the EU youth policy measures do not define youth by a specific age. Nevertheless, it is generally considered to cover persons between the age of 15 and 24, sometimes up to the age of 29[30] and, in statistical data, even up to the age of 34.[31] Yet the more important feature of this group is

[22] See TFEU Art 6(e), which enlists education, vocational training, youth and sport.

[23] TFEU Art 165(4) concludes with 'excluding any harmonisation of the law and regulations of the Member States'.

[24] See TFEU Art 288 for their definitions.

[25] For an overview, see European Commission, 'EU Youth Strategy'. Available at: htpp//ec.europa.eu/youth/policy/youth-strategy_en.

[26] Council Resolution on a Renewed Framework for European Cooperation in the Youth Field (2010–2018) [2009] OJ C311/1.

[27] ibid 2.

[28] ibid.

[29] B Laffan and C Shaw, 'Classifying and Mapping OMC in Different Policy Areas' (2005) *New GOV Working Paper* 02/D09; more specifically, Commission Communication, An EU Strategy for Youth – Investing and empowering a renewed open method of coordination to address youth challenges and opportunities, COM(2009) 200 final.

[30] European Commission, *EU Youth Report. An EU Strategy for Youth – Investing and Empowering*, SEC (2009) 549 final, 17.

[31] Statistics on young people neither in employment nor in education or training (*eurostat*, 27 July 2017). Available at: http//ec.europa.eu/eurostat/statistics-explained/index.php/Statistics_on_young_people_neither_in_employment_nor_in_education_or_training.

its possible disadvantage, particularly in the labour market. As Sargeant points out, such disadvantage comes in different forms.[32] There is, for example, disadvantage related to the type of job with which young people enter the labour market. These are often temporary jobs (e.g. fixed-term contracts, on-call work, zero-hour contracts, etc)[33]

Other forms of disadvantage or vulnerability result from long-term unemployment, low levels of qualification and educational achievements, health problems and disabilities and ethnic background.[34] Research indicates that young people are more often at risk of being subjected to one or more of these disadvantages than workers above 25.[35] This is reflected in the higher levels of unemployment among young people. For example, in 2013 the general unemployment rate in the 28 EU Member States was 11 per cent, whereas for young people this was more than double at 24 per cent.[36] In some countries, the difference is not that drastic. For instance in 2014, the general unemployment rate in Germany was 5.2 per cent; for young people it was 7.7 per cent. In other countries both levels are relatively low. For example, in the Netherlands the general level of unemployment was 7.4 per cent and for young people 12.4 per cent. Nevertheless, in most of the Member States, the difference between the general unemployment rate and that of young people is considerable. In Greece, the general unemployment rate was 26 per cent but that for young people was 52 per cent. In Spain it was 24.5 per cent versus 53.2 per cent respectively, while in Italy the general unemployment rate was 12.7 per cent compared to the nearly four times higher rate of 42.7 per cent for young people.[37]

The risk of becoming unemployed is particularly high for young people, since they have to transition from education into the labour market. Statistical data from the EU Labour Force Survey (LFS) shows a connection between the time

[32] Sargeant (n 4) 6.

[33] For precarious contracts through the lens of EU anti-discrimination law, see chapter by M Bell in the present volume. In this context, see also Sargeant (n 4) 6, who refers to research that identified 12 different forms of flexible work; S Dex and A McCulloch, *Flexible Employment in Britain: A Statistical Analysis* (Manchester, Equal Opportunities Commission, 1995). See also Eurofound, *NEETs. Young People Not in Employment, Education or Training: Characteristics, Costs and Policy Responses in Europe.* (Luxembourg, Publications Office of the European Union, 2012) 2.

[34] Sargeant (n 4) 4. See also J O'Reilly et al., 'Five Characteristics of Youth Unemployment in Europe: Flexibility, Education, Migration, Family Legacies, and EU Policy' (2015) *SAGE Open* 1.

[35] ibid. See on this also M Sargeant and E Tucker, 'Health and Safety of Vulnerable Workers: Case Studies from Canada and the UK' (2009) 7 *Policy and Practice in Health and Safety* 51. Although this study is on migrant workers, Sargeant argues that the idea of 'layers of vulnerability' applies *mutatis mutandis* also to young people.

[36] Eurostat defines youth unemployment as 'all the youth (i.e. people between the ages of 15 and 24, inclusive) who are unemployed' and the youth unemployment rate as 'the percentage of the unemployed in the age group 15 to 24 years old compared to the total labour force (both employed and unemployed) in that age group'. See 'Glossary: Youth unemployment' (*eurostat*, 6 August 2014). Available at: http//ec.europa.eu/eurostat/statistics-explained/index.php/Glossary:Youth_unemployment_rate.

[37] Check for these data at 'Unemployment statistics' (*eurostat*, 16 January 2018) Available at: http//ec.europa.eu/eurostat/statistics-explained/index.php/Unemployment_statistics. For other data substantiating the same conclusions, see Sargeant (n 4) 5.

young people need to enter the labour market on the one hand, and their level of education, on the other. In general, the time required for this transition is significantly longer for young people with a low level or a poor quality of education (10 months on average) than it is for young people with a high level or a good quality of education (five months on average).[38] Unfortunately, 'young people who face unemployment or a slow transition may experience long-term adverse effects in terms of future labour market success, earnings or family formation'.[39] The importance of obtaining a good educational qualification is further emphasised, since statistical data also indicate a correlation between unemployment rates and the attained level of education. The data distinguish three levels of educational attainment[40] and three age groups.[41] On average, in all three age groups, the rate for young people who were neither in employment nor in education or training (NEET) was the highest among those with a low educational attainment level and the lowest among young those with the highest educational attainment level.[42]

C. EU Youth Strategy

Young people have been a target group of EU measures not only since the economic and financial crisis in 2008, but from the early days of the European Economic Community.[43] For example, in 1963 the Council adopted a decision on a common vocational training policy in which young people were one of the target groups;[44] in 1976, a mixed resolution was adopted 'concerning measures to be taken to improve the preparation of young people for work and to facilitate their transition from education to working life'.[45] Youth policy has been top of the EU's political agenda since the 1980s when the core of the baby-boom generation

[38] See 'Figure 2 – Average length of transition from school to work by education attainment level, 2009' (*eurostat*, 5 February 2013). Available at: http//ec.europa.eu/eurostat/statistics-explained/index.php/File:Figure_2-_Average_length_of_transition_from_school_to_work_by_educational_attainment_level,_2009.png. Note that a transition is considered successful after obtaining a first job of at least three months.

[39] Council conclusions on the employability of graduates from education and training, 3164th EDUCATION, YOUTH, CULTURE and SPORT Council meeting, Brussels, 10 and 11 May 2012.

[40] These are: (1) less than primary, primary, lower secondary; (2) upper secondary or post-secondary non-tertiary education; and (3) tertiary education.

[41] These are: 20–24 years; 25–29 years; and 30–34 years.

[42] Statistics on young people neither in employment nor in education or training (*eurostat*, 27 July 2015) Available at: http//ec.europa.eu/eurostat/statistics-explained/index.php/Statistics_on_young_people_neither_in_employment_nor_in_education_or_training.

[43] See in more detail, P Copeland and BP ter Haar, 'The Open Methods of Coordination as Amplifier for EU Soft Law: The Case of EU Youth Policy' (2015) *Acta Juridica Hungarica* 14.

[44] 63/266/EEC Council Decision laying down general principles for implementing a common vocational training policy [1963] OJ 63/1338.

[45] Resolution of the Council and of the Ministers of Education, meeting within the Council, concerning measures to be taken to improve the preparation of young people for work and to facilitate their transition from education to working life [1976] OJ C308/1.

entered the labour market.[46] By 2010, the EU had adopted approximately 100 measures within all eight action fields identified in the 2009 Framework Resolution,[47] collectively referred to as the EU Youth Strategy (EUYS).

The culmination of Europe's youth measures in the EUYS did not happen overnight. The first step can be traced back to the 2001 Commission White Paper 'New Impetus for European Youth'[48] which mainly dealt with active citizenship of young people.[49] In this context, employment constitutes an essential resource for the autonomy of young people since it enables them to fulfil their role in society.[50] Another important step towards the EUYS was the 2005 Youth Pact.[51] In that pact, the policy discourse shifts slightly from the emphasis on the role and importance of young persons in society to the recognition of the vulnerability of young people in society.[52] Since 2009, when the signs of the impact of the economic and financial crisis on youth employment first emerged, the policy discourse has been shifting towards investment in young people to improve their circumstances, especially in the labour market.[53] Hence the focus of the first policy cycle of the EUYS was on youth employment.[54] Thereto, Annex I to the Framework Resolution lists 11 possible policy initiatives, *inter alia*, the option to take the special situation of young people into account when devising flexicurity strategies.[55] The policy focus of the Framework Resolution is amplified by one of the flagship initiatives of Europe 2020,[56] namely Youth on the Move.[57] The aim of Youth on the Move has been to improve the education and employability of young people, to reduce high youth unemployment and to increase the youth-employment rate in line with the wider

[46] Eurofound (n 33) 4.

[47] Council Resolution on European Cooperation in the Youth Field (n 26). *cf* BP ter Haar, *Open Method of Coordination. An analysis of its meaning for the development of a social Europe*, Dissertation Leiden University (2012), 189–193 (Annex 7.1).

[48] European Commission White Paper of 21 November 2001 – A new impetus for European youth, COM(2001) 681 final.

[49] For an elaboration on this, see T Barber, "Choice, Voice and Engagement'. An Exploration of Models and Methods which Promote Active Youth Citizenship in the New Europe', Seminar Young People and Active European Citizenship, 2006.

[50] European Commission White Paper (n 48) 4. For an elaboration on the historical development of content of the EUYS, see BP ter Haar, 'Youth OMC: Coordination of Governance to Deal with the NEET's Needs', Ius Commune conference – OMC workshop, 2016.

[51] European Council, *Presidency Conclusions*, Brussels, 22 and 23 March 2005 (7619/05), Annex 1.

[52] Commission Communication, Addressing the concerns of young people in Europe – implementing the European Youth Pact and promoting active citizenship, COM(2005) 206 final, 2–3.

[53] COM(2009) 200 final (n 29), 5.

[54] ibid, Annex 1.

[55] ibid.

[56] Europe 2020 is the successor of the Lisbon Strategy and is 'the EU's agenda for growth and jobs for the current decade. It emphasises smart, sustainable and inclusive growth as a way to overcome the structural weaknesses in Europe's economy, improve its competitiveness and productivity and underpin a sustainable social market economy. *cf* Europe 2020 Strategy (*European Commission*). Available at: http//ec.europa.eu/info/strategy/european-semester/framework/europe-2020-strategy_en.

[57] Commission Communication, Youth on the Move. An initiative to unleash the potential of young people to achieve smart, sustainable and inclusive growth in the European Union, COM(2010) 477 final.

EU target of achieving a 75 per cent employment rate for the working-age population (20–64 years).[58]

In 2011, the Commission launched the Youth Opportunities Initiative.[59] Within that initiative, it identified the following factors as challenges and root causes for youth unemployment: leaving school early without qualifications; lack of relevant skills and work experience; precarious employment followed by spells of unemployment; limited training opportunities; and insufficient/inappropriate active labour market policies.[60] To address these factors, the Commission encouraged Member States to take decisive measures to prevent early school leaving, to develop skills relevant for the labour market, to support a first work experience and on-the-job training, and to improve access to the labour market.[61] The latter includes measures to reform employment protection legislation, to reduce excessive rigidities of permanent contracts, and to ease labour market access for those left outside.[62]

The EU supports the Member States in their activities with financial assistance and policy guidance. The latter focuses on the promotion of innovative approaches facilitating the transition from school into work.[63] Over the years, the Commission has launched various initiatives.[64] The 2016 Youth Package brought these initiatives together in three strands of action, with the latter two extending beyond employment: (1) better opportunities to access employment; (2) better opportunities through education and training; and (3) better opportunities for solidarity, learning mobility, and participation.[65] The first strand of action includes the Youth Guarantee,[66] which is financially supported by the Youth Employment Initiative.[67] It is a political commitment from the Member States to give every young person under the age of 25 an offer of employment of good quality, continual education, and an apprenticeship or a traineeship within a period of four months after becoming unemployed or having left formal education.[68]

Measures promoted by the EUYS encourage Member States to undertake activities that entail differential treatment on grounds of age or at least distinguishing young people (roughly aged between 18 and 29) from all other age groups.

[58] ibid 3.

[59] Commission Communication, *Youth Opportunities Initiative*, COM(2011) 933.

[60] ibid 6.

[61] ibid 7–8.

[62] ibid 8.

[63] ibid 9–10.

[64] For a full overview, see Copeland and ter Haar (n 43).

[65] Commission Communication, *Investing in Europe's Youth*, COM(2016) 940 final.

[66] Council Recommendation on establishing a Youth Guarantee [2013] OJ C120/01; Commission Communication, Working together for Europe's young people: A call to action on youth unemployment, COM(2013) 447 final; Commission Communication, The Youth Guarantee and Youth Employment Initiative three years on, COM(2016) 646 final.

[67] Commission Communication, Youth Employment Initiative COM(2013) 144 final.

[68] ibid 5.

For instance, as part of the Youth Guarantee, France adopted the *Emplois d'avenir* scheme aiming to deliver subsidised jobs for low-skilled young people living in disadvantaged areas,[69] and Croatia established eleven centres for Lifelong Career Guidance for all its citizens, with a focus on young people.[70] In other Member States, this has resulted in the adoption of measures specifically distinguishing on the basis of age. For example, the Latvian *Know and Do* project aims to identify, motivate and activate non-registered young people aged between 15 and 29 to return to education, employment or training.[71] The Dutch Work–Study Right entitles young people between the ages of 18 and 27, who are not in employment, education or training, to receive a personalised plan guiding them to employment or back to education or training.[72]

The EUYS thus explicitly invites Member States to differentiate between age groups, which is potentially at odds with EU anti-discrimination law on the grounds of age. At times, EU age-discrimination law can be considered a blessing for EUYS, for instance when it enables a measure favouring young people and similarly, when it does not allow for a measure to benefit another age-group while placing young people at a disadvantage. In both situations, young people benefit, as the FED offers them protection. The FED could also be a blessing when a measure serves a legitimate aim but is ill-designed, and consequently fails the test of appropriateness and necessity. However, at other times, EU anti-discrimination law can turn into a curse (e.g. when a measure favouring young people cannot be justified due to the negative impact on another age group). The extent to which EU anti-discrimination law is a blessing or a curse will be analysed in the following sections. Section III provides a short description of the approach of the Framework Equality Directive regarding age discrimination and Section IV provides a description of five cases of the CJEU on age discrimination regarding young people.[73] Section V analyses the case law of the CJEU and draws conclusions about the utility of EU anti-discrimination law for EU youth employment policies.

III. EU Age-discrimination Law

The inclusion of age amongst the protected grounds in the FED is not as self-evident as it may first appear. Therefore, this section starts with an exploration of age as a protected ground. and then discusses how age as a discrimination ground is treated in the Framework Equality Directive.

[69] ibid.
[70] ibid 6.
[71] ibid.
[72] ter Haar (2016) (n 50).
[73] Namely Case C-88/08 *Hütter* (n 8), Case C-555/07 *Kücükdeveci* (n 15), Case C-432/14 *O* (n 16), Case C-548/15 *De Lange* (n 17), Case C-143/16 *Abercrombie & Fitch* (n 18).

A. Age as a Protected Ground

Chapter 12 by Rachel Horton in this volume elaborately discusses the two most dominant arguments that justify the inclusion of age as a protected ground.[74] In brief, the first is the 'complete life view', which argues that when age is taken as a criterion to determine access to goods, resources, work, etc., this does not create inequality because over the course of a lifetime everyone will be eligible for the same benefits and subject to the same burdens, provided the criterion is used consistently.[75] The second is the 'fair innings argument', which refers to the fact that discrimination on the grounds of age is sometimes necessary either to avoid inequality or to achieve substantive equality between generations.[76] Both arguments consider age discrimination not in terms of protection against discrimination of a particular group, but as a necessity generated by the passage of time.[77] Both arguments have also been criticised for their reliance on false presumptions. For example, the fair innings argument presumes that mandatory retirement is an effective way of improving youth employment.[78] The complete life argument builds on the presumption that everyone will have the same opportunities in life, which is generally not the case. Consequently, not everyone is able to gain the same advantages and benefits.[79] Moreover, excluding people from access to valuable resources today may result in a lifetime of inequality because of the impact on a person's dignity or autonomy among other things. Exactly these types of interests are often regarded as the fundamental aims to be protected by anti-discrimination law.[80]

It is unclear which argument underpins the EU's prohibition of discrimination on grounds of age.[81] However, it should be noted that at the time the negotiations for the Framework Equality Directive (FED) took place, there were serious concerns about the ageing workforce of Europe.[82] This issue creates serious challenges for employment, pensions, health care, social cohesion and intergenerational solidarity, among others[83] and has resulted in for example

[74] See also A Numhauser-Henning, 'The EU Ban on Age-Discrimination and Older Workers: Potentials and Pitfalls' (2013) 29 *The International Journal of Comparative Labour Law and Industrial Relations* 391.

[75] See chapter by Horton in the present volume, where she also refers to D McKerlie, 'Equality and Time' (1989) 99 *Ethics* 475; G Cupit, 'Justice, Age, and Veneration' (1998) 108 *Ethics* 702.

[76] See the chapter by Horton in the present volume.

[77] ibid.

[78] ibid. See on this presumption, among many others R Böheim, 'The Effect of Early Retirement Schemes on Youth Employment' (2014) *IZA World of Labor* No 70.

[79] See the chapter by Horton in the present volume.

[80] ibid. See also Framework Equality Directive, Preamble recital 11.

[81] For an analysis of the approach of the CJEU, see the chapter by Horton in the present volume.

[82] Framework Equality Directive, Preamble recital 8. See also C Barnard, *EU Employment Law* (Oxford, Oxford University Press, 2012) 343.

[83] S Bisom-Rapp and M Sargeant, 'Increasing the Employment Rate of Older Workers' (2011) 27 *The International Journal of Comparative Labour Law and Industrial Relations* 301.

a policy on active aging,[84] with the elderly as specific target group in the European Employment Strategy.[85] The prohibition of age discrimination is considered an essential tool for achieving these goals.[86]

Nevertheless, the FED also protects young people.[87] Recital 25 of its Preamble refers to the guidelines of the European Employment Strategy, which encompass specific policy guidelines addressing young people.[88] Article 6(1)(a) FED refers to young people (and older workers) who may be treated differently in certain aspects of employment.[89] Furthermore, 'age' also includes 'relative age',[90] which refers to a differentiation based on a period of time that is related to the age of another person. An example of such a distinction is an 'age-gap clause' in a survivor's pensions scheme stipulating that if the surviving partner is more than 15 years younger than the deceased employee, (s)he will not be entitled to the pension.[91]

B. Article 6 of the Framework Equality Directive

Due to its specific nature, age as a discriminatory ground is treated differently from other protected categories. In addition to the general derogations in Article 5(2) (indirect discrimination) and Article 4 (genuine job requirement), Article 6 FED provides a special regime for objectively justifying both direct and indirect differential treatment based on age.[92] More specifically, Article 6 provides a list of reasons related to employment policies, labour market policies and vocational training, which could be accepted as a legitimate aim to justify direct as well as indirect age discrimination. However, this list is not exhaustive, leaving it to the CJEU to clarify what could further be accepted as a legitimate aim. Objectives that have been accepted so far include policies based on intergenerational solidarity,[93]

[84] Active Ageing (*European Commission*). Available at: http//ec.europa.eu/social/main.jsp?catId=1062. See also ter Haar and Rönnmar (n 10).

[85] D Kasneci, 'Active Ageing: the EU Policy Response to the Challenge of Population Ageing' (2007) 8 *European Papers On The New Welfare* 1.

[86] Framework Equality Directive, Preamble recitals 8 and 25.

[87] K Riesenhuber, *European Employment Law: A Systematic Exposition* (Antwerp, Intersentia, 2012) 332; C O'Cinneide, 'Age Discrimination and European Law' (Luxembourg, Office for Official Publications of the European Communities, 2005).

[88] See, eg Council Resolution on the 1999 Employment Guidelines [1999] OJ C62/02, Guidelines 1 and 7.

[89] See below section III B.

[90] Riesenhuber (n 87) 332.

[91] Case C-427/06 *Birgit Bartsch v Bosch und Siemens Hausgeräte (BSH) Altersfürsorge GmbH* EU:C:2008:517. On this case, see also C Kilpatrick, 'The CJEU and Labour Law: A 2008 Retrospective' (2009) 38 *Industrial Law Journal* 180.

[92] See FED, Preamble recital 25. For an elaborate description of Article 2(5) and Article 4 as derogations, see Barnard (n 82) 369–371.

[93] Riesenhuber (n 87) 334 with reference to Case C-341/08 *Domnica Petersen v Berufungsausschuss für Zahnärzte für den Bezirk Westfalen-Lippe* EU:C:2010:4, paras 65 *et seq*.; Case C-250/09 *Vasil Ivanov Georgiev v Tehnicheski universitet – Sofia, filial Plovdiv* EU:C:2010:699; Joined Cases C-159/10 and C-160/10 *Fuchs and Köhler* (n 11) para 50.

wage policies including measures to reward experience,[94] and measures to protect established rights during a transitional period[95,96]

As regards this list of accepted objectives, it is remarkable that they all serve a public interest rather than that of an individual employer.[97] In its judgment in the Joined Cases *Fuchs* and *Köhler* (2011), the CJEU explicitly stated that aims which may be considered 'legitimate' must have a public interest nature distinguishable from purely individual reasons particular to the employer's situation, such as cost reduction or improving competitiveness.[98] Nevertheless, Member States may be entitled to raise cost reduction as an aim in pursuit of public interest aims such as (labour) cost reduction.[99]

Article 6 FED lays down four criteria that need to be strictly complied with for a differentiation on grounds of age not to amount to a prohibited discrimination.[100] These are:

(a) Member States may provide that differences of treatment on grounds of age shall not constitute discrimination, if
(b) within the context of the law,
(c) they are objectively and reasonably justified by a legitimate aim, and
(d) if the means of achieving that aim are proportionate and necessary.

With respect to (c), the CJEU has held that Member States have a broad discretion in their choice of legitimate aims and the definition of measures to achieve it.[101] However, the means to pursue such policies are subject to a proportionality test requiring that the measures are both appropriate and necessary. Analysis of the CJEU's case law concerning older workers indicates that the appropriateness of the national measure is rather easily accepted by the Court as long as it does not appear to be manifestly inappropriate to attain the legitimate aim.[102] The necessity of the measure seems to be assessed in greater detail. However, with a case-by-case approach, it is not possible to draw a general conclusion about this.[103] Nevertheless, the CJEU seems to apply a more lenient 'control' standard with regard to more

[94] ibid, with reference to Joined Cases C-297/10 and C-198/10 *Sabine Hennigs v Eisenbahn-Bundesamt and Land Berlin v Alexander Mai* EU:C:2011:560, para 71; Case C-17/05 *B F Cadman v Health & Safety Executive* EU:C:2006:633, para 34; and Case C-88/08 *Hütter* (n 8) para 47.

[95] ibid, with reference to Joined Cases C-297/10 and C-198/10 *Hennigs* (n 94) paras 88 ff; C-456/05 *Commission of the European Communities v Federal Republic of Germany* EU:C:2007:755, paras 63 and 65.

[96] See also Barnard (n 82) 371–372.

[97] Riesenhuber (n 87) 334.

[98] Joined Cases C-159/10 and C-160/10 *Fuchs and Köhler* (n 11) para 52.

[99] ibid.

[100] See further: Barnard (n 82) 372, with reference to Case C-388/07 *Age Concern* EU:C:2009:128, para 62.

[101] Case C-411/05 *Palacios de la Villa* EU:C:2007:604, para 68.

[102] ter Haar and Rönnmar (n 10).

[103] Barnard (n 82) 374.

general systems of mandatory retirement, while employing a stricter standard for early mandatory retirement of specific professional groups.[104] The strictest standards seem to be applied to cases related to collective dismissals and discrimination against younger workers.[105] If the latter is the case, this would potentially put EU Youth Policy even more at odds with EU anti-discrimination law than, for example, the EU's Active Ageing Policy. However, the indication needs to be nuanced, because it is based on merely two cases – *Hütter*[106] and *Kücükdeveci*.[107] Recently, the CJEU ruled on three more cases dealing with age discrimination and young people – *O*,[108] *De Lange*,[109] and *Abercrombie*.[110] The next section analyses the strictness of the review adopted by the CJEU in these five cases.

IV. Age Discrimination of Young People in CJEU's Case Law

The five cases of *Hütter*, *Kücükdeveci*, *O*, *De Lange*, and *Abercrombie* will be analysed in chronological order. Central to the analysis is the CJEU's assessment of what amounts to a legitimate aim and the appropriateness and necessity of the measure to achieve that aim. Other issues, such as the exclusionary effect of EU general principles of law, among which the right not to be discriminated on the grounds of age,[111] will not be addressed.

A. *Hütter*

The case of *Hütter* tested an Austrian provision of the Law on Contractual Public Servants (*Vertragsbedienstetengesetz VBG*). The provision states that only persons above the age of 15 can be recruited as public servants. Furthermore, it excludes periods of service completed before the age of 18 from entitlements related to the length of service or professional experience. This includes periods of service completed by way of vocational training at a university or college.[112]

The case was initiated by Mr. Hütter (born in 1986), who together with a colleague completed an apprenticeship from September 2001 to March 2005 as

[104] ter Haar and Rönnmar (n 10).
[105] ibid.
[106] Case C-88/08 *Hütter* (n 8).
[107] Case C-555/07 *Kücükdeveci* (n 15).
[108] Case C-432/14 *O* (n 16).
[109] Case C-548/15 *JJ de Lange* (n 17).
[110] Case C-143/16 *Abercrombie & Fitch* (n 18).
[111] On this in relation to the *Kücükdeveci* case see, e.g. M de Mol, 'The Novel Approach of the CJEU on the Horizontal Direct Effect of the EU Principle of Non-Discrimination: (Unbridled) Expansionism of EU Law?' (2011) 18 *Maastricht Journal of European and Comparative Law* 109.
[112] Case C-88/08 *Hütter* (n 8) paras 9–11.

a laboratory technician with a public body (TUG). After his apprenticeship, he and his colleague were recruited for an additional period of three months. However, Hütter's colleague was placed on a higher incremental wage step. For Hütter, only 6.5 months of the apprenticeship were taken into account (i.e. the months after he turned 18) whereas 28.5 months were taken into account for his colleague. Hütter brought an action before the Graz Regional Court for Civil Matters and sought payment of compensation equivalent to the difference in treatment he received due to his age, because he considered that treatment to be unjustified and in breach of both the Austrian and EU anti-discrimination laws.[113]

With regard to the legitimacy of the aim pursued by the legislation, the CJEU acknowledged two objectives. First, it encourages pupils to pursue a general secondary education rather than vocational education; and second, it seeks to promote the recruitment of persons who have had a vocational education rather than of persons with a general secondary education.[114] The CJEU considered that such a measure could serve a legitimate aim within the meaning of Article 6 FED.[115]

With respect to the appropriateness and the necessity of the measure, the Court noted that Member States unarguably enjoy broad discretion in their choice of measures capable of attaining the pursued objectives.[116] However, at first glance, the measure at hand appears contradictory: it aims to promote general secondary education over vocational training, but then seems to favour vocational training over general secondary education.[117] Due to this inconsistency, the Court ruled that the measure cannot be appropriate or necessary.[118] Regarding the content of the measure, the CJEU considered that using criteria of previous professional experience for the determination of the pay scale can be proportionate and necessary to serve such an aim. However, the additional requirement linking the accreditation of experience to a certain age in this measure results in an unequal award of experience.[119] Thus, in addition to the inconsistency of the aim of the measure, the explicit condition of the age of 18 also renders the measure inappropriate for achieving the aim.[120]

Furthermore, the CJEU pointed out that 'non-accreditation of experience acquired before the age of 18 applies without distinction to all contractual public servants, whatever the age at which they are recruited'.[121] Thus, this criterion does not single out a group of persons defined by their young age to promote their integration into the labour market by granting special conditions

[113] ibid paras 13–15.
[114] ibid paras 40 and 46.
[115] ibid paras 39–41.
[116] ibid para 45.
[117] ibid para 46.
[118] ibid.
[119] ibid para 47.
[120] ibid para 48.
[121] ibid para 49.

of recruitment.[122] Hence, the Court did not deem the measure at hand appropriate for the purpose of promoting the entry into the labour market of a category of workers defined by their (young) age,[123] implying that the measure constitutes unjustified prohibited discrimination on grounds of age.

B. *Kücükdeveci*

The *Kücükdeveci* case challenged a German measure on notice periods, where '[i]n calculating the length of employment, periods prior to the completion of the employee's 25th year of age are not taken into account'.[124] The case was initiated by Ms Kücükdeveci, who had been employed by Swedex since June 1996. In December 2016, Swedex dismissed her with an effective date of 31 January 2007, taking into account the statutory notice period. In accordance with the national legislation, the statutory notice period was calculated as if the employee had three years of service (i.e. from the age of 25 to 28). However, Kücükdeveci had worked for Swedex for ten years, since she was 18.[125] Kücükdeveci contested her dismissal, claiming that her notice period should have been four months – a period that corresponded to ten years of service.[126] She argued that the measure stipulating that years served before the age of 25 are not to be calculated is discriminatory on the grounds of age, contrary to EU law, and should therefore be disapplied.[127]

The CJEU held that the national measure disadvantages younger workers in comparison to older workers. The effect of the measure is to exclude young workers from benefiting from the progressive extension of notice periods (in the case of dismissal according to the length of the employment relationship) whereas older workers with comparable seniority will, by contrast, be able to benefit from it.[128] Therefore, the CJEU concluded that the measure constitutes discrimination on grounds of age, and went on to assess the objective justification for the measure.[129]

As for the legitimate aim of this measure, the CJEU accepted the following arguments of the German Government – the law, which originated in 1926 and sets the threshold at 25,

> was the outcome of a compromise between, first, the government of the time, which wanted a uniform extension by three months of the notice period for the dismissal of workers aged over 40, second, the supporters of a progressive extension of that period for all workers, and, third, the supporters of a progressive extension of the notice

[122] ibid.
[123] ibid.
[124] Case C-555/07 *Kücükdeveci* (n 15).
[125] ibid paras 12–13.
[126] ibid para 14.
[127] ibid para 15.
[128] ibid para 30.
[129] ibid paras 31–32.

> period without taking the period of employment into account, the purpose of the rule being to give employers partial relief from lengthy periods of notice for workers aged under 25.[130]

The underlying idea of the legislation was that young workers generally react more easily and more rapidly to the loss of their jobs, hence, greater flexibility can be demanded from them.[131] Furthermore, it was reasoned that a shorter notice period for younger workers facilitates their recruitment by increasing the flexibility of personnel management.[132] More specifically, the legitimate aim is 'to afford employers greater flexibility in personnel management by alleviating the burden on them in respect of the dismissal of young workers'.[133]

Based on these arguments, the CJEU concluded that the objectives mentioned clearly belong to employment and labour market policy within the meaning of Article 6(1) FED.[134] When ascertaining whether the measure is also appropriate and necessary, the Court opined that the extension of the notice period is not appropriate for achieving the legitimate aim, because it applies to all employees who start working before the age of 25, whatever their age at the time of dismissal.[135] Additionally, the CJEU considered that the measure affects young people unequally due to its impact on those who enter the labour market early in life, often after little or no vocational training, and not workers who enter the labour market after a long period of training.[136] The measure challenged in this case thus results in unequal treatment of young workers, especially of those who enter the labour market at an early age. Consequently, the measure constitutes unjustified prohibited discrimination on grounds of age.

C. *O*

The case of *O* challenged the French dismissal legislation, more specifically the provision which stipulated as follows:[137]

> The end-of-contract payment shall not be payable:
>
> […]
>
> 2 Where the contract is entered into with a young person for a period falling within the school holidays or university vacations
>
> […]

[130] ibid para 34.
[131] ibid para 35.
[132] ibid.
[133] ibid para 39.
[134] ibid para 36.
[135] ibid paras 40–41.
[136] ibid para 42.
[137] Case C-432/14 *O* (n 16) para 6.

During the Christmas break, Mr. O, a student, was recruited by Bio Philippe Auguste SARL under a fixed-term contract for a period from 21 December 2010 to 24 December 2010. On the expiry of his contract, pursuant to the French legislation, Mr. O was not paid the end-of-contract payment. Mr. O brought an action before the Court claiming that the legislative provision concerned was contrary to the provisions of the French Constitution guaranteeing the principle of equal treatment and the principle of non-discrimination on the grounds of age.[138]

The main question in this case is not whether the national provision can be justified under Article 6(1) FED, but rather if the provision is discriminatory under Article 2 FED. Therefore, the CJEU examined whether the situation of a student like Mr O employed under a fixed-term employment contract during his university holidays is objectively comparable to that of workers who are entitled to the end-of-contract payment under that provision.[139] The aim of the end-of-contract payment is to compensate for the insecurity of the employee's situation when the contractual relationship is not continued.[140] However, employees like Mr O do not experience job insecurity after the expiry of their contract since they return to school or university.[141] Additionally, the CJEU considered that other categories of employees in situations comparable to that of Mr O also do not receive end-of-contract payment (e.g. replacements for seasonal workers).[142] Therefore, the Court concluded that Mr O was not in a situation objectively comparable to that of workers who are entitled to the end-of-contract payment, and thus the measure did not constitute discrimination on the grounds of age.[143]

D. *De Lange*

The case of *De Lange* tested a Dutch tax measure. The latter reads as follows:[144]

> Training expenditure is deductible if the combined amount exceeds EUR 500 and [for training undertaken] beyond the standard period of study, if the combined amount does not exceed EUR 15 000.
>
> The standard period of study is the period not exceeding 16 calendar quarters [...] during which, after reaching the age of 18 but before reaching the age of 30, he devotes the time available for work largely to a training course with a total workload of such a magnitude that [, in addition to the training,] full-time employment is not possible.

[138] ibid paras 9–10. An interesting detail in this case is that Mr O was related to one of the managers of defendant and that the dispute had been provoked solely and exclusively to challenge the provisions at issue (para 15).

[139] ibid para 33.

[140] ibid para 34.

[141] ibid paras 34–35.

[142] ibid para 38.

[143] ibid, para 39.

[144] Case C-548/15 *De Lange* (n 17) para 8.

The consequence of this measure is that, under certain conditions, persons under the age of 30 can deduct the full costs of vocational training from their taxable income, whereas this is limited to an amount of €15,000 for persons who have reached the age of 30.[145]

Mr De Lange started his training as a commercial airline pilot at the age of 32. Therefore, the Netherlands tax authorities limited his right to tax reduction to €15,000 instead of the full amount of €44,057.[146] In the reference for a preliminary ruling, the Supreme Court of the Netherlands first asked whether a tax scheme, such as the one at issue in the main proceedings, falls within the material scope of Article 3 FED. According to the CJEU, the aim of the measure is to promote the access of young people to training and to improve their position in the labour market. The right to deduct from income tax is, thus, designed to help young people by offering them tax concessions that will make it easier for them to study during the defined period and, therefore, gain a firm position on the labour market.[147] Accordingly, the tax scheme falls within the material scope of Article 3(1)(b) FED.[148]

The aim of the tax scheme (i.e. promoting the position of young people on the labour market to advance their vocational integration or to ensure their protection) can be regarded as legitimate for the purpose of Article 6(1) FED.[149] With regard to appropriateness and necessity, the CJEU considered it common ground that such a tax scheme 'is capable of improving the position of young people on the labour market', functioning as 'an incentive to pursue vocational training'.[150] Furthermore, the CJEU found that given the broad discretion enjoyed by the Member States, the taxation scheme did not go beyond what is necessary to attain the objective.[151] Decisive to this conclusion was the clarification provided by the Dutch Government that persons over the age of 30 generally have 'had the opportunity to undertake prior training and to pursue a professional activity, with the result that, being in a better financial position than young people who have recently left the school system, they are able to bear at least in part the financial burden of new training'.[152]

E. *Abercrombie*

Central to the *Abercrombie* case is the Italian legislation concerning on-call contracts (i.e. flexible employment contracts whereby an employee makes

[145] ibid para 10.
[146] ibid para 11.
[147] ibid para 19.
[148] ibid para 20.
[149] ibid para 27.
[150] ibid para 29.
[151] ibid para 34.
[152] ibid para 33.

her/himself available to the needs of the employer).[153] In general, such a contract is subject to objective conditions related to the intermittent nature of the services and requirements specified in collective agreements. However, the same contract may be offered in all circumstance to workers up to the age of 25 and over the age of 45.[154] Mr Bordonaro was employed by Abercrombie under such an on-call contract for over a year and a half. When he turned 25, his employment contract was automatically terminated due to the fact that the age condition ceased to be fulfilled.[155] Bordonaro brought an action before the Italian courts seeking a ruling that both his fixed-term on-call contract and his dismissal were unlawful due to age discrimination.[156]

Firstly, the CJEU examined whether Bordonaro had been treated differently because of his age. Thereto, the Court held that the Italian measure established two regimes: one concerned with the access to and conditions of employment; the other with the dismissal of on-call workers. Both regimes are conditioned by the age category to which those workers belong.[157] Thus, on-call contracts for workers aged 25 or more and up to 45 are only allowed under certain conditions. On-call contracts with workers aged under 25 or over 45 are not subject to such conditions.[158] Therefore, the CJEU held that young workers are comparable to other workers, meaning that the contested measure constitutes a difference in treatment on the grounds of age.[159]

Secondly, the CJEU examined whether the difference in treatment can be justified. With regard to the legitimate aim, it noted that the provision forms a part of a legal framework intended to make the employment market more flexible to increase employment levels.[160] The measures facilitate the entry of young people to the labour market.[161] In a labour market as difficult as in Italy, a lack of professional experience is a factor that hampers young people. Gaining experience, even if it is through flexible work and for a limited time, could constitute a springboard towards new employment opportunities.[162] The measure thus serves the aim of creating special conditions for access to employment (i.e. encouraging recruitment). This falls within a legitimate aim covered by Article 6 FED.[163] Therefore, it is necessary to examine whether the measure is appropriate and necessary to achieve that aim.[164]

[153] Case C-143/16 *Abercrombie* (n 18) para 6.
[154] ibid.
[155] ibid para 11.
[156] ibid para 12. Note that the CJEU first considers whether Bordonaro is a worker within the meaning of Article 45 TFEU, concluding that he is (paras 19–23).
[157] ibid para 26.
[158] ibid.
[159] ibid para 27–28.
[160] ibid para 32.
[161] ibid para 33.
[162] ibid and similar para 34.
[163] ibid para 37, with reference to Joined Cases C-159/10 and C-160/10 *Fuchs and Köhler* (n 11).
[164] ibid paras 39–40.

The CJEU considered the measure appropriate, since this less onerous and costly instrument (i.e. an on-call contract) may indeed encourage employers to respond more to job applications from young people.[165] As regards the necessity of the provision, the CJEU observed that in the context of a persistent economic crisis and weak growth, the situation of a worker aged under 25 years, who can access the labour market through a flexible and temporary employment contract, is preferable to the situation of someone without such a possibility who is unemployed as a result.[166] Additionally, the Italian Government explained that the measure is necessary because it provides access to the labour market for people at risk of social exclusion and helps to eliminate forms of illegal work.[167] It also clarified that on-call workers enjoy a number of guarantees (e.g. they are protected against less favourable treatment than other workers at equivalent level).[168] Hence, the CJEU held it reasonable for the Italian Government to regard the measure as necessary.[169]

V. Analysis of EU Age-discrimination Case Law: Its Implications for EU Youth Policy

The outcome of the cases described in section IV are summarised in Table 13.1.

Table 13.1 Outcome of the five cases on age discrimination involving young people

Case	Discrimination	Discriminatory effect of the measure	Justifiable
Hütter	Yes	Distinction by age results in unequal treatment between young people with similar work experience.	No
Kücükdeveci	Yes	Distinction by age results in unequal treatment between young people who enter the labour market after a short period of education and young people who enter the labour market after a long(er) period of education.	No
O	No	Different treatment is not based on age but on the need to protect against insecurity of income after loss of employment.	n.a.

(continued)

[165] ibid para 41.
[166] ibid para 42.
[167] ibid para 43.
[168] ibid para 45.
[169] ibid para 46.

Table 13.1 (*Continued*)

Case	Discrimination	Discriminatory effect of the measure	Justifiable
De Lange	Yes	Different treatment based on age in order to promote educational opportunities for young people, which people above 30 have already enjoyed.	Yes
Abercrombie	Yes	Different treatment based on age to gain work experience to improve opportunities for regular employment.	Yes

In four of the five cases, the CJEU found that the measure constituted a difference in treatment on grounds of age. Only in *O* was no differentiation found, obviating the need to assess the measure further. With respect to the four cases, the CJEU repeated that Member States enjoy a broad discretion in their choice to pursue a particular aim and in the definition of measures capable of achieving it.[170] Even in *Hütter*, the Court accepted the legitimate aim despite its inconsistency (i.e. promotion of secondary education in favour of vocational training) while the effect of the measure is that vocational training is favoured over secondary training. Unsurprisingly, the CJEU did consider the inconsistent measure in *Hütter* inappropriate for achieving the legitimate aim. Furthermore, the CJEU confirmed that the reward of experience can be appropriate for determining the wage scale. Nonetheless, the Court concluded that the measure could not be justified, because the additional age threshold of 25 resulted in unequal treatment between two persons with similar experience. A similar conclusion was reached in *Kücükdeveci* – the years of service can be appropriate as a condition for establishing notice periods; however, the additional condition of age cannot, because that would affect young people who enter the labour market early and not those who enter the labour market after a long period of education.

In the remaining two cases, *De Lange* and *Abercrombie*, the CJEU concluded that the measures at stake were appropriate and necessary to achieve the legitimate aim. In *De Lange*, the Court considered the tax scheme appropriate for improving the position of young people in the labour market and providing an incentive to pursue vocational training. Furthermore, the measure was deemed necessary, since persons over the age of 30 (who are excluded from the scheme) already had the opportunity to undertake prior training and to pursue a professional activity. They are therefore in a better financial position and able to bear the financial burden of new training. In *Abercrombie*, the CJEU held the measure appropriate since the on-call contracts may indeed encourage employers to hire young people. It seems that the fact that on-call work is in principle a form of precarious

[170] The CJEU held this for the first time in Case C-144/04 *Mangold* EU:C:2005:709 and Case C-411/05 *Palacios de la Villa* (n 101).

work was not an issue for the CJEU. Its conclusion is most likely influenced by the temporary nature of the on-call contract as it is available only until the age of 25, and because it is intended to provide work experience which could constitute a springboard towards new employment, and thus a steady entry into the labour market. Furthermore, misgivings about precariousness are mitigated, since the young persons concerned are protected against being treated less favourably than other workers at the same level. In the assessment of the necessity, the CJEU took into account the Italian economic and social situation, especially the risk of social exclusion of young people unable to enter the labour market, and the objective of eliminating illegal work.

The measures in *De Lange* and *Abercrombie* fit perfectly with the EUYS. The tax scheme in *De Lange* is clearly designed to ease the access of young people to vocational training to facilitate their transition into the labour market. The on-call contract in *Abercrombie* is an example of utilising flexible forms of employment to improve the position of young people in the labour market. These are the only two measures the CJEU accepted as being appropriate and necessary to achieve the legitimate aim pursued. As such, the Framework Equality Directive confirms the legality of differentiating rules which favour young people.

The legislation in *Hütter* could, in principle, have fitted within the EUYS, since it aims to encourage young people to achieve an educational level that will improve their opportunities to enter the labour market. However, due to its inconsistency, it is an ill-designed measure, and its benefits for young people should be questioned. It can thus be concluded that the FED protects young people against poorly designed measures that may hamper their situation rather than benefitting them.

In *Kücükdeveci,* the rule primarily favoured older workers over younger workers by granting a longer notice period for workers above 45. The fact that younger workers also benefit from the measure is incidental. Since the years of service before the age of 25 were not considered when calculating the notice period, young workers were cheaper to dismiss. This enabled employers to increase the flexibility in personnel management, encouraging the recruitment of young workers. In line with previous judgments, the Court held that the length of service as a condition for differential treatment can be appropriate and necessary. It is the condition of age that makes the measure unjustifiable. The fact that the years of service between the age of 18 and 25 are not calculated for the notice period results in a difference in treatment, not between older workers (45 plus) and younger workers, but between young workers aged 25 plus and 18 to 24. The age distinction puts young people who enter the labour market at a young age and consequently have limited education in a less favourable position compared to young people who stay in education for longer and therefore enter the labour market at a later age. Thus, while the FED allows for a difference in treatment between older workers (45 plus) and younger workers based on the length of service, it protects young people against unnecessary further disadvantage based on age.

The *O* case differed from the others as there was no situation of unequal treatment. Nonetheless, the relevant measure affects young people, since the termination of work engaged in during holidays is treated differently from regular work. An interesting aspect of this case is the Court's conclusion that the challenged measure is acceptable because the aim of the end-of-contract payment is to compensate for the insecurity of the employee's situation when the contractual relationship discontinues. Yet employees like Mr O will go back to school or university and are thus not in a situation of job insecurity when their contract expires. Using this reasoning, a similarity can be found with the CJEU's judgments on mandatory retirement which is considered acceptable because of the consequences following from the termination of the employment contract, namely alternative income.

With regard to the claim that the CJEU is more lenient in accepting discrimination against older workers than against younger workers, the following can be observed based on the five cases discussed in this study. The measures that affected young people negatively – as was the situation in *Hütter* and *Kücükdeveci* – could not stand the proportionality test and were found to be inappropriate and unnecessary. The measures that affect young people positively, but older people negatively – such as in *De Lange* and *Abercrombie* – could stand the proportionality test and were found to be appropriate and necessary. The commonality between the four cases is that the position of young people is protected. The CJEU shows consistency in its approach of being more sympathetic to the situation of young people than older workers.

Although the CJEU seems sympathetic to the situation of young people, one point of critique can be made. In *Abercrombie*, the Court could have been stricter in applying the proportionality test. In this case, the Italian Government argued that on-call contracts were essential for young people to gain professional experience which would significantly improve their chances of getting a regular job. This leads to the question of why an age criterion is needed. As in *Hütter*, the Court could have reasoned that the age requirement was unnecessary to achieve the aim, since it could be achieved by allowing the use of on-call contracts for a certain period after the completion of education. Such an approach would be more just towards young people who enter the labour market after a long(er) period of education. With a more strict application of the proportionality test, the CJEU could offer even better protection for young people against discrimination on the grounds of age.

With respect to the main question of this chapter, embraced in the title, it can be concluded that the Framework Equality Directive provides measures that protect (*De Lange* and *Abercrombie)* and prohibits measures that negatively affect young people (*Hütter* and *Kücükdeveci*). Hence, from the perspective of EU Youth Policy, the Framework Equality Directive has been rather more of a help than a hindrance.

PART VI

Disability

14

Breaking Down Barriers? The Judicial Interpretation of 'Disability' and 'Reasonable Accommodation' in EU Anti-Discrimination Law

LUÍSA LOURENÇO AND PEKKA POHJANKOSKI

I. Introduction

The adoption by the European Union (EU or Union) of a number of legislative measures in the field of disability law in the past 20 years represents an undoubted achievement for the advancement of human rights in Europe. The Framework Equality Directive (FED) 2000,[1] sectoral legislation on accessibility, as well as the EU's conclusion of its first international human rights treaty, the United Nations Convention on the Rights of Persons with Disabilities (UN Disability Convention),[2] are milestones in that regard. However, with the arrival of this new normative framework, novel legal challenges have also arisen. Although the case law of the Court of Justice of the European Union (CJEU)[3] has, to some extent, clarified the concepts of 'disability' and 'reasonable accommodation' for the purposes of the FED, the judicial interpretation of those concepts continues to present a host of thorny issues.

The CJEU has defined 'disability' under the FED as a 'limitation which results in particular from physical, mental or psychological impairments which in

[1] Council Directive 2000/78/EC establishing a general framework for equal treatment in employment and occupation [2000] OJ L303/16 (Framework Equality Directive).

[2] 2515 UNTS 3. See also Council Decision 2010/48/EC concerning the conclusion, by the European Community, of the United Nations Convention on the Rights of Persons with Disabilities [2010] OJ L23/35; and Council Decision (EC) 7407/07 on the signing, on behalf of the European Community, of the United Nations' Convention on the Rights of Persons with Disabilities. On the UN Disability Convention, see the chapter by L Waddington in the present volume.

[3] Pursuant to Art 19 of the Treaty on the European Union (TEU), the Court of Justice of the European Union includes the Court of Justice, the General Court and specialised courts. The case law cited in this chapter is exclusively that of the Court of Justice.

interaction with various barriers may hinder the full and effective participation of the person concerned in professional life on an equal basis with other workers'.[4] As such, the CJEU has taken note of the paradigm shift from the medical model to the social model of disability, drawing inspiration from the UN Disability Convention.[5] However, the definition of 'persons with disabilities' under the UN Disability Convention is so vast as to cover nearly every hardship of human life.[6] Likewise, the definition of 'disability' adopted on that basis by the CJEU is remarkably broad. Yet, further interpretation of that definition is a delicate exercise, since a restrictive judicial reading of its various elements may easily become a barrier in itself for persons with disabilities to availing themselves of the protection against discrimination under EU law.

With a wide definition of disability that refers to barriers in participation, the interpretation of the concept of reasonable accommodation becomes all the more essential. According to the CJEU, reasonable accommodation means the 'elimination of the various barriers that hinder the full and effective participation of persons with disabilities in professional life on an equal basis with other workers'.[7] The *raison d'être* of the duty of accommodation is to translate the abstract rights of persons with disabilities into concrete life-facilitating measures. The key question is, however, what measures are to be considered reasonable? Such analysis remains essentially a case-by-case exercise, which means that the difficult task of defining the precise content of the required measures falls on employers and public authorities, and ultimately on judicial decision-makers.

This chapter aims to present an overview of EU disability law, as well as the relevant case law of the CJEU on the concepts of disability and reasonable accommodation – two key notions both under the FED and more generally in this field. The uncertainties and difficulties that national courts in EU Member States face in the application of these concepts are also explored. While an increasing number of decisions have emerged in recent years from the CJEU, several important issues still await judicial clarification.

II. EU Disability Law: An Overview

The issue of disability is most prominently regulated under EU law by way of anti-discrimination provisions.[8] To this end, the most important legislative measure

[4] See, e.g. Joined Cases C-335/11 and C-337/11 *HK Danmark, acting on behalf of Jette Ring v Dansk almennyttigt Boligselskab and HK Danmark, acting on behalf of Lone Skouboe Werge v Dansk Arbejdsgiverforening, acting on behalf of Pro Display A/S* EU:C:2013:222, para 38. See further section III below.

[5] On the medical and social models of disability, see respectively n 41 and n 42 below.

[6] See Art 1 of the UN Disability Convention.

[7] See Joined Cases C-335/11 and C-337/11 *Ring and others* (n 4) para 54. See further section IV below.

[8] The power to adopt anti-discrimination legislation was conferred on the EU with the adoption of the Treaty of Amsterdam in 1997. For the development of EU disability law, see L Waddington,

is the FED, which prohibits discrimination in employment and occupation on a number of grounds, including disability. Considerations for persons with disabilities nevertheless pervade all fields of EU law, as required by the 'mainstreaming' provision (Article 10 TFEU), according to which the EU legislature shall aim to combat discrimination based on disability in defining and implementing the EU's policies and activities. Similarly, the EU institutions must observe Articles 21 and 26 of the Charter of Fundamental Rights of the European Union (Charter)[9] on the non-discrimination and integration of persons with disabilities, particularly when enacting legislation.[10] That being so, EU law regulates matters affecting persons with disabilities in various fields, such as transport,[11] internal market,[12] judicial cooperation in criminal matters[13] and border checks, asylum and immigration,[14] to name but a few. While the adoption of anti-discrimination acts requires unanimity of the Member States' representatives in the Council of the European Union,[15] most sectoral legislation is enacted following the ordinary legislative procedure.[16]

From Rome to Nice in a Wheelchair: The Development of the European Disability Policy (Groningen, European Law Publishing, 2006).

[9] Charter of Fundamental Rights of the European Union [2016] OJ C202/393 (consolidated version) (CFR).

[10] The EU's policy on disability is set out in the 'European Disability Strategy 2010–2020: A Renewed Commitment to a Barrier-Free Europe', which identifies eight priority areas of action: accessibility, participation, equality, employment, education and training, social protection, health and external action. See COM(2010) 636 final, 4.

[11] See Regulation (EC) No 1107/2006 of the European Parliament and of the Council concerning the rights of disabled persons and persons with reduced mobility when travelling by air [2006] OJ L204/1; Regulation (EU) No 181/2011 of the European Parliament and of the Council concerning the rights of passengers in bus and coach transport and amending Regulation (EC) No 2006/2004 [2011] OJ L55/1; Regulation (EC) No 1371/2007 of the European Parliament and of the Council on rail passengers' rights and obligations [2007] OJ L315/14; Regulation (EU) No 1177/2010 of the European Parliament and of the Council concerning the rights of passengers when travelling by sea and inland waterway and amending Regulation (EC) No 2006/2004 [2010] OJ L334/1.

[12] See, e.g. European Parliament and Council Directive 95/16/EC on the approximation of the laws of the Member States relating to lifts [1995] OJ L213/1; Commission Regulation (EU) No 651/2014 declaring certain categories of aid compatible with the internal market in application of Articles 107 and 108 of the Treaty [2014] OJ L187/1 (notably concerning aid for employment of workers with disabilities); Directive 2014/24/EU of the European Parliament and of the Council on public procurement and repealing Directive 2004/18/EC [2014] OJ L94/65; Directive 2014/25/EU of the European Parliament and of the Council on procurement by entities operating in the water, energy, transport and postal services sectors and repealing Directive 2004/17/EC [2014] OJ L94/243 (see, in particular, Art 38 on reserved contracts to sheltered employment programmes).

[13] See Arts 3 and 22 of Directive 2012/29/EU of the European Parliament and of the Council establishing minimum standards on the rights, support and protection of victims of crime, and replacing Council Framework Decision 2001/220/JHA [2012] OJ L315/57.

[14] See Art 21 of Directive 2013/33/EU of the European Parliament and of the Council laying down standards for the reception of applicants for international protection [2013] OJ L180/96.

[15] Pursuant to Art 19 TFEU.

[16] On choosing the appropriate legal basis for measures dealing only incidentally with disability, see, e.g. Case C-130/10 *Parliament v Council* EU:C:2012:472, para 43 (citing case law under which measures incidental to the main component of an EU Act may be adopted on the legal basis appropriate for enacting the main component).

The UN Disability Convention, the first human rights treaty to which the EU is a contracting party in its own right, is an important source of EU disability law.[17] As both the EU and its Member States have powers in the fields covered by the UN Disability Convention, it was concluded as a 'mixed' agreement.[18] From the perspective of judicial interpretation, the UN Disability Convention brings flesh to the bones of EU disability law. Although the CJEU has concluded that the UN Disability Convention may not be relied on directly by individuals,[19] its potential importance as a source of interpretation is considerable. Indeed, EU secondary law must be given an interpretation that is consistent with its international commitments.[20] The UN Disability Convention also plays a role in negotiations with candidate countries for accession into the EU, as the situation of fundamental rights protection in those countries is evaluated.[21] This follows logically from the fact that the promotion of human rights, including those of persons with disabilities, is an EU external policy goal and the EU treaties instruct the Union actors to take the rights of persons with disabilities into account when acting on the international scene.[22] As for the EU's other international engagements in the field of disability law, mention should be made of the Marrakesh Treaty to Facilitate Access to Published Works for Persons who are Blind, Visually Impaired, or Otherwise Print Disabled, which, in particular, establishes international rules limiting copyright for the benefit of persons with disabilities.[23]

Sectoral EU legislation on disability is primarily concerned with different forms of accessibility.[24] Accessibility refers to ensuring in advance a level

[17] On the history of the treaty negotiations from the EU's perspective, see G De Búrca, 'The EU in the Negotiation of the UN Disability Convention' (2010) 35 *European Law Review* 174.

[18] See Council Decision 2010/48/EC (n 2). Annex II of the Decision lists EU acts on matters governed by the UN Disability Convention. See also Code of Conduct between the Council, the Member States and the Commission setting out internal arrangements for the implementation by and representation of the European Union relating to the United Nations Convention on the Rights of Persons with Disabilities [2010] OJ C340/8. On mixed agreements generally, see J Heliskoski, *Mixed Agreements as a Technique for Organizing the International Relations of the European Community and its Member States* (The Hague, Kluwer Law International, 2001).

[19] Case C-363/12 *Z v A Government Department and the Board of Management of a Community School* EU:C:2014:159, para 90.

[20] See, e.g. Case C-61/94 *Commission v Germany* EU:C:1996:313, para 52.

[21] See, e.g. the Former Yugoslav Republic of Macedonia 2008 Progress Report, Accompanying the Communication from the Commission to the European Parliament and the Council: Enlargement Strategy and Main Challenges 2008–2009, SEC(2008) 2695, 52 ('Little progress has been made in the area of anti-discrimination. … Moreover, the country has not signed the UN Convention on the rights of people with disabilities.').

[22] See Art 21 TEU. On the EU's commitment to protect persons with disabilities under public international law, see also P Pohjankoski, 'UN Disability Convention through the Prism of EU Law: Boosting Human Rights but Blurring Responsibilities?' (2017) 2 *Anti-Discrimination Law Review* 28.

[23] See Council Decision on the signing, on behalf of the European Union, of the Marrakesh Treaty to Facilitate Access to Published Works for Persons who are Blind, Visually Impaired, or otherwise Print Disabled [2014] OJ L115/1. See also Opinion 3/15 of the Court EU:C:2017:114 (holding that conclusion of the Marrakesh Treaty falls within EU's exclusive competence).

[24] The Proposal for a European Accessibility Act defines accessible products and services as those that are 'perceptible, operable and understandable for persons with functional limitations, including

playing field for persons with disabilities as beneficiaries of rights under EU law concerning, for example, freedom of movement, participation in economic life, or voting rights in EU elections. Provisions on accessibility feature in numerous EU Acts.[25] Furthermore, the European Commission has proposed the adoption of a 'European Accessibility Act' which seeks to harmonise accessibility requirements for products and services.[26] This legislation is also designed to improve the functioning of the internal market, as divergent accessibility requirements concerning products and services in Member States' national legislation create barriers to cross-border trade. Further, the UN Disability Convention obliges the EU to adopt, within its competences, appropriate measures to enable equal access for persons with disabilities to the physical environment, to transportation, to information and communications, and to other facilities and services open or provided to the public.[27] Similarly, Article 26 of the Charter, which requires that the EU recognises and respects the right of persons with disabilities to 'benefit from measures designed to ensure their independence, social and occupational integration and participation in the life of the community', highlights the importance of accessibility.[28] Although the CJEU has held that this provision does not require the EU legislature to adopt any specific measure,[29] its prescriptions are to be taken into account notably when enacting any form of legislation potentially affecting persons with disabilities.

Finally, it can be argued that EU law encompasses a general principle of non-discrimination on grounds of disability. According to the CJEU, the general principle of non-discrimination may be a source of directly applicable rights in relationships between private parties, permitting to set aside Member State legislation not in conformity with such a principle, when that national legislation

persons with disabilities, on an equal basis with others'. See Article 2(1) of Proposal for a Directive of the European Parliament and of the Council on the approximation of the laws, regulations and administrative provisions of the Member States as regards the accessibility requirements for products and services, COM(2015) 615 final. According to its Recital 24, accessibility should be defined by reference to this Directive when other EU legislation establishes accessibility obligations without providing specific requirements.

[25] See, e.g. Directive (EU) 2016/2102 of the European Parliament and of the Council on the accessibility of the websites and mobile applications of public sector bodies [2016] OJ L327/1; Directive 2004/27/EC of the European Parliament and of the Council amending Directive 2001/83/EC on the Community code relating to medicinal products for human use [2004] OJ L136/34 (requiring in particular that packaging of medicinal products include labels in Braille); Directive 2002/22/EC of the European Parliament and of the Council on universal service and users' rights relating to electronic communications networks and services (Universal Service Directive) [2002] OJ L108/51 (requiring Member States to provide access for persons with disabilities to publicly available telephone services, including emergency services); Directive 2006/126/EC of the European Parliament and of the Council on driving licences (Recast) [2006] OJ L403/18 (providing for the possibility of issuing driving licences for specifically adapted vehicles to persons with locomotory disabilities).

[26] Proposal for a European Accessibility Act (n 24).

[27] See Art 9 of the UN Disability Convention.

[28] See also Recital 9 of the Proposal for a European Accessibility Act (n 24).

[29] Case C-356/12 *Wolfgang Glatzel v Freistaat Bayern* EU:C:2014:350, para 78.

falls within the scope of EU law.[30] Further, according to case law, the FED gives concrete expression to the general principle of non-discrimination as it exists in international instruments, the constitutional traditions common to the Member States, and the Charter.[31] Disability is expressly referred to in that Directive, as well as in Article 19 TFEU and Article 21 of the Charter. As regards international law, the European Court of Human Rights (ECtHR) has held that disability constitutes a prohibited ground of discrimination under the European Convention on Human Rights (ECHR).[32] Moreover, the UN Disability Convention, which provides a comprehensive framework for ensuring equal treatment of persons with disabilities, has not only been concluded by the EU, but also signed by all of its Member States and ratified by all but one of them.[33] The CJEU stated in *Kaltoft* (2014) that no general principle of non-discrimination on grounds of obesity exists, but that obesity could constitute a disability in certain situations.[34] The referring national Court did not specifically enquire about the general principle of non-discrimination on grounds of disability and the CJEU did not frame its decision in such terms. Nevertheless, having regard to primary EU law and the relevant international instruments, it seems that the prohibition of discrimination on grounds of disability should be entitled to the status of a general principle of EU law.

III. Who is 'Disabled'? The Definition of Disability in EU Law

The first time the CJEU was faced with the challenge of defining disability for EU law purposes was in *Chacón Navas*.[35] Ms Chacón Navas was dismissed from her position with the catering company Eurest while she was absent from work

[30] See Case C-144/04 *Werner Mangold v Rüdiger Helm* EU:C:2005:709; Case C-555/07 *Seda Kücükdeveci v Swedex GmbH & Co KG*. EU:C:2010:21; Case C-441/14 *Dansk Industri (DI), acting on behalf of Ajos A/S v Estate of Karsten Eigil Rasmussen* EU:C:2016:278. On the rejection of the doctrine, see Judgment of the Danish Supreme Court of 6 December 2016 in Case 15/2014 (on the basis of CJEU decision in Case C-441/14). On general principles of EU law, see generally T Tridimas, *The General Principles of EU Law*, 2nd edn (Oxford, Oxford University Press, 2007).

[31] About the general principle of non-discrimination on grounds of age, see, eg Case C-441/14 *Dansk Industri* (n 30) para 22.

[32] Convention for the Protection of Human Rights and Fundamental Freedoms, signed in Rome on 4 November 1950. See Judgment of 30 April 2009 in *Glor v Switzerland* (13444/04) CE:ECHR:2009:0430JUD001344404, para 80 ('As the list of grounds of distinction given in Article 14 is not exhaustive …, there is no doubt that the scope of this provision includes discrimination based on disability.'). Protocol No 12 to the ECHR establishes a general prohibition of discrimination, but it has not been ratified by all EU Member States.

[33] See Council Decision concerning the conclusion of the UN Disability Convention (n 2). To date, Ireland has not yet ratified the UN Disability Convention. See also the chapter by L Waddington in the present volume.

[34] Case C-354/13 *Fag og Arbejde (FOA), acting on behalf of Karsten Kaltoft, v Kommunernes Landsforening (KL), acting on behalf of the Municipality of Billund* EU:C:2014:2463.

[35] Case C-13/05 *Sonia Chacón Navas v Eurest Colectividades SA* EU:C:2006:456.

due to a prolonged period of sickness, spanning eight months. The dismissal was challenged before a Spanish Social Affairs Court, which referred a question on the interpretation of the concept of disability to the CJEU: Did the Framework Equality Directive 2000 afford protection against dismissal on grounds of sickness? The CJEU noted that the Directive did not itself define 'disability' or refer to Member States' national laws for guidance on how to define it.[36] Considering that a definition of disability was necessary to assess whether Ms Chacón Navas's situation was covered by the protection afforded by the Directive, the CJEU held that the concept must be understood as referring to a 'limitation which results in particular from physical, mental or psychological impairments and which hinders the participation of the person concerned in professional life'.[37] The CJEU further observed that as the EU legislature had deliberately used the term 'disability' and not 'sickness', these concepts could not simply be treated as being the same.[38] Thus, protection against dismissal was not available for persons 'as soon as they develop any type of sickness'.[39] As for the definition itself, many external observers perceived the CJEU as endorsing the so-called 'medical model' of disability, which likens a physical impairment to disability.[40] Indeed, under this definition, 'disability' was essentially equated with the impairment of the person in question. The CJEU was criticised for ignoring the 'social model' of disability, under which disability results not from the impairment itself, but from its interaction with various systemic barriers in society.[41]

A few years after *Chacón Navas*, the conclusion of the UN Disability Convention by the EU in 2010 prompted a shift in the CJEU's approach to defining disability.[42] In *Ring and others* (2013), the claimants had been dismissed from employment upon returning to work after a period of sick leave.[43] Ms Ring suffered from constant severe lumbar pain, while Ms Skouboe Werge had whiplash injuries from

[36] ibid para 39.

[37] ibid para 43.

[38] ibid para 44.

[39] ibid para 46.

[40] See, e.g. L Waddington, 'Equal to the Task? Re-examining EU Equality Law in Light of the UN Convention on the Rights of Persons with Disabilities' in L Waddington, J Quinn and E Flynn (eds) *European Yearbook of Disability Law, Volume 4* (The Netherlands, Intersentia, 2013) 186; A Hendriks and O Lewis, 'Disability' in Y Jolly and BM Knoppers (eds), *Routledge Handbook of Medical Law and Ethics* (Abingdon, Routledge, 2015) 80.

[41] The social model seems to have emerged in the UK in the 1970s, developed by members of the Union of the Physically Impaired against Segregation. See, further, e.g. S Favalli and D Ferri, 'Defining Disability in the EU Non-Discrimination Legislation: Judicial Activism and Legislative Restraints' (2016) 22 *European Public Law* 541, 542 ff.

[42] In the meantime, the CJEU held in 2008 that the protection against discrimination on grounds of disability also extends to discrimination 'by association'. See Case C-303/06 *S Coleman v Attridge Law and Steve Law* EU:C:2008:415, para 56 (holding that the FED prohibits discrimination of an employee's child on grounds of disability). To that effect, see also Judgment of 22 March 2016 in *Guberina v Croatia* (23682/13) CE:ECHR:2016:0322JUD002368213, para 79 ('the alleged discriminatory treatment of the applicant on account of the disability of his child, with whom he has close personal links and for whom he provides care, is a form of disability-based discrimination covered by Article 14 of the [ECHR]').

[43] Joined Cases C-335/11 and C-337/11 *Ring and others* (n 4).

a traffic accident. The employers of the claimants submitted that the employees could not be considered disabled merely because they could not work full-time. Addressing the relationship between illness and disability, the CJEU noted that the UN Disability Convention now formed part of the EU legal order. As work and employment were fields covered by the UN Disability Convention, the FED was to be interpreted in light of its provisions. This led the CJEU to refashion the definition of disability it had put forward in *Chacón Navas*, considering that for the purposes of the FED, 'disability' should from now on instead be interpreted as a 'limitation which results in particular from physical, mental or psychological impairments which in interaction with various barriers may hinder the full and effective participation of the person concerned in professional life on an equal basis with other workers'.[44] It added that limiting the scope of the Directive by reference to the origin of the disability at issue would counteract its effectiveness and objectives. As such, disabilities caused by an illness – if they entailed long-term effects – should be covered by its provisions.[45] The definition given in *Ring and others* has since become established in the anti-discrimination case law on disability, both in relation to the FED and Article 21 of the Charter.[46]

However, that definition does not seem to be valid in other regulatory contexts. Advocate General Mengozzi in *Oxycure Belgium* (2017) opined that the definition developed in the employment context of the FED should be applied to other fields, such as the VAT treatment of products intended for disabled persons, so as to maintain a coherent approach, especially with regard to the difficult distinction between illness and disability.[47] The CJEU did not, however, address this issue in its judgment.[48] Furthermore, in the context of the EU's Customs Nomenclature,[49] the CJEU has explicitly refused to adopt the definition of 'disability' in the FED and the Charter and, by contrast, interpreted the concept of 'disabled persons' as having a narrower scope.[50] As such, this expression covers only 'persons affected by a non-marginal limit on their ability to walk, the duration of that limitation and the existence of other limitations relating to the capacities of those persons being irrelevant'.[51] Similarly, in the field of transport regulation, the definition is more restrictive and anchored to physical impairments which relate to mobility. Thus,

[44] ibid para 38.

[45] ibid para 41.

[46] See Cases C-312/11 *Commission v Italy* EU:C:2013:446, para 56; Case C-363/12 *Z.* (n 19) para 76; C-354/13 *Kaltoft* (n 34) para 53; Case C-356/12 *Glatzel* (n 29) paras 44–46.

[47] Case C-573/15 *Oxycure Belgium* EU:C:2016:792, Opinion of AG Mengozzi, paras 23–24 (referring to Case C-360/11 *Commission v Spain* EU:C:2013:17) and paras 27–28.

[48] Case C-573/15 *Oxycure Belgium* EU:C:2017:189.

[49] Combined Nomenclature of the Common Customs Tariff in Annex I to Council Regulation (EEC) No 2658/87 on the tariff and statistical nomenclature and on the Common Customs Tariff [1987] OJ L256/1, as amended by Commission Regulation (EC) No 1810/2004 [2004] OJ L327/1.

[50] Case C-198/15 *Invamed Group Ltd and others v Commissioners for Her Majesty's Revenue & Customs* EU:C:2016:362, para 33.

[51] ibid para 34.

Regulation 1371/2007 on the rights and obligations of rail passengers equates 'disabled persons' with 'persons with reduced mobility', that is:

> any person whose mobility when using transport is reduced due to any physical disability (sensory or locomotory, permanent or temporary), intellectual disability or impairment, or any other cause of disability, or as a result of age, and whose situation needs appropriate attention and adaptation to his or her particular needs of the service made available to all passengers.[52]

The Commission's Proposal for a European Accessibility Act also uses two different definitions: that of 'persons with functional limitations' encompassing 'persons who have any physical, mental, intellectual or sensory impairment, age related impairment, or other human body performance related causes, permanent or temporary, which in interaction with various barriers result in their reduced access to products and services, leading to a situation that requires adaptation to their particular needs of those products and services'; and that of 'persons with disabilities' which covers persons who have 'long-term physical, mental, intellectual or sensory impairments which in interaction with various barriers may hinder their full and effective participation in society on an equal basis with others'.[53] Finally, Member States retain different definitions of disability in their legislation and in some contexts, EU-wide rules refer back to these national definitions. For example, the Recommendation on an EU format and mutual recognition of parking cards for disabled persons explicitly allows the Member States to determine who should be regarded as having a disability for the purpose of the Recommendation.[54]

In light of the various formulations adopted by the EU legislature, currently there appears to be no 'one-size-fits-all' approach to defining disability. At the same time, it is also unclear whether the definition in the UN Disability Convention, taken up by the CJEU in the anti-discrimination context, may serve as a broader frame of reference. Having different definitions for different regulatory contexts may not be problematic as such. Nevertheless, considering that the definition of 'persons with disabilities' in Article 1 of the UN Disability Convention should inform the EU legislature's action in the field of disability law, it would be helpful if reasons were provided when derogating from that understanding of the concept.

As for the FED, the broad definition of disability endorsed in *Ring and others* is, in itself, rather difficult to apply in practice. To recall, this definition refers to multiple criteria for establishing a 'limitation' notably resulting from 'impairments' which, in interaction with various 'barriers' may hinder the 'full and effective' participation of the person concerned in professional life on an equal basis with

[52] See Art 3(15) Regulation (EC) No 1371/2007 (n 11). The same definition has been taken up by Arts 3(a) Regulation (EU) 1177/2010 and 3(j) Regulation (EU) No 181/2011 (n 11).

[53] See Proposal for a European Accessibility Act (n 24), Art 2, points 3 and 4.

[54] Council Recommendation 98/376/EC on a parking card for people with disabilities, [1998] OJ L167/25, Recital 7 ('the definition of disability and the rules for assigning parking cards to persons with disabilities are the responsibility of the Member States').

other workers. In addition, such a limitation must be 'long-term'.[55] Even if the reference to 'a limitation' does not seem problematic, several questions arise regarding the different elements in the wording. How to define 'impairment'? What is meant by 'full and effective participation in professional life'? Last, but not least, how long is 'long term'? Some indicators can be gleaned from the CJEU's case law.

First, it appears from the definition established in *Ring and others* that all disabilities stem from 'impairments'. Advocate General Jääskinen has defended the view that the 'abstract medical or social insurance classifications concerning the degree of the impairment as such' should not affect the applicability of the concept of disability.[56] Thus, the seriousness of the impairment should not matter for the purposes of this definition. Yet, the fact remains that, although the seriousness of the impairment is not material, medical data may still be required to establish the existence of any impairment. Here, caution is required to not equate impairment with disability. The EU legislature has used the terms interchangeably elsewhere. In the field of transport, for example, the regulations seem to equate (intellectual) impairment with (intellectual) disability, by referring to 'any physical disability (sensory or locomotory, permanent or temporary), *intellectual disability or impairment*, or any other cause of disability'.[57] Were this approach to be used in interpreting the FED, it could risk reintroducing the medical model of disability into the definition.

Second, with regard to 'full and effective participation in professional life', it must be recalled that this criterion reflects the scope of the FED, which covers only situations related to employment and occupation. The CJEU made this clear in *Z*, where the Irish Equality Tribunal asked whether the refusal to provide paid maternity leave or adoption leave to a female worker, who had recourse to a surrogacy arrangement to have a child due to her lack of uterus, could be regarded as discrimination on grounds of disability.[58] In his Opinion, Advocate General Wahl did not rule out that, in certain circumstances, the condition at issue might hinder full and effective participation *in society*, but concluded that in the situation at hand, full and effective participation *in professional life* was not prevented.[59] Endorsing the view of the Advocate General, the CJEU confirmed that the inability to have a child via conventional means, while being a limitation resulting from a physical impairment, does not *per se* make it impossible for the person to 'carry out her work or constitut[e] a hindrance to the exercise of her professional activity'.[60]

[55] Joined Cases C-335/11 and C-337/11 *Ring and others* (n 4) paras 37 and 39.

[56] Case C-354/13 *Kaltoft* EU:C:2014:2106 (n 34) Opinion of AG Jääskinen, para 44.

[57] This definition is used, as mentioned above, in Art 3(j) Regulation (EU) No 181/2011, Art 3(15) Regulation (EC) No 1371/2007 and Art 3(a) Regulation (EU) 1177/2010 (n 11). Emphasis added.

[58] Case C-363/12 *Z.* (n 19).

[59] Case C-363/12 *Z.* EU:C:2013:604, Opinion of AG Wahl, paras 93 and 95.

[60] Case C-363/12 *Z.* (n 19) para 81.

In this judgment, the CJEU's reading of the 'full and effective participation' criterion is quite narrow. Granted, since the FED was enacted to regulate situations concerning employment and occupation, the EU legislature may not have contemplated surrogacy childbirth arrangements and, hence, the situation of Ms Z could be seen as falling outside the scope of the Directive. Nonetheless, the right to paid leave on grounds of childbirth is arguably an essential component of the rights provided to workers for successfully combining their working life and family obligations. As such, one wonders whether it can be categorically excluded that the impossibility to benefit from such leave, rather than the impossibility to have children by conventional means, might hinder a person's full and effective participation also *in professional life* on an equal basis with others.

Third, as for the 'long-term' requirement, the CJEU has provided more detailed guidance. The preliminary reference in *Daouidi* (2016) concerned the situation of a kitchen worker, Mr Daouidi, whose elbow was dislocated as a result of a slip-and-fall accident.[61] Six months after the accident, his elbow was still in plaster, leading the national Court to enquire whether the limitation in Mr Daouidi's case was 'long-term' in nature. The CJEU considered that a limitation should be evaluated in light of the clarity of the prognosis and its short-term progress as well as the likelihood of a prolonged incapacity.[62] It further reiterated that disabilities caused by accidents are not excluded from the notion of disability under the FED.[63] This requirement is of paramount importance for the distinction between illness and disability. The CJEU understands that illnesses, whether curable or incurable, may entail limitations covered by the definition of disability.[64] Similarly, the Committee on the Rights of Persons with Disabilities (CRPD committee)[65] has established that the difference between illness and disability is a difference in degree and not in kind.[66]

[61] Case C-395/15 *Mohamed Daouidi v Bootes Plus SL and others* EU:C:2016:917.

[62] ibid para 56. Advocate General Mengozzi stressed in his Opinion in *Oxycure* (n 48) that 'the characteristic feature of the concept of "disability" is its long-term nature, as opposed to the diminution of certain faculties as a result of, in particular, a sporadic or temporary illness' (para 29). In his view, and in spite of the lack of clarity stemming from the Court's case law, 'both the physical, mental, intellectual or psychological incapacities and the limitation which they cause for individuals affected by them that must be long-term and that allow a distinction to be drawn between the concept of "disability" and the concept of "illness".' Footnote 16 of the Opinion.

[63] Case C-395/15 *Daouidi* (n 61) paras 44–45.

[64] Joined Cases C-335/11 and C-337/11 *Ring and others* (n 4) para 41.

[65] The CRPD committee, established pursuant to Art 34 of the UN Convention, is a body of independent experts which monitors the implementation of the UN Convention. Under the Optional Protocol, it has competence to examine individual complaints with regard to alleged violations of the Convention by States parties to the Protocol. The EU has not signed the Optional Protocol. On the Optional Protocol, see also P Pohjankoski, 'UN Disability Convention through the Prism of EU Law: Boosting Human Rights but Blurring Responsibilities?' (n 22).

[66] See *SC v Brazil*, CRPD/C/12/D/10/2013, 2 October 2014, at 8 ('the difference between illness and disability is a difference of degree and not a difference of kind. A health impairment which initially is conceived of as illness can develop into an impairment in the context of disability as a consequence of its duration or its chronicity').

Although the CJEU has clarified many aspects of the definition of 'disability' under the FED, several issues remain open. An individual analysis of the various components of the definition can constitute a *de facto* standing requirement for litigants and hinder access to justice.[67] The complex definition of disability under the *Ring* case law could become a source of litigation in itself, potentially creating problems for those attempting to enforce their rights under the FED. With regard to other grounds of discrimination, such as age or sex, the question of definition is usually avoided, since in most cases this will be either apparent or easily established.[68] However, where discrimination on grounds of disability arises, the qualification of the individual as 'disabled' is a preliminary requirement. A rigid analysis of the different components of the definition could hence become a barrier in itself.

To avoid this, the definition of disability established in *Ring and others* should be read broadly, with a view to respecting the spirit of the UN Disability Convention, which aims to guarantee equal enjoyment of all human rights to all persons. That being said, such an approach shifts the legal analysis from assessing who to deem 'persons with disabilities' to what accommodation measures can reasonably be provided. The duty to provide reasonable accommodation is thus the subject of the next section.

IV. What is *Reasonable*? The Duty of Reasonable Accommodation in EU Law

The ultimate aim of the duty of reasonable accommodation is to guarantee that persons with disabilities are treated on an equal basis with others. The UN Disability Convention specifies that a denial of such accommodation constitutes a prohibited form of discrimination.[69] In EU secondary law, the obligation of reasonable accommodation features explicitly in the FED. Moreover, the UN Disability Convention also contains a general duty of reasonable accommodation, which must be taken into account when interpreting EU legislation.[70] Therefore,

[67] On the judicial backlash in interpreting the Americans with Disabilities Act, see V Perju, 'Impairment, Discrimination, and the Legal Construction of Disability in the European Union and the United States' (2011) 44 *Cornell International Law Journal* 279, 311 ff.

[68] However, with regard to discrimination on grounds of racial or ethnic origin, see Case C-83/14 *"CHEZ Razpredelenie Bulgaria" AD v Komisia za zashtita ot diskriminatsia* EU:C:2015:480, para 46 (defining ethnicity as '[having] its origin in the idea of societal groups marked in particular by common nationality, religious faith, language, cultural and traditional origins and backgrounds'); Case C-668/15 *Jyske Finans A/S v Ligebehandlingsnævnet, acting on behalf of Ismar Huskic* EU:C:2017:278, paras 18–19 (holding that ethnic origin cannot be determined on the sole basis of birthplace).

[69] See Arts 2 and 5 of the UN Disability Convention.

[70] According to Art 2 of the UN Disability Convention, reasonable accommodation means 'necessary and appropriate modification and adjustments not imposing a disproportionate or undue burden, where needed in a particular case, to ensure to persons with disabilities the enjoyment or exercise on

questions relating to the duty may also arise under EU law in other regulatory contexts besides employment.[71]

Under Article 5 of the FED, reasonable accommodation in the work context requires that employers take appropriate measures, where needed in a particular case, to 'enable a person with a disability to have access to, participate in, or advance in employment, or to undergo training'.[72] As is apparent from the wording of the provision, this refers to the duty to take appropriate measures 'where needed in a particular case', as opposed to obligations requiring that employers provide accessible environments as a general matter and before specifically being requested to do so. It may be noted that, pursuant to the FED, the obligation of reasonable accommodation applies specifically in connection with discriminatory treatment on grounds of disability, not in respect of the other prohibited grounds of discrimination, namely those of religion or belief, age, or sexual orientation.[73] This particularity should not, however, be confused with the possibility to adopt so-called positive (affirmative) action, which exists in respect of all grounds of discrimination.[74]

The duty to provide reasonable accommodation under the FED applies to all employers and is mandatory. Although Recital 17 of the Directive's preamble states that its provisions do not require the 'recruitment, promotion, maintenance in employment or training' of an individual who is 'not competent, capable and available to perform the essential functions of the post concerned or to undergo the relevant training', this general rule is importantly without prejudice to the obligation to provide reasonable accommodation. Thus, when requested, employers must, in principle, adapt the workplace to the particular disability of an employee. The CJEU has held that accommodation measures, such as the use of special

an equal basis with others of all human rights and fundamental freedoms'. On the duty of consistent interpretation with the UN Disability Convention, see, eg Case C-395/15 *Daouidi* (n 61) para 41. See also the chapter by L Waddington in the present volume.

[71] See, e.g. Recital 3 of Directive 2014/24/EU of the European Parliament and of the Council of on public procurement and repealing Directive 2004/18/EC [2014] OJ L94/65, which provides that '[w]hen implementing this Directive, the [UN Disability Convention] should be taken into account, in particular in connection with the choice of means of communications, technical specifications, award criteria and contract performance conditions'.

[72] For a European Commission infringement action against Italy on the incomplete implementation of that provision, see Case C-312/11 *Commission v Italy* (n 46).

[73] FED, Art 5. In the United States, the statutory obligation of reasonable accommodation extends to discrimination on grounds of religion. See in particular *EEOC v Abercrombie & Fitch Stores, Inc* 575 US (2015) (holding that an employer with a neutral clothing policy must accommodate Muslim headgear under Title VII of Civil Rights Act of 1964). Cf. Case C-157/15 *Samira Achbita and Centrum voor gelijkheid van kansen en voor racismebestrijding v G4S Secure Solutions NV* EU:C:2017:203, para 43 (holding that an employer should examine the possibility of accommodating a Muslim headscarf when possible without incurring additional burden).

[74] See Art 7 of Framework Equality Directive 2000; Art 5 of Council Directive 2000/43/EC implementing the principle of equal treatment between persons irrespective of racial or ethnic origin [2000] OJ L180/22. On the former, see Case C-406/15 *Petya Milkova v Izpalnitelen direktor na Agentsiata za privatizatsia i sledprivatizatsionen control* EU:C:2017:198.

equipment, are a consequence of disability.[75] As such, the definition of the concept of 'disability' within the meaning of Article 1 of FED comes before the determination and assessment of the appropriate accommodation measures referred to in its Article 5.[76]

That being said, EU anti-discrimination law does not require that all forms of employment be made available to everyone and the duty of reasonable accommodation does not alter this premise. Indeed, under the FED, Member States may provide that certain characteristics linked to prohibited grounds of discrimination are, by reason of the nature of the work or of the context in which it is carried out, 'genuine and determining' occupational requirements.[77] Thus, employers cannot be required to hire, for example, blind persons to fly aircraft, because eyesight is an essential requirement for being a pilot.[78] Similarly, fire-fighters may be expected to have a high level of physical fitness, a characteristic which may be precluded by certain disabilities.[79] Such characteristics must, however, be objectively necessary for carrying out the work in question. Whereas age is a prohibited ground of discrimination in its own right under the FED, it should also be noted that there is a connection between old age and certain disabilities, which may be relevant for assessing the requirements for certain types of work.[80] However, the circumstances where such characteristics are essential for certain types of work are limited. The Member State providing for such requirements must ensure that the regulatory objective is legitimate and that the requirement is proportionate to its aim.[81]

The CJEU has held that the duty of reasonable accommodation must be interpreted broadly in light of the UN Disability Convention. As such, the concept should be understood as referring to the 'elimination of the various barriers that hinder the full and effective participation of persons with disabilities in professional life on an equal basis with other workers'.[82] According to the CRPD committee, the duty to provide reasonable accommodation under the UN Disability Convention

[75] Joined Cases C-335/11 and C-337/11 *Ring and others* (n 4) paras 45–46. Cf. US Supreme Court in *Sutton v United Air Lines Inc*, 527 US 471 (1999) (myopic twin sisters applying for commercial airline pilot post not considered disabled because vision can be corrected).

[76] Joined Cases C-335/11 and C-337/11 *Ring and others* (n 4) para 45.

[77] FED, Art 4(1).

[78] On the requirement of eyesight for commercial airline pilots, see Case C-447/09 *Reinhard Prigge and ors v Deutsche Lufthansa AG* EU:C:2011:573, para 67. On the importance of necessary eyesight for operating lorries in road traffic, see also Case C-356/12 *Glatzel* (n 29). See also Framework Equality Directive 2000, Art 3(4), according to which Member States may provide that the directive, in so far as it relates to discrimination on the ground of disability, shall not apply to the armed forces.

[79] On the connection between physical fitness and age, see Case C-229/08 *Colin Wolf v Stadt Frankfurt am Main* EU:C:2010:3, para 40.

[80] On the relationship between age and disability, see e.g. Case C-152/11 *Johann Odar v Baxter Deutschland GmbH* EU:C:2012:772, para 69 ('severely disabled people … generally face greater difficulties in finding new employment, … those risks tend to become exacerbated as they approach retirement age').

[81] See Recital 23 of the Framework Equality Directive 2000.

[82] Joined Cases C-335/11 and C-337/11 *Ring and others* (n 4) paras 53–54.

is immediately applicable and not subject to progressive realisation.[83] Under the FED, the accommodation measures should be 'effective and practical', which could be understood as emphasising functional results over formal compliance.[84] Measures listed therein include 'adapting premises and equipment, patterns of working time, the distribution of tasks or the provision of training or integration resources'.[85] The adaptation of the physical working environment may require, for example, the installation of specific equipment or rearranging the working area. According to the CJEU, patterns of working time refer to the rhythm or speed at which the work is done, therefore an adjustment may involve scheduling regular breaks in the work.[86] The CJEU has held that a reduction in working hours may also constitute an appropriate measure of reasonable accommodation.[87]

When do accommodation measures become 'unreasonable'? According to the FED, the employer is relieved of the duty of reasonable accommodation if the solicited measures would constitute a disproportionate burden.[88] Relevant factors in assessing whether given accommodation measures constitute a disproportionate burden on the employer include the size or the financial resources of the employer.[89] Article 5 of the Directive specifies that the burden cannot be considered disproportionate when it is 'sufficiently remedied by measures existing within the framework of the disability policy of the Member State concerned'. On this basis, it can be assumed that when the disability policy of a Member State provides, for example, for financial aid to employers hiring persons with disabilities, such an employer may only justify a refusal to put in place accommodation measures when that financial aid is plainly insufficient to remedy the costs of their implementation. However, even such cases will require an analysis of other factors to determine whether the remainder of the burden placed on the employer (i.e. the cost which is not remedied by public support) is disproportionate.

That said, the extent of appropriate accommodation measures cannot be determined in advance and the finding of a disproportionate burden is inherently a case-by-case analysis. To date, there is relatively little CJEU case law on the concept of reasonable accommodation. However, some guidelines for assessing the proportionality of the burden caused by accommodation may be distilled from the practice of the CRPD committee and the ECtHR. While their interpretations of the UN Disability Convention are not directly binding on the EU, their decisions may nonetheless have some persuasive value. Indeed, all the EU Member States are parties to the ECHR and a number of them have ratified the Optional

[83] CRPD/C/ESP/CO/1 (consideration of education-related aspects of the report submitted by Spain under Art 35 of the UN Disability Convention), 6. On the CRPD Committee, see n 65.

[84] FED, recital 20.

[85] ibid.

[86] Joined Cases C-335/11 and C-337/11 *Ring and others* (n 4) para 55.

[87] ibid, paras 56 and 64. See also Case C-312/11 *Commission v Italy* (n 46) para 60.

[88] The UN Disability Convention uses the term 'undue burden', but the difference in terminology is not considered material. In any event, the FED predates the conclusion of the UN Disability Convention and should be read consistently with its obligations.

[89] FED, recital 21.

Protocol to the UN Disability Convention, establishing the individual complaints mechanism before the CRPD committee.[90]

The CRPD committee considered the notion of undue burden in the employment context in *Marie-Louise Jungelin v Sweden* (2014), where the complainant was a job-seeker with a severe visual impairment.[91] According to the decision, the Swedish Social Insurance Agency could not be required to employ the person in question as responsible for handling social security applications. She would not have been able to perform all the duties of the position without an assistant, because the available IT software could not convert handwritten documents into Braille and the handling of such documents formed a significant part of the work. The estimated costs of the required changes to the IT systems were around 10-15 million Swedish *kronar* (circa €1–1.5 million) which amounted to approximately 2 per cent of the agency's IT budget. As such, the CRPD committee agreed with the earlier decision of the Swedish Labour Court that the support and adaptation measures required would constitute an undue burden for the Social Insurance Agency.

Conversely, in *HM v Sweden* (2012), the CRPD committee considered that no undue burden existed where the city planning office refused to grant a building permission for the construction of a rehabilitative hydrotherapy pool because the extension to the person's house was claimed to be incompatible with the city's development plan.[92] The person in question suffered from a hereditary condition severely limiting her physical mobility. Medical certificates showed that the only type of rehabilitation that could stop its progress was hydrotherapy, which in the person's particular circumstances would only be practicable in an indoor pool at her house. For the construction of the pool, planning permission for an extension of approximately 63 square metres to the house on privately owned land was requested. However, this extension would, to a large extent, have been on land where building was not allowed and permission was denied. In its decision, the CRPD committee underlined that the planning authorities had not addressed the specific circumstances and the particular disability-related needs of the person in the decision-making process.[93] It further noted that the Swedish Planning and Building Act allowed for departures from the development plan.[94] Therefore, allowing the extension would not be an undue burden for the planning authorities.[95] While this decision was not taken in an employment context, it highlights the importance of assessing the individual needs of the person requesting accommodation.

[90] The ECHR enjoys special status under EU law pursuant to Article 6(3) TEU and Article 52(3) of the Charter. On the CRPD committee, see n 65 above.

[91] *Marie-Louise Jungelin v Sweden*, CRPD/C/12/D/5/2011, 2 October 2014.

[92] *HM v Sweden*, CRPD/C/7/D/3/2011, 21 May 2012. On a violation of the duty of reasonable accommodation in prison conditions, see *Mr X v Argentina*, CRPD/C/11/D/8/2012, 11 April 2014.

[93] ibid at 13.

[94] ibid at 12.

[95] ibid at 13.

In fact, it appears practically impossible to justify a refusal of accommodation measures if the requested measures have not been given any consideration. In *Çam v Turkey* (2006), the ECtHR held that the failure of a music conservatory to consider reasonable accommodation measures to allow a person with a visual disability to attend a programme in the performance studies of bağlama (Turkish lute) was discriminatory.[96] The ECtHR took into account the current developments in international law and, in particular, the duty of reasonable accommodation for persons with disabilities as expressed in the UN Disability Convention.[97] Considering that the music conservatory had failed to even consider the possibility of accommodating the disability of the applicant, the ECtHR held that the denial of reasonable accommodation constituted a violation of the rights to anti-discrimination and education under the ECHR.[98]

V. Conclusion

The past 20 years have witnessed great progress as regards the equal treatment of persons with disabilities in EU law. The conclusion of the UN Disability Convention by the EU has mandated further mainstreaming of the protection of persons with disabilities in secondary legislation. Specifically, in the field of anti-discrimination, the CJEU has endorsed the ideology of the UN Disability Convention, interpreting the concepts of disability and reasonable accommodation in light of its provisions.

Nonetheless, the judicial interpretation of these concepts continues to raise questions, notably in the context of the FED. The definition of disability adopted by the CJEU in *Ring and others* appears, on the one hand, very broad and of little definitional value. On the other hand, a restrictive judicial interpretation of the various components required to qualify an individual as 'disabled' under this definition can become an unnecessary barrier for litigants to enforcing their rights. The range of disability-related definitions used in secondary legislation does little to clarify matters. As for the duty of reasonable accommodation, its nature mandates a case-by-case proportionality analysis. The CJEU has established some elements of guidance regarding the concept, but relevant case law remains scarce. In the meantime, the practice of the ECtHR and the CRPD committee may provide some interpretative guidance for assessing the scope of this duty.

As the broad definition of disability is of little help in resolving concrete disputes, the interpretation and application of the duty of reasonable accommodation assumes a primordial role for the judiciary. It is expected that national courts will seek to clarify the limits of that duty by further references to the CJEU.

[96] See Judgment of 23 February 2016 in Case *Çam v Turkey* (51500/08) CE:ECHR:2016:0223JUD005150008,.

[97] ibid paras 64–65.

[98] ibid para 69.

15

The Influence of the UN Convention on the Rights of Persons with Disabilities on EU Anti-Discrimination Law

LISA WADDINGTON

I. Introduction

Some ten years after adopting the Framework Equality Directive (Directive 2000/78),[1] and two years after proposing a new equality directive which extends beyond the field of employment (2008 proposal),[2] the European Union (EU) became a party to the UN Convention on the Rights of Persons with Disabilities (CRPD or Convention). As a result, the EU is bound by the Convention to the extent of its competences which, as demonstrated by Article 19 TFEU and the adoption of the Framework Equality Directive (FED), include combatting discrimination on the ground of disability.[3] Disability discrimination is addressed extensively in the CRPD and, in some respects, the Convention is more precise, and certainly has a far broader scope, than the Framework Equality Directive and the 2008 proposal. This chapter explores the consequences of the conclusion of the CRPD for EU anti-discrimination law and focuses on three issues.

Firstly, whilst the Framework Equality Directive was not adopted with a view to implementing the Convention, the Court of Justice of the European Union (CJEU) is bound to take the CRPD into account in interpreting secondary EU law, because of its acquired status as EU law. The chapter considers how the CRPD has influenced the Court's interpretation of the concept of disability under the Directive in particular.

[1] Council Directive 2000/78/EC establishing a general framework for equal treatment in employment and occupation [2000] OJ L303/16 (Framework Equality Directive).

[2] European Commission, 'Proposal for a Council Directive on implementing the principle of equal treatment between persons irrespective of religion or belief, disability, age or sexual orientation' COM(2008) 426 final.

[3] Treaty on the Functioning of the European Union [2016] OJ C202/1 (consolidated version), Art 19 (TFEU).

Secondly, in 2008 the Commission proposed a broad anti-discrimination directive covering a number of grounds, including disability, and extending beyond employment. Whilst this directive has not been adopted to date, it has been subject to a number of revisions, in light, *inter alia*, of the EU's conclusion of the CRPD in 2010. The chapter will consider how the CRPD has influenced the proposal and make comparisons between the original proposal and the latest publicly available version of the proposal to identify changes linked to the CRPD.[4]

Lastly, the EU, as a State Party to the Convention, is obliged to submit itself to the reporting procedure foreseen in Articles 35 and 36 CRPD. The Commission, on behalf of the EU, submitted its state report to the UN Committee on the Rights of Persons with Disabilities in 2014[5] and the Committee also received 'alternative' or 'shadow' reports from civil society organisations in the EU.[6] In April 2015, the Committee produced a List of Issues[7] which the EU responded to;[8] in October 2015, it published its Concluding Observations for the EU.[9] Some of the observations address anti-discrimination, and this chapter reflects on these.

Prior to examining these three issues, the chapter sets the scene and discusses the CRPD, and the EU's conclusion of the CRPD.

II. Setting the Scene

The Convention, as is appropriate for a human rights instrument, strongly reflects the social-contextual model[10] of disability.[11] Explicit recognition is made of the fact that 'disability results from the interaction between persons with impairments

[4] At the time of writing (Spring 2017), the latest publicly available version was 'Proposal for a Council Directive on implementing the principle of equal treatment between persons irrespective of religion or belief, disability, age or sexual orientation' Version of 14 December 2016, 14500/16. I am grateful to Janina Arsenjeva for helping me track down recent Council documents identifying the state of negotiations and the proposal. Information in this chapter relates to Spring 2017 and subsequent developments have not been incorporated.

[5] Commission Staff Working Document, 'Report on the implementation of the UN Convention on the Rights of Persons with Disabilities (CRPD) by the European Union' SWD(2014) 182 final.

[6] See, eg the European Disability Forum Alternative Report to the EU Committee on the Rights of Persons with Disabilities, available via the EDF homepage. Available at: www.edf-feph.org/default.asp.

[7] Committee on the Rights of Persons with Disabilities, 'List of issues in relation to the initial report of the European Union' (2015) CRPD/C/EU/Q/1.

[8] Commission Staff Working Document, 'Reply of the European Union to the list of issues in relation to the initial report of the European Union on the implementation of the UN Convention on the Rights of Persons with Disabilities' SWD(2015) 127 final.

[9] Committee on the Rights of Persons with Disabilities, 'Concluding observations on the initial report of the European Union' (2015) CRPD/C/EU/CO/1.

[10] See on models of disability eg M Priestley, 'Constructions and Creations: Idealism, Materialism and Disability Theory' (1998) 13 *Disability and Society* 75.

[11] This section draws on text in L Waddington, 'The European Union and the United Nations Convention on the Rights of Persons with Disabilities: A Story of Exclusive and Shared Competences' (2011) 18 *Maastricht Journal of European and Comparative Law* 431.

and attitudinal and environmental barriers that hinders their full and effective participation in society on an equal basis with others'.[12] The Convention therefore reflects the reality that disability stems primarily from the failure of the social environment to meet the needs and aspirations of people with impairments. It is the highest legal manifestation and confirmation of the social-contextual model of disability on the international stage.

The scope of the Convention is extremely broad.[13] It does not simply prohibit disability discrimination, nor does it only cover civil or political rights or economic, cultural or social rights. Instead, the Convention is underpinned by the principles of anti-discrimination and equality, which embrace the right to a reasonable accommodation, and these are linked to a broad group of rights, including both civil and political rights, such as the right to liberty,[14] as well as more substantive rights, such as the right to education.[15]

The principles of equality and anti-discrimination run through the Convention like a red thread. They find their anchor in Article 3 CRPD, which Quinn has described as providing the 'moral compass for change' which the Convention embraces.[16] This article refers not only to anti-discrimination and equality of opportunity, but also to a series of other principles which 'animate' the Convention, including dignity; individual autonomy; full and active participation and inclusion; respect for difference; and accessibility. The principles of anti-discrimination and equality find repeated reference elsewhere in the Convention. In light of this, Article 2 CRPD, which elaborates on key terms used in the Convention, contains a broad definition of 'discrimination on the basis of disability', and specifies that such discrimination includes the denial of a reasonable accommodation.

The principles of equality and anti-discrimination also receive specific attention in Article 5 CRPD. This article embraces both a formal approach to equality ('equal before and under the law');[17] and a more substantive approach ('prohibit discrimination on the basis of disability';[18] provision of 'reasonable accommodation';[19] and positive action measures 'shall not be considered discrimination'[20]). States Parties are under an obligation to recognise and ensure protection of these rights. Elsewhere, the Convention is 'sprinkled' liberally with

[12] Preamble, recital (e). See also Art 1.

[13] G Quinn, 'The UN Convention on the Human Rights of Persons with Disabilities' (2007) 9, paper on file with author; and TJ Melish, 'Perspectives on the UN Convention on the Rights of Persons with Disabilities: The UN Disability Convention: Historic Process, Strong Prospects, and Why the U.S. Should Ratify' (2007) 14 *Human Rights Brief* 37, fn 11, who describes the Convention as adopting a 'hybrid approach'.

[14] CRPD Art 14.

[15] ibid Art 24.

[16] Quinn (n 13) 3.

[17] CRPD Art 5(1).

[18] ibid Art 5(2).

[19] ibid Art 5(3).

[20] The Convention does not refer to positive action, but instead Art 5(4) speaks of '[s]pecific measures which are necessary to accelerate or achieve de facto equality'.

references to anti-discrimination, equality and reasonable accommodation. Eliminating discrimination, in the sense of removing obstacles and barriers to accessibility, also lies at the heart of Article 9 CRPD.

Lastly, Article 4 of the Convention sets out the general obligations of the States Parties, which include the requirement 'to adopt all appropriate legislative, administrative and other measures for the implementation of the rights recognised in the present Convention'.[21] Quinn has concisely stated that this article 'converts the convention into a trigger for worldwide disability law reform'.[22]

The European Community, represented by the European Commission, played an active role in the negotiations that led to the adoption of the Convention. Following the adoption of the CRPD in 2006, the European Community, along with all of its Member States, signed the Convention. The 2007 Council Decision[23] on the signing of the Convention by the Community has as its legal basis both Articles 13 EC (now Article 19 TFEU) and 95 EC (now Article 114 TFEU).[24] The former article addresses combatting discrimination on the grounds of, *inter alia*, disability, whilst the latter covers the establishment and functioning of the internal market.

In November 2009, the Council adopted a Decision concerning the conclusion by the European Community of the CRPD.[25] This provided for the depositing of instruments of formal confirmation with the Secretary General of the United Nations.[26] The European Union proceeded to conclude the CRPD in December 2010, with the Convention coming into force in January 2011.[27]

The Council Decision specified that when depositing the instruments of formal confirmation the President of the Council would deposit a Declaration of Competence, as foreseen in Article 44 CRPD which concerns regional integration organisations. As a result, an appendix was attached to the Council Decision to conclude the Convention, entitled 'Declaration concerning the Competence of the European Community with regard to matters governed by the United Nations Convention and the Rights of Persons with Disabilities'. The Declaration of Competence 'indicates' the competences transferred to the Community (now Union) by the Member States in the areas covered by the Convention under the previous EC Treaty and identifies those areas of exclusive and shared competence. Combatting discrimination on the ground of disability is listed as an area falling

[21] Given that the purpose of this chapter is to not to explore the implications of the Convention in full, the description of its contents has necessarily been brief and selective. Many important provisions have not been touched on in this overview.

[22] Quinn (n 13) 5.

[23] Council Decision (EC) on the signing, on behalf of the European Community, of the United Nations' Convention on the Rights of Persons with Disabilities, 20 March 2007, 7407/07.

[24] A third legal basis was Art 300(2) EC (now Art 218 TFEU). This article addresses the procedure to be followed when the Community concludes agreements with international organisations.

[25] Council Decision concerning the conclusion, by the European Community, of the United Nations Convention on the Rights of Persons with Disabilities (2010/48/EC) [2010] OJ L23/35.

[26] ibid Art 2(1).

[27] For further information on the process of the EU conclusion of the CRPD see Waddington (n 11).

within competences which are shared between the EU and the Member States. One of the recommendations of the CRPD Committee to the EU in its Concluding Observations was that the EU 'regularly update the declaration of competence and its list of instruments to include recently adopted instruments and instruments that may not specifically refer to persons with disabilities, but that are relevant to persons with disabilities'.[28]

III. The Influence of the CRPD on the CJEU'S Interpretation of the Framework Equality Directive

A. The Status of International Agreements Concluded by the EU

The Court of Justice of the European Union (CJEU or the Court) has held as early as 1974 that international agreements concluded by the EU 'form an integral part of the Community [now Union] legal system'[29] and that the Court has the jurisdiction to interpret the provisions of such agreements.[30,31] The TFEU also briefly addresses the status of international agreements to which the EU is a party in Article 216(2), which provides that '[a]greements concluded by the Union are binding upon the institutions of the Union and on its Member States'. This does not explicitly indicate the hierarchy of such agreements and treaties within the EU legal order. However, the CJEU has addressed this lacuna in its case law. The Court has therefore established a hierarchy of norms, whereby international agreements concluded by the EU are inferior to primary law but superior to secondary law.[32]

Given this hierarchy, the CJEU is bound to interpret secondary EU law which falls within the scope of an international agreement concluded by the EU in a manner which is consistent with that agreement to the extent that this is possible.[33] The Court established this in *Commission v Germany* (1996), in which it held 'the primacy of international agreements concluded by the Community over provisions of secondary Community legislation means that such provisions must, so far as is possible, be interpreted in a manner that is consistent with those

[28] Committee on the Rights of Persons with Disabilities (n 9) para 17.

[29] Case 181/73 *Haegeman v Belgium* EU:C:1974:41, para 5.

[30] This section draws on text in L Waddington, 'Chapter on the European Union' in L Waddington and A Lawson (eds), *The UN Convention on the Rights of Persons with Disabilities in Practice: A Comparative Analysis of the Role of Courts* (Oxford University Press, 2018).

[31] Case 181/73 *Haegeman* (n 29) para 6; Case 12/86 *Demirel v Stadt Schwäbisch Gmünd* EU:C:1987:400.

[32] For a fairly recent restatement of this principle, see Case C-366/10 *Air Transport Association of America and Others* EU:C:2011:864, para 50. See also Joined Cases C-335/11 and C-337/11 *HK Danmark (Ring and Skouboe Werge)* EU:C:2013:222, paras 28-9.

[33] Case C-61/94 *Commission v Germany* EU:C:1996:313, para 52; Case C-341/95 *Bettati v Safety Hi-Tech* EU:C:1998:353, para 20.

agreements'.[34] In *Bettati* (1998), the Court reiterated this statement, and stressed this obligation with regard to EU instruments designed to give effect to international agreements. The Court therefore held: '[i]t is settled law that Community legislation must, so far as possible, be interpreted in a manner that is consistent with international law, in particular where its provisions are intended specifically to give effect to an international agreement concluded by the Community'.[35]

B. The Case Law of the CJEU and the CRPD: The Definition of Disability

The definition of disability[36] for the purposes of the Framework Equality Directive (FED) has proved particularly problematic for national courts, and has resulted in a number of preliminary references to the CJEU.[37] The issue first arose in the pre-CRPD case of *Chacón Navas* (2006).[38] In this case, the Court produced its first definition of disability, stating that the FED was designed to combat employment discrimination and defined disability in that context as 'a limitation which results in particular from physical, mental or psychological impairments and which hinders the participation of the person concerned in professional life'.[39]

The definition developed by the Court in *Chacón Navas* was based on the individual or medical model of disability. According to the definition, the cause of the disadvantage (or the 'limitation') is the 'impairment' which an individual has, and it is the 'impairment' which hinders participation in professional life. Therefore, the problem lies in the impaired individual, not in the reaction of society to the impairment or the organisation of society.

This model can be contrasted with a social-contextual model of disability which, as noted above, lies at the heart of the CRPD. According to this model, disability is the result of an interaction between an impairment and an inaccessible and discriminatory environment, rather than being the consequence of a medical condition which results in reduced ability.[40]

[34] Case C-61/94 *Commission v Germany* (n 33) para 52.

[35] Case C-341/95 *Bettati v Safety Hi-Tech* (n 33) para 20. In addition to interpreting provisions of EU secondary legislation in a manner which is compatible with an international agreement, the Court may also hold that provisions of an international agreement concluded by the EU have direct effect. Space precludes a further discussion of this issue here.

[36] The Court has also referred to the CRPD in judgments concerning other provisions and elements of the FED. However, this chapter focuses only on the issue of the definition of disability for the purposes of the Directive as, arguably, the CRPD has had the greatest impact here.

[37] This section draws on text in L Waddington, 'Saying All the Right Things and Still Getting it Wrong: The Court of Justice's Definition of Disability and Non-Discrimination Law' (2015) 22 *Maastricht Journal of European and Comparative Law* 576. For further discussion of the Court's case law on the concept of disability, see the chapter by L Lourenço and P Pohjankoski in the present volume.

[38] Case C-13/05 *Chacón Navas v Eurest Colectividades SA* EU:C:2006:456.

[39] ibid para 43.

[40] For a pre-CRPD discussion on the models of disability, see Priestley (n 10).

The CJEU only had the chance to review its '*Chacón Navas*' definition of disability in 2013, by which time the Convention had come into force for the EU. In *HK Danmark (Ring and Skouboe Werge)* (2013), the referring Danish court submitted an elaborate set of questions related to the concept of disability and essentially sought clarification as to the meaning of this concept in light of the *Chacón Navas* judgment.[41] In the judgment, the Court noted as a preliminary observation that under Article 216(2) TFEU, international agreements concluded by the EU are part of EU law and are binding on its institutions and prevail over acts of the EU.[42] In addition, given the primacy of international agreements over instruments of EU secondary law, the latter must be interpreted in a way which is consistent with international agreements as far as possible.[43] Based on this, the Court stated that the UN Convention forms 'an integral part of the European Union legal order'[44] and the FED must be interpreted 'in a manner consistent with that Convention'.[45]

The Court recalled its judgment in *Chacón Navas* which, it stressed, was decided before the EU became a party to the CRPD.[46] It then proceeded to refer to provisions in the Convention which elaborate on the concept of disability, including Article 1, which states that 'Persons with disabilities include those who have long-term physical, mental, intellectual or sensory impairments which in interaction with various barriers may hinder their full and effective participation in society on an equal basis with others'.[47] Drawing closely on Article 1 CRPD, the Court held that the concept of 'disability' must be understood as:

> a limitation which results in particular from physical, mental or psychological impairments which in interaction with various barriers may hinder the full and effective participation of the person concerned in professional life on an equal basis with other workers.[48]

One can conclude that the CRPD, and its Article 1 in particular, set the tone for how disability was defined by the Court in this case. Unlike the individual or medical view, which underlay the judgment in *Chacón Navas*, disability is not assessed purely in terms of the existence of an impairment, which restricts the functional ability of an individual, but the relevance of social and environmental factors in limiting – or disabling – people are to be taken into account. In short, one could expect the definition embraced by the Court in *HK Danmark (Ring and Skouboe Werge)* to lead to a reconceptualisation of what disability is for the purposes of

[41] Joined Cases C-335/11 and C-337/11 *HK Danmark (Ring and Skouboe Werge)* (n 32).

[42] ibid para 28.

[43] ibid para 29. See also D Ferri, 'The Conclusion of the UN Convention on the Rights of Persons with Disabilities by the EC/EU: A Constitutional Perspective' in L Waddington and G Quinn (eds), *European Yearbook of Disability Law*, vol 2 (Antwerp, Intersentia, 2010) 66–68 in particular.

[44] Joined Cases C-335/11 and C-337/11 *HK Danmark* (n 32) para 30.

[45] ibid para 32.

[46] ibid para 37.

[47] ibid.

[48] ibid para 38.

the FED, and a movement away from a narrow impairment-based perspective. Indeed, Advocate General Wahl has described the judgment in *HK Danmark (Ring and Skouboe Werge)* as marking 'a paradigm shift in the Court's case-law'.[49] However, it is worth noting that unlike the CRPD, which uses participation in society as a reference point, the Court's judgment in *HK Danmark (Ring and Skouboe Werge)* requires a person to be hindered in participation in the more limited field of professional life. The implications of this requirement became apparent in the case of *Z* which is discussed below.

This definition of disability for the purposes of the FED has since been repeated three times by the Court in *Z v A Government Department and the Board of Management of a Community School* (2014),[50] *Kaltoft* (2014)[51] and, most recently, in *Daouidi* (2016).[52] The definition therefore seems to be rather set. However, an examination of these cases shows that the Court may not be embracing or fully comprehending the significance of a definition of disability based on the social–contextual model found in the CRPD.

Z concerned a woman who had no uterus and was unable to become pregnant. Ms Z and her husband arranged for a surrogate mother to carry their genetic child. Following the birth of the child, Ms Z's employer in Ireland refused her a period of paid leave equivalent to maternity or adoption leave on the grounds that she qualified for neither and the law did not provide for paid leave following the birth of a child through surrogacy. Ms Z argued that this amounted to, *inter alia*, disability discrimination, and was prohibited under the Directive.

The Court in *Z* reiterated the importance of interpreting EU law in a manner compatible with the CRPD, and restated its definition of disability set out in *HK Danmark (Ring and Skouboe Werge)*. It recognised that Ms Z's lack of a uterus and the inability to give birth naturally amounted to an impairment and stated that:

> it is not disputed that such a condition constitutes a limitation which results in particular from physical, mental or psychological impairments, or that it is of a long-term nature.[53]

However, implicitly recalling its own definition of disability, the Court noted, 'the concept of "disability" within the meaning of Directive 2000/78 presupposes that the limitation from which the person suffers, in interaction with various barriers, may hinder that person's full and effective participation in professional

[49] Case C-363/12 *Z v A Government Department and the Board of Management of a Community School* EU:C:2013:604, Opinion of AG Wahl, para 88.

[50] Case C-363/12 *Z v A Government Department and the Board of Management of a Community School* EU:C:2014:159. For a discussion of the inter-sectional nature of this case, see the chapter by R Xenidis in the present volume.

[51] Case C-354/13 *FOA v Kommunernes Landsforening (KL) (Kaltoft)* EU:C:2014:2463.

[52] Case C-395/15 *Mohamed Daouidi v Bootes Plus SL and Others* EU:C:2016:917.

[53] Case C-363/12 *Z* (n 50) para 79.

life on an equal basis with other workers'.[54] It proceeded to agree with its Advocate General,[55] finding that:

> the inability to have a child by conventional means does not in itself, in principle, prevent the commissioning mother from having access to, participating in or advancing in employment. In the present case, it is not apparent from the order for reference that Ms Z's condition by itself made it impossible for her to carry out her work or constituted a hindrance to the exercise of her professional activity.[56]

As a result, Ms Z was held not to have a 'disability' within the meaning of the Directive.[57] It seems that the Court recognised that Ms Z may have been disabled, and indeed implied that she may have been recognised as being disabled under the CRPD,[58] but did not find that her condition amounted to a disability for the purposes of the FED, because it did not impact on her ability to work. In spite of embracing the CRPD-based definition of disability developed in *HK Danmark (Ring and Skouboe Werge)*, it is submitted that the Court, once again, resorted to an individual or medical model of disability in practice.[59] Looked at from a limited individual or medical perspective, it is undoubtedly true that Ms Z's impairment had no direct impact on her ability to work. However, in taking this approach, the Court arguably failed to take into account the fields in which discrimination is prohibited under the Directive and the impact Ms Z's impairment had on her access to employment-related benefits. The Directive prohibits disability-based discrimination with regard to, *inter alia*, 'employment and working conditions, including dismissals and pay'.[60] This is part of the material scope of the FED. Taking this into account, one can see that Ms Z did experience a limitation (indirectly) resulting from an impairment in interaction with various barriers, and was consequently disabled within the meaning of the Court's definition. Those barriers were the absence of a statutory regime providing for a period of paid leave following the birth of a child through surrogacy, which relates to employment conditions. This barrier was particularly likely to affect someone in Ms Z's position who was unable to have a child naturally, and could therefore be regarded as indirectly discriminatory.

A subsequent judgment of the CJEU concerned Mr Kaltoft, who was dismissed from his job as a childminder, after 15 years of employment, by a Danish local authority.[61] Mr Kaltoft was obese, weighing over 150 kilos,[62] and he claimed

[54] ibid para 80.
[55] See Case C-363/12 *Z* (Opinion of AG Wahl) (n 49) paras 82–98.
[56] Case C-363/12 *Z* (n 50) para 81.
[57] ibid para 82.
[58] This was also recognised by AG Wahl in his Opinion in Case C-363/12 *Z* (n 49) para 93.
[59] As in Case C-13/05 *Chacón Navas* (n 38).
[60] Article 3(1)(c). This was quoted in Case C-363/12 *Z* (n 50) para 23.
[61] Case C-354/13 *Kaltoft* (n 51).
[62] B Waterfield and J Huggler, '"I don't feel my weight is a big problem' says Dane in EU obesity ruling' *Daily Telegraph* (London, 18 December 2014). Available at: www.telegraph.co.uk/health/dietandfitness/11302442/I-dont-feel-my-weight-is-a-big-problem-says-Dane-in-EU-obesity-ruling.html.

that he was dismissed because he was obese and that this was contrary to the Directive.

With regard to the definition of disability and the question of whether obesity could be regarded as a particular form of disability, the Court ultimately repeated its definition of disability first given in *HK Danmark (Ring and Skouboe Werge)*. It held that obesity does not, in itself, constitute a 'disability' since it does not necessarily involve a limitation which results from an impairment and which, in interaction with various barriers, hinders participation in professional life.[63] However, where obesity does lead to such a limitation, it should be regarded as a disability. The Court said this would be the case, for example, if an obese worker was affected by reduced mobility or medical conditions related to his obesity which prevented him from carrying out his work or caused him discomfort when working.[64] The Court concluded by holding that obesity constitutes a 'disability' within the context of the FED, where 'it entails a limitation resulting in particular from long-term physical, mental or psychological impairments which in interaction with various barriers may hinder the full and effective participation of the person concerned in professional life on an equal basis with other workers'.[65]

The CJEU's definition of disability once again refers to a limitation resulting from an impairment which, in interaction with other barriers, hinders professional participation. The examples of hindrances given by the Court in this case concern physical limitations directly caused by the obesity. Mr Kaltoft claimed that he had no such limitations, and was perfectly capable of doing his job.[66] However, if this is true, and he was nevertheless dismissed because of his obesity, then he clearly did face a barrier – in the form of the negative attitude and prejudice of his employer. Many disabled people face such barriers – in essence discrimination resulting from false assumptions about ability and stigma – and it is clear that the CRPD, to which the EU is a party, is designed to address this.[67]

The CJEU did not state in its judgment that the 'various barriers [which] may hinder the full and effective participation of the person concerned in professional life' include or exclude such discriminatory attitudes.[68] However, as in *Z*, the Court's approach places an emphasis on the need for limitations resulting from impairments (which in interaction with various barriers hinder participation in professional life). The examples given of such limitations in the context of obesity are clearly physical and directly connected to obesity or a related medical condition. This seems to render it difficult to interpret the Court's definition of disability as embracing individuals who experience no physical limitation, but who are

[63] Case C-354/13 *Kaltoft* (n 51) para 58.

[64] ibid para 60.

[65] ibid para 64.

[66] Waterfield and Huggler (n 62).

[67] In line with this, Art 8(1)(b) CRPD requires 'States Parties to undertake to adopt immediate, effective and appropriate measures' 'to combat stereotypes, prejudices and harmful practices relating to persons with disabilities'.

[68] Case C-354/13 *Kaltoft* (n 51) para 53.

only hampered by the discriminatory attitudes of others, discriminatory rules, or provisions.[69] In essence, it seems that an individual who is 'disabled' by the false assumptions and prejudice of others – by discrimination – but who does not experience a physical limitation, may be excluded from protection from disability discrimination.[70] Such individuals would only be protected if they did experience a limitation in combination with various barriers which hindered their participation in professional life. This is reflected in the finding of Advocate General Jääskinin in *Kaltoft* where he stated that:

> absence of a bodily function or organ, or an illness requiring particular attention, continuous medication and control may be a physiological or psychological burden to the person concerned, but not render impossible the full and effective carrying out of work, or hinder participation on an equal basis in professional life in general.[71]

In brief, *Z* seems to demonstrate a failure to appreciate the relevance or importance of the role which environmental or socially constructed features play in creating disability, whilst *Kaltoft* shows that it may not always be easy for national Courts to work with the Court's definition, and nor may the definition always be 'fit for purpose', given that a goal of the FED is to combat *discrimination* on the ground of disability. The Court's approach to disability in *Kaltoft* may exclude individuals who do not have an actual limitation directly related to their impairment, but who nevertheless experience disability discrimination, from protection under the Directive.[72] Lastly, in *Daouidi*, the Court placed an emphasis on the provision of medical evidence to establish the likely duration of a person's incapacity; this reliance on medical evidence may reflect the CJEU's overall discomfort with the social-contextual model of disability.[73]

In conclusion, the CJEU has certainly taken seriously the EU's and thus its own obligations under the CRPD. The Court has amended its definition of disability for the purposes of the FED quite radically, ostensibly to bring it into line with the Convention. The definition first developed in *HK Danmark (Ring and Skouboe Werge)* and repeated in the cases of *Z*, *Kaltoft* and *Daouidi* indeed moves away from the individual or medical model of disability reflected in the *Chacón Navas* judgment, and seemingly embraces the social-contextual model of disability. However, as noted above, unlike the CRPD, which uses participation

[69] The role of discrimination and prejudice with regard to people who are obese was raised by Mr Kaltoft. Mr Kaltoft's argument was noted by AG Jääskinen in his Opinion: '[obesity] can equally entail limitations on the employment market by reason of prejudice on the basis of physical appearance' – Case C-354/13 *Kaltoft* ECLI:EU:C:2014:2106, Opinion of AG Jääskinen, para 52.

[70] One way around this problem would be interpret the Directive as providing protection to individuals who are discriminated on the grounds that they are assumed or perceived to have a disability. For reasons of space, this is not explored further in this chapter.

[71] Case C-354/13 *Kaltoft* (Opinion of AG Jääskinen) (n 69) para 34.

[72] In such a case, the discrimination would result from the discriminator's false assumption about the individual's limited abilities.

[73] Case C-395/15 *Daouidi* (n 52). For a more detailed discussion see L Waddington, 'HvJ EU 01-12-12016, C-395/15 *Daouidi* (met noot)' (2017) *European Human Rights Cases* issue 2, 92.

in society as a reference point, the Court's definition of disability requires that a person is hindered in participation in the more limited field of professional life. As a result, an individual who has an impairment which impacts on some activity other than professional life, but who nevertheless experiences disadvantage or exclusion with regard to their professional life for a reason linked to their impairment, as Ms Z did, will be excluded from the protection from disability discrimination offered by the Directive.

Moreover, the second key element of the CJEU's definition of disability, namely that the limitation (impairment) in interaction with 'various barriers' hinders professional participation, is repeatedly stated by the Court in its definition, but it seems reluctant to regard as disabled an individual whose 'disability' is the result of those socially created barriers. An individual may be impaired without this impacting on their ability to work – but this does not mean that such a person is able to participate in the labour market and access all employment-related benefits on an equal basis with others. They may still face discrimination, prejudice, stigma and an inaccessible environment in their professional life, all of which serve to exclude them or limit their options. In short, the CJEU is clearly 'talking the talk' of the social-contextual model of disability found in the CRPD, but it is arguably struggling to 'walk the walk' and apply that model in practice.

IV. The Influence of the CRPD on the 2008 Proposal for a New EU Equality Directive

In 2008, the Commission proposed a new anti-discrimination directive[74] to complement the Framework Equality Directive (FED) and extend protection from discrimination to areas beyond employment.[75] The proposal covers the same grounds as the FED and, whilst the EU was not yet a party to the CRPD at the time the proposal was published, the Convention was already exerting an influence. The Impact Assessment in the Commission staff working document accompanying the proposal pointed out that:

> the Member States will have to implement [the Convention] whatever action is taken at EU level to tackle discrimination based on disability. Member States would implement the UN Convention through adopting new legislation or amending existing national legislation. An EC Directive can therefore be seen as a way of facilitating implementation of parts of the Convention.[76]

[74] Proposal for Council Directive (n 2).

[75] This text draws on, and significantly updates, the text in L Waddington, 'Future Prospects for EU Equality Law. Lessons to be Learnt from the Proposed Equal Treatment Directive' (2011) 2 *European Law Review* 163.

[76] Commission staff working document accompanying the proposal for a Council Directive on implementing the principle of equal treatment between persons irrespective of religion or belief, disability, age or sexual orientation – Summary of the Impact Assessment, COM(2008) 426 final, 24.

The related summary of the impact assessment also noted:

> The [Impact Assessment] also explains that a directive which prohibited discrimination based on disability, as well as other grounds, could be an effective and coherent way for the Member States to implement parts of the UN Convention on the rights of persons with disabilities.[77]

Moreover, in the first half of 2015, in response to a questionnaire circulated by the Latvian Presidency, various Member States 'stressed the need to ensure compatibility' between the proposed directive and the CRPD.[78] However, in response a Commission representative reminded delegates that:

> the EU legal order was autonomous in character, regardless of the fact that the EU and its Member States had signed and ratified the UNCRPD. Thus the basic principle and concepts of the UNCRPD would have to be respected by the Directive and a degree of alignment was required, but neither the scope of the Directive nor its detailed provisions and implementation procedure would have to be slavishly copied from the UNCRPD. Thus for example, the scope of the draft Directive was not determined by the UNCRPD but by the competences of the Union as defined in the Treaties, which in turn meant that it would be legally impossible to implement the entire UNCRPD by means of an EU Directive. Indeed, if the Member States decided to reject the proposed Directive, they would still be obliged to implement the UNCRPD. Conversely, the Directive could, if the Member States so decided, go further that the UNCRPD in certain ways – for example, by setting a deadline for implementation (as indeed has been requested by the UN Committee on the Rights of Persons with Disabilities).[79]

Meanwhile, progress reports on the proposal from the previous three Council presidencies (the Netherlands, Slovakia and Luxembourg) have noted that 'several delegations have underlined the significance of the proposal in the context of the implementation of the UN Convention on the Rights of Persons with Disabilities (UNCRPD). However, some delegations would have preferred more ambitious provisions in regard to disability'.[80]

The latest version of the proposal contains six references to the CRPD whereas the original version contained three such references. All references are found in the preamble. However, the most significant influence of the Convention arguably relates to the wording and definitions included in the proposal, and how that tracks equivalent terms or articles in the Convention rather than explicit references to the CRPD. In that respect, the influence of the CRPD on the proposal can be identified in at least three areas, which are considered below: the definition of/guidance on the concept of disability; reasonable accommodation and discrimination; and accessibility.

[77] ibid 6.

[78] Progress Report from the Presidency to the Permanent Representatives Committee/Council (2015) 13877/1/15 REV 1, 6.

[79] ibid 7.

[80] See, e.g. the Progress Report from the Presidency to the Permanent Representatives Committee/Council (2016) 14284/16, 2.

A. The Concept of Disability

As noted above, the CRPD provides guidance on the concept of disability. Article 1 of the Convention specifies as follows:

> Persons with disabilities includes those who have long-term physical, mental, intellectual or sensory impairments which in interaction with various barriers may hinder their full and effective participation in society on an equal basis with others.

In addition, Recital (e) of the Preamble states the following:

> Recognising that disability is an evolving concept and that disability results from the interaction between persons with impairments and attitudinal and environmental barriers that hinders their full and effective participation in society on an equal basis with others.

In spite of the guidance on the concept of disability found in the Preamble and Article 1 of the Convention, the original 2008 proposal for the Directive did not contain any such guidance. However, the European Parliament subsequently proposed inserting a recital based on the relevant provision in Article 1 of the Convention,[81] and this was taken over and is included in the current version of the proposal:

> Persons with disabilities include those who have long-term physical, mental, intellectual or sensory impairments which, in interaction with various barriers, may hinder their full and effective participation in society on an equal basis with others.[82]

This amendment was inserted into the proposal at a fairly early stage in the negotiations and has remained unchanged.

B. Reasonable Accommodation

Article 2 of the Convention provides that discrimination 'includes denial of reasonable accommodation', and this is repeated in Article 5. Article 2 also defines 'reasonable accommodation' as meaning 'necessary and appropriate modification and adjustments not imposing a disproportionate or undue burden, where needed in a particular case, to ensure to persons with disabilities the enjoyment or exercise on an equal basis with others of all human rights and fundamental freedoms'.

[81] European Parliament legislative resolution of 2 April 2009 on the proposal for a Council directive on implementing the principle of equal treatment between persons irrespective of religion or belief, disability, age or sexual orientation (COM(2008)0426 – C6-0291/2008 – 2008/0140(CNS)), amendment 17. Amendment 3 of the resolution also proposed that the following text be included in the preamble: 'This Directive is one means by which the Community is complying with its obligations under the UN Convention on the Rights of Persons with Disabilities, and should be interpreted in that light.' The latest publicly available version of the full proposal (Version of 14 December 2016, 14500/16) does not include this amendment.

[82] Recital 19a. Version of 14 December 2016, 14500/16.

The Impact Assessment in the Commission staff working document accompanying the proposal, as noted above, identified the 2008 proposal as an effective way of implementing the CRPD and stated that 'by defining what is expected in terms of "reasonable accommodation" a directive would provide greater legal certainty than the Convention'.[83]

In line with the CRPD, the Commission's original 2008 proposal clearly defined an unjustified failure to make a reasonable accommodation as a form of discrimination, and linked this to the Convention. The original proposal therefore provided in Article 2(5):

> Denial of reasonable accommodation … as regards persons with disabilities shall be deemed to be discrimination.

Furthermore, Recital 2 specified:

> In particular, the UN Convention on the Rights of Persons with Disabilities includes the denial of reasonable accommodation in its definition of discrimination.[84]

The latest version of the proposal adopts a slightly different approach, but maintains the link between reasonable accommodation and discrimination. Article 2(1) now lists six kinds of discrimination which are to be prohibited, including 'denial of reasonable accommodation for persons with disabilities'.[85] Moreover Article 4a of the latest version, entitled reasonable accommodation for persons with disabilities, contains the following definition of reasonable accommodation:

> [R]easonable accommodation means necessary and appropriate modification and adjustments not imposing a disproportionate burden, where needed in a particular case, to accommodate the specific needs of a person with a disability so as to allow that person access on an equal basis with others to the specific social protection measure, educational activity, good or service concerned.[86]

This definition of reasonable accommodation was not found in the original proposal, leading to concern amongst some Member States as to the exact nature of the obligation. This led Bell to note in 2010 that '[g]iven that denial of reasonable accommodation is to become a form of unlawful discrimination, it is surprising that the proposed Directive remains somewhat elusive on what constitutes reasonable accommodation'.[87] Part of the definition that was eventually included in the proposal was taken word for word from Article 2 CRPD, indicating that the EU drew on the Convention when addressing this issue. This also goes some way to

[83] Commission staff working document (n 76) 6.

[84] This provision is unchanged in the latest publicly available version (Version of 14 December 2016, 14500/16).

[85] ibid.

[86] ibid Art 4a(2).

[87] M Bell, 'Advancing EU Anti-Discrimination Law: the European Commission's 2008 Proposal for a New Directive' (2009) 3 *The Equal Rights Review* 7, 10.

explain the difference between the definition of reasonable accommodation found in the 2008 proposal and the definition of the same term in the FED. The scope of the proposed definition – relating as it does only to access to social protection measures, educational activities, and goods and services – is narrower than the scope found in the definition of reasonable accommodation in the CRPD, which relates to 'enjoyment or exercise of all human rights and fundamental freedoms'.[88]

C. Accessibility

Lastly, it is worth noting that the CRPD pays a lot of attention to securing accessibility for people with disabilities. Accessibility is one of the central principles of the Convention found in Article 3, and eliminating discrimination, in the sense of removing obstacles and barriers to accessibility, also lies at the heart of Article 9. That article requires States Parties to:

> take appropriate measures to ensure to persons with disabilities access, on an equal basis with others, to the physical environment, to transportation, to information and communications, including information and communications technologies and systems, and to other facilities and services open or provided to the public.[89]

These measures include the 'identification and elimination of obstacles and barriers to accessibility'[90] in a wide range of areas, and could certainly be interpreted as requiring, *inter alia*, measures to combat discrimination.

The Commission's original 2008 proposal also contained extensive and controversial provisions relating to accessibility. In Article 4(1)(a), it provided as follows:

> The measures necessary to enable persons with disabilities to have effective non-discriminatory access to social protection, social advantages, health care, education and access to and supply of goods and services which are available to the public, including housing and transport, shall be provided by anticipation, including through appropriate modifications and adjustments. Such measures should not impose a disproportionate burden, nor require fundamental alteration of the social protection, social advantages, health care, education, or goods and services in question or require the provision of alternatives thereto.

This provision was much criticised by Member States, *inter alia*, on the grounds that it was too vague and uncertain. The original proposal does not clarify on whom this duty falls, but the implication is that Member States and service providers must take action to ensure equal access for people with disabilities. As a result of the perceived lack of clarity, the proposal was greatly amended and there were

[88] CRPD Art 2.
[89] ibid Art 9(1).
[90] ibid.

attempts to clarify what is meant by 'effective non-discriminatory access'. Later versions of the proposal simply refer to 'accessibility for persons with disabilities, on an equal basis as others' and when such accessibility can legitimately be refused.[91] The current version of the proposal provides:

> Member States shall take the necessary and appropriate measures to ensure accessibility for persons with disabilities on an equal basis with others, within the areas set out in Article 3 [which identifies the material scope of the proposal LW]. However, these measures should not impose a disproportionate burden.[92]

and

> Accessibility includes general anticipatory measures to ensure the effective implementation of the principle of equal treatment for persons with disabilities in the areas set out in Article 3.[93]

In addition, Recital 19b of the current version, partially mirroring the language of Article 9(1) CRPD, reads:

> Measures to ensure accessibility for persons with disabilities, on an equal basis with others, to the areas covered by this Directive play an important part in ensuring full equality in practice. Such measures should comprise the identification and elimination of obstacles and barriers to accessibility, as well as the prevention of new obstacles and barriers. Measures to ensure accessibility for persons with disabilities should not impose a disproportionate burden.[94]

Recitals 19c, 19d and 19e of the current version of the proposal also address accessibility, with Recital 19d referring explicitly to the CRPD:

> Improvements of accessibility can be provided by a variety of means, including application of the 'universal design' principle. According to the United Nations Convention on the Rights of Persons with Disabilities, 'universal design' means the design of products, environments, programmes and services to be usable by all people, to the greatest possible extent, without the need for adaption or specialised design. 'Universal design' should not exclude assistive devices for particular groups where this is needed. Member States should undertake or promote research and development of universally designed goods and services falling within the scope of this Directive, with the aim of meeting the specific needs of persons with disabilities while reducing the need for adaptation and the cost as much as possible, and to promote their availability and use. Member States

[91] European Parliament legislative resolution (n 81) Amendment 14: 'Persons with disabilities frequently face discrimination in the form of inaccessible public transport and the built environment, as well as inaccessible communications and information. Member States must take measures to ensure accessibility in these areas in order to put into effect the principle of equal treatment.' However, this amendment is not reflected in the latest version of the proposal available via the Council's homepage (Version of 14 December 2016, 14500/16).

[92] Version of 14 December 2016, 14500/16, Art 4(1).

[93] ibid Art 4(1)(a).

[94] Additional text in Recital 19b of the current proposal which is included in brackets is not included in the above quote.

should also promote universal design in the development of standards and guidelines so as to progressively ensure accessibility of goods and services.[95]

It is clear that the intention is to involve more than an individualised response to the needs of a particular person, as and when those needs arise and require anticipation of the likely access needs of the group of people with disabilities as a whole, and the taking of steps to meet those needs, as well as 'universal design'. Moreover, as is apparent from the three most recent 'Progress Reports from the Presidencies of the Council', significant attention is currently being paid to the relationship between the proposal's provisions on accessibility on the one hand and other EU legislation, including the proposed European Accessibility Act,[96] on the other. This matter still needs to be clarified.

In reaction to the responses received to the Latvian questionnaire noted above, the Council Working Party on Social Questions, under the Luxembourg Presidency, considered ensuring the accessibility provisions in the proposal were in line with the CRPD, which itself contains no disproportionate burden criterion linked to accessibility. This could mean that accessibility should always be pursued even if implementation was gradual. In response, the Commission representative emphasised that the disproportionate burden criterion in the context of accessibility was an important element of the proposed directive, and reflected a balance between 'a binding approach (including implementation deadlines) and compensatory elements (including the concept of a disproportionate burden and the idea of progressive implementation)'.[97]

In conclusion, agreement amongst most Member States seems to exist in principle on the inclusion of a provision addressing accessibility, although no agreement has been reached on how this provision should be framed or on the relationship between the accessibility provisions in this instrument, the European Accessibility Act and other EU measures setting accessibility standards. However, the key point is that the proposal does pay attention to ensuring accessibility by anticipation, and is not simply confining itself to requiring that reasonable accommodations be made for specific individuals. If adopted, this would be a potentially far-reaching and important contribution to complying with the CRPD by the EU and its Member States. Moreover, in general, the 2008 proposal reveals a strong desire amongst both the Commission and some Member States to implement the anti-discrimination provisions of the CRPD, and to do this through EU law, although this desire has not yet resulted in the adoption of the proposal.

[95] Version of 14 December 2016, 14500/16, Recital 19d. The recital includes a reference in a footnote to CRPD Art 2.

[96] Proposal for a Directive of the European Parliament and of the Council on the approximation of the laws, regulations and administrative provisions of the Member States as regards the accessibility requirements for products and services, COM(2015) 615 final.

[97] Progress report from the Presidency to the Permanent Representatives Committee/Council (2015) 13877/1/15 REV 1, 6-7.

V. The UN CRPD Committee's Concluding Observations on the EU

Like all States Parties to the CRPD, the European Union is obliged to report periodically to the UN Committee on the Rights of Persons with Disabilities on the steps which it has taken to comply with the Convention. Under Article 35 of the CRPD, all States Parties are required to submit to the Committee 'a comprehensive report on measures taken to give effect to its obligations under the present Convention and on the progress made in that regard'. Article 36 CRPD further establishes:

> Each report shall be considered by the Committee, which shall make such suggestions and general recommendations on the report as it may consider appropriate and shall forward these to the State Party concerned. The State Party may respond with any information it chooses to the Committee. The Committee may request further information from States Parties relevant to the implementation of the present Convention.

The European Union submitted its report, which was written by the European Commission, to the Committee in 2014.[98] The Committee also received 'alternative' or 'shadow' reports from civil society, such as the European Disability Forum,[99] in which they expressed their views on the actions and compliance of the EU.

At its April 2015 meeting in Geneva, the Committee made a first consideration of these reports, and adopted a 'List of issues in relation to the initial report of the European Union'.[100] In essence, this was a long list of questions linked to individual articles and topics in the Convention, to which the European Commission, on behalf of the EU, was expected to respond. The questions related to EU legislation and policy, as well as the internal policy of the institutions. With regard to Article 5 CRPD on equality and anti-discrimination, the Committee asked the EU, *inter alia*:

> Please provide the intended timescale for the adoption by the Council of the additional equal treatment directive to extend the existing European Union anti-discrimination legal framework to areas outside the field of employment.[101]

The EU's response to the list of issues addressed this question in the following way:[102]

> Negotiations continue in the Council where the adoption of the Commission's proposal requires Member States' unanimous approval. The current stage of the legislative procedure has no time limit so the adoption date cannot be predicted. The Commission identified as a political priority the directive's adoption to complete the protection

[98] Commission Staff Working Document (n 5).
[99] The European Disability Forum Alternative Report (n 6).
[100] Committee on the Rights of Persons with Disabilities (n 7).
[101] ibid para 9.
[102] Commission Staff Working Document (n 8) para 36.

> under EU law against discrimination on grounds of religion or belief, disability, age and sexual orientation. The Commission is seeking to convince Member States to abandon their current resistance. The Commission aims to have it adopted under its current mandate.
>
> In its Resolution of 20 May 2015, the Parliament deplored the lack of progress within the Council and urged Member States to adopt a common position without delay.[103]

In October 2015, the CRPD Committee adopted its Concluding Observations on the EU report based on proposals from the two Committee members who were rapporteurs.[104] In line with Concluding Observations directed to other State Parties, the observations begin with a couple of paragraphs of praise for the EU. The Committee notes with appreciation 'that the EU is the first regional organisation to ratify a human rights treaty concluded under the auspices of the UN, thus setting a positive precedent in public international law'[105] and that regulations covering the European Structural and Investment Funds contain provisions that reflect the Convention.[106] However, the majority of the 12-page document reflects the Committee's concerns and recommendations. In total, the Concluding Observations contain 42 recommendations to the EU, all highlighted in bold. These address the full range of Convention rights and are identified on an article-by-article basis. The recommendations relate to, *inter alia*, conducting a review of EU legislation to ensure full harmonisation with the Convention, adopting proposed legislation, mainstreaming disability issues, awareness raising and campaigns on disability, ensuring accessibility, prohibiting disability discrimination, budget allocation and EU staff matters.

With regard to equality and anti-discrimination (Article 5 CRPD), the CRPD Committee made the following remark (para 18) and recommendation (para 19).

> 18. The Committee is concerned that Directives 2000/43, 2004/113 and 2006/54 failed to explicitly prohibit discrimination based on disability and prescribe for duty to provide reasonable accommodation to persons with disabilities in the areas of social protection, health care, (re)habilitation, education and provisions of goods and services, such as housing transport and insurance.
>
> 19. The Committee recommends that the European Union adopt its proposed horizontal Equal Treatment Directive extending protection from discrimination to persons with disabilities, including by the provision of reasonable accommodation, to all areas of competence. Furthermore, the Committee recommends that the European Union ensure discrimination in all aspects based on disability is prohibited, including multiple and intersectional discrimination.

[103] ibid paras 36–37.
[104] Committee on the Rights of Persons with Disabilities (n 9).
[105] ibid para 4.
[106] ibid para 5.

Directives 2006/54[107] and 2004/113[108] address sex discrimination with regard to employment and beyond employment respectively, whilst Directive 2000/43[109] addresses discrimination on the grounds of race/ethnic origin in both areas.

It is worth noting that many Member States already support the adoption of the Commission's 2008 proposal. This is evident from the introduction to a note from the General Secretariat of the Council accompanying an earlier version of the proposal which highlights that:

> several delegations have underlined the significance of the proposal in the context of the UN Convention on the Rights of Persons with Disabilities (UNCRPD). BE, FI, NL, SK, SI, BG, HU and Cion have stressed the need to maintain consistency with the UNCRPD. ES, AT, PT and SI would have preferred more ambitious provisions in regard to disability.[110]

With regard to these delegations and the Commission, the Committee's Concluding Observations are therefore 'preaching to the converted'. However, the same note goes on to state 'DE has maintained a general reservation and expressed various concerns', reflecting the well know opposition of Germany to the adoption of the proposal.[111] It seems unlikely that the Committee's non-binding recommendation will influence Germany's position.

The Concluding Observations also recommend that the EU ensures that multiple and intersectional discrimination related to disability is prohibited. The Commission's proposal cannot be regarded as achieving this and, to date, the EU has not legislated explicitly to prohibit such forms of discrimination on any of the grounds covered by the Treaty in its various equality directives.[112] Given the challenges to the adoption of the current proposal, it seems doubtful that the proposal will be amended in this respect and, even more unlikely, that the Commission will produce a new legislative proposal addressing multiple and intersectional discrimination.

[107] Directive 2006/54/EC of the European Parliament and of the Council on the implementation of the principle of equal opportunities and equal treatment of men and women in matters of employment and occupation (recast) [2006] OJ L204/23.

[108] Council Directive 2004/113/EC implementing the principle of equal treatment between men and women in the access to and supply of goods and services [2004] OJ L373/37.

[109] Council Directive 2000/43/EC implementing the principle of equal treatment between persons irrespective of racial or ethnic origin [2000] OJ L180/22.

[110] See Note from General Secretariat of the Council, 11 December 2014, Council (EPSCO), Proposal for Council Directive on implementing the principle of equal treatment between persons irrespective of religion or belief, disability, age or sexual orientation (2014) 15705/14, ADD 1 REV 2. Underlining and footnotes not included.

[111] ibid.

[112] For a broader picture on multiple discrimination in EU law and the current pitfalls, see the chapter by R Xenidis in the present volume.

VI. Conclusion

The conclusion of the CRPD has certainly influenced EU anti-discrimination law on disability. The most tangible influence is to be seen in the case law of the CJEU and its interpretation of the concept of disability for the purposes of the FED. The interpretation by the CJEU is, of course, binding throughout the EU. However, this is not to say that the definition of disability found in the various pieces of national legislation transposing the Directive, which were adopted prior to the judgment of *HK Danmark (Ring and Skouboe Werge)* and before the EU and its Member States became a party to the Convention,[113] are compatible with the Court's post-CRPD view of disability. This may potentially open the door to initiating infringement procedures by the Commission against Member States which apply an individual or medical-based definition of disability although, as of yet, there are no signs that this is on the cards. Moreover, for the reasons outlined in this chapter, the Court's definition and approach may themselves be failing to meet the standard of the Convention.

The influence of the Convention can also be seen in the amended 2008 proposal for a new anti-discrimination directive and the *de facto* incorporation of text from the Convention within the proposal. Key terms found in the proposal, such as 'disability' and 'reasonable accommodation', have explicitly been defined in line with the CRPD. This reflects a desire amongst the Commission and some Member States to implement the Convention in the equality field through EU legislation; however, the proposal remains stalled in the Council.

Lastly, the Concluding Observations on the EU of the CRPD Committee reinforce the calls being made by many to secure the adoption of the 2008 proposal for a new anti-discrimination directive. However, the Concluding Observations are unlikely to tip the balance in favour of adoption, and the proposal remains highly contested within the Council.

The picture is also rather mixed in terms of the overall progress made by EU law in protecting persons with disabilities from discrimination since 2000. The FED led to the adoption of disability anti-discrimination law for the first time in most Member States. Furthermore, in many States, such legislation extends protection beyond the field of employment, although that is not required under EU law. However, the number of disability-related cases reaching the CJEU is low and to date focused mostly, but not exclusively, on the issue of the definition of disability. In some Member States, case law concerning disability discrimination is also highly limited, whilst others reveal a gradually increasing awareness of disability discrimination linked to increased case law. Nevertheless, discrimination in all its forms continues to hamper the participation of persons with disabilities in society. The CRPD adds a further dimension to this complicated picture. The EU's policy and legislative agenda has undoubtedly been influenced by the CRPD to

[113] At the time of writing, Ireland is the only EU Member State which has not ratified the CRPD.

some degree. Moreover, the EU's conclusion of the CRPD significantly allows for an outside body – the UN Committee linked to the Convention – to bring critical pressure to bear on the EU. The Committee has raised a number of issues in its Concluding Observations to the EU. However, while the influence of the CRPD is evident in the CJEU's case law, the Committee did not comment on this in its Concluding Observations. Its insight into the compatibility of that case law, and particularly the Court's application of its CRPD-inspired definition of disability, would have been welcome.

Epilogue

The Limits of a Transformative Change in European Equality Law

BRUNO DE WITTE

The creation of a broad anti-discrimination competence by the Treaty of Amsterdam (in what was then Article 13 EC, now Article 19 Treaty on the Functioning of the European Union (TFEU)), and the almost immediate adoption, on that legal basis, of the 'twin directives' of 2000 (Directives 2000/43 and 2000/78) has often been seen as a transformative moment for the European Union's role in combating discrimination, and for the evolution of equality law in Europe more generally. Within EU law, discrimination law ceased to be a 'side show', that is, an ancillary part of broader economic and social objectives of the EU and became a self-standing policy of the European Union: the EU's institutions were called to 'combat discrimination' in Europe, quite apart from any cross-border or market-hindering impact that discrimination might have. The grounds that were then identified as 'suspect classifications' remained limited but were broader than just gender and nationality and included some grounds, such as age and sexual orientation, that had not been seen as requiring legal action in the EU before that time. Next to this change in EU constitutional law, the adoption of the two directives, in 2000, also caused major changes in the domestic law of many EU member states – changes which were often stubbornly resisted, for example in Germany where the implementation of the directives took much longer than the allowed deadline. Indeed, whereas all EU states had a general constitutional principle of equality, not many of them were familiar, outside the domain of gender equality, with the kind of detailed substantive norms and procedural requirements that those two directives imposed on them.

The concrete formulation of rights and obligations in the twin directives owed a lot to advances in the field of gender equality that had occurred in the previous decades through EU legislation and jurisprudence, for example with the inclusion of the prohibition of indirect discrimination (and its definition in the text of the directives) and the partial shift of the burden of proof to the benefit of victims of discrimination. But the directives of 2000 were also innovative compared to the pre-existing *acquis* of gender equality; for example, they introduced the notion of reasonable accommodation into EU law (albeit limited to the ground of disability), they added harassment as a separate form of discrimination, and they innovated on the procedural side through a series of requirements which aim at facilitating the effective access to justice for victims of discrimination. The latter element contrasted with early EU equality law (i.e. the laws dealing with nationality and sex discrimination) whose enforcement happened through the general compliance instruments of European law, namely direct infringement actions by the Commission against the states that failed to comply with EU equality law, and the duty for national courts to disapply, if necessary, any contrasting national norms.

The transformations accomplished by, and through, the twin directives are carefully documented in the contributions to this book. Yet, many of those contributions also highlight the limits of this transformative process. I will conclude this volume by some reflections on the nature of those limits.

A first limit is one of *material scope*. EU anti-discrimination law is still, by and large, confined to the employment sphere and, to that extent, can still be seen as essentially a branch of labour law. The Race Equality Directive 2000/43 has a much broader remit, but there is not much evidence that it has played an important role in areas other than employment; in the case law of the CJEU, at any rate, the only non-employment discrimination judgment so far was *CHEZ* (if we leave aside gender equality). Ten years ago, the Commission proposed a directive to complete the project contained in Article 19 TFEU by extending anti-discrimination on grounds of age, religion, disability and sexual orientation beyond the sphere of employment, but it seems that the political momentum to pursue the programme of combating discrimination has weakened, and is no longer strong enough to overcome the major hurdle of the requirement of unanimity within the EU Council. So, it seems that EU anti-discrimination law will continue to be mostly confined to the employment sphere.

A second limit is that of the *uneven application* of EU anti-discrimination law even within the sphere of employment law. The invocation of EU law norms is still, 15 years after the deadline for the implementation of the directives, quite uneven between the grounds and between the countries. Whereas the Court of Justice received numerous preliminary questions about age discrimination, it only very recently received the first ones on religion; whereas German, Belgian, Danish, Irish and Spanish courts frequently found their way to the Court of Justice, there have been hardly any references from countries such as France, Italy or Poland. Does this mean that, in the latter group of countries, EU equality law is implemented and applied in such an excellent manner that no questions of interpretation arise that should be submitted to the CJEU, or does this rather indicate a lack of legal mobilisation or lack of interest from the side of the courts of those countries?

A third limit, brought out in many of the contributions of this book, concerns the continuing *uncertainty about the meaning of central concepts* of anti-discrimination law. The crucial concept of indirect discrimination is a case in point. Although the Luxembourg Court's case law on gender discrimination had managed to configure relatively clear contours of the prohibition of indirect discrimination against women, its case law on the 'new grounds' does not show the same clarity. The CJEU, as well as national courts, is still struggling with the distinction between direct and indirect discrimination, and even with the apparently simple question of whether these two forms are mutually exclusive in relation to the same facts. This question is highlighted, for instance, in many of the critical comments (including in two chapters of this book) on the recent headscarf judgments of the CJEU. The Court has also failed, so far, to get to grips with the notion of multiple or intersectional discrimination, as shown in Raphaële Xenidis' contribution and the sharing of the burden of proof continues to be an elusive concept, as shown in the chapter by Kristin Henrard.

A fourth limit extends beyond the text of the twin directives, and of Article 19 TFEU, and relates to the fact that there seems to be an irreducible *gap between legal proclamation and effective social change*. Anti-discrimination law is a governance tool that can change the lives of some persons, in some situations, and in some parts of Europe; but does it actually reduce discriminatory behaviour overall, and does it – more generally – produce greater social justice? We do not have conclusive answers to those questions, despite the rich legal and extra-legal scholarship spawned by the development of EU anti-discrimination law, including the excellent contributions in this book. Morag Goodwin points to this in her contribution about the Roma, where the gap between anti-discrimination law in the books, and social marginalisation on the ground, seems particularly egregious; but this kind of gap arises for other disadvantaged groups than the Roma and for other suspect grounds than race. Judgments of the Court of Justice on anti-discrimination law always give rise to many interesting and critical comments, but the literature on the application of anti-discrimination law at the national level is more limited, and the literature on the non-judicial forms of advancing the anti-discrimination agenda even less so. This leaves ample scope for further investigation of the practical role played by EU anti-discrimination law in furthering social justice in Europe.

INDEX